EQUITY AND FIXED INCOME

CFA® Program Curriculum
2015 • LEVEL I • VOLUME 5

Please visit our website at
www.WileyGlobalFinance.com.

WILEY

FSC
www.fsc.org

MIX
Paper from
responsible sources

FSC® C005928

CONTENTS

Equity

indicates an optional segment

indicates an optional segment

◘ indicates an optional segment

◙ indicates an optional segment

indicates an optional segment

◙ indicates an optional segment

◘ indicates an optional segment

How to Use the CFA Program Curriculum

Congratulations on your decision to enter the Chartered Financial Analyst (CFA®) Program. This exciting and rewarding program of study reflects your desire to become a serious investment professional. You are embarking on a program noted for its high ethical standards and the breadth of knowledge, skills, and abilities it develops. Your commitment to the CFA Program should be educationally and professionally rewarding.

The credential you seek is respected around the world as a mark of accomplishment and dedication. Each level of the program represents a distinct achievement in professional development. Successful completion of the program is rewarded with membership in a prestigious global community of investment professionals. CFA charterholders are dedicated to life-long learning and maintaining currency with the ever-changing dynamics of a challenging profession. The CFA Program represents the first step toward a career-long commitment to professional education.

The CFA examination measures your mastery of the core skills required to succeed as an investment professional. These core skills are the basis for the Candidate Body of Knowledge (CBOK™). The CBOK consists of four components:

- A broad topic outline that lists the major top-level topic areas (www. cfainstitute.org/cbok);
- Topic area weights that indicate the relative exam weightings of the top-level topic areas (www.cfainstitute.org/level_I);
- Learning outcome statements (LOS) that advise candidates about the specific knowledge, skills, and abilities they should acquire from readings covering a topic area (LOS are provided in candidate study sessions and at the beginning of each reading); and
- The CFA Program curriculum, readings, and end-of-reading questions, which candidates receive upon exam registration.

Therefore, the key to your success on the CFA examinations is studying and understanding the CBOK. The following sections provide background on the CBOK, the organization of the curriculum, and tips for developing an effective study program.

CURRICULUM DEVELOPMENT PROCESS

The CFA Program is grounded in the practice of the investment profession. Using the Global Body of Investment Knowledge (GBIK) collaborative website, CFA Institute performs a continuous practice analysis with investment professionals around the world to determine the knowledge, skills, and abilities (competencies) that are relevant to the profession. Regional expert panels and targeted surveys are conducted annually to verify and reinforce the continuous feedback from the GBIK collaborative website. The practice analysis process ultimately defines the CBOK. The CBOK contains the competencies that are generally accepted and applied by investment professionals. These competencies are used in practice in a generalist context and are expected to be demonstrated by a recently qualified CFA charterholder.

A committee consisting of practicing charterholders, in conjunction with CFA Institute staff, designs the CFA Program curriculum in order to deliver the CBOK to candidates. The examinations, also written by practicing charterholders, are designed to allow you to demonstrate your mastery of the CBOK as set forth in the CFA Program curriculum. As you structure your personal study program, you should emphasize mastery of the CBOK and the practical application of that knowledge. For more information on the practice analysis, CBOK, and development of the CFA Program curriculum, please visit www.cfainstitute.org.

ORGANIZATION OF THE CURRICULUM

The Level I CFA Program curriculum is organized into 10 topic areas. Each topic area begins with a brief statement of the material and the depth of knowledge expected.

Each topic area is then divided into one or more study sessions. These study sessions—18 sessions in the Level I curriculum—should form the basic structure of your reading and preparation.

Each study session includes a statement of its structure and objective and is further divided into specific reading assignments. An outline illustrating the organization of these 18 study sessions can be found at the front of each volume.

The reading assignments are the basis for all examination questions and are selected or developed specifically to teach the knowledge, skills, and abilities reflected in the CBOK. These readings are drawn from content commissioned by CFA Institute, textbook chapters, professional journal articles, research analyst reports, and cases. All readings include problems and solutions to help you understand and master the topic areas.

Reading-specific Learning Outcome Statements (LOS) are listed at the beginning of each reading. These LOS indicate what you should be able to accomplish after studying the reading. The LOS, the reading, and the end-of-reading questions are dependent on each other, with the reading and questions providing context for understanding the scope of the LOS.

You should use the LOS to guide and focus your study because each examination question is based on an assigned reading and one or more LOS. The readings provide context for the LOS and enable you to apply a principle or concept in a variety of scenarios. The candidate is responsible for the entirety of the required material in a study session, which includes the assigned readings as well as the end-of-reading questions and problems.

We encourage you to review the information about the LOS on our website (www.cfainstitute.org/programs/cfaprogram/courseofstudy/Pages/study_sessions.aspx), including the descriptions of LOS "command words" (www.cfainstitute.org/programs/Documents/cfa_and_cipm_los_command_words.pdf).

FEATURES OF THE CURRICULUM

Required vs. Optional Segments   You should read all of an assigned reading. In some cases, though, we have reprinted an entire chapter or article and marked certain parts of the reading as "optional." The CFA examination is based only on the required segments, and the optional segments are included only when it is determined that they might help you to better understand the required segments (by seeing the required material in its full context). When an optional segment begins, you will see an icon and a dashed vertical bar in the outside margin that will continue until the optional segment ends, accompanied by another icon. *Unless the material is specifically marked as optional, you should assume it is required.* You should rely on the required segments and the reading-specific LOS in preparing for the examination.

END OPTIONAL
SEGMENT

Problems/Solutions   *All questions and problems in the readings as well as their solutions (which are provided directly following the problems) are part of the curriculum and are required material for the exam.* When appropriate, we have included problems within and after the readings to demonstrate practical application and reinforce your understanding of the concepts presented. The questions and problems are designed to help you learn these concepts and may serve as a basis for exam questions. Many of these questions are adapted from past CFA examinations.

Glossary and Index   For your convenience, we have printed a comprehensive glossary in each volume. Throughout the curriculum, a **bolded** word in a reading denotes a term defined in the glossary. The curriculum eBook is searchable, but we also publish an index that can be found on the CFA Institute website with the Level I study sessions.

Source Material   The authorship, publisher, and copyright owners are given for each reading for your reference. We recommend that you use the CFA Institute curriculum rather than the original source materials because the curriculum may include only selected pages from outside readings, updated sections within the readings, and problems and solutions tailored to the CFA Program.

LOS Self-Check   We have inserted checkboxes next to each LOS that you can use to track your progress in mastering the concepts in each reading.

DESIGNING YOUR PERSONAL STUDY PROGRAM

Create a Schedule   An orderly, systematic approach to exam preparation is critical. You should dedicate a consistent block of time every week to reading and studying. Complete all reading assignments and the associated problems and solutions in each study session. Review the LOS both before and after you study each reading to ensure that you have mastered the applicable content and can demonstrate the knowledge, skill, or ability described by the LOS and the assigned reading. Use the LOS self-check to track your progress and highlight areas of weakness for later review.

As you prepare for your exam, we will e-mail you important exam updates, testing policies, and study tips. Be sure to read these carefully. Curriculum errata are periodically updated and posted on the study session page at www.cfainstitute.org. You can also sign up for an RSS feed to alert you to the latest errata update.

Successful candidates report an average of more than 300 hours preparing for each exam. Your preparation time will vary based on your prior education and experience. For each level of the curriculum, there are 18 study sessions. So, a good plan is to devote 15–20 hours per week for 18 weeks to studying the material. Use the final four to six weeks before the exam to review what you have learned and practice with topic and mock exams. This recommendation, however, may underestimate the hours needed for appropriate examination preparation depending on your individual circumstances, relevant experience, and academic background. You will undoubtedly adjust your study time to conform to your own strengths and weaknesses and to your educational and professional background.

You will probably spend more time on some study sessions than on others, but on average you should plan on devoting 15–20 hours per study session. You should allow ample time for both in-depth study of all topic areas and additional concentration on those topic areas for which you feel the least prepared.

An interactive study planner is available in the candidate resources area of our website to help you plan your study time. The interactive study planner recommends completion dates for each topic of the curriculum. Dates are determined based on study time available, exam topic weights, and curriculum weights. As you progress through the curriculum, the interactive study planner dynamically adjusts your study plan when you are running off schedule to help you stay on track for completion prior to the examination.

CFA Institute Topic Exams   The CFA Institute topic exams are intended to assess your mastery of individual topic areas as you progress through your studies. After each test, you will receive immediate feedback noting the correct responses and indicating the relevant assigned reading so you can identify areas of weakness for further study. The topic exams reflect the question formats and level of difficulty of the actual CFA examinations. For more information on the topic tests, please visit www.cfainstitute.org.

CFA Institute Mock Exams   Mock examinations mimic the actual CFA examinations not only in question format and level of difficulty, but also in length and topic weight. The three-hour mock exams simulate the morning and afternoon sessions of the actual CFA examination, and are intended to be taken after you complete your study of the full curriculum so you can test your understanding of the curriculum and your readiness for the exam. You will receive feedback at the end of the mock exam, noting the correct responses and indicating the relevant assigned readings so you can assess areas of weakness for further study during your review period. We recommend that you take mock exams during the final stages of your preparation for the actual CFA examination. For more information on the mock examinations, please visit www.cfainstitute.org.

Preparatory Providers   After you enroll in the CFA Program, you may receive numerous solicitations for preparatory courses and review materials. When considering a prep course, make sure the provider is in compliance with the CFA Institute Prep Provider Guidelines Program (www.cfainstitute.org/partners/examprep/Pages/cfa_prep_provider_guidelines.aspx). Just remember, there are no shortcuts to success on the CFA examinations; reading and studying the CFA curriculum is the key to success on the examination. The CFA examinations reference only the CFA Institute assigned curriculum—no preparatory course or review course materials are consulted or referenced.

SUMMARY

Every question on the CFA examination is based on the content contained in the required readings and on one or more LOS. Frequently, an examination question is based on a specific example highlighted within a reading or on a specific end-of-reading question and/or problem and its solution. To make effective use of the CFA Program curriculum, please remember these key points:

1 All pages printed in the curriculum are required reading for the examination except for occasional sections marked as optional. You may read optional pages as background, but you will not be tested on them.

2 All questions, problems, and their solutions—printed at the end of readings—are part of the curriculum and are required study material for the examination.

3 You should make appropriate use of the topic and mock examinations and other resources available at www.cfainstitute.org.

4 Use the interactive study planner to create a schedule and commit sufficient study time to cover the 18 study sessions, review the materials, and take topic and mock examinations.

5 Some of the concepts in the study sessions may be superseded by updated rulings and/or pronouncements issued after a reading was published. Candidates are expected to be familiar with the overall analytical framework contained in the assigned readings. Candidates are not responsible for changes that occur after the material was written.

FEEDBACK

At CFA Institute, we are committed to delivering a comprehensive and rigorous curriculum for the development of competent, ethically grounded investment professionals. We rely on candidate and member feedback as we work to incorporate content, design, and packaging improvements. You can be assured that we will continue to listen to your suggestions. Please send any comments or feedback to info@cfainstitute.org. Ongoing improvements in the curriculum will help you prepare for success on the upcoming examinations and for a lifetime of learning as a serious investment professional.

Equity

TOPIC LEVEL LEARNING OUTCOME

The candidate should be able to describe characteristics of equity investments, security markets, and indices. The candidate should also be able to analyze industries, companies, and equity securities and to describe and demonstrate the use of basic equity valuation models.

13

Equity

Market Organization, Market Indices, and Market Efficiency

This study session explains important characteristics of the markets in which equities, fixed-income instruments, derivatives, and alternative investments trade. The reading on market organization and structure describes market classifications, types of assets and market participants, and how assets are traded. The reading on security market indices explains how indices are constructed, managed, and used in investments. The reading on market efficiency discusses the degree to which market prices reflect information. It also explains implications of different degrees of market efficiency for security analysis and portfolio management.

READING ASSIGNMENTS

Reading 45	Market Organization and Structure by Larry Harris, CFA
Reading 46	Security Market Indices by Paul D. Kaplan, CFA, and Dorothy C. Kelly, CFA
Reading 47	Market Efficiency by W. Sean Cleary, CFA, Howard J. Atkinson, CFA, and Pamela Peterson Drake, CFA

Market Organization and Structure

by Larry Harris, CFA

LEARNING OUTCOMES

Mastery	The candidate should be able to:
☐	a. explain the main functions of the financial system;
☐	b. describe classifications of assets and markets;
☐	c. describe the major types of securities, currencies, contracts, commodities, and real assets that trade in organized markets, including their distinguishing characteristics and major subtypes;
☐	d. describe types of financial intermediaries and services that they provide;
☐	e. compare positions an investor can take in an asset;
☐	f. calculate and interpret the leverage ratio, the rate of return on a margin transaction, and the security price at which the investor would receive a margin call;
☐	g. compare execution, validity, and clearing instructions;
☐	h. compare market orders with limit orders;
☐	i. define primary and secondary markets and explain how secondary markets support primary markets;
☐	j. describe how securities, contracts, and currencies are traded in quote-driven, order-driven, and brokered markets;
☐	k. describe characteristics of a well-functioning financial system;
☐	l. describe objectives of market regulation.

1   INTRODUCTION

Financial analysts gather and process information to make investment decisions, including those related to buying and selling assets. Generally, the decisions involve trading securities, currencies, contracts, commodities, and real assets such as real estate. Consider several examples:

- Fixed income analysts evaluate issuer credit-worthiness and macroeconomic prospects to determine which bonds and notes to buy or sell to preserve capital while obtaining a fair rate of return.

- Stock analysts study corporate values to determine which stocks to buy or sell to maximize the value of their stock portfolios.

- Corporate treasurers analyze exchange rates, interest rates, and credit conditions to determine which currencies to trade and which notes to buy or sell to have funds available in a needed currency.

- Risk managers work for producers or users of commodities to calculate how many commodity futures contracts to buy or sell to manage inventory risks.

Financial analysts must understand the characteristics of the markets in which their decisions will be executed. This reading, by examining those markets from the analyst's perspective, provides that understanding.

This reading is organized as follows. Section 2 examines the functions of the financial system. Section 3 introduces assets that investors, information-motivated traders, and risk managers use to advance their financial objectives and presents ways practitioners classify these assets into markets. These assets include such financial instruments as securities, currencies, and some contracts; certain commodities; and real assets. Financial analysts must know the distinctive characteristics of these trading assets.

Section 4 is an overview of financial intermediaries (entities that facilitate the functioning of the financial system). Section 5 discusses the positions that can be obtained while trading assets. You will learn about the benefits and risks of long and short positions, how these positions can be financed, and how the financing affects their risks. Section 6 discusses how market participants order trades and how markets process those orders. These processes must be understood to achieve trading objectives while controlling transaction costs.

Section 7 focuses on describing primary markets. Section 8 describes the structures of secondary markets in securities. Sections 9 and 10 close the reading with discussions of the characteristics of a well-functioning financial system and of how regulation helps make financial markets function better. A summary reviews the reading's major ideas and points, and practice problems conclude.

2   THE FUNCTIONS OF THE FINANCIAL SYSTEM

The financial system includes markets and various financial intermediaries that help transfer financial assets, real assets, and financial risks in various forms from one entity to another, from one place to another, and from one point in time to another. These transfers take place whenever someone exchanges one asset or financial contract for another. The assets and contracts that people (people act on behalf of themselves, companies, charities, governments, etc., so the term "people" has a broad definition in this reading) trade include notes, bonds, stocks, exchange-traded funds, currencies, forward contracts, futures contracts, option contracts, swap contracts, and certain commodities. When the buyer and seller voluntarily arrange their trades, as is usually the case, the buyer and the seller both expect to be better off.

People use the financial system for six main purposes:

1   to save money for the future;

2   to borrow money for current use;

3   to raise equity capital;

4   to manage risks;

5   to exchange assets for immediate and future deliveries; and

6   to trade on information.

The main functions of the financial system are to facilitate:

1   the achievement of the purposes for which people use the financial system;

2   the discovery of the rates of return that equate aggregate savings with aggregate borrowings; and

3   the allocation of capital to the best uses.

These functions are extremely important to economic welfare. In a well-functioning financial system, transaction costs are low, analysts can value savings and investments, and scarce capital resources are used well.

Sections 2.1 through 2.3 expand on these three functions. The six subsections of Section 2.1 cover the six main purposes for which people use the financial system and how the financial system facilitates the achievement of those purposes. Sections 2.2 and 2.3 discuss determining rates of return and capital allocation efficiency, respectively.

2.1 Helping People Achieve Their Purposes in Using the Financial System

People often arrange transactions to achieve more than one purpose when using the financial system. For example, an investor who buys the stock of an oil producer may do so to move her wealth from the present to the future, to hedge the risk that she will have to pay more for energy in the future, and to exploit insightful research that she conducted that suggests the company's stock is undervalued in the marketplace. If the investment proves to be successful, she will have saved money for the future, managed her energy risk exposure, and obtained a return on her research.

The separate discussions of each of the six main uses of the financial system by people will help you better identify the reasons why people trade. Your ability to identify the various uses of the financial system will help you avoid confusion that often leads to poor financial decisions. The financial intermediaries that are mentioned in these discussions are explained further in Section 4.

2.1.1 Saving

People often have money that they choose not to spend now and that they want available in the future. For example, workers who save for their retirements need to move some of their current earnings into the future. When they retire, they will use their savings to replace the wages that they will no longer be earning. Similarly, companies save money from their sales revenue so that they can pay vendors when their bills come due, repay debt, or acquire assets (for example, other companies or machinery) in the future.

To move money from the present to the future, savers buy notes, certificates of deposit, bonds, stocks, mutual funds, or real assets such as real estate. These alternatives generally provide a better expected rate of return than simply storing money.

Savers then sell these assets in the future to fund their future expenditures. When savers commit money to earn a financial return, they commonly are called investors. They invest when they purchase assets, and they divest when they sell them.

Investors require a fair rate of return while their money is invested. The required fair rate of return compensates them for the use of their money and for the risk that they may lose money if the investment fails or if inflation reduces the real value of their investments.

The financial system facilitates savings when institutions create investment vehicles, such as bank deposits, notes, stocks, and mutual funds, that investors can acquire and sell without paying substantial transaction costs. When these instruments are fairly priced and easy to trade, investors will use them to save more.

2.1.2 *Borrowing*

People, companies, and governments often want to spend money now that they do not have. They can obtain money to fund projects that they wish to undertake now by borrowing it. Companies can also obtain funds by selling ownership or equity interests (covered in Section 2.1.3). Banks and other investors provide those requiring funds with money because they expect to be repaid with interest or because they expect to be compensated with future disbursements, such as dividends and capital gains, as the ownership interest appreciates in value.

People may borrow to pay for such items as vacations, homes, cars, or education. They generally borrow through mortgages and personal loans, or by using credit cards. People typically repay these loans with money they earn later.

Companies often require money to fund current operations or to engage in new capital projects. They may borrow the needed funds in a variety of ways, such as arranging a loan or a line of credit with a bank, or selling fixed income securities to investors. Companies typically repay their borrowing with income generated in the future. In addition to borrowing, companies may raise funds by selling ownership interests.

Governments may borrow money to pay salaries and other expenses, to fund projects, to provide welfare benefits to their citizens and residents, and to subsidize various activities. Governments borrow by selling bills, notes, or bonds. Governments repay their debt using future revenues from taxes and in some instances from the projects funded by these debts.

Borrowers can borrow from lenders only if the lenders believe that they will be repaid. If the lenders believe, however, that repayment in full with interest may not occur, they will demand higher rates of interest to cover their expected losses and to compensate them for the discomfit they experience wondering whether they will lose their money. To lower the costs of borrowing, borrowers often pledge assets as collateral for their loans. The assets pledged as collateral often include those that will be purchased by the proceeds of the loan. If the borrowers do not repay their loans, the lenders can sell the collateral and use the proceeds to settle the loans.

Lenders often will not loan to borrowers who intend to invest in risky projects, especially if the borrowers cannot pledge other collateral. Investors may still be willing to supply capital for these risky projects if they believe that the projects will likely produce valuable future cash flows. Rather than lending money, however, they will contribute capital in exchange for equity in the projects.

The financial system facilitates borrowing. Lenders aggregate from savers the funds that borrowers require. Borrowers must convince lenders that they can repay their loans, and that, in the event they cannot, lenders can recover most of the funds lent. Credit bureaus, credit rating agencies, and governments promote borrowing; credit bureaus and credit rating agencies do so by collecting and disseminating information that lenders need to analyze credit prospects and governments do so by establishing bankruptcy codes and courts that define and enforce the rights of borrowers and lenders. When the transaction costs of loans (i.e., the costs of arranging, monitoring, and collecting them) are low, borrowers can borrow more to fund current expenditures with credible promises to return the money in the future.

2.1.3 *Raising Equity Capital*

Companies often raise money for projects by selling (issuing) ownership interests (e.g., corporate common stock or partnership interests). Although these equity instruments legally represent ownership in companies rather than loans to the companies, selling equity to raise capital is simply another mechanism for moving money from the future to the present. When shareholders or partners contribute capital to a company, the company obtains money in the present in exchange for equity instruments that will be entitled to distributions in the future. Although the repayment of the money is not scheduled as it would be for loans, equity instruments also represent potential claims on money in the future.

The financial system facilitates raising equity capital. Investment banks help companies issue equities, analysts value the securities that companies sell, and regulatory reporting requirements and accounting standards attempt to ensure the production of meaningful financial disclosures. The financial system helps promote capital formation by producing the financial information needed to determine fair prices for equity. Liquid markets help companies raise capital. In these markets, shareholders can easily divest their equities as desired. When investors can easily value and trade equities, they are more willing to fund reasonable projects that companies wish to undertake.

EXAMPLE 1

Financing Capital Projects

As a chief financial officer (CFO) of a large industrial firm, you need to raise cash within a few months to pay for a project to expand existing and acquire new manufacturing facilities. What are the primary options available to you?

Solution:

Your primary options are to borrow the funds or to raise the funds by selling ownership interests. If the company borrows the funds, you may have the company pledge some or all of the project as collateral to reduce the cost of borrowing.

2.1.4 *Managing Risks*

Many people, companies, and governments face financial risks that concern them. These risks include default risk and the risk of changes in interest rates, exchange rates, raw material prices, and sale prices, among many other risks. These risks are often managed by trading contracts that serve as hedges for the risks.

For example, a farmer and a food processor both face risks related to the price of grain. The farmer fears that prices will be lower than expected when his grain is ready for sale whereas the food processor fears that prices will be higher than expected when she has to buy grain in the future. They both can eliminate their exposures to these risks if they enter into a binding forward contract for the farmer to sell a specified quantity of grain to the food processor at a future date at a mutually agreed upon price. By entering into a forward contract that sets the future trade price, they both eliminate their exposure to changing grain prices.

In general, hedgers trade to offset or insure against risks that concern them. In addition to forward contracts, they may use futures contracts, option contracts, or insurance contracts to transfer risk to other entities more willing to bear the risks (these contracts will be covered in Section 3.4). Often the hedger and the other entity face exactly the opposite risks, so the transfer makes both more secure, as in the grain example.

The financial system facilitates risk management when liquid markets exist in which risk managers can trade instruments that are correlated (or inversely correlated) with the risks that concern them without incurring substantial transaction costs. Investment banks, exchanges, and insurance companies devote substantial resources to designing such contracts and to ensuring that they will trade in liquid markets. When such markets exist, people are better able to manage the risks that they face and often are more willing to undertake risky activities that they expect will be profitable.

2.1.5 Exchanging Assets for Immediate Delivery (Spot Market Trading)

People and companies often trade one asset for another that they rate more highly or, equivalently, that is more useful to them. They may trade one currency for another currency, or money for a needed commodity or right. Following are some examples that illustrate these trades:

■   Volkswagen pays its German workers in euros, but the company receives dollars when it sells cars in the United States. To convert money from dollars to euros, Volkswagen trades in the foreign exchange markets.

■   A Mexican investor who is worried about the prospects for peso inflation or a potential devaluation of the peso may buy gold in the spot gold market. (This transaction may hedge against the risk of devaluation of the peso because the value of gold may increase with inflation.)

■   A plastic producer must buy carbon credits to emit carbon dioxide when burning fuel to comply with environmental regulations. The carbon credit is a legal right that the producer must have to engage in activities that emit carbon dioxide.

In each of these cases, the trades are considered spot market trades because the instruments trade for immediate delivery. The financial system facilitates these exchanges when liquid spot markets exist in which people can arrange and settle trades without substantial transaction costs.

2.1.6 Information-Motivated Trading

Information-motivated traders trade to profit from information that they believe allows them to predict future prices. Like all other traders, they hope to buy at low prices and sell at higher prices. Unlike pure investors, however, they expect to earn a return on their information in addition to the normal return expected for bearing risk through time.

Active investment managers are information-motivated traders who collect and analyze information to identify securities, contracts, and other assets that their analyses indicate are under- or overvalued. They then buy those that they consider undervalued and sell those that they consider overvalued. If successful, they obtain a greater return than the unconditional return that would be expected for bearing the risk in their positions. The return that they expect to obtain is a conditional return earned on the basis of the information in their analyses. Practitioners often call this process active portfolio management.

Note that the distinction between pure investors and information-motivated traders depends on their motives for trading and not on the risks that they take or their expected holding periods. Investors trade to move wealth from the present to the future whereas information-motivated traders trade to profit from superior information about future values. When trading to move wealth forward, the time period may be short or long. For example, a bank treasurer may only need to move money overnight and might use money market instruments trading in an interbank funds market to accomplish that. A pension fund, however, may need to move money 30 years forward and might do that by using shares trading in a stock market. Both are investors although their expected holding periods and the risks in the instruments that they trade are vastly different.

In contrast, information-motivated traders trade because their information-based analyses suggest to them that prices of various instruments will increase or decrease in the future at a rate faster than others without their information or analytical models would expect. After establishing their positions, they hope that prices will change quickly in their favor so that they can close their positions, realize their profits, and redeploy their capital. These price changes may occur almost instantaneously, or they may take years to occur if information about the mispricing is difficult to obtain or understand.

The two categories of traders are not mutually exclusive. Investors also are often information-motivated traders. Many investors who want to move wealth forward through time collect and analyze information to select securities that will allow them to obtain conditional returns that are greater than the unconditional returns expected for securities in their assets classes. If they have rational reasons to expect that their efforts will indeed produce superior returns, they are information-motivated traders. If they consistently fail to produce such returns, their efforts will be futile, and they would have been better off simply buying and holding well-diversified portfolios.

EXAMPLE 2

Investing versus Information-Motivated Trading

The head of a large labor union with a pension fund asks you, a pension consultant, to distinguish between investing and information-motivated trading. You are expected to provide an explanation that addresses the financial problems that she faces. How would you respond?

Solution:

The object of investing for the pension fund is to move the union's pension assets from the present to the future when they will be needed to pay the union's retired pensioners. The pension fund managers will typically do this by buying stocks, bonds, and perhaps other assets. The pension fund managers expect to receive a fair rate of return on the pension fund's assets without paying excessive transaction costs and management fees. The return should compensate the fund for the risks that it bears and for the time that other people are using the fund's money.

The object of information-motivated trading is to earn a return in excess of the fair rate of return. Information-motivated traders analyze information that they collect with the hope that their analyses will allow them to predict better than others where prices will be in the future. They then buy assets that they think will produce excess returns and sell those that they think will underperform. Active investment managers are information-motivated traders.

The characteristic that most distinguishes investors from information-motivated traders is the return that they expect. Although both types of traders hope to obtain extraordinary returns, investors rationally expect to receive only fair returns during the periods of their investments. In contrast, information-motivated traders expect to make returns in excess of required fair rates of return. Of course, not all investing or information-motivated trading is successful (in other words, the actual returns may not equal or exceed the expected returns).

The financial system facilitates information-motivated trading when liquid markets allow active managers to trade without significant transaction costs. Accounting standards and reporting requirements that produce meaningful financial disclosures reduce the costs of being well informed, but do not necessarily help informed traders profit because they often compete with each other. The most profitable well-informed traders are often those that have the most unique insights into future values.

2.1.7 *Summary*

People use the financial system for many purposes, the most important of which are saving, borrowing, raising equity capital, managing risk, exchanging assets in spot markets, and information-motivated trading. The financial system best facilitates these uses when people can trade instruments that interest them in liquid markets, when institutions provide financial services at low cost, when information about assets and about credit risks is readily available, and when regulation helps ensure that everyone faithfully honors their contracts.

2.2 Determining Rates of Return

Saving, borrowing, and selling equity are all means of moving money through time. Savers move money from the present to the future whereas borrowers and equity issuers move money from the future to the present.

Because time machines do not exist, money can travel forward in time only if an equal amount of money is travelling in the other direction. This equality always occurs because borrowers and equity sellers create the securities in which savers invest. For example, the bond sold by a company that needs to move money from the future to the present is the same bond bought by a saver who needs to move money from the present to the future.

The aggregate amount of money that savers will move from the present to the future is related to the expected rate of return on their investments. If the expected return is high, they will forgo current consumption and move more money to the future. Similarly, the aggregate amount of money that borrowers and equity sellers will move from the future to the present depends on the costs of borrowing funds or of giving up ownership. These costs can be expressed as the rate of return that borrowers and equity sellers are expected to deliver in exchange for obtaining current funds. It is the same rate that savers expect to receive when delivering current funds. If this rate is low, borrowers and equity sellers will want to move more money to the present from the future. In other words, they will want to raise more funds.

Because the total money saved must equal the total money borrowed and received in exchange for equity, the expected rate of return depends on the aggregate supply of funds through savings and the aggregate demand for funds. If the rate is too high, savers will want to move more money to the future than borrowers and equity issuers will want to move to the present. The expected rate will have to be lower to discourage the savers and to encourage the borrowers and equity issuers. Conversely, if the rate is too low, savers will want to move less money forward than borrowers and equity issuers will want to move to the present. The expected rate will have to be higher to encourage the savers and to discourage the borrowers and equity issuers. Between rates too high and too low, an expected rate of return exists, in theory, in which the aggregate supply of funds for investing (supply of funds saved) and the aggregate demand for funds through borrowing and equity issuing are equal.

Economists call this rate the equilibrium interest rate. It is the price for moving money through time. Determining this rate is one of the most important functions of the financial system. The equilibrium interest rate is the only interest rate that would exist if all securities were equally risky, had equal terms, and were equally liquid. In fact, the required rates of return for securities vary by their risk characteristics, terms, and liquidity. For a given issuer, investors generally require higher rates of return for equity than for debt, for long-term securities than for short-term securities, and for illiquid securities than for liquid ones. Financial analysts recognize that all required rates of return depend on a common equilibrium interest rate plus adjustments for risk.

EXAMPLE 3

Interest Rates

For a presentation to private wealth clients by your firm's chief economist, you are asked to prepare the audience by explaining the most fundamental facts concerning the role of interest rates in the economy. You agree. What main points should you try to convey?

Solution:

Savers have money now that they will want to use in the future. Borrowers want to use money now that they do not have, but they expect that they will have money in the future. Borrowers are loaned money by savers and promise to repay it in the future.

The interest rate is the return that lenders, the savers, expect to receive from borrowers for allowing borrowers to use the savers' money. The interest rate is the price of using money.

Interest rates depend on the total amount of money that people want to borrow and the total amount of money that people are willing to lend. Interest rates are high when, in aggregate, people value having money now substantially more than they value having money in the future. In contrast, if many people with money want to use it in the future and few people presently need more money than they have, interest rates will be low.

2.3 Capital Allocation Efficiency

Primary capital markets (primary markets) are the markets in which companies and governments raise capital (funds). Companies may raise funds by borrowing money or by issuing equity. Governments may raise funds by borrowing money.

Economies are said to be allocationally efficient when their financial systems allocate capital (funds) to those uses that are most productive. Although companies may be interested in getting funding for many potential projects, not all projects are worth funding. One of the most important functions of the financial system is to ensure that only the best projects obtain scarce capital funds; the funds available from savers should be allocated to the most productive uses.

In market-based economies, savers determine, directly or indirectly, which projects obtain capital. Savers determine capital allocations directly by choosing which securities they will invest in. Savers determine capital allocations indirectly by giving funds to financial intermediaries that then invest the funds. Because investors fear the loss of their money, they will lend at lower interest rates to borrowers with the best credit prospects or the best collateral, and they will lend at higher rates to other borrowers with less secure prospects. Similarly, they will buy only those equities that they believe have the best prospects relative to their prices and risks.

To avoid losses, investors carefully study the prospects of the various investment opportunities available to them. The decisions that they make tend to be well informed, which helps ensure that capital is allocated efficiently. The fear of losses by investors and by those raising funds to invest in projects ensures that only the best projects tend to be funded. The process works best when investors are well informed about the prospects of the various projects.

In general, investors will fund an equity project if they expect that the value of the project is greater than its cost, and they will not fund projects otherwise. If the investor expectations are accurate, only projects that should be undertaken will be funded and all such projects will be funded. Accurate market information thus leads to efficient capital allocation.

EXAMPLE 4

Primary Market Capital Allocation

How can poor information about the value of a project result in poor capital allocation decisions?

Solution:

Projects should be undertaken only if their value is greater than their cost. If investors have poor information and overestimate the value of a project in which its true value is less than its cost, a wealth-diminishing project may be undertaken. Alternatively, if investors have poor information and underestimate the value of a project in which its true value is greater than its cost, a wealth-enhancing project may not be undertaken.

3　ASSETS AND CONTRACTS

People, companies, and governments use many different assets and contracts to further their financial goals and to manage their risks. The most common assets include financial assets (such as bank deposits, certificates of deposit, loans, mortgages, corporate and government bonds and notes, common and preferred stocks, real estate investment trusts, master limited partnership interests, pooled investment products, and exchange-traded funds), currencies, certain commodities (such as gold and oil), and real assets (such as real estate). The most common contracts are option, futures, forward, swap, and insurance contracts. People, companies, and governments use these assets and contracts to raise funds, to invest, to profit from information-motivated trading, to hedge risks, and/or to transfer money from one form to another.

3.1 Classifications of Assets and Markets

Practitioners often classify assets and the markets in which they trade by various common characteristics to facilitate communications with their clients, with each other, and with regulators.

The most actively traded assets are securities, currencies, contracts, and commodities. In addition, real assets are traded. Securities generally include debt instruments, equities, and shares in pooled investment vehicles. **Currencies** are monies issued by national monetary authorities. Contracts are agreements to exchange securities, currencies, commodities or other contracts in the future. Commodities include precious metals, energy products, industrial metals, and agricultural products. Real assets are tangible properties such as real estate, airplanes, or machinery. Securities, currencies, and contracts are classified as financial assets whereas commodities and real assets are classified as physical assets.

Securities are further classified as debt or equity. Debt instruments (also called fixed-income instruments) are promises to repay borrowed money. Equities represent ownership in companies. Pooled investment vehicle shares represent ownership of an undivided interest in an investment portfolio. The portfolio may include securities, currencies, contracts, commodities, or real assets. Pooled investment vehicles, such as exchange-traded funds, which exclusively own shares in other companies, generally are also considered equities.

Securities are also classified by whether they are public or private securities. Public securities are those registered to trade in public markets, such as on exchanges or through dealers. In most jurisdictions, issuers must meet stringent minimum regulatory standards, including reporting and corporate governance standards, to issue publicly traded securities.

Private securities are all other securities. Often, only specially qualified investors can purchase private equities and private debt instruments. Investors may purchase them directly from the issuer or indirectly through an investment vehicle specifically formed to hold such securities. Issuers often issue private securities when they find public reporting standards too burdensome or when they do not want to conform to the regulatory standards associated with public equity. Venture capital is private equity that investors supply to companies when or shortly after they are founded. Private securities generally are illiquid. In contrast, many public securities trade in liquid markets in which sellers can easily find buyers for their securities.

Contracts are derivative contracts if their values depend on the prices of other underlying assets. Derivative contracts may be classified as physical or financial depending on whether the underlying instruments are physical products or financial securities. Equity derivatives are contracts whose values depend on equities or indices of equities. Fixed-income derivatives are contracts whose values depend on debt securities or indices of debt securities.

Practitioners classify markets by whether the markets trade instruments for immediate delivery or for future delivery. Markets that trade contracts that call for delivery in the future are forward or futures markets. Those that trade for immediate delivery are called **spot markets** to distinguish them from forward markets that trade contracts on the same underlying instruments. Options markets trade contracts that deliver in the future, but delivery takes place only if the holders of the options choose to exercise them.

When issuers sell securities to investors, practitioners say that they trade in the **primary market**. When investors sell those securities to others, they trade in the **secondary market**. In the primary market, funds flow to the issuer of the security from the purchaser. In the secondary market, funds flow between traders.

Practitioners classify financial markets as money markets or capital markets. **Money markets** trade debt instruments maturing in one year or less. The most common such instruments are repurchase agreements (defined in Section 3.2.1), negotiable certificates of deposit, government bills, and commercial paper. In contrast, **capital markets** trade instruments of longer duration, such as bonds and equities, whose values depend on the credit-worthiness of the issuers and on payments of interest or dividends that will be made in the future and may be uncertain. Corporations generally finance their operations in the capital markets, but some also finance a portion of their operations by issuing short-term securities, such as commercial paper.

Finally, practitioners distinguish between **traditional investment markets** and **alternative investment markets**. Traditional investments include all publicly traded debts and equities and shares in pooled investment vehicles that hold publicly traded debts and/or equities. Alternative investments include **hedge funds**, private equities (including venture capital), commodities, real estate securities and real estate properties, securitized debts, operating leases, machinery, collectibles, and precious gems. Because these investments are often hard to trade and hard to value, they may sometimes trade at substantial deviations from their intrinsic values. The discounts compensate investors for the research that they must do to value these assets and for their inability to easily sell the assets if they need to liquidate a portion of their portfolios.

The remainder of this section describes the most common assets and contracts that people, companies, and governments trade.

EXAMPLE 5

Asset and Market Classification

The investment policy of a mutual fund only permits the fund to invest in public equities traded in secondary markets. Would the fund be able to purchase:

1 Common stock of a company that trades on a large stock exchange?

2 Common stock of a public company that trades only through dealers?

3 A government bond?

4 A single stock futures contract?

5 Common stock sold for the first time by a properly registered public company?

6 Shares in a privately held bank with €10 billion of capital?

Solution to 1:

Yes. Common stock is equity. Those common stocks that trade on large exchanges invariably are public equities that trade in secondary markets.

Solution to 2:

Yes. Dealer markets are secondary markets and the security is a public equity.

Solution to 3:

No. Although government bonds are public securities, they are not equities. They are debt securities.

Solution to 4:

No. Although the underlying instruments for single stock futures are invariably public equities, single stock futures are derivative contracts, not equities.

Solution to 5:

No. The fund would not be able to buy these shares because a purchase from the issuer would be in the primary market. The fund would have to wait until it could buy the shares from someone other than the issuer.

Solution to 6:

No. These shares are private equities, not public equities. The public prominence of the company does not make its securities public securities unless they have been properly registered as public securities.

3.2 Securities

People, companies, and governments sell securities to raise money. Securities include bonds, notes, commercial paper, mortgages, common stocks, preferred stocks, warrants, mutual fund shares, unit trusts, and depository receipts. These can be classified broadly as fixed-income instruments, equities, and shares in pooled investment vehicles. Note that the legal definition of a security varies by country and may or may not coincide with the usage here. Securities that are sold to the public or that can be resold to the public are called issues. Companies and governments are the most common issuers.

3.2.1 *Fixed Income*

Fixed-income instruments contractually include predetermined payment schedules that usually include interest and principal payments. Fixed-income instruments generally are promises to repay borrowed money but may include other instruments with payment schedules, such as settlements of legal cases or prizes from lotteries. The payment amounts may be pre-specified or they may vary according to a fixed formula that depends on the future values of an interest rate or a commodity price. Bonds, notes, bills, certificates of deposit, commercial paper, repurchase agreements, loan agreements, and mortgages are examples of promises to repay money in the future. People, companies, and governments create fixed-income instruments when they borrow money.

Corporations and governments issue bonds and notes. Fixed-income securities with shorter maturities are called "notes," those with longer maturities are called "bonds." The cutoff is usually at 10 years. In practice, however, the terms are generally used interchangeably. Both become short-term instruments when the remaining time until maturity is short, usually taken to be one year or less.

Some corporations issue convertible bonds, which are typically convertible into stock, usually at the option of the holder after some period. If stock prices are high so that conversion is likely, convertibles are valued like stock. Conversely, if stock prices are low so that conversion is unlikely, convertibles are valued like bonds.

Bills, certificates of deposit, and commercial paper are respectively issued by governments, banks, and corporations. They usually mature within a year of being issued; certificates of deposit sometimes have longer initial maturities.

Repurchase agreements (repos) are short-term lending instruments. The term can be as short as overnight. A borrower seeking funds will sell an instrument—typically a high quality bond—to a lender with an agreement to repurchase it later at a slightly higher price based on an agreed upon interest rate.

Practitioners distinguish between short-term, intermediate-term, and long-term fixed-income securities. No general consensus exists about the definition of short-term, intermediate-term, and long-term. Instruments that mature in less than one to two years are considered short-term instruments whereas those that mature in more than five to ten years are considered long-term instruments. In the middle are intermediate-term instruments.

Instruments trading in money markets are called money market instruments. Such instruments are traded debt instruments maturing in one year or less. Money market funds and corporations seeking a return on their short-term cash balances typically hold money market instruments.

3.2.2 *Equities*

Equities represent ownership rights in companies. These include common and pre-ferred shares. Common shareholders own residual rights to the assets of the company. They have the right to receive any dividends declared by the boards of directors, and in the event of liquidation, any assets remaining after all other claims are paid. Acting through the boards of directors that they elect, common shareholders usually can select the managers who run the corporations.

Preferred shares are equities that have preferred rights (relative to common shares) to the cash flows and assets of the company. Preferred shareholders generally have the right to receive a specific dividend on a regular basis. If the preferred share is a cumulative preferred equity, the company must pay the preferred shareholders any previously omitted dividends before it can pay dividends to the common shareholders.

Preferred shareholders also have higher claims to assets relative to common share-holders in the event of corporate liquidation. For valuation purposes, financial analysts generally treat preferred stocks as fixed-income securities when the issuers will clearly be able to pay their promised dividends in the foreseeable future.

Warrants are securities issued by a corporation that allow the warrant holders to buy a security issued by that corporation, if they so desire, usually at any time before the warrants expire or, if not, upon expiration. The security that warrant holders can buy usually is the issuer's common stock, in which case the warrants are considered equities because the warrant holders can obtain equity in the company by exercising their warrants. The warrant **exercise price** is the price that the warrant holder must pay to buy the security.

EXAMPLE 6

Securities

What factors distinguish fixed-income securities from equities?

Solution:

Fixed-income securities generate income on a regular schedule. They derive their value from the promise to pay a scheduled cash flow. The most common fixed-income securities are promises made by people, companies, and governments to repay loans.

Equities represent residual ownership in companies after all other claims—including any fixed-income liabilities of the company—have been satisfied. For corporations, the claims of preferred equities typically have priority over the claims of common equities. Common equities have the residual ownership in corporations.

3.2.3 Pooled Investments

Pooled investment vehicles are mutual funds, trusts, depositories, and hedge funds, that issue securities that represent shared ownership in the assets that these entities hold. The securities created by mutual funds, trusts, depositories, and hedge fund are respectively called *shares*, *units*, *depository receipts*, and *limited partnership interests* but practitioners often use these terms interchangeably. People invest in pooled investment vehicles to benefit from the investment management services of their managers and from diversification opportunities that are not readily available to them on an individual basis.

Mutual funds are investment vehicles that pool money from many investors for investment in a portfolio of securities. They are often legally organized as investment trusts or as corporate investment companies. Pooled investment vehicles may be open-ended or closed-ended. Open-ended funds issue new shares and redeem existing shares on demand, usually on a daily basis. The price at which a fund redeems and sells the fund's shares is based on the net asset value of the fund's portfolio, which is the difference between the fund's assets and liabilities, expressed on a per share basis. Investors generally buy and sell open-ended mutual funds by trading with the mutual fund.

In contrast, closed-end funds issue shares in primary market offerings that the fund or its investment bankers arrange. Once issued, investors cannot sell their shares of the fund back to the fund by demanding redemption. Instead, investors in closed-end funds must sell their shares to other investors in the secondary market. The secondary market prices of closed-end funds may differ—sometimes quite significantly—from their net asset values. Closed-end funds generally trade at a discount to their net asset values. The discount reflects the expenses of running the fund and sometimes investor concerns about the quality of the management. Closed-end funds may also trade at a discount or a premium to net asset value when investors believe that the portfolio securities are overvalued or undervalued. Many financial analysts thus believe that discounts and premiums on closed-end funds measure market sentiment.

Exchange-traded funds (ETFs) and exchange-traded notes (ETNs) are open-ended funds that investors can trade among themselves in secondary markets. The prices at which ETFs trade rarely differ much from net asset values because a class of investors, known as authorized participants (APs), has the option of trading directly with the ETF. If the market price of an equity ETF is sufficiently below its net asset value, APs will buy shares in the secondary market at market price and redeem shares at net asset value with the fund. Conversely, if the price of an ETF is sufficiently above its net asset value, APs will buy shares from the fund at net asset value and sell shares in the secondary market at market price. As a result, the market price and net asset values of ETFs tend to converge.

Many ETFs permit only in-kind deposits and redemptions. Buyers who buy directly from such a fund pay for their shares with a portfolio of securities rather than with cash. Similarly, sellers receive a portfolio of securities. The transaction portfolio generally is very similar—often essentially identical—to the portfolio held by the fund. Practitioners sometimes call such funds "depositories" because they issue depository receipts for the portfolios that traders deposit with them. The traders then trade the receipts in the secondary market. Some warehouses holding industrial materials and precious metals also issue tradable warehouse receipts.

Asset-backed securities are securities whose values and income payments are derived from a pool of assets, such as mortgage bonds, credit card debt, or car loans. These securities typically pass interest and principal payments received from the pool of assets through to their holders on a monthly basis. These payments may depend on formulas that give some classes of securities—called tranches—backed by the pool more value than other classes.

Hedge funds are investment funds that generally organize as limited partnerships. The hedge fund managers are the general partners. The limited partners are qualified investors who are wealthy enough and well informed enough to tolerate and accept substantial losses, should they occur. The regulatory requirements to participate in a hedge fund and the regulatory restrictions on hedge funds vary by jurisdiction. Most hedge funds follow only one investment strategy, but no single investment strategy characterizes hedge funds as a group. Hedge funds exist that follow almost every imaginable strategy ranging from long–short arbitrage in the stock markets to direct investments in exotic alternative assets.

The primary distinguishing characteristic of hedge funds is their management compensation scheme. Almost all funds pay their managers with an annual fee that is proportional to their assets and with an additional performance fee that depends on the wealth that the funds generate for their shareholders. A secondary distinguishing characteristic of many hedge funds is the use of leverage to increase risk exposure and to hopefully increase returns.

3.3 Currencies

Currencies are monies issued by national monetary authorities. Approximately 175 currencies are currently in use throughout the world. Some of these currencies are regarded as reserve currencies. Reserve currencies are currencies that national central banks and other monetary authorities hold in significant quantities. The primary reserve currencies are the US dollar and the euro. Secondary reserve currencies include the British pound, the Japanese yen, and the Swiss franc.

Currencies trade in foreign exchange markets. In spot currency transactions, one currency is immediately or almost immediately exchanged for another. The rate of exchange is called the spot exchange rate. Traders typically negotiate institutional trades in multiples of large quantities, such as US$1 million or ¥100 million. Institutional trades generally settle in two business days.

Retail currency trades most commonly take place through commercial banks when their customers exchange currencies at a location of the bank, use ATM machines when travelling to withdraw a different currency than the currency in which their bank accounts are denominated, or use credit cards to buy items priced in different currencies. Retail currency trades also take place at airport kiosks, at store front currency exchanges, or on the street.

3.4 Contracts

A contract is an agreement among traders to do something in the future. Contracts include forward, futures, swap, option, and insurance contracts. The values of most contracts depend on the value of an **underlying** asset. The underlying asset may be a commodity, a security, an index representing the values of other instruments, a currency pair or basket, or other contracts.

Contracts provide for some physical or cash settlement in the future. In a physically settled contract, settlement occurs when the parties to the contract physically exchange some item, such as tomatoes, pork bellies, or gold bars. Physical settlement also includes the delivery of such financial instruments as bonds, equities, or futures contracts even though the delivery is electronic. In contrast, cash settled contracts settle through cash payments. The amount of the payment depends on formulas specified in the contracts.

Financial analysts classify contracts by whether they are physical or financial based on the nature of the underlying asset. If the underlying asset is a physical product, the contract is a physical; otherwise, the contract is a financial. Examples of assets classified as physical include contracts for the delivery of petroleum, lumber, and gold. Examples of assets classified as financial include option contracts, and contracts on interest rates, stock indices, currencies, and credit default swaps.

Contracts that call for immediate delivery are called spot contracts, and they trade in spot markets. Immediate delivery generally is three days or less, but depends on each market. All other contracts involve what practitioners call futurity. They derive their values from events that will take place in the future.

EXAMPLE 7

Contracts for Difference

Contracts for difference (CFD) allow people to speculate on price changes for an underlying asset, such as a common stock or an index. Dealers generally sell CFDs to their clients. When the clients sell the CFDs back to their dealer, they receive any appreciation in the underlying asset's price between the time of purchase and sale (open and close) of the contract. If the underlying asset's price drops over this interval, the client pays the dealer the difference.

1　Are contracts for difference derivative contracts?

2　Are contracts for difference based on copper prices cash settled or physically settled?

Solution to 1:

Contracts for difference are derivative contracts because their values are derived from changes in the prices of the underlying asset on which they are based.

Solution to 2:

All contracts for difference are cash settled contracts regardless of the underlying asset on which they are based because they settle in cash and not in the underlying asset.

3.4.1 *Forward Contracts*

A **forward contract** is an agreement to trade the underlying asset in the future at a price agreed upon today. For example, a contract for the sale of wheat after the harvest is a forward contract. People often use forward contracts to reduce risk. Before planting wheat, farmers like to know the price at which they will sell their crop. Similarly, before committing to sell flour to bakers in the future, millers like to know the prices that they will pay for wheat. The farmer and the miller both reduce their operating risks by agreeing to trade wheat forward.

Practitioners call such traders hedgers because they use their contractual commitments to hedge their risks. If the price of wheat falls, the wheat farmer's crop will drop in value on the spot market but he has a contract to sell wheat in the future at a higher fixed price. The forward contract has become more valuable to the farmer. Conversely, if the price of wheat rises, the miller's future obligation to sell flour will become more burdensome because of the high price he would have to pay for wheat on the spot market, but the miller has a contract to buy wheat at a lower fixed price. The forward contract has become more valuable to the miller. In both cases, fluctuations in the spot price are hedged by the forward contract. The forward contract offsets the operating risks that the hedgers face.

Consider a simple example of hedging. A tomato farmer in southern Ontario, Canada, grows tomatoes for processing into tomato sauce. The farmer expects to harvest 250,000 bushels and that the price at harvest will be $1.03. That price, however, could fluctuate significantly before the harvest. If the price of tomatoes drops to $0.75, the farmer would lose $0.28 per bushel ($1.03 – $0.75) relative to his expectations, or a total of $70,000. Now, suppose that the farmer can sell tomatoes forward to Heinz at $1.01 for delivery at the harvest. If the farmer sells 250,000 bushels forward, and the price of tomatoes drops to $0.75, the farmer would still be able to sell his tomatoes for $1.01, and thus would not suffer from the drop in price of tomatoes.

EXAMPLE 8

Hedging Gold Production

An Indonesian gold producer invests in a mine expansion project on the expectation that gold prices will remain at or above 35,000 rupiah per gram when the new project starts producing ore.

1 What risks does the gold producer face with respect to the price of gold?

2 How might the gold producer hedge its gold price risk?

Solution to 1:

The gold producer faces the risk that the price of gold could fall below 35,000 rupiah before it can sell its new production. If so, the investment in the expansion project will be less profitable than expected, and may even generate losses for the mine.

> **Solution to 2:**
>
> The gold producer could hedge the gold price risk by selling gold forward, hopefully at a price near 35,000 rupiah. Even if the price of gold falls, the gold producer would get paid the contract price.

Forward contracts are very common, but two problems limit their usefulness for many market participants. The first problem is counterparty risk. **Counterparty risk** is the risk that the other party to a contract will fail to honor the terms of the contract. Concerns about counterparty risk ensure that generally only parties who have long-standing relationships with each other execute forward contracts. Trustworthiness is critical when prices are volatile because, after a large price change, one side or the other may prefer not to settle the contract.

The second problem is liquidity. Trading out of a forward contract is very difficult because it can only be done with the consent of the other party. The liquidity problem ensures that forward contracts tend to be executed only among participants for whom delivery is economically efficient and quite certain at the time of contracting so that both parties will want to arrange for delivery.

The counterparty risk problem and the liquidity problem often make it difficult for market participants to obtain the hedging benefits associated with forward contracting. Fortunately, futures contracts have been developed to mitigate these problems.

3.4.2 *Futures Contracts*

A **futures contract** is a standardized forward contract for which a clearinghouse guarantees the performance of all traders. The buyer of a futures contract is the side that will take physical delivery or its cash equivalent. The seller of a futures contract is the side that is liable for the delivery or its cash equivalent. A **clearinghouse** is an organization that ensures that no trader is harmed if another trader fails to honor the contract. In effect, the clearinghouse acts as the buyer for every seller and as the seller for every buyer. Buyers and sellers, therefore, can trade futures without worrying whether their counterparties are creditworthy. Because futures contracts are standardized, a buyer can eliminate his obligation to buy by selling his contract to anyone. A seller similarly can eliminate her obligation to deliver by buying a contact from anyone. In either case, the clearinghouse will release the trader from all future obligations if his or her long and short positions exactly offset each other.

To protect against defaults, futures clearinghouses require that all participants post with the clearinghouse an amount of money known as **initial margin** when they enter a contract. The clearinghouse then settles the margin accounts on a daily basis. All participants who have lost on their contracts that day will have the amount of their losses deducted from their margin by the clearinghouse. The clearinghouse similarly increases margins for all participants who gained on that day. Participants whose margins drop below the required **maintenance margin** must replenish their accounts. If a participant does not provide sufficient additional margin when required, the participant's broker will immediately trade to offset the participant's position. These **variation margin** payments ensure that the liabilities associated with futures contracts do not grow large.

EXAMPLE 9

Futures Margin

NYMEX's Light Sweet Crude Oil futures contract specifies the delivery of 1,000 barrels of West Texas Intermediate (WTI) Crude Oil when the contract finally settles. A broker requires that its clients post an initial overnight margin of $7,763 per contract and an overnight maintenance margin of $5,750 per contract. A client buys ten contracts at $75 per barrel through this broker. On the next day, the contract settles for $72 per barrel. How much additional margin will the client have to provide to his broker?

Solution:

The client lost three dollars per barrel (he is the side committed to take delivery or its cash equivalent at $75 per barrel).This results in a $3,000 loss on each of his 10 contracts, and a total loss of $30,000. His initial margin of $77,630 is reduced by $30,000 leaving $47,630 in his margin account. Because his account has dropped below the maintenance margin requirement of $57,500, the client will get a margin call. The client must provide an additional $30,000 = $77,630 − $47,630 to replenish his margin account; the account is replenished to the amount of the initial margin. The client will only receive another margin call if his account drops to below $57,500 again.

Futures contracts have vastly improved the efficiency of forward contracting markets. Traders can trade standardized futures contracts with anyone without worrying about counterparty risk, and they can close their positions by arranging offsetting trades. Hedgers for whom the terms of the standard contract are not ideal generally still use the futures markets because the contracts embody most of the price risk that concerns them. They simply offset (close out) their futures positions, at the same time they enter spot contracts on which they make or take ultimate delivery.

EXAMPLE 10

Forward and Futures Contracts

What feature most distinguishes futures contracts from forward contracts?

Solution:

A futures contract is a standardized forward contract for which a clearinghouse guarantees the performance of all buyers and sellers. The clearinghouse reduces the counterparty risk problem. The clearinghouse allows a buyer who has bought a contract from one person and sold the same contract to another person to net out the two obligations so that she is no longer liable for either side of the contract; the positions are closed. The ability to trade futures contracts provides liquidity in futures contracts compared with forward contracts.

3.4.3 *Swap Contracts*

A **swap contract** is an agreement to exchange payments of periodic cash flows that depend on future asset prices or interest rates. For example, in a typical **interest rate swap**, at periodic intervals, one party makes fixed cash payments to the counterparty in exchange for variable cash payments from the counterparty. The variable payments are based on a pre-specified variable interest rate such as the London Interbank Offered

Rate (Libor). This swap effectively exchanges fixed interest payments for variable interest payments. Because the variable rate is set in the future, the cash flows for this contract are uncertain when the parties enter the contract.

Investment managers often enter interest rate swaps when they own a fixed long-term income stream that they want to convert to a cash flow that varies with current short-term interest rates, or vice versa. The conversion may allow them to substantially reduce the total interest rate risk to which they are exposed. Hedgers often use swap contracts to manage risks.

In a **commodity swap**, one party typically makes fixed payments in exchange for payments that depend on future prices of a commodity such as oil. In a **currency swap**, the parties exchange payments denominated in different currencies. The payments may be fixed, or they may vary depending on future interest rates in the two countries. In an **equity swap**, the parties exchange fixed cash payments for payments that depend on the returns to a stock or a stock index.

EXAMPLE 11

Swap and Forward Contracts

What feature most distinguishes a swap contract from a cash-settled forward contract?

Solution:

Both contracts provide for the exchange of cash payments in the future. A forward contract only has a single cash payment at the end that depends on an underlying price or index at the end. In contrast, a swap contract has several scheduled periodic payments, each of which depends on an underlying price or index at the time of the payment.

3.4.4 Option Contracts

An **option contract** allows the holder (the purchaser) of the **option** to buy or sell, depending on the type of option, an underlying instrument at a specified price at or before a specified date in the future. Those that do buy or sell are said to **exercise** their contracts. An option to buy is a **call option**, and an option to sell is a **put** option. The specified price is called the strike price (exercise price). If the holders can exercise their contracts only when they mature, they are **European-style** contracts. If they can exercise the contracts earlier, they are **American-style** contracts. Many exchanges list standardized option contracts on individual stocks, stock indices, futures contracts, currencies, swaps, and precious metals. Institutions also trade many customized option contracts with dealers in the over-the-counter derivative market.

Option holders generally will exercise call options if the strike price is below the market price of the underlying instrument, in which case, they will be able to buy at a lower price than the market price. Similarly, they will exercise put options if the strike price is above the underlying instrument price so that they sell at a higher price than the market price. Otherwise, option holders allow their options to expire as worthless.

The price that traders pay for an option is the option premium. Options can be quite expensive because, unlike forward and futures contracts, they do not impose any liability on the holder. The premium compensates the sellers of options—called option writers—for giving the call option holders the right to potentially buy below market prices and put option holders the right to potentially sell above market prices. Because the writers must trade if the holders exercise their options, option contracts may impose substantial liabilities on the writers.

> **EXAMPLE 12**
>
> ## Option and Forward Contracts
>
> What feature most distinguishes option contracts from forward contracts?
>
> **Solution:**
>
> The holder of an option contract has the right, but not the obligation, to buy (for a call option) or sell (for a put option) the underlying instrument at some time in the future. The writer of an option contract must trade the underlying instrument if the holder exercises the option.
>
> In contrast, the two parties to a forward contract must trade the underlying instrument (or its equivalent value for a cash-settled contract) at some time in the future if either party wants to settle the contract.

3.4.5 Other Contracts

Insurance contracts pay their beneficiaries a cash benefit if some event occurs. Life, liability, and automobile insurance are examples of insurance contracts sold to retail clients. People generally use insurance contracts to compensate for losses that they will experience if bad things happen unexpectedly. Insurance contracts allow them to hedge risks that they face.

Credit default swaps (CDS) are insurance contracts that promise payment of principal in the event that a company defaults on its bonds. Bondholders use credit default swaps to convert risky bonds into more secure investments. Other creditors of the company may also buy them to hedge against the risk they will not be paid if the company goes bankrupt.

Well-informed traders who believe that a corporation will default on its bonds may buy credit default swaps written on the corporation's bonds if the swap prices are sufficiently low. If they are correct, the traders will profit if the payoff to the swap is more than the cost of buying and maintaining the swap position.

People sometimes also buy insurance contracts as investments, especially in jurisdictions where payouts from insurance contracts are not subject to as much taxation as are payouts to other investment vehicles. They may buy these contracts directly from insurance companies, or they may buy already issued contracts from their owners. For example, the life settlements market trades life insurance contracts that people sell to investors when they need cash.

3.5 Commodities

Commodities include precious metals, energy products, industrial metals, agricultural products, and carbon credits. Spot commodity markets trade commodities for immediate delivery whereas the forward and futures markets trade commodities for future delivery. Managers seeking positions in commodities can acquire them directly by trading in the spot markets or indirectly by trading forward and futures contracts.

The producers and processors of industrial metals and agricultural products are the primary users of the spot commodity markets because they generally are best able to take and make delivery and to store physical products. They undertake these activities in the normal course of operating their businesses. Their ability to handle physical products and the information that they gather operating businesses also gives them substantial advantages as information-motivated traders in these markets. Many producers employ financial analysts to help them analyze commodity market conditions so that they can best manage their inventories to hedge their operational risks and to speculate on future price changes.

Commodities also interest information-motivated traders and investment managers because they can use them as hedges against risks that they hold in their portfolios or as vehicles to speculate on future price changes. Most such traders take positions in the futures markets because they usually do not have facilities to handle most physical products nor can they easily obtain them. They also cannot easily cope with the normal variation in qualities that characterizes many commodities. Information-motivated traders and investment managers also prefer to trade in futures markets because most futures markets are more liquid than their associated spot markets and forward markets. The liquidity allows them to easily close their positions before delivery so that they can avoid handling physical products.

Some information-motivated traders and investment managers, however, trade in the spot commodity markets, especially when they can easily contract for low-cost storage. Commodities for which delivery and storage costs are lowest are nonperishable products for which the ratio of value to weight is high and variation in quality is low. These generally include precious metals, industrial diamonds, such high-value industrial metals as copper, aluminum, and mercury, and carbon credits.

3.6 Real Assets

Real assets include such tangible properties as real estate, airplanes, machinery, or lumber stands. These assets normally are held by operating companies, such as real estate developers, airplane leasing companies, manufacturers, or loggers. Many institutional investment managers, however, have been adding real assets to their portfolios as direct investments (involving direct ownership of the real assets) and indirect investments (involving indirect ownership, for example, purchase of securities of companies that invest in real assets or real estate investment trusts). Investments in real assets are attractive to them because of the income and tax benefits that they often generate, and because changes in their values may have a low correlation with other investments that the managers hold.

Direct investments in real assets generally require substantial management to ensure that the assets are maintained and used efficiently. Investment managers investing in such assets must either hire personnel to manage them or hire outside management companies. Either way, management of real assets is quite costly.

Real assets are unique properties in the sense that no two assets are alike. An example of a unique property is a real estate parcel. No two parcels are the same because, if nothing else, they are located in different places. Real assets generally differ in their conditions, remaining useful lives, locations, and suitability for various purposes. These differences are very important to the people who use them, so the market for a given real asset may be very limited. Thus, real assets tend to trade in very illiquid markets.

The heterogeneity of real assets, their illiquidity, and the substantial costs of managing them are all factors that complicate the valuation of real assets and generally make them unsuitable for most investment portfolios. These same problems, however, often cause real assets to be misvalued in the market, so astute information-motivated traders may occasionally identify significantly undervalued assets. The benefits from purchasing such assets, however, are often offset by the substantial costs of searching for them and by the substantial costs of managing them.

Many financial intermediaries create entities, such as real estate investment trusts (REITs) and master limited partnerships (MLPs), to securitize real assets and to facilitate indirect investment in real assets. The financial intermediaries manage the assets and pass through the net benefits after management costs to the investors who hold these securities. Because these securities are much more homogenous and divisible than the real assets that they represent, they tend to trade in much more liquid markets. Thus, they are much more suitable as investments than the real assets themselves.

Of course, investors seeking exposure to real assets can also buy shares in corporations that hold and operate real assets. Although almost all corporations hold and operate real assets, many specialize in assets that particularly interest investors seeking exposure to specific real asset classes. For example, investors interested in owning aircraft can buy an aircraft leasing company such as Waha Capital (Abu Dhabi Securities Exchange) and Aircastle Limited (NYSE).

EXAMPLE 13

Assets and Contracts

Consider the following assets and contracts:

Bank deposits	Hedge funds
Certificates of deposit	Master limited partnership interests
Common stocks	Mortgages
Corporate bonds	Mutual funds
Currencies	Stock option contracts
Exchange-traded funds	Preferred stocks
Lumber forward contracts	Real estate parcels
Crude oil futures contracts	Interest rate swaps
Gold	Treasury notes

1   Which of these represent ownership in corporations?

2   Which of these are debt instruments?

3   Which of these are created by traders rather than by issuers?

4   Which of these are pooled investment vehicles?

5   Which of these are real assets?

6   Which of these would a home builder most likely use to hedge construction costs?

7   Which of these would a corporation trade when moving cash balances among various countries?

Solution to 1:

Common and preferred stocks represent ownership in corporations.

Solution to 2:

Bank deposits, certificates of deposit, corporate bonds, mortgages, and Treasury notes are all debt instruments. They respectively represent loans made to banks, corporations, mortgagees (typically real estate owners), and the Treasury.

Solution to 3:

Lumber forward contracts, crude oil futures contracts, stock option contracts, and interest rate swaps are created when the seller sells them to a buyer.

Solution to 4:

Exchange-traded funds, hedge funds, and mutual funds are pooled investment vehicles. They represent shared ownership in a portfolio of other assets.

Solution to 5:

Real estate parcels are real assets.

Solution to 6:

A builder would buy lumber forward contracts to lock in the price of lumber needed to build homes.

Solution to 7:

Corporations often trade currencies when moving cash from one country to another.

4 FINANCIAL INTERMEDIARIES

Financial intermediaries help entities achieve their financial goals. These intermediaries include commercial, mortgage, and investment banks; credit unions, credit card companies, and various other finance corporations; brokers and exchanges; dealers and arbitrageurs; clearinghouses and depositories; mutual funds and hedge funds; and insurance companies. The services and products that financial intermediaries provide allow their clients to solve the financial problems that they face more efficiently than they could do so by themselves. Financial intermediaries are essential to well-functioning financial systems.

Financial intermediaries are called intermediaries because the services and products that they provide help connect buyers to sellers in various ways. Whether the connections are easy to identify or involve complex financial structures, financial intermediaries stand between one or more buyers and one or more sellers and help them transfer capital and risk between them. Financial intermediaries' activities allow buyers and sellers to benefit from trading, often without any knowledge of the other.

This section introduces the main financial intermediaries that provide services and products in well-developed financial markets. The discussion starts with those intermediaries whose services most obviously connect buyers to sellers and then proceeds to those intermediaries whose services create more subtle connections. Because many financial intermediaries provide many different types of services, some are mentioned more than once. The section concludes with a general characterization of the various ways in which financial intermediaries add value to the financial system.

4.1 Brokers, Exchanges, and Alternative Trading Systems

Brokers are agents who fill orders for their clients. They do not trade with their clients. Instead, they search for traders who are willing to take the other side of their clients' orders. Individual brokers may work for large brokerage firms, the brokerage arm of banks, or at exchanges. Some brokers match clients to clients personally. Others use specialized computer systems to identify potential trades and help their clients fill their orders. Brokers help their clients trade by reducing the costs of finding counterparties for their trades.

Block brokers provide brokerage service to large traders. Large orders are hard to fill because finding a counterparty willing to do a large trade is often quite difficult. A large buy order generally will trade at a premium to the current market price, and a large sell order generally will trade at a discount to the current market price. These price concessions encourage other traders to trade with the large traders. They also make large traders reluctant, however, to expose their orders to the public before their trades are arranged because they do not want to move the market. Block brokers, therefore, carefully manage the exposure of the orders entrusted to them, which makes filling them difficult.

Investment banks provide advice to their mostly corporate clients and help them arrange transactions such as initial and seasoned securities offerings. Their corporate finance divisions help corporations finance their business by issuing securities, such as common and preferred shares, notes, and bonds. Another function of corporate finance divisions is to help companies identify and acquire other companies (i.e., in mergers and acquisitions).

Exchanges provide places where traders can meet to arrange their trades. Historically, brokers and dealers met on an exchange floor to negotiate trades. Increasingly, exchanges arrange trades for traders based on orders that brokers and dealers submit to them. Such exchanges essentially act as brokers. The distinction between exchanges and brokers has become quite blurred. Exchanges and brokers that use electronic order matching systems to arrange trades among their clients are functionally indistinguishable in this respect. Examples of exchanges include the NYSE-Euronext, Eurex, Deutsche Börse, the Chicago Mercantile Exchange, the Tokyo Stock Exchange, and the Singapore Exchange.

Exchanges are easily distinguished from brokers by their regulatory operations. Most exchanges regulate their members' behavior when trading on the exchange, and sometimes away from the exchange.

Many securities exchanges regulate the issuers that list their securities on the exchange. These regulations generally require timely financial disclosure. Financial analysts use this information to value the securities traded at the exchange. Without such disclosure, valuing securities could be very difficult and market prices might not reflect the fundamental values of the securities. In such situations, well-informed participants may profit from less-informed participants. To avoid such losses, the less-informed participants may withdraw from the market, which can greatly increase corporate costs of capital.

Some exchanges also prohibit issuers from creating capital structures that would concentrate voting rights in the hands of a few owners who do not own a commensurate share of the equity. These regulations attempt to ensure that corporations are run for the benefit of all shareholders and not to promote the interests of controlling shareholders who do not have significant economic stakes in the company.

Exchanges derive their regulatory authority from their national or regional governments, or through the voluntary agreements of their members and issuers to subject themselves to the exchange regulations. In most countries, government regulators oversee the exchange rules and the regulatory operations. Most countries also impose financial disclosure standards on public issuers. Examples of government regulatory bodies include the Japanese Financial Services Agency, the Hong Kong Securities and Futures Commission, the British Financial Services Authority, the German Bundesanstalt für Finanzdienstleistungsaufsicht, the US Securities and Exchange Commission, the Ontario Securities Commission, and the Mexican Comisión Nacional Bancaria y de Valores.

Alternative trading systems (ATSs), also known as **electronic communications networks** (ECNs) or **multilateral trading facilities** (MTFs) are trading venues that function like exchanges but that do not exercise regulatory authority over their subscribers except with respect to the conduct of their trading in their trading systems. Some ATSs operate electronic trading systems that are otherwise indistinguishable from the trading systems operated by exchanges. Others operate innovative trading systems that suggest trades to their customers based on information that their customers share with them or that they obtain through research into their customers' preferences. Many ATSs are known as **dark pools** because they do not display the orders that their clients send to them. Large investment managers especially like these systems because market prices often move to their disadvantage when other traders know about their large orders. ATSs may be owned and operated by broker–dealers, exchanges, banks, or by companies organized solely for this purpose, many of which may be owned by a consortia of brokers–dealers and banks. Examples of ATSs include PureTrading (Canada), the Order Machine (Netherlands), Chi-X Europe, BATS (United States), POSIT (United States), Liquidnet (United States), Baxter-FX (Ireland), and Turquoise (Europe). Many of these ATSs provide services in many markets besides the ones in which they are domiciled.

4.2 Dealers

Dealers fill their clients' orders by trading with them. When their clients want to sell securities or contracts, dealers buy the instruments for their own accounts. If their clients want to buy securities, dealers sell securities that they own or have borrowed. After completing a transaction, dealers hope to reverse the transaction by trading with another client on the other side of the market. When they are successful, they effectively connect a buyer who arrived at one point in time with a seller who arrived at another point in time.

The service that dealers provide is liquidity. **Liquidity** is the ability to buy or sell with low transactions costs when you want to trade. By allowing their clients to trade when they want to trade, dealers provide liquidity to them. In over-the-counter markets, dealers offer liquidity when their clients ask them to trade with them. In exchange markets, dealers offer liquidity to anyone who is willing to trade at the prices that the dealers offer at the exchange. Dealers profit when they can buy at prices that on average are lower than the prices at which they sell.

Dealers may organize their operations within proprietary trading houses, investment banks, and hedge funds, or as sole proprietorships. Some dealers are traditional dealers in the sense that individuals make trading decisions. Others use computerized trading to make all trading decisions. Examples of companies with large dealing operations include Deutsche Securities (Germany), RBC Capital Markets (Canada), Nomura (Japan), Timber Hill (United States), Knight Securities (United States), Goldman Sachs (United States), and IG Group plc (United Kingdom). Almost all investment banks have large dealing operations.

Most dealers also broker orders, and many brokers deal to their customers. Accordingly, practitioners often use the term **broker–dealer** to refer to dealers and brokers. Broker–dealers have a conflict of interest with respect to how they fill their customers' orders. When acting as a broker, they must seek the best price for their customers' orders. When acting as dealers, however, they profit most when they sell to their customers at high prices or buy from their customers at low prices. The problem is most serious when the customer allows the broker–dealer to decide whether to trade the order with another trader or to fill it as a dealer. Consequently, when trading with a broker–dealer, some customers specify how they want their orders filled. They may also trade only with pure agency brokers who do not also deal.

Primary dealers are dealers with whom central banks trade when conducting monetary policy. They buy bills, notes, and bonds when the central banks sell them to decrease the money supply. The dealers then sell these instruments to their clients. Similarly, when the central banks want to increase the money supply, the primary dealers buy these instruments from their clients and sell them to the central banks.

EXAMPLE 14

Brokers and Dealers

What characteristic *most likely* distinguishes brokers from dealers?

> **Solution:**
>
> Brokers are agents that arrange trades on behalf of their clients. They do not trade with their clients. In contrast, dealers are proprietary traders who trade with their clients.

4.3 Securitizers

Banks and investment companies create new financial products when they buy and repackage securities or other assets. For example, mortgage banks commonly originate hundreds or thousands of residential mortgages by lending money to homeowners. They then place the mortgages in a pool and sell shares of the pool to investors as mortgage pass-through securities, which are also known as mortgage-backed securities. All payments of principal and interest are passed through to the investors each month, after deducting the costs of servicing the mortgages. Investors who purchase these pass-through securities obtain securities that in aggregate have the same net cash flows and associated risks as the pool of mortgages.

The process of buying assets, placing them in a pool, and then selling securities that represent ownership of the pool is called securitization.

Mortgage-backed securities have the advantage that default losses and early repayments are much more predictable for a diversified portfolio of mortgages than they are for individual mortgages. They are also attractive to investors who cannot efficiently service mortgages but wish to invest in mortgages. By securitizing mortgage pools, the mortgage banks allow investors who are not large enough to buy hundreds of mortgages to obtain the benefits of diversification and economies of scale in loan servicing.

Securitization greatly improves liquidity in the mortgage markets because it allows investors in the pass-through securities to buy mortgages indirectly that they otherwise would not buy. Because the financial risks associated with mortgage-backed securities (debt securities with specified claims on the cash flows of a portfolio of mortgages) are much more predictable than those of individual mortgages, mortgage-backed securities are easier to price and thus easier to sell when investors need to raise cash. These characteristics make the market for mortgage-backed securities much more liquid than the market for individual mortgages. Because investors value liquidity—the ability to sell when they want to—they will pay more for securitized mortgages than for individual mortgages. The homeowners benefit because higher mortgage prices imply lower interest rates.

The mortgage bank is a financial intermediary because it connects investors who want to buy mortgages to homeowners who want to borrow money. The homeowners sell mortgages to the bank when the bank lends them money.

Some mortgage banks form mortgage pools from mortgages that they buy from other banks that originate the loans. These mortgage banks are also financial intermediaries because they connect sellers of mortgages to buyers of mortgage-backed securities. Although the sellers of the mortgages are the originating lenders and not the borrowers, the benefits of creating liquid mortgage-backed securities ultimately flow back to the borrowers.

The creation of the pass-through securities generally takes place on the accounts of the mortgage bank. The bank buys mortgages and sells pass-through securities whose values depend on the mortgage pool. The mortgages appear on the bank's accounts as assets and the mortgage-backed securities appear as liabilities.

In many securitizations, the financial intermediary avoids placing the assets and liabilities on its balance sheet by setting up a special corporation or trust that buys the assets and issues the securities. That corporation or trust is called a **special purpose vehicle** (SPV) or alternatively a **special purpose entity** (SPE). Conducting a securitization through a special purpose vehicle is advantageous to investors because their interests in the asset pool are better protected in an SPV than they would be on the balance sheet of the financial intermediary if the financial intermediary were to go bankrupt.

Financial intermediaries securitize many assets. Besides mortgages, banks securitize car loans, credit card receivables, bank loans, and airplane leases, to name just a few assets. As a class, these securities are called asset-backed securities.

When financial intermediaries securitize assets, they often create several classes of securities, called tranches, that have different rights to the cash flows from the asset pool. The tranches are structured so that some produce more predictable cash flows than do others. The senior tranches have first rights to the cash flow from the asset pool. Because the overall risk of a given asset pool cannot be changed, the more junior tranches bear a disproportionate share of the risk of the pool. Practitioners often call the most junior tranche toxic waste because it is so risky. The complexity associated with slicing asset pools into tranches can make the resulting securities difficult to value. Mistakes in valuing these securities contributed to the financial crisis that started in 2007.

Investment companies also create pass-through securities based on investment pools. For example, an exchange-traded fund is an asset-backed security that represents ownership in the securities and contracts held by the fund. The shareholders benefit from the securitization because they can buy or sell an entire portfolio in a single transaction. Because the transaction cost savings are quite substantial, exchange-traded funds often trade in very liquid markets. The investment companies (and sometimes the arbitrageurs) that create exchange-traded funds are financial intermediaries because they connect the buyers of the funds to the sellers of the assets that make up the fund portfolios.

More generally, the creators of all pooled investment vehicles are financial intermediaries that transform portfolios of securities and contracts into securities that represent undivided ownership of the portfolios. The investors in these funds thus indirectly invest in the securities held by the fund. They benefit from the expertise of the investment manager and from obtaining a portfolio that may be more diversified than one they might otherwise be able to hold.

4.4 Depository Institutions and Other Financial Corporations

Depository institutions include commercial banks, savings and loan banks, credit unions, and similar institutions that raise funds from depositors and other investors and lend it to borrowers. The banks give their depositors interest and transaction services, such as check writing and check cashing, in exchange for using their money. They may also raise funds by selling bonds or equity in the bank.

These banks are financial intermediaries because they transfer funds from their depositors and investors to their borrowers. The depositors and investors benefit because they obtain a return (in interest, transaction services, dividends, or capital appreciation) on their funds without having to contract with the borrowers and manage their loans. The borrowers benefit because they obtain the funds that they need without having to search for investors who will trust them to repay their loans.

Many other financial corporations provide credit services. For example, acceptance corporations, discount corporations, payday advance corporations, and factors provide credit to borrowers by lending them money secured by such assets as consumer loans, machinery, future paychecks, or accounts receivables. They finance these loans by selling commercial paper, bonds, and shares to investors. These corporations are intermediaries because they connect investors to borrowers. The investors obtain investments secured by a diversified portfolio of loans while the borrowers obtain funds without having to search for investors.

Brokers also act as financial intermediaries when they lend funds to clients who want to buy securities on margin. They generally obtain the funds from other clients who deposit them in their accounts. Brokers who provide these services to hedge funds and other similar institutions are called prime brokers.

Banks, financial corporations, and brokers can only raise money from depositors and other lenders because their equity owners retain residual interests in the performance of the loans that they make. If the borrowers default, the depositors and other lenders have priority claims over the equity owners. If insufficient money is collected from the borrowers, shareholders' equity is used to pay their depositors and other lenders. The risk of losing capital focuses the equity owners' and management's attention so that credit is not offered foolishly.

Because the ability of these companies to cover their credit losses is limited by the capital that their owners invest in them, the depositors and other investors who lend them money pay close attention to how much money the owners have at risk. For example, if a finance corporation is poorly capitalized, its shareholders will lose little if its clients default on the loans that the finance corporation makes to them. In that case, the finance corporation will have little incentive to lend only to creditworthy borrowers and to effectively manage collection on those loans once they have been made. Worse, it may even choose to lend to borrowers with poor credit because the interest rates that they can charge such borrowers are higher. Until those loans default, the higher income will make the corporation appear to be more profitable than it actually is. Depositors and other investors are aware of these problems and generally pay close attention to them. Accordingly, poorly capitalized financial institutions cannot easily borrow money to finance their operations at favorable rates.

Depository banks and financial corporations are similar to securitized asset pools that issue pass-through securities. Their depositors and investors own securities that ultimately are backed by an asset pool consisting of their loan portfolios. The depositors generally hold the most senior tranche, followed by the other creditors. The shareholders hold the most junior tranche. In the event of bankruptcy, they are paid only if everyone else is paid.

EXAMPLE 15

Commercial Banks

What services do commercial banks provide that make them financial intermediaries?

Solution:

Commercial banks collect deposits from investors and lend them to borrowers. They are intermediaries because they connect lenders to borrowers. Commercial banks also provide transaction services that make it easier for the banks' depository customers to pay bills and collect funds from their own customers.

4.5 Insurance Companies

Insurance companies help people and companies offset risks that concern them. They do this by creating insurance contracts (policies) that provide a payment in the event that some loss occurs. The insured buy these contracts to hedge against potential losses. Common examples of insurance contracts include auto, fire, life, liability, medical, theft, and disaster insurance contracts.

Credit default swaps are also insurance contracts, but historically they have not been subject to the same reserve requirements that most governments apply to more traditional insurance contracts. They may be sold by insurance companies or by other financial entities, such as investment banks or hedge funds.

Insurance contracts transfer risk from those who buy the contracts to those who sell them. Although insurance companies occasionally broker trades between the insured and the insurer, they more commonly provide the insurance themselves. In that case, the insurance company's owners and creditors become the indirect insurers of the risks that the insurance company assumes. Insurance companies also often transfer risks that they do not wish to bear by buying reinsurance policies from reinsurers.

Insurers are financial intermediaries because they connect the buyers of their insurance contracts with investors, creditors, and reinsurers who are willing to bear the insured risks. The buyers benefit because they can easily obtain the risk transfers that they seek without searching for entities that would be willing to assume those risks.

The owners, creditors, and reinsurers of the insurance company benefit because the company allows them to sell their tolerance for risk easily without having to manage the insurance contracts. Instead, the company manages the relationships with the insured—primarily collections and claims—and hopefully controls the various problems—fraud, moral hazard, and adverse selection—that often plague insurance markets. Fraud occurs when people deliberately cause or falsely report losses to collect on insurance. Moral hazard occurs when people are less careful about avoiding insured losses than they would be if they were not insured so that losses occur more often than they would otherwise. Adverse selection occurs when only those who are most at risk buy insurance so that insured losses tend to be greater than average.

Everyone benefits because insurance companies hold large diversified portfolios of policies. Loss rates for well-diversified portfolios of insurance contracts are much more predictable than for single contracts. For such contracts as auto insurance in which losses are almost uncorrelated across policies, diversification ensures that the financial performance of a large portfolio of contracts will be quite predictable and so holding the portfolio will not be very risky. The insured benefit because they do not have to pay the insurers much to compensate them for bearing risk (the expected loss is quite predictable so the risk is relatively low). Instead, their insurance premiums primarily reflect the expected loss rate in the portfolio plus the costs of running and financing the company.

4.6 Arbitrageurs

Arbitrageurs trade when they can identify opportunities to buy and sell identical or essentially similar instruments at different prices in different markets. They profit when they can buy in one market for less than they sell in another market. Arbitrageurs are financial intermediaries because they connect buyers in one market to sellers in another market.

The purest form of arbitrage involves buying and selling the same instrument in two different markets. Arbitrageurs who do such trades sell to buyers in one market and buy from sellers in the other market. They provide liquidity to the markets because they make it easier for buyers and sellers to trade when and where they want to trade.

Because dealers and arbitrageurs both provide liquidity to other traders, they compete with each other. The dealers connect buyers and sellers who arrive in the same market at different times whereas the arbitrageurs connect buyers and sellers who arrive at the same time in different markets. In practice, traders who profit from offering liquidity rarely are purely dealers or purely arbitrageurs. Instead, most traders attempt to identify and exploit every opportunity they can to manage their inventories profitably.

If information about prices is readily available to market participants, pure arbitrages involving the same instrument will be quite rare. Traders who are well informed about market conditions usually route their orders to the market offering the best price so that arbitrageurs will have few opportunities to match traders across markets when they want to trade the exact same instrument.

Arbitrageurs often trade securities or contracts whose values depend on the same underlying factors. For example, dealers in equity option contracts often sell call options in the contract market and buy the underlying shares in the stock market. Because the values of the call options and of the underlying shares are closely correlated (the value of the call increases with the value of the shares), the long stock position hedges the risk in the short call position so that the dealer's net position is not too risky.

Similar to the pure arbitrage that involves the same instrument in different markets, these arbitrage trades connect buyers in one market to sellers in another market. In this case, however, the buyers and sellers are interested in different instruments whose values are closely related. In the example, the buyer is interested in buying a call options contract, the value of which is a nonlinear function of the value of the underlying stock; the seller is interested in selling the underlying stock.

Options dealers buy stock and sell calls when calls are overpriced relative to the underlying stocks. They use complicated financial models to value options in relation to underlying stock values, and they use financial engineering techniques to control the risk of their portfolios. Successful arbitrageurs must know valuation relations well and they must manage the risk in their portfolios well to trade profitably. They profit by buying the relatively undervalued instrument and selling the relatively overvalued instrument.

Buying a risk in one form and selling it another form involves a process called replication. Arbitrageurs use various trading strategies to replicate the returns to securities and contracts. If they can substantially replicate those returns, they can use the replication trading strategy to offset the risk of buying or selling the actual securities and contracts. The combined effect of their trading is to transform risk from one form to another. This process allows them to create or eliminate contracts in response to the excess demand for, and supply of, contracts.

For example, when traders want to buy more call contracts than are presently available, they push the call contract prices up so that calls become overvalued relative to the underlying stock. The arbitrageurs replicate calls by using a particular financial engineering strategy to buy the underlying stock, and then create the desired call option contracts by selling them short. In contrast, if more calls have been created than traders want to hold, call prices will fall so that calls become undervalued relative to the underlying stock. The arbitrageurs will trade stocks and contracts to absorb the excess contracts. Arbitrageurs who use these strategies are financial intermediaries because they connect buyers and sellers who want to trade the same underlying risks but in different forms.

EXAMPLE 16

Dealers and Arbitrageurs

With respect to providing liquidity to market participants, what characteristics most clearly distinguish dealers from arbitrageurs?

> **Solution:**
>
> Dealers provide liquidity to buyers and sellers who arrive at the same market at different times. They move liquidity through time. Arbitrageurs provide liquidity to buyers and sellers who arrive at different markets at the same time. They move liquidity across markets.

4.7 Settlement and Custodial Services

In addition to connecting buyers to sellers through a variety of direct and indirect means, financial intermediaries also help their customers settle their trades and ensure that the resulting positions are not stolen or pledged more than once as collateral.

Clearinghouses arrange for final settlement of trades. In futures markets, they guarantee contract performance. In other markets, they may act only as escrow agents, transferring money from the buyer to the seller while transferring securities from the seller to the buyer.

The members of a clearinghouse are the only traders for whom the clearinghouse will settle trades. To ensure that their members settle the trades that they present to the clearinghouse, clearinghouses require that their members have adequate capital and post-performance bonds (margins). Clearinghouses also limit the aggregate net (buy minus sell) quantities that their members can settle.

Brokers and dealers who are not members of the clearinghouse must arrange to have a clearinghouse member settle their trades. To ensure that the non-member brokers and dealers can settle their trades, clearinghouse members require that their customers (the non-member brokers and dealers) have adequate capital and post-margins. They also limit the aggregate net quantities that their customers can settle and they monitor their customers' trading to ensure that they do not arrange trades that they cannot settle.

Brokers and dealers similarly monitor the trades made by their retail and institutional customers, and regulate their customers to ensure that they do not arrange trades that they cannot settle.

This hierarchical system of responsibility generally ensures that traders settle their trades. The brokers and dealers guarantee settlement of the trades they arrange for their retail and institutional customers. The clearinghouse members guarantee settlement of the trades that their customers present to them, and clearinghouses guarantee settlement of all trades presented to them by their members. If a clearinghouse member fails to settle a trade, the clearinghouse settles the trade using its own capital or capital drafted from the other members.

Reliable settlement of all trades is extremely important to a well-functioning financial system because it allows strangers to confidently contract with each other without worrying too much about **counterparty risk**, the risk that their counterparties will not settle their trades. A secure clearinghouse system thus greatly increases liquidity because it greatly increases the number of counterparties with whom a trader can safely arrange a trade.

In many national markets, clearinghouses clear all securities trades so that traders can trade securities through any exchange, broker, alternative trading system, or dealer. These clearinghouse systems promote competition among these exchange service providers.

In contrast, most futures exchanges have their own clearinghouses. These clearinghouses usually will not accept trades arranged away from their exchanges so that a competing exchange cannot trade another exchange's contracts. Competing exchanges may create similar contracts, but moving traders from one established market to a new market is extraordinarily difficult because traders prefer to trade where other traders trade.

Depositories or custodians hold securities on behalf of their clients. These services, which are often offered by banks, help prevent the loss of securities through fraud, oversight, or natural disaster. Broker–dealers also often hold securities on behalf of their customers so that the customers do not have to hold the securities in certificate form. To avoid problems with lost certificates, securities increasingly are issued only in electronic form.

EXAMPLE 17

Financial Intermediaries

As a relatively new member of the business community, you decide it would be advantageous to join the local lunch club to network with businessmen. Upon learning that you are a financial analyst, club members soon enlist you to give a lunch speech. During the question and answer session afterwards, a member of the audience asks, "I keep reading in the newspaper about the need to regulate 'financial intermediaries', but really don't understand exactly what they are. Can you tell me?" How do you answer?

Solution:

Financial intermediaries are companies that help their clients achieve their financial goals. They are called intermediaries because, in some way or another, they stand between two or more people who would like to trade with each other, but for various reasons find it difficult to do so directly. The intermediary arranges the trade for them, or more often, trades with both sides.

For example, a commercial bank is an intermediary that connects investors with money to borrowers who need money. The investors buy certificates of deposit from the bank, buy bonds or stock issued by the bank, or simply are depositors in the bank. The borrowers borrow this money from the bank when they arrange loans. Without the bank's intermediation, the investors would have to find trustworthy borrowers themselves, which would be difficult, and the borrowers would have to find trusting lenders, which would also be difficult.

Similarly, an insurance company is an intermediary because it connects customers who want to insure risks with investors who are willing to bear those risks. The investors own shares or bonds issued by the insurance company, or they have sold reinsurance contracts to the insurance company. The insured benefit because they can more easily buy a policy from an insurance company than they can find counterparties who would be willing to bear their risks. The investors benefit because the insurance company creates a diversified portfolio of risks by selling insurance to thousands or millions of customers. Diversification ensures that the net risk borne by the insurance company and its investors will be predictable and thus financially manageable.

In both cases, the financial intermediary also manages the relationships with its customers and investors so that neither side has to worry about the credit-worthiness or trust-worthiness of its counterparties. For example, the bank manages credit quality and collections on its loans and the insurance company manages risk exposure and collections on its policies. These services benefit both sides by reducing the costs of connecting investors to borrowers or of insured to insurers.

These are only two examples of financial intermediation. Many others involve firms engaged in brokerage, dealing, arbitrage, securitization, investment management, and the clearing and settlement of trades. In all cases, the financial intermediary stands between a buyer and a seller, offering them services that allow them to better achieve their financial goals in a cost effective and efficient manner.

4.8 Summary

By facilitating transactions among buyers and sellers, financial intermediaries provide services essential to a well-functioning financial system. They facilitate transactions the following ways:

1 Brokers, exchanges, and various alternative trading systems match buyers and sellers interested in trading the same instrument at the same place and time. These financial intermediaries specialize in discovering and organizing information about who wants to trade.

2 Dealers and arbitrageurs connect buyers to sellers interested in trading the same instrument but who are not present at the same place and time. Dealers connect buyers to sellers who are present at the same place but at different times whereas arbitrageurs connect buyers to sellers who are present at the same time but in different places. These financial intermediaries trade for their own accounts when providing these services. Dealers buy or sell with one client and hope to do the offsetting transaction later with another client. Arbitrageurs buy from a seller in one market while simultaneously selling to a buyer in another market.

3 Many financial intermediaries create new instruments that depend on the cash flows and associated financial risks of other instruments. The intermediaries provide these services when they securitize assets, manage investment funds, operate banks and other finance corporations that offer investments to investors and loans to borrowers, and operate insurance companies that pool risks. The instruments that they create generally are more attractive to their clients than the instruments on which they are based. The new instruments also may be differentiated to appeal to diverse clienteles. Their efforts connect buyers of one or more instruments to sellers of other instruments, all of which in aggregate provide the same cash flows and risk exposures. Financial intermediaries thus effectively arrange trades among traders who otherwise would not trade with each other.

4 Arbitrageurs who conduct arbitrage among securities and contracts whose values depend on common factors convert risk from one form to another. Their trading connects buyers and sellers who want to trade similar risks expressed in different forms.

5 Banks, clearinghouses, and depositories provide services that ensure traders settle their trades and that the resulting positions are not stolen or pledged more than once as collateral.

5   POSITIONS

People generally solve their financial and risk management problems by taking positions in various assets or contracts. A **position** in an asset is the quantity of the instrument that an entity owns or owes. A portfolio consists of a set of positions.

People have **long positions** when they own assets or contracts. Examples of long positions include ownership of stocks, bonds, currencies, contracts, commodities, or real assets. Long positions benefit from an appreciation in the prices of the assets or contracts owned.

People have **short positions** when they have sold assets that they do not own, or when they write and sell contracts. Short positions benefit from a decrease in the prices of the assets or contracts sold. Short sellers profit by selling at high prices and repurchasing at lower prices. Information-motivated traders sell assets and contracts short positions when they believe that prices will fall.

Hedgers also often sell instruments short. They short securities and contracts when the financial risks inherent in the instruments are positively correlated with the risks to which they are exposed. For example, to hedge the risk associated with holding copper inventories, a wire manufacturer would sell short copper futures. If the price of copper falls, the manufacturer will lose on his copper inventories but gain on his short futures position. (If the risk in an instrument is inversely correlated with a risk to which hedgers are exposed, the hedgers will hedge with long positions.)

Contracts have long sides and short sides. The long side of a forward or futures contract is the side that will take physical delivery or its cash equivalent. The short side of such contracts is the side that is liable for the delivery. The long side of a futures contract increases in value when the value of the underlying asset increases in value.

The identification of the two sides can be confusing for option contracts. The long side of an option contract is the side that holds the right to exercise the option. The short side is the side that must satisfy the obligation. Practitioners say that that the long side *holds* the option and the short side *writes* the option, so the long side is the holder and the short side is the writer. The put contracts are the source of the potential confusion. The put contract holder has the right to sell the underlying to the writer. The holder will benefit if the price of the underlying falls, in which case the price of the put contract will rise. The holder is long the put contract and has an indirect short position in the underlying instrument. Analysts call the indirect short position short exposure to the underlying. The put contract holders have long exposure to their option contract and short exposure to the underlying instrument.

Exhibit 1   Option Positions and Their Associated Underlying Risk Exposures

Type of Option	Option Position	Exposure to Underlying Risk
Call	Long	Long
Call	Short	Short
Put	Long	Short
Put	Short	Long

The identification of the long side in a swap contract is often arbitrary because swap contracts call for the exchange of contractually determined cash flows rather than for the purchase (or the cash equivalent) of some underlying instrument. In general, the side that benefits from an increase in the quoted price is the long side.

The identification of the long side in currency contracts also may be confusing. In this case, the confusion stems from symmetry in the contracts. The buyer of one currency is the seller of the other currency, and vice versa for the seller. Thus, a long forward position in one currency is a short forward position in the other currency. When practitioners describe a position, they generally will say, "I'm long the dollar against the yen," which means they have bought dollars and sold yen.

5.1 Short Positions

Short sellers create short positions in contracts by selling contracts that they do not own. In a sense, they become the issuers of the contract when they create the liabilities associated with their contracts. This analogy will also help you better understand risk when you study corporate finance: Corporations create short positions in their bonds when they issue bonds in exchange for cash. Although bonds are generally considered to be securities, they are also contracts between the issuer and the bondholder.

Short sellers create short positions in securities by borrowing securities from security lenders who are long holders. The short sellers then sell the borrowed securities to other traders. Short sellers close their positions by repurchasing the securities and returning them to the security lenders. If the securities drop in value, the short sellers profit because they repurchase the securities at lower prices than the prices at which they sold the securities. If the securities rise in value, they will lose. Short sellers who buy to close their positions are said to cover their positions.

The potential gains in a long position generally are unbounded. For example, the stock prices of such highly successful companies as Yahoo! have increased more than 50-fold since they were first publicly traded. The potential losses on long positions, however, are limited to no more than 100 percent—a complete loss—for long positions without any associated liabilities.

In contrast, the potential gains on a short position are limited to no more than 100 percent whereas the potential losses are unbounded. The unbounded potential losses on short positions make short positions very risky in volatile instruments. For example, if you shorted 100 shares of Yahoo! in July 1996 at $20 and you kept your position open for four years, you would have lost $148,000 on your $2,000 initial short position. During this period, Yahoo! rose 75-fold to $1,500 on a split-adjusted equivalent basis.

Although security lenders generally believe that they are long the securities that they lend, in fact, they do not actually own the securities during the periods of their loans. Instead, they own promises made by the short sellers to return the securities. These promises are memorialized in security lending agreements. These agreements specify that the short sellers will pay the long sellers all dividends or interest that they otherwise would have received had they not lent their securities. These payments are called payments-in-lieu of dividends (or of interest), and they may have different tax treatments than actual dividends and interest. The security lending agreements also protect the lenders in the event of a stock split.

To secure the security loans, lenders require that the short seller leave the proceeds of the short sale on deposit with them as collateral for the stock loan. They invest the collateral in short-term securities, and they rebate the interest to the short sellers at rates called short rebate rates. The short rebate rates are determined in the market and generally are available only to institutional short-sellers and some large retail traders. If a security is hard to borrow, the rebate rate may be very small or even negative. Such securities are said to be on special. Otherwise, the rebate rate is usually 10 basis points less than the overnight rate in the interbank funds market. Most security lending agreements require various margin payments to keep the credit risk among the parties from growing when prices change.

Securities lenders lend their securities because the short rebate rates they pay on the collateral are lower than the interest rates they receive from investing the collateral. The difference is because of the implicit loan fees that they receive from the borrowers for borrowing the stock. The difference also compensates lenders for risks that the lenders take when investing the collateral and for the risk that the borrowers will default if prices rise significantly.

> **EXAMPLE 18**
>
> ## Short Positions in Securities and Contracts
>
> How is the process of short selling shares of Siemens different from that of short selling a Siemens equity call option contract?
>
> **Solution:**
>
> To short sell shares of Siemens, the seller (or his broker) must borrow the shares from a long holder so that he can deliver them to the buyer. To short sell a Siemens equity call option contract, the seller simply creates the contract when he sells it to the buyer.

5.2 Leveraged Positions

In many markets, traders can buy securities by borrowing some of the purchase price. They usually borrow the money from their brokers. The borrowed money is called the **margin loan**, and they are said to buy on margin. The interest rate that the buyers pay for their margin loan is called the **call money rate**. The call money rate is above the government bill rate and is negotiable. Large buyers generally obtain more favorable rates than do retail buyers. For institutional-size buyers, the call money rate is quite low because the loans are generally well secured by securities held as collateral by the lender.

Trader's equity is that portion of the security price that the buyer must supply. Traders who buy securities on margin are subject to minimum margin requirements. The **initial margin requirement** is the minimum fraction of the purchase price that must be trader's equity. This requirement may be set by the government, the exchange, or the exchange clearinghouse. For example, in the United States, the Federal Reserve Board sets the initial margin requirement through Regulation T. In Hong Kong, the Securities and Futures Commission sets the margin requirements. In all markets, brokers often require more equity than the government-required minimum from their clients when lending to them.

Many markets allow brokers to lend their clients more money if the brokers use risk models to measure and control the overall risk of their clients' portfolios. This system is called portfolio margining.

Buying securities on margin can greatly increase the potential gains or losses for a given amount of equity in a position because the trader can buy more securities on margin than he could otherwise. The buyer thus earns greater profits when prices rise and suffers greater losses when prices fall. The relation between risk and borrowing is called **financial leverage** (often simply called leverage). Traders leverage their positions when they borrow to buy more securities. A highly leveraged position is large relative to the equity that supports it.

The leverage ratio is the ratio of the value of the position to the value of the equity investment in it. The leverage ratio indicates how many times larger a position is than the equity that supports it. The maximum leverage ratio associated with a position financed by the minimum margin requirement is one divided by the minimum margin requirement. If the requirement is 40 percent, then the maximum leverage ratio is 2.5 = 100% position ÷ 40% equity.

The leverage ratio indicates how much more risky a leveraged position is relative to an unleveraged position. For example, if a stock bought on 40 percent margin rises 10 percent, the buyer will experience a 25 percent (2.5 × 10%) return on the equity investment in her leveraged position. But if the stock falls by 10 percent, the return on the equity investment will be −25 percent (before the interest on the margin loan and before payment of commissions).

Financial analysts must be able to compute the total return to the equity investment in a leveraged position. The total return depends on the price change of the purchased security, the dividends or interest paid by the security, the interest paid on the margin loan, and the commissions paid to buy and sell the security. The following example illustrates the computation of the total return to a leveraged purchase of stock that pays a dividend.

EXAMPLE 19

Computing Total Return to a Leveraged Stock Purchase

A buyer buys stock on margin and holds the position for exactly one year, during which time the stock pays a dividend. For simplicity, assume that the interest on the loan and the dividend are both paid at the end of the year.

Purchase price	$20/share
Sale price	$15/share
Shares purchased	1,000
Leverage ratio	2.5
Call money rate	5%
Dividend	$0.10/share
Commission	$0.01/share

1   What is the total return on this investment?

2   Why is the loss greater than the 25 percent decrease in the market price?

Solution to 1:

To find the return on this investment, first determine the initial equity and then determine the equity remaining after the sale. The total purchase price is $20,000. The leverage ratio of 2.5 indicates that the buyer's equity financed 40 percent = (1 ÷ 2.5) of the purchase price. Thus, the equity investment is $8,000 = 40% of $20,000. The $12,000 remainder is borrowed. The actual investment is slightly higher because the buyer must pay a commission of $10 = $0.01/share × 1,000 shares to buy the stock. The total initial investment is $8,010.

At the end of the year, the stock price has declined by $5/share. The buyer lost $5,000 = $5/share × 1,000 shares as a result of the price change. In addition, the buyer has to pay interest at 5 percent on the $12,000 loan, or $600. The buyer also receives a dividend of $0.10/share, or $100. The trader's equity remaining after the sale is computed from the initial equity investment as follows:

Initial investment	$8,010
Purchase commission	−10
Trading gains/losses	−5,000
Margin interest paid	−600
Dividends received	100
Sales commission paid	−10
Remaining equity	$2,490

or

Proceeds on sale	$15,000
Payoff loan	−12,000

Margin interest paid	−600
Dividends received	100
Sales commission paid	−10
Remaining equity	$2,490

so that the return on the initial investment of $8,010 is $(2{,}490 - 8{,}010)/8{,}010 =$ −68.9%.

Solution to 2:

The realized loss is substantially greater than the stock price return of ($15 − $20)/$20 = −25%. Most of the difference is because of the leverage with the remainder primarily the result of the interest paid on the loan. Based on the leverage alone and ignoring the other cash flows, we would expect that the return on the equity would be −62.5% = 2.5 leverage times the −25% stock price return.

In the above example, if the stock dropped more than the buyer's original 40 percent margin (ignoring commissions, interest, and dividends), the trader's equity would have become negative. In that case, the investor would owe his broker more than the stock is worth. Brokers often lose money in such situations if the buyer does not repay the loan out of other funds.

To prevent such losses, brokers require that margin buyers always have a minimum amount of equity in their positions. This minimum is called the **maintenance margin requirement**. It is usually 25 percent of the current value of the position, but it may be higher or lower depending on the volatility of the instrument and the policies of the broker.

If the value of the equity falls below the maintenance margin requirement, the buyer will receive a **margin call**, or request for additional equity. If the buyer does not deposit additional equity with the broker in a timely manner, the broker will close the position to prevent further losses and thereby secure repayment of the margin loan.

When you buy securities on margin, you must know the price at which you will receive a margin call if prices drop. The answer to this question depends on your initial equity and on the maintenance margin requirement.

EXAMPLE 20

Margin Call Price

A trader buys stock on margin posting 40 percent of the initial stock price of $20 as equity. The maintenance margin requirement for the position is 25 percent. Below what price will a margin call occur?

Solution:

The trader's initial equity is 40 percent of the initial stock price of $20, or $8 per share. Subsequent changes in equity per share are equal to the share price change so that equity per share is equal to $8 + ($P$ − 20) where P is the current share price. The margin call takes place when equity drops below the 25 percent maintenance margin requirement. The price below which a margin call will take place is the solution to the following equation:

$$\frac{\text{Equity/share}}{\text{Price/share}} = \frac{\$8 + P - 20}{P} = 25\%$$

> which occurs at P = 16. When the price drops below $16, the equity will be under $4/share, which is less than 25 percent of the price.

Traders who sell securities short are also subject to margin requirements because they have borrowed securities. Initially, the trader's equity supporting the short position must be at least equal to the margin requirement times the initial value of the short position. If prices rise, equity will be lost. At some point, the short seller will have to contribute additional equity to meet the maintenance margin requirement. Otherwise, the broker will buy the security back to cover the short position to prevent further losses and thereby secure repayment of the stock loan.

6   ORDERS

Buyers and sellers communicate with the brokers, exchanges, and dealers that arrange their trades by issuing **orders**. All orders specify what instrument to trade, how much to trade, and whether to buy or sell. Most orders also have other instructions attached to them. These additional instructions may include execution instructions, validity instructions, and clearing instructions. **Execution instructions** indicate how to fill the order, **validity instructions** indicate when the order may be filled, and **clearing instructions** indicate how to arrange the final settlement of the trade.

In this section, we introduce various order instructions and explain how traders use them to achieve their objectives. We discuss execution mechanisms—how exchanges, brokers and dealers fill orders—in the next section. To understand the concepts in this section, however, you need to know a little about order execution mechanisms.

In most markets, dealers and various other proprietary traders often are willing to buy from, or sell to, other traders seeking to sell or buy. The prices at which they are willing to buy are called **bid** prices and those at which they are willing to sell are called **ask** prices, or sometimes **offer** prices. The ask prices are invariably higher than the bid prices.

The traders who are willing to trade at various prices may also indicate the quantities that they will trade at those prices. These quantities are called **bid sizes** and **ask sizes** depending on whether they are attached to bids or offers.

Practitioners say that the traders who offer to trade make a market. Those who trade with them take the market.

The highest bid in the market is the **best bid**, and the lowest ask in the market is the **best offer**. The difference between the best bid and the best offer is the **market bid–ask spread**. When traders ask, "What's the market?" they want to know the best bid and ask prices and their associated sizes. Bid–ask spreads are an implicit cost of trading. Markets with small bid–ask spreads are markets in which the costs of trading are small, at least for the sizes quoted. Dealers often quote both bid and ask prices, and in that case, practitioners say that they quote a two-sided market. The market spread is never more than any dealer spread.

6.1 Execution Instructions

Market and limit orders convey the most common execution instructions. A **market order** instructs the broker or exchange to obtain the best price immediately available when filling the order. A **limit order** conveys almost the same instruction: Obtain the best price immediately available, but in no event accept a price higher than a specified limit price when buying or accept a price lower than a specified limit price when selling.

Many people mistakenly believe that limit orders specify the prices at which the orders will trade. Although limit orders do often trade at their limit prices, remember that the first instruction is to obtain the best price available. If better prices are available than the limit price, brokers and exchanges should obtain those prices for their clients.

Market orders generally execute immediately if other traders are willing to take the other side of the trade. The main drawback with market orders is that they can be expensive to execute, especially when the order is placed in a market for a thinly traded security, or more generally, when the order is large relative to the normal trading activity in the market. In that case, a market buy order may fill at a high price, or a market sell order may fill at a low price if no traders are willing to trade at better prices. High purchase prices and low sale prices represent price concessions given to other traders to encourage them to take the other side of the trade. Because the sizes of price concessions can be difficult to predict, and because prices often change between when a trader submits an order and when the order finally fills, the execution prices for market orders are often uncertain.

Buyers and sellers who are concerned about the possibility of trading at unacceptable prices add limit price instructions to their orders. The main problem with limit orders is that they may not execute. Limit orders do not execute if the limit price on a buy order is too low, or if the limit price on a sell order is too high. For example, if an investment manager submits a limit order to buy at the limit price of 20 (buy limit 20) and nobody is willing to sell at or below 20, the order will not trade. If prices never drop to 20, the manager will never buy. If the price subsequently rises, the manager will have lost the opportunity to profit from the price rise.

Whether traders use market orders or limit orders when trying to arrange trades depends on their concerns about price, trading quickly, and failing to trade. On average, limit orders trade at better prices than do market orders, but they often do not trade. Traders generally regret when their limit orders fail to trade because they usually would have profited if they had traded. Limit buy orders do not fill when prices are rising, and limit sell orders do not fill when prices are falling. In both cases, traders would be better off if their orders had filled.

The probability that a limit order will execute depends on where the order is placed relative to market prices. An aggressively priced order is more likely to trade than is a less aggressively priced order. A limit buy order is aggressively priced when the limit price is high relative to the market bid and ask prices. If the limit price is placed above the best offer, the buy order generally will partially or completely fill at the best offer price, depending on the size available at the best offer. Such limit orders are called **marketable limit orders** because at least part of the order can trade immediately. A limit buy order with a very high price relative to the market is essentially a market order.

If the buy order is placed above the best bid but below the best offer, traders say the order makes a new market because it becomes the new best bid. Such orders generally will not immediately trade, but they may attract sellers who are interested in trading. A buy order placed at the best bid is said to make market. It may have to wait until all other buy orders at that price trade first. Finally, a buy order placed below the best bid is **behind the market**. It will not execute unless market prices drop. Traders call limit orders that are waiting to trade **standing limit orders**.

Sell limit orders are aggressively priced if the limit price is low relative to market prices. The limit price of a marketable sell limit order is below the best bid. A limit sell order placed between the best bid and the best offer makes a new market on the sell side, one placed at the best offer makes market, and one placed above the best offer is behind the market.

Exhibit 2 presents a simplified **limit order book** in which orders are presented ranked by their limit prices for a hypothetical market. The market is "26 bid, offered at 28" because the best bid is 26 and the best offer (ask) is 28.

Exhibit 2   Terms Traders Use to Describe Standing Limit Orders

Order Prices

Bids	Offers (Asks)	
	33	The least aggressively priced sell orders are far from the market.
	32	
	31	These sell orders are *behind the market*. We also say that they are *away from the market*.
	30	
	29	
	28	The *best offer* is *at the market*.
		The space between the current best bid and offer is *inside the market*. If a new limit order arrives here, it *makes a new market*.
26		The *best bid* is *at the market*.
25		
24		These buy orders *are behind the market*. We also say that they are *away from the market*.
23		
22		
21		The least aggressively priced buy orders are *far from the market*.

The best bid and best offer *make the market*.

Source: Trading and Exchanges.
Harris, Larry. 2003. *Trading and Exchanges: Market Microstructure for Practitioners*. New York: Oxford University Press.

EXAMPLE 21

Making and Taking

1   What is the difference between making a market and taking a market?

2   What order types are most likely associated with making a market and taking a market?

Solution to 1:

A trader makes a market when the trader offers to trade. A trader takes a market when the trader accepts an offer to trade.

Solution to 2:

Traders place standing limit orders to give other traders opportunities to trade. Standing limit orders thus make markets. In contrast, traders use market orders or marketable limit orders to take offers to trade. These marketable orders take the market.

A trade-off exists between how aggressively priced an order is and the ultimate trade price. Although aggressively priced orders fill faster and with more certainty then do less aggressively priced limit orders, the prices at which they execute are inferior. Buyers seeking to trade quickly must pay higher prices to increase the probability of trading quickly. Similarly, sellers seeking to trade quickly must accept lower prices to increase the probability of trading quickly.

Some order execution instructions specify conditions on size. For example, **all-or-nothing (AON) orders** can only trade if their entire sizes can be traded. Traders can similarly specify minimum fill sizes. This specification is common when settlement costs depend on the number of trades made to fill an order and not on the aggregate size of the order.

Exposure instructions indicate whether, how, and perhaps to whom orders should be exposed. **Hidden orders** are exposed only to the brokers or exchanges that receive them. These agencies cannot disclose hidden orders to other traders until they can fill them. Traders use hidden orders when they are afraid that other traders might behave strategically if they knew that a large order was in the market. Traders can discover hidden size only by submitting orders that will trade with that size. Thus, traders can only learn about hidden size after they have committed to trading with it.

Traders also often indicate a specific **display size** for their orders. Brokers and exchanges then expose only the display size for these orders. Any additional size is hidden from the public but can be filled if a suitably large order arrives. Traders sometimes call such orders **iceberg orders** because most of the order is hidden. Traders specify display sizes when they do not want to display their full sizes, but still want other traders to know that someone is willing to trade at the displayed price. Traders on the opposite side who wish to trade additional size at that price can discover the hidden size only if they trade the displayed size, at which point the broker or exchange will display any remaining size up to the display size. They also can discover the hidden size by submitting large orders that will trade with that size.

EXAMPLE 22

Market versus Limit and Hidden versus Displayed Orders

You are the buy-side trader for a very clever investment manager. The manager has hired a commercial satellite firm to take regular pictures of the parking lots in which new car dealers store their inventories. It has also hired some part-time workers to count the cars on the lots. With this information and some econometric analyses, the manager can predict weekly new car sale announcements more accurately than can most analysts. The manager typically makes a quarter percent each week on this strategy. Once a week, a day before the announcements are made, the manager gives you large orders to buy or sell car manufacturers based on his insights into their dealers' sales. What primary issues should you consider when deciding whether to:

1 use market or limit orders to fill his orders?

2 display the orders or hide them?

Solution to 1:

The manager's information is quite perishable. If his orders are not filled before the weekly sales are reported to the public, the manager will lose the opportunity to profit from the information as prices immediately adjust to the news. The manager, therefore, needs to get the orders filled quickly. This consideration suggests that the orders should be submitted as market orders. If submitted as limit orders, the orders might not execute and the firm would lose the opportunity to profit.

Large market orders, however, can be very expensive to execute, especially if few people are willing to trade significant size on the other side of the market. Because transaction costs can easily exceed the expected quarter percent return, you should submit limit orders to limit the execution prices that you are willing to accept. It is better to fail to trade than to trade at losing prices.

Solution to 2:

Your large orders could easily move the market if many people were aware of them, and even more so if others were aware that you are trading on behalf of a successful information-motivated trader. You thus should consider submitting hidden orders. The disadvantage of hidden orders is that they do not let people know that they can trade the other side if they want to.

6.2 Validity Instructions

Validity instructions indicate when an order may be filled. The most common validity instruction is the **day order**. A day order is good for the day on which it is submitted. If it has not been filled by the close of business, the order expires unfilled.

Good-till-cancelled orders (GTC) are just that. In practice, most brokers limit how long they will manage an order to ensure that they do not fill orders that their clients have forgotten. Such brokers may limit their GTC orders to a few months.

Immediate or cancel orders (IOC) are good only upon receipt by the broker or exchange. If they cannot be filled in part or in whole, they cancel immediately. In some markets these orders are also known as **fill or kill** orders. When searching for hidden liquidity, electronic algorithmic trading systems often submit thousands of these IOC orders for every order that they fill.

Good-on-close orders can only be filled at the close of trading. These orders often are market orders, so traders call them **market-on-close** orders. Traders often use on-close orders when they want to trade at the same prices that will be published as the closing prices of the day. Mutual funds often like to trade at such prices because they value their portfolios at closing prices. Many traders also use **good-on-open** orders.

6.2.1 Stop Orders

A **stop order** is an order in which a trader has specified a stop price condition. The stop order may not be filled until the stop price condition has been satisfied. For a sell order, the stop price condition suspends execution of the order until a trade occurs at or below the stop price. After that trade, the stop condition is satisfied and the order becomes valid for execution, subject to all other execution instructions attached to it. If the market price subsequently rises above the sell order's stop price before the order trades, the order remains valid. Similarly, a buy order with a stop condition becomes valid only after a price rises above the specified stop price.

Traders often call stop orders **stop-loss orders** because many traders use them with the hope of stopping losses on positions that they have established. For example, a trader who has bought stock at 40 may want to sell the stock if the price falls below 30. In that case, the trader might submit a "GTC, stop 30, market sell" order. If the price falls to or below 30, the market order becomes valid and it should immediately execute at the best price then available in the market. That price may be substantially lower than 30 if the market is falling quickly. The stop-loss order thus does not guarantee a stop to losses at the stop price. If potential sellers are worried about trading at too low of a price, they can attach stop instructions to limit orders instead of market orders. In this example, if the trader is unwilling to sell below 25, the trader would submit a "GTC, stop 30, limit 25 sell" order.

If a trader wants to guarantee that he can sell at 30, the trader would buy a put option contract struck at 30. The purchase price of the option would include a premium for the insurance that the trader is buying. Option contracts can be viewed as limit orders for which execution is guaranteed at the strike price. A trader similarly might use a stop-buy order or a call option to limit losses on a short position.

A portfolio manager might use a stop-buy order when the manager believes that a security is undervalued but is unwilling to trade without market confirmation. For example, suppose that a stock currently trades for 50 RMB and a manager believes that it should be worth 100 RMB. Further, the manager believes that the stock will much more likely be worth 100 RMB if other traders are willing to buy it above 65 RMB. To best take advantage of this information, the manager would consider issuing a "GTC, stop 65 RMB, limit 100 RMB buy" order. Note that if the manager relies too much on the market when making this trading decision, however, he may violate CFA Standard of Professional Conduct V.A.2, which requires that all investment actions have a reasonable and adequate basis supported by appropriate research and investigation.

Because stop-sell orders become valid when prices are falling and stop-buy orders become valid when prices are rising, traders using stop orders contribute to market momentum as their sell orders push prices down further and their buy orders push prices up. Execution prices for stop orders thus are often quite poor.

EXAMPLE 23

Limit and Stop Instructions

In what ways do limit and stop instructions differ?

Solution:

Although both limit and stop instructions specify prices, the role that these prices play in the arrangement of a trade are completely different. A limit price places a limit on what trade prices will be acceptable to the trader. A buyer will accept prices only at or lower than the limit price whereas a seller will accept prices only at or above the limit price.

In contrast, a stop price indicates when an order can be filled. A buy order can only be filled once the market has traded at a price at or above the stop price. A sell order can only be filled once the market has traded at a price at or below the stop price.

Both order instructions may delay or prevent the execution of an order. A buy limit order will not execute until someone is willing to sell at or below the limit price. Similarly, a sell limit order will not execute until someone is willing to buy at or above the limit sell price. In contrast, a stop-buy order will not execute if the market price never rises to the stop price. Similarly, a stop-sell order will not execute if the market price never falls to the stop price.

6.3 Clearing Instructions

Clearing instructions tell brokers and exchanges how to arrange final settlement of trades. Traders generally do not attach these instructions to each order—instead they provide them as standing instructions. These instructions indicate what entity is responsible for clearing and settling the trade. For retail trades, that entity is the customer's broker. For institutional trades, that entity may be a custodian or another broker. When a client uses one broker to arrange trades and another broker to settle trades, traders say that the first broker gives up the trade to the other broker, who is often known as the prime broker. Institutional traders provide these instructions so they can obtain specialized execution services from different brokers while maintaining a single account for custodial services and other prime brokerage services, such as margin loans.

An important clearing instruction that must appear on security sale orders is an indication of whether the sale is a long sale or a short sale. In either case, the broker representing the sell order must ensure that the trader can deliver securities for settlement. For a long sale, the broker must confirm that the securities held are available for delivery. For a short sale, the broker must either borrow the security on behalf of the client or confirm that the client can borrow the security.

7 PRIMARY SECURITY MARKETS

When issuers first sell their securities to investors, practitioners say that the trades take place in the **primary markets**. An issuer makes an **initial public offering** (IPO)—sometimes called a placing—of a security issue when it sells the security to the public for the first time. A seasoned security is a security that an issuer has already issued. If the issuer wants to sell additional units of a previously issued security, it makes a **seasoned offering** (sometimes called a secondary offering). Both types of offerings occur in the **primary market** where issuers sell their securities to investors. Later, if investors trade these securities among themselves, they trade in **secondary markets**. This section discusses primary markets and the procedures that issuers use to offer their securities to the public.

7.1 Public Offerings

Corporations generally contract with an investment bank to help them sell their securities to the public. The investment bank then lines up subscribers who will buy the security. Investment bankers call this process **book building**. In London, the book builder is called the book runner. The bank tries to build a book of orders to which they can sell the offering. Investment banks often support their book building by providing investment information and opinion about the issuer to their clients and to the public. Before the offering, the issuer generally makes a very detailed disclosure of its business, of the risks inherent in it, and of the uses to which the new funds will be placed.

When time is of the essence, issuers in Europe may issue securities through an **accelerated book build**, in which the investment bank arranges the offering in only one or two days. Such sales often occur at discounted prices.

The first public offering of common stock in a company consists of newly issued shares to be sold by the company. It may also include shares that the founders and other early investors in the company seek to sell. The initial public offering provides these investors with a means of liquidating their investments.

In an **underwritten offering**—the most common type of offering—the investment bank guarantees the sale of the issue at an offering price that it negotiates with the issuer. If the issue is undersubscribed, the bank will buy whatever securities it cannot sell at the offering price. In the case of an IPO, the underwriter usually also promises to make a market in the security for about a month to ensure that the secondary market will be liquid and to provide price support, if necessary. For large issues, a syndicate of investment banks and broker–dealers helps the **lead underwriter** build the book. The issuer usually pays an underwriting fee of about 7 percent for these various services. The underwriting fee is a placement cost of the offering.

In a **best effort offering**, the investment bank acts only as broker. If the offering is undersubscribed, the issuer will not sell as much as it hoped to sell.

For both types of offerings, the issuer and the bank usually jointly set the offering price following a negotiation. If they set a price that buyers consider too high, the offering will be undersubscribed, and they will fail to sell the entire issue. If they set the price too low, the offering will be oversubscribed, in which case the securities are often allocated to preferred clients or on a pro-rata basis.

(Note that CFA Standard of Professional Conduct III.B—fair dealing—requires that the allocation be based on a written policy disclosed to clients and suggests that the securities be offered on a pro-rata basis among all clients who have comparable relationships with their broker–dealers.)

Investment banks have a conflict of interest with respect to the offering price in underwritten offerings. As agents for the issuers, they generally are supposed to select the offering price that will raise the most money. But as underwriters, they have strong incentives to choose a low price. If the price is low, the banks can allocate valuable shares to benefit their clients and thereby indirectly benefit the banks. If the price is too high, the underwriters will have to buy overvalued shares in the offering and perhaps also during the following month if they must support the price in the secondary market, which directly costs the banks. These considerations tend to lower initial offering prices so that prices in the secondary market often rise immediately following an IPO. They are less important in a seasoned offering because trading in the secondary market helps identify the proper price for the offering.

First time issuers generally accept lower offering prices because they and many others believe that an undersubscribed IPO conveys very unfavorable information to the market about the company's prospects at a time when it is most vulnerable to public opinion about its prospects. They fear that an undersubscribed initial public offering will make it substantially harder to raise additional capital in subsequent seasoned offerings.

EXAMPLE 24

The Playtech Initial Public Offering

Playtech is a designer, developer, and licensor of software for the gambling industry. On 28 March 2006, Playtech raised approximately £265 million gross through an initial public offering of 103,142,466 ordinary shares at £2.57 per ordinary share. After the initial public offering, Playtech had 213,333,333 ordinary shares issued and outstanding.

Playtech received gross proceeds of approximately £34.3 million and net proceeds of £31.8 million. The ordinary shares that were sold to the public represented approximately 48 percent of Playtech's total issued ordinary shares.

The shares commenced trading at 8:00 AM on the AIM market of the London Stock Exchange where Playtech opened at £2.74, traded 37 million shares between £2.68 and £2.74, and closed at £2.73.

1   Approximately how many new shares were issued by the company and how many shares were sold by the company's founders? What fraction of their holdings in the company did the founders sell?

2   Approximately what return did the subscribers who participated in the IPO make on the first day it traded?

3   Approximately how much did Playtech pay in placement costs as a percentage of the new funds raised?

Solution to 1:

Playtech received gross proceeds of £34.3 million at £2.57 per share so the company issued and sold 13,346,304 shares (= £34.3 million/£2.57 per share). The total placement was for 103,142,466 shares, so the founders sold 89,796,162 shares (= 103,142,466 shares − 13,346,304 shares). Because approximately 200 million = 213.3 million − 13.3 million shares were outstanding before the placement, the founders sold approximately 45 percent (= 90 million/200 million) of the company.

Solution to 2:

The subscribers bought the stock for £2.57 per share and it closed at £2.73. The first day return thus was $6.2\% = \dfrac{2.73 - 2.57}{2.57} \times 100$.

Solution to 3:

Playtech obtained gross proceeds of £34.3 million, but only raised net proceeds of £31.8 million. The £2.5 million difference was the total cost of the placement to the firm, which is 7.9 percent of £31.8 million net proceeds.

7.2 Private Placements and Other Primary Market Transactions

Corporations sometimes issue their securities in private placements. In a **private placement**, corporations sell securities directly to a small group of qualified investors, usually with the assistance of an investment bank. Qualified investors have sufficient knowledge and experience to recognize the risks that they assume, and sufficient wealth to assume those risks responsibly. Most countries allow corporations to do private placements without nearly as much public disclosure as is required for public offerings. Private placements, therefore, may be cheaper than public offerings, but the buyers generally require higher returns (lower purchase prices) because they cannot subsequently trade the securities in an organized secondary market.

Corporations sometimes sell new issues of seasoned securities directly to the public on a piecemeal basis via a shelf registration. In a **shelf registration**, the corporation makes all public disclosures that it would for a regular offering, but it does not sell the shares in a single transaction. Instead, it sells the shares directly into the secondary market over time, generally when it needs additional capital. Shelf registrations provide corporations with flexibility in the timing of their capital transactions, and they can alleviate the downward price pressures often associated with large secondary offerings.

Many corporations may also issue shares via dividend reinvestment plans (DRPs or DRIPs, for short) that allow their shareholders to reinvest their dividends in newly issued shares of the corporation (in particular, DRPs specify that the corporation issue new shares for the plan rather than purchase them on the open market). These plans sometimes also allow existing shareholders and other investors to buy additional stock at a slight discount to current prices.

Finally, corporations can issue new stock via a rights offering. In a rights offering, the corporation distributes rights to buy stock at a fixed price to existing shareholders in proportion to their holdings. Because the rights need not be exercised, they are options. The exercise price, however, is set below the current market price of the stock so that buying stock with the rights is immediately profitable. Consequently, shareholders will experience dilution in the value of their existing shares. They can offset the dilution loss by exercising their rights or by selling the rights to others who will exercise them. Shareholders generally do not like rights offerings because they must provide additional capital (or sell their rights) to avoid losses through dilution. Financial analysts recognize that these securities, although called rights, are actually short-term stock warrants and value them accordingly.

The national governments of financially strong countries generally issue their bonds, notes, and bills in public auctions organized by a government agency (usually associated with the finance ministry). They may also sell them directly to dealers.

Smaller and less financially secure national governments and most regional governments often contract with investment banks to help them sell and distribute their securities. The laws of many governments, however, require that they auction their securities.

EXAMPLE 25

Private and Public Placements

In what ways do private placements differ from public placements?

Solution:

Issuers make private placements to a limited number of investors that generally are financially sophisticated and well informed about risk. The investors generally have some relationship to the issuer. Issuers make public placements when they sell securities to the general public. Public placements generally require substantially more financial disclosure than do private placements.

7.3 Importance of Secondary Markets to Primary Markets

Corporations and governments can raise money in the primary markets at lower cost when their securities will trade in liquid secondary markets. In a **liquid market**, traders can buy or sell with low transaction costs and small price concessions when they want to trade. Buyers value liquidity because they may need to sell their securities to meet liquidity needs. Investors thus will pay more for securities that they can easily sell than for those that they cannot easily sell. Higher prices translate into lower costs of capital for the issuers.

SECONDARY SECURITY MARKET AND CONTRACT MARKET STRUCTURES

8

Trading is the successful outcome to a bilateral search in which buyers look for sellers and sellers look for buyers. Many market structures have developed to reduce the costs of this search. Markets are liquid when the costs of finding a suitable counterparty to a trade are low.

Trading in securities and contracts takes place in a variety of market structures. The structures differ by when trades can be arranged, who arranges the trades, how they do so, and how traders learn about possible trading opportunities and executed trades. This section introduces the various market structures used to trade securities and contracts. We first consider trading sessions, then execution mechanisms, and finally market information systems.

8.1 Trading Sessions

Markets are organized as call markets or as continuous trading markets. In a **call market**, trades can be arranged only when the market is called at a particular time and place. In contrast in a **continuous trading market**, trades can be arranged and executed anytime the market is open.

Buyers can easily find sellers and vice versa in call markets because all traders interested in trading (or orders representing their interests) are present at the same time and place. Call markets thus have the potential to be very liquid when they are called. But they are completely illiquid between trading sessions. In contrast, traders can arrange and execute their trades at anytime in continuous trading markets, but doing so can be difficult if the buyers and sellers (or their orders) are not both present at the same time.

Most call markets use single price auctions to match buyers to sellers. In these auctions, the market constructs order books representing all buy orders and all seller orders. The market then chooses a single trade price that will maximize the total volume of trade. The order books are supply and demand schedules, and the point at which they cross determines the trade price.

Call markets usually are organized just once a day, but some markets organize calls at more frequent intervals.

Many continuous trading markets start their trading with a call market auction. During a pre-opening period, traders submit their orders for the market call. At the opening, any possible trades are arranged and then trading continues in the continuous trading session. Some continuous trading markets also close their trading with a call. In these markets, traders who are only interested in trading in the closing call submit market- or limit-on-close orders.

EXAMPLE 26

Call Markets and Continuous Trading Markets

1 What is the main advantage of a call market compared with a continuous trading market?

2 What is the main advantage of a continuous trading market compared with a call market?

Solution to 1:

By gathering all traders to the same place at the same time, a call market makes it easier for buyers to find sellers and vice versa. In contrast, if buyers and sellers (or their orders) are not present at the same time in a continuous market, they cannot trade.

Solution to 2:

In a continuous trading market, a willing buyer and seller can trade at anytime the market is open. In contrast, in a call market trading can take place only when the market is called.

8.2 Execution Mechanisms

The three main types of market structures are quote-driven markets (sometimes called price-driven or dealer markets), order-driven markets, and brokered markets. In **quote-driven markets**, customers trade with dealers. In **order-driven markets**, an order matching system run by an exchange, a broker, or an alternative trading system uses rules to arrange trades based on the orders that traders submit. Most exchanges and ECNs organize order-driven markets. In **brokered markets**, brokers arrange trades between their customers. Brokered markets are common for transactions of unique instruments, such as real estate properties, intellectual properties, or large blocks of securities. Many trading systems use more than one type of market structure.

8.2.1 *Quote-Driven Markets*

Worldwide, most trading, other than in stocks, takes place in quote-driven markets. Almost all bonds and currencies and most spot commodities trade in quote-driven markets. Traders call them quote-driven (or price-driven or dealer) because customers trade at the prices quoted by dealers. Depending on the instrument traded, the dealers work for commercial banks, for investment banks, for broker–dealers, or for proprietary trading houses.

Quote-driven markets also often are called over-the-counter (OTC) markets because securities used to be literally traded over the dealer's counter in the dealer's office. Now, most trades in OTC markets are conducted over proprietary computer communications networks, by telephone, or sometimes over instant messaging systems.

8.2.2 *Order-Driven Markets*

Order-driven markets arrange trades using rules to match buy orders to sell orders. The orders may be submitted by customers or by dealers. Almost all exchanges use order-driven trading systems, and every automated trading system is an order-driven system.

Because rules match buyers to sellers, traders often trade with complete strangers. Order-driven markets thus must have procedures to ensure that buyers and sellers perform on their trade contracts. Otherwise, dishonest traders would enter contracts that they would not settle if a change in market conditions made settlement unprofitable.

Two sets of rules characterize order-driven market mechanisms: Order matching rules and trade pricing rules. The order matching rules match buy orders to sell orders. The trade pricing rules determine the prices at which the matched trades take place.

8.2.2.1 Order Matching Rules

Order-driven trading systems match buyers to sellers using rules that rank the buy orders and the sell orders based on price, and often along with other secondary criteria. The systems then match the highest ranking buy order with the highest ranking sell order. If the buyer is willing to pay at least as much as the seller is willing to receive, the system will arrange a trade for the minimum of the buy and sell quantities. The remaining size, if any, is then matched with the next order on the other side and the process continues until no further trades can be arranged.

The **order precedence hierarchy** determines which orders go first. The first rule is **price priority**: The highest priced buy orders and the lowest priced sell orders go first. They are the most aggressively priced orders. **Secondary precedence rules** determine how to rank orders at the same price. Most trading systems use time precedence to rank orders at the same price. The first order to arrive has precedence over other orders. In trading systems that permit hidden and partially hidden orders, displayed quantities at a given price generally have precedence over the undisplayed quantities. So the complete precedence hierarchy is given by price priority, display precedence at a given price, and finally time precedence among all orders with the same display status at a given price. These rules give traders incentives to improve price, display their orders, and arrive early if they want to trade quickly. These incentives increase market liquidity.

8.2.2.2 Trade Pricing Rules After the orders are matched, the trading system then uses its trade pricing rule to determine the trade price. The three rules that various order-driven markets use to price their trades are the uniform pricing rule, the discriminatory pricing rule, and the derivative pricing rule.

Call markets commonly use the uniform pricing rule. Under this rule, all trades execute at the same price. The market chooses the price that maximizes the total quantity traded.

Continuous trading markets use the **discriminatory pricing rule**. Under this rule, the limit price of the order or quote that first arrived—the standing order—determines the trade price. This rule allows a large arriving trader to discriminate among standing limit orders by filling the most aggressively priced orders first at their limit prices and then filling less aggressively priced orders at their less favorable (from the point of view of the arriving trader) limit prices. If trading systems did not use this pricing rule, large traders would break their orders into pieces to price discriminate on their own.

EXAMPLE 27

Filling a Large Order in a Continuous Trading Market

Before the arrival of a large order, a market has the following limit orders standing on its book:

Buyer	Bid Size	Limit Price(¥)	Offer Size	Seller
Takumi	15	100.1		
Hiroto	8	100.2		
Shou	10	100.3		
		100.4	4	Hina
		100.5	6	Sakur
		100.6	12	Miku

Buyer Tsubasa submits a day order to buy 15 contracts, limit ¥100.5. With whom does he trade, what is his average trade price, and what does the limit order book look like afterward?

Solution:

Tsubasa's buy order first fills with the most aggressively priced sell order, which is Hina's order for four contracts. A trade takes place at ¥100.4 for four contracts, Hina's order fills completely, and Tsubasa still has 11 more contracts remaining.

The next most aggressively priced sell order is Sakur's order for six contracts. A second trade takes place at ¥100.5 for six contracts, Sakur's order fills completely, and Tsubasa still has five more contracts remaining.

The next most aggressively priced sell order is Miku's order at ¥100.6. No further trade is possible, however, because her limit sell price is above Tsubasa's limit buy price. Tsubasa's average trade price is $¥100.46 = \dfrac{4 \times ¥100.4 + 6 \times ¥100.5}{4 + 6}$.

Because Tsubasa issued a day order, the remainder of his order is placed on the book on the buy side at ¥100.5. The following orders are then on the book:

Buyer	Bid Size	Limit Price (¥)	Offer Size	Seller
Takumi	15	100.1		
Hiroto	8	100.2		
Shou	10	100.3		

Buyer	Bid Size	Limit Price (¥)	Offer Size	Seller
		100.4		
Tsubasa	5	100.5		
		100.6	12	Miku

If Tsubasa had issued an immediate-or-cancel order, the remaining five contracts would have been cancelled.

Crossing networks use the derivative pricing rule. **Crossing networks** are trading systems that match buyers and sellers who are willing to trade at prices obtained from other markets. Most systems cross their trades at the midpoint of the best bid and ask quotes published by the exchange at which the security primarily trades. This pricing rule is called a **derivative pricing rule** because the price is derived from another market. In particular, the price does not depend on the orders submitted to the crossing network. Some crossing networks are organized as call markets and others as continuously trading markets. The most important crossing market is the equity trading system POSIT.

8.2.3 *Brokered Markets*

The third execution mechanism is the **brokered market**, in which brokers arrange trades among their clients. Brokers organize markets for instruments for which finding a buyer or a seller willing to trade is difficult because the instruments are unique and thus of interest only to a limited number of people or institutions. These instruments generally are also infrequently traded and expensive to carry in inventory. Examples of such instruments include very large blocks of stock, real estate properties, fine art masterpieces, intellectual properties, operating companies, liquor licenses, and taxi medallions. Because dealers generally are unable or unwilling to hold these assets in their inventories, they will not make markets in them. Organizing order-driven markets for these instruments is not sensible because too few traders would submit orders to them.

Successful brokers in these markets try to know everyone who might now or in the future be willing to trade. They spend most of their time on the telephone and in meetings building their networks.

EXAMPLE 28

Quote-Driven, Order-Driven, and Brokered Markets

What are the primary advantages of quote-driven, order-driven, and brokered markets?

Solution:

In a quote-driven market, dealers generally are available to supply liquidity. In an order-driven market, traders can supply liquidity to each other. In a brokered market, brokers help find traders who are willing to trade when dealers would not be willing to make markets and when traders would not be willing to post orders.

8.3 Market Information Systems

Markets vary in the type and quantity of data that they disseminate to the public. Traders say that a market is pre-trade transparent if the market publishes real-time data about quotes and orders. Markets are post-trade transparent if the market publishes trade prices and sizes soon after trades occur.

Buy-side traders value transparency because it allows them to better manage their trading, understand market values, and estimate their prospective and actual transaction costs. In contrast, dealers prefer to trade in opaque markets because, as frequent traders, they have an information advantage over those who know less than they do. Bid–ask spreads tend to be wider and transaction costs tend to be higher in opaque markets because finding the best available price is harder for traders in such markets.

9   WELL-FUNCTIONING FINANCIAL SYSTEMS

The financial system allows traders to solve financing and risk management problems. In a well-functioning financial system:

- investors can easily move money from the present to the future while obtaining a fair rate of return for the risks that they bear;

- borrowers can easily obtain funds that they need to undertake current projects if they can credibly promise to repay the funds in the future;

- hedgers can easily trade away or offset the risks that concern them; and

- traders can easily trade currencies for other currencies or commodities that they need.

If the assets or contracts needed to solve these problems are available to trade, the financial system has **complete markets**. If the costs of arranging these trades are low, the financial system is **operationally efficient**. If the prices of the assets and contracts reflect all available information related to fundamental values, the financial system is informationally efficient.

Well-functioning financial systems are characterized by:

- the existence of well-developed markets that trade instruments that help people solve their financial problems (complete markets);

- liquid markets in which the costs of trading—commissions, bid–ask spreads, and order price impacts—are low (operationally efficient markets);

- timely financial disclosures by corporations and governments that allow market participants to estimate the fundamental values of securities (support **informationally efficient markets**); and

- prices that reflect fundamental values so that prices vary primarily in response to changes in fundamental values and not to demands for liquidity made by uninformed traders (informationally efficient markets).

Such complete and operationally efficient markets are produced by financial intermediaries who:

- organize exchanges, brokerages, and alternative trading systems that match buyers to sellers;

- provide liquidity on demand to traders;

- securitize assets to produce investment instruments that are attractive to investors and thereby lower the costs of funds for borrowers;

- run banks that match investors to borrowers by taking deposits and making loans;

- run insurance companies that pool uncorrelated risks;

- provide investment advisory services that help investors manage and grow their assets at low cost;

- organize clearinghouses that ensure everyone settles their trades and contracts; and

- organize depositories that ensure nobody loses their assets.

The benefits of a well-functioning financial system are huge. In such systems, investors who need to move money to the future can easily connect with entrepreneurs who need money now to develop new products and services. Similarly, producers who would otherwise avoid valuable projects because they are too risky can easily transfer those risks to others who can better bear them. Most importantly, these transactions generally can take place among strangers so that the benefits from trading can be derived from an enormous number of potential matches.

In contrast, economies that have poorly functioning financial systems have great difficulties allocating capital among the many companies who could use it. Financial transactions tend to be limited to arrangements within families when people cannot easily find trustworthy counterparties who will honor their contracts. In such economies, capital is allocated inefficiently, risks are not easily shared, and production is inefficient.

An extraordinarily important byproduct of an operationally efficient financial system is the production of informationally efficient prices. Prices are informationally efficient when they reflect all available information about fundamental values. Informative prices are crucially important to the welfare of an economy because they help ensure that resources go where they are most valuable. Economies that use resources where they are most valuable are **allocationally efficient**. Economies that do not use resources where they are most valuable waste their resources and consequently often are quite poor.

Well-informed traders make prices informationally efficient. When they buy assets and contracts that they think are undervalued, they tend to push the assets' prices up. Similarly, when they sell assets and contracts that they think are overvalued, they tend to push the assets' prices down. The effect of their trading thus causes prices to reflect their information about values.

How accurately prices reflect fundamental information depends on the costs of obtaining fundamental information and on the liquidity available to well-informed traders. Accounting standards and reporting requirements that produce meaningful and timely financial disclosures reduce the costs of obtaining fundamental information and thereby allow analysts to form more accurate estimates of fundamental values. Liquid markets allow well-informed traders to fill their orders at low cost. If filling orders is very costly, informed trading may not be profitable. In that case, information-motivated traders will not commit resources to collect and analyze data and they will not trade. Without their research and their associated trading, prices would be less informative.

EXAMPLE 29

Well-Functioning Financial Systems

As a financial analyst specializing in emerging market equities, you understand that a well-functioning financial system contributes to the economic prosperity of a country. You are asked to start covering a new small market country. What factors will you consider when characterizing the quality of its financial markets?

Solution:

In general, you will consider whether:

- the country has markets that allow its companies and residents to finance projects, save for the future, and exchange risk;
- the costs of trading in those markets is low; and
- prices reflect fundamental values.

You may specifically check to see whether:

- fixed income and stock markets allow borrowers to easily obtain capital from investors;
- corporations disclose financial and operating data on a timely basis in conformity to widely respected reporting standards, such as IFRS;
- forward, futures, and options markets trade instruments that companies need to hedge their risks;
- dealers and arbitrageurs allow traders to trade when they want to;
- bid–ask spreads are small;
- trades and contracts invariably settle as expected;
- investment managers provide high-quality management services for reasonable fees;
- banks and other financing companies are well capitalized and thus able to help investors provide capital to borrowers;
- securitized assets are available and represent reasonable credit risks;
- insurance companies are well capitalized and thus able to help those exposed to risks insure against them; and
- price volatility appears consistent with changes in fundamental values.

10   MARKET REGULATION

Government agencies and practitioner organizations regulate many markets and the financial intermediaries that participate in them. The regulators generally seek to promote fair and orderly markets in which traders can trade at prices that accurately reflect fundamental values without incurring excessive transaction costs. This section identifies the problems that financial regulators hope to solve and the objectives of their regulations.

Regrettably, some people will steal from each other if given a chance, especially if the probability of detection is low or if the penalty for being caught is low. The number of ways that people can steal or misappropriate wealth generally increases with the complexity of their relationships and with asymmetries in their knowledge. Because financial markets tend to be complex, and because customers are often much less sophisticated than the professionals that serve them, the potential for losses through various frauds can be unacceptably high in unregulated markets.

Regulators thus ensure that systems are in place to protect customers from fraud. In principle, the customers themselves would demand such systems as a condition of doing business. When customers are unsophisticated or poorly informed, however, they may not know how to protect themselves. When the costs of learning are large—as they often are in complex financial markets—having regulators look out for the public interest can be economically efficient.

More customer money is probably lost in financial markets through negligence than through outright fraud. Most customers in financial markets use various agents to help them solve problems that they do not understand well. These agents include securities brokers, financial advisers, investment managers, and insurance agents. Because customers generally do not have much information about market conditions, they find it extremely difficult to measure the added value they obtain from their agents. This problem is especially challenging when performance has a strong random component. In that case, determining whether agents are skilled or lucky is very difficult. Moreover, if the agent is a good salesman, the customer may not critically evaluate their agent's performance. These conditions, which characterize most financial markets, ensure that customers cannot easily determine whether their agents are working faithfully for them. They tend to lose if their agents are unqualified or lazy, or if they unconsciously favor themselves and their friends over their clients, as is natural for even the most honest people.

Regulators help solve these agency problems by setting minimum standards of competence for agents and by defining and enforcing minimum standards of practice. CFA Institute provides significant standard setting leadership in the areas of investment management and investment performance reporting through its Chartered Financial Analyst Program, in which you are studying, and its Global Investment Performance Standards. In principle, regulation would not be necessary if customers could identify competent agents and effectively measure their performance. In the financial markets, doing so is very difficult.

Regulators often act to level the playing field for market participants. For example, in many jurisdictions, insider trading in securities is illegal. The rule prevents corporate insiders and others with access to corporate information from trading on material information that has not been released to the public. The purpose of the rule is to reduce the profits that insiders could extract from the markets. These profits would come from other traders who would lose when they trade with well-informed insiders. Because traders tend to withdraw from markets when they lose, rules against insider trading help keep markets liquid. They also keep corporate insiders from hoarding information.

Many situations arise in financial markets in which common standards benefit everyone involved. For example, having all companies report financial results on a common basis allows financial analysts to easily compare companies. Accordingly, the International Accounting Standards Board (IASB) and the US-based Financial Accounting Standards Board, among many others, promulgate common financial standards to which all companies must report. The benefits of having common reporting standards has led to a very successful and continuing effort to converge all accounting standards to a single worldwide standard. Without such regulations, investors might eventually refuse to invest in companies that do not report to a common standard, but such market-based discipline is a very slow regulator of behavior, and it would have little effect on companies that do not need to raise new capital.

Regulators generally require that financial firms maintain minimum levels of capital. These capital requirements serve two purposes. First, they ensure that the companies will be able to honor their contractual commitments when unexpected market movements or poor decisions cause them to lose money. Second, they ensure that the owners of financial firms have substantial interest in the decisions that they make. Without a substantial financial interest in the decisions that they make, companies often take too many risks and exercise poor judgment about extending credit to others. When such companies fail, they impose significant costs on others. Minimum capital requirements reduce the probability that financial firms will fail and they reduce the disruptions associated with those failures that do occur. In principle, a firm's customers and counterparties could require minimum capital levels as a condition of doing business with the firm, but they have more difficulty enforcing their contracts than do governments who can imprison people.

Regulators similarly regulate insurance companies and pension funds that make long-term promises to their clients. Such entities need to maintain adequate reserves to ensure that they can fund their liabilities. Unfortunately, their managers have a tendency to underestimate these reserves if they will not be around when the liabilities come due. Again, in principle, policyholders and employees could regulate the behavior of their insurance funds and their employers by refusing to contract with them if they do not promise to adequately fund their liabilities. In practice, however, the sophistication, information, and time necessary to write and enforce contracts that control these problems are beyond the reach of most people. The government thus is a sensible regulator of such problems.

Many regulators are self-regulating organizations (SROs) that regulate their members. Exchanges, clearinghouses, and dealer trade organizations are examples of self-regulating organizations. In some cases, the members of these organizations voluntarily subject themselves to the SRO's regulations to promote the common good. In other cases, governments delegate regulatory and enforcement authorities to SROs, usually subject to the supervision of a government agency, such as a national securities and exchange authority. Exchanges, dealer associations, and clearing agencies often regulate their members with these delegated powers.

By setting high standards of behavior, SROs help their members obtain the confidence of their customers. They also reduce the chance that members of the SRO will incur losses when dealing with other members of the SRO.

When regulators fail to solve the problems discussed here, the financial system does not function well. People who lose money stop saving and borrowers with good ideas cannot fund their projects. Similarly, hedgers withdraw from markets when the costs of hedging are high. Without the ability to hedge, producers become reluctant to specialize because specialization generally increases risk. Because specialization also decreases costs, however, production becomes less efficient as producers chose safer technologies. Economies that cannot solve the regulatory problems described in this section tend to operate less efficiently than do better regulated economies, and they tend to be less wealthy.

To summarize, the objectives of market regulation are to:

1   control fraud;

2   control agency problems;

3   promote fairness;

4   set mutually beneficial standards;

5   prevent undercapitalized financial firms from exploiting their investors by making excessively risky investments; and

6   ensure that long-term liabilities are funded.

Regulation is necessary because regulating certain behaviors through market-based mechanisms is too costly for people who are unsophisticated and uninformed. Effectively regulated markets allow people to better achieve their financial goals.

> ### EXAMPLE 30
>
> ## Bankrupt Traders
>
> You are the chief executive officer of a brokerage that is a member of a clearinghouse. A trader who clears through your firm is bankrupt at midday, but you do not yet know it even though your clearing agreement with him explicitly requires that he immediately report significant losses. The trader knows that if he takes a large position, prices might move in his favor so that he will no longer be bankrupt. The trader attempts to do so and succeeds. You find out about this later in the evening.
>
> 1 Why does the clearinghouse regulate its members?
>
> 2 What should you do about the trader?
>
> 3 Why would the clearinghouse allow you to keep his trading profits?
>
> **Solution to 1:**
>
> The clearinghouse regulates its members to ensure that no member imposes costs on another member by failing to settle a trade.
>
> **Solution to 2:**
>
> You should immediately end your clearing relationship with the trader and confiscate his trading profits. The trader was trading with your firm's capital after he became bankrupt. Had he lost, your firm would have borne the loss.
>
> **Solution to 3:**
>
> If the clearinghouse did not permit you to keep his trading profits, other traders similarly situated might attempt the same strategy.

SUMMARY

This reading introduces how the financial system operates and explains how well-functioning financial systems lead to wealthy economies. Financial analysts need to understand how the financial system works because their analyses often lead to trading decisions.

The financial system consists of markets and the financial intermediaries that operate in them. These institutions allow buyers to connect with sellers. They may trade directly with each other when they trade the same instrument or they only may trade indirectly when a financial intermediary connects the buyer to the seller through transactions with each that appear on the intermediary's balance sheet. The buyer and seller may exchange instruments, cash flows, or risks.

The following points, among others, were made in this reading:

- The financial system consists of mechanisms that allow strangers to contract with each other to move money through time, to hedge risks, and to exchange assets that they value less for those that they value more.

- Investors move money from the present to the future when they save. They expect a normal rate of return for bearing risk through time. Borrowers move money from the future to the present to fund current projects and expenditures. Hedgers trade to reduce their exposure to risks they prefer not to take. Information-motivated traders are active investment managers who try to identify under- and overvalued instruments.

- Securities are first sold in primary markets by their issuers. They then trade in secondary markets.

- People invest in pooled investment vehicles to benefit from the investment management services of their managers.

- Forward contracts allow buyers and sellers to arrange for future sales at predetermined prices. Futures contracts are forward contracts guaranteed by clearinghouses. The guarantee ensures that strangers are willing to trade with each other and that traders can offset their positions by trading with anybody. These features of futures contract markets make them highly attractive to hedgers and information-motivated traders.

- Many financial intermediaries connect buyers to sellers in a given instrument, acting directly as brokers and exchanges or indirectly as dealers and arbitrageurs.

- Financial intermediaries create instruments when they conduct arbitrage, securitize assets, borrow to lend, manage investment funds, or pool insurance contracts. These activities all transform cash flows and risks from one form to another. Their services allow buyers and sellers to connect with each other through instruments that meet their specific needs.

- Financial markets work best when strangers can contract with each other without worrying about whether their counterparts are able and willing to honor their contract. Clearinghouses, variation margins, maintenance margins, and settlement guarantees made by creditworthy brokers on behalf of their clients help manage credit risk and ultimately allow strangers to contract with each other.

- Information-motivated traders short sell when they expect that prices will fall. Hedgers short sell to reduce the risks of a long position in a related contract or commodity.

- Margin loans allow people to buy more securities than their equity would otherwise permit them to buy. The larger positions expose them to more risk so that gains and losses for a given amount of equity will be larger. The leverage ratio is the value of a position divided by the value of the equity supporting it. The returns to the equity in a position are equal to the leverage ratio times the returns to the unleveraged position.

- To protect against credit losses, brokers demand maintenance margin payments from their customers who have borrowed cash or securities when adverse price changes cause their customer's equity to drop below the maintenance margin ratio. Brokers close positions for customers who do not satisfy these margin calls.

- Orders are instructions to trade. They always specify instrument, side (buy or sell), and quantity. They usually also provide several other instructions.

- Market orders tend to fill quickly but often at inferior prices. Limit orders generally fill at better prices if they fill, but they may not fill. Traders choose order submission strategies on the basis of how quickly they want to trade, the prices they are willing to accept, and the consequences of failing to trade.

- Stop instructions are attached to other orders to delay efforts to fill them until the stop condition is satisfied. Although stop orders are often used to stop losses, they are not always effective.

- Issuers sell their securities using underwritten public offerings, best efforts public offerings, private placements, shelf registrations, dividend reinvestment programs, and rights offerings. Investment banks have a conflict of interests when setting the initial offering price in an IPO.

- Well-functioning secondary markets are essential to raising capital in the primary markets because investors value the ability to sell their securities if they no longer want to hold them or if they need to disinvest to raise cash. If they cannot trade their securities in a liquid market, they will not pay as much for them.

- Matching buyers and sellers in call markets is easy because the traders (or their orders) come together at the same time and place.

- Dealers provide liquidity in quote-driven markets. Public traders as well as dealers provide liquidity in order-driven markets.

- Order-driven markets arrange trades by ranking orders using precedence rules. The rules generally ensure that traders who provide the best prices, display the most size, and arrive early trade first. Continuous order-driven markets price orders using the discriminatory pricing rule. Under this rule, standing limit orders determine trade prices.

- Brokers help people trade unique instruments or positions for which finding a buyer or a seller is difficult.

- Transaction costs are lower in transparent markets than in opaque markets because traders can more easily determine market value and more easily manage their trading in transparent markets.

- A well-functioning financial system allows people to trade instruments that best solve their wealth and risk management problems with low transaction costs. Complete and liquid markets characterize a well-functioning financial system. Complete markets are markets in which the instruments needed to solve investment and risk management problems are available to trade. Liquid markets are markets in which traders can trade when they want to trade at low cost.

- The financial system is operationally efficient when its markets are liquid. Liquid markets lower the costs of raising capital.

- A well-functioning financial system promotes wealth by ensuring that capital allocation decisions are well made. A well-functioning financial system also promotes wealth by allowing people to share the risks associated with valuable products that would otherwise not be undertaken.

- Prices are informationally efficient when they reflect all available information about fundamental values. Information-motivated traders make prices informationally efficient. Prices will be most informative in liquid markets because information-motivated traders will not invest in information and research if establishing positions based on their analyses is too costly.

- Regulators generally seek to promote fair and orderly markets in which traders can trade at prices that accurately reflect fundamental values without incurring excessive transaction costs. Governmental agencies and self-regulating organizations of practitioners provide regulatory services that attempt to make markets safer and more efficient.

- Mandated financial disclosure programs for the issuers of publicly traded securities ensure that information necessary to estimate security values is available to financial analysts on a consistent basis.

PRACTICE PROBLEMS

1   Akihiko Takabe has designed a sophisticated forecasting model, which predicts the movements in the overall stock market, in the hope of earning a return in excess of a fair return for the risk involved. He uses the predictions of the model to decide whether to buy, hold, or sell the shares of an index fund that aims to replicate the movements of the stock market. Takabe would *best* be characterized as a(n):

    A   hedger.

    B   investor.

    C   information-motivated trader.

2   James Beach is young and has substantial wealth. A significant proportion of his stock portfolio consists of emerging market stocks that offer relatively high expected returns at the cost of relatively high risk. Beach believes that investment in emerging market stocks is appropriate for him given his ability and willingness to take risk. Which of the following labels *most appropriately* describes Beach?

    A   Hedger.

    B   Investor.

    C   Information-motivated trader.

3   Lisa Smith owns a manufacturing company in the United States. Her company has sold goods to a customer in Brazil and will be paid in Brazilian real (BRL) in three months. Smith is concerned about the possibility of the BRL depreciating more than expected against the US dollar (USD). Therefore, she is planning to sell three-month futures contracts on the BRL. The seller of such contracts generally gains when the BRL depreciates against the USD. If Smith were to sell these future contracts, she would *most appropriately* be described as a(n):

    A   hedger.

    B   investor.

    C   information-motivated trader.

4   Which of the following is *not* a function of the financial system?

    A   To regulate arbitrageurs' profits (excess returns).

    B   To help the economy achieve allocational efficiency.

    C   To facilitate borrowing by businesses to fund current operations.

5   An investor primarily invests in stocks of publicly traded companies. The investor wants to increase the diversification of his portfolio. A friend has recommended investing in real estate properties. The purchase of real estate would *best* be characterized as a transaction in the:

    A   derivative investment market.

    B   traditional investment market.

    C   alternative investment market.

6   A hedge fund holds its excess cash in 90-day commercial paper and negotiable certificates of deposit. The cash management policy of the hedge fund is *best described* as using:

    A   capital market instruments.

B money market instruments.

C intermediate-term debt instruments.

7 An oil and gas exploration and production company announces that it is offering 30 million shares to the public at $45.50 each. This transaction is *most likely* a sale in the:

A futures market.

B primary market.

C secondary market.

8 Consider a mutual fund that invests primarily in fixed-income securities that have been determined to be appropriate given the fund's investment goal. Which of the following is *least likely* to be a part of this fund?

A Warrants.

B Commercial paper.

C Repurchase agreements.

9 A friend has asked you to explain the differences between open-end and closed-end funds. Which of the following will you *most likely* include in your explanation?

A Closed-end funds are unavailable to new investors.

B When investors sell the shares of an open-end fund, they can receive a discount or a premium to the fund's net asset value.

C When selling shares, investors in an open-end fund sell the shares back to the fund whereas investors in a closed-end fund sell the shares to others in the secondary market.

10 The usefulness of a forward contract is limited by some problems. Which of the following is *most likely* one of those problems?

A Once you have entered into a forward contract, it is difficult to exit from the contract.

B Entering into a forward contract requires the long party to deposit an initial amount with the short party.

C If the price of the underlying asset moves adversely from the perspective of the long party, periodic payments must be made to the short party.

11 Tony Harris is planning to start trading in commodities. He has heard about the use of futures contracts on commodities and is learning more about them. Which of the following is Harris *least likely* to find associated with a futures contract?

A Existence of counterparty risk.

B Standardized contractual terms.

C Payment of an initial margin to enter into a contract.

12 A German company that exports machinery is expecting to receive $10 million in three months. The firm converts all its foreign currency receipts into euros. The chief financial officer of the company wishes to lock in a minimum fixed rate for converting the $10 million to euro but also wants to keep the flexibility to use the future spot rate if it is favorable. What hedging transaction is *most likely* to achieve this objective?

A Selling dollars forward.

B Buying put options on the dollar.

C Selling futures contracts on dollars.

13 A book publisher requires substantial quantities of paper. The publisher and a paper producer have entered into an agreement for the publisher to buy and the producer to supply a given quantity of paper four months later at a price agreed upon today. This agreement is a:

    A futures contract.

    B forward contract.

    C commodity swap.

14 The Standard & Poor's Depositary Receipts (SPDRs) is an investment that tracks the S&P 500 stock market index. Purchases and sales of SPDRs during an average trading day are *best* described as:

    A primary market transactions in a pooled investment.

    B secondary market transactions in a pooled investment.

    C secondary market transactions in an actively managed investment.

15 The Standard & Poor's Depositary Receipts (SPDRs) is an exchange-traded fund in the United States that is designed to track the S&P 500 stock market index. The current price of a share of SPDRs is $113. A trader has just bought call options on shares of SPDRs for a premium of $3 per share. The call options expire in five months and have an exercise price of $120 per share. On the expiration date, the trader will exercise the call options (ignore any transaction costs) if and only if the shares of SPDRs are trading:

    A below $120 per share.

    B above $120 per share.

    C above $123 per share.

16 Which of the following statements about exchange-traded funds is *most correct*?

    A Exchange-traded funds are not backed by any assets.

    B The investment companies that create exchange-traded funds are financial intermediaries.

    C The transaction costs of trading shares of exchange-traded funds are substantially greater than the combined costs of trading the underlying assets of the fund.

17 Jason Schmidt works for a hedge fund and he specializes in finding profit opportunities that are the result of inefficiencies in the market for convertible bonds—bonds that can be converted into a predetermined amount of a company's common stock. Schmidt tries to find convertibles that are priced inefficiently relative to the underlying stock. The trading strategy involves the simultaneous purchase of the convertible bond and the short sale of the underlying common stock. The above process could best be described as:

    A hedging.

    B arbitrage.

    C securitization.

18 Pierre-Louis Robert just purchased a call option on shares of the Michelin Group. A few days ago he wrote a put option on Michelin shares. The call and put options have the same exercise price, expiration date, and number of shares underlying. Considering both positions, Robert's exposure to the risk of the stock of the Michelin Group is:

    A long.

    B short.

    C neutral.

19 An online brokerage firm has set the minimum margin requirement at 55 percent. What is the maximum leverage ratio associated with a position financed by this minimum margin requirement?

A 1.55.

B 1.82.

C 2.22.

20 A trader has purchased 200 shares of a non-dividend-paying firm on margin at a price of $50 per share. The leverage ratio is 2.5. Six months later, the trader sells these shares at $60 per share. Ignoring the interest paid on the borrowed amount and the transaction costs, what was the return to the trader during the six-month period?

A 20 percent.

B 33.33 percent.

C 50 percent.

21 Jason Williams purchased 500 shares of a company at $32 per share. The stock was bought on 75 percent margin. One month later, Williams had to pay interest on the amount borrowed at a rate of 2 percent per month. At that time, Williams received a dividend of $0.50 per share. Immediately after that he sold the shares at $28 per share. He paid commissions of $10 on the purchase and $10 on the sale of the stock. What was the rate of return on this investment for the one-month period?

A −12.5 percent.

B −15.4 percent.

C −50.1 percent.

22 Caroline Rogers believes the price of Gamma Corp. stock will go down in the near future. She has decided to sell short 200 shares of Gamma Corp. at the current market price of €47. The initial margin requirement is 40 percent. Which of the following is an appropriate statement regarding the margin requirement that Rogers is subject to on this short sale?

A She will need to contribute €3,760 as margin.

B She will need to contribute €5,640 as margin.

C She will only need to leave the proceeds from the short sale as deposit and does not need to contribute any additional funds.

23 The current price of a stock is $25 per share. You have $10,000 to invest. You borrow an additional $10,000 from your broker and invest $20,000 in the stock. If the maintenance margin is 30 percent, at what price will a margin call first occur?

A $9.62.

B $17.86.

C $19.71.

24 You have placed a sell market-on-open order—a market order that would automatically be submitted at the market's open tomorrow and would fill at the market price. Your instruction, to sell the shares at the market open, is a(n):

A execution instruction.

B validity instruction.

C clearing instruction.

25 A market has the following limit orders standing on its book for a particular stock. The bid and ask sizes are number of shares in hundreds.

Bid Size	Limit Price (€)	Offer Size
5	9.73	
12	9.81	
4	9.84	
6	9.95	
	10.02	5
	10.10	12
	10.14	8

What is the market?

A   9.73 bid, offered at 10.14.

B   9.81 bid, offered at 10.10.

C   9.95 bid, offered at 10.02.

26 Consider the following limit order book for a stock. The bid and ask sizes are number of shares in hundreds.

Bid Size	Limit Price (¥)	Offer Size
3	122.80	
8	123.00	
4	123.35	
	123.80	7
	124.10	6
	124.50	7

A new buy limit order is placed for 300 shares at ¥123.40. This limit order is said to:

A   take the market.

B   make the market.

C   make a new market.

27 Currently, the market in a stock is "$54.62 bid, offered at $54.71." A new sell limit order is placed at $54.62. This limit order is said to:

A   take the market.

B   make the market.

C   make a new market.

28 Jim White has sold short 100 shares of Super Stores at a price of $42 per share. He has also simultaneously placed a "good-till-cancelled, stop 50, limit 55 buy" order. Assume that if the stop condition specified by White is satisfied and the order becomes valid, it will get executed. Excluding transaction costs, what is the maximum possible loss that White can have?

A $800.

B $1,300.

C   Unlimited.

29 You own shares of a company that are currently trading at $30 a share. Your technical analysis of the shares indicates a support level of $27.50. That is, if the price of the shares is going down, it is more likely to stay above this level rather than fall below it. If the price does fall below this level, however, you believe that the price may continue to decline. You have no immediate intent to sell the

shares but are concerned about the possibility of a huge loss if the share price declines below the support level. Which of the following types of orders could you place to most appropriately address your concern?

A Short sell order.

B Good-till-cancelled stop sell order.

C Good-till-cancelled stop buy order.

30 In an underwritten offering, the risk that the entire issue may not be sold to the public at the stipulated offering price is borne by the:

A issuer.

B investment bank.

C buyers of the part of the issue that is sold.

31 A British company listed on the Alternative Investment Market of the London Stock Exchange, announced the sale of 6,686,665 shares to a small group of qualified investors at £0.025 per share. Which of the following *best describes* this sale?

A Shelf registration.

B Private placement.

C Initial public offering.

32 A German publicly traded company, to raise new capital, gave its existing shareholders the opportunity to subscribe for new shares. The existing shareholders could purchase two new shares at a subscription price of €4.58 per share for every 15 shares held. This is an example of a(n):

A rights offering.

B private placement.

C initial public offering.

33 Consider an order-driven system that allows hidden orders. The following four sell orders on a particular stock are currently in the system's limit order book. Based on the commonly used order precedence hierarchy, which of these orders will have precedence over others?

Order	Time of Arrival (HH:MM:SS)	Limit Price (€)	Special Instruction (If any)
I	9:52:01	20.33	
II	9:52:08	20.29	Hidden order
III	9:53:04	20.29	
IV	9:53:49	20.29	

A Order I (time of arrival of 9:52:01).

B Order II (time of arrival of 9:52:08).

C Order III (time of arrival of 9:53:04).

34 Zhenhu Li has submitted an immediate-or-cancel buy order for 500 shares of a company at a limit price of CNY 74.25. There are two sell limit orders standing in that stock's order book at that time. One is for 300 shares at a limit price of CNY 74.30 and the other is for 400 shares at a limit price of CNY 74.35. How many shares in Li's order would get cancelled?

A None (the order would remain open but unfilled).

B 200 (300 shares would get filled).

C 500 (there would be no fill).

35 A market has the following limit orders standing on its book for a particular stock:

Buyer	Bid Size (Number of Shares)	Limit Price (£)	Offer Size (Number of Shares)	Seller
Keith	1,000	19.70		
Paul	200	19.84		
Ann	400	19.89		
Mary	300	20.02		
		20.03	800	Jack
		20.11	1,100	Margaret
		20.16	400	Jeff

Ian submits a day order to sell 1,000 shares, limit £19.83. Assuming that no more buy orders are submitted on that day after Ian submits his order, what would be Ian's average trade price?

A £19.70.

B £19.92.

C £20.05.

36 A financial analyst is examining whether a country's financial market is well functioning. She finds that the transaction costs in this market are low and trading volumes are high. She concludes that the market is quite liquid. In such a market:

A traders will find it hard to make use of their information.

B traders will find it easy to trade and their trading will make the market less informationally efficient.

C traders will find it easy to trade and their trading will make the market more informationally efficient.

37 The government of a country whose financial markets are in an early stage of development has hired you as a consultant on financial market regulation. Your first task is to prepare a list of the objectives of market regulation. Which of the following is *least likely* to be included in this list of objectives?

A Minimize agency problems in the financial markets.

B Ensure that financial markets are fair and orderly.

C Ensure that investors in the stock market achieve a rate of return that is at least equal to the risk-free rate of return.

SOLUTIONS

1   C is correct. Takabe is best characterized as an information-motivated trader. Takabe believes that his model provides him superior information about the movements in the stock market and his motive for trading is to profit from this information.

2   B is correct. Beach is an investor. He is simply investing in risky assets consistent with his level of risk aversion. Beach is not hedging any existing risk or using information to identify and trade mispriced securities. Therefore, he is not a hedger or an information-motivated trader.

3   A is correct. Smith is a hedger. The short position on the BRL futures contract offsets the BRL long position in three months. She is hedging the risk of the BRL depreciating against the USD. If the BRL depreciates, the value of the cash inflow goes down in USD terms but there is a gain on the futures contracts.

4   A is correct. Regulation of arbitrageurs' profits is not a function of the financial system. The financial system facilitates the allocation of capital to the best uses and the purposes for which people use the financial system, including borrowing money.

5   C is correct. The purchase of real estate properties is a transaction in the alternative investment market.

6   B is correct. The 90-day commercial paper and negotiable certificates of deposit are money market instruments.

7   B is correct. This transaction is a sale in the primary market. It is a sale of shares from the issuer to the investor and funds flow to the issuer of the security from the purchaser.

8   A is correct. Warrants are least likely to be part of the fund. Warrant holders have the right to buy the issuer's common stock. Thus, warrants are typically classified as equity and are least likely to be a part of a fixed-income mutual fund. Commercial paper and repurchase agreements are short-term fixed-income securities.

9   C is correct. When investors want to sell their shares, investors of an open-end fund sell the shares back to the fund whereas investors of a closed-end fund sell the shares to others in the secondary market. Closed-end funds are available to new investors but they must purchase shares in the fund in the secondary market. The shares of a closed-end fund trade at a premium or discount to net asset value.

10   A is correct. Once you have entered into a forward contract, it is difficult to exit from the contract. As opposed to a futures contract, trading out of a forward contract is quite difficult. There is no exchange of cash at the origination of a forward contract. There is no exchange on a forward contract until the maturity of the contract.

11   A is correct. Harris is least likely to find counterparty risk associated with a futures contract. There is limited counterparty risk in a futures contract because the clearinghouse is on the other side of every contract.

12   B is correct. Buying a put option on the dollar will ensure a minimum exchange rate but does not have to be exercised if the exchange rate moves in a favorable direction. Forward and futures contracts would lock in a fixed rate but would not allow for the possibility to profit in case the value of the dollar three months later in the spot market turns out to be greater than the value in the forward or futures contract.

13 B is correct. The agreement between the publisher and the paper supplier to respectively buy and supply paper in the future at a price agreed upon today is a forward contract.

14 B is correct. SPDRs trade in the secondary market and are a pooled investment vehicle.

15 B is correct. The holder of the call option will exercise the call options if the price is above the exercise price of $120 per share. Note that if the stock price is above $120 but less than $123, the option would be exercised even though the net result for the option buyer after considering the premium is a loss. For example, if the stock price is $122, the option buyer would exercise the option to make $2 = $122 – $120 per share, resulting in a loss of $1 = $3 – $2 after considering the premium. It is better to exercise and have a loss of only $1, however, rather than not exercise and lose the entire $3 premium.

16 B is correct. The investment companies that create exchange-traded funds (ETFs) are financial intermediaries. ETFs are securities that represent ownership in the assets held by the fund. The transaction costs of trading shares of ETFs are substantially lower than the combined costs of trading the underlying assets of the ETF.

17 B is correct. The process can best be described as arbitrage because it involves buying and selling instruments, whose values are closely related, at different prices in different markets.

18 A is correct. Robert's exposure to the risk of the stock of the Michelin Group is long. The exposure as a result of the long call position is long. The exposure as a result of the short put position is also long. Therefore, the combined exposure is long.

19 B is correct. The maximum leverage ratio is 1.82 = 100% position ÷ 55% equity. The maximum leverage ratio associated with a position financed by the minimum margin requirement is one divided by the minimum margin requirement.

20 C is correct. The return is 50 percent. If the position had been unleveraged, the return would be 20% = (60 – 50)/50. Because of leverage, the return is 50% = 2.5 × 20%.

Another way to look at this problem is that the equity contributed by the trader (the minimum margin requirement) is 40% = 100% ÷ 2.5. The trader contributed $20 = 40% of $50 per share. The gain is $10 per share, resulting in a return of 50% = 10/20.

21 B is correct. The return is –15.4 percent.

Total cost of the purchase = $16,000 = 500 × $32

Equity invested = $12,000 = 0.75 × $16,000

Amount borrowed = $4,000 = 16,000 – 12,000

Interest paid at month end = $80 = 0.02 × $4,000

Dividend received at month end = $250 = 500 × $0.50

Proceeds on stock sale = $14,000 = 500 × $28

Total commissions paid = $20 = $10 + $10

Net gain/loss = –$1,850 = –16,000 – 80 + 250 + 14,000 – 20

Initial investment including commission on purchase = $12,010

Return = –15.4% = –$1,850/$12,010

22 A is correct. She will need to contribute €3,760 as margin. In view of the possibility of a loss, if the stock price goes up, she will need to contribute €3,760 = 40% of €9,400 as the initial margin. Rogers will need to leave the proceeds from the short sale (€9,400 = 200 × €47) on deposit.

23 B is correct. A margin call will first occur at a price of $17.86. Because you have contributed half and borrowed the remaining half, your initial equity is 50 percent of the initial stock price, or $12.50 = 0.50 × $25. If P is the subsequent price, your equity would change by an amount equal to the change in price. So, your equity at price P would be 12.50 + (P – 25). A margin call will occur when the percentage margin drops to 30 percent. So, the price at which a margin call will occur is the solution to the following equation.

$$\frac{Equity \ / \ Share}{Price \ / \ Share} = \frac{12.50 + P - 25}{P} = 30\%$$

The solution is P = $17.86.

24 B is correct. An instruction regarding when to fill an order is considered a validity instruction.

25 C is correct. The market is 9.95 bid, offered at 10.02. The best bid is at €9.95 and the best offer is €10.02.

26 C is correct. This order is said to make a new market. The new buy order is at ¥123.40, which is better than the current best bid of ¥123.35. Therefore, the buy order is making a new market. Had the new order been at ¥123.35, it would be said to make the market. Because the new buy limit order is at a price less than the best offer of ¥123.80, it will not immediately execute and is not taking the market.

27 A is correct. This order is said to take the market. The new sell order is at $54.62, which is at the current best bid. Therefore, the new sell order will immediately trade with the current best bid and is taking the market.

28 B is correct. The maximum possible loss is $1,300. If the stock price crosses $50, the stop buy order will become valid and will get executed at a maximum limit price of $55. The maximum loss per share is $13 = $55 – $42, or $1,300 for 100 shares.

29 B is correct. The most appropriate order is a good-till-cancelled stop sell order. This order will be acted on if the stock price declines below a specified price (in this case, $27.50). This order is sometimes referred to as a good-till-cancelled stop loss sell order. You are generally bullish about the stock, as indicated by no immediate intent to sell, and would expect a loss on short selling the stock. A stop buy order is placed to buy a stock when the stock is going up.

30 B is correct. The investment bank bears the risk that the issue may be undersubscribed at the offering price. If the entire issue is not sold, the investment bank underwriting the issue will buy the unsold securities at the offering price.

31 B is correct. This sale is a private placement. As the company is already publicly traded, the share sale is clearly not an initial public offering. The sale also does not involve a shelf registration because the company is not selling shares to the public on a piecemeal basis.

32 A is correct. This offering is a rights offering. The company is distributing rights to buy stock at a fixed price to existing shareholders in proportion to their holdings.

33 C is correct. Order III (time of arrival of 9:53:04) has precedence. In the order precedence hierarchy, the first rule is price priority. Based on this rule, sell orders II, III, and IV get precedence over order I. The next rule is display precedence at a given price. Because order II is a hidden order, orders III and IV get precedence. Finally, order III gets precedence over order IV based on time priority at same price and same display status.

34 C is correct. The order for 500 shares would get cancelled; there would be no fill. Li is willing to buy at CNY 74.25 or less but the minimum offer price in the book is CNY 74.30; therefore, no part of the order would be filled. Because Li's order is immediate-or-cancel, it would be cancelled.

35 B is correct. Ian's average trade price is:

$$£19.92 = \frac{300 \times £20.02 + 400 \times £19.89 \ + \ 200 \times £19.84}{300 + 400 + 200}$$

Ian's sell order first fills with the most aggressively priced buy order, which is Mary's order for 300 shares at £20.02. Ian still has 700 shares for sale. The next most aggressively priced buy order is Ann's order for 400 shares at £19.89. This order is filled. Ian still has 300 shares for sale. The next most aggressively priced buy order is Paul's order for 200 shares at £19.84. A third trade takes place. Ian still has 100 shares for sale.

The next buy order is Keith's order for 1,000 shares at £19.70. However, this price is below Ian's limit price of £19.83. Therefore, no more trade is possible.

36 C is correct. In such a market, well-informed traders will find it easy to trade and their trading will make the market more informationally efficient. In a liquid market, it is easier for informed traders to fill their orders. Their trading will cause prices to incorporate their information and the prices will be more in line with the fundamental values.

37 C is correct. Ensure that investors in the stock market achieve a rate of return that is at least equal to the risk-free rate of return is least likely to be included as an objective of market regulation. Stocks are risky investments and there would be occasions when a stock market investment would not only have a return less than the risk-free rate but also a negative return. Minimizing agency costs and ensuring that financial markets are fair and orderly are objectives of market regulation.

Security Market Indices

by Paul D. Kaplan, CFA, and Dorothy C. Kelly, CFA

LEARNING OUTCOMES

Mastery	The candidate should be able to:
☐	a. describe a security market index;
☐	b. calculate and interpret the value, price return, and total return of an index;
☐	c. describe the choices and issues in index construction and management;
☐	d. compare the different weighting methods used in index construction;
☐	e. calculate and analyze the value and return of an index given its weighting method;
☐	f. describe rebalancing and reconstitution of an index;
☐	g. describe uses of security market indices;
☐	h. describe types of equity indices;
☐	i. describe types of fixed-income indices;
☐	j. describe indices representing alternative investments;
☐	k. compare types of security market indices.

INTRODUCTION

1

Investors gather and analyze vast amounts of information about security markets on a continual basis. Because this work can be both time consuming and data intensive, investors often use a single measure that consolidates this information and reflects the performance of an entire security market.

Security market indices were first introduced as a simple measure to reflect the performance of the US stock market. Since then, security market indices have evolved into important multi-purpose tools that help investors track the performance of various security markets, estimate risk, and evaluate the performance of investment managers. They also form the basis for new investment products.

> **in·dex**, *noun* (*pl.* **in·dex·es** *or* **in·di·ces**) Latin *indic-, index,* from *indicare* to indicate: an indicator, sign, or measure of something.

ORIGIN OF MARKET INDICES

Investors had access to regularly published data on individual security prices in London as early as 1698, but nearly 200 years passed before they had access to a simple indicator to reflect security market information.[1] To give readers a sense of how the US stock market in general performed on a given day, publishers Charles H. Dow and Edward D. Jones introduced the Dow Jones Average, the world's first security market index, in 1884.[2] The index, which appeared in *The Customers' Afternoon Letter*, consisted of the stocks of nine railroads and two industrial companies. It eventually became the Dow Jones Transportation Average.[3] Convinced that industrial companies, rather than railroads, would be "the great speculative market" of the future, Dow and Jones introduced a second index in May 1896—the Dow Jones Industrial Average (DJIA). It had an initial value of 40.94 and consisted of 12 stocks from major US industries.[4,5] Today, investors can choose from among thousands of indices to measure and monitor different security markets and asset classes.

This reading is organized as follows. Section 2 defines a security market index and explains how to calculate the price return and total return of an index for a single period and over multiple periods. Section 3 describes how indices are constructed and managed. Section 4 discusses the use of market indices. Sections 5, 6, and 7 discuss various types of indices, and the final section summarizes the reading. Practice problems follow the conclusions and summary.

2   INDEX DEFINITION AND CALCULATIONS OF VALUE AND RETURNS

A **security market index** represents a given security market, market segment, or asset class. Most indices are constructed as portfolios of marketable securities.

The value of an index is calculated on a regular basis using either the actual or estimated market prices of the individual securities, known as **constituent securities**, within the index. For each security market index, investors may encounter two versions of the same index (i.e., an index with identical constituent securities and weights): one version based on price return and one version based on total return. As the name suggests, a **price return index**, also known as a **price index**, reflects *only* the prices of the constituent securities within the index. A **total return index**, in contrast, reflects not only the prices of the constituent securities but also the reinvestment of all income received since inception.

1 London Stock Exchange, "Our History" (2009): www.londonstockexchange.com.
2 Dow Jones & Company, "Dow Jones Industrial Average Historical Components," (2008):2.
3 Dow Jones & Company, "Dow Jones History" (2009): www.dowjones.com/history.asp.
4 Dow Jones & Company, *The Market's Measure*, edited by John A. Presbo (1999):11.
5 Dow Jones & Company, "Dow Jones Industrial Average Historical Components" (2008):2.

At inception, the values of the price and total return versions of an index are equal. As time passes, however, the value of the total return index, which includes the reinvestment of all dividends and/or interest received, will exceed the value of the price return index by an increasing amount. A look at how the values of each version are calculated over multiple periods illustrates why.

The value of a price return index is calculated as:

$$V_{PRI} = \frac{\sum_{i=1}^{N} n_i P_i}{D} \tag{1}$$

where

V_{PRI} = the value of the price return index
n_i = the number of units of constituent security i held in the index portfolio
N = the number of constituent securities in the index
P_i = the unit price of constituent security i
D = the value of the divisor

The **divisor** is a number initially chosen at inception. It is frequently chosen so that the price index has a convenient initial value, such as 1,000. The index provider then adjusts the value of the divisor as necessary to avoid changes in the index value that are unrelated to changes in the prices of its constituent securities. For example, when changing index constituents, the index provider may adjust the divisor so that the value of the index with the new constituents equals the value of the index prior to the changes.

Index return calculations, like calculations of investment portfolio returns, may measure price return or total return. **Price return** measures only price appreciation or percentage change in price. **Total return** measures price appreciation plus interest, dividends, and other distributions.

2.1 Calculation of Single-Period Returns

For a security market index, price return can be calculated in two ways: either the percentage change in value of the price return index, or the weighted average of price returns of the constituent securities. The price return of an index can be expressed as:

$$PR_I = \frac{V_{PRI1} - V_{PRI0}}{V_{PRI0}} \tag{2}$$

where

PR_I = the price return of the index portfolio (as a decimal number, i.e., 12 percent is 0.12)
V_{PRI1} = the value of the price return index at the end of the period
V_{PRI0} = the value of the price return index at the beginning of the period

Similarly, the price return of each constituent security can be expressed as:

$$PR_i = \frac{P_{i1} - P_{i0}}{P_{i0}} \tag{3}$$

where

PR_i = the price return of constituent security i (as a decimal number)
P_{i1} = the price of constituent security i at the end of the period
P_{i0} = the price of constituent security i at the beginning of the period

Because the price return of the index equals the weighted average of price returns of the individual securities, we can write:

$$PR_I = \sum_{i=1}^{N} w_i PR_i = \sum_{i=1}^{N} w_i \left(\frac{P_{i1} - P_{i0}}{P_{i0}} \right) = 1 \tag{4}$$

where:

PR_I = the price return of index portfolio (as a decimal number)

PR_i = the price return of constituent security i (as a decimal number)

N = the number of individual securities in the index

w_i = the weight of security i (the fraction of the index portfolio allocated to security i)

P_{i1} = the price of constituent security i at the end of the period

P_{i0} = the price of constituent security i at the beginning of the period

Equation 4 can be rewritten simply as:

$$PR_I = w_1 PR_1 + w_2 PR_2 + \ldots + w_N PR_N \tag{5}$$

where

PR_I = the price return of index portfolio (as a decimal number)

PR_i = the price return of constituent security i (as a decimal number)

w_i = the weight of security i (the fraction of the index portfolio allocated to security i)

N = the number of securities in the index

Total return measures price appreciation plus interest, dividends, and other distributions. Thus, the **total return** of an index is the price appreciation, or change in the value of the price return index, plus income (dividends and/or interest) over the period, expressed as a percentage of the beginning value of the price return index. The total return of an index can be expressed as:

$$TR_I = \frac{V_{PRI1} - V_{PRI0} + Inc_I}{V_{PRI0}} \tag{6}$$

where

TR_I = the total return of the index portfolio (as a decimal number)

V_{PRI1} = the value of the price return index at the end of the period

V_{PRI0} = the value of the price return index at the beginning of the period

Inc_I = the total income (dividends and/or interest) from all securities in the index held over the period

The total return of an index can also be calculated as the weighted average of total returns of the constituent securities. The total return of each constituent security in the index is calculated as:

$$TR_i = \frac{P_{1i} - P_{0i} + Inc_i}{P_{0i}} \tag{7}$$

where

TR_i = the total return of constituent security i (as a decimal number)

P_{1i} = the price of constituent security i at the end of the period

P_{0i} = the price of constituent security i at the beginning of the period

Inc_i = the total income (dividends and/or interest) from security i over the period

Because the total return of an index can be calculated as the weighted average of total returns of the constituent securities, we can express total return as:

$$\text{TR}_I = \sum_{i=1}^{N} w_i \text{TR}_i = \sum_{i=1}^{N} w_i \left(\frac{P_{1i} - P_{0i} + Inc_i}{P_{0i}} \right) \tag{8}$$

Equation 8 can be rewritten simply as

$$\text{TR}_I = w_1 \text{TR}_1 + w_2 \text{TR}_2 + \dots + w_N \text{TR}_N \tag{9}$$

where

TR_I = the total return of the index portfolio (as a decimal number)

TR_i = the total return of constituent security i (as a decimal number)

w_i = the weight of security i (the fraction of the index portfolio allocated to security i)

N = the number of securities in the index

2.2 Calculation of Index Values over Multiple Time Periods

The calculation of index values over multiple time periods requires geometrically linking the series of index returns. With a series of price returns for an index, we can calculate the value of the price return index with the following equation:

$$V_{PRIT} = V_{PRI0} \, (1+PR_{I1})(1+PR_{I2})\dots(1+PR_{IT}) \tag{10}$$

where

V_{PRI0} = the value of the price return index at inception

V_{PRIT} = the value of the price return index at time t

PR_{IT} = the price return (as a decimal number) on the index over period t, $t = 1, 2, \dots, T$

For an index with an inception value set to 1,000 and price returns of 5 percent and 3 percent for Periods 1 and 2 respectively, the values of the price return index would be calculated as follows:

Period	Return (%)	Calculation	Ending Value
0		1,000(1.00)	1,000.00
1	5.00	1,000(1.05)	1,050.00
2	3.00	1,000(1.05)(1.03)	1,081.50

Similarly, the series of total returns for an index is used to calculate the value of the total return index with the following equation:

$$V_{TRIT} = V_{TRI0} \, (1+TR_{I1})(1+TR_{I2})\dots(1+TR_{IT}) \tag{11}$$

where

V_{TRI0} = the value of the index at inception

V_{TRIT} = the value of the total return index at time t

TR_{IT} = the total return (as a decimal number) on the index over period t, $t = 1, 2, \dots, T$

Suppose that the same index yields an additional 1.5 percent return from income in Period 1 and an additional 2.0 percent return from income in Period 2, bringing the total returns for Periods 1 and 2, respectively, to 6.5 percent and 5 percent. The values of the total return index would be calculated as follows:

Period	Return (%)	Calculation	Ending Value
0		1,000(1.00)	1,000.00
1	6.50	1,000(1.065)	1,065.00
2	5.00	1,000(1.065)(1.05)	1,118.25

As illustrated above, as time passes, the value of the total return index, which includes the reinvestment of all dividends and/or interest received, exceeds the value of the price return index by an increasing amount.

3   INDEX CONSTRUCTION AND MANAGEMENT

Constructing and managing a security market index is similar to constructing and managing a portfolio of securities. Index providers must decide the following:

1   Which target market should the index represent?

2   Which securities should be selected from that target market?

3   How much weight should be allocated to each security in the index?

4   When should the index be rebalanced?

5   When should the security selection and weighting decision be re-examined?

3.1 Target Market and Security Selection

The first decision in index construction is identifying the target market, market segment, or asset class that the index is intended to represent. The target market may be defined very broadly or narrowly. It may be based on asset class (e.g., equities, fixed income, real estate, commodities, hedge funds); geographic region (e.g., Japan, South Africa, Latin America, Europe); the exchange on which the securities are traded (e.g., Shanghai, Toronto, Tokyo), and/or other characteristics (e.g., economic sector, company size, investment style, duration, or credit quality).

The target market determines the investment universe and the securities available for inclusion in the index. Once the investment universe is identified, the number of securities and the specific securities to include in the index must be determined. The constituent securities could be nearly all those in the target market or a representative sample of the target market. Some equity indices, such as the S&P 500 Index and the FTSE 100, fix the number of securities included in the index and indicate this number in the name of the index. Other indices allow the number of securities to vary to reflect changes in the target market or to maintain a certain percentage of the target market. For example, the Tokyo Stock Price Index (TOPIX) represents and includes all of the largest stocks, known as the First Section, listed on the Tokyo Stock Exchange. To be included in the First Section—and thus the TOPIX—stocks must meet certain criteria, such as the number of shares outstanding, the number of shareholders, and market capitalization. Stocks that no longer meet the criteria are removed from the First Section and also the TOPIX. Objective or mechanical rules determine the constituent securities of most, but not all, indices. The Sensex of Bombay and the S&P 500, for example, use a selection committee and more subjective decision-making rules to determine constituent securities.

3.2 Index Weighting

The weighting decision determines how much of each security to include in the index and has a substantial impact on an index's value. Index providers use a number of methods to weight the constituent securities in an index. Indices can be price weighted, equal weighted, market-capitalization weighted, or fundamentally weighted. Each weighting method has its advantages and disadvantages.

3.2.1 Price Weighting

The simplest method to weight an index and the one used by Charles Dow to construct the Dow Jones Industrial Average is **price weighting**. In price weighting, the weight on each constituent security is determined by dividing its price by the sum of all the prices of the constituent securities. The weight is calculated using the following formula:

$$w_i^P = \frac{P_i}{\sum\limits_{i=1}^{N} P_i} \qquad\qquad (12)$$

Exhibit 1 illustrates the values, weights, and single-period returns following inception of a price-weighted equity index with five constituent securities. The value of the price-weighted index is determined by dividing the sum of the security values (101.50) by the divisor, which is typically set at inception to equal the initial number of securities in the index. Thus, in our example, the divisor is 5 and the initial value of the index is calculated as 101.50 ÷ 5 = 20.30.

As illustrated in this exhibit, Security A, which has the highest price, also has the highest weighting and thus will have the greatest impact on the return of the index. Note how both the price return and the total return of the index are calculated on the basis of the corresponding returns on the constituent securities.

A property unique to price-weighted indices is that a stock split on one constituent security changes the weights on all the securities in the index.[6] To prevent the stock split and the resulting new weights from changing the value of the index, the index provider must adjust the value of the divisor as illustrated in Exhibit 2. Given a 2-for-1 split in Security A, the divisor is adjusted by dividing the sum of the constituent prices *after* the split (77.50) by the value of the index *before* the split (21.00). This adjustment results in changing the divisor from 5 to 3.69 so that the index value is maintained at 21.00.

The primary advantage of price weighting is its simplicity. The main disadvantage of price weighting is that it results in arbitrary weights for each security. In particular, a stock split in any one security causes arbitrary changes in the weights of all the constituents' securities.

3.2.2 Equal Weighting

Another simple index weighting method is **equal weighting**. This method assigns an equal weight to each constituent security at inception. The weights are calculated as:

$$w_i^E = \frac{1}{N} \qquad\qquad (13)$$

where

w_i = fraction of the portfolio that is allocated to security i or weight of security i

---

6 A stock split is an increase in the number of shares outstanding and a proportionate decrease in the price per share such that the total market value of equity, as well as investors' proportionate ownership in the company, does not change.

Exhibit 1 Example of a Price-Weighted Equity Index

Security	Shares in Index	BOP Price	Value (Shares × BOP Price)	BOP Weight (%)	EOP Price	Dividends Per Share	Value (Shares × EOP Price)	Total Dividends	Price Return (%)	Total Return (%)	BOP Weight × Price Return (%)	BOP Weight × Total Return (%)	EOP Weight (%)
A	1	50.00	50.00	49.26	55.00	0.75	55.00	0.75	10.00	11.50	4.93	5.66	52.38
B	1	25.00	25.00	24.63	22.00	0.10	22.00	0.10	-12.00	-11.60	-2.96	-2.86	20.95
C	1	12.50	12.50	12.32	8.00	0.00	8.00	0.00	-36.00	-36.00	-4.43	-4.43	7.62
D	1	10.00	10.00	9.85	14.00	0.05	14.00	0.05	40.00	40.50	3.94	3.99	13.33
E	1	4.00	4.00	3.94	6.00	0.00	6.00	0.00	50.00	50.00	1.97	1.97	5.72
Total			101.50	100.00			105.00	0.90			3.45	4.33	100.00
Index Value			20.30				21.00	0.18	3.45	4.33			

Divisor = 5

BOP = Beginning of period

EOP = End of period

Type of Index	BOP Value	Return (%)	EOP Value
Price Return	20.30	3.45	21.00
Total Return	20.30	4.33	21.18

Exhibit 2   Impact of 2-for-1 Split in Security A

Security	Price before Split	Weight before Split (%)	Price after Split	Weight after Split (%)
A	55.00	52.38	27.50	35.48
B	22.00	20.95	22.00	28.39
C	8.00	7.62	8.00	10.32
D	14.00	13.33	14.00	18.07
E	6.00	5.72	6.00	7.74
Total	105.00	100.00	77.50	100.00
Divisor	5.00		3.69	
Index Value	21.00		21.00	

N = number of securities in the index

To construct an equal-weighted index from the five securities in Exhibit 1, the index provider allocates one-fifth (20 percent) of the value of the index (at the beginning of the period) to each security. Dividing the value allocated to each security by each security's individual share price determines the number of shares of each security to include in the index. Unlike a price-weighted index, where the weights are arbitrarily determined by the market prices, the weights in an equal-weighted index are arbitrarily assigned by the index provider.

Exhibit 3 illustrates the values, weights, and single-period returns following inception of an equal-weighted index with the same constituent securities as those in Exhibit 1. This example assumes a beginning index portfolio value of 10,000 (i.e., an investment of 2,000 in each security). To set the initial value of the index to 1,000, the divisor is set to 10 (10,000 ÷ 10 = 1,000).

Exhibits 1 and 3 demonstrate how different weighting methods result in different returns. The 10.4 percent price return of the equal-weighted index shown in Exhibit 3 differs significantly from the 3.45 percent price return of the price-weighted index in Exhibit 1.

Like price weighting, the primary advantage of equal weighting is its simplicity. Equal weighting, however, has a number of disadvantages. First, securities that constitute the largest fraction of the target market value are underrepresented, and securities that constitute a small fraction of the target market value are overrepresented. Second, after the index is constructed and the prices of constituent securities change, the index is no longer equally weighted. Therefore, maintaining equal weights requires frequent adjustments (rebalancing) to the index.

3.2.3 Market-Capitalization Weighting

In **market-capitalization weighting**, or value weighting, the weight on each constituent security is determined by dividing its market capitalization by the total market capitalization (the sum of the market capitalization) of all the securities in the index. Market capitalization or value is calculated by multiplying the number of shares outstanding by the market price per share.

The market-capitalization weight of security i is:

$$w_i^M = \frac{Q_i P_i}{\sum_{j=1}^{N} Q_j P_j} \tag{14}$$

where

   w_i = fraction of the portfolio that is allocated to security i or weight of
        security i
   Q_i = number of shares outstanding of security i
   P_i = share price of security i
   N = number of securities in the index

Exhibit 4 illustrates the values, weights, and single-period returns following inception of a market-capitalization-weighted index for the same five-security market. Security A, with 3,000 shares outstanding and a price of 50 per share, has a market capitalization of 150,000 or 26.29 percent (150,000/570,500) of the entire index portfolio. The resulting index weights in the exhibit reflect the relative value of each security as measured by its market capitalization.

As shown in Exhibits 1, 3, and 4, the weighting method affects the index's returns. The price and total returns of the market-capitalization index in Exhibit 4 (1.49 percent and 2.13 percent, respectively) differ significantly from those of the price-weighted

Exhibit 3 Example of an Equal-Weighted Equity Index

Security	Shares in Index	BOP Price	Value (Shares × BOP Price)	Weight (%)	EOP Price	Dividends Per Share	Value (Shares × EOP Price)	Total Dividends	Price Return (%)	Total Return (%)	Weight × Price Return (%)	Weight × Total Return (%)	EOP Weight (%)
A	40	50.00	2,000	20.00	55.00	0.75	2,200	30	10.00	11.50	2.00	2.30	19.93
B	80	25.00	2,000	20.00	22.00	0.10	1,760	8	-12.00	-11.60	-2.40	-2.32	15.94
C	160	12.50	2,000	20.00	8.00	0.00	1,280	0	-36.00	-36.00	-7.20	-7.20	11.60
D	200	10.00	2,000	20.00	14.00	0.05	2,800	10	40.00	40.50	8.00	8.10	25.36
E	500	4.00	2,000	20.00	6.00	0.00	3,000	0	50.00	50.00	10.00	10.00	27.17
Total			10,000	100.00			11,040	48			10.40	10.88	100.00
Index Value			1,000				1,104	4.80	10.40	10.88			

Divisor = 10

BOP = Beginning of period

EOP = End of period

Type of Index	BOP Value	Return (%)	EOP Value
Price Return	1,000.00	10.40	1,104.00
Total Return	1,000.00	10.88	1,108.80

Exhibit 4 Example of a Market-Capitalization-Weighted Equity Index

Stock	Shares Out-standing	BOP Price	BOP Market Cap	BOP Weight (%)	EOP Price	Dividends Per Share	EOP Market Cap	Total Dividends	Price Return (%)	Total Return (%)	BOP Weight × Price Return (%)	BOP Weight × Total Return (%)	EOP Weight (%)
A	3,000	50.00	150,000	26.29	55.00	0.75	165,000	2,250	10.00	11.50	2.63	3.02	28.50
B	10,000	25.00	250,000	43.82	22.00	0.10	220,000	1,000	−12.00	−11.60	−5.26	−5.08	38.00
C	5,000	12.50	62,500	10.96	8.00	0.00	40,000	0	−36.00	−36.00	−3.95	−3.95	6.91
D	8,000	10.00	80,000	14.02	14.00	0.05	112,000	400	40.00	40.50	5.61	5.68	19.34
E	7,000	4.00	28,000	4.91	6.00	0.00	42,000	0	50.00	50.00	2.46	2.46	7.25
Total			570,500	100.00			579,000	3,650			1.49	2.13	100.00
Index Value			1,000				1,014.90	6.40	1.49	2.13			

Divisor = 570.50

BOP = Beginning of period

EOP = End of period

Type of Index	BOP Value	Return (%)	EOP Value
Price Return	1,000.00	1.49	1,014.90
Total Return	1,000.00	2.13	1,021.30

(3.45 percent and 4.33 percent, respectively) and equal-weighted (10.40 percent and 10.88 percent respectively) indices. To understand the source and magnitude of the difference, compare the weights and returns of each security under each of the weighting methods. The weight of Security A, for example, ranges from 49.26 percent in the price-weighted index to 20 percent in the equal-weighted index. With a price return of 10 percent, Security A contributes 4.93 percent to the price return of the price-weighted index, 2.00 percent to the price return of the equal-weighted index, and 2.63 percent to the price return of the market-capitalization-weighted index. With a total return of 11.50 percent, Security A contributes 5.66 percent to the total return of the price-weighted index, 2.30 percent to the total return of the equal-weighted index, and 3.02 percent to the total return of the market-capitalization-weighted index.

3.2.3.1 Float-Adjusted Market-Capitalization Weighting

In **float-adjusted market-capitalization weighting**, the weight on each constituent security is determined by adjusting its market capitalization for its **market float**. Typically, market float is the number of shares of the constituent security that are available to the investing public. For companies that are closely held, only a portion of the shares outstanding are available to the investing public (the rest are held by a small group of controlling investors). In addition to excluding shares held by controlling shareholders, most float-adjusted market-capitalization-weighted indices also exclude shares held by other corporations and governments. Some providers of indices that are designed to represent the investment opportunities of global investors further reduce the number of shares included in the index by excluding shares that are not available to foreigner investors. The index providers may refer to these indices as "free-float-adjusted market-capitalization-weighted indices."

Float-adjusted market-capitalization-weighted indices reflect the shares available for public trading by multiplying the market price per share by the number of shares available to the investing public (i.e., the float-adjusted market capitalization) rather than the total number of shares outstanding (total market capitalization). Currently, most market-capitalization-weighted indices are float adjusted. Therefore, unless otherwise indicated, for the remainder of this reading, "market-capitalization" weighting refers to float-adjusted market-capitalization weighting.

The float-adjusted market-capitalization weight of security i is calculated as:

$$w_i^M = \frac{f_i Q_i P_i}{\sum\limits_{j=1}^{N} f_j Q_j P_j} \tag{15}$$

where

f_i = fraction of shares outstanding in the market float

w_i = fraction of the portfolio that is allocated to security i or weight of security i

Q_i = number of shares outstanding of security i

P_i = share price of security i

N = number of securities in the index

Exhibit 5 illustrates the values, weights, and single-period returns following inception of a float-adjusted market-capitalization-weighted equity index using the same five securities as before. The low percentage of shares of Security D in the market float compared with the number of shares outstanding indicates that the security is closely held.

The primary advantage of market-capitalization weighting (including float adjusted) is that constituent securities are held in proportion to their value in the target market. The primary disadvantage is that constituent securities whose prices have risen

Exhibit 5 Example of Float-Adjusted Market-Capitalization-Weighted Equity Index

Stock	Shares Out-standing	% Shares in Market Float	Shares in Index	BOP Price	BOP Float-Adjusted Market Cap	BOP Weight (%)	EOP Price	Dividends Per Share	Ending Float-Adjusted Market Cap	Total Dividends	Price Return (%)	Total Return (%)	BOP Weight × Price Return (%)	BOP Weight × Total Return (%)	EOP Weight (%)
A	3,000	100	3,000	50.00	150,000	35.40	55.00	0.75	165,000	2,250	10.00	11.50	3.54	4.07	39.61
B	10,000	70	7,000	25.00	175,000	41.31	22.00	0.10	154,000	700	−12.00	−11.60	−4.96	−4.79	36.97
C	5,000	90	4,500	12.50	56,250	13.28	8.00	0.00	36,000	0	−36.00	−36.00	−4.78	−4.78	8.64
D	8,000	25	2,000	10.00	20,000	4.72	14.00	0.05	28,000	100	40.00	40.50	1.89	1.91	6.72
E	7,000	80	5,600	4.00	22,400	5.29	6.00	0.00	33,600	0	50.00	50.00	2.65	2.65	8.06
Total					423,650	100.00			416,600	3,050			−1.66	−0.94	100.00
Index Value					1,000				983.36	7.20	−1.66	−0.94			

Divisor = 423.65

BOP = Beginning of period

EOP = End of period

Type of Index	Initial Value	Return (%)	Ending Value
Price Return	1,000.00	−1.66	983.36
Total Return	1,000.00	−0.94	990.56

the most (or fallen the most) have a greater (or lower) weight in the index (i.e., as a security's price rises relative to other securities in the index, its weight increases; and as its price decreases in value relative to other securities in the index, its weight decreases). This weighting method leads to overweighting stocks that have risen in price (and may be overvalued) and underweighting stocks that have declined in price (and may be undervalued). The effect of this weighting method is similar to a momentum investment strategy in that over time, the securities that have risen in price the most will have the largest weights in the index.

3.2.4 Fundamental Weighting

Fundamental weighting attempts to address the disadvantages of market-capitalization weighting by using measures of a company's size that are independent of its security price to determine the weight on each constituent security. These measures include book value, cash flow, revenues, earnings, dividends, and number of employees.

Some fundamental indices use a single measure, such as total dividends, to weight the constituent securities, whereas others combine the weights from several measures to form a composite value that is used for weighting.

Letting F_i denote a given fundamental size measure of company i, the fundamental weight on security i is:

$$w_i^F = \frac{F_i}{\sum\limits_{j=1}^{N} F_j} \tag{16}$$

Relative to a market-capitalization-weighted index, a fundamental index with weights based on such an item as earnings will result in greater weights on constituent securities with earnings yields (earnings divided by price) that are higher than the earnings yield of the overall market-weighted portfolio. Similarly, stocks with earnings yields less than the yield on the overall market-weighted portfolio will have lower weights. For example, suppose there are two stocks in an index. Stock A has a market capitalization of €200 million, Stock B has a market capitalization of €800 million, and their aggregate market capitalization is €1 billion (€1,000 million). Both companies have earnings of €20 million and aggregate earnings of €40 million. Thus, Stock A has an earnings yield of 10 percent (20/200) and Stock B has an earnings yield of 2.5 percent (20/800). The earnings weight of Stock A is 50 percent (20/40), which is higher than its market-capitalization weight of 20 percent (200/1,000). The earnings weight of Stock B is 50 percent (20/40), which is less than its market-capitalization weight of 80 percent (800/1,000). Relative to the market-cap-weighted index, the earnings-weighted index over-weights the high-yield Stock A and under-weights the low-yield Stock B.

The most important property of fundamental weighting is that it leads to indices that have a "value" tilt. That is, a fundamentally weighted index has ratios of book value, earnings, dividends, etc. to market value that are higher than its market-capitalization-weighted counterpart. Also, in contrast to the momentum "effect" of market-capitalization-weighted indices, fundamentally weighted indices generally will have a contrarian "effect" in that the portfolio weights will shift away from securities that have increased in relative value and toward securities that have fallen in relative value whenever the portfolio is rebalanced.

3.3 Index Management: Rebalancing and Reconstitution

So far, we have discussed index construction. Index management entails the two remaining questions:

- When should the index be rebalanced?
- When should the security selection and weighting decisions be re-examined?

3.3.1 Rebalancing

Rebalancing refers to adjusting the weights of the constituent securities in the index. To maintain the weight of each security consistent with the index's weighting method, the index provider rebalances the index by adjusting the weights of the constituent securities on a regularly scheduled basis (rebalancing dates)—usually quarterly. Rebalancing is necessary because the weights of the constituent securities change as their market prices change. Note, for example, that the weights of the securities in the equal-weighted index (Exhibit 3) at the end of the period are no longer equal (i.e., 20 percent):

Security A	19.93%
Security B	15.94
Security C	11.60
Security D	25.36
Security E	27.17

In rebalancing the index, the weights of Securities D and E (which had the highest returns) would be decreased and the weights of Securities A, B, and C (which had the lowest returns) would be increased. Thus, rebalancing creates turnover within an index.

Price-weighted indices are not rebalanced because the weight of each constituent security is determined by its price. For market-capitalization-weighted indices, rebalancing is less of a concern because the indices largely rebalance themselves. In our market-capitalization index, for example, the weight of Security C automatically declined from 10.96 percent to 6.91 percent, reflecting the 36 percent decline in its market price. Market-capitalization weights are only adjusted to reflect mergers, acquisitions, liquidations, and other corporate actions between rebalancing dates.

3.3.2 Reconstitution

Reconstitution is the process of changing the constituent securities in an index. It is similar to a portfolio manager deciding to change the securities in his or her portfolio. Reconstitution is part of the rebalancing cycle. The reconstitution date is the date on which index providers review the constituent securities, re-apply the initial criteria for inclusion in the index, and select which securities to retain, remove, or add. Constituent securities that no longer meet the criteria are replaced with securities that do meet the criteria. Once the revised list of constituent securities is determined, the weighting method is re-applied. Indices are reconstituted to reflect changes in the target market (bankruptcies, de-listings, mergers, acquisitions, etc.) and/or to reflect the judgment of the selection committee.

Reconstitution creates turnover in a number of different ways, particularly for market-capitalization-weighted indices. When one security is removed and another is added, the index provider has to change the weights of the other securities in order to maintain the market-capitalization weighting of the index.

The frequency of reconstitution is a major issue for widely used indices and their constituent securities. The Russell 2000 Index, for example, reconstitutes annually. It is used as a benchmark by numerous investment funds, and each year, prior to the index's reconstitution, the managers of these funds buy stocks they think will be added to the index—driving those stocks' prices up—and sell stocks they think will be deleted from the index—driving those stocks' prices down. Exhibit 6 illustrates the potential impact of these decisions. Beginning in late April 2009, some managers began acquiring and bidding up the price of Uranium Energy Corporation (UEC) because they believed that it would be included in the reconstituted Russell 2000 Index. On 12 June, Russell listed UEC as a preliminary addition to the Russell 2000 Index and the Russell 3000 Index.[7] By that time, the stock value had increased by more than 300 percent. Investors continued to bid up the stock price in the weeks following the announcement, and the stock closed on the reconstitution date of 30 June at USD2.90, up nearly 400 percent for the quarter.

Exhibit 6   Three-Month Performance of Uranium Energy Corporation and NASDAQ April through June 2009

Source: Yahoo! Finance and Capital IQ.

USES OF MARKET INDICES

4

Indices were initially created to give a sense of how a particular security market performed on a given day. With the development of modern financial theory, their uses in investment management have expanded significantly. Some of the major uses of indices include:

- gauges of market sentiment;
- proxies for measuring and modeling returns, systematic risk, and risk-adjusted performance;
- proxies for asset classes in asset allocation models;

---

7 According to the press release, final membership in the index would be published after market close on Friday, 26 June.

- benchmarks for actively managed portfolios; and
- model portfolios for such investment products as index funds and exchange-traded funds (ETFs).

Investors using security market indices must be familiar with how various indices are constructed in order to select the index or indices most appropriate for their needs.

4.1 Gauges of Market Sentiment

The original purpose of stock market indices was to provide a gauge of investor confidence or market sentiment. As indicators of the collective opinion of market participants, indices reflect investor attitudes and behavior. The Dow Jones Industrial Average has a long history, is frequently quoted in the media, and remains a popular gauge of market sentiment. It may not accurately reflect the overall attitude of investors or the "market," however, because the index consists of only 30 of the thousands of US stocks traded each day.

4.2 Proxies for Measuring and Modeling Returns, Systematic Risk, and Risk-Adjusted Performance

The capital asset pricing model (CAPM) defines beta as the systematic risk of a security with respect to the entire market. The market portfolio in the CAPM consists of all risky securities. To represent the performance of the market portfolio, investors use a broad index. For example, the Tokyo Price Index (TOPIX) and the S&P 500 often serve as proxies for the market portfolio in Japan and the United States, respectively, and are used for measuring and modeling systematic risk and market returns.

Security market indices also serve as market proxies when measuring risk-adjusted performance. The beta of an actively managed portfolio allows investors to form a passive alternative with the same level of systematic risk. For example, if the beta of an actively managed portfolio of global stocks is 0.95 with respect to the MSCI World Index, investors can create a passive portfolio with the same systematic risk by investing 95 percent of their portfolio in a MSCI World Index fund and holding the remaining 5 percent in cash. Alpha, the difference between the return of the actively managed portfolio and the return of the passive portfolio, is a measure of risk-adjusted return or investment performance. Alpha can be the result of manager skill (or lack thereof), transaction costs, and fees.

4.3 Proxies for Asset Classes in Asset Allocation Models

Because indices exhibit the risk and return profiles of select groups of securities, they play a critical role as proxies for asset classes in asset allocation models. They provide the historical data used to model the risks and returns of different asset classes.

4.4 Benchmarks for Actively Managed Portfolios

Investors often use indices as benchmarks to evaluate the performance of active portfolio managers. The index selected as the benchmark should reflect the investment strategy used by the manager. For example, an active manager investing in global small-capitalization stocks should be evaluated using a benchmark index, such as the FTSE Global Small Cap Index, which includes 4,600 small-capitalization stocks across 48 countries.

The choice of an index to use as a benchmark is important because an inappropriate index could lead to incorrect conclusions regarding an active manager's investment performance. Suppose that the small-cap manager underperformed the small-cap index but outperformed a broad equity market index. If investors use the broad market index as a benchmark, they might conclude that the small-cap manager is earning his or her fees and should be retained or given additional assets to invest. Using the small-cap index as a benchmark might lead to a very different conclusion.

4.5 Model Portfolios for Investment Products

Indices also serve as the basis for the development of new investment products. Using indices as benchmarks for actively managed portfolios has led some investors to conclude that they should invest in the benchmarks instead. Based on the CAPM's conclusion that investors should hold the market portfolio, broad market index funds have been developed to function as proxies for the market portfolio.

Investment management firms initially developed and managed index portfolios for institutional investors. Eventually, mutual fund companies introduced index funds for individual investors. Subsequently, investment management firms introduced exchange-traded funds, which are managed the same way as index mutual funds but trade like stocks.

The first ETFs were based on existing indices. As the popularity of ETFs increased, index providers created new indices for the specific purpose of forming ETFs, leading to the creation of numerous narrowly defined indices with corresponding ETFs. The Market Vectors Vietnam ETF, for example, allows investors to invest in the equity market of Vietnam.

The choice of indices to meet the needs of investors is extensive. Index providers are constantly looking for opportunities to develop indices to meet the needs of investors.

EQUITY INDICES $\qquad$ 5

A wide variety of equity indices exist, including broad market, multi-market, sector, and style indices.

5.1 Broad Market Indices

A broad equity market index, as its name suggests, represents an entire given equity market and typically includes securities representing more than 90 percent of the selected market. For example, the Shanghai Stock Exchange Composite Index (SSE) is a market-capitalization-weighted index of all shares that trade on the Shanghai Stock Exchange. In the United States, the Wilshire 5000 Total Market Index is a market-capitalization-weighted index that includes more than 6,000 equity securities and is designed to represent the entire US equity market.[8] The Russell 3000, consisting of the largest 3,000 stocks by market capitalization, represents 99 percent of the US equity market.

---

8 Despite its name, the Wilshire 5000 has no constraint on the number of securities that can be included. It included approximately 5,000 securities at inception.

5.2 Multi-Market Indices

Multi-market indices usually comprise indices from different countries and are designed to represent multiple security markets. Multi-market indices may represent multiple national markets, geographic regions, economic development groups, and, in some cases, the entire world. World indices are of importance to investors who take a global approach to equity investing without any particular bias toward a particular country or region. A number of index providers publish families of multi-market equity indices.

MSCI Barra offers a number of multi-market indices. As shown in Exhibit 7, MSCI Barra classifies countries along two dimensions: level of economic development and geographic region. Developmental groups, which MSCI Barra refers to as market classifications, include developed markets, emerging markets, and frontier markets. The geographic regions are largely divided by longitudinal lines of the globe: the Americas, Europe with Africa, and Asia with the Pacific. MSCI Barra provides country-specific indices for each of the developed and emerging market countries within its multi-market indices. MSCI Barra periodically reviews the market classifications of countries in its indices for movement from frontier markets to emerging markets and from emerging markets to developed markets and reconstitutes the indices accordingly.

Exhibit 7   MSCI International Equity Indices—Country and Market Coverage (as of June 2009)

Developed Markets		
Americas	**Europe**	**Pacific**
Canada, United States	Austria, Belgium, Denmark, Finland, France, Germany, Greece, Ireland, Italy, Netherlands, Norway, Portugal, Spain, Sweden, Switzerland, United Kingdom	Australia, Hong Kong, Japan, New Zealand, Singapore

Emerging Markets		
Americas	**Europe, Middle East, Africa**	**Asia**
Argentina[1], Brazil, Chile, Colombia, Mexico, Peru	Czech Republic, Egypt, Hungary, Israel, Jordan, Morocco, Poland, Russia, South Africa, Turkey	China, India, Indonesia, South Korea, Malaysia, Pakistan[2], Philippines, Taiwan, Thailand

Frontier Markets				
Americas	**Central & Eastern Europe & CIS**	**Africa**	**Middle East**	**Asia**
Jamaica[3], Trinidad & Tobago[3]	Bulgaria, Croatia, Estonia, Lithuania, Kazakhstan, Romania, Serbia, Slovenia, Ukraine	Botswana[4], Ghana[4], Kenya, Mauritius, Nigeria, Tunisia	Lebanon, Bahrain, Kuwait, Oman, Qatar, United Arab Emirates, Saudi Arabia[5]	Sri Lanka, Vietnam

[1]The MSCI Argentina Index was reclassified from the MSCI Emerging Markets Index to the MSCI Frontier Markets Index at the end of May 2009 to coincide with the May 2009 Semi-Annual Index Review.

[2]The MSCI Pakistan Index was removed from the MSCI Emerging Markets Index as of the close of December 31, 2008 to reflect the deterioration of investability conditions in the Pakistani equity market. In May 2009, the MSCI Pakistan Index was added to the MSCI Frontier Markets Index to coincide with the May 2009 Semi-Annual Index Review.

[3]In May 2009, the MSCI Trinidad & Tobago Index was added to the MSCI Frontier Markets Index. However, the MSCI Jamaica Index continues to be maintained as a stand-alone country index because it does not meet the liquidity requirements of the Frontiers Market Index.

[4]Botswana and Ghana currently stand-alone and are not included in the MSCI Frontier Markets Index. The addition of these two countries to the MSCI Frontier Market Index is under consideration.

Exhibit 7	**(Continued)**

[5]Saudi Arabia is currently not included in the MSCI Frontier Markets Index but is part of the MSCI GCC Countries Index.
Source: MSCI Barra (www.mscibarra.com/products/indices/equity/index.jsp), June 2009.

5.2.1 *Fundamental Weighting in Multi-Market Indices*

Some index providers weight the securities within each country by market capitalization and then weight each country in the overall index in proportion to its relative GDP, effectively creating fundamental weighting in multi-market indices. GDP-weighted indices were some of the first fundamentally weighted indices created. Introduced in 1987 by MSCI to address the 60 percent weight of Japanese equities in the market-capitalization-weighted MSCI EAFE Index at the time, GDP-weighted indices reduced the allocation to Japanese equities by half.[9]

5.3 Sector Indices

Sector indices represent and track different economic sectors—such as consumer goods, energy, finance, health care, and technology—on either a national, regional, or global basis. Because different sectors of the economy behave differently over the course of the business cycle, some investors may seek to overweight or underweight their exposure to particular sectors.

Sector indices are organized as families; each index within the family represents an economic sector. Typically, the aggregation of a sector index family is equivalent to a broad market index. Economic sector classification can be applied on a global, regional, or country-specific basis, but no universally agreed upon sector classification method exists.

Sector indices play an important role in performance analysis because they provide a means to determine whether a portfolio manager is more successful at stock selection or sector allocation. Sector indices also serve as model portfolios for sector-specific ETFs and other investment products.

5.4 Style Indices

Style indices represent groups of securities classified according to market capitalization, value, growth, or a combination of these characteristics. They are intended to reflect the investing styles of certain investors, such as the growth investor, value investor, and small-cap investor.

5.4.1 *Market Capitalization*

Market-capitalization indices represent securities categorized according to the major capitalization categories: large cap, midcap, and small cap. With no universal definition of these categories, the indices differ on the distinctions between large cap and midcap and between midcap and small cap, as well as the minimum market-capitalization size required to be included in a small-cap index. Classification into categories can be based on absolute market capitalization (e.g., below €100 million) or relative market capitalization (e.g., the smallest 2,500 stocks).

---

9 Steven A. Schoenfeld, *Active Index Investing* (Hoboken, NJ: John Wiley & Sons, 2004):220.

5.4.2 *Value/Growth Classification*

Some indices represent categories of stocks based on their classifications as either value or growth stocks. Different index providers use different factors and valuation ratios (low price-to-book ratios, low price-to-earnings ratios, high dividend yields, etc.) to distinguish between value and growth equities.

5.4.3 *Market Capitalization and Value/Growth Classification*

Combining the three market-capitalization groups with value and growth classifications results in six basic style index categories:

- Large-Cap Value   ■ Large-Cap Growth
- Mid-Cap Value   ■ Mid-Cap Growth
- Small-Cap Value   ■ Small-Cap Growth

Because indices use different size and valuation classifications, the constituents of indices designed to represent a given style, such as small-cap value, may differ—sometimes substantially.

Because valuation ratios and market capitalizations change over time, stocks frequently migrate from one style index category to another on reconstitution dates. As a result, style indices generally have much higher turnover than do broad market indices.

6   FIXED-INCOME INDICES

A wide variety of fixed-income indices exists, but the nature of the fixed-income markets and fixed-income securities leads to some very important challenges to fixed-income index construction and replication. These challenges are the number of securities in the fixed-income universe, the availability of pricing data, and the liquidity of the securities.

6.1 Construction

The fixed-income universe includes securities issued by governments, government agencies, and corporations. Each of these entities may issue a variety of fixed-income securities with different characteristics. As a result, the number of fixed-income securities is many times larger than the number of equity securities. To represent a specific fixed-income market or segment, indices may include thousands of different securities. Over time, these fixed-income securities mature, and issuers offer new securities to meet their financing needs, leading to turnover in fixed-income indices.

Another challenge in index construction is that fixed-income markets are predominantly dealer markets. This means that firms (dealers) are assigned to specific securities and are responsible for creating liquid markets for those securities by purchasing and selling them from their inventory. In addition, many securities do not trade frequently and, as a result, are relatively illiquid. As a result, index providers must contact dealers to obtain current prices on constituent securities to update the index or they must estimate the prices of constituent securities using the prices of traded fixed-income securities with similar characteristics.

These challenges can result in indices with dissimilar numbers of bonds representing the same markets. As seen in Exhibit 8, the differences can be large. The large number of fixed-income securities—combined with the lack of liquidity of some securities—has made it more costly and difficult, compared with equity indices, for investors to replicate fixed-income indices and duplicate their performance.

Exhibit 8   Comparison of Minimum Issue Size and Bond Holdings by Index

Index	Barclays Capital		Markit iBoxx		Morningstar	
	Min (Thousands)	No. of Bonds	Min (Thousands)	No. of Bonds	Min (Thousands)	No. of Bonds
US agency	250,000	988	500,000	435	1,000,000	193
US corporate	250,000	3,134	500,000	1,694	500,000	1,862
UK corporate	250,000	916	100,000	713	225,000	303
Euro corporate	300,000	1,285	500,000	1,167	325,000	829

Source: Morningstar.

6.2 Types of Fixed-Income Indices

The wide variety of fixed-income securities, ranging from zero-coupon bonds to bonds with embedded options (i.e., callable or putable bonds), results in a number of different types of fixed-income indices. Similar to equities, fixed-income securities can be categorized according to the issuer's economic sector, the issuer's geographic region, or the economic development of the issuer's geographic region. Fixed-income securities can also be classified along the following dimensions:

- type of issuer (government, government agency, corporation);
- type of financing (general obligation, collateralized);
- currency of payments;
- maturity;
- credit quality (investment grade, high yield, credit agency ratings); and
- absence or presence of inflation protection.

Fixed-income indices are based on these various dimensions and can be categorized as follows:

- aggregate or broad market indices;
- market sector indices;
- style indices;
- economic sector indices; and
- specialized indices such as high-yield, inflation-linked, and emerging market indices.

The first fixed-income index created, the Barclays Capital US Aggregate Bond Index (formerly the Lehman Brothers Aggregate Bond Index), is an example of a single-country aggregate index. Designed to represent the broad market of US fixed-income securities, it comprises more than 9,200 securities, including US Treasury, government-related, corporate, mortgage-backed, asset-backed, and commercial mortgage-backed securities.

Aggregate indices can be subdivided by market sector (government, government agency, collateralized, corporate); style (maturity, credit quality); economic sector, or some other characteristic to create more narrowly defined indices. A common distinction reflected in indices is between investment grade (e.g., those with a Standard & Poor's credit rating of BBB– or better) and high-yield securities. Investment-grade indices are typically further subdivided by maturity (i.e., short, intermediate, or long) and by credit rating (e.g., AAA, BBB, etc.).[10] The wide variety of fixed-income indices reflects the partitioning of fixed-income securities on the basis of a variety of dimensions.

Exhibit 9 illustrates how the major types of fixed-income indices can be organized on the basis of various dimensions.

Exhibit 9	Dimensions of Fixed-Income Indices			
Market	Global			
	Regional			
	Country or currency zone			
Type	Corporate	Collateralized *Securitized* Mortgage-backed	Government agency	Government
Maturity	For example, 1–3, 3–5, 5–7, 7–10, 10+ years; short-term, medium-term, or long-term			
Credit quality	For example, AAA, AA, A, BBB, etc.; Aaa, Aa, A, Baa, etc.; investment grade, high yield			

All aggregate indices include a variety of market sectors and credit ratings. The breakdown of the Barclays Capital Global Aggregate Bond Index by market sectors and by credit rating is shown in Exhibit 10 and Exhibit 11, respectively.

Exhibit 10	Market Sector Breakdown of the Barclays Capital Global Aggregate Bond Index

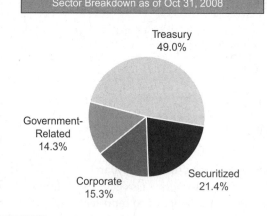

Source: Barclays Capital, "The Benchmark in Fixed Income: Barclays Capital Indices" (December 2008).

---

10 The credit rating categories vary based on the credit rating agency used by the index provider.

Exhibit 11   Credit Breakdown of the Barclays Capital Global Aggregate Bond Index

Quality Breakdown as of Oct 31, 2008

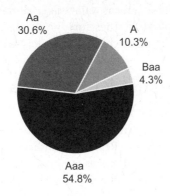

Aa
30.6%

A
10.3%

Baa
4.3%

Aaa
54.8%

Source: Barclays Capital, "The Benchmark in Fixed Income: Barclays Capital Indices" (December 2008).

INDICES FOR ALTERNATIVE INVESTMENTS

7

Many investors seek to lower the risk or enhance the performance of their portfolios by investing in assets classes other than equities and fixed income. Interest in alternative assets and investment strategies has led to the creation of indices designed to represent broad classes of alternative investments. Three of the most widely followed alternative investment classes are commodities, real estate, and hedge funds.

7.1 Commodity Indices

Commodity indices consist of futures contracts on one or more commodities, such as agricultural products (rice, wheat, sugar), livestock (cattle, hogs), precious and common metals (gold, silver, copper), and energy commodities (crude oil, natural gas).

Although some commodity indices may include the same commodities, the returns of these indices may differ because each index may use a different weighting method. Because commodity indices do not have an obvious weighting mechanism, such as market capitalization, commodity index providers create their own weighting methods. Some indices, such as the Commodity Research Bureau (CRB) Index, contain a fixed number of commodities that are weighted equally. The S&P GSCI uses a combination of liquidity measures and world production values in its weighting scheme and allocates more weight to commodities that have risen in price. Other indices have fixed weights that are determined by a committee.

The different weighting methods can also lead to large differences in exposure to specific commodities. The S&P GSCI, for example, has approximately double the energy-sector weighting and one-third the agriculture sector weighting of the CRB Index. These differences result in indices with very different risk and return profiles. Unlike commodity indices, broad equity and fixed-income indices that target the same markets share similar risk and return profiles.

The performance of commodity indices can also be quite different from their underlying commodities because the indices consist of futures contracts on the commodities rather than the actual commodities. Index returns are affected by factors other than changes in the prices of the underlying commodities because futures contracts must be continually "rolled over" (i.e., replacing a contract nearing expiration with a new contract). Commodity index returns reflect the risk-free interest rate, the changes in future prices, and the roll yield. Therefore, a commodity index return can be quite different from the return based on changes in the prices of the underlying commodities.

7.2 Real Estate Investment Trust Indices

Real estate indices represent not only the market for real estate securities but also the market for real estate—a highly illiquid market and asset class with infrequent transactions and pricing information. Real estate indices can be categorized as appraisal indices, repeat sales indices, and real estate investment trust (REIT) indices.

REIT indices consist of shares of publicly traded REITs. REITS are public or private corporations organized specifically to invest in real estate, either through ownership of properties or investment in mortgages. Shares of public REITs are traded on the world's various stock exchanges and are a popular choice for investing in commercial real estate properties. Because REIT indices are based on publicly traded REITs with continuous market pricing, the value of REIT indices is calculated continuously.

The FTSE EPRA/NAREIT global family of REIT indices shown in Exhibit 12 seeks to represent trends in real estate stocks worldwide and includes representation from the European Real Estate Association (EPRA) and the National Association of Real Estate Investment Trusts (NAREIT).

Exhibit 12   The FTSE EPRA/NAREIT Global REIT Index Family

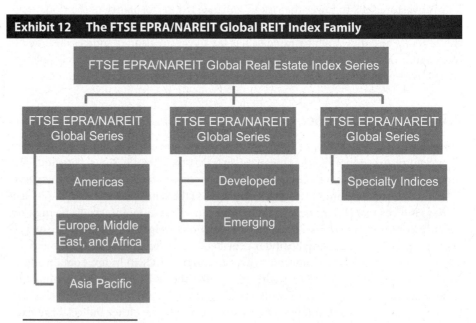

Source: FTSE International, "FTSE EPRA/NAREIT Global & Global Ex US Indices" Factsheet 2009). "FTSE®" is a trade mark of the London Stock Exchange Plc, "NAREIT®" is the a trade mark of the National Association of Real Estate Investment Trusts ("NAREIT") and "EPRA®" is a trade mark of the European Public Real Estate Association ("EPRA") and all are used by FTSE International Limited ("FTSE") under license.

7.3 Hedge Fund Indices

Hedge fund indices reflect the returns on hedge funds. **Hedge funds** are private investment vehicles that typically use leverage and long and short investment strategies.

A number of research organizations maintain databases of hedge fund returns and summarize these returns into indices. These database indices are designed to represent the performance of the hedge funds on a very broad global level (hedge funds in general) or the strategy level. Most of these indices are equal weighted and represent the performance of the hedge funds within a particular database.

Most research organizations rely on the voluntary cooperation of hedge funds to compile performance data. As unregulated entities, however, hedge funds are not required to report their performance to any party other than their investors. Therefore, each hedge fund decides to which database(s) it will report its performance. As a result, rather than index providers determining the constituents, the constituents determine the index.

Frequently, a hedge fund reports its performance to only one database. The result is little overlap of funds covered by the different indices. With little overlap between their constituents, different global hedge fund indices may reflect very different performance for the hedge fund industry over the same period of time.

Another consequence of the voluntary performance reporting is the potential for survivorship bias and, therefore, inaccurate performance representation. This means that hedge funds with poor performance may be less likely to report their performance to the database or may stop reporting to the database, so their returns may be excluded when measuring the return of the index. As a result, the index may not accurately reflect actual hedge fund performance so much as the performance of hedge funds that are performing well.

REPRESENTATIVE INDICES WORLDWIDE

As indicated in this reading, the choice of indices to meet the needs of investors is extensive. Investors using security market indices must be careful in their selection of the index or indices most appropriate for their needs. The following table illustrates the variety of indices reflecting different asset classes, markets, and weighting methods.

Index	Representing	Number of Securities	Weighting Method	Comments
Dow Jones Industrial Average	US blue chip companies	30	Price	The oldest and most widely known US equity index. *Wall Street Journal* editors choose 30 stocks from among large, mature blue-chip companies.
Nikkei Stock Average	Japanese blue chip companies	225	Modified price	Known as the Nikkei 225 and originally formulated by Dow Jones & Company. Because of extreme variation in price levels of component securities, some high-priced shares are weighted as a fraction of share price. Index contains some illiquid stocks.
TOPIX	All companies listed on the Tokyo Stock Exchange First Section	Varies	Float-adjusted market cap	Represents about 93 percent of the market value of all Japanese equities. Contains a large number of very small, illiquid stocks, making exact replication difficult.

(continued)

Index	Representing	Number of Securities	Weighting Method	Comments
MSCI All Country World Index	Stocks of 23 developed and 22 emerging markets	Varies	Free-float-adjusted market cap	Composed of companies representative of the market structure of developed and emerging market countries in the Americas, Europe/Middle East, and Asia/Pacific regions. Price return and total return versions available in both USD and local currencies.
S&P Developed Ex-US BMI Energy Sector Index	Energy sector of developed global markets outside the United States	Varies	Float-adjusted market cap	Serves as a model portfolio for the SPDR® S&P Energy Sector Exchange-Traded Fund (ETF).
Barclays Capital Global Aggregate Bond Index	Investment-grade bonds in the North American, European, and Asian markets	Varies	Market cap	Formerly known as Lehman Brothers Global Aggregate Bond Index.
Markit iBoxx Euro High-Yield Bond Indices	Sub-investment-grade euro-denominated corporate bonds	Varies	Market cap and variations	Rebalanced monthly. Represents tradable part of market. Price and total return versions available with such analytical values as yield, duration, modified duration, and convexity. Provides platform for research and structured products.
FTSE EPRA/NAREIT Global Real Estate Index	Real estate securities in the North American, European, and Asian markets	335	Float-adjusted market cap	The stocks of REITs that constitute the index trade on public stock exchanges and may be constituents of equity market indices.
HFRX Global Hedge Fund Index	Overall composition of the HFR database	Varies	Asset weighted	Comprises all eligible hedge fund strategies. Examples include convertible arbitrage, distressed securities, market neutral, event driven, macro, and relative value arbitrage. Constituent strategies are asset weighted on the basis of asset distribution within the hedge fund industry.
HFRX Equal Weighted Strategies EUR Index	Overall composition of the HFR database	Varies	Equal weighted	Denominated in euros and is constructed from the same strategies as the HFRX Global Hedge Fund Index.
Morningstar Style Indices	US stocks classified by market cap and value/growth orientation	Varies	Float-adjusted market cap	The nine indices defined by combinations of market cap (large, mid, and small) and value/growth orientation (value, core, growth) have mutually exclusive constituents and are exhaustive with respect to the Morningstar US Market Index. Each is a model portfolio for one of the iShares Morningstar ETFs.

SUMMARY

This reading explains and illustrates the construction, management, and uses of security market indices. It also discusses various types of indices. Security market indices are invaluable tools for investors, who can select from among thousands of indices representing a variety of security markets, market segments, and asset classes. These indices range from those representing the global market for major asset classes to those representing alternative investments in specific geographic markets. To benefit from the use of security market indices, investors must understand their construction and determine whether the selected index is appropriate for their purposes. Frequently, an index that is well suited for one purpose may not be well suited for other purposes. Users of indices must be familiar with how various indices are constructed in order to select the index or indices most appropriate for their needs.

Among the key points made in this reading are the following:

- Security market indices are intended to measure the values of different target markets (security markets, market segments, or asset classes).

- The constituent securities selected for inclusion in the security market index are intended to represent the target market.

- A price return index reflects only the prices of the constituent securities.

- A total return index reflects not only the prices of the constituent securities but also the reinvestment of all income received since the inception of the index.

- Methods used to weight the constituents of an index range from the very simple, such as price and equal weightings, to the more complex, such as market-capitalization and fundamental weightings.

- Choices in index construction—in particular, the choice of weighting method—affect index valuation and returns.

- Index management includes 1) periodic rebalancing to ensure that the index maintains appropriate weightings and 2) reconstitution to ensure the index represents the desired target market.

- Rebalancing and reconstitution create turnover in an index. Reconstitution can dramatically affect prices of current and prospective constituents.

- Indices serve a variety of purposes. They gauge market sentiment and serve as benchmarks for actively managed portfolios. They act as proxies for measuring systematic risk and risk-adjusted performance. They also serve as proxies for asset classes in asset allocation models and as model portfolios for investment products.

- Investors can choose from security market indices representing various asset classes, including equity, fixed-income, commodity, real estate, and hedge fund indices.

- Within most asset classes, index providers offer a wide variety of indices, ranging from broad market indices to highly specialized indices based on the issuer's geographic region, economic development group, or economic sector or other factors.

- Proper use of security market indices depends on understanding their construction and management.

PRACTICE PROBLEMS

1   A security market index represents the:

   A   risk of a security market.

   B   security market as a whole.

   C   security market, market segment, or asset class.

2   Security market indices are:

   A   constructed and managed like a portfolio of securities.

   B   simple interchangeable tools for measuring the returns of different asset classes.

   C   valued on a regular basis using the actual market prices of the constituent securities.

3   When creating a security market index, an index provider must first determine the:

   A   target market.

   B   appropriate weighting method.

   C   number of constituent securities.

4   One month after inception, the price return version and total return version of a single index (consisting of identical securities and weights) will be equal if:

   A   market prices have not changed.

   B   capital gains are offset by capital losses.

   C   the securities do not pay dividends or interest.

5   The values of a price return index and a total return index consisting of identical equal-weighted dividend-paying equities will be equal:

   A   only at inception.

   B   at inception and on rebalancing dates.

   C   at inception and on reconstitution dates.

6   An analyst gathers the following information for an equal-weighted index comprised of assets Able, Baker, and Charlie:

Security	Beginning of Period Price (€)	End of Period Price (€)	Total Dividends (€)
Able	10.00	12.00	0.75
Baker	20.00	19.00	1.00
Charlie	30.00	30.00	2.00

   The price return of the index is:

   A   1.7%.

   B   5.0%.

   C   11.4%.

7   An analyst gathers the following information for an equal-weighted index comprised of assets Able, Baker, and Charlie:

Security	Beginning of Period Price (€)	End of Period Price (€)	Total Dividends (€)
Able	10.00	12.00	0.75
Baker	20.00	19.00	1.00
Charlie	30.00	30.00	2.00

The total return of the index is:

A 5.0%.

B 7.9%.

C 11.4%.

8 An analyst gathers the following information for a price-weighted index comprised of securities ABC, DEF, and GHI:

Security	Beginning of Period Price (£)	End of Period Price (£)	Total Dividends (£)
ABC	25.00	27.00	1.00
DEF	35.00	25.00	1.50
GHI	15.00	16.00	1.00

The price return of the index is:

A −4.6%.

B −9.3%.

C −13.9%.

9 An analyst gathers the following information for a market-capitalization-weighted index comprised of securities MNO, QRS, and XYZ:

Security	Beginning of Period Price (¥)	End of Period Price (¥)	Dividends per Share (¥)	Shares Outstanding
MNO	2,500	2,700	100	5,000
QRS	3,500	2,500	150	7,500
XYZ	1,500	1,600	100	10,000

The price return of the index is:

A −9.33%.

B −10.23%.

C −13.90%.

10 An analyst gathers the following information for a market-capitalization-weighted index comprised of securities MNO, QRS, and XYZ:

Security	Beginning of Period Price (¥)	End of Period Price (¥)	Dividends Per Share (¥)	Shares Outstanding
MNO	2,500	2,700	100	5,000
QRS	3,500	2,500	150	7,500
XYZ	1,500	1,600	100	10,000

The total return of the index is:

A 1.04%.

B −5.35%.

    C −10.23%.

11 When creating a security market index, the target market:

    A determines the investment universe.

    B is usually a broadly defined asset class.

    C determines the number of securities to be included in the index.

12 An analyst gathers the following data for a price-weighted index:

	Beginning of Period		**End of Period**	
Security	**Price (€)**	**Shares**	**Price (€)**	**Shares**
A	20.00	300	22.00	300
B	50.00	300	48.00	300
C	26.00	2,000	30.00	2,000

    The price return of the index over the period is:

    A 4.2%.

    B 7.1%.

    C 21.4%.

13 An analyst gathers the following data for a value-weighted index:

	Beginning of Period		**End of Period**	
Security	**Price (£)**	**Shares**	**Price (£)**	**Shares**
A	20.00	300	22.00	300
B	50.00	300	48.00	300
C	26.00	2,000	30.00	2,000

    The return on the value-weighted index over the period is:

    A 7.1%.

    B 11.0%.

    C 21.4%.

14 An analyst gathers the following data for an equally-weighted index:

	Beginning of Period		**End of Period**	
Security	**Price (¥)**	**Shares**	**Price (¥)**	**Shares**
A	20.00	300	22.00	300
B	50.00	300	48.00	300
C	26.00	2,000	30.00	2,000

    The return on the index over the period is:

    A 4.2%.

    B 6.8%.

    C 7.1%.

15 Which of the following index weighting methods requires an adjustment to the divisor after a stock split?

    A Price weighting.

    B Fundamental weighting.

    C Market-capitalization weighting.

16 If the price return of an equal-weighted index exceeds that of a market-capitalization-weighted index comprised of the same securities, the *most likely* explanation is:

A stock splits.

B dividend distributions.

C outperformance of small-market-capitalization stocks.

17 A float-adjusted market-capitalization-weighted index weights each of its constituent securities by its price and:

A its trading volume.

B the number of its shares outstanding.

C the number of its shares available to the investing public.

18 Which of the following index weighting methods is most likely subject to a value tilt?

A Equal weighting.

B Fundamental weighting.

C Market-capitalization weighting.

19 Rebalancing an index is the process of periodically adjusting the constituent:

A securities' weights to optimize investment performance.

B securities to maintain consistency with the target market.

C securities' weights to maintain consistency with the index's weighting method.

20 Which of the following index weighting methods requires the most frequent rebalancing?

A Price weighting.

B Equal weighting.

C Market-capitalization weighting.

21 Reconstitution of a security market index reduces:

A portfolio turnover.

B the need for rebalancing.

C the likelihood that the index includes securities that are not representative of the target market.

22 Security market indices are used as:

A measures of investment returns.

B proxies to measure unsystematic risk.

C proxies for specific asset classes in asset allocation models.

23 Uses of market indices do not include serving as a:

A measure of systematic risk.

B basis for new investment products.

C benchmark for evaluating portfolio performance.

24 Which of the following statements regarding sector indices is *most* accurate? Sector indices:

A track different economic sectors and cannot be aggregated to represent the equivalent of a broad market index.

B provide a means to determine whether an active investment manager is more successful at stock selection or sector allocation.

C   apply a universally agreed upon sector classification system to identify the constituent securities of specific economic sectors, such as consumer goods, energy, finance, health care.

25   Which of the following is an example of a style index? An index based on:

A   geography.

B   economic sector.

C   market capitalization.

26   Which of the following statements regarding fixed-income indices is *most* accurate?

A   Liquidity issues make it difficult for investors to easily replicate fixed-income indices.

B   Rebalancing and reconstitution are the only sources of turnover in fixed-income indices.

C   Fixed-income indices representing the same target market hold similar numbers of bonds.

27   An aggregate fixed-income index:

A   comprises corporate and asset-backed securities.

B   represents the market of government-issued securities.

C   can be subdivided by market or economic sector to create more narrowly defined indices.

28   Fixed-income indices are *least likely* constructed on the basis of:

A   maturity.

B   type of issuer.

C   coupon frequency.

29   Commodity index values are based on:

A   futures contract prices.

B   the market price of the specific commodity.

C   the average market price of a basket of similar commodities.

30   Which of the following statements is *most* accurate?

A   Commodity indices all share similar weighting methods.

B   Commodity indices containing the same underlying commodities offer similar returns.

C   The performance of commodity indices can be quite different from that of the underlying commodities.

31   Which of the following is *not* a real estate index category?

A   Appraisal index.

B   Initial sales index.

C   Repeat sales index.

32   A unique feature of hedge fund indices is that they:

A   are frequently equal weighted.

B   are determined by the constituents of the index.

C   reflect the value of private rather than public investments.

33   The returns of hedge fund indices are *most likely*:

A   biased upward.

B   biased downward.

C similar across different index providers.

34 In comparison to equity indices, the constituent securities of fixed-income indices are:

A more liquid.

B easier to price.

C drawn from a larger investment universe.

SOLUTIONS

1 C is correct. A security market index represents the value of a given security market, market segment, or asset class.

2 A is correct. Security market indices are constructed and managed like a portfolio of securities.

3 A is correct. The first decision is identifying the target market that the index is intended to represent because the target market determines the investment universe and the securities available for inclusion in the index.

4 C is correct. The difference between a price return index and a total return index consisting of identical securities and weights is the income generated over time by the underlying securities. If the securities in the index do not generate income, both indices will be identical in value.

5 A is correct. At inception, the values of the price return and total return versions of an index are equal.

6 B is correct. The price return is the sum of the weighted returns of each security. The return of Able is 20 percent [(12 − 10)/10]; of Baker is −5 percent [(19 − 20)/20]; and of Charlie is 0 percent [(30 − 30)/30]. The price return index assigns a weight of 1/3 to each asset; therefore, the price return is 1/3 × [20% + (−5%) + 0%] = 5%.

7 C is correct. The total return of an index is calculated on the basis of the change in price of the underlying securities plus the sum of income received or the sum of the weighted total returns of each security. The total return of Able is 27.5 percent; of Baker is 0 percent; and of Charlie is 6.7 percent:

    Able: (12 − 10 + 0.75)/10 = 27.5%

    Baker: (19 − 20 + 1)/20 = 0%

    Charlie: (30 − 30 + 2)/30 = 6.7%

An equal-weighted index applies the same weight (1/3) to each security's return; therefore, the total return = 1/3 × (27.5% + 0% + 6.7%) = 11.4%.

8 B is correct. The price return of the price-weighted index is the percentage change in price of the index: (68 − 75)/75 = −9.33%.

Security	Beginning of Period Price (£)	End of Period Price (£)
ABC	25.00	27.00
DEF	35.00	25.00
GHI	15.00	16.00
TOTAL	75.00	68.00

9 B is correct. The price return of the index is (48,250,000 − 53,750,000)/53,750,000 = −10.23%.

Security	Beginning of Period Price (¥)	Shares Outstanding	Beginning of Period Value (¥)	End of Period Price (¥)	End of Period Value (¥)
MNO	2,500	5,000	12,500,000	2,700	13,500,000
QRS	3,500	7,500	26,250,000	2,500	18,750,000

Security	Beginning of Period Price (¥)	Shares Outstanding	Beginning of Period Value (¥)	End of Period Price (¥)	End of Period Value (¥)
XYZ	1,500	10,000	15,000,000	1,600	16,000,000
Total			53,750,000		48,250,000

10 B is correct. The total return of the market-capitalization-weighted index is calculated below:

Security	Beginning of Period Value (¥)	End of Period Value (¥)	Total Dividends (¥)	Total Return (%)
MNO	12,500,000	13,500,000	500,000	12.00
QRS	26,250,000	18,750,000	1,125,000	−24.29
XYZ	15,000,000	16,000,000	1,000,000	13.33
Total	53,750,000	48,250,000	2,625,000	−5.35

11 A is correct. The target market determines the investment universe and the securities available for inclusion in the index.

12 A is correct. The sum of prices at the beginning of the period is 96; the sum at the end of the period is 100. Regardless of the divisor, the price return is $100/96 − 1 = 0.042$ or 4.2 percent.

13 B is correct. It is the percentage change in the market value over the period:

Market value at beginning of period: $(20 \times 300) + (50 \times 300) + (26 \times 2,000) = 73,000$

Market value at end of period: $(22 \times 300) + (48 \times 300) + (30 \times 2,000) = 81,000$

Percentage change is $81,000/73,000 − 1 = 0.1096$ or 11.0 percent with rounding.

14 C is correct. With an equal-weighted index, the same amount is invested in each security. Assuming $1,000 is invested in each of the three stocks, the index value is $3,000 at the beginning of the period and the following number of shares is purchased for each stock:

Security A: 50 shares

Security B: 20 shares

Security C: 38.46 shares.

Using the prices at the beginning of the period for each security, the index value at the end of the period is $3,213.8: $(\$22 \times 50) + (\$48 \times 20) + (\$30 \times 38.46)$. The price return is $\$3,213.8/\$3,000 − 1 = 7.1\%$.

15 A is correct. In the price weighting method, the divisor must be adjusted so the index value immediately after the split is the same as the index value immediately prior to the split.

16 C is correct. The main source of return differences arises from outperformance of small-cap securities or underperformance of large-cap securities. In an equal-weighted index, securities that constitute the largest fraction of the market are underrepresented and securities that constitute only a small fraction of the market are overrepresented. Thus, higher equal-weighted index returns will occur if the smaller-cap equities outperform the larger-cap equities.

17 C is correct. "Float" is the number of shares available for public trading.

18 B is correct. Fundamental weighting leads to indices that have a value tilt.

19 C is correct. Rebalancing refers to adjusting the weights of constituent securities in an index to maintain consistency with the index's weighting method.

20 B is correct. Changing market prices will cause weights that were initially equal to become unequal, thus requiring rebalancing.

21 C is correct. Reconstitution is the process by which index providers review the constituent securities, re-apply the initial criteria for inclusion in the index, and select which securities to retain, remove, or add. Constituent securities that no longer meet the criteria are replaced with securities that do. Thus, reconstitution reduces the likelihood that the index includes securities that are not representative of the target market.

22 C is correct. Security market indices play a critical role as proxies for asset classes in asset allocation models.

23 A is correct. Security market indices are used as proxies for measuring market or systematic risk, not as measures of systematic risk.

24 B is correct. Sector indices provide a means to determine whether a portfolio manager is more successful at stock selection or sector allocation.

25 C is correct. Style indices represent groups of securities classified according to market capitalization, value, growth, or a combination of these characteristics.

26 A is correct. The large number of fixed-income securities—combined with the lack of liquidity of some securities—makes it costly and difficult for investors to replicate fixed-income indices.

27 C is correct. An aggregate fixed-income index can be subdivided by market sector (government, government agency, collateralized, corporate), style (maturity, credit quality), economic sector, or some other characteristic to create more narrowly defined indices.

28 C is correct. Coupon frequency is not a dimension on which fixed-income indices are based.

29 A is correct. Commodity indices consist of futures contracts on one or more commodities.

30 C is correct. The performance of commodity indices can be quite different from that of the underlying commodities because the indices consist of futures contracts on the commodities rather than the actual commodities.

31 B is correct. It is not a real estate index category.

32 B is correct. Hedge funds are not required to report their performance to any party other than their investors. Therefore, each hedge fund decides to which database(s) it will report its performance. Thus, for a hedge fund index, constituents determine the index rather than index providers determining the constituents.

33 A is correct. Voluntary performance reporting may lead to survivorship bias, and poorer performing hedge funds will be less likely to report their performance.

34 C is correct. The fixed-income market has more issuers and securities than the equity market.

Market Efficiency

*by W. Sean Cleary, CFA, Howard J. Atkinson, CFA, and
Pamela Peterson Drake, CFA*

LEARNING OUTCOMES

Mastery	The candidate should be able to:
☐	**a.** describe market efficiency and related concepts, including their importance to investment practitioners;
☐	**b.** distinguish between market value and intrinsic value;
☐	**c.** explain factors that affect a market's efficiency;
☐	**d.** contrast weak-form, semi-strong-form, and strong-form market efficiency;
☐	**e.** explain the implications of each form of market efficiency for fundamental analysis, technical analysis, and the choice between active and passive portfolio management;
☐	**f.** describe selected market anomalies;
☐	**g.** contrast the behavioral finance view of investor behavior to that of traditional finance.

INTRODUCTION

Market efficiency concerns the extent to which market prices incorporate available information. If market prices do not fully incorporate information, then opportunities may exist to make a profit from the gathering and processing of information. The subject of market efficiency is, therefore, of great interest to investment managers, as illustrated in Example 1.

Market Efficiency and Active Manager Selection

The chief investment officer (CIO) of a major university endowment fund has listed eight steps in the active manager selection process that can be applied both to traditional investments (e.g., common equity and fixed-income securities) and to alternative investments (e.g., private equity, hedge funds, and real assets). The first step specified is the evaluation of market opportunity:

> What is the opportunity and why is it there? To answer this question we start by studying capital markets and the types of managers operating within those markets. We identify market inefficiencies and try to understand their causes, such as regulatory structures or behavioral biases. We can rule out many broad groups of managers and strategies by simply determining that the degree of market inefficiency necessary to support a strategy is implausible. Importantly, we consider the past history of active returns meaningless unless we understand why markets will allow those active returns to continue into the future.[1]

The CIO's description underscores the importance of not assuming that past active returns that might be found in a historical dataset will repeat themselves in the future. **Active returns** refer to returns earned by strategies that do *not* assume that all information is fully reflected in market prices.

Governments and market regulators also care about the extent to which market prices incorporate information. Efficient markets imply informative prices—prices that accurately reflect available information about fundamental values. In market-based economies, market prices help determine which companies (and which projects) obtain capital. If these prices do not efficiently incorporate information about a company's prospects, then it is possible that funds will be misdirected. By contrast, prices that are informative help direct scarce resources and funds available for investment to their highest-valued uses.[2] Informative prices thus promote economic growth. The efficiency of a country's capital markets (in which businesses raise financing) is an important characteristic of a well-functioning financial system.

The remainder of this reading is organized as follows. Section 2 provides specifics on how the efficiency of an asset market is described and discusses the factors affecting (i.e., contributing to and impeding) market efficiency. Section 3 presents an influential three-way classification of the efficiency of security markets and discusses its implications for fundamental analysis, technical analysis, and portfolio management. Section 4 presents several market anomalies (apparent market inefficiencies that have received enough attention to be individually identified and named) and describes how these anomalies relate to investment strategies. Section 5 introduces behavioral finance and how that field of study relates to market efficiency. A summary concludes the reading.

---

1 The CIO is Christopher J. Brightman, CFA, of the University of Virginia Investment Management Company, as reported in Yau, Schneeweis, Robinson, and Weiss (2007, pp. 481–482).
2 This concept is known as allocative efficiency.

THE CONCEPT OF MARKET EFFICIENCY

2

2.1 The Description of Efficient Markets

An **informationally efficient market** (an **efficient market**) is a market in which asset prices reflect new information quickly and rationally. An efficient market is thus a market in which asset prices reflect all past and present information.[3]

In this section we expand on this definition by clarifying the time frame required for an asset's price to incorporate information as well as describing the elements of information releases assumed under market efficiency. We discuss the difference between market value and intrinsic value and illustrate how inefficiencies or discrepancies between these values can provide profitable opportunities for active investment. As financial markets are generally not considered being either completely efficient or inefficient, but rather falling within a range between the two extremes, we describe a number of factors that contribute to and impede the degree of efficiency of a financial market. Finally, we conclude our overview of market efficiency by illustrating how the costs incurred by traders in identifying and exploiting possible market inefficiencies affect how we interpret market efficiency.

Investment managers and analysts, as noted, are interested in market efficiency because the extent to which a market is efficient affects how many profitable trading opportunities (market inefficiencies) exist. Consistent, superior, risk-adjusted returns (net of all expenses) are not achievable in an efficient market.[4] In a highly efficient market, a **passive investment** strategy (i.e., buying and holding a broad market portfolio) that does not seek superior risk-adjusted returns is preferred to an **active investment** strategy because of lower costs (for example, transaction and information-seeking costs). By contrast, in a very inefficient market, opportunities may exist for an active investment strategy to achieve superior risk-adjusted returns (net of all expenses in executing the strategy) as compared with a passive investment strategy. In inefficient markets, an active investment strategy may outperform a passive investment strategy on a risk-adjusted basis. Understanding the characteristics of an efficient market and being able to evaluate the efficiency of a particular market are important topics for investment analysts and portfolio managers.

An efficient market is a market in which asset prices reflect information quickly. But what is the time frame of "quickly"? Trades are the mechanism by which information can be incorporated into asset transaction prices. The time needed to execute trades to exploit an inefficiency may provide a baseline for judging speed of adjustment.[5] The time frame for an asset's price to incorporate information must be at least as long as the shortest time a trader needs to execute a transaction in the asset. In certain markets, such as foreign exchange and developed equity markets, market efficiency relative to certain types of information has been studied using time frames as short as one minute or less. If the time frame of price adjustment allows many traders to earn profits with little risk, then the market is relatively inefficient. These considerations lead to the observation that market efficiency can be viewed as falling on a continuum.

---

3 This definition is convenient for making several instructional points. The definition that most simply explains the sense of the word *efficient* in this context can be found in Fama (1976): "An efficient capital market is a market that is efficient in processing information" (p. 134).

4 The technical term for *superior* in this context is *positive abnormal* in the sense of higher than expected given the asset's risk (as measured, according to capital market theory, by the asset's contribution to the risk of a well-diversified portfolio).

5 Although the original theory of market efficiency does not quantify this speed, the basic idea is that it is sufficiently swift to make it impossible to consistently earn abnormal profits. Chordia, Roll, and Subrahmanyam (2005) suggest that the adjustment to information on the New York Stock Exchange (NYSE) is between 5 and 60 minutes.

Finally, an important point is that in an efficient market, prices should be expected to react only to the elements of information releases that are not anticipated fully by investors—that is, to the "unexpected" or "surprise" element of such releases. Investors process the unexpected information and revise expectations (for example, about an asset's future cash flows, risk, or required rate of return) accordingly. The revised expectations enter or get incorporated in the asset price through trades in the asset. Market participants who process the news and believe that at the current market price an asset does not offer sufficient compensation for its perceived risk will tend to sell it or even sell it short. Market participants with opposite views should be buyers. In this way the market establishes the price that balances the various opinions after expectations are revised.

EXAMPLE 2

Price Reaction to the Default on a Bond Issue

Suppose that a speculative-grade bond issuer announces, just before bond markets open, that it will default on an upcoming interest payment. In the announcement, the issuer confirms various reports made in the financial media in the period leading up to the announcement. Prior to the issuer's announcement, the financial news media reported the following: 1) suppliers of the company were making deliveries only for cash payment, reducing the company's liquidity; 2) the issuer's financial condition had probably deteriorated to the point that it lacked the cash to meet an upcoming interest payment; and 3) although public capital markets were closed to the company, it was negotiating with a bank for a private loan that would permit it to meet its interest payment and continue operations for at least nine months. If the issuer defaults on the bond, the consensus opinion of analysts is that bondholders will recover approximately $0.36 to $0.38 per dollar face value.

1   If the market for the bond is highly efficient, the bond's market price is *most likely* to fully reflect the bond's value after default:

   A   in the period leading up to the announcement.

   B   in the first trade prices after the market opens on the announcement day.

   C   when the issuer actually misses the payment on the interest payment date.

2   If the market for the bond is highly efficient, the piece of information that bond investors *most likely* focused on in the issuer's announcement was that the issuer:

   A   had failed in its negotiations for a bank loan.

   B   lacked the cash to meet the upcoming interest payment.

   C   had been required to make cash payments for supplier deliveries.

Solution to 1:

B is correct. The announcement removed any uncertainty about default. In the period leading up to the announcement, the bond's market price incorporated a probability of default but the price would not have fully reflected the bond's value after default. The possibility that a bank loan might permit the company to avoid default was not eliminated until the announcement.

> **Solution to 2:**
>
> A is correct. The failure of the loan negotiations first becomes known in this announcement. The failure implies default.

2.2 Market Value versus Intrinsic Value

Market value is the price at which an asset can currently be bought or sold. **Intrinsic value** (sometimes called **fundamental value**) is, broadly speaking, the value that would be placed on it by investors if they had a complete understanding of the asset's investment characteristics.[6] For a bond, for example, such information would include its interest (coupon) rate, principal value, the timing of its interest and principal payments, the other terms of the bond contract (indenture), a precise understanding of its default risk, the liquidity of its market, and other issue-specific items. In addition, market variables such as the term structure of interest rates and the size of various market premiums applying to the issue (for default risk, etc.) would enter into a discounted cash flow estimate of the bond's intrinsic value (discounted cash flow models are often used for such estimates). The word *estimate* is used because in practice, intrinsic value can be estimated but is not known for certain.

If investors believe a market is highly *efficient*, they will usually accept market prices as accurately reflecting intrinsic values. Discrepancies between market price and intrinsic value are the basis for profitable active investment. Active investors seek to own assets selling below perceived intrinsic value in the marketplace and to sell or sell short assets selling above perceived intrinsic value.

If investors believe an asset market is relatively *inefficient*, they may try to develop an independent estimate of intrinsic value. The challenge for investors and analysts is estimating an asset's intrinsic value. Numerous theories and models, including the dividend discount model, can be used to estimate an asset's intrinsic value, but they all require some form of judgment regarding the size, timing, and riskiness of the future cash flows associated with the asset. The more complex an asset's future cash flows, the more difficult it is to estimate its intrinsic value. These complexities and the estimates of an asset's market value are reflected in the market through the buying and selling of assets. The market value of an asset represents the intersection of supply and demand—the point that is low enough to induce at least one investor to buy while being high enough to induce at least one investor to sell. Because information relevant to valuation flows continually to investors, estimates of intrinsic value change, and hence, market values change.

> **EXAMPLE 3**
>
> ## Intrinsic Value
>
> 1 An analyst estimates that a security's intrinsic value is lower than its market value. The security appears to be:
>
>   A undervalued.
>
>   B fairly valued.
>
>   C overvalued.
>
> 2 A market in which assets' market values are, on average, equal to or nearly equal to intrinsic values is *best described* as a market that is attractive for:

---

6 Intrinsic value is often defined as the present value of all expected future cash flows of the asset.

A active investment.

B passive investment.

C both active and passive investment.

3 Suppose that the future cash flows of an asset are accurately estimated. The asset trades in a market that you believe is highly efficient based on most evidence. But your intrinsic value estimate exceeds market value by a moderate amount. The *most likely* conclusion is that you have:

A overestimated the asset's risk.

B underestimated the asset's risk.

C identified a market inefficiency.

Solution to 1:

C is correct. The market is valuing the asset at more than its true worth.

Solution to 2:

B is correct because an active investment is not expected to earn superior risk-adjusted returns. The additional costs of active investment are not justified in such a market.

Solution to 3:

B is correct. If risk is underestimated, the discount rate being applied to find the present value of the expected cash flows (estimated intrinsic value) will be too low and the intrinsic value estimate will be too high.

2.3 Factors Contributing to and Impeding a Market's Efficiency

For markets to be efficient, prices should adjust quickly and rationally to the release of new information. In other words, prices of assets in an efficient market should "fully reflect" all information. Financial markets, however, are generally not classified at the two extremes as either completely inefficient or completely efficient but, rather, as exhibiting various degrees of efficiency. In other words, market efficiency should be viewed as falling on a continuum between extremes of completely efficient, at one end, and completely inefficient, at the other. Asset prices in a highly efficient market, by definition, reflect information more quickly and more accurately than in a less-efficient market. These degrees of efficiency also vary through time, across geographical markets, and by type of market. A number of factors contribute to and impede the degree of efficiency in a financial market.

2.3.1 *Market Participants*

One of the most critical factors contributing to the degree of efficiency in a market is the number of market participants. Consider the following example that illustrates the relationship between the number of market participants and market efficiency.

EXAMPLE 4

Illustration of Market Efficiency

Assume that the shares of a small market capitalization (cap) company trade on a public stock exchange. Because of its size, it is not considered "blue-chip" and not many professional investors follow the activities of the company.[7] A small-cap fund analyst reports that the most recent annual operating performance of the company has been surprisingly good, considering the recent slump in its industry. The company's share price, however, has been slow to react to the positive financial results because the company is not being recommended by the majority of research analysts. This mispricing implies that the market for this company's shares is less than fully efficient. The small-cap fund analyst recognizes the opportunity and immediately recommends the purchase of the company's shares. The share price gradually increases as more investors purchase the shares once the news of the mispricing spreads through the market. As a result, it takes a few days for the share price to fully reflect the information.

Six months later, the company reports another solid set of interim financial results. But because the previous mispricing and subsequent profit opportunities have become known in the market, the number of analysts following the company's shares has increased substantially. As a result, as soon as unexpected information about the positive interim results are released to the public, a large number of buy orders quickly drive up the stock price, thereby making the market for these shares more efficient than before.

A large number of investors (individual and institutional) follow the major financial markets closely on a daily basis, and if mispricings exist in these markets, as illustrated by the example, investors will act so that these mispricings disappear quickly. Besides the number of investors, the number of financial analysts who follow or analyze a security or asset should be positively related to market efficiency. The number of market participants and resulting trading activity can vary significantly through time. A lack of trading activity can cause or accentuate other market imperfections that impede market efficiency. In fact, in many of these markets, such as China, trading in many of the listed stocks is restricted for foreigners. By nature, this limitation reduces the number of market participants, restricts the potential for trading activity, and hence reduces market efficiency.

EXAMPLE 5

Factors Affecting Market Efficiency

The expected effect on market efficiency of opening a securities market to trading by foreigners would be to:

A   decrease market efficiency.

B   leave market efficiency unchanged.

C   increase market efficiency.

---

7 A "blue-chip" share is one from a well-recognized company that is considered to be high quality but low risk. This term generally refers to a company that has a long history of earnings and paying dividends.

> **Solution:**
>
> C is correct. The opening of markets as described should increase market efficiency by increasing the number of market participants.

2.3.2 *Information Availability and Financial Disclosure*

Information availability (e.g., an active financial news media) and financial disclosure should promote market efficiency. Information regarding trading activity and traded companies in such markets as the New York Stock Exchange, the London Stock Exchange, and the Tokyo Stock Exchange is readily available. Many investors and analysts participate in these markets, and analyst coverage of listed companies is typically substantial. As a result, these markets are quite efficient. In contrast, trading activity and material information availability may be lacking in smaller securities markets, such as those operating in some emerging markets.

Similarly, significant differences may exist in the efficiency of different types of markets. For example, many securities trade primarily or exclusively in dealer or over-the-counter (OTC) markets, including bonds, money market instruments, currencies, mortgage-backed securities, swaps, and forward contracts. The information provided by the dealers that serve as market makers for these markets can vary significantly in quality and quantity, both through time and across different product markets.

Treating all market participants fairly is critical for the integrity of the market and explains why regulators place such an emphasis on "fair, orderly, and efficient markets."[8] A key element of this fairness is that all investors have access to the information necessary to value securities that trade in the market. Rules and regulations that promote fairness and efficiency in a market include those pertaining to the disclosure of information and illegal insider trading.

For example, US Securities and Exchange Commission's (SEC's) Regulation FD (Fair Disclosure) requires that if security issuers provide nonpublic information to some market professionals or investors, they must also disclose this information to the public.[9] This requirement helps provide equal and fair opportunities, which is important in encouraging participation in the market. A related issue deals with illegal insider trading. The SEC's rules, along with court cases, define illegal insider trading as trading in securities by market participants who are considered insiders "while in possession of material, nonpublic information about the security."[10,11] Although these rules cannot guarantee that some participants will not have an advantage over others and that insiders will not trade on the basis of inside information, the civil and criminal penalties associated with breaking these rules are intended to discourage illegal insider trading and promote fairness.

---

8 "The Investor's Advocate: How the SEC Protects Investors, Maintains Market Integrity, and Facilitates Capital Formation," US Securities and Exchange Commission (www.sec.gov/about/whatwedo.shtml).

9 Regulation FD, "Selective Disclosure and Insider Trading," 17 CFR Parts 240, 243, and 249, effective 23 October 2000.

10 Although not the focus of this particular reading, it is important to note that a party is considered an insider not only when the individual is a corporate insider, such as an officer or director, but also when the individual is aware that the information is nonpublic information [Securities and Exchange Commission, Rules 10b5-1 ("Trading on the Basis of Material Nonpublic Information in Insider Trading Cases") and Rule 10b5-2 "Duties of Trust or Confidence in Misappropriation Insider Trading Cases")].

11 In contrast to the situation in the United States, in other developed markets, the insider trading laws are generally promulgated by the courts, although the definition of "insider trading" is generally through statutes. See, for example, the European Community's (EC's) Insider Trading Directive, *Council Directive Coordinating Regulations on Insider Dealing*, Directive 89/592, article 32, 1989 OJ (L 334) 30, 1.

2.3.3 *Limits to Trading*

Arbitrage is a set of transactions that produces riskless profits. Arbitrageurs are traders who engage in such trades to benefit from pricing discrepancies (inefficiencies) in markets. Such trading activity contributes to market efficiency. For example, if an asset is traded in two markets but at different prices, the actions of buying the asset in the market in which it is underpriced and selling the asset in the market in which it is overpriced will eventually bring these two prices together. The presence of these arbitrageurs helps pricing discrepancies disappear quickly. Obviously, market efficiency is impeded by any limitation on arbitrage resulting from operating inefficiencies, such as difficulties in executing trades in a timely manner, prohibitively high trading costs, and a lack of transparency in market prices.

Some market experts argue that restrictions on short selling limit arbitrage trading, which impedes market efficiency. **Short selling** is the transaction whereby an investor sells shares that he or she does not own by borrowing them from a broker and agreeing to replace them at a future date. Short selling allows investors to sell securities they believe to be overvalued, much in the same way they can buy those they believe to be undervalued. In theory, such activities promote more efficient pricing. Regulators and others, however, have argued that short selling may exaggerate downward market movements, leading to crashes in affected securities. In contrast, some researchers report evidence indicating that when investors are unable to borrow securities, that is to short the security, or when costs to borrow shares are high, market prices may deviate from intrinsic values.[12] Furthermore, research suggests that short selling is helpful in price discovery (that is, it facilitates supply and demand in determining prices).[13]

2.4 Transaction Costs and Information-Acquisition Costs

The costs incurred by traders in identifying and exploiting possible market inefficiencies affect the interpretation of market efficiency. The two types of costs to consider are transaction costs and information-acquisition costs.

- *Transaction costs*: Practically, transaction costs are incurred in trading to exploit any perceived market inefficiency. Thus, "efficient" should be viewed as efficient within the bounds of transaction costs. For example, consider a violation of the principle that two identical assets should sell for the same price in different markets. Such a violation can be considered to be a rather simple possible exception to market efficiency because prices appear to be inconsistently processing information. To exploit the violation, a trader could arbitrage by simultaneously shorting the asset in the higher-price market and buying the asset in the lower-price market. If the price discrepancy between the two markets is smaller than the transaction costs involved in the arbitrage for the lowest cost traders, the arbitrage will not occur, and both prices are in effect efficient within the bounds of arbitrage. These bounds of arbitrage are relatively narrow in highly liquid markets, such as the market for US Treasury bills, but could be wide in illiquid markets.

- *Information-acquisition costs*: Practically, expenses are always associated with gathering and analyzing information. New information is incorporated in transaction prices by traders placing trades based on their analysis of information. Active investors who place trades based on information they have gathered and analyzed play a key role in market prices adjusting to reflect new information.

---

12 A significant amount of research supports this view, including Jones and Lamont (2002) and Duffie, Garleanu, and Pederson (2002).
13 See Bris, Goetzmann, and Zhu (2009).

The classic view of market efficiency is that active investors incur information acquisition costs but that money is wasted because prices already reflect all relevant information. This view of efficiency is very strict in the sense of viewing a market as inefficient if active investing can recapture any part of the costs, such as research costs and active asset selection. Grossman and Stiglitz (1980) argue that prices must offer a return to information acquisition; in equilibrium, if markets are efficient, returns net of such expenses are just fair returns for the risk incurred. The modern perspective views a market as inefficient if, after deducting such costs, active investing can earn superior returns. Gross of expenses, a return should accrue to information acquisition in an efficient market.

In summary, a modern perspective calls for the investor to consider transaction costs and information-acquisition costs when evaluating the efficiency of a market. A price discrepancy must be sufficiently large to leave the investor with a profit (adjusted for risk) after taking account of the transaction costs and information-acquisition costs to reach the conclusion that the discrepancy may represent a market inefficiency. Prices may somewhat less than fully reflect available information without there being a true market opportunity for active investors.

3   FORMS OF MARKET EFFICIENCY

Eugene Fama developed a framework for describing the degree to which markets are efficient.[14] In his efficient market hypothesis, markets are efficient when prices reflect *all* relevant information at any point in time. This means that the market prices observed for securities, for example, reflect the information available at the time.

In his framework, Fama defines three forms of efficiency: weak, semi-strong, and strong. Each form is defined with respect to the available information that is reflected in prices.

Forms of Market Efficiency	Market Prices Reflect:		
	Past Market Data	Public Information	Private Information
Weak form of market efficiency	✓		
Semi-strong form of market efficiency	✓	✓	
Strong form of market efficiency	✓	✓	✓

A finding that investors can consistently earn **abnormal returns** by trading on the basis of information is evidence contrary to market efficiency. In general, abnormal returns are returns in excess of those expected given a security's risk and the market's return. In other words, abnormal return equals actual return less expected return.

---

14 Fama (1970).

3.1 Weak Form

In the **weak-form efficient market hypothesis**, security prices fully reflect *all past market data*, which refers to all historical price and trading volume information. If markets are weak-form efficient, past trading data are already reflected in current prices and investors cannot predict future price changes by extrapolating prices or patterns of prices from the past.[15]

Tests of whether securities markets are weak-form efficient require looking at patterns of prices. One approach is to see whether there is any serial correlation in security returns, which would imply a predictable pattern.[16] Although there is some weak correlation in daily security returns, there is not enough correlation to make this a profitable trading rule after considering transaction costs.

An alternative approach to test weak-form efficiency is to examine specific trading rules that attempt to exploit historical trading data. If any such trading rule consistently generates abnormal risk-adjusted returns after trading costs, this evidence will contradict weak-form efficiency. This approach is commonly associated with **technical analysis**, which involves the analysis of historical trading information (primarily pricing and volume data) in an attempt to identify recurring patterns in the trading data that can be used to guide investment decisions. Many technical analysts, also referred to as "technicians," argue that many movements in stock prices are based, in large part, on psychology. Many technicians attempt to predict how market participants will behave, based on analyses of past behavior, and then trade on those predictions. Technicians often argue that simple statistical tests of trading rules are not conclusive because they are not applied to the more sophisticated trading strategies that can be used and that the research excludes the technician's subjective judgment. Thus, it is difficult to definitively refute this assertion because there are an unlimited number of possible technical trading rules.

Can technical analysts profit from trading on past trends? Overall, the evidence indicates that investors cannot consistently earn abnormal profits using past prices or other technical analysis strategies in developed markets.[17] Some evidence suggests, however, that there are opportunities to profit on technical analysis in countries with developing markets, including China, Hungary, Bangladesh, and Turkey.[18]

3.2 Semi-Strong Form

In a **semi-strong-form efficient market**, prices reflect all publicly known and available information. Publicly available information includes financial statement data (such as earnings, dividends, corporate investments, changes in management, etc.) and financial market data (such as closing prices, shares traded, etc.). Therefore, the semi-strong form of market efficiency encompasses the weak form. In other words, if a market is semi-strong efficient, then it must also be weak-form efficient. A market that quickly incorporates all publicly available information into its prices is semi-strong efficient.

In a semi-strong market, efforts to analyze publicly available information are futile. That is, analyzing earnings announcements of companies to identify underpriced or overpriced securities is pointless because the prices of these securities already reflect all publicly available information. If markets are semi-strong efficient, no single investor has access to information that is not already available to other market participants,

---

15 Market efficiency should not be confused with the random walk hypothesis, in which price changes over time are independent of one another. A random walk model is one of many alternative expected return generating models. Market efficiency does not require that returns follow a random walk.

16 Serial correlation is a statistical measure of the degree to which the returns in one period are related to the returns in another period.

17 Bessembinder and Chan (1998) and Fifield, Power, and Sinclair (2005).

18 Fifield, Power, and Sinclair (2005), Chen and Li (2006), and Mobarek, Mollah, and Bhuyan (2008).

and as a consequence, no single investor can gain an advantage in predicting future security prices. In a semi-strong efficient market, prices adjust quickly and accurately to new information. Suppose a company announces earnings that are higher than expected. In a semi-strong efficient market, investors would not be able to act on this announcement and earn abnormal returns.

A common empirical test of investors' reaction to information releases is the event study. Suppose a researcher wants to test whether investors react to the announcement that the company is paying a special dividend. The researcher identifies a sample period and then those companies that paid a special dividend in the period and the date of the announcement. Then, for each company's stock, the researcher calculates the expected return on the share for the event date. This expected return may be based on many different models, including the capital asset pricing model, a simple market model, or a market index return. The researcher calculates the excess return as the difference between the actual return and the expected return. Once the researcher has calculated the event's excess return for each share, statistical tests are conducted to see whether the abnormal returns are statistically different from zero. The process of an event study is outlined in Exhibit 1.

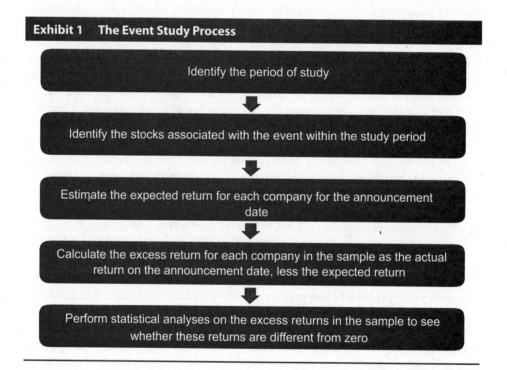

Exhibit 1   The Event Study Process

Identify the period of study

Identify the stocks associated with the event within the study period

Estimate the expected return for each company for the announcement date

Calculate the excess return for each company in the sample as the actual return on the announcement date, less the expected return

Perform statistical analyses on the excess returns in the sample to see whether these returns are different from zero

How do event studies relate to efficient markets? In a semi-strong efficient market, share prices react quickly and accurately to public information. Therefore, if the information is good news, such as better-than-expected earnings, one would expect the company's shares to increase immediately at the time of the announcement; if it is bad news, one would expect a swift, negative reaction. If actual returns exceed what is expected in absence of the announcement and these returns are confined to the announcement period, then they are consistent with the idea that market prices react quickly to new information. In other words, the finding of excess returns at the time of the announcement does not necessarily indicate market inefficiency. In contrast, the finding of consistent excess returns following the announcement would suggest a trading opportunity. Trading on the basis of the announcement—that is, once the announcement is made—would not, on average, yield abnormal returns.

EXAMPLE 6

Information Arrival and Market Reaction

Consider an example of a news item and its effect on a share's price. In June 2008, the US Federal Trade Commission (FTC) began an investigation of Intel Corporation regarding non-competitiveness, and on 16 December 2009, the FTC announced that it was suing Intel over non-competitive issues. This announcement was made before the market opened for trading on 16 December.

Intel stock closed at $19.78 on 15 December 2009 but opened at $19.50 on 16 December. The stock then traded in the range from $19.45 to $19.68 within the first half hour as the news of the suit and Intel's initial response were spreading among investors. Exhibit 2 illustrates the price of Intel for the first 90 minutes of trading on 16 December.

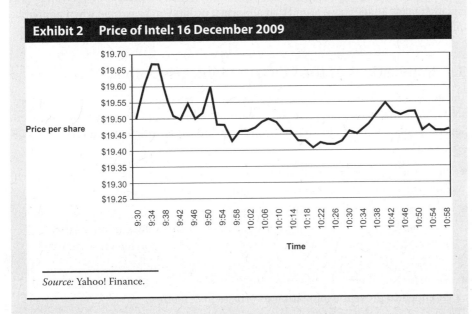

Exhibit 2   Price of Intel: 16 December 2009

Source: Yahoo! Finance.

Is the fact that the price of Intel moves up immediately and then comes down indicative of an inefficiency regarding information? Not necessarily. Does it mean that investors overreacted? Not necessarily. During the morning, both before and after the market opened, news flowed about the lawsuit and the company's reaction to the lawsuit. The price of the shares reflects investors' reactions to this news. Why didn't Intel's shares simply move to a new level and stay there? Because 1) information continued to flow during the day on Intel and investors' estimate of the importance of this news on Intel's stock value continued to change, and 2) other news, related to other events and issues (such as the economy), affected stock prices.

Researchers have examined many different company-specific information events, including stock splits, dividend changes, and merger announcements, as well as economy-wide events, such as regulation changes and tax rate changes. The results of most research are consistent with the view that developed securities markets might be semi-strong efficient. But some evidence suggests that the markets in developing countries may not be semi-strong efficient.[19]

---

19 See Gan, Lee, Hwa, and Zhang (2005) and Raja, Sudhahar, and Selvam (2009).

3.3 Strong Form

In a **strong-form efficient market**, security prices fully reflect both public and private information. A market that is strong-form efficient is, by definition, also semi-strong- and weak-form efficient. In the case of a strong-form efficient market, insiders would not be able to earn abnormal returns from trading on the basis of private information. A strong-form efficient market also means that prices reflect all private information, which means that prices reflect everything that the management of a company knows about the financial condition of the company that has not been publicly released. However, this is not likely because of the strong prohibitions against insider trading that are found in most countries. If a market is strong-form efficient, those with insider information cannot earn abnormal returns.

Researchers test whether a market is strong-form efficient by testing whether investors can earn abnormal profits by trading on nonpublic information. The results of these tests are consistent with the view that securities markets are not strong-form efficient; many studies have found that abnormal profits can be earned when nonpublic information is used.[20]

3.4 Implications of the Efficient Market Hypothesis

The implications of efficient markets to investment managers and analysts are important because they affect the value of securities and how these securities are managed. Several implications can be drawn from the evidence on efficient markets for developed markets:

- Securities markets are weak-form efficient, and therefore, investors cannot earn abnormal returns by trading on the basis of past trends in price.

- Securities markets are semi-strong efficient, and therefore, analysts who collect and analyze information must consider whether that information is already reflected in security prices and how any new information affects a security's value.[21]

- Securities markets are not strong-form efficient because securities laws are intended to prevent exploitation of private information.

3.4.1 Fundamental Analysis

Fundamental analysis is the examination of publicly available information and the formulation of forecasts to estimate the intrinsic value of assets. Fundamental analysis involves the estimation of an asset's value using company data, such as earnings and sales forecasts, and risk estimates as well as industry and economic data, such as economic growth, inflation, and interest rates. Buy and sell decisions depend on whether the current market price is less than or greater than the estimated intrinsic value.

The semi-strong form of market efficiency says that all available public information is reflected in current prices. So, what good is fundamental analysis? Fundamental analysis is necessary in a well-functioning market because this analysis helps the market participants understand the value implications of information. In other words, fundamental analysis facilitates a semi-strong efficient market by disseminating

---

20 Evidence that finds that markets are not strong-form efficient include Jaffe (1974) and Rozeff and Zaman (1988).

21 In the case of the Intel example, this implication would mean estimating how the actual filing of the lawsuit and the company's reaction to the lawsuit affect the value of Intel, while keeping in mind that the expectation of a lawsuit was already impounded in Intel's stock price.

value-relevant information. And, although fundamental analysis requires costly information, this analysis can be profitable in terms of generating abnormal returns if the analyst creates a comparative advantage with respect to this information.[22]

3.4.2 *Technical Analysis*

Investors using **technical analysis** attempt to profit by looking at patterns of prices and trading volume. Although some price patterns persist, exploiting these patterns may be too costly and, hence, would not produce abnormal returns.

Consider a situation in which a pattern of prices exists. With so many investors examining prices, this pattern will be detected. If profitable, exploiting this pattern will eventually affect prices such that this pattern will no longer exist; it will be arbitraged away. In other words, by detecting and exploiting patterns in prices, technical analysts assist markets in maintaining weak-form efficiency. Does this mean that technical analysts cannot earn abnormal profits? Not necessarily, because there may be a possibility of earning abnormal profits from a pricing inefficiency. But would it be possible to earn abnormal returns on a consistent basis from exploiting such a pattern? No, because the actions of market participants will arbitrage this opportunity quickly, and the inefficiency will no longer exist.

3.4.3 *Portfolio Management*

If securities markets are weak-form and semi-strong-form efficient, the implication is that active trading, whether attempting to exploit price patterns or public information, is not likely to generate abnormal returns. In other words, portfolio managers cannot beat the market on a consistent basis, so therefore, passive portfolio management should outperform active portfolio management. Researchers have observed that mutual funds do not, on average, outperform the market on a risk-adjusted basis.[23] Mutual funds perform, on average, similar to the market before considering fees and expenses and perform worse than the market, on average, once fees and expenses are considered. Even if a mutual fund is not actively managed, there are costs to managing these funds, which reduces net returns.

So, what good are portfolio managers? The role of a portfolio manager is not necessarily to beat the market but, rather, to establish and manage a portfolio consistent with the portfolio's objectives, with appropriate diversification and asset allocation, while taking into consideration the risk preferences and tax situation of the investor.

MARKET PRICING ANOMALIES

4

Although considerable evidence shows that markets are efficient, researchers have also reported a number of potential inefficiencies, or anomalies, that result in the mispricing of securities. These market anomalies, if persistent, are exceptions to the notion of market efficiency. In other words, a **market anomaly** occurs if a change in the price of an asset or security cannot directly be linked to current relevant information known in the market or to the release of new information into the market. Although the list is far from exhaustive, in this section, several well-known anomalies in financial markets are discussed.

---

22 Brealey (1983).
23 See Malkiel (1995). One of the challenges to evaluating mutual fund performance is that the researcher must control for survivorship bias.

The validity of any evidence supporting the existence of such market inefficiencies must be *consistent* over reasonably long periods. Otherwise, a detected market anomaly may largely be an artifact of the sample period chosen. In the widespread search for discovering profitable anomalies, many findings could simply be the product of a process called **data mining**, also known as **data snooping**. In generally accepted research practice, an initial hypothesis is developed which is based on economic rationale, followed by tests conducted on objectively selected data to either confirm or reject the original hypothesis. However, with data mining the process is reversed where data is often examined with the intent to develop a hypothesis, instead of developing a hypothesis first. This is done by analyzing data in various manners, and even utilizing different empirical approaches until you find support for a desired result, in this case a profitable anomaly. Can researchers look back on data and find a trading strategy that would have yielded abnormal returns? Absolutely. Will this trading strategy provide abnormal returns in the future? Perhaps not. It is always possible that enough data snooping can detect a trading strategy that would have worked in the past, and it is always possible that some trading strategy can produce abnormal returns simply by chance. But in an efficient market, such a strategy is unlikely to generate abnormal returns on a consistent basis in the future. Although identified anomalies may frequently appear to produce excess returns, it is generally difficult to profitably exploit the anomalies after accounting for risk, trading costs, and so on.

Several anomalies are listed in Exhibit 3. This list is by no means exhaustive, but it provides information on the breadth of the anomalies. A few of these anomalies are discussed in more detail in the following sections. The anomalies are placed into categories based on the research method that identified the anomaly. Time-series anomalies were identified using time series of data. Cross-sectional anomalies were identified based on analyzing a cross section of companies that differ on some key characteristics. Other anomalies were identified by a variety of means, including event studies.

Exhibit 3	Sampling of Observed Pricing Anomalies	
Time Series	**Cross-Sectional**	**Other**
January effect	Size effect	Closed-end fund discount
Day-of-the-week effect	Value effect	Earnings surprise
Weekend effect	Book-to-market ratios	Initial public offerings
Turn-of-the-month effect	P/E ratio effect	Distressed securities effect
Holiday effect	Value Line enigma	Stock splits
Time-of-day effect		Super Bowl
Momentum		
Overreaction		

4.1 Time-Series Anomalies

Two of the major categories of time-series anomalies that have been documented are 1) calendar anomalies and 2) momentum and overreaction anomalies.

4.1.1 *Calendar Anomalies*

In the 1980s, a number of researchers reported that stock market returns in January were significantly higher compared to the rest of the months of the year, with most of the abnormal returns reported during the first five trading days in January. Since its first documentation in the 1980s, this pattern, known as the **January effect**, has been observed in most equity markets around the world. This anomaly is also known as the **turn-of-the-year effect**, or even often referred to as the "small firm in January effect" because it is most frequently observed for the returns of small market capitalization stocks.[24]

The January effect contradicts the efficient market hypothesis because excess returns in January are not attributed to any new and relevant information or news. A number of reasons have been suggested for this anomaly, including tax-loss selling. Researchers have speculated that, in order to reduce their tax liabilities, investors sell their "loser" securities in December for the purpose of creating capital losses, which can then be used to offset any capital gains. A related explanation is that these losers tend to be small-cap stocks with high volatility.[25] This increased supply of equities in December depresses their prices, and then these shares are bought in early January at relatively attractive prices. This demand then drives their prices up again. Overall, the evidence indicates that tax-loss selling may account for a portion of January abnormal returns, but it does not explain all of it.

Another possible explanation for the anomaly is so-called "window dressing", a practice in which portfolio managers sell their riskier securities prior to 31 December. The explanation is as follows: many portfolio managers prepare the annual reports of their portfolio holdings as of 31 December. Selling riskier securities is an attempt to make their portfolios appear less risky. After 31 December, a portfolio manager would then simply purchase riskier securities in an attempt to earn higher returns. However, similar to the tax-loss selling hypothesis, the research evidence in support of the window dressing hypothesis explains some, but not all, of the anomaly.

Recent evidence for both stock and bond returns suggests that the January effect is not persistent and, therefore, is not a pricing anomaly. Once an appropriate adjustment for risk is made, the January "effect" does not produce abnormal returns.[26]

Several other calendar effects, including the day-of-the-week and the weekend effects,[27] have been found. These anomalies are summarized in Exhibit 4.[28] But like the size effect, which will be described later, most of these anomalies have been eliminated over time. One view is that the anomalies have been exploited such that the effect has been arbitraged away. Another view, however, is that increasingly sophisticated statistical methodologies fail to detect pricing inefficiencies.

Exhibit 4 Calendar-Based Anomalies	
Anomaly	**Observation**
Turn-of-the-month effect	Returns tend to be higher on the last trading day of the month and the first three trading days of the next month.
Day-of-the-week effect	The average Monday return is negative and lower than the average returns for the other four days, which are all positive.

(continued)

---

24 There is also evidence of a January effect in bond returns that is more prevalent in high-yield corporate bonds, similar to the small-company effect for stocks.
25 See Roll (1983).
26 See, for example, Kim (2006).
27 For a discussion of several of these anomalous patterns, see Jacobs and Levy (1988).
28 The weekend effect consists of a pattern of returns around the weekend: abnormal positive returns on Fridays followed by abnormally negative returns on Mondays. This is a day-of-the-week effect that specifically links Friday and Monday returns. It is interesting to note that in 2009, the weekend effect in the United States was inverted, with 80 percent of the gains from March 2009 onward coming from the first trading day of the week.

Exhibit 4	(Continued)
Anomaly	**Observation**
Weekend effect	Returns on weekends tend to be lower than returns on weekdays.
Holiday effect	Returns on stocks in the day prior to market holidays tend to be higher than other days.

4.1.2 *Momentum and Overreaction Anomalies*

Momentum anomalies relate to short-term share price patterns. One of the earliest studies to identify this type of anomaly was conducted by Werner DeBondt and Richard Thaler, who argued that investors overreact to the release of unexpected public information.[29] Therefore, stock prices will be inflated (depressed) for those companies releasing good (bad) information. This anomaly has become known as the overreaction effect. Using the overreaction effect, they proposed a strategy that involved buying "loser" portfolios and selling "winner" portfolios. They defined stocks as winners or losers based on their total returns over the previous three- to five-year period. They found that in a subsequent period, the loser portfolios outperformed the market, while the winner portfolios underperformed the market. Similar patterns have been documented in many, but not all, global stock markets as well as in bond markets. One criticism is that the observed anomaly may be the result of statistical problems in the analysis.

A contradiction to weak-form efficiency occurs when securities that have experienced high returns in the short term tend to continue to generate higher returns in subsequent periods.[30] Empirical support for the existence of momentum in stock returns in most stock markets around the world is well documented. If investors can trade on the basis of momentum and earn abnormal profits, then this anomaly contradicts the weak form of the efficient market hypothesis because it represents a pattern in prices that can be exploited by simply using historical price information.[31]

Researchers have argued that the existence of momentum is rational and not contrary to market efficiency because it is plausible that there are shocks to the expected growth rates of cash flows to shareholders and that these shocks induce a serial correlation that is rational and short lived.[32] In other words, having stocks with some degree of momentum in their security returns may not imply irrationality but, rather, may reflect prices adjusting to a shock in growth rates.

4.2 Cross-Sectional Anomalies

Two of the most researched cross-sectional anomalies in financial markets are the size effect and the value effect.

---

29 DeBondt and Thaler (1985).
30 Notice that this pattern lies in sharp contrast to DeBondt and Thaler's reversal pattern that is displayed over longer periods of time. In theory, the two patterns could be related. In other words, it is feasible that prices are bid up extremely high, perhaps too high, in the short term for companies that are doing well. In the longer term (three-to-five years), the prices of these short-term winners correct themselves and they do poorly.
31 Jegadeesh and Titman (2001).
32 Johnson (2002).

4.2.1 *Size Effect*

The size effect results from the observation that equities of small-cap companies tend to outperform equities of large-cap companies on a risk-adjusted basis. Many researchers documented a small-company effect soon after the initial research was published in 1981. This effect, however, was not apparent in subsequent studies.[33] Part of the reason that the size effect was not confirmed by subsequent studies may be because of the fact that if it were truly an anomaly, investors acting on this effect would reduce any potential returns. But some of the explanation may simply be that the effect as originally observed was a chance outcome and, therefore, not actually an inefficiency.

4.2.2 *Value Effect*

A number of global empirical studies have shown that value stocks, which are generally referred to as stocks that have below-average price-to-earnings (P/E) and market-to-book (M/B) ratios, and above-average dividend yields, have consistently outperformed growth stocks over long periods of time.[34] If the effect persists, the value stock anomaly contradicts semi-strong market efficiency because all the information used to categorize stocks in this manner is publicly available.

Fama and French developed a three-factor model to predict stock returns.[35] In addition to the use of market returns as specified by the capital asset pricing model (CAPM), the Fama and French model also includes the size of the company as measured by the market value of its equity and the company's book value of equity divided by its market value of equity, which is a value measure. The Fama and French model captures risk dimensions related to stock returns that the CAPM model does not consider. Fama and French find that when they apply the three-factor model instead of the CAPM, the value stock anomaly disappears.

4.3 Other Anomalies

A number of additional anomalies has been documented in the financial markets, including the existence of closed-end investment fund discounts, price reactions to the release of earnings information, returns of initial public offerings, and the predictability of returns based on prior information.

4.3.1 *Closed-End Investment Fund Discounts*

A closed-end investment fund issues a fixed number of shares at inception and does not sell any additional shares after the initial offering. Therefore, the fund capitalization is fixed unless a secondary public offering is made. The shares of closed-end funds trade on stock markets like any other shares in the equity market (i.e., their prices are determined by supply and demand).

Theoretically, these shares should trade at a price approximately equal to their net asset value (NAV) per share, which is simply the total market value of the fund's security holdings less any liabilities divided by the number of shares outstanding. An abundance of research, however, has documented that, on average, closed-end funds

---

33 Although a large number of studies documents a small-company effect, these studies are concentrated in a period similar to that of the original research and, therefore, use a similar data set. The key to whether something is a true anomaly is persistence in out-of-sample tests. Fama and French (2008) document that the size effect is apparent only in microcap stocks but not in small- and large-cap stocks and these microcap stocks may have a significant influence in studies that document a size effect.

34 For example, see Capaul, Rowley, and Sharpe (1993) and Fama and French (1998).

35 Fama and French (1995).

trade at a discount from NAV. Most studies have documented average discounts in the 4–10 percent range, although individual funds have traded at discounts exceeding 50 percent and others have traded at large premiums.[36]

The closed-end fund discount presents a puzzle because conceptually, an investor could purchase all the shares in the fund, liquidate the fund, and end up making a profit. Some researchers have suggested that these discounts are attributed to management fees or expectations of the managers' performance, but these explanations are not supported by the evidence.[37] An alternative explanation for the discount is that tax liabilities are associated with unrealized capital gains and losses that exist prior to when the investor bought the shares, and hence, the investor does not have complete control over the timing of the realization of gains and losses.[38] Although the evidence supports this hypothesis to a certain extent, the tax effect is not large enough to explain the entire discount. Finally, it has often been argued that the discounts exist because of liquidity problems and errors in calculating NAV. The illiquidity explanation is plausible if shares are recorded at the same price as more liquid, publicly traded stocks; some evidence supports this assertion. But as with tax reasons, liquidity issues explain only a portion of the discount effect.

Can these discounts be exploited to earn abnormal returns if transaction costs are taken into account? No. First, the transaction costs involved in exploiting the discount—buying all the shares and liquidating the fund—would eliminate any profit.[39] Second, these discounts tend to revert to zero over time. Hence, a strategy to trade on the basis of these discounts would not likely be profitable.[40]

4.3.2 *Earnings Surprise*

Although most event studies have supported semi-strong market efficiency, some researchers have provided evidence that questions semi-strong market efficiency. One of these studies relates to the extensively examined adjustment of stock prices to earnings announcements.[41] The unexpected part of the earnings announcement, or **earnings surprise**, is the portion of earnings that is unanticipated by investors and, according to the efficient market hypothesis, merits a price adjustment. Positive (negative) surprises should cause appropriate and rapid price increases (decreases). Several studies have been conducted using data from numerous markets around the world. Most of the results indicate that earnings surprises are reflected quickly in stock prices, but the adjustment process is not always efficient. In particular, although a substantial adjustment occurs prior to and at the announcement date, an adjustment also occurs after the announcement.[42]

As a result of these slow price adjustments, companies that display the largest positive earnings surprises subsequently display superior stock return performance, whereas poor subsequent performance is displayed by companies with low or negative

---

36 See Dimson and Minio-Kozerski (1999) for a review of this literature.

37 See Lee, Sheifer, and Thaler (1990).

38 The return to owners of closed-end fund shares has three parts: 1) the price appreciation or depreciation of the shares themselves, 2) the dividends earned and distributed to owners by the fund, and 3) the capital gains and losses earned by the fund that are distributed by the fund. The explanation of the anomalous pricing has to do with the timing of the distribution of capital gains.

39 See, for example, the study by Pontiff (1996), which shows how the cost of arbitraging these discounts eliminates the profit.

40 See Pontiff (1995).

41 See Jones, Rendleman, and Latané (1984).

42 Not surprisingly, it is often argued that this slow reaction contributes to a momentum pattern.

earnings surprises.[43] This finding implies that investors could earn abnormal returns using publicly available information by buying stocks of companies that had positive earnings surprises and selling those with negative surprises.

Although there is support for abnormal returns associated with earnings surprises, and some support for such returns beyond the announcement period, there is also evidence indicating that these observed abnormal returns are an artifact of studies that do not sufficiently control for transaction costs and risk.[44]

4.3.3 *Initial Public Offerings (IPOs)*

When a company offers shares of its stock to the public for the first time, it does so through an initial public offering (or IPO). This offering involves working with an investment bank that helps price and market the newly issued shares. After the offering is complete, the new shares trade on a stock market for the first time. Given the risk that investment bankers face in trying to sell a new issue for which the true price is unknown, it is perhaps not surprising to find that, on average, the initial selling price is set too low and that the price increases dramatically on the first trading day. The percentage difference between the issue price and the closing price at the end of the first day of trading is often referred to as the degree of underpricing.

The evidence suggests that, on average, investors who are able to buy the shares of an IPO at their offering price may be able to earn abnormal profits. For example, during the internet bubble of 1995–2000, many IPOs ended their first day of trading up by more than 100 percent. Such performance, however, is not always the case. Sometimes the issues are priced too high, which means that share prices drop on their first day of trading. In addition, the evidence also suggests that investors buying after the initial offering are not able to earn abnormal profits because prices adjust quickly to the "true" values, which supports semi-strong market efficiency. In fact, the subsequent long-term performance of IPOs is generally found to be below average. Taken together, the IPO underpricing and the subsequent poor performance suggests that the markets are overly optimistic initially (i.e., investors overreact).

Some researchers have examined closely why IPOs may appear to have anomalous returns. Because of the small size of the IPO companies and the method of equally weighting the samples, what appears to be an anomaly may simply be an artifact of the methodology.[45]

4.3.4 *Predictability of Returns Based on Prior Information*

A number of researchers have documented that equity returns are related to prior information on such factors as interest rates, inflation rates, stock volatility, and dividend yields.[46] But finding that equity returns are affected by changes in economic fundamentals is not evidence of market inefficiency and would not result in abnormal trading returns.[47]

---

43 A similar pattern has been documented in the corporate bond market, where bond prices react too slowly to new company earnings announcements as well as to changes in company debt ratings.
44 See Brown (1997) for a summary of evidence supporting the existence of this anomaly. See Zarowin (1989) for evidence regarding the role of size in explaining abnormal returns to surprises; Alexander, Goff, and Peterson (1989) for evidence regarding transaction costs and unexpected earnings strategies; and Kim and Kim (2003) for evidence indicating that the anomalous returns can be explained by risk factors.
45 See Brav and Gompers (1997) and Brav, Geczy, and Gompers (1995).
46 See, for example, Fama and Schwert (1977) and Fama and French (1988).
47 See Fama and French (2008).

Furthermore, the relationship between stock returns and the prior information is not consistent over time. For example, in one study, the relationship between stock prices and dividend yields changed from positive to negative in different periods.[48] Hence, a trading strategy based on dividend yields would not yield consistent abnormal returns.

4.4 Implications for Investment Strategies

Although it is interesting to consider the anomalies just described, attempting to benefit from them in practice is not easy. In fact, most researchers conclude that observed anomalies are not violations of market efficiency but, rather, are the result of statistical methodologies used to detect the anomalies. As a result, if the methodologies are corrected, most of these anomalies disappear.[49] Another point to consider is that in an efficient market, overreactions may occur, but then so do under-reactions.[50] Therefore, on average, the markets are efficient. In other words, investors face challenges when they attempt to translate statistical anomalies into economic profits. Consider the following quote regarding anomalies from the *Economist* ("Frontiers of Finance Survey," 9 October 1993):

> Many can be explained away. When transactions costs are taken into account, the fact that stock prices tend to over-react to news, falling back the day after good news and bouncing up the day after bad news, proves unexploitable: price reversals are always within the bid-ask spread. Others such as the small-firm effect, work for a few years and then fail for a few years. Others prove to be merely proxies for the reward for risk taking. Many have disappeared since (and because) attention has been drawn to them.

It is difficult to envision entrusting your retirement savings to a manager whose strategy is based on buying securities on Mondays, which tends to have negative returns on average, and selling them on Fridays. For one thing, the negative Monday returns are merely an average, so on any given week, they could be positive. In addition, such a strategy would generate large trading costs. Even more importantly, investors would likely be uncomfortable investing their funds in a strategy that has no compelling underlying economic rationale.

5   BEHAVIORAL FINANCE

Behavioral finance is a field of financial thought that examines investor behavior and how this behavior affects what is observed in the financial markets. The behavior of individuals, in particular their cognitive biases, has been offered as a possible explanation for a number of pricing anomalies. In a broader sense, behavioral finance attempts to explain why individuals make the decisions that they do, whether these decisions are rational or irrational. The focus of much of the work in this area is on the cognitive biases that affect investment decisions.

Most asset-pricing models assume that markets are rational and that the intrinsic value of a security reflects this rationality. But market efficiency and asset-pricing models do not require that each individual is rational—rather, only that the market is

---

48 Schwert (2003, Chapter 15).
49 Fama (1998).
50 This point is made by Fama (1998).

rational. This leaves a lot of room for individual behavior to deviate from rationality. Even if individuals deviate from rationality, however, there may still be no room for profitable arbitrage for any observed mispricing in the financial markets.

5.1 Loss Aversion

In most financial models, the assumption is that investors are risk averse. **Risk aversion** implies that, although investors dislike risk, they are willing to assume risk if adequately compensated in the form of higher expected returns. In the most general models, researchers assume that investors do not like risk, whether the risk is that the returns are higher than expected or lower than expected. Behavioralists, however, allow for the possibility that this dislike for risk is not symmetrical. For example, some argue that behavioral theories of loss aversion can explain observed overreaction in markets, such that investors dislike losses more than they like comparable gains.[51] If loss aversion is more important than risk aversion, researchers should observe that investors overreact.[52] Although this can explain the overreaction anomaly, evidence also suggests that under reaction is just as prevalent as overreaction, which counters these arguments.

5.2 Overconfidence

One of the behavioral biases offered to explain pricing anomalies is overconfidence. If investors are overconfident, they place too much emphasis on their ability to process and interpret information about a security. Overconfident investors do not process information appropriately, and if there is a sufficient number of these investors, stocks will be mispriced.[53] But most researchers argue that this mispricing is temporary, with prices correcting eventually. The issues, however, are how long it takes prices to become correctly priced, whether this mispricing is predictable, and whether investors can consistently earn abnormal profits.

Evidence has suggested that overconfidence results in mispricing for US, UK, German, French, and Japanese markets.[54] This overconfidence, however, is predominantly in higher-growth companies, whose prices react slowly to new information.[55]

5.3 Other Behavioral Biases

Other behavioral theories that have been put forth as explaining investor behavior include the following:

- **representativeness**, with investors assessing probabilities of outcomes depending on how similar they are to the current state;
- **gambler's fallacy**, in which recent outcomes affect investors' estimates of future probabilities;
- **mental accounting**, in which investors keep track of the gains and losses for different investments in separate mental accounts;
- **conservatism**, where investors tend to be slow to react to changes;

---

[51] See DeBondt and Thaler (1985) and Tversky and Kahneman (1981).

[52] See Fama (1998).

[53] Another aspect to overconfidence is that investors who are overconfident in their ability to select investments and manage a portfolio tend to use less diversification, investing in what is most familiar. Therefore, investor behavior may affect investment results—returns and risk—without implications for the efficiency of markets.

[54] Scott, Stumpp, and Xu (2003) and Boujelbene Abbes, Boujelbene, and Bouri (2009).

[55] Scott, Stumpp, and Xu (2003).

- **disposition effect**, in which investors tend to avoid realizing losses but, rather, seek to realize gains; and

- **narrow framing**, in which investors focus on issues in isolation.[56]

The basic idea of these theories is that investors are humans and, therefore, imperfect and that the beliefs they have about a given asset's value may not be homogeneous. These behaviors help explain observed pricing anomalies. But the issue, which is controversial, is whether these insights help exploit any mispricing. In other words, researchers can use investor behavior to explain pricing, but can investors use it to predict how asset prices will be affected?

5.4 Information Cascades

One application of behavioral theories to markets and pricing focuses on the role of personal learning in markets, where personal learning is what investors learn by observing trading outcomes and what they learn from "conversations"—ideas shared among investors about specific assets and the markets.[57] This approach argues that social interaction and the resultant contagion is important in pricing and can explain such phenomena as price changes without accompanying news and mistakes in valuation.

Biases that investors possess, such as framing or mental accounting, can lead to herding behavior or information cascades. Herding and information cascades are related but not identical concepts. **Herding** is clustered trading that may or may not be based on information.[58] An **information cascade**, in contrast, is the transmission of information from those participants who act first and whose decisions influence the decisions of others. Those who are acting on the choices of others may be ignoring their own preferences in favor of imitating the choices of others. In particular, information cascades may occur with respect to the release of accounting information because accounting information is noisy. For example, the release of earnings is noisy because it is uncertain what the current earnings imply about future earnings.

Information cascades may result in serial correlation of stock returns, which is consistent with overreaction anomalies. Do information cascades result in correct pricing? Some argue that if a cascade is leading toward an incorrect value, this cascade is "fragile" and will be corrected because investors will ultimately give more weight to public information or the trading of a recognized informed trader.[59] Information cascades, although documented in markets, do not necessarily mean that investors can exploit them as profitable trading opportunities.

Are information cascades rational? If the informed traders act first and uninformed traders imitate the informed traders, this behavior is consistent with rationality. The imitation trading by the uninformed traders helps the market incorporate relevant information and improves market efficiency.[60] The empirical evidence is consistent with the idea that information cascades are greater for a stock when the information quality regarding the company is poor.[61] Hence, information cascades are enhancing the information available to traders.

---

56 For a review of these behavioral issues, see Hirshleifer (2001).

57 Hirshleifer and Teoh (2009).

58 The term used when there is herding without information is "spurious herding."

59 Avery and Zemsky (1999).

60 Another alternative is that the uninformed traders are the majority of the market participants and the imitators are imitating not because they agree with the actions of the majority but because they are looking to act on the actions of the uninformed traders.

61 Avery and Zemsky (1999) and Bikhchandani, Hirshleifer, and Welch (1992).

5.5 Behavioral Finance and Efficient Markets

The use of behavioral theories to explain observed pricing is an important part of the understanding of how markets function and how prices are determined. Whether there is a behavioral explanation for market anomalies remains a debate. Pricing anomalies are continually being uncovered, and then statistical and behavioral explanations are offered to explain these anomalies.

On the one hand, if investors must be rational for efficient markets to exist, then all the foibles of human investors suggest that markets cannot be efficient. On the other hand, if all that is required for markets to be efficient is that investors cannot consistently beat the market on a risk-adjusted basis, then the evidence does support market efficiency.

SUMMARY

This reading has provided an overview of the theory and evidence regarding market efficiency and has discussed the different forms of market efficiency as well as the implications for fundamental analysis, technical analysis, and portfolio management. The general conclusion drawn from the efficient market hypothesis is that it is not possible to beat the market on a consistent basis by generating returns in excess of those expected for the level of risk of the investment.

Additional key points include the following:

- The efficiency of a market is affected by the number of market participants and depth of analyst coverage, information availability, and limits to trading.

- There are three forms of efficient markets, each based on what is considered to be the information used in determining asset prices. In the weak form, asset prices fully reflect all market data, which refers to all past price and trading volume information. In the semi-strong form, asset prices reflect all publicly known and available information. In the strong form, asset prices fully reflect all information, which includes both public and private information.

- Intrinsic value refers to the true value of an asset, whereas market value refers to the price at which an asset can be bought or sold. When markets are efficient, the two should be the same or very close. But when markets are not efficient, the two can diverge significantly.

- Most empirical evidence supports the idea that securities markets in developed countries are semi-strong-form efficient; however, empirical evidence does not support the strong form of the efficient market hypothesis.

- A number of anomalies have been documented that contradict the notion of market efficiency, including the size anomaly, the January anomaly, and the winners–losers anomalies. In most cases, however, contradictory evidence both supports and refutes the anomaly.

- Behavioral finance uses human psychology, such as cognitive biases, in an attempt to explain investment decisions. Whereas behavioral finance is helpful in understanding observed decisions, a market can still be considered efficient even if market participants exhibit seemingly irrational behaviors, such as herding.

REFERENCES

Alexander, John C., Delbert Goff, and Pamela P. Peterson. 1989. "Profitability of a Trading Strategy Based on Unexpected Earnings." *Financial Analysts Journal*, vol. 45, no. 4:65–71.

Avery, Christopher, and Peter Zemsky. 1998. "Multi-Dimensional Uncertainty and Herding in Financial Markets." *American Economic Review*, vol. 88, no. 4:724–748.

Bessembinder, Hendrik, and Kalok Chan. 1998. "Market Efficiency and the Returns to Technical Analysis." *Financial Management*, vol. 27, no. 2:5–17.

Bikhchandani, Sushil, David Hirshleifer, and Ivo Welch. 1992. "A Theory of Fads, Fashion, Custom, and Cultural Change as Informational Cascades." *Journal of Political Economy*, vol. 100, no. 5:992–1026.

Bouljelbene Abbes, Mouna, Younes Boujelbene, and Abdelfettah Bouri. 2009. "Overconfidence Bias: Explanation of Market Anomalies French Market Case." *Journal of Applied Economic Sciences*, vol. 4, no. 1:12–25.

Brav, Alon, and Paul A. Gompers. 1997. "Myth or Reality? The Long-Run Underperformance of Initial Public Offerings: Evidence from Venture and Nonventure Capital-Backed Companies." *Journal of Finance*, vol. 52, no. 5:1791–1821.

Brav, Alon, Christopher Geczy, and Paul A. Gompers. 1995. "The Long-Run Underperformance of Seasoned Equity Offerings Revisited." Working paper, Harvard University.

Brealey, Richard. 1983. "Can Professional Investors Beat the Market?" *An Introduction to Risk and Return from Common Stocks*, 2nd edition. Cambridge, MA: MIT Press.

Bris, Arturo, William N. Goetzmann, and Ning Zhu. 2009. "Efficiency and the Bear: Short Sales and Markets around the World." *Journal of Finance*, vol. 62, no. 3:1029–1079.

Brown, Laurence D. 1997. "Earning Surprise Research: Synthesis and Perspectives." *Financial Analysts Journal*, vol. 53, no. 2:13–19.

Capaul, Carlo, Ian Rowley, and William Sharpe. 1993. "International Value and Growth Stock Returns." *Financial Analysts Journal*, vol. 49:27–36.

Chen, Kong-Jun, and Xiao-Ming Li. 2006. "Is Technical Analysis Useful for Stock Traders in China? Evidence from the Szse Component A-Share Index." *Pacific Economic Review*, vol. 11, no. 4:477–488.

Chordia, Tarun, Richard Roll, and Avanidhar Subrahmanyam. 2005. "Evidence on the Speed of Convergence to Market Efficiency." *Journal of Financial Economics*, vol. 76, no. 2:271–292.

DeBondt, Werner, and Richard Thaler. 1985. "Does the Stock Market Overreact?" *Journal of Finance*, vol. 40, no. 3:793–808.

Dimson, Elroy, and Carolina Minio-Kozerski. 1999. "Closed-End Funds: A Survey." *Financial Markets, Institutions & Instruments*, vol. 8, no. 2:1–41.

Duffie, Darrell, Nicholae Garleanu, and Lasse Heje Pederson. 2002. "Securities Lending, Shorting and Pricing." *Journal of Financial Economics*, vol. 66, no. Issue 2–3:307–339.

Fama, Eugene F. 1970. "Efficient Capital Markets: A Review of Theory and Empirical Work." *Journal of Finance*, vol. 25, no. 2:383–417.

Fama, Eugene F. 1976. *Foundations of Finance*. New York: Basic Books.

Fama, Eugene F. 1998. "Market Efficiency, Long-Term Returns, and Behavioral Finance." *Journal of Financial Economics*, vol. 50, no. 3:283–306.

Fama, Eugene F., and G. William Schwert. 1977. "Asset Returns and Inflation." *Journal of Financial Economics*, vol. 5, no. 2:115–146.

Fama, Eugene F., and Kenneth R. French. 1988. "Dividend Yields and Expected Stock Returns." *Journal of Financial Economics*, vol. 22, no. 1:3–25.

Fama, Eugene F., and Kenneth R. French. 1995. "Size and Book-to-Market Factors in Earnings and Returns." *Journal of Finance*, vol. 50, no. 1:131–155.

Fama, Eugene F., and Kenneth R. French. 1998. "Value versus Growth: The International Evidence." *Journal of Finance*, vol. 53:1975–1999.

Fama, Eugene F., and Kenneth R. French. 2008. "Dissecting Anomalies." *Journal of Finance*, vol. 63, no. 4:1653–1678.

Fifield, Suzanne, David Power, and C. Donald Sinclair. 2005. "An Analysis of Trading Strategies in Eleven European Stock Markets." *European Journal of Finance*, vol. 11, no. 6:531–548.

Gan, Christopher, Minsoo Lee, Au Yong Hue Hwa, and Jun Zhang. 2005. "Revisiting Share Market Efficiency: Evidence from the New Zealand, Australia, US and Japan Stock Indices." *American Journal of Applied Sciences*, vol. 2, no. 5:996–1002.

Grossman, Sanford J., and Joseph E. Stiglitz. 1980. "On the Impossibility of Informationally Efficient Markets." *American Economic Review*, vol. 70, no. 3:393–408.

Hirshleifer, David. 2001. "Investor Psychology and Asset Pricing." *Journal of Finance*, vol. 56, no. 4:1533–1597.

Hirshleifer, David, and Siew Hong Teoh. 2009. "Thought and Behavior Contagion in Capital Markets." In *Handbook of Financial Markets: Dynamics and Evolution*. Edited by Klaus Reiner Schenk-Hoppe and Thorstein Hens. Amsterdam: North Holland.

Jacobs, Bruce I., and Kenneth N. Levy. 1988. "Calendar Anomalies: Abnormal Returns at Calendar Turning Points." *Financial Analysts Journal*, vol. 44, no. 6:28–39.

Jaffe, Jeffrey. 1974. "Special Information and Insider Trading." *Journal of Business*, vol. 47, no. 3:410–428.

Jegadeesh, Narayan, and Sheridan Titman. 2001. "Profitability of Momentum Strategies: An Evaluation of Alternative Explanations." *Journal of Finance*, vol. 56:699–720.

Johnson, Timothy C. 2002. "Rational Momentum Effects." *Journal of Finance*, vol. 57, no. 2:585–608.

Jones, Charles M., and Owen A. Lamont. 2002. "Short-Sale Constraints and Stock Returns." *Journal of Financial Economics*, vol. 66, no. 2–3:207–239.

Jones, Charles P., Richard J. Rendleman, and Henry. A. Latané. 1984. "Stock Returns and SUEs during the 1970's." *Journal of Portfolio Management*, vol. 10:18–22.

Kim, Donchoi, and Myungsun Kim. 2003. "A Multifactor Explanation of Post-Earnings Announcement Drift." *Journal of Financial and Quantitative Analysis*, vol. 38, no. 2:383–398.

Kim, Dongcheol. 2006. "On the Information Uncertainty Risk and the January Effect." *Journal of Business*, vol. 79, no. 4:2127–2162.

Lee, Charles M.C., Andrei Sheifer, and Richard H. Thaler. 1990. "Anomalies: Closed-End Mutual Funds." *Journal of Economic Perspectives*, vol. 4, no. 4:153–164.

Malkiel, Burton G. 1995. "Returns from Investing in Equity Mutual Funds 1971 to 1991." *Journal of Finance*, vol. 50:549–572.

Mobarek, Asma, A. Sabur Mollah, and Rafiqul Bhuyan. 2008. "Market Efficiency in Emerging Stock Market." *Journal of Emerging Market Finance*, vol. 7, no. 1:17–41.

Pontiff, Jeffrey. 1995. "Closed-End Fund Premia and Returns: Implications for Financial Market Equilibrium." *Journal of Financial Economics*, vol. 37:341–370.

Pontiff, Jeffrey. 1996. "Costly Arbitrage: Evidence from Closed-End Funds." *Quarterly Journal of Economics*, vol. 111, no. 4:1135–1151.

Raja, M., J. Clement Sudhahar, and M. Selvam. 2009. "Testing the Semi-Strong Form Efficiency of Indian Stock Market with Respect to Information Content of Stock Split Announcement—A Study of IT Industry." *International Research Journal of Finance and Economics*, vol. 25:7–20.

Roll, Richard. 1983. "On Computing Mean Returns and the Small Firm Premium." *Journal of Financial Economics*, vol. 12:371–386.

Rozeff, Michael S., and Mir A. Zaman. 1988. "Market Efficiency and Insider Trading: New Evidence." *Journal of Business*, vol. 61:25–44.

Schwert, G. William. 2003. "Anomalies and Market Efficiency." *Handbook of the Economics of Finance*. Edited by George M. Constantinides, M. Harris, and Rene Stulz. Amsterdam: Elsevier Science, B. V.

Scott, James, Margaret Stumpp, and Peter Xu. 2003. "Overconfidence Bias in International Stock Prices." *Journal of Portfolio Management*, vol. 29, no. 2:80–89.

Tversky, Amos, and Daniel Kahneman. 1981. "The Framing of Decisions and the Psychology of Choice." *Science*, vol. 211, no. 30:453–458.

Yau, Jot, Thomas Schneeweis, Thomas Robinson, and Lisa Weiss. 2007. "Alternative Investments Portfolio Management." *Managing Investment Portfolios: A Dynamic Process*. Hoboken, NJ: John Wiley & Sons.

Zarowin, P. 1989. "Does the Stock Market Overreact to Corporate Earnings Information?" *Journal of Finance*, vol. 44:1385–1399.

PRACTICE PROBLEMS

1   In an efficient market, the change in a company's share price is *most likely* the result of:

    A   insiders' private information.

    B   the previous day's change in stock price.

    C   new information coming into the market.

2   Regulation that restricts some investors from participating in a market will *most likely*:

    A   impede market efficiency.

    B   not affect market efficiency.

    C   contribute to market efficiency.

3   With respect to efficient market theory, when a market allows short selling, the efficiency of the market is *most likely* to:

    A   increase.

    B   decrease.

    C   remain the same.

4   Which of the following regulations will *most likely* contribute to market efficiency? Regulatory restrictions on:

    A   short selling.

    B   foreign traders.

    C   insiders trading with nonpublic information.

5   Which of the following market regulations will *most likely* impede market efficiency?

    A   Restricting traders' ability to short sell.

    B   Allowing unrestricted foreign investor trading.

    C   Penalizing investors who trade with nonpublic information.

6   If markets are efficient, the difference between the intrinsic value and market value of a company's security is:

    A   negative.

    B   zero.

    C   positive.

7   The intrinsic value of an undervalued asset is:

    A   less than the asset's market value.

    B   greater than the asset's market value.

    C   the value at which the asset can currently be bought or sold.

8   The market value of an undervalued asset is:

    A   greater than the asset's intrinsic value.

    B   the value at which the asset can currently be bought or sold.

    C   equal to the present value of all the asset's expected cash flows.

9   With respect to the efficient market hypothesis, if security prices reflect *only* past prices and trading volume information, then the market is:

    A   weak-form efficient.

B strong-form efficient.

C semi-strong-form efficient.

10 Which one of the following statements *best* describes the semi-strong form of market efficiency?

A Empirical tests examine the historical patterns in security prices.

B Security prices reflect all publicly known and available information.

C Semi-strong-form efficient markets are not necessarily weak-form efficient.

11 If markets are semi-strong efficient, standard fundamental analysis will yield abnormal trading profits that are:

A negative.

B equal to zero.

C positive.

12 If prices reflect all public and private information, the market is *best* described as:

A weak-form efficient.

B strong-form efficient.

C semi-strong-form efficient.

13 If markets are semi-strong-form efficient, then passive portfolio management strategies are *most likely* to:

A earn abnormal returns.

B outperform active trading strategies.

C underperform active trading strategies.

14 If a market is semi-strong-form efficient, the risk-adjusted returns of a passively managed portfolio relative to an actively managed portfolio are *most likely*:

A lower.

B higher.

C the same.

15 Technical analysts assume that markets are:

A weak-form efficient.

B weak-form inefficient.

C semi-strong-form efficient.

16 Fundamental analysts assume that markets are:

A weak-form inefficient.

B semi-strong-form efficient.

C semi-strong-form inefficient.

17 If a market is weak-form efficient but semi-strong-form inefficient, then which of the following types of portfolio management is *most likely* to produce abnormal returns?

A Passive portfolio management.

B Active portfolio management based on technical analysis.

C Active portfolio management based on fundamental analysis.

18 An increase in the time between when an order to trade a security is placed and when the order is executed *most likely* indicates that market efficiency has:

A decreased.

B remained the same.

C increased.

19 With respect to efficient markets, a company whose share price reacts gradually to the public release of its annual report *most likely* indicates that the market where the company trades is:

A semi-strong-form efficient.

B subject to behavioral biases.

C receiving additional information about the company.

20 Which of the following is *least likely* to explain the January effect anomaly?

A Tax-loss selling.

B Release of new information in January.

C Window dressing of portfolio holdings.

21 If a researcher conducting empirical tests of a trading strategy using time series of returns finds statistically significant abnormal returns, then the researcher has *most likely* found:

A a market anomaly.

B evidence of market inefficiency.

C a strategy to produce future abnormal returns.

22 Which of the following market anomalies is inconsistent with weak-form market efficiency?

A Earnings surprise.

B Momentum pattern.

C Closed-end fund discount.

23 Researchers have found that value stocks have consistently outperformed growth stocks. An investor wishing to exploit the value effect should purchase the stock of companies with above-average:

A dividend yields.

B market-to-book ratios.

C price-to-earnings ratios.

24 With respect to rational and irrational investment decisions, the efficient market hypothesis requires:

A only that the market is rational.

B that all investors make rational decisions.

C that some investors make irrational decisions.

25 Observed overreactions in markets can be explained by an investor's degree of:

A risk aversion.

B loss aversion.

C confidence in the market.

26 Like traditional finance models, the behavioral theory of loss aversion assumes that investors dislike risk; however, the dislike of risk in behavioral theory is assumed to be:

A leptokurtic.

B symmetrical.

C asymmetrical.

SOLUTIONS

1 C is correct. Today's price change is independent of the one from yesterday, and in an efficient market, investors will react to new, independent information as it is made public.

2 A is correct. Reducing the number of market participants can accentuate market imperfections and impede market efficiency (e.g., restrictions on foreign investor trading).

3 A is correct. According to theory, reducing the restrictions on trading will allow for more arbitrage trading, thereby promoting more efficient pricing. Although regulators argue that short selling exaggerates downward price movements, empirical research indicates that short selling is helpful in price discovery.

4 C is correct. Regulation to restrict unfair use of nonpublic information encourages greater participation in the market, which increases market efficiency. Regulators (e.g., US SEC) discourage illegal insider trading by issuing penalties to violators of their insider trading rules.

5 A is correct. Restricting short selling will reduce arbitrage trading, which promotes market efficiency. Permitting foreign investor trading increases market participation, which makes markets more efficient. Penalizing insider trading encourages greater market participation, which increases market efficiency.

6 B is correct. A security's intrinsic value and market value should be equal when markets are efficient.

7 B is correct. The intrinsic value of an undervalued asset is greater than the market value of the asset, where the market value is the transaction price at which an asset can be currently bought or sold.

8 B is correct. The market value is the transaction price at which an asset can be currently bought or sold.

9 A is correct. The weak-form efficient market hypothesis is defined as a market where security prices fully reflect all market data, which refers to all past price and trading volume information.

10 B is correct. In semi-strong-form efficient markets, security prices reflect all publicly available information.

11 B is correct. If all public information should already be reflected in the market price, then the abnormal trading profit will be equal to zero when fundamental analysis is used.

12 B is correct. The strong-form efficient market hypothesis assumes all information, public or private, has already been reflected in the prices.

13 B is correct. Costs associated with active trading strategies would be difficult to recover; thus, such active trading strategies would have difficulty outperforming passive strategies on a consistent after-cost basis.

14 B is correct. In a semi-strong-form efficient market, passive portfolio strategies should outperform active portfolio strategies on a risk-adjusted basis.

15 B is correct. Technical analysts use past prices and volume to predict future prices, which is inconsistent with the weakest form of market efficiency (i.e., weak-form market efficiency). Weak-form market efficiency states that investors cannot earn abnormal returns by trading on the basis of past trends in price and volume.

16 C is correct. Fundamental analysts use publicly available information to estimate a security's intrinsic value to determine if the security is mispriced, which is inconsistent with the semi-strong form of market efficiency. Semi-strong-form market efficiency states that investors cannot earn abnormal returns by trading based on publicly available information.

17 C is correct. If markets are not semi-strong-form efficient, then fundamental analysts are able to use publicly available information to estimate a security's intrinsic value and identify misvalued securities. Technical analysis is not able to earn abnormal returns if markets are weak-form efficient. Passive portfolio managers outperform fundamental analysis if markets are semi-strong-form efficient.

18 A is correct. Operating inefficiencies reduce market efficiency.

19 C is correct. If markets are efficient, the information from the annual report is reflected in the stock prices; therefore, the gradual changes must be from the release of additional information.

20 B is correct. The excess returns in January are not attributed to any new information or news; however, research has found that part of the seasonal pattern can be explained by tax-loss selling and portfolio window dressing.

21 A is correct. Finding significant abnormal returns does not necessarily indicate that markets are inefficient or that abnormal returns can be realized by applying the strategy to future time periods. Abnormal returns are considered market anomalies because they may be the result of the model used to estimate the expected returns or may be the result of underestimating transaction costs or other expenses associated with implementing the strategy, rather than because of market inefficiency.

22 B is correct. Trading based on historical momentum indicates that price patterns exist and can be exploited by using historical price information. A momentum trading strategy that produces abnormal returns contradicts the weak form of the efficient market hypothesis, which states that investors cannot earn abnormal returns on the basis of past trends in prices.

23 A is correct. Higher than average dividend yield is a characteristic of a value stock, along with low price-to-earnings and low market-to-book ratios. Growth stocks are characterized by low dividend yields and high price-to-earnings and high market-to-book ratios.

24 A is correct. The efficient market hypothesis and asset-pricing models only require that the market is rational. Behavioral finance is used to explain *some* of the market anomalies as irrational decisions.

25 B is correct. Behavioral theories of loss aversion can explain observed overreaction in markets, such that investors dislike losses more than comparable gains (i.e., risk is not symmetrical).

26 C is correct. Behavioral theories of loss aversion allow for the possibility that the dislike for risk is not symmetrical, which allows for loss aversion to explain observed overreaction in markets such that investors dislike losses more than they like comparable gains.

Equity Analysis and Valuation

This study session focuses on the characteristics, analysis, and valuation of equity securities. The first reading discusses various types and features of equity securities and their roles in investment management. The second reading explains how to conduct industry and company analyses; the reading's major focus is on understating a company's competitive position. The first two readings constitute necessary background knowledge for the third reading, which introduces the subject of equity valuation.

READING ASSIGNMENTS

Overview of Equity Securities

by Ryan C. Fuhrmann, CFA, and Asjeet S. Lamba, CFA

LEARNING OUTCOMES

Mastery	The candidate should be able to:
☐	**a.** describe characteristics of types of equity securities;
☐	**b.** describe differences in voting rights and other ownership characteristics among different equity classes;
☐	**c.** distinguish between public and private equity securities;
☐	**d.** describe methods for investing in non-domestic equity securities;
☐	**e.** compare the risk and return characteristics of different types of equity securities;
☐	**f.** explain the role of equity securities in the financing of a company's assets;
☐	**g.** distinguish between the market value and book value of equity securities;
☐	**h.** compare a company's cost of equity, its (accounting) return on equity, and investors' required rates of return.

INTRODUCTION

1

Equity securities represent ownership claims on a company's net assets. As an asset class, equity plays a fundamental role in investment analysis and portfolio management because it represents a significant portion of many individual and institutional investment portfolios.

The study of equity securities is important for many reasons. First, the decision on how much of a client's portfolio to allocate to equities affects the risk and return characteristics of the entire portfolio. Second, different types of equity securities have different ownership claims on a company's net assets, which affect their risk and return characteristics in different ways. Finally, variations in the features of equity securities are reflected in their market prices, so it is important to understand the valuation implications of these features.

This reading provides an overview of equity securities and their different features and establishes the background required to analyze and value equity securities in a global context. It addresses the following questions:

■   What distinguishes common shares from preference shares, and what purposes do these securities serve in financing a company's operations?

■   What are convertible preference shares, and why are they often used to raise equity for unseasoned or highly risky companies?

■   What are private equity securities, and how do they differ from public equity securities?

■   What are depository receipts and their various types, and what is the rationale for investing in them?

■   What are the risk factors involved in investing in equity securities?

■   How do equity securities create company value?

■   What is the relationship between a company's cost of equity, its return on equity, and investors' required rate of return?

The remainder of this reading is organized as follows. Section 2 provides an overview of global equity markets and their historical performance. Section 3 examines the different types and characteristics of equity securities, and Section 4 outlines the differences between public and private equity securities. Section 5 provides an overview of the various types of equity securities listed and traded in global markets. Section 6 discusses the risk and return characteristics of equity securities. Section 7 examines the role of equity securities in creating company value and the relationship between a company's cost of equity, its return on equity, and investors' required rate of return. The final section summarizes the reading.

2   EQUITY SECURITIES IN GLOBAL FINANCIAL MARKETS

This section highlights the relative importance and performance of equity securities as an asset class. We examine the total market capitalization and trading volume of global equity markets and the prevalence of equity ownership across various geographic regions. We also examine historical returns on equities and compare them to the returns on government bonds and bills.

Exhibit 1 summarizes the contributions of selected countries and geographic regions to global gross domestic product (GDP) and global equity market capitalization. Analysts can examine the relationship between equity market capitalization and GDP as an indicator of whether the global equity market (or a specific country's or region's equity market) is under, over, or fairly valued. Global equity markets expanded at twice the rate of global GDP between 1993 and 2004. At the beginning of 2008, global GDP and equity market capitalization were nearly equal at approximately US$55 trillion.[1] This implies an equity market capitalization to GDP ratio of 100 percent, which was almost twice the long-run average of 50 percent and indicates that global equity markets were overvalued at that time.

Exhibit 1 illustrates the significant value that investors attach to publicly traded equities relative to the sum of goods and services produced globally every year. It shows the continued significance, and the potential over-representation, of US equity markets relative to their contribution to global GDP. That is, while US equity markets contribute around 43 percent to the total capitalization of global equity markets, their

---

1 EconomyWatch.Com http://www.economywatch.com/gdp/world-gdp/.

contribution to the global GDP is only around 21 percent. Following the stock market turmoil in 2008, however, the market capitalization to GDP ratio of the United States fell to 59 percent, which is significantly lower than its long-run average of 79 percent.[2]

As equity markets outside the United States develop and become increasingly global, their total capitalization levels are expected to grow closer to their respective world GDP contributions. Therefore, it is important to understand and analyze equity securities from a global perspective.

Exhibit 1 **Country and Regional Contributions to Global GDP and Equity Market Capitalization (2007)**

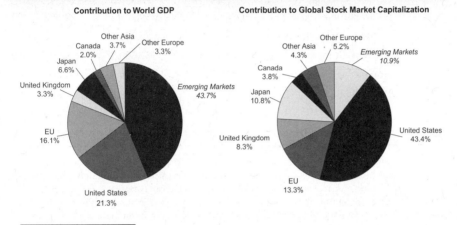

Source: MacroMavens, *IMF World Economic Outlook 2008*, Standard & Poor's BMI Global Index weights.

Exhibit 2 lists the top 10 equity markets at the end of 2008 based on total market capitalization (in billions of US dollars), trading volume, and the number of listed companies.[3] Note that the rankings differ based on the criteria used. For example, the top three markets based on total market capitalization are the NYSE Euronext (US), Tokyo Stock Exchange Group, and NASDAQ OMX; however, the top three markets based on total US dollar trading volume are the Nasdaq OMX, NYSE Euronext (US), and London Stock Exchange, respectively.[4] A relatively new entrant to this top 10 list is China's Shanghai Stock Exchange, which is the only emerging equity market represented on this list.

---

2 For further details, see Bary (2008).

3 The market capitalization of an individual stock is computed as the share price multiplied by the number of shares outstanding. The total market capitalization of an equity market is the sum of the market capitalizations of each individual stock listed on that market. Similarly, the total trading volume of an equity market is computed by value weighting the total trading volume of each individual stock listed on that market. Total dollar trading volume is computed as the average share price multiplied by the number of shares traded.

4 NASDAQ is the acronym for the National Association of Securities Dealers Automated Quotations.

Exhibit 2	Equity Markets Ranked by Total Market Capitalization at the End of 2008 (Billions of US Dollars)			
Rank	Name of Market	Total US Dollar Market Capitalization	Total US Dollar Trading Volume	Number of Listed Companies
1	NYSE Euronext (US)	$9,208.9	$33,638.9	3,011
2	Tokyo Stock Exchange Group	$3,115.8	$5,607.3	2,390
3	NASDAQ OMX	$2,396.3	$36,446.5	2,952
4	NYSE Euronext (Europe)	$2,101.7	$4,411.2	1,002
5	London Stock Exchange	$1,868.2	$6,271.5	3,096
6	Shanghai Stock Exchange	$1,425.4	$2,600.2	864
7	Hong Kong Exchanges	$1,328.8	$1,629.8	1,261
8	Deutsche Börse	$1,110.6	$4,678.8	832
9	TSX Group	$1,033.4	$1,716.2	3,841
10	BME Spanish Exchanges	$948.4	$2,410.7	3,576

Source: Adapted from the *World Federation of Exchanges 2008 Report* (see http://www.world-exchanges.org). Note that market capitalization by company is calculated by multiplying its stock price by the number of shares outstanding. The market's overall capitalization is the aggregate of the market capitalizations of all companies traded on that market. The number of listed companies includes both domestic and foreign companies whose shares trade on these markets.

Exhibit 3 compares the *real* (or inflation-adjusted) compounded returns on government bonds, government bills, and equity securities in 19 countries plus the world index ("Wld"), the world ex-US ("WxU"), and Europe ("Eur") during the 112 years 1900–2011.[5] In real terms, government bonds and bills have essentially kept pace with the inflation rate, earning annualized real returns of less than 2 percent in most countries.[6] By comparison, real returns in equity markets have generally been above 3.5 percent per year in most markets—with a world average return just over 5 percent and a world average return excluding the United States just under 5 percent. During this period, Australia and South Africa were the best performing markets followed by the United States, Sweden, and New Zealand.

---

5 The real return for a security is approximated by taking the nominal return and subtracting the observed inflation rate in that country.
6 The exceptions are Belgium, Italy, Germany, France, Japan, and England—where the average real returns on government bonds and/or bills have been negative. In general, that performance reflects the very high inflation rates in these countries during the World War years.

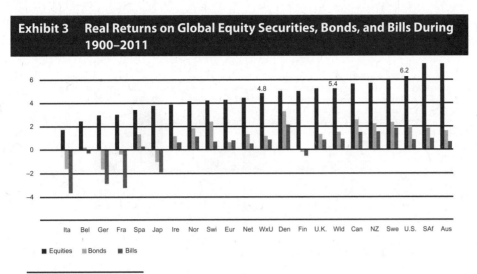

Exhibit 3   Real Returns on Global Equity Securities, Bonds, and Bills During 1900–2011

Source: Dimson, Marsh, and Staunton (2012a). This chart is updated annually and can be found at www.tinyurl.com/DMSsourcebook.

Exhibit 4 focuses on the real compounded rates of return on equity securities in the same 19 countries over 1900–2011 Only the South African and Australian equity markets were better investments in real terms for the US investor than their own equity market.

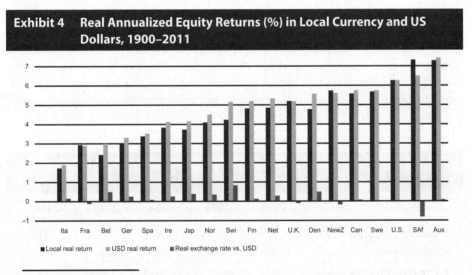

Exhibit 4   Real Annualized Equity Returns (%) in Local Currency and US Dollars, 1900–2011

Source: Dimson, Marsh, and Staunton (2012a). This chart is updated annually and can be found at www.tinyurl.com/DMSsourcebook.

The volatility in equity market returns is further highlighted in Exhibit 5, which shows the average performance of the worldwide equity index (in US dollars), bonds, and bills (bonds and bills are based on US data).

These observations and historical data are consistent with the concept that the return on securities is directly related to risk level. That is, equity securities have higher risk levels when compared with government bonds and bills, they earn higher rates of return to compensate investors for these higher risk levels, and they also tend to be more volatile over time.

Exhibit 5   Returns and Risk of Major Asset Classes since 1900

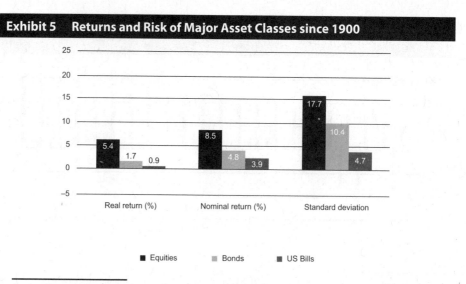

Source: Dimson, Marsh, and Staunton (2012a). This chart is updated annually and can be found at www.tinyurl.com/DMSsourcebook.

Given the high risk levels associated with equity securities, it is reasonable to expect that investors' tolerance for risk will tend to differ across equity markets. This is illustrated in Exhibit 6, which shows the results of a series of studies conducted by the Australian Securities Exchange on international differences in equity ownership. During the 2000–2008 period, equity ownership as a percentage of the population was lowest in South Korea (averaging 7.5 percent), followed by Germany (16.6 percent) and Sweden (21 percent). In contrast, Australia, Canada, and the United States had the highest equity ownership as a percentage of the population (averaging almost 50 percent). In addition, there has been a relative decline in share ownership in several countries over recent years, which is not surprising given the recent overall uncertainty in global economies and the volatility in equity markets that this uncertainty has created.

Exhibit 6   International Comparisons of Stock Ownership in Selected Countries: 2000–2008[7]

	2000	2002	2004	2006	2008
Australia – Direct/Indirect	52%	50%	55%	46%	41%
Canada – Shares/Funds	49	46	49	N/A	N/A
Germany – Shares/Funds	19	18	16	16	14
Hong Kong – Shares	22	20	24	N/A	22
New Zealand	24	N/A	23	26	N/A
South Korea – Shares	7	8	8	7	N/A
Switzerland – Shares/Funds	34	25	21	21	21
Sweden – Shares	22	23	22	20	18

---

7 The percentages reported in the exhibit are based on samples of the adult population in each country who own equity securities either directly or indirectly through investment or retirement funds. For example, 41 percent of the adult population of Australia in 2008 (approximately 6.7 million people) owned equity securities either directly or indirectly. As noted in the study, it is not appropriate to make absolute comparisons across countries given the differences in methodology, sampling, timing, and definitions that have been used in different countries. However, trends across different countries can be identified.

Exhibit 6	(Continued)				
	2000	**2002**	**2004**	**2006**	**2008**
United Kingdom – Shares/Funds	26	25	22	20	18
United States – Direct/Indirect	N/A	50	49	N/A	45

Source: Adapted from the *2008 Australian Share Ownership Study* conducted by the Australian Securities Exchange (see http://www.asx.com.au). For Australia and the United States, the data pertain to direct and indirect ownership in equity markets; for other countries, the data pertain to direct ownership in shares and share funds. Data not available in specific years are shown as "N/A."

An important implication from the above discussion is that equity securities represent a key asset class for global investors because of their unique return and risk characteristics. We next examine the various types of equity securities traded on global markets and their salient characteristics.

TYPES AND CHARACTERISTICS OF EQUITY SECURITIES

3

Companies finance their operations by issuing either debt or equity securities. A key difference between these securities is that debt is a liability of the issuing company, whereas equity is not. This means that when a company issues debt, it is contractually obligated to repay the amount it borrows (i.e., the principal or face value of the debt) at a specified future date. The cost of using these funds is called interest, which the company is contractually obligated to pay until the debt matures or is retired.

When the company issues equity securities, it is not contractually obligated to repay the amount it receives from shareholders, nor is it contractually obligated to make periodic payments to shareholders for the use of their funds. Instead, shareholders have a claim on the company's assets after all liabilities have been paid. Because of this residual claim, equity shareholders are considered to be owners of the company. Investors who purchase equity securities are seeking total return (i.e., capital or price appreciation and dividend income), whereas investors who purchase debt securities (and hold until maturity) are seeking interest income. As a result, equity investors expect the company's management to act in their best interest by making operating decisions that will maximize the market price of their shares (i.e., shareholder wealth).

In addition to common shares (also known as ordinary shares or common stock), companies may also issue preference shares (also known as preferred stock), the other type of equity security. The following sections discuss the different types and characteristics of common and preference securities.

3.1 Common Shares

Common shares represent an ownership interest in a company and are the predominant type of equity security. As a result, investors share in the operating performance of the company, participate in the governance process through voting rights, and have a claim on the company's net assets in the case of liquidation. Companies may choose to pay out some, or all, of their net income in the form of cash dividends to common shareholders, but they are not contractually obligated to do so.[8]

Voting rights provide shareholders with the opportunity to participate in major corporate governance decisions, including the election of its board of directors, the decision to merge with or take over another company, and the selection of outside auditors. Shareholder voting generally takes place during a company's annual meeting. As a result of geographic limitations and the large number of shareholders, it is often not feasible for shareholders to attend the annual meeting in person. For this reason, shareholders may **vote by proxy**, which allows a designated party—such as another shareholder, a shareholder representative, or management—to vote on the shareholders' behalf.

Regular shareholder voting, where each share represents one vote, is referred to as **statutory voting**. Although it is the common method of voting, it is not always the most appropriate one to use to elect a board of directors. To better serve shareholders who own a small number of shares, **cumulative voting** is often used. Cumulative voting allows shareholders to direct their total voting rights to specific candidates, as opposed to having to allocate their voting rights evenly among all candidates. Total voting rights are based on the number of shares owned multiplied by the number of board directors being elected. For example, under cumulative voting, if four board directors are to be elected, a shareholder who owns 100 shares is entitled to 400 votes and can either cast all 400 votes in favor of a single candidate or spread them across the candidates in any proportion. In contrast, under statutory voting, a shareholder would be able to cast only a maximum of 100 votes for each candidate.

The key benefit to cumulative voting is that it allows shareholders with a small number of shares to apply all of their votes to one candidate, thus providing the opportunity for a higher level of representation on the board than would be allowed under statutory voting.

Exhibit 7 describes the rights of Viacom Corporation's shareholders. In this case, a dual-share arrangement allows the founding chairman and his family to control more than 70 percent of the voting rights through the ownership of Class A shares. This arrangement gives them the ability to exert control over the board of director election process, corporate decision making, and other important aspects of managing the company. A cumulative voting arrangement for any minority shareholders of Class A shares would improve their board representation.

Exhibit 7   Share Class Arrangements at Viacom Corporation[9]

Viacom has two classes of common stock: Class A, which is the voting stock, and Class B, which is the non-voting stock. There is no difference between the two classes except for voting rights; they generally trade within a close price range of each other. There are, however, far more shares of Class B outstanding, so most of the trading occurs in that class.

Voting Rights—Holders of Class A common stock are entitled to one vote per share. Holders of Class B common stock do not have any voting rights, except as required by Delaware law. Generally, all matters to be voted on by Viacom

---

8 It is also possible for companies to pay more than the current period's net income as dividends. Such payout policies are, however, generally not sustainable in the long run.
9 This information has been adapted from Viacom's investor relations website and its 10-K filing with the US Securities and Exchange Commission; see www.viacom.com.

Exhibit 7 (Continued)

stockholders must be approved by a majority of the aggregate voting power of the shares of Class A common stock present in person or represented by proxy, except as required by Delaware law.

Dividends—Stockholders of Class A common stock and Class B common stock will share ratably in any cash dividend declared by the Board of Directors, subject to any preferential rights of any outstanding preferred stock. Viacom does not currently pay a cash dividend, and any decision to pay a cash dividend in the future will be at the discretion of the Board of Directors and will depend on many factors.

Conversion—So long as there are 5,000 shares of Class A common stock outstanding, each share of Class A common stock will be convertible at the option of the holder of such share into one share of Class B common stock.

Liquidation Rights—In the event of liquidation, dissolution or winding-up of Viacom, all stockholders of common stock, regardless of class, will be entitled to share ratably in any assets available for distributions to stockholders of shares of Viacom common stock subject to the preferential rights of any outstanding preferred stock.

Split, Subdivisions or Combination—In the event of a split, subdivision or combination of the outstanding shares of Class A common stock or Class B common stock, the outstanding shares of the other class of common stock will be divided proportionally.

Preemptive Rights—Shares of Class A common stock and Class B common stock do not entitle a stockholder to any preemptive rights enabling a stockholder to subscribe for or receive shares of stock of any class or any other securities convertible into shares of stock of any class of Viacom.

As seen in Exhibit 7, companies can issue different classes of common shares (Class A and Class B shares), with each class offering different ownership rights.[10] For example, as shown in Exhibit 8, the Ford Motor Company has Class A shares ("Common Stock"), which are owned by the investing public. It also has Class B shares, which are owned only by the Ford family. The exhibit contains an excerpt from Ford's *2008 Annual Report* (p. 115). Class A shareholders have 60 percent voting rights, whereas Class B shareholders have 40 percent. In the case of liquidation, however, Class B shareholders will not only receive the first US$0.50 per share that is available for distribution (as will Class A shareholders), but they will also receive the next US$1.00 per share that is available for distribution before Class A shareholders receive anything else. Thus, Class B shareholders have an opportunity to receive a larger proportion of distributions upon liquidation than do Class A shareholders.[11]

---

10 In some countries, including the United States, companies can issue different classes of shares, with Class A shares being the most common. The role and function of different classes of shares is described in more detail in Exhibit 8.

11 For example, if US$2.00 per share is available for distribution, the Common Stock (Class A) shareholders will receive US$0.50 per share, while the Class B shareholders will receive US$1.50 per share. However, if there is US$3.50 per share available for distribution, the Common Stock shareholders will receive a total of US$1.50 per share and the Class B shareholders will receive a total of US$2.00 per share.

Exhibit 8　Share Class Arrangements at Ford Motor Company[12]

NOTE 21. CAPITAL STOCK AND AMOUNTS PER SHARE

All general voting power is vested in the holders of Common Stock and Class B Stock. Holders of our Common Stock have 60% of the general voting power and holders of our Class B Stock are entitled to such number of votes per share as will give them the remaining 40%. Shares of Common Stock and Class B Stock share equally in dividends when and as paid, with stock dividends payable in shares of stock of the class held. As discussed in Note 16, we are prohibited from paying dividends (other than dividends payable in stock) under the terms of the Credit Agreement.

If liquidated, each share of Common Stock will be entitled to the first $0.50 available for distribution to holders of Common Stock and Class B Stock, each share of Class B Stock will be entitled to the next $1.00 so available, each share of Common Stock will be entitled to the next $0.50 so available and each share of Common and Class B Stock will be entitled to an equal amount thereafter.

Common shares may also be callable or putable. **Callable common shares** (also known as redeemable common shares) give the issuing company the option (or right), but not the obligation, to buy back shares from investors at a call price that is specified when the shares are originally issued. It is most common for companies to call (or redeem) their common shares when the market price is above the pre-specified call price. The company benefits because it can buy back its shares below the current market price and later resell them at a higher market price, and it can also reduce dividend payments to preserve capital, if required. Investors benefit because they receive a guaranteed return when their shares are called. Exhibit 9 provides an example of callable common shares issued by Genomic Solutions in the US market. The exhibit provides details on the creation of callable common shares used to consummate a strategic alliance between PerkinElmer and Genomic Solutions. The arrangement contains provisions more favorable to PerkinElmer because at the time it was a more established and better capitalized company than Genomic Solutions.

Exhibit 9　Callable Stock Arrangement from Genomic Solutions[13]

The following information assumes that the underwriters do not exercise the over-allotment option granted by us to purchase additional shares in the offering:

Callable common stock offered by us:	7,000,000 shares
Callable common stock to be outstanding after the offering:	22,718,888 shares
Common stock to be outstanding after the offering:	1,269,841 shares
Proposed NASDAQ National Market symbol:	GNSL
Use of proceeds:	General corporate purposes and possible future acquisitions

For two years from the completion of this offering, we may require all holders of our callable common stock to sell their shares back to us. We must exercise this right at PerkinElmer's direction. The price for repurchase of our callable

---

12 Extracted from Ford Motor Company's *2008 Annual Report* (virtual.stivesonline.com/publication/?i=14030).

13 Genomic Solutions Form S-1 as filed with the US SEC (14 May 2000); see www.edgar-online.com.

Exhibit 9   (Continued)

common stock generally will be 20% over the market price. PerkinElmer also has a right to match any third party offer for our callable common stock or our business that our board of directors is prepared to accept.

Putable common shares give investors the option or right to sell their shares (i.e., "put" them) back to the issuing company at a price that is specified when the shares are originally issued. Investors will generally sell their shares back to the issuing company when the market price is below the pre-specified put price. Thus, the put option feature limits the potential loss for investors. From the issuing company's perspective, the put option facilitates raising capital because the shares are more appealing to investors.

Exhibit 10 provides an example of putable common shares issued by Dreyer's, now a subsidiary of Switzerland-based Nestlé. In this case, shareholders had the right to sell their shares to Dreyer's for US$83.10, the pre-specified put price.

Exhibit 10   Putable Stock Arrangement for Dreyer's Grand Ice Cream[14]

Dreyer's Grand Ice Cream Holdings, Inc. ("Dreyer's") (NNM: DRYR) announced today that the period during which holders of shares of Dreyer's Class A Callable Putable Common Stock (the "Class A Shares") could require Dreyer's to purchase their Class A Shares (the "Put Right") for a cash payment of $83.10 per Class A Share (the "Purchase Price") expired at 5:00 p.m. New York City time on January 13, 2006 (the "Expiration Time"). According to the report of the depositary agent for the Put Right, holders of an aggregate of 30,518,885 Class A Shares (including 1,792,193 shares subject to guaranteed delivery procedures) properly exercised the Put Right.

3.2 Preference Shares

Preference shares (or preferred stock) rank above common shares with respect to the payment of dividends and the distribution of the company's net assets upon liquidation.[15] However, preference shareholders do not share in the operating performance of the company and generally do not have any voting rights, unless explicitly allowed for at issuance. Preference shares have characteristics of both debt securities and common shares. Similar to the interest payments on debt securities, the dividends on preference shares are fixed and are generally higher than the dividends on common shares. However, unlike interest payments, preference dividends are not contractual obligations of the company. Similar to common shares, preference shares can be perpetual (i.e., no fixed maturity date), can pay dividends indefinitely, and can be callable or putable.

Exhibit 11 provides an example of callable preference shares issued by Goldman Sachs to raise capital during the credit crisis of 2008. In this case, Berkshire Hathaway, the purchaser of the shares, will receive an ongoing dividend from Goldman Sachs. If Goldman Sachs chooses to buy back the shares, it must do so at a 10 percent premium above their par value.

---

14 "Dreyer's Announces Expiration of Put Period and Anticipated Merger with Nestle," *Business Wire* (14 January 2006): www.findarticles.com/p/articles/mi_m0EIN/is_2006_Jan_14/ai_n16001349.

15 Preference shares have a lower priority than debt in the case of liquidation. That is, debt holders have a higher claim on a firm's assets in the event of liquidation and will receive what is owed to them first, followed by preference shareholders and then common shareholders.

Exhibit 11	Callable Stock Arrangement between Goldman Sachs and Berkshire Hathaway[16]

New York, NY—September 23, 2008—The Goldman Sachs Group, Inc. (NYSE: GS) announced today that it has reached an agreement to sell $5 billion of perpetual preferred stock to Berkshire Hathaway, Inc. in a private offering. The preferred stock has a dividend of 10 percent and is callable at any time at a 10 percent premium. In conjunction with this offering, Berkshire Hathaway will also receive warrants to purchase $5 billion of common stock with a strike price of $115 per share, which are exercisable at any time for a five year term. In addition, Goldman Sachs is raising at least $2.5 billion in common equity in a public offering.

Dividends on preference shares can be cumulative, non-cumulative, participating, non-participating, or some combination thereof (i.e., cumulative participating, cumulative non-participating, non-cumulative participating, non-cumulative non-participating).

Dividends on **cumulative preference shares** accrue so that if the company decides not to pay a dividend in one or more periods, the unpaid dividends accrue and must be paid in full before dividends on common shares can be paid. In contrast, **non-cumulative preference shares** have no such provision. This means that any dividends that are not paid in the current or subsequent periods are forfeited permanently and are not accrued over time to be paid at a later date. However, the company is still not permitted to pay any dividends to common shareholders in the current period unless preferred dividends have been paid first.

Participating preference shares entitle the shareholders to receive the standard preferred dividend plus the opportunity to receive an additional dividend if the company's profits exceed a pre-specified level. In addition, participating preference shares can also contain provisions that entitle shareholders to an additional distribution of the company's assets upon liquidation, above the par (or face) value of the preference shares. **Non-participating preference shares** do not allow shareholders to share in the profits of the company. Instead, shareholders are entitled to receive only a fixed dividend payment and the par value of the shares in the event of liquidation. The use of participating preference shares is much more common for smaller, riskier companies where the possibility of future liquidation is more of a concern to investors.

Preference shares can also be convertible. **Convertible preference shares** entitle shareholders to convert their shares into a specified number of common shares. This conversion ratio is determined at issuance. Convertible preference shares have the following advantages:

■ They allow investors to earn a higher dividend than if they invested in the company's common shares.

■ They allow investors the opportunity to share in the profits of the company.

■ They allow investors to benefit from a rise in the price of the common shares through the conversion option.

■ Their price is less volatile than the underlying common shares because the dividend payments are known and more stable.

---

16 Goldman Sachs, "Berkshire Hathaway to Invest $5 Billion in Goldman Sachs," (23 September 2008): www.goldmansachs.com/our-firm/press/press-releases/archived/2008/berkshire-hathaway-invest.html.

As a result, the use of convertible preference shares is a popular financing option in venture capital and private equity transactions in which the issuing companies are considered to be of higher risk and when it may be years before the issuing company "goes public" (i.e., issues common shares to the public).

Exhibit 12 provides examples of the types and characteristics of preference shares as issued by DBS Bank of Singapore.

Exhibit 12   Examples of Preference Shares Issued by DBS Bank[17]

SINGAPORE, MAY 12—DBS Bank said today it plans to offer S$700 million in preference shares and make it available to both retail and institutional investors in Singapore. Called the DBS Preferred Investment Issue, it will yield investors a fixed non-cumulative gross dividend rate of 6% for the first ten years and a floating rate thereafter. The DBS Preferred Investment Issue will be offered in two tranches, consisting of a S$100 million tranche to retail investors via ATMs and a S$600 million placement tranche available to both retail and institutional investors. Depending on investor demand, DBS could increase the offering amount.

Jackson Tai, President and Chief Operating Officer of DBS Group Holdings, said that following the success of the hybrid Tier 1 issue in March, DBS decided to make this new issue available to the local retail investors. "We consider these issues as an important capital management tool. We were pleased with the success of our hybrid Tier 1 issue for institutional investors and wanted to introduce a capital instrument that would be available to retail investors as well."

DBS Preferred Investment Issues are perpetual securities, redeemable after ten years at the option of DBS Bank and at every dividend date thereafter subject to certain redemption conditions. They are issued by DBS Bank and are considered to be core Tier 1 capital under the Monetary Authority of Singapore and Bank of International Settlement's guidelines. They will be listed on the Singapore Exchange Securities Trading Limited and can be traded on the secondary market through a broker. Holders of the DBS Preferred Investment Issue will receive the dividend net of the 24.5% income tax. Investors may claim the tax credit in their tax returns.

PRIVATE VERSUS PUBLIC EQUITY SECURITIES

4

Our discussion so far has focused on equity securities that are issued and traded in public markets and on exchanges. Equity securities can also be issued and traded in private equity markets. **Private equity securities** are issued primarily to institutional investors via non-public offerings, such as private placements. Because they are not listed on public exchanges, there is no active secondary market for these securities. As a result, private equity securities do not have "market determined" quoted prices, are highly illiquid, and require negotiations between investors in order to be traded. In addition, financial statements and other important information needed to determine the fair value of private equity securities may be difficult to obtain because the issuing companies are typically not required by regulatory authorities to publish this information.

---

17 DBS Bank, "DBS Follows US$850 Million Offering of Subordinated Notes to International Markets with Singapore Dollar Market Financing" (12 May 2001): www.dbs.com/newsroom/2001/Pages/press010512.aspx.

There are three primary types of private equity investments: venture capital, leveraged buyouts, and private investment in public equity. **Venture capital** investments provide "seed" or start-up capital, early-stage financing, or mezzanine financing to companies that are in the early stages of development and require additional capital for expansion. These funds are then used to finance the company's product development and growth. Venture capitalists range from family and friends to wealthy individuals and private equity funds. Because the equity securities issued to venture capitalists are not publicly traded, they generally require a commitment of funds for a relatively long period of time; the opportunity to "exit" the investment is typically within 3 to 10 years from the initial start-up. The exit return earned by these private equity investors is based on the price that the securities can be sold for if and when the start-up company first goes public, either via an **initial public offering** (IPO) on the stock market or by being sold to other investors.

A **leveraged buyout** (LBO) occurs when a group of investors (such as the company's management or a private equity partnership) uses a large amount of debt to purchase all of the outstanding common shares of a publicly traded company. In cases where the group of investors acquiring the company is primarily comprised of the company's existing management, the transaction is referred to as a **management buyout** (MBO). After the shares are purchased, they cease to trade on an exchange and the investor group takes full control of the company. In other words, the company is taken "private" or has been privatized. Companies that are candidates for these types of transactions generally have large amounts of undervalued assets (which can be sold to reduce debt) and generate high levels of cash flows (which are used to make interest and principal payments on the debt). The ultimate objective of a buyout (LBO or MBO) is to restructure the acquired company and later take it "public" again by issuing new shares to the public in the primary market.

The third type of private investment is a **private investment in public equity**, or PIPE.[18] This type of investment is generally sought by a public company that is in need of additional capital quickly and is willing to sell a sizeable ownership position to a private investor or investor group. For example, a company may require a large investment of new equity funds in a short period of time because it has significant expansion opportunities, is facing high levels of indebtedness, or is experiencing a rapid deterioration in its operations. Depending on how urgent the need is and the size of the capital requirement, the private investor may be able to purchase shares in the company at a significant discount to the publicly-quoted market price. Exhibit 13 contains a recent PIPE transaction for the electronics retailer hhgregg, which also included the issuance of additional common shares to the public.

Exhibit 13   Example of a PIPE Transaction[19]

On July 20, 2009, hhgregg completed a public stock offering of 4,025,000 shares of its common stock at $16.50 per share. Concurrently with the public offering, investment funds affiliated with Freeman Spogli & Co. purchased an additional 1,000,000 shares of common stock, in a private placement transaction, at the price per share paid by the public in the offering. Proceeds, net of underwriting fees, from the public stock offering and private placement, totaled approximately $78.6 million. These proceeds will be used for general corporate purposes, including funding the Company's accelerated new store growth plans.

---

18 The term PIPE is widely used in the United States and is also used internationally, including in emerging markets.
19 This information was obtained from hhgregg's first quarter fiscal 2009 earnings report (http://ir.hhgregg.com/releasedetail.cfm?ReleaseID=401980).

While the global private equity market is relatively small in comparison to the global public equity market, it has experienced considerable growth over the past three decades. According to a study of the private equity market sponsored by the *World Economic Forum* and spanning the period 1970–2007, approximately US$3.6 trillion in debt and equity were acquired in leveraged buyouts. Of this amount, approximately 75 percent or US$2.7 trillion worth of transactions occurred during 2001–2007.[20] While the US and the UK markets were the focus of most private equity investments during the 1980s and 1990s, private equity investments outside of these markets have grown substantially in recent years. In addition, the number of companies operating under private equity ownership has also grown. For example, during the mid-1990s, fewer than 2,000 companies were under LBO ownership compared to close to 14,000 companies that were under LBO ownership globally at the beginning of 2007. The holding period for private equity investments has also increased during this time period from 3 to 5 years (1980s and 1990s) to approximately 10 years.[21]

The move to longer holding periods has given private equity investors the opportunity to more effectively and patiently address any underlying operational issues facing the company and to better manage it for long-term value creation. Because of the longer holding periods, more private equity firms are issuing convertible preference shares because they provide investors with greater total return potential through their dividend payments and the ability to convert their shares into common shares during an IPO.

In operating a publicly traded company, management often feels pressured to focus on short-term results[22] (e.g., meeting quarterly sales and earnings targets from analysts biased toward near-term price performance) instead of operating the company to obtain long-term sustainable revenue and earnings growth. By "going private," management can adopt a more long-term focus and can eliminate certain costs that are necessary to operate a publicly traded company—such as the cost of meeting regulatory and stock exchange filing requirements, the cost of maintaining investor relations departments to communicate with shareholders and the media, and the cost of holding quarterly analyst conference calls.

As described above, public equity markets are much larger than private equity networks and allow companies more opportunities to raise capital that is subsequently actively traded in secondary markets. By operating under public scrutiny, companies are incentivized to be more open in terms of corporate governance and executive compensation to ensure that they are acting for the benefit of shareholders. In fact, some studies have shown that private equity firms score lower in terms of corporate governance effectiveness, which may be attributed to the fact that shareholders, analysts, and other stakeholders are able to influence management when corporate governance and other policies are public.

INVESTING IN NON-DOMESTIC EQUITY SECURITIES

5

Technological innovations and the growth of electronic information exchanges (electronic trading networks, the internet, etc.) have accelerated the integration and growth of global financial markets. As detailed previously, global capital markets have expanded at a much more rapid rate than global GDP in recent years; both primary and secondary international markets have benefited from the enhanced ability to

---

20 Stromberg (2008).
21 See, for example, Bailey, Wirth, and Zapol (2005).
22 For further information, see "Overcoming Short-Termism: A Call for a More Responsible Approach to Investment and Business Management" (www.aspeninstitute.org/bsp/cvsg/policy2009).

rapidly and openly exchange information. Increased integration of equity markets has made it easier and less expensive for companies to raise capital and to expand their shareholder base beyond their local market. Integration has also made it easier for investors to invest in companies that are located outside of their domestic markets. This has enabled investors to further diversify and improve the risk and return characteristics of their portfolios by adding a class of assets with lower correlations to local country assets.

One barrier to investing globally is that many countries still impose "foreign restrictions" on individuals and companies from other countries that want to invest in their domestic companies. There are three primary reasons for these restrictions. The first is to limit the amount of control that foreign investors can exert on domestic companies. For example, some countries prevent foreign investors from acquiring a majority interest in domestic companies. The second is to give domestic investors the opportunity to own shares in the foreign companies that are conducting business in their country. For example, the Swedish home furnishings retailer IKEA abandoned efforts to invest in parts of the Asia/Pacific region because local governments did not want IKEA to maintain complete ownership of its stores. The third reason is to reduce the volatility of capital flows into and out of domestic equity markets. For example, one of the main consequences of the Asian Financial Crisis in 1997–98 was the large outflow of capital from such emerging market countries as Thailand, Indonesia, and South Korea. These outflows led to dramatic declines in the equity markets of these countries and significant currency devaluations and resulted in many governments placing restrictions on capital flows. Today, many of these same markets have built up currency reserves to better withstand capital outflows inherent in economic contractions and periods of financial market turmoil.

Studies have shown that reducing restrictions on foreign ownership has led to improved equity market performance over the long term.[23] Although restrictions vary widely, more countries are allowing increasing levels of foreign ownership. For example, Australia has sought tax reforms as a means to encourage international demand for its managed funds in order to increase its role as an international financial center. China recently announced plans to allow designated foreign institutional investors to invest up to US$1 billion in its domestic yuan-denominated A shares (up from a previous US$800 million) as it seeks to slowly liberalize its stock markets.

Over the past two decades, three trends have emerged: a) an increasing number of companies have issued shares in markets outside of their home country; b) the number of companies whose shares are traded in markets outside of their home has increased; and c) an increasing number of companies are dual listed, which means that their shares are simultaneously issued and traded in two or more markets. Companies located in emerging markets have particularly benefited from these trends because they no longer have to be concerned with capital constraints or lack of liquidity in their domestic markets. These companies have found it easier to raise capital in the markets of developed countries because these markets generally have higher levels of liquidity and more stringent financial reporting requirements and accounting standards. Being listed on an international exchange has a number of benefits. It can increase investor awareness about the company's products and services, enhance the liquidity of the company's shares, and increase corporate transparency because of the additional market exposure and the need to meet a greater number of filing requirements.

Technological advancements have made it easier for investors to trade shares in foreign markets. The German insurance company Allianz SE recently delisted its shares from the NYSE and certain European markets because international investors

---

23 See, for example, Henry and Chari (2004).

increasingly traded its shares on the Frankfurt Stock Exchange. Exhibit 14 illustrates the extent to which the institutional shareholder base at BASF, a large German chemical corporation, has become increasingly global in nature.

Exhibit 14 Example of Increased Globalization of Share Ownership[24]

BASF is one of the largest publicly owned companies with around 460,000 shareholders and a high free float. An analysis of the shareholder structure carried out in September 2008 showed that, at 22% of share capital, the United States and Canada made up the largest regional group of institutional investors. Institutional investors from Germany made up 13%. Shareholders from Great Britain and Ireland held 14% of BASF shares, while a further 14% are held by institutional investors from the rest of Europe. Around 28% of the company's share capital is held by private investors, most of whom are resident in Germany.

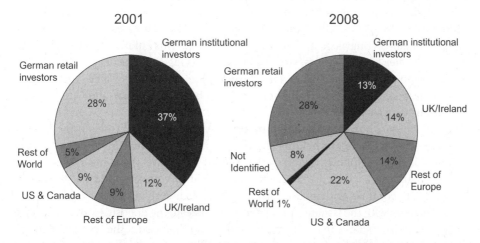

5.1 Direct Investing

Investors can use a variety of methods to invest in the equity of companies outside of their local market. The most obvious is to buy and sell securities directly in foreign markets. However, this means that all transactions—including the purchase and sale of shares, dividend payments, and capital gains—are in the company's, not the investor's, domestic currency. In addition, investors must be familiar with the trading, clearing, and settlement regulations and procedures of that market. Investing directly often results in less transparency and more volatility because audited financial information may not be provided on a regular basis and the market may be less liquid. Alternatively, investors can use such securities as depository receipts and global registered shares, which represent the equity of international companies and are traded on local exchanges and in the local currencies. With these securities, investors have to worry less about currency conversions (price quotations and dividend payments are in the investor's local currency), unfamiliar market practices, and differences in accounting standards. The sections that follow discuss various securities that investors can invest in outside of their home market.

---

24 Adapted from BASF's investor relations website (www.basf.com). **Free float** refers to the extent that shares are readily and freely tradable in the secondary market.

5.2 Depository Receipts

A **depository receipt**[25] (DR) is a security that trades like an ordinary share on a local exchange and represents an economic interest in a foreign company. It allows the publicly listed shares of a foreign company to be traded on an exchange outside its domestic market. A depository receipt is created when the equity shares of a foreign company are deposited in a bank (i.e., the depository) in the country on whose exchange the shares will trade. The depository then issues receipts that represent the shares that were deposited. The number of receipts issued and the price of each DR is based on a ratio, which specifies the number of depository receipts to the underlying shares. Consequently, a DR may represent one share of the underlying stock, many shares of the underlying stock, or a fractional share of the underlying stock. The price of each DR will be affected by factors that affect the price of the underlying shares, such as company fundamentals, market conditions, analysts' recommendations, and exchange rate movements. In addition, any short-term valuation discrepancies between shares traded on multiple exchanges represent a quick arbitrage profit opportunity for astute traders to exploit. The responsibilities of the **depository bank** that issues the receipts include acting as custodian and as a registrar. This entails handling dividend payments, other taxable events, stock splits, and serving as the transfer agent for the foreign company whose securities the DR represents. The Bank of New York Mellon is the largest depository bank; however, Deutsche Bank, JPMorgan, and Citibank also offer depository services.[26]

A DR can be **sponsored** or **unsponsored**. A sponsored DR is when the foreign company whose shares are held by the depository has a direct involvement in the issuance of the receipts. Investors in sponsored DRs have the same rights as the direct owners of the common shares (e.g., the right to vote and the right to receive dividends). In contrast, with an unsponsored DR, the underlying foreign company has no involvement with the issuance of the receipts. Instead, the depository purchases the foreign company's shares in its domestic market and then issues the receipts through brokerage firms in the depository's local market. In this case, the depository bank, not the investors in the DR, retains the voting rights. Sponsored DRs are generally subject to greater reporting requirements than unsponsored DRs. In the United States, for example, sponsored DRs must be registered (meet the reporting requirements) with the US Securities and Exchange Commission (SEC). Exhibit 15 contains an example of a sponsored DR issued by Japan Airlines.

Exhibit 15   Sponsored versus Unsponsored Depository Receipts[27]

The Japan Airlines (JAL) Group, Asia's biggest airline grouping, has picked the Bank of New York as the depository bank to make its previously unsponsored American depository receipts (ADRs) sponsored. By taking this action and by boosting investor relations activities in the United States, the JAL group aims to increase the number of overseas shareholders. The JAL Group's sponsored ADRs became effective on August 19th, 2004 and dealing will start on August 25th. The JAL Group's American depository receipts had been previously issued in the United States as unsponsored ADRs by several US depository banks since the 1970s. However, as unsponsored ADRs are issued without the involvement of the company itself, the company has difficulty in identifying ADR holders

---

25 Note that the spellings *depositary* and *depository* are used interchangeably in financial markets. In this reading, we use the spelling *depository* throughout.

26 Boubakri, Cosset, and Samet (2008).

27 Adapted from Japan Airlines Group's investor relations website (www.jal.com/en/press/2004/082301/img/ADRS.pdf).

Exhibit 15   (Continued)

and controlling ADRs. From now, the JAL Group will be able to better serve its ADR holders and, at the same time, the JAL Group intends to increase its overseas investors.

There are two types of depository receipts: Global depository receipts (GDRs) and American depository receipts (ADRs), which are described below.

5.2.1 *Global Depository Receipts*

A **global depository receipt** (GDR) is issued outside of the company's home country and outside of the United States. The depository bank that issues GDRs is generally located (or has branches) in the countries on whose exchanges the shares are traded. A key advantage of GDRs is that they are not subject to the foreign ownership and capital flow restrictions that may be imposed by the issuing company's home country because they are sold outside of that country. The issuing company selects the exchange where the GDR is to be traded based on such factors as investors' familiarity with the company or the existence of a large international investor base. The London and Luxembourg exchanges were the first ones to trade GDRs. Other stock exchanges trading GDRs are the Dubai International Financial Exchange, the Singapore Stock Exchange, and the Hong Kong Stock Exchange. Currently, the London and Luxembourg exchanges are where most GDRs are traded because they can be issued in a more timely manner and at a lower cost. Regardless of the exchange they are traded on, the majority of GDRs are denominated in US dollars, although the number of GDRs denominated in pound sterling and euros is increasing. Note that although GDRs cannot be listed on US exchanges, they can be privately placed with institutional investors based in the United States.

5.2.2 *American Depository Receipts*

An **American depository receipt** (ADR) is a US dollar-denominated security that trades like a common share on US exchanges. First created in 1927, ADRs are the oldest type of depository receipts and are currently the most commonly traded depository receipts. They enable foreign companies to raise capital from US investors. Note that an ADR is one form of a GDR; however, not all GDRs are ADRs because GDRs cannot be publicly traded in the United States. The term **American depository share** (ADS) is often used in tandem with the term ADR. A depository share is a security that is actually traded in the issuing company's domestic market. That is, while American depository receipts are the certificates that are traded on US markets, American depository shares are the underlying shares on which these receipts are based.

There are four primary types of ADRs, with each type having different levels of corporate governance and filing requirements. Level I Sponsored ADRs trade in the over-the-counter (OTC) market and do not require full registration with the Securities and Exchange Commission (SEC). Level II and Level III Sponsored ADRs can trade on the New York Stock Exchange (NYSE), NASDAQ, and American Stock Exchange (AMEX). Level II and III ADRs allow companies to raise capital and make acquisitions using these securities. However, the issuing companies must fulfill all SEC requirements.

The fourth type of ADR, an SEC Rule 144A or a Regulation S depository receipt, does not require SEC registration. Instead, foreign companies are able to raise capital by privately placing these depository receipts with qualified institutional investors or to offshore non-US investors. Exhibit 16 summarizes the main features of ADRs.

Exhibit 16	Summary of the Main Features of American Depository Receipts

	Level I (Unlisted)	Level II (Listed)	Level III (Listed)	Rule 144A (Unlisted)
Objectives	Develop and broaden US investor base with existing shares	Develop and broaden US investor base with existing shares	Develop and broaden US investor base with existing/new shares	Access qualified institutional buyers (QIBs)
Raising capital on US markets?	No	No	Yes, through public offerings	Yes, through private placements to QIBs
SEC registration	Form F-6	Form F-6	Forms F-1 and F-6	None
Trading	Over the counter (OTC)	NYSE, NASDAQ, or AMEX	NYSE, NASDAQ, or AMEX	Private offerings, resales, and trading through automated linkages such as PORTAL
Listing fees	Low	High	High	Low
Size and earnings requirements	None	Yes	Yes	None

Source: Adapted from Boubakri, Cosset, and Samet (2008): Table 1.

More than 2,000 DRs, from over 80 countries, currently trade on US exchanges. Based on current statistics, the total market value of DRs issued and traded is estimated at approximately US$2 trillion, or 15 percent of the total dollar value of equities traded in US markets.[28]

5.2.3 *Global Registered Share*

A **global registered share** (GRS) is a common share that is traded on different stock exchanges around the world in different currencies. Currency conversions are not needed to purchase or sell them, because identical shares are quoted and traded in different currencies. Thus, the same share purchased on the Swiss exchange in Swiss francs can be sold on the Tokyo exchange for Japanese yen. As a result, GRSs offer more flexibility than depository receipts because the shares represent an actual ownership interest in the company that can be traded anywhere and currency conversions are not needed to purchase or sell them. GRSs were created and issued by Daimler Chrysler in 1998.

5.2.4 *Basket of Listed Depository Receipts*

Another type of global security is a **basket of listed depository receipts** (BLDR), which is an exchange-traded fund (ETF) that represents a portfolio of depository receipts. An ETF is a security that tracks an index but trades like an individual share on an exchange. An equity-ETF is a security that contains a portfolio of equities that tracks an index. It trades throughout the day and can be bought, sold, or sold short, just like an individual share. Like ordinary shares, ETFs can also be purchased on margin and used in hedging or arbitrage strategies. The BLDR is a specific class of ETF security that consists of an underlying portfolio of DRs and is designed to track the price performance of an underlying DR index. For example, the Asia 50 ADR Index Fund is a capitalization-weighted ETF designed to track the performance of 50 Asian market-based ADRs.

---

28 *JPMorgan Depositary Receipt Guide* (2005):4.

RISK AND RETURN CHARACTERISTICS OF EQUITY SECURITIES

6

Different types of equity securities have different ownership claims on a company's net assets. The type of equity security and its features affect its risk and return characteristics. The following sections discuss the different return and risk characteristics of equity securities.

6.1 Return Characteristics of Equity Securities

There are two main sources of equity securities' total return: price change (or capital gain) and dividend income. The price change represents the difference between the purchase price (P_{t-1}) and the sale price (P_t) of a share at the end of time $t-1$ and t, respectively. Cash or stock dividends (D_t) represent distributions that the company makes to its shareholders during period t. Therefore, an equity security's total return is calculated as:

$$\text{Total return, } R_t = (P_t - P_{t-1} + D_t)/P_{t-1} \qquad (1)$$

For non-dividend-paying stocks, the total return consists of price appreciation only. Companies that are in the early stages of their life cycle generally do not pay dividends because earnings and cash flows are reinvested to finance the company's growth. In contrast, companies that are in the mature phase of their life cycle may not have as many profitable growth opportunities; therefore, excess cash flows are often returned to investors via the payment of regular dividends or through share repurchases.

For investors who purchase depository receipts or foreign shares directly, there is a third source of return: **foreign exchange gains (or losses)**. Foreign exchange gains arise because of the change in the exchange rate between the investor's currency and the currency that the foreign shares are denominated in. For example, US investors who purchase the ADRs of a Japanese company will earn an additional return if the yen appreciates relative to the US dollar. Conversely, these investors will earn a lower total return if the yen depreciates relative to the US dollar. For example, if the total return for a Japanese company was 10 percent in Japan and the yen depreciated by 10 percent against the US dollar, the total return of the ADR would be (approximately) 0 percent. If the yen had instead appreciated by 10 percent against the US dollar, the total return of the ADR would be (approximately) 20 percent.

Investors that only consider price appreciation overlook an important source of return: the compounding that results from reinvested dividends. Reinvested dividends are cash dividends that the investor receives and uses to purchase additional shares. As Exhibit 17 shows, in the long run total returns on equity securities are dramatically influenced by the compounding effect of reinvested dividends. Between 1900 and 2011, US$1 invested in US equities in 1900 would have grown in *real* terms to US$834 with dividends reinvested, but to just US$8.1 when taking only the price appreciation or capital gain into account. This corresponds to a real compounded return of 6.2 percent per year with dividends reinvested, versus only 1.9 percent per year without dividends reinvested. The comparable ending real wealth for bonds and bills are US$9.30 and US$2.80, respectively. These ending real wealth figures correspond to annualized real compounded returns of 2.0 percent on bonds and 0.9 percent on bills.

Exhibit 17   Impact of Reinvested Dividends on Cumulative Real Returns in the US and UK Equity Market: 1900–2011

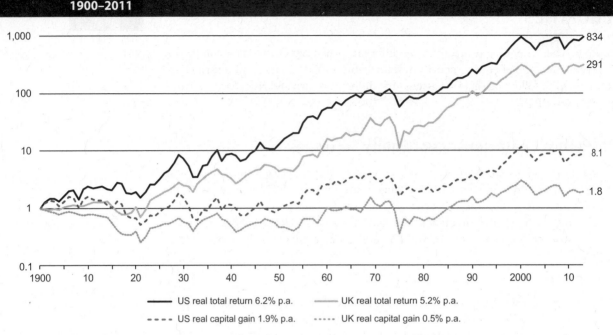

Source: Dimson, Marsh, and Staunton (2012b). This chart is updated annually and can be found at www.tinyurl.com/DMSsourcebook.

6.2 Risk of Equity Securities

The risk of any security is based on the uncertainty of its future cash flows. The greater the uncertainty of its future cash flows, the greater the risk and the more variable or volatile the security's price. As discussed above, an equity security's total return is determined by its price change and dividends. Therefore, the risk of an equity security can be defined as the uncertainty of its expected (or future) total return. Risk is most often measured by calculating the standard deviation of the equity's expected total return.

A variety of different methods can be used to estimate an equity's expected total return and risk. One method uses the equity's average historical return and the standard deviation of this return as proxies for its expected future return and risk. Another method involves estimating a range of future returns over a specified period of time, assigning probabilities to those returns, and then calculating an expected return and a standard deviation of return based on this information.

The type of equity security, as well as its characteristics, affects the uncertainty of its future cash flows and therefore its risk. In general, preference shares are less risky than common shares for three main reasons:

1   Dividends on preference shares are known and fixed, and they account for a large portion of the preference shares' total return. Therefore, there is less uncertainty about future cash flows.

2   Preference shareholders receive dividends and other distributions before common shareholders.

3   The amount preference shareholders will receive if the company is liquidated is known and fixed as the par (or face) value of their shares. However, there is no guarantee that investors will receive that amount if the company experiences financial difficulty.

With common shares, however, a larger portion of shareholders' total return (or all of their total return for non-dividend shares) is based on future price appreciation and future dividends are unknown. If the company is liquidated, common shareholders will receive whatever amount (if any) is remaining after the company's creditors and preference shareholders have been paid. In summary, because the uncertainty surrounding the total return of preference shares is less than common shares, preference shares have lower risk and lower expected return than common shares.

It is important to note that some preference shares and common shares can be riskier than others because of their associated characteristics. For example, from an investor's point of view, putable common or preference shares are less risky than their callable or non-callable counterparts because they give the investor the option to sell the shares to the issuer at a pre-determined price. This pre-determined price establishes a minimum price that investors will receive and reduces the uncertainty associated with the security's future cash flow. As a result, putable shares generally pay a lower dividend than non-putable shares.

Because the major source of total return for preference shares is dividend income, the primary risk affecting all preference shares is the uncertainty of future dividend payments. Regardless of the preference shares' features (callable, putable, cumulative, etc.), the greater the uncertainty surrounding the issuer's ability to pay dividends, the greater risk. Because the ability of a company to pay dividends is based on its future cash flows and net income, investors try to estimate these amounts by examining past trends or forecasting future amounts. The more earnings and the greater amount of cash flow that the company has had, or is expected to have, the lower the uncertainty and risk associated with its ability to pay future dividends.

Callable common or preference shares are riskier than their non-callable counterparts because the issuer has the option to redeem the shares at a pre-determined price. Because the call price limits investors' potential future total return, callable shares generally pay a higher dividend to compensate investors for the risk that the shares could be called in the future. Similarly, putable preference shares have lower risk than non-putable preference shares. Cumulative preference shares have lower risk than non-cumulative preference shares because the cumulative feature gives investors the right to receive any unpaid dividends before any dividends can be paid to common shareholders.

EQUITY SECURITIES AND COMPANY VALUE

7

Companies issue equity securities on primary markets to raise capital and increase liquidity. This additional liquidity also provides the corporation an additional "currency" (its equity), which it can use to make acquisitions and provide stock option-based incentives to employees. The primary goal of raising capital is to finance the company's revenue-generating activities in order to increase its net income and maximize the wealth of its shareholders. In most cases, the capital that is raised is used to finance the purchase of long-lived assets, capital expansion projects, research and development, the entry into new product or geographic regions, and the acquisition of other companies. Alternatively, a company may be forced to raise capital to ensure that it continues to operate as a going concern. In these cases, capital is raised to fulfill regulatory requirements, improve capital adequacy ratios, or to ensure that debt covenants are met.

The ultimate goal of management is to increase the book value (shareholders' equity on a company's balance sheet) of the company and maximize the market value of its equity. Although management actions can directly affect the book value of the company (by increasing net income or by selling or purchasing its own shares), they can only indirectly affect the market value of its equity. The book value of a company's equity—the difference between its total assets and total liabilities—increases when the company retains its net income. The more net income that is earned and retained, the greater the company's book value of equity. Because management's decisions directly influence a company's net income, they also directly influence its book value of equity.

The market value of the company's equity, however, reflects the collective and differing expectations of investors concerning the amount, timing, and uncertainty of the company's future cash flows. Rarely will book value and market value be equal. Although management may be accomplishing its objective of increasing the company's book value, this increase may not be reflected in the market value of the company's equity because it does not affect investors' expectations about the company's future cash flows. A key measure that investors use to evaluate the effectiveness of management in increasing the company's book value is the accounting return on equity.

7.1 Accounting Return on Equity

Return on equity (ROE) is the primary measure that equity investors use to determine whether the management of a company is effectively and efficiently using the capital they have provided to generate profits. It measures the total amount of net income available to common shareholders generated by the total equity capital invested in the company. It is computed as net income available to ordinary shareholders (i.e., after preferred dividends have been deducted) divided by the average total book value of equity (BVE). That is:

$$\text{ROE}_t = \frac{\text{NI}_t}{\text{Average BVE}_t} = \frac{\text{NI}_t}{(\text{BVE}_t + \text{BVE}_{t-1})\,/\,2} \tag{2}$$

where NI_t is the net income in year t and the average book value of equity is computed as the book values at the beginning and end of year t divided by 2. Return on equity assumes that the net income produced in the current year is generated by the equity existing at the beginning of the year and any new equity that was invested during the year. Note that some formulas only use shareholders' equity at the beginning of year t (that is, the end of year $t - 1$) in the denominator. This assumes that only the equity existing at the beginning of the year was used to generate the company's net income during the year. That is:

$$\text{ROE}_t = \frac{\text{NI}_t}{\text{BVE}_{t-1}} \tag{3}$$

Both formulas are appropriate to use as long as they are applied consistently. For example, using beginning of the year book value is appropriate when book values are relatively stable over time or when computing ROE for a company annually over a period of time. Average book value is more appropriate if a company experiences more volatile year-end book values or if the industry convention is to use average book values in calculating ROE.

One caveat to be aware of when computing and analyzing ROE is that net income and the book value of equity are directly affected by management's choice of accounting methods, such as those relating to depreciation (straight line versus accelerated methods) or inventories (first in, first out versus weighted average cost). Different accounting methods can make it difficult to compare the return on equity of companies even if they operate in the same industry. It may also be difficult to compare the ROE of the same company over time if its accounting methods have changed during that time.

Exhibit 18 contains information on the net income and total book value of shareholders' equity for three **blue chip** (widely held large market capitalization companies that are considered financially sound and are leaders in their respective industry or local stock market) pharmaceutical companies: Pfizer, Novartis AG, and GlaxoSmithKline. The data are for their financial years ending December 2006 through December 2008.[29]

Exhibit 18	Net Income and Book Value of Equity for Pfizer, Novartis AG, and GlaxoSmithKline (in Thousands of US Dollars)		
	Financial Year Ending		
	31 Dec 2008	**31 Dec 2007**	**31 Dec 2006**
Pfizer			
Net income	$8,104,000	$8,144,000	$19,337,000
Total stockholders' equity	$57,556,000	$65,010,000	$71,358,000
Novartis AG			
Net income	$8,233,000	$11,968,000	$5,264,000
Total stockholders' equity	$50,437,000	$49,396,000	$41,670,000
GlaxoSmithKline			
Net income	$6,822,505	$10,605,663	$8,747,382
Total stockholders' equity	$11,483,295	$19,180,072	$67,888,692

Using the average book value of equity, the return on equity for Pfizer for the years ending December 2007 and 2008 can be calculated as:

Return on equity for the year ending December 2007

$$ROE_{2007} = \frac{NI_{2007}}{(BVE_{2006} + BVE_{2007}) / 2} = \frac{8,144,000}{(71,358,000 + 65,010,000) / 2} = 11.9\%$$

Return on equity for the year ending December 2008

$$ROE_{2008} = \frac{NI_{2008}}{(BVE_{2007} + BVE_{2008}) / 2} = \frac{8,104,000}{(65,010,000 + 57,556,000) / 2} = 13.2\%$$

Exhibit 19 summarizes the return on equity for Novartis and GlaxoSmithKline in addition to Pfizer for 2007 and 2008.

Exhibit 19	Return on Equity for Pfizer, Novartis AG, and GlaxoSmithKline	
	31 Dec 2008 (%)	**31 Dec 2007 (%)**
Pfizer	13.2	11.9
Novartis AG	16.5	26.3
GlaxoSmithKline	44.5	24.4

---

29 Pfizer uses US GAAP to prepare its financial statements; Novartis and GlaxoSmithKline use International Financial Reporting Standards. Therefore, it would be inappropriate to compare the ROE of Pfizer to that of Novartis or GlaxoSmithKline.

In the case of Novartis, the ROE of 26.3 percent in 2007 indicates that the company was able to generate a return (profit) of US$0.263 on every US$1.00 of capital invested by shareholders. In 2008, its operating performance deteriorated because it was only able to generate a 16.5 percent return on its equity. In contrast, GlaxoSmithKline almost doubled its return on equity over this period, from 24.4 percent to 44.5 percent. Pfizer's ROE remained relatively unchanged.

ROE can increase if net income increases at a faster rate than shareholders' equity or if net income decreases at a slower rate than shareholders' equity. In the case of Novartis, ROE fell in 2008 because its net income decreased by over 30 percent while shareholders' equity remained relatively stable. Stated differently, Novartis was less effective in using its equity capital to generate profits in 2008 than in 2007. In the case of GlaxoSmithKline, its ROE increased dramatically from 24.4 percent to 44.5 percent in 2007 versus 2008 even though its net income fell over 35 percent because its average shareholder equity decreased dramatically from 2006–2007 to 2007–2008.

An important question to ask is whether an increasing ROE is always good. The short answer is, "it depends." One reason ROE can increase is if net income decreases at a slower rate than shareholders' equity, which is not a positive sign. In addition, ROE can increase if the company issues debt and then uses the proceeds to repurchase some of its outstanding shares. This action will increase the company's leverage and make its equity riskier. Therefore, it is important to examine the source of changes in the company's net income *and* shareholders' equity over time. The DuPont formula, which is discussed in a separate reading, can be used to analyze the sources of changes in a company's ROE.

The book value of a company's equity reflects the historical operating and financing decisions of its management. The market value of the company's equity reflects these decisions as well as investors' collective assessment and expectations about the company's future cash flows generated by its positive net present value investment opportunities. If investors believe that the company has a large number of these future cash flow-generating investment opportunities, the market value of the company's equity will exceed its book value. Exhibit 20 shows the market price per share, the total number of shares outstanding, and the total book value of shareholders' equity for Pfizer, Novartis AG, and GlaxoSmithKline at the end of December 2008. This exhibit also shows the total market value of equity (or market capitalization) computed as the number of shares outstanding multiplied by the market price per share.

Exhibit 20	Market Information for Pfizer, Novartis AG, and GlaxoSmithKline (in Thousands of US Dollars except market price)		
	Pfizer	**Novartis AG**	**GlaxoSmithKline**
Market price	$16.97	$47.64	$35.84
Total shares outstanding	6,750,000	2,260,000	2,530,000
Total shareholders' equity	$57,556,000	$50,437,000	$11,483,295
Total market value of equity	$114,547,500	$107,666,400	$90,675,200

Note that in Exhibit 20, the total market value of equity for Pfizer is computed as:

Market value of equity = Market price per share × Shares outstanding

Market value of equity = US$16.97 × 6,750,000 = US$114,547,500.

The book value of equity per share for Pfizer can be computed as:

Book value of equity per share = Total shareholders' equity/Shares outstanding

Book value of equity per share = US$57,556,000/6,750,000 = US$8.53.

A useful ratio to compute is a company's price-to-book ratio, which is also referred to as the market-to-book ratio. This ratio provides an indication of investors' expectations about a company's future investment and cash flow-generating opportunities. The larger the price-to-book ratio (i.e., the greater the divergence between market value per share and book value per share), the more favorably investors will view the company's future investment opportunities. For Pfizer the price-to-book ratio is:

Price-to-book ratio = Market price per share/Book value of equity per share

Price-to-book ratio = US$16.97/US$8.53 = 1.99.

Exhibit 21 contains the market price per share, book value of equity per share, and price-to-book ratios for Novartis and GlaxoSmithKline in addition to Pfizer.

Exhibit 21	Pfizer, Novartis AG, and GlaxoSmithKline		
	Pfizer	**Novartis AG**	**GlaxoSmithKline**
Market price per share	$16.97	$47.64	$35.84
Book value of equity per share	$8.53	$22.32	$4.54
Price-to-book ratio	1.99	2.13	7.89

The market price per share of all three companies exceeds their respective book values, so their price-to-book ratios are all greater than 1.00. However, there are significant differences in the sizes of their price-to-book ratios. GlaxoSmithKline has the largest price-to-book ratio, while the price-to-book ratios of Pfizer and Novartis are similar to each other. This suggests that investors believe that GlaxoSmithKline has substantially higher future growth opportunities than either Pfizer or Novartis.

It is not appropriate to compare the price-to-book ratios of companies in different industries because their price-to-book ratios also reflect investors' outlook for the industry. Companies in high growth industries, such as technology, will generally have higher price-to-book ratios than companies in slower growth (i.e., mature) industries, such as heavy equipment. Therefore, it is more appropriate to compare the price-to-book ratios of companies in the same industry. A company with relatively high growth opportunities compared to its industry peers would likely have a higher price-to-book ratio than the average price-to-book ratio of the industry.

Book value and return on equity are useful in helping analysts determine value but can be limited as a primary means to estimate a company's true or intrinsic value, which is the present value of its future projected cash flows. In Exhibit 22, Warren Buffett, one of the most successful investors in the world and CEO of Berkshire Hathaway, provides an explanation of the differences between the book value of a company and its intrinsic value in a letter to shareholders. As discussed above, market value reflects the collective and differing expectations of investors concerning the amount, timing, and uncertainty of a company's future cash flows. A company's intrinsic value can only be estimated because it is impossible to predict the amount and timing of its future cash flows. However, astute investors—such as Buffett—have been able to profit from discrepancies between their estimates of a company's intrinsic value and the market value of its equity.

Exhibit 22   Book Value versus Intrinsic Value[30]

We regularly report our per-share book value, an easily calculable number, though one of limited use. Just as regularly, we tell you that what counts is intrinsic value, a number that is impossible to pinpoint but essential to estimate.

For example, in 1964, we could state with certitude that Berkshire's per-share book value was $19.46. However, that figure considerably overstated the stock's intrinsic value since all of the company's resources were tied up in a sub-profitable textile business. Our textile assets had neither going-concern nor liquidation values equal to their carrying values. In 1964, then, anyone inquiring into the soundness of Berkshire's balance sheet might well have deserved the answer once offered up by a Hollywood mogul of dubious reputation: "Don't worry, the liabilities are solid."

Today, Berkshire's situation has reversed: Many of the businesses we control are worth far more than their carrying value. (Those we don't control, such as Coca-Cola or Gillette, are carried at current market values.) We continue to give you book value figures, however, because they serve as a rough, understated, tracking measure for Berkshire's intrinsic value.

We define intrinsic value as the discounted value of the cash that can be taken out of a business during its remaining life. Anyone calculating intrinsic value necessarily comes up with a highly subjective figure that will change both as estimates of future cash flows are revised and as interest rates move. Despite its fuzziness, however, intrinsic value is all-important and is the only logical way to evaluate the relative attractiveness of investments and businesses.

To see how historical input (book value) and future output (intrinsic value) can diverge, let's look at another form of investment, a college education. Think of the education's cost as its "book value." If it is to be accurate, the cost should include the earnings that were foregone by the student because he chose college rather than a job.

For this exercise, we will ignore the important non-economic benefits of an education and focus strictly on its economic value. First, we must estimate the earnings that the graduate will receive over his lifetime and subtract from that figure an estimate of what he would have earned had he lacked his education. That gives us an excess earnings figure, which must then be discounted, at an appropriate interest rate, back to graduation day. The dollar result equals the intrinsic economic value of the education.

7.2 The Cost of Equity and Investors' Required Rates of Return

When companies issue debt (or borrow from a bank) or equity securities, there is a cost associated with the capital that is raised. In order to maximize profitability and shareholder wealth, companies attempt to raise capital efficiently so as to minimize these costs.

When a company issues debt, the cost it incurs for the use of these funds is called the cost of debt. The cost of debt is relatively easy to estimate because it reflects the periodic interest (or coupon) rate that the company is contractually obligated to pay to its bondholders (lenders). When a company raises capital by issuing equity, the cost it incurs is called the cost of equity. Unlike debt, however, the company is not contractually obligated to make any payments to its shareholders for the use of their funds. As a result, the cost of equity is more difficult to estimate.

---

30 Extracts from Berkshire Hathaway's *2008 Annual Report* (www.berkshirehathaway.com).

Investors require a return on the funds they provide to the company. This return is called the investor's minimum required rate of return. When investors purchase the company's debt securities, their minimum required rate of return is the periodic rate of interest they charge the company for the use of their funds. Because all of the bondholders receive the same periodic rate of interest, their required rate of return is the same. Therefore, the company's cost of debt and the investors' minimum required rate of return on the debt are the same.

When investors purchase the company's equity securities, their minimum required rate of return is based on the future cash flows they expect to receive. Because these future cash flows are both uncertain and unknown, the investors' minimum required rate of return must be estimated. In addition, the minimum required return may differ across investors based on their expectations about the company's future cash flows. As a result, the company's cost of equity may be different from the investors' minimum required rate of return on equity.[31] Because companies try to raise capital at the lowest possible cost, the company's cost of equity is often used as a proxy for the investors' *minimum* required rate of return.

In other words, the cost of equity can be thought of as the minimum expected rate of return that a company must offer its investors to purchase its shares in the primary market and to maintain its share price in the secondary market. If this expected rate of return is not maintained in the secondary market, then the share price will adjust so that it meets the minimum required rate of return demanded by investors. For example, if investors require a higher rate of return on equity than the company's cost of equity, they would sell their shares and invest their funds elsewhere resulting in a decline in the company's share price. As the share price declined, the cost of equity would increase to reach the higher rate of return that investors require.

Two models commonly used to estimate a company's cost of equity (or investors' minimum required rate of return) are the dividend discount model (DDM) and the capital asset pricing model (CAPM). These models are discussed in detail in other curriculum readings.

The cost of debt (after tax) and the cost of equity (i.e., the minimum required rates of return on debt and equity) are integral components of the capital budgeting process because they are used to estimate a company's weighted average cost of capital (WACC). Capital budgeting is the decision-making process that companies use to evaluate potential long-term investments. The WACC represents the minimum required rate of return that the company must earn on its long-term investments to satisfy all providers of capital. The company then chooses among those long-term investments with expected returns that are greater than its WACC.

SUMMARY

Equity securities play a fundamental role in investment analysis and portfolio management. The importance of this asset class continues to grow on a global scale because of the need for equity capital in developed and emerging markets, technological innovation, and the growing sophistication of electronic information exchange. Given their absolute return potential and ability to impact the risk and return characteristics of portfolios, equity securities are of importance to both individual and institutional investors.

---

31 Another important factor that can cause a firm's cost of equity to differ from investors' required rate of return on equity is the flotation cost associated with equity.

This reading introduces equity securities and provides an overview of global equity markets. A detailed analysis of their historical performance shows that equity securities have offered average real annual returns superior to government bills and bonds, which have provided average real annual returns that have only kept pace with inflation. The different types and characteristics of common and preference equity securities are examined, and the primary differences between public and private equity securities are outlined. An overview of the various types of equity securities listed and traded in global markets is provided, including a discussion of their risk and return characteristics. Finally, the role of equity securities in creating company value is examined as well as the relationship between a company's cost of equity, its accounting return on equity, investors' required rate of return, and the company's intrinsic value.

We conclude with a summary of the key components of this reading:

- Common shares represent an ownership interest in a company and give investors a claim on its operating performance, the opportunity to participate in the corporate decision-making process, and a claim on the company's net assets in the case of liquidation.

- Callable common shares give the issuer the right to buy back the shares from shareholders at a price determined when the shares are originally issued.

- Putable common shares give shareholders the right to sell the shares back to the issuer at a price specified when the shares are originally issued.

- Preference shares are a form of equity in which payments made to preference shareholders take precedence over any payments made to common stockholders.

- Cumulative preference shares are preference shares on which dividend payments are accrued so that any payments omitted by the company must be paid before another dividend can be paid to common shareholders. Non-cumulative preference shares have no such provisions, implying that the dividend payments are at the company's discretion and are thus similar to payments made to common shareholders.

- Participating preference shares allow investors to receive the standard preferred dividend plus the opportunity to receive a share of corporate profits above a pre-specified amount. Non-participating preference shares allow investors to simply receive the initial investment plus any accrued dividends in the event of liquidation.

- Callable and putable preference shares provide issuers and investors with the same rights and obligations as their common share counterparts.

- Private equity securities are issued primarily to institutional investors in private placements and do not trade in secondary equity markets. There are three types of private equity investments: venture capital, leveraged buyouts, and private investments in public equity (PIPEs).

- The objective of private equity investing is to increase the ability of the company's management to focus on its operating activities for long-term value creation. The strategy is to take the "private" company "public" after certain profit and other benchmarks have been met.

- Depository receipts are securities that trade like ordinary shares on a local exchange but which represent an economic interest in a foreign company. They allow the publicly listed shares of foreign companies to be traded on an exchange outside their domestic market.

- American depository receipts are US dollar-denominated securities trading much like standard US securities on US markets. Global depository receipts are similar to ADRs but contain certain restrictions in terms of their ability to be resold among investors.

- Underlying characteristics of equity securities can greatly affect their risk and return.

- A company's accounting return on equity is the total return that it earns on shareholders' book equity.

- A company's cost of equity is the minimum rate of return that stockholders require the company to pay them for investing in its equity.

REFERENCES

Bailey, Elizabeth, Meg Wirth, and David Zapol. 2005. "Venture Capital and Global Health." *Financing Global Health Ventures*, Discussion Paper (September 2005): http://www.commonscapital.com/downloads/Venture_Capital_and_Global_Health.pdf

Bary, Andrew. 2008. "Does Extreme Stress Signal an Economic Snapback?" *Barron's* (24 November 2008): online.barrons.com/article/SB122732177515750213.html.

Boubakri, Narjess, Jean-Claude Cosset, and Anis Samet. 2008. "The Choice of ADRs." Finance International Meeting AFFI – EUROFIDAI, December 2007. (http://ssrn.com/abstract=1006839).

Dimson, Elroy, Paul Marsh, and Mike Staunton. 2012a. *Credit Suisse Global Investment Returns Sourcebook 2012*. Credit Suisse Research Institute.

Dimson, Elroy, Paul Marsh, and Mike Staunton. 2012b. *Credit Suisse Global Investment Returns Yearbook 2012*. Credit Suisse Research Institute.

Henry, Peter Blair, and Anusha Chari. 2004. "Risk Sharing and Asset Prices: Evidence from a Natural Experiment." *Journal of Finance*, vol. 59, no. 3:1295–1324.

Strömberg, Per. 2008. "The New Demography of Private Equity." The *Global Economic Impact of Private Equity Report 2008*, World Economic Forum.

PRACTICE PROBLEMS

1 Which of the following is *not* a characteristic of common equity?

  A It represents an ownership interest in the company.

  B Shareholders participate in the decision-making process.

  C The company is obligated to make periodic dividend payments.

2 The type of equity voting right that grants one vote for each share of equity owned is referred to as:

  A proxy voting.

  B statutory voting.

  C cumulative voting.

3 All of the following are characteristics of preference shares *except*:

  A They are either callable or putable.

  B They generally do not have voting rights.

  C They do not share in the operating performance of the company.

4 Participating preference shares entitle shareholders to:

  A participate in the decision-making process of the company.

  B convert their shares into a specified number of common shares.

  C receive an additional dividend if the company's profits exceed a pre-determined level.

5 Which of the following statements about private equity securities is *incorrect*?

  A They cannot be sold on secondary markets.

  B They have market-determined quoted prices.

  C They are primarily issued to institutional investors.

6 Venture capital investments:

  A can be publicly traded.

  B do not require a long-term commitment of funds.

  C provide mezzanine financing to early-stage companies.

7 Which of the following statements *most accurately* describes one difference between private and public equity firms?

  A Private equity firms are focused more on short-term results than public firms.

  B Private equity firms' regulatory and investor relations operations are less costly than those of public firms.

  C Private equity firms are incentivized to be more open with investors about governance and compensation than public firms.

8 Emerging markets have benefited from recent trends in international markets. Which of the following has *not* been a benefit of these trends?

  A Emerging market companies do not have to worry about a lack of liquidity in their home equity markets.

  B Emerging market companies have found it easier to raise capital in the markets of developed countries.

C Emerging market companies have benefited from the stability of foreign exchange markets.

9 When investing in unsponsored depository receipts, the voting rights to the shares in the trust belong to:

A the depository bank.

B the investors in the depository receipts.

C the issuer of the shares held in the trust.

10 With respect to Level III sponsored ADRs, which of the following is *least likely* to be accurate? They:

A have low listing fees.

B are traded on the NYSE, NASDAQ, and AMEX.

C are used to raise equity capital in US markets.

11 A basket of listed depository receipts, or an exchange-traded fund, would *most likely* be used for:

A gaining exposure to a single equity.

B hedging exposure to a single equity.

C gaining exposure to multiple equities.

12 Calculate the total return on a share of equity using the following data:

Purchase price: $50

Sale price: $42

Dividend paid during holding period: $2

A −12.0%

B −14.3%

C −16.0%

13 If a US-based investor purchases a euro-denominated ETF and the euro subsequently depreciates in value relative to the dollar, the investor will have a total return that is:

A lower than the ETF's total return.

B higher than the ETF's total return.

C the same as the ETF's total return.

14 Which of the following is *incorrect* about the risk of an equity security? The risk of an equity security is:

A based on the uncertainty of its cash flows.

B based on the uncertainty of its future price.

C measured using the standard deviation of its dividends.

15 From an investor's point of view, which of the following equity securities is the *least* risky?

A Putable preference shares.

B Callable preference shares.

C Non-callable preference shares.

16 Which of the following is *least likely* to be a reason for a company to issue equity securities on the primary market?

A To raise capital.

B To increase liquidity.

C To increase return on equity.

17 Which of the following is *not* a primary goal of raising equity capital?

   A   To finance the purchase of long-lived assets.

   B   To finance the company's revenue-generating activities.

   C   To ensure that the company continues as a going concern.

18 Which of the following statements is *most accurate* in describing a company's book value?

   A   Book value increases when a company retains its net income.

   B   Book value is usually equal to the company's market value.

   C   The ultimate goal of management is to maximize book value.

19 Calculate the book value of a company using the following information:

Number of shares outstanding	100,000
Price per share	€52
Total assets	€12,000,000
Total liabilities	€7,500,000
Net Income	€2,000,000

   A   €4,500,000.

   B   €5,200,000.

   C   €6,500,000.

20 Which of the following statements is *least accurate* in describing a company's market value?

   A   Management's decisions do not influence the company's market value.

   B   Increases in book value may not be reflected in the company's market value.

   C   Market value reflects the collective and differing expectations of investors.

21 Calculate the 2009 return on equity (ROE) of a stable company using the following data:

Total sales	£2,500,000
Net income	£2,000,000
Beginning of year total assets	£50,000,000
Beginning of year total liabilities	£35,000,000
Number of shares outstanding at the end of 2009	1,000,000
Price per share at the end of 2009	£20

   A   10.0%.

   B   13.3%.

   C   16.7%.

22 Holding all other factors constant, which of the following situations will *most likely* lead to an increase in a company's return on equity?

   A   The market price of the company's shares increases.

   B   Net income increases at a slower rate than shareholders' equity.

   C   The company issues debt to repurchase outstanding shares of equity.

23 Which of the following measures is the *most difficult* to estimate?

   A   The cost of debt.

   B   The cost of equity.

   C   Investors' required rate of return on debt.

24 A company's cost of equity is often used as a proxy for investors':

    A   average required rate of return.

    B   minimum required rate of return.

    C   maximum required rate of return.

SOLUTIONS

1 C is correct. The company is not obligated to make dividend payments. It is at the discretion of the company whether or not it chooses to pay dividends.

2 B is correct. Statutory voting is the type of equity voting right that grants one vote per share owned.

3 A is correct. Preference shares do not have to be either callable or putable.

4 C is correct. Participating preference shares entitle shareholders to receive an additional dividend if the company's profits exceed a pre-determined level.

5 B is correct. Private equity securities do not have market-determined quoted prices.

6 C is correct. Venture capital investments can be used to provide mezzanine financing to companies in their early stage of development.

7 B is correct. Regulatory and investor relations costs are lower for private equity firms than for public firms. There are no stock exchange, regulatory, or shareholder involvements with private equity, whereas for public firms these costs can be high.

8 C is correct. The trends in emerging markets have not led to the stability of foreign exchange markets.

9 A is correct. In an unsponsored DR, the depository bank owns the voting rights to the shares. The bank purchases the shares, places them into a trust, and then sells shares in the trust—not the underlying shares—in other markets.

10 A is correct. The listing fees on Level III sponsored ADRs are high.

11 C is correct. An ETF is used to gain exposure to a basket of securities (equity, fixed income, commodity futures, etc.).

12 A is correct. The formula states $R_t = (P_t - P_{t-1} + D_t)/P_t$. Therefore, total return = (42 − 50 + 2)/50 = −12.0%.

13 A is correct. The depreciated value of the euro will create an additional loss in the form of currency return that is lower than the ETF's return.

14 C is correct. Some equity securities do not pay dividends, and therefore the standard deviation of dividends cannot be used to measure the risk of all equity securities.

15 A is correct. Putable shares, whether common or preference, give the investor the option to sell the shares back to the issuer at a pre-determined price. This pre-determined price creates a floor for the share's price that reduces the uncertainty of future cash flows for the investor (i.e., lowers risk relative to the other two types of shares listed).

16 C is correct. Issuing shares in the primary (and secondary) market *reduces* a company's return on equity because it increases the total amount of equity capital invested in the company (i.e., the denominator in the ROE formula).

17 C is correct. Capital is raised to ensure the company's existence only when it is required. It is not a typical goal of raising capital.

18 A is correct. A company's book value increases when a company retains its net income.

19 A is correct. The book value of the company is equal to total assets minus total liabilities, which is €12,000,000 − €7,500,000 = €4,500,000.

20 A is correct. A company's market value is affected by management's decisions. Management's decisions can directly affect the company's *book* value, which can then affect its market value.

21 B is correct. A company's ROE is calculated as (NI_t/BVE_{t-1}). For 2009, the BVE_{t-1} is equal to the beginning total assets minus the beginning total liabilities, which equals £50,000,000 – £35,000,000 = £15,000,000. Therefore, ROE_{2009} = £2,000,000/£15,000,000 = 13.3%.

22 C is correct. A company's ROE will increase if it issues debt to repurchase outstanding shares of equity.

23 B is correct. The cost of equity is not easily determined. It is dependent on investors' required rate of return on equity, which reflects the different risk levels of investors and their expectations about the company's future cash flows.

24 B is correct. Companies try to raise funds at the lowest possible cost. Therefore, cost of equity is used as a proxy for the minimum required rate of return.

Introduction to Industry and Company Analysis

by Patrick W. Dorsey, CFA, Anthony M. Fiore, CFA, and Ian Rossa O'Reilly, CFA

LEARNING OUTCOMES

Mastery	*The candidate should be able to:*
☐	**a.** explain uses of industry analysis and the relation of industry analysis to company analysis;
☐	**b.** compare methods by which companies can be grouped, current industry classification systems, and classify a company, given a description of its activities and the classification system;
☐	**c.** explain the factors that affect the sensitivity of a company to the business cycle and the uses and limitations of industry and company descriptors such as "growth," "defensive," and "cyclical";
☐	**d.** explain how "peer group" as used in equity valuation relates to a company's industry classification;
☐	**e.** describe the elements that need to be covered in a thorough industry analysis;
☐	**f.** describe the principles of strategic analysis of an industry;
☐	**g.** explain the effects of barriers to entry, industry concentration, industry capacity, and market share stability on pricing power and return on capital;
☐	**h.** describe product and industry life cycle models, classify an industry as to life cycle phase (embryonic, growth, shakeout, maturity, and decline), and describe limitations of the life-cycle concept in forecasting industry performance;
☐	**i.** compare characteristics of representative industries from the various economic sectors;
☐	**j.** describe demographic, governmental, social, and technological influences on industry growth, profitability, and risk;
☐	**k.** describe the elements that should be covered in a thorough company analysis.

1   INTRODUCTION

Industry analysis is the analysis of a specific branch of manufacturing, service, or trade. Understanding the industry in which a company operates provides an essential framework for the analysis of the individual company—that is, **company analysis**. Equity analysis and credit analysis are often conducted by analysts who concentrate on one or several industries, which results in synergies and efficiencies in gathering and interpreting information.

Among the questions we address in this reading are the following:

- What are the similarities and differences among industry classification systems?
- How does an analyst go about choosing a peer group of companies?
- What are the key factors to consider when analyzing an industry?
- What advantages are enjoyed by companies in strategically well-positioned industries?

After discussing the uses of industry analysis in the next section, Sections 3 and 4 discuss, respectively, approaches to identifying similar companies and industry classification systems. Section 5 covers the description and analysis of industries. Also, Section 5, which includes an introduction to competitive analysis, provides a background to Section 6, which introduces company analysis. The reading ends with a summary, and practice problems follow the text.

2   USES OF INDUSTRY ANALYSIS

Industry analysis is useful in a number of investment applications that make use of fundamental analysis. Its uses include the following:

- *Understanding a company's business and business environment.* Industry analysis is often a critical early step in stock selection and valuation because it provides insights into the issuer's growth opportunities, competitive dynamics, and business risks. For a credit analyst, industry analysis provides insights into the appropriateness of a company's use of debt financing and into its ability to meet its promised payments during economic contractions.

- *Identifying active equity investment opportunities.* Investors taking a top-down investing approach use industry analysis to identify industries with positive, neutral, or negative outlooks for profitability and growth. Generally, investors will then overweight, market weight, or underweight those industries (as appropriate to their outlooks) relative to the investor's benchmark if the investor judges that the industry's perceived prospects are not fully incorporated in market prices. Apart from security selection, some investors attempt to outperform their benchmarks by industry or sector rotation—that is, timing investments in industries in relation to an analysis of industry fundamentals and/or business-cycle conditions (technical analysis may also play a role in such strategies). Several studies have underscored the importance of industry analysis by suggesting that the industry factor in stock returns is at least as important as the country factor (e.g., Cavaglia, Diermeier, Moroz, and De Zordo, 2004). In addition, industry membership has been found to account for about 20 percent of the variability of a company's profitability in the United States (McGahan and Porter 1995).

- *Portfolio performance attribution.* Performance attribution, which addresses the sources of a portfolio's returns, usually in relation to the portfolio's benchmark, includes industry or sector selection. Industry classification schemes play a role in such performance attribution.

Later in this reading we explore the considerations involved in understanding a company's business and business environment. The next section addresses how companies may be grouped into industries.

APPROACHES TO IDENTIFYING SIMILAR COMPANIES

3

Industry classification attempts to place companies into groups on the basis of commonalities. In the following sections, we discuss the three major approaches to industry classification:

- products and/or services supplied;
- business-cycle sensitivities; and
- statistical similarities.

3.1 Products and/or Services Supplied

Modern classification schemes are most commonly based on grouping companies by similar products and/or services. According to this perspective, an **industry** is defined as a group of companies offering similar products and/or services. For example, major companies in the global heavy truck industry include Volvo, Daimler AG, Paccar, and Navistar, all of which make large commercial vehicles for the on-highway truck market. Similarly, some of the large players in the global automobile industry are Toyota, General Motors, Volkswagen, Ford, Honda, Nissan, PSA Peugeot Citroën, and Hyundai, all of which produce light vehicles that are close substitutes for one another.

Industry classification schemes typically provide multiple levels of aggregation. The term **sector** is often used to refer to a group of related industries. The health care sector, for example, consists of a number of related industries, including the pharmaceutical, biotechnology, medical device, medical supply, hospital, and managed care industries.

These classification schemes typically place a company in an industry on the basis of a determination of its principal business activity. A company's **principal business activity** is the source from which the company derives a majority of its revenues and/or earnings. For example, companies that derive a majority of their revenues from the sale of pharmaceuticals include Novartis AG, Pfizer Inc., Roche Holding AG, GlaxoSmithKline, and Sanofi-aventis S.A., all of which could be grouped together as part of the global pharmaceutical industry. Companies that engage in more than one significant business activity usually report the revenues (and, in many cases, operating profits) of the different business segments in their financial statements.[1]

Examples of classification systems based on products and/or services include the commercial classification systems that will be discussed later, namely, the Global Industry Classification Standard (GICS), Russell Global Sectors (RGS), and Industry

---

[1] For more information, see International Financial Reporting Standard (IFRS) 8: Operating Segments. In IFRS 8, *business segments* are called *operating segments*.

Classification Benchmark. In addition to grouping companies by product and/or service, some of the major classification systems, including GICS and RGS, group consumer-related companies into cyclical and non-cyclical categories depending on the company's sensitivity to the business cycle. The next section addresses how companies can be categorized on the basis of economic sensitivity.

3.2 Business-Cycle Sensitivities

Companies are sometimes grouped on the basis of their relative sensitivity to the business cycle. This method often results in two broad groupings of companies—cyclical and non-cyclical.

A **cyclical** company is one whose profits are strongly correlated with the strength of the overall economy. Such companies experience wider-than-average fluctuations in demand—high demand during periods of economic expansion and low demand during periods of economic contraction—and/or are subject to greater-than-average profit variability related to high operating leverage (i.e., high fixed costs). Concerning demand, cyclical products and services are often relatively expensive and/or represent purchases that can be delayed if necessary (e.g., because of declining disposable income). Examples of cyclical industries are autos, housing, basic materials, industrials, and technology. A **non-cyclical** company is one whose performance is largely independent of the business cycle. Non-cyclical companies produce goods or services for which demand remains relatively stable throughout the business cycle. Examples of non-cyclical industries are food and beverage, household and personal care products, health care, and utilities.

Although the classification systems we will discuss do not label their categories as cyclical or non-cyclical, certain sectors tend to experience greater economic sensitivity than others. Sectors that tend to exhibit a relatively high degree of economic sensitivity include consumer discretionary, energy, financials, industrials, technology, and materials. In contrast, sectors that exhibit relatively less economic sensitivity include consumer staples, health care, telecommunications, and utilities.

EXAMPLE 1

Descriptions Related to the Cyclical/Noncyclical Distinction

Analysts commonly encounter a number of labels related to the cyclical/non-cyclical distinction. For example, non-cyclical industries have sometimes been sorted into defensive (or stable) versus growth. Defensive industries and companies are those whose revenues and profits are least affected by fluctuations in overall economic activity. These industries/companies tend to produce staple consumer goods (e.g., bread), to provide basic services (grocery stores, drug stores, fast food outlets), or to have their rates and revenues determined by contracts or government regulation (e.g., cost-of-service, rate-of-return regulated public utilities). Growth industries would include industries with specific demand dynamics that are so strong that they override the significance of broad economic or other external factors and generate growth regardless of overall economic conditions, although their rates of growth may slow during an economic downturn.[2]

---

2 Sometimes the "growth" label is attached to countries or regions in which economic growth is so strong that the fluctuations in local economic activity do not produce an actual decline in economic output, merely variation from high to low rates of real growth (e.g., China, India).

The usefulness of industry and company labels such as cyclical, growth, and defensive is limited. Cyclical industries as well as growth industries often have growth companies within them. A cyclical industry itself, although exposed to the effects of fluctuations in overall economic activity, may grow at an above-average rate for periods spanning multiple business cycles.[3] Furthermore, when fluctuations in economic activity are large, as in the deep recession of 2008–2009, few companies escape the effects of the cyclical weakness in overall economic activity.

The defensive label is also problematic. Industries may include both companies that are growth and companies that are defensive in character, making the choice between a "growth" and a "defensive" label difficult. Moreover, "defensive" cannot be understood as necessarily being descriptive of investment characteristics. Food supermarkets, for example, would typically be described as defensive but can be subject to profit-damaging price wars. So-called defensive industries/companies may sometimes face industry dynamics that make them far from defensive in the sense of preserving shareholders' capital.

One limitation of the cyclical/non-cyclical classification is that business-cycle sensitivity is a continuous spectrum rather than an "either/or" issue, so placement of companies in one of the two major groups is somewhat arbitrary. The impact of severe recessions usually reaches all parts of the economy, so non-cyclical is better understood as a relative term.

Another limitation of a business-cycle classification for global investing is that different countries and regions of the world frequently progress through the various stages of the business cycle at different times. While one region of the world may be experiencing economic expansion, other regions or countries may be in recession, which complicates the application of a business-cycle approach to industry analysis. For example, a jewelry retailer (i.e., a cyclical company) that is selling domestically into a weak economy will exhibit markedly different fundamental performance relative to a jewelry company operating in an environment where demand is robust. Comparing these two companies—that is, similar companies that are currently exposed to different demand environments—could suggest investment opportunities. Combining fundamental data from such companies, however, to establish industry benchmark values would be misleading.

3.3 Statistical Similarities

Statistical approaches to grouping companies are typically based on the correlations of past securities' returns. For example, using the technique known as cluster analysis, companies are separated (on the basis of historical correlations of stock returns) into groups *in which* correlations are relatively high but *between which* correlations are relatively low. This method of aggregation often results in non-intuitive groups of companies, and the composition of the groups may vary significantly by time period and region of the world. Moreover, statistical approaches rely on historical data, but analysts have no guarantee that past correlation values will continue in the future. In addition, such approaches carry the inherent dangers of all statistical methods, namely, 1) falsely indicating a relationship that arose because of chance or 2) falsely excluding a relationship that actually is significant.

---

3 The label **growth cyclical** is sometimes used to describe companies that are growing rapidly on a long-term basis but that still experience above-average fluctuation in their revenues and profits over the course of a business cycle.

4   INDUSTRY CLASSIFICATION SYSTEMS

A well-designed classification system often serves as a useful starting point for industry analysis. It allows analysts to compare industry trends and relative valuations among companies in a group. Classification systems that take a global perspective enable portfolio managers and research analysts to make global comparisons of companies in the same industry. For example, given the global nature of the automobile industry, a thorough analysis of the industry would include auto companies from many different countries and regions of the world.

4.1 Commercial Industry Classification Systems

Major index providers, including Standard & Poor's, MSCI Barra, Russell Investments, Dow Jones, and FTSE, classify companies in their equity indices into industry groupings. Most classification schemes used by these index providers contain multiple levels of classification that start at the broadest level with a general sector grouping, then, in several further steps, subdivide or disaggregate the sectors into more "granular" (i.e., more narrowly defined) sub-industry groups.

4.1.1 *Global Industry Classification Standard*

GICS was jointly developed by Standard & Poor's and MSCI Barra, two of the largest providers of global equity indices, in 1999. As the name implies, GICS was designed to facilitate global comparisons of industries, and it classifies companies in both developed and developing economies. Each company is assigned to a sub-industry according to its principal business activity. Each sub-industry belongs to a particular industry; each industry belongs to an industry group; and each group belongs to a sector. In June 2009, the GICS classification structure comprised four levels of detail consisting of 154 sub-industries, 68 industries, 24 industry groups, and 10 sectors. The composition of GICS has historically been adjusted over time to reflect changes in the global equity markets.

4.1.2 *Russell Global Sectors*

The RGS classification system uses a three-tier structure to classify companies globally on the basis of the products or services a company produces. In June 2009, the RGS classification system consisted of 9 sectors, 32 subsectors, and 141 industries. Besides the number of tiers, another difference between the RGS and GICS classification systems is that the RGS system contains nine sectors, whereas GICS consists of ten. For example, the RGS system does not provide a separate sector for telecommunication service companies. Many companies that GICS classifies as "Telecommunication Services," including China Mobile Ltd., AT&T, and Telefonica, are assigned by RGS to its more broadly defined "Utilities" sector.

4.1.3 *Industry Classification Benchmark*

The Industry Classification Benchmark (ICB), which was jointly developed by Dow Jones and FTSE, uses a four-tier structure to categorize companies globally on the basis of the source from which a company derives the majority of its revenue. In June 2009, the ICB classification system consisted of 10 industries, 19 supersectors, 41 sectors, and 114 subsectors. Although the ICB is similar to GICS in the number of tiers and the method by which companies are assigned to particular groups, the two systems use significantly different nomenclature. For example, whereas GICS uses the term "sector" to describe its broadest grouping of companies, ICB uses the term "industry." Another difference between the two systems is that ICB distinguishes between consumer goods and consumer services companies, whereas both GICS and the RGS systems group consumer products companies and consumer services companies together into sectors on the basis of economic sensitivity. These stylistic distinctions tend to be less obvious at the more granular levels of the different hierarchies.

Despite these subtle differences, the three commercial classification systems use common methodologies for assigning companies to groups. Also, the broadest level of grouping for all three systems is quite similar. Specifically, GICS, the RGS, and the ICB each identify 9 or 10 broad groupings below which all other categories reside. Next, we describe sectors that are fairly representative of how the broadest level of industry classification is viewed by GICS, RGS, and ICB.

4.1.4 Description of Representative Sectors

Basic Materials and Processing: companies engaged in the production of building materials, chemicals, paper and forest products, containers and packaging, and metal, mineral, and mining companies.

Consumer Discretionary: companies that derive a majority of revenue from the sale of consumer-related products or services for which demand tends to exhibit a relatively high degree of economic sensitivity. Examples of business activities that frequently fall into this category are automotive, apparel, hotel, and restaurant businesses.

Consumer Staples: consumer-related companies whose business tends to exhibit less economic sensitivity than other companies; for example, manufacturers of food, beverage, tobacco, and personal care products.

Energy: companies whose primary line of business involves the exploration, production, or refining of natural resources used to produce energy; companies that derive a majority of revenue from the sale of equipment or through the provision of services to energy companies would also fall into this category.

Financial Services: companies whose primary line of business involves banking, finance, insurance, real estate, asset management, and/or brokerage services.

Health Care: manufacturers of pharmaceutical and biotech products, medical devices, health care equipment, and medical supplies and providers of health care services.

Industrial/Producer Durables: manufacturers of capital goods and providers of commercial services; for example, business activities would include heavy machinery and equipment manufacture, aerospace and defense, transportation services, and commercial services and supplies.

Technology: companies involved in the manufacture or sale of computers, software, semiconductors, and communications equipment; other business activities that frequently fall into this category are electronic entertainment, internet services, and technology consulting and services.

Telecommunications: companies that provide fixed-line and wireless communication services; some vendors prefer to combine telecommunication and utility companies together into a single "utilities" category.

Utilities: electric, gas, and water utilities; telecommunication companies are sometimes included in this category.

To classify a company accurately in a particular classification scheme requires definitions of the classification categories, a statement about the criteria used in classification, and detailed information about the subject company. Example 2 introduces an exercise in such classification. In addressing the question, the reader can make use of the widely applicable sector descriptions just given and familiarity with available business products and services.

EXAMPLE 2

Classifying Companies into Industries

The text defines 10 representative sectors, repeated here in Exhibit 1. Suppose the classification system is based on the criterion of a company's principal business activity as judged primarily by source of revenue.

Exhibit 1   Ten Sectors
Sector
Basic Materials and Processing
Consumer Discretionary
Consumer Staples
Energy
Financial Services
Health Care
Industrial/Producer Durables
Technology
Telecommunications
Utilities

Based on the information given, determine an appropriate industry membership for each of the following hypothetical companies:

1   A natural gas transporter and marketer

2   A manufacturer of heavy construction equipment

3   A provider of regional telephone services

4   A semiconductor company

5   A manufacturer of medical devices

6   A chain of supermarkets

7   A manufacturer of chemicals and plastics

8   A manufacturer of automobiles

9   An investment management company

10   A manufacturer of luxury leather goods

11   A regulated supplier of electricity

12   A provider of wireless broadband services

13   A manufacturer of soaps and detergents

14   A software development company

15   An insurer

16   A regulated provider of water/wastewater services

17   A petroleum (oil) service company

18 A manufacturer of pharmaceuticals

19 A provider of rail transportation services

20 A metals mining company

Solution:

Sector	Company Number
Basic Materials and Processing	7, 20
Consumer Discretionary	8, 10
Consumer Staples	6, 13
Energy	1, 17
Financial Services	9, 15
Health Care	5, 18
Industrial/Producer Durables	2, 19
Technology	4, 14
Telecommunications	3, 12
Utilities	11, 16

Example 3 reviews some major concepts in industry classification.

EXAMPLE 3

Industry Classification Schemes

1 The GICS classification system classifies companies on the basis of a company's primary business activity as measured primarily by:

A assets.

B income.

C revenue.

2 Which of the following is *least likely* to be accurately described as a cyclical company? A(n):

A automobile manufacturer.

B producer of breakfast cereals.

C apparel company producing the newest trendy clothes for teenage girls.

3 Which of the following is the *most accurate* statement? A statistical approach to grouping companies into industries:

A is based on historical correlations of the securities' returns.

B frequently produces industry groups whose composition is similar worldwide.

C emphasizes the descriptive statistics of industries consisting of companies producing similar products and/or services.

Solution to 1:

C is correct.

> **Solution to 2:**
>
> B is correct. A producer of staple foods such as cereals is a classic example of a non-cyclical company. Demand for automobiles is cyclical—that is, relatively high during economic expansions and relatively low during economic contractions. Also, demand for teenage fashions is likely to be more sensitive to the business cycle than demand for standard food items such as breakfast cereals. When budgets have been reduced, families may try to avoid expensive clothing or extend the life of existing wardrobes.
>
> **Solution to 3:**
>
> A is correct.

4.2 Governmental Industry Classification Systems

A number of classification systems in use by various governmental agencies today organize statistical data according to type of industrial or economic activity. A common goal of each government classification system is to facilitate the comparison of data—both over time and among countries that use the same system. Continuity of the data is critical to the measurement and evaluation of economic performance over time.

4.2.1 *International Standard Industrial Classification of All Economic Activities*

The International Standard Industrial Classification of All Economic Activities (ISIC) was adopted by the United Nations in 1948 to address the need for international comparability of economic statistics. ISIC classifies entities into various categories on the basis of the principal type of economic activity the entity performs. ISIC is organized into 11 categories, 21 sections, 88 divisions, 233 groups, and more than 400 classes. According to the United Nations, a majority of the countries around the world have either used ISIC as their national activity classification system or have developed national classifications derived from ISIC. Some of the organizations currently using the ISIC are the UN and its specialized agencies, the International Monetary Fund, the World Bank, and other international bodies.

4.2.2 *Statistical Classification of Economic Activities in the European Community*

Often regarded as the European version of ISIC, Statistical Classification of Economic Activities in the European Community (NACE) is the classification of economic activities that correspond to ISIC at the European level. Similar to ISIC, NACE classification is organized according to economic activity. NACE is composed of four levels—namely, sections (identified by alphabetical letters A through U), divisions (identified by two-digit numerical codes 01 through 99), groups (identified by three-digit numerical codes 01.1 through 99.0), and classes (identified by four-digit numerical codes 01.11 through 99.00).

4.2.3 *Australian and New Zealand Standard Industrial Classification*

The Australian and New Zealand Standard Industrial Classification (ANZSIC) was jointly developed by the Australian Bureau of Statistics and Statistics New Zealand in 1993 to facilitate the comparison of industry statistics of the two countries and comparisons with the rest of the world. International comparability was achieved by aligning ANZSIC with the international standards used by ISIC. ANZSIC has a structure comprising five levels—namely, divisions (the broadest level), subdivisions, groups, classes, and at the most granular level, subclasses (New Zealand only).

4.2.4 *North American Industry Classification System*

Jointly developed by the United States, Canada, and Mexico, the North American Industry Classification System (NAICS) replaced the Standard Industrial Classification (SIC) system in 1997. NAICS distinguishes between establishments and enterprises. NAICS classifies establishments into industries according to the primary business activity of the establishment. In the NAICS system, an *establishment* is defined as "a single physical location where business is conducted or where services or industrial operations are performed" (e.g., factory, store, hotel, movie theater, farm, office). An *enterprise* may consist of more than one location performing the same or different types of economic activities. Each establishment of that enterprise is assigned a NAICS code on the basis of its own primary business activity.[4]

NAICS uses a two-digit through six-digit code to structure its categories into five levels of detail. The greater the number of digits in the code, the more narrowly defined the category. The five levels of categories, from broadest to narrowest, are sector (signified by the first two digits of the code), subsector (third digit of the code), industry group (fourth digit), NAICS industry (fifth digit), and national industry (sixth digit). The five-digit code is the level of greatest amount of comparability among countries; a six-digit code provides for more country-specific detail.

Although differences exist, the structures of ISIC, NACE, ANZSIC, and NAICS are similar enough that many of the categories from each of the different classification systems are compatible with one another. The US Census Bureau has published tables showing how the various categories of the classification systems relate to one another.[5]

4.3 Strengths and Weaknesses of Current Systems

Unlike commercial classification systems, most government systems do not disclose information about a specific business or company, so an analyst cannot know all of the constituents of a particular category. For example, in the United States, federal law prohibits the Census Bureau from disclosing individual company activities, so, their NAICS and SIC codes are unknown.

Most government and commercial classification systems are reviewed and, if necessary, updated from time to time. Generally, commercial classification systems are adjusted more frequently than government classification systems, which may be updated only every five years or so. NAICS, for example, is reviewed for potential revisions every five years.

Government classification systems generally do not distinguish between small and large businesses, between for-profit and not-for-profit organizations, or between public and private companies. Many commercial classification systems have the ability to distinguish between large and small companies by virtue of association with a particular equity index, and these systems include only for-profit and publicly traded organizations.

Another limitation of current systems is that the narrowest classification unit assigned to a company generally cannot be assumed to be its peer group for the purposes of detailed fundamental comparisons or valuation. A **peer group** is a group of companies engaged in similar business activities whose economics and valuation are influenced by closely related factors. Comparisons of a company in relation to a well-defined peer group can provide valuable insights into the company's performance and its relative valuation.

---

4 For more information, see www.census.gov/eos/www/naics/faqs/faqs.html#q2.

5 For more information, see www.census.gov/eos/www/naics/concordances/concordances.html.

4.4 Constructing a Peer Group

The construction of a peer group is a subjective process; the result often differs significantly from even the most narrowly defined categories given by the commercial classification systems. However, commercial classification systems do provide a starting point for the construction of a relevant peer group because, by using such systems, an analyst can quickly discover the public companies operating in the chosen industry.

In fact, one approach to constructing a peer group is to start by identifying other companies operating in the same industry. Analysts who subscribe to one or more of the commercial classification systems that were discussed in Section 4.1 can quickly generate a list of other companies in the industry in which the company operates according to that particular service provider's definition of the industry. An analyst can then investigate the business activities of these companies and make adjustments as necessary to ensure that the businesses truly are comparable. The following lists of suggested steps and questions are given as practical aids to analysts in identifying peer companies.

Steps in constructing a preliminary list of peer companies

- Examine commercial classification systems, if available to the analyst. These systems often provide a useful starting point for identifying companies operating in the same industry.
- Review the subject company's annual report for a discussion of the competitive environment. Companies frequently cite specific competitors.
- Review competitors' annual reports to identify other potential comparable companies.
- Review industry trade publications to identify comparable companies.
- Confirm that each comparable company derives a significant portion of its revenue and operating profit from a business activity similar to the primary business of the subject company.

Questions that may improve the list of peer companies

- What proportion of revenue and operating profit is derived from business activities similar to those of the subject company? In general, a higher percentage results in a more meaningful comparison.
- Does a potential peer company face a demand environment similar to that of the subject company? For example, a comparison of growth rates, margins, and valuations may be of limited value when comparing companies that are exposed to different stages of the business cycle. (As mentioned, such differences may be the result of conducting business in geographically different markets.)
- Does a potential company have a finance subsidiary? Some companies operate a finance division to facilitate the sale of their products (e.g., Caterpillar Inc. and John Deere). To make a meaningful comparison of companies, the analyst should make adjustments to the financial statements to lessen the impact that the finance subsidiaries have on the various financial metrics being compared.

Example 4 illustrates the process of identifying a peer group of companies and shows some of the practical hurdles to determining a peer group.

EXAMPLE 4

An Analyst Researches the Peer Group of Brink's Home Security

Suppose that an analyst needs to identify the peer group of companies for Brink's Home Security for use in the valuation section of a company report. Brink's is a provider of electronic security and alarm monitoring services primarily to residential customers in North America. The analyst starts by looking at Brink's industry classification according to GICS. As previously discussed, the most narrowly defined category that GICS uses is the sub-industry level, and in June 2009, Brink's was in the GICS sub-industry called Specialized Consumer Services, together with the companies listed here:

GICS Sector: Consumer Discretionary

 GICS Industry Group: Consumer Services

  GICS Industry: Diversified Consumer Services

   GICS Sub-Industry: Specialized Consumer Services

    Brink's Home Security Holdings, Inc.

    Coinstar, Inc.

    H&R Block, Inc.

    Hillenbrand Inc.

    Mathews International Corporation

    Pre-Paid Legal Services Inc.

    Regis Corporation

    Service Corporation International

    Sotheby's

After looking over the list of companies, the analyst quickly realizes that some adjustments need to be made to the list to end up with a peer group of companies that are comparable to Brink's. For example, Brink's has little in common with the hair care salon services of Regis or, for that matter, with the funeral service operations of Hillenbrand, Mathews, or Service Corporation. In fact, after careful inspection, the analyst concludes that none of the other companies included in the GICS sub-industry are particularly good "comparables" for Brink's.

Next, the analyst reviews the latest annual report for Brink's to find management statements concerning its competitors. On p. 6 of Brink's 2008 10-K, in the section titled "Industry Trends and Competition," is a list of other companies with comparable business activities: "We believe our primary competitors with national scope include: ADT Security Services, Inc., (part of Tyco International, Ltd.), Protection One, Inc., Monitronics International, Inc. and Stanley Security Solutions, (part of The Stanley Works)." The analyst notes that Protection One on this list is another publicly held security services company and a likely candidate for inclusion in the peer group for Brink's. Monitronics International is privately held, so the analyst excludes it from the peer group; up-to-date, detailed fundamental data are not available for it.

The analyst discovers that ADT represents a significant portion of Tyco International's sales and profits (more than 40 percent of 2008 sales and profits); therefore, an argument could be made to include Tyco International in the peer group. The analyst might also consider including Stanley Works in the peer group because that company derived roughly a third of its revenue and close to half of its operating profit from its security division in 2008. Just as the analyst reviewed the latest annual report for Brink's to identify additional potential comparables, the analyst should also scan the annual reports of the other companies listed to see if other comparables exist. In checking these three companies' annual reports, the analyst finds that Protection One is the only one that cites specific competitors; Tyco and Stanley Works discuss competition only broadly.

After scanning all of the annual reports, the analyst finds no additional comparables.

The analyst decides that Brink's peer group consists of ADT Security Services, Protection One, and Stanley Security Solutions but also decides to give extra weight to the comparison with Protection One in valuation because the comparison with Protection One has the fewest complicating factors.

In connection with this discussion, note that International Financial Reporting Standards and US GAAP require companies to disclose financial information about their operating segments (subject to certain qualifications). Such disclosures provide analysts with operational and financial information that can be helpful in peer-group determination.

Although companies with limited lines of business may neatly be categorized into a single peer group, companies with multiple divisions may be included in more than one category. For example, Belgium-based Anheuser-Busch InBev primarily makes and sells various brands of beer. It can easily be grouped together with other beverage companies (the theme park business constitutes a relatively immaterial part of total revenue). However, US-based Hewlett-Packard Company (HP), a global provider of technology and software solutions, might reasonably be included in more than one category. Investors interested in the personal computer (PC) industry, for example, would probably include HP in their peer group, but investors constructing a peer group of providers of information technology services would probably include HP in that group also.

In summary, analysts must distinguish between a company's industry—as defined by one or more of the various classification systems—and its peer group. A company's peer group should consist of companies with similar business activities whose economic activity depends on similar drivers of demand and similar factors related to cost structure and access to financial capital. In practice, these necessities frequently result in a smaller group (even a different group) of companies than the most narrowly defined categories used by the common commercial classification systems. Example 5 illustrates various aspects of developing and using peer groups.

EXAMPLE 5

The Semiconductor Industry: Business-Cycle Sensitivity and Peer-Group Determination

The GICS semiconductor and semiconductor equipment industry (453010) has two sub-industries—the semiconductor equipment sub-industry (45301010) and the semiconductors sub-industry (45301020). Members of the semiconductor equipment sub-industry include equipment suppliers such as Lam Research Corporation and ASML Holdings NV; the semiconductors sub-industry includes integrated circuit manufacturers Intel Corporation and Taiwan Semiconductor Manufacturing Company Ltd.

Lam Research is a leading supplier of wafer fabrication equipment and services to the world's semiconductor industry. Lam also offers wafer-cleaning equipment that is used after many of the individual steps required to manufacture a finished wafer. Often, the technical advances that Lam introduces in its wafer-etching and wafer-cleaning products are also available as upgrades to its installed base. This benefit provides customers with a cost-effective way to extend the performance and capabilities of their existing wafer fabrication lines.

ASML describes itself as the world's leading provider of lithography systems (etching and printing on wafers) for the semiconductor industry. ASML manufactures complex machines that are critical to the production of integrated circuits or microchips. ASML designs, develops, integrates, markets, and services these advanced systems, which help chip makers reduce the size and increase the functionality of microchips and consumer electronic equipment. The machines are costly and thus represent a substantial capital investment for a purchaser.

Based on revenue, Intel is the world's largest semiconductor chip maker and has the dominant share of microprocessors for the personal computer market. Intel has made significant investments in research and development (R&D) to introduce and produce new chips for new applications.

Established in 1987, Taiwan Semiconductor Manufacturing (TSM) is the world's largest dedicated semiconductor foundry (a semiconductor fabrication plant that executes the designs of other companies). TSM describes itself as offering cutting-edge process technologies, pioneering design services, manufacturing efficiency, and product quality. The company's revenues represent about 50 percent of the dedicated foundry segment in the semiconductor industry.

The questions that follow take the perspective of early 2009, when many economies around the world were in a recession. Based only on the information given, answer the following questions:

1   If the weak economy of early 2009 were to recover within the next 12–18 months, which of the two sub-industries of the semiconductor and semiconductor equipment industry would most likely be the first to experience a positive improvement in business?

2   Explain whether Intel and TSM should be considered members of the same peer group.

3   Explain whether Lam Research and ASML should be considered members of the same peer group.

Solution to 1:

In the most likely scenario, improvement in the business of the equipment makers (Lam and ASML) would lag that of semiconductor companies (Intel and TSM). Because of the weak economy of early 2009, excess manufacturing capacity should be available to meet increased demand for integrated circuits in the near term without additional equipment, which is a major capital investment. When semiconductor manufacturers believe the longer-term outlook has improved, they should begin to place orders for additional equipment.

Solution to 2:

Intel and TSM are not likely to be considered comparable members of the same peer group because they have different sets of customers and different business models. Intel designs and produces its own proprietary semiconductors for direct sale to customers, such as personal computer makers. TSM provides design and production services to a diverse group of integrated circuit suppliers that generally do not have their own in-house manufacturing capabilities. In mid-2009, Standard & Poor's did not group Intel and TSM in the same peer group; Intel was in the Semiconductors, Logic, Larger Companies group and TSM was in the Semiconductors, Foundry Services group.

Solution to 3:

Both Lam Research and ASML are leading companies that design and manufacture equipment to produce semiconductor chips. The companies are comparable because they both depend on the same economic factors that drive demand for their products. Their major customers are the semiconductor chip companies. In mid-2009, Standard & Poor's grouped both companies in the same peer group—Semiconductor Equipment, Larger Front End.

The next section addresses fundamental skills in describing and analyzing an industry.

5 DESCRIBING AND ANALYZING AN INDUSTRY

In their work, analysts study statistical relationships between industry trends and a range of economic and business variables. Analysts use economic, industry, and business publications and internet resources as sources of information. They also seek information from industry associations, from the individual subject companies they are analyzing, and from these companies' competitors, suppliers, and customers. An analyst with a superior knowledge about an industry's characteristics, conditions, and trends has a competitive edge in evaluating the investment merits of the companies in the industry.

Analysts attempt to develop practical, reliable industry forecasts by using various approaches to forecasting. They often estimate a range of projections for a variable reflecting various possible scenarios. Analysts may seek to compare their projections with the projections of other analysts, partly to study differences in methodology and conclusions but also to identify differences between their forecasts and consensus forecasts. These latter differences are extremely important for uncovering investment opportunities because, to be the basis for superior investment performance, the forecast for a value-relevant variable must be both correct and sufficiently different from the consensus reflected in the price of publicly traded securities. Note that, although some information on analysts' revenue projections, EPS estimates, and ratings are accessible in some markets, analysts may have limited access to details about other analysts' work and assumptions because such details are kept confidential for competitive reasons.

Investment managers and analysts also examine industry performance 1) in relation to other industries to identify industries with superior/inferior returns and 2) over time to determine the degree of consistency, stability, and risk in the returns in the industry over time. The objective of this analysis is to identify industries that offer the highest potential for investment returns on a risk-adjusted basis. The investment time horizon can be either long or short, as is the case for a rotation strategy in which portfolios are rotated into the industry groups that are expected to benefit from the next stage in the business cycle.

Often, analysts examine **strategic groups** (groups sharing distinct business models or catering to specific market segments in an industry) almost as separate industries within industries. Criteria for selecting a strategic group might include the complexity of the product or service, its mode of delivery, and "barriers to entry." For example, charter airlines form a strategic group among "airlines" that is quite distinct from scheduled airlines; full-service hotels form a strategic group that is separate from limited-service or budget hotels; and companies that sell proprietary drugs (which are protected by patents) would be in a separate group from companies that sell generic drugs (which do not have patent protection) partly because the two groups pursue different strategies and use different business models.

Analysts often consider and classify industries according to industry **life-cycle stage**. The analyst determines whether an industry is in the embryonic, growth, shake-out, mature, or declining stage of the industry life cycle. During the stages of the life cycle of a product or industry, its position on the experience curve is often analyzed. The **experience curve** shows direct cost per unit of good or service produced or delivered as a typically declining function of cumulative output. The curve declines 1) because as the utilization of capital equipment increases, fixed costs (administration, overhead, advertising, etc.) are spread over a larger number of units of production, 2) because of improvements in labor efficiency and management of facilities, and 3) because of advances in production methods and product design. Examples exist in virtually all industries, but the experience curve is especially important in industries with high fixed overhead costs and/or repetitive production operations, such as electronics and appliance, automobile, and aircraft manufacturing. The industry life cycle is discussed in depth later in this reading.

Exhibit 2 provides a framework designed to help analysts check that they have considered the range of forces that may affect the evolution of an industry. It shows, at the macro level, macroeconomic, demographic, governmental, social, and technological influences affecting the industry. It then depicts how an industry is affected by the forces driving industry competition (threat of new entrants, substitution threats, customer and supplier bargaining forces), the competitive forces in the industry, life-cycle issues, business-cycle considerations, and position of the industry on the experience curve. Exhibit 2 summarizes and brings together pictorially topics and concepts discussed in this section.

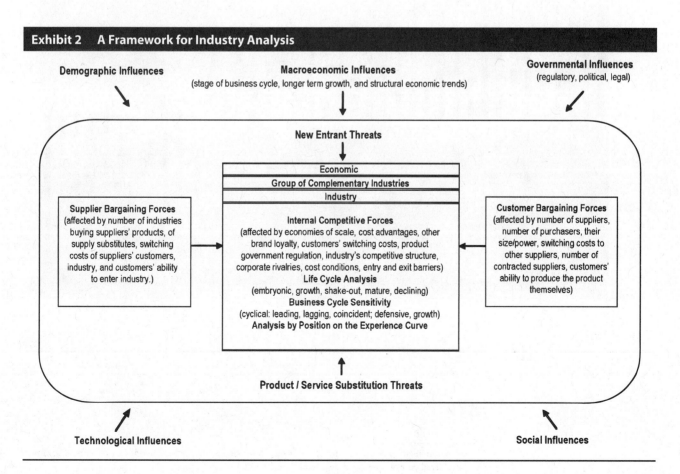

Exhibit 2   A Framework for Industry Analysis

5.1 Principles of Strategic Analysis

When analyzing an industry, the analyst must recognize that the economic fundamentals can vary markedly among industries. Some industries are highly competitive, with most players struggling to earn adequate returns on capital, whereas other industries have attractive characteristics that allow almost all industry participants to generate healthy profits. Exhibit 3 makes this point graphically. It shows the average spread between return on invested capital (ROIC) and the cost of capital for 54 industries from 2006 through 2008.[6] Industries earning positive spreads appear to be earning **economic profits**, in the sense that they are achieving returns on investment above the opportunity cost of funds. This result should create value—that is, should increase the wealth of the investors, who are the providers of capital. In contrast, industries that are realizing negative spreads are destroying value. As can be seen, some industries struggled to generate positive economic returns (i.e., to create value) even during this period of synchronized global growth, while other industries did very well in earning such returns.

Exhibit 3   Some Industries Create Value, Others Destroy It

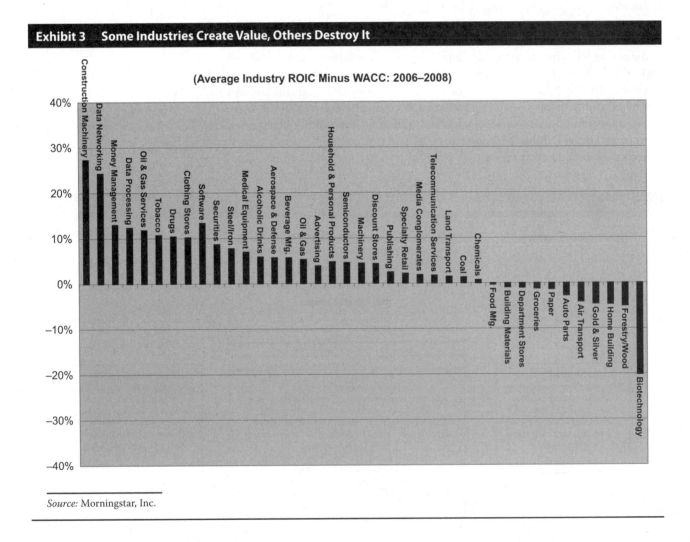

Source: Morningstar, Inc.

---

6 Return on invested capital can be defined as net operating profit after tax divided by the sum of common and preferred equity, long-term debt, and minority interests.

Differing competitive environments are often tied to the structural attributes of an industry, which is one reason industry analysis is a vital complement to company analysis. To thoroughly analyze a company itself, the analyst needs to understand the context in which the company operates. Needless to say, industry analysis must be forward looking. Many of the industries in Exhibit 3 were very different 10 or 15 years ago and would have been placed differently with respect to value creation; many will look very different 10 or 15 years from now. As analysts examine the competitive structure of an industry, they should always be thinking about what attributes could change in the future.

Analysis of the competitive environment with an emphasis on the implications of the environment for corporate strategy is known as **strategic analysis**. Michael Porter's "five forces" framework is the classic starting point for strategic analysis;[7] although it was originally aimed more at internal managers of businesses than at external security analysts, the framework is useful to both.[8]

Porter focused on five determinants of the intensity of competition in an industry:

- The **threat of substitute products**, which can negatively affect demand if customers choose other ways of satisfying their needs. For example, consumers may trade down from premium beers to discount brands during recessions. Low-priced brands may be close substitutes for premium brands, which, when consumer budgets are constrained, reduces the ability of premium brands to maintain or increase prices.

- The **bargaining power of customers**, which can affect the intensity of competition by exerting influence on suppliers regarding prices (and possibly other factors such as product quality). For example, auto parts companies generally sell to a small number of auto manufacturers, which allows those customers, the auto manufacturers, to be tough negotiators when it comes to setting prices.

- The **bargaining power of suppliers**, which may be able to raise prices or restrict the supply of key inputs to a company. For example, workers at a heavily unionized company may have greater bargaining power as suppliers of labor than workers at a comparable non-unionized company. Suppliers of scarce or limited parts or elements often possess significant pricing power.

- The **threat of new entrants** to the industry, which depends on barriers to entry, or how difficult it would be for new competitors to enter the industry. Industries that are easy to enter will generally be more competitive than industries with high barriers to entry.

- The **intensity of rivalry** among incumbent companies (i.e., the current companies in the industry), which is a function of the industry's competitive structure. Industries that are fragmented among many small competitors, have high fixed costs, provide undifferentiated (commodity-like) products, or have high exit barriers usually experience more intense rivalry than industries without these characteristics.

Although all five of these forces merit attention, the fourth and fifth are particularly recommended as a first focus for analysis. The two factors are broadly applicable because all companies have competitors and must worry about new entrants to their industries. Also, in investigating these two forces, the analyst may become familiar in detail with an industry's incumbents and potential entrants, and all these companies' relative competitive prospects.

---

7 See Porter (2008) for a recent presentation.
8 What aspects of a company are important may be different for internal and external analysts. Whether information about competitive positions is accurately reflected in market prices, for example, would be relatively more important to external analysts.

Addressing the following questions should help the analyst evaluate the threat of new entrants and the level of competition in an industry and thereby provide an effective base for describing and analyzing the industry:

- What are the barriers to entry? Is it difficult or easy for a new competitor to challenge incumbents? Relatively high (low) barriers to entry imply that the threat of new entrants is relatively low (high).

- How concentrated is the industry? Do a small number of companies control a relatively large share of the market, or does the industry have many players, each with a small market share?

- What are capacity levels? That is, based on existing investment, how much of the goods or services can be delivered in a given time frame? Does the industry suffer chronic over- or under-capacity, or do supply and demand tend to come into balance reasonably quickly in the industry?

- How stable are market shares? Do companies tend to rapidly gain or lose share, or is the industry stable?

- Where is the industry in its life cycle? Does it have meaningful growth prospects, or is demand stagnant/declining?

- How important is price to the customer's purchase decision?

The answers to these questions are elements of any thorough industry analysis.

5.1.1 *Barriers to Entry*

When a company is earning economic profits, the chances that it will be able to sustain them through time are greater, all else being equal, if the industry has high barriers to entry. The ease with which new competitors can challenge incumbents is often an important factor in determining the competitive landscape of an industry. If new competitors can easily enter the industry, the industry is likely to be highly competitive because high returns on invested capital will quickly be competed away by new entrants eager to grab their share of economic profits. As a result, industries with low barriers to entry often have little pricing power because price increases that raise companies' returns on capital will eventually attract new competitors to the industry.

If incumbents are protected by barriers to entry, the threat of new entrants is lower, and incumbents may enjoy a more benign competitive environment. Often, these barriers to entry can lead to greater pricing power, because potential competitors would find it difficult to enter the industry and undercut incumbents' prices. Of course, high barriers to entry do not guarantee pricing power, because incumbents may compete fiercely among each other.

A classic example of an industry with low barriers to entry is restaurants. Anyone with a modest amount of capital and some culinary skill can open a restaurant, and popular restaurants quickly attract competition. As a result, the industry is very competitive, and many restaurants fail in their first few years of business.

At the other end of the spectrum of barriers to entry are the global credit card networks such as MasterCard and Visa, both of which often post operating margins greater than 30 percent. Such high profits should attract competition, but the barriers to entry are extremely high. Capital costs are one hurdle; also, building a massive data-processing network would not be cheap. Imagine for a moment that a venture capitalist was willing to fund the construction of a network that would replicate the physical infrastructure of the incumbents—the new card-processing company would have to convince millions of consumers to use the new card and convince thousands of merchants to accept the card. Consumers would not want to use a card that merchants did not accept, and merchants would not want to accept a card that few consumers carried. This problem would be difficult to solve, which is why the barriers to entering this industry are quite high. The barriers help preserve the profitability of the incumbent players.

One way of understanding barriers to entry is simply by thinking about what it would take for new players to compete in an industry. How much money would they need to spend? What kind of intellectual capital would they need to acquire? How easy would it be to attract enough customers to become successful?

Another way to investigate the issue is by looking at historical data. How often have new companies tried to enter the industry? Is a list of industry participants today markedly different from what it was five or ten years ago? These kinds of data can be very helpful because the information is based on the real-world experience of many entrepreneurs and businesses making capital allocation decisions. If an industry has seen a flood of new entrants over the past several years, odds are good that the barriers are low; conversely, if the same ten companies that dominate an industry today dominated it ten years ago, barriers to entry are probably fairly high.

Do not confuse barriers to *entry*, however, with barriers to *success*. In some industries, entering may be easy but becoming successful enough to threaten the incumbents might be quite hard. For example, in the United States, starting a mutual fund requires a capital investment of perhaps US$150,000—not much of a barrier to an industry with historically high returns on capital. But once one has started a mutual fund, how does the company gather assets? Financial intermediaries are unlikely to sell a mutual fund with no track record. So, the fund may need to incur operational losses for a few years until it has established a good track record. Even with a track record, the fund will be competing in a crowded marketplace against companies with massive advertising budgets and well-paid salespeople. In this industry, good distribution can be even more valuable than good performance. So, although entering the asset management industry may be relatively easy, succeeding is another thing altogether.

Also, high barriers to entry do not automatically lead to good pricing power and attractive industry economics. Consider the cases of auto making, commercial aircraft manufacturing, and refining industries. Starting up a new company in any of these industries would be tremendously difficult. Aside from the massive capital costs, there would be significant other barriers to entry: A new automaker would need manufacturing expertise and a dealer network; an aircraft manufacturer would need a tremendous amount of intellectual capital; and a refiner would need process expertise and regulatory approvals.

Yet, all of these industries are quite competitive, with limited or nonexistent pricing power, and few industry participants reliably generate returns on capital in excess of their costs of capital. Among the reasons for this seeming paradox of high barriers to entry plus poor pricing power, two stand out.

- First, price is a large component of the customer's purchase decision when buying from these companies in these industries. In some cases, the reason is that the companies (e.g., refiners) sell a commodity; in some cases, the product is expensive but has easily available substitutes. For example, most airlines choose between purchasing Boeing and Airbus airplanes not on brand but on cost-related considerations: Airlines need to transport people and cargo at the lowest possible cost per mile because the airlines have limited ability to pass along higher costs to customers. That consideration makes price a huge component of their purchase decision. Most airlines purchase whichever plane is the most cost efficient at any point in time. The result is that the Boeing Company and Airbus have limited ability to price their planes at a level that generates good returns on invested capital.[9]

■ Second, these industries all have high barriers to exit, which means they are prone to overcapacity. A refinery or automobile plant cannot be used for anything other than, respectively, refining oil or producing cars, which makes it hard to redeploy the capital elsewhere and exit the industry if conditions become unprofitable. This barrier gives owners of these types of assets a strong incentive to attempt to keep those loss-making plants operating, which, of course, prolongs conditions of overcapacity.

A final consideration when analyzing barriers to entry is that they can change over time. Years ago, a potential new entrant to the semiconductor industry would have needed the capital and expertise to build a "fab" (the industry term for a semi-conductor manufacturing plant). Chip fabs are hugely expensive and technologically complex, which deterred potential new entrants. Starting in the mid-1990s, however, the outsourcing of chip making to contract semiconductor manufacturers became feasible, which meant that designers of chips could challenge the manufacturers without the need to build their own plants. As a result, the industry became much more fragmented through the late 1990s and into the first decade of the 21st century.

So, in general, high barriers to entry can lead to better pricing and less competitive industry conditions, but important exceptions are worth bearing in mind.

5.1.2 *Industry Concentration*

Much like industries with barriers to entry, industries that are concentrated among a relatively small number of players often experience relatively less price competition. Again, there are important exceptions, so the reader should not automatically assume that concentrated industries always have pricing power or that fragmented industries do not.

An analysis of industry concentration should start with market share: What percentage of the market does each of the largest players have, and how large are those shares relative to each other and relative to the remainder of the market? Often, the *relative* market shares of competitors matter as much as their *absolute* market shares.

For example, the global market for long-haul commercial aircraft is extremely concentrated—only Boeing and Airbus manufacture these types of planes. The two companies have roughly similar market shares, however, and control essentially the entire market. Because neither enjoys a scale advantage relative to its competitor and because any business gained by one is lost by the other, competition tends to be fierce.

This situation contrasts with the market for home improvement products in the United States, which is dominated by Home Depot and Lowe's. These two companies have 11 percent and 7 percent market share, respectively, which doesn't sound very large. However, the next largest competitor has only 2 percent of the market, and most market participants are tiny with miniscule market shares. Both Home Depot and Lowe's have historically posted high returns on invested capital, in part because they could profitably grow by targeting smaller competitors rather than engaging in fierce competition with each other.

Fragmented industries tend to be highly price competitive for several reasons. First, the large number of companies makes coordination difficult because there are too many competitors for each industry member to monitor effectively. Second, each player has such a small piece of the market that even a small gain in market share can

---

9 Neither company's commercial aircraft segment has reliably generated returns on capital comfortably in excess of the company's cost of capital for many years. Boeing's returns on capital have been respectable overall, but the company's military segment is much more profitable than its commercial aircraft segment.

make a meaningful difference to its fortunes, which increases the incentive of each company to undercut prices and attempt to steal share. Finally, the large number of players encourages industry members to think of themselves individualistically rather than as members of a larger group, which can lead to fierce competitive behavior.

In concentrated industries, in contrast, each player can relatively easily keep track of what its competitors are doing, which makes tacit coordination much more feasible. Also, leading industry members are large, which means they have more to lose—and proportionately less to gain—by destructive price behavior. Large companies are also more tied to the fortunes of the industry as a whole, making them more likely to consider the long-run effects of a price war on overall industry economics.

As with barriers to entry, the level of industry concentration is a guideline rather than a hard and fast rule when thinking about the level of pricing power in an industry. For example, Exhibit 4 shows a rough classification of industries compiled by Morningstar after asking its equity analysts whether industries were characterized by strong or weak pricing power and whether those industries were concentrated or fragmented. Examples of companies in industries are included in parentheses. In the upper right quadrant ("concentrated with weak pricing power"), those industries that are capital intensive and sell commodity-like products are shown in boldface.

Exhibit 4   A Two-Factor Analysis of Industries

Concentrated with Strong Pricing Power

Soft Drinks (Coca-Cola Co., PepsiCo)
Orthopedic Devices (Zimmer, Smith & Nephew)
Laboratory Services (Quest Diagnostics, LabCorp)
Biotech (Amgen, Genzyme)
Pharmaceuticals (Merck & Co., Novartis)
Microprocessors (Intel, Advanced Micro Devices)
Industrial Gases (Praxair, Air Products and Chemicals)
Enterprise Storage (EMC)
Enterprise Networking (Cisco Systems)
Integrated Shippers (UPS, FedEx, DHL International)
US Railroads (Burlington Northern)
US Defense (General Dynamics)
Heavy Construction Equipment (Caterpillar, Komatsu)
Seaborne Iron Ore (Vale, Rio Tinto)
Confections (Cadbury, Mars/Wrigley)
Credit Card Networks (MasterCard, Visa)
Custody & Asset Administration (BNY Mellon, State Street)
Investment Banking /Mergers &Acquisitions (Goldman Sachs, UBS)
Futures Exchanges (Chicago Mercantile Exchange, Intercontinental Exchange)
Canadian Banking (RBC Bank, TD Bank)
Australian Banking
Tobacco (Philip Morris, British American Tobacco)
Alcoholic Beverages (Diageo, Pernod Ricard)

Concentrated with Weak Pricing Power

Commercial Aircraft (Boeing, Airbus)
Automobiles (General Motors, Toyota, Daimler)
Memory (DRAM & Flash Product, Samsung, Hynix)
Semiconductor Equipment (Applied Materials, Tokyo Electron)
Generic Drugs (Teva Pharmaceutical Industries, Sandoz)
Consumer Electronics (Sony Electronics, Koninklijke Philips Electronics)
PCs (Dell, Acer, Lenovo)
Printers/Office Machines (HP, Lexmark)
Refiners (Valero, Marathon Oil)
Major Integrated Oil (BP, ExxonMobil)
Equity Exchanges (NYSE, Deutsche Börse Group)

(continued)

Exhibit 4   (Continued)

Fragmented with Strong Pricing Power	Fragmented with Weak Pricing Power
Asset Management (BlackRock, Fidelity)	Consumer Packaged Goods (Procter & Gamble,
For-Profit Education (Apollo Group, DeVry University)	Unilever)
Analog Chips (Texas Instruments, STMicroelectronics)	Retail (Walmart, Carrefour Group)
Industrial Distribution (Fastenal, W.W. Grainger)	Marine Transportation (Maersk Line, Frontline)
Propane Distribution (AmeriGas, Ferrellgas)	Solar Panels
Private Banking (Northern Trust, Credit Suisse)	Homebuilding
	Airlines
	Mining (metals)
	Chemicals
	Engineering & Construction
	Metal Service Centers
	Commercial Printing
	Restaurants
	Radio Broadcasting
	Oil Services
	Life Insurance
	Reinsurance
	Exploration & Production (E&P)
	US Banking
	Specialty Finance
	Property/Casualty Insurance
	Household and Personal Products

Source: Morningstar Equity Research.

The industries in the top right quadrant defy the "concentration is good for pricing" guideline. We discussed the commercial aircraft manufacturing example in the preceding section, but many other industries are dominated by a small number of players yet have difficult competitive environments and limited pricing power.

When we examine these concentrated-yet-competitive industries, a clear theme emerges: Many industries in this quadrant (the boldface ones) are highly capital intensive and sell commodity-like products. As we saw in the discussion of exit barriers, capital-intensive industries can be prone to overcapacity, which mitigates the benefits of industry concentration. Also, if the industry sells a commodity product that is difficult—or impossible—to differentiate, the incentive to compete on price increases because a lower price frequently results in greater market share.[10]

The computer memory market is a perfect example of a concentrated-yet-competitive industry. Dynamic random access memory (DRAM) is widely used in PCs, and the industry is concentrated, with about three-quarters of global market share held by the top four companies. The industry is also highly capital intensive; a new fab costs upwards of US$3 billion. But one DRAM chip is much like another, and players in this market have a huge economic incentive to capture market share because of the large scale economies involved in running a semiconductor manufacturing plant. As a result, price competition tends to be extremely fierce and industry concentration is essentially a moot point in the face of these other competitive dynamics.

---

10 There are a small number of concentrated and rational commodity industries, such as potash (a type of fertilizer) and seaborne iron ore. What sets these industries apart is that they are *hyper*-concentrated: The top two players control 60 percent of the global potash market, and the top three players control two-thirds of the global market for seaborne iron ore.

The global soft drink market is also highly concentrated, of course, but capital requirements are relatively low and industry participants sell a differentiated product. Pepsi and Coca-Cola do not own their own bottling facilities, so a drop in market share does not affect them as much as it would a memory-chip maker. Moreover, although memory-chip companies are assured of gaining market share and increasing sales volumes by cutting prices, a sizable proportion of consumers would not switch from Pepsi to Coke (or vice-versa) even if one cost much less than the other.

Generally, industry concentration is a good indicator that an industry has pricing power and rational competition, but other factors may override the importance of concentration. Industry fragmentation is a much stronger signal that the industry is competitive with limited pricing power. Notice how few fragmented industries are in the bottom left quadrant in Exhibit 4.

The industry characteristics discussed here are guidelines meant to steer the analyst in a particular direction, not rules that should cause the analyst to ignore other relevant analytical factors.

5.1.3 *Industry Capacity*

The effect on pricing of industry capacity (the maximum amount of a good or service that can be supplied in a given time period) is clear: Tight, or limited, capacity gives participants more pricing power as demand for the product or service exceeds supply, whereas overcapacity leads to price cutting and a very competitive environment as excess supply chases demand. An analyst should think about not only current capacity conditions but future changes in capacity levels. How quickly can companies in the industry adjust to fluctuations in demand? How flexible is the industry in bringing supply and demand into balance? What will be the effect of that process on industry pricing power or on industry margins?

Generally, capacity is fixed in the short term and variable in the long term because capacity can be increased—e.g., new factories can be built—if time is sufficient. What is considered "sufficient" time—and, therefore, the duration of the short term, in which capacity cannot be increased—may vary dramatically among industries. Sometimes, adding capacity takes years to complete, as in the case of the construction of a "greenfield" (new) manufacturing plant for pharmaceuticals or for paper, which is complex and subject to regulatory requirements (e.g., relating to the plant's waste). In other situations, capacity may be added or reduced relatively quickly, as is the case with service industries, such as advertising. In cyclical markets, such as commercial paper and paperboard, capacity conditions can change rapidly. Strong demand in the early stages of an economic recovery can result in the addition of supply. Given the long lead times to build manufacturing plants, new supply may reach the market just as demand slows, rapidly changing capacity conditions from tight to loose. Such considerations underscore the importance of forecasting long-term industry demand in evaluating industry investments in capacity.

One of the more dramatic examples of this process in recent years occurred in the market for maritime dry-bulk shipping during the commodity boom of 2003–2008. Rapid industrialization in China—combined with synchronized global economic growth—increased demand for cargo ships that could transport iron ore, coal, grains, and other high-volume/low-value commodities. Given that the supply of cargo ships could not be increased very quickly (because ships take time to build and large commercial shipyards typically have multi-year backlogs), shippers naturally raised prices to take advantage of the tight global cargo capacity. In fact, the price to charter the largest type of dry-bulk vessel—a Capesize-class ship too big to fit through the Panama Canal—increased more than fivefold in only a year, from approximately US$30,000 per day in early 2006 to almost US$160,000 per day by late 2007.

As one would expect, orders for new dry-bulk carriers skyrocketed during this period as the industry scrambled to add shipping capacity to take advantage of seemingly insatiable demand and very favorable pricing. In early 2006, the number of dry-bulk carriers on order from shipyards represented approximately 20 percent of the worldwide fleet. By late 2008, the number of bulk ships on order represented almost 70 percent of the global bulk fleet.[11] Of course, the prospect of this additional capacity, combined with a dramatic slump in aggregate global demand for commodities, caused a massive decline in shipping rates. Capesize charter rates plummeted from the US$160,000/day high of late 2007 to a low of under US$10,000 per day just one year later.

In this example, the conditions of tight supply that were driving strong dry-bulk pricing were quite clear, and these high prices drove attractive returns on capital—and share-price performance—for dry-bulk-shipping companies. However, the careful analyst would have looked at future additions to supply in the form of new ships on order and would have forecasted that the tight supply conditions were not sustainable and thus that the pricing power of dry-bulk shippers was short-lived. These predictions are, in fact, precisely what occurred.

Note that capacity need not be physical. After Hurricane Katrina caused enormous damage to the southeastern United States in 2005, reinsurance rates quickly spiked as customers sought to increase their financial protection from future hurricanes. However, these high reinsurance rates enticed a flood of fresh capital into the reinsurance market, and a number of new reinsurance companies were founded, which brought rates back down.

Generally, if new capacity is physical—for example, an auto manufacturing plant or a massive cargo ship—it will take longer for new capacity to come on line to meet an increase in demand, resulting in a longer period of tight conditions. Unfortunately, capacity additions frequently overshoot long-run demand, and because physical capital is often hard to re-deploy, industries reliant on physical capacity may get stuck in conditions of excess capacity and diminished pricing power for an extended period.

Financial and human capital, in contrast, can be quickly shifted to new uses. In the reinsurance example, for instance, financial capital was quick to enter the reinsurance market and take advantage of tight capacity conditions, but if too much capital had entered the market, some portion of that capital could easily have left to seek higher returns elsewhere. Money can be used for many things, but massive bulk cargo vessels are not useful for much more than transporting heavy goods across oceans.

5.1.4 *Market Share Stability*

Examining the stability of industry market shares over time is similar to thinking about barriers to entry and the frequency with which new players enter an industry. In fact, barriers to entry and the frequency of new product introductions, together with such factors as product differentiation—all affect market shares. Stable market shares typically indicate less competitive industries; unstable market shares often indicate highly competitive industries that have limited pricing power.

A comparison of two non-commodity markets in the health care sector illustrates this point. Over the past decade, the orthopedic device industry—mainly artificial hips and knees—has been a relatively stable global oligopoly. As Exhibit 5 indicates, five companies control about 95 percent of the worldwide market, and the market shares of those companies have changed by only small amounts over the past several years.

---

11 From "RS Platou Monthly" (November 2008): www.platou.com/loadfileservlet/loadfiledb?id=1228989312093PUBLISHER&key=1228989321421.

Exhibit 5	Market Share Stability in Global Orthopedic Devices (Entries Are Market Share)			
Worldwide Knee/Hip Market Share	**2005 (%)**	**2006 (%)**	**2007 (%)**	**2008 (%)**
Zimmer	27.9	27.5	27.2	26.0
Johnson & Johnson (DePuy)	24.0	23.9	22.9	22.9
Stryker	21.6	21.4	21.5	21.3
Smith & Nephew	9.4	9.8	11.5	12.6
Biomet	11.5	10.9	10.9	11.3

Source: Company reports and Morningstar estimates.

In contrast, although the US market for stents—small metal mesh devices used to prop open blocked arteries—is also controlled by a handful of companies, market shares recently have gone from being very stable to being marked by rapid change. Johnson & Johnson, which together with Boston Scientific, dominated the US stent market for many years, went from having about half the market in 2007 to having only 15 percent in early 2009; over the same period, Abbott Laboratories increased its market share from zero to 25 percent. The reason for this change was the launch of new stents by Abbott and Medtronic, which took market share from Johnson & Johnson and Boston Scientific's established stents.

Orthopedic device companies have experienced more stability in their market shares for two reasons. First, artificial hips and knees are complicated to implant, and each manufacturer's products are slightly different. As a result, orthopedic surgeons become proficient at using one or several companies' devices and may be reluctant to incur the time and cost of learning how to implant products from a competing company. The second reason is the relatively slow pace of innovation in the orthopedic device industry, which tends to be evolutionary rather than revolutionary, making the benefit of switching among product lines relatively low. In addition, the number of orthopedic device companies has remained fairly static over many years.

In contrast, the US stent market has experienced rapid shifts in market shares because of several factors. First, interventional cardiologists seem to be more open than orthopedic surgeons to implanting stents from different manufacturers; that tendency may reflect lower switching costs for stents relative to orthopedic devices. More importantly, however, the pace of innovation in the stent market has become quite rapid, giving cardiologists added incentive to switch to newer stents, with potentially better patient outcomes, as they became available.

Low switching costs plus a relatively high benefit from switching caused market shares to change quickly in the stent market. High switching costs for orthopedic devices coupled with slow innovation resulted in a lower benefit from switching, which led to greater market share stability in orthopedic devices.

5.1.5 *Industry Life Cycle*

An industry's life-cycle position often has a large impact on its competitive dynamics, making this position an important component of the strategic analysis of an industry.

5.1.5.1 Description of an Industry Life-Cycle Model
Industries, like individual companies, tend to evolve over time, and usually experience significant changes in the rate of growth and levels of profitability along the way. Just as an investment in an individual company requires careful monitoring, industry analysis is a continuous process to identify changes that may be occurring or be likely to occur. A useful framework for

analyzing the evolution of an industry is an industry life-cycle model, which identifies the sequential stages that an industry typically goes through. The five stages of an industry life-cycle model are embryonic, growth, shakeout, mature, and decline. Each stage is characterized by different opportunities and threats.[12] Exhibit 6 shows the model as a curve illustrating the level and growth rate of demand at each stage.

Exhibit 6   An Industry Life-Cycle Model

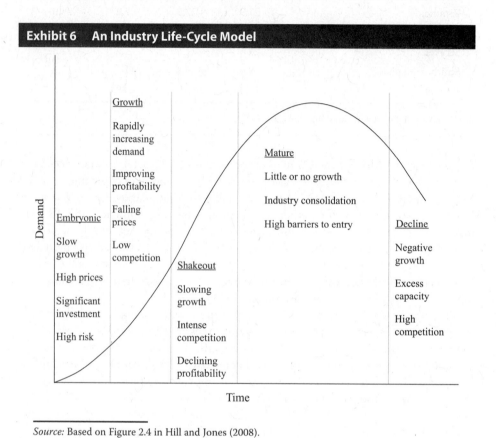

Source: Based on Figure 2.4 in Hill and Jones (2008).

Embryonic   An embryonic industry is one that is just beginning to develop. For example, in the 1960s, the global semiconductor industry was in the embryonic stage (it has grown to become a US$249 billion industry in 2008)[13] and in the early 1980s, the global mobile phone industry was in the embryonic stage (it now produces and sells more than a billion handsets annually). Characteristics of the embryonic stage include slow growth and high prices because customers tend to be unfamiliar with the industry's product and volumes are not yet sufficient to achieve meaningful economies of scale. Increasing product awareness and developing distribution channels are key strategic initiatives of companies during this stage. Substantial investment is generally required, and the risk of failure is high. A majority of start-up companies do not succeed.

Growth   A growth industry tends to be characterized by rapidly increasing demand, improving profitability, falling prices, and relativity low competition among companies in the industry. Demand is fueled by new customers entering the market, and prices fall as economies of scale are achieved and as distribution channels develop. The threat

---

12 Much of the discussion that follows regarding life-cycle stages owes a debt to the discussion in Hill and Jones (2008).

13 Semiconductor Industry Association Factsheet: www.sia-online.org/cs/industry_resources/industry_fact_sheet.

of new competitors entering the industry is usually highest during the growth stage, when barriers to entry are relatively low. Competition tends to be relatively limited, however, because rapidly expanding demand provides companies with an opportunity to grow without needing to capture market share from competitors. Industry profitability improves as volumes rise and economies of scale are attained.

Shakeout The shakeout stage is usually characterized by slowing growth, intense competition, and declining profitability. During the shakeout stage, demand approaches market saturation levels because few new customers are left to enter the market. Competition is intense as growth becomes increasingly dependent on market share gains. Excess industry capacity begins to develop as the rate at which companies continue to invest exceeds the overall growth of industry demand. In an effort to boost volumes to fill excess capacity, companies often cut prices, so industry profitability begins to decline. During the shakeout stage, companies increasingly focus on reducing their cost structure (restructuring) and building brand loyalty. Marginal companies may fail or merge with others.

Mature Characteristics of a mature industry include little or no growth, industry consolidation, and relatively high barriers to entry. Industry growth tends to be limited to replacement demand and population expansion because the market at this stage is completely saturated. As a result of the shakeout, mature industries often consolidate and become oligopolies. The surviving companies tend to have brand loyalty and relatively efficient cost structures, both of which are significant barriers to entry. During periods of stable demand, companies in mature industries tend to recognize their interdependence and try to avoid price wars. Periodic price wars do occur, however, most notably during periods of declining demand (such as during economic downturns). Companies with superior products or services are likely to gain market share and experience above-industry-average growth and profitability.

Decline During the decline stage, industry growth turns negative, excess capacity develops, and competition increases. Industry demand at this stage may decline for a variety of reasons, including technological substitution (for example, the newspaper industry has been declining for years as more people turn to the internet and 24-hour cable news networks for information), social changes, and global competition (for example, low-cost foreign manufacturers pushing the US textile industry into decline). As demand falls, excess capacity in the industry forms and companies respond by cutting prices, which often leads to price wars. The weaker companies often exit the industry at this point, merge, or redeploy capital into different products and services.

When overall demand for an industry's products or services is declining, the opportunity for individual companies to earn above-average returns on invested capital tends to be less than when demand is stable or increasing, because of price cutting and higher per-unit costs as production is cut back. Example 6 deals with industry life cycles.

EXAMPLE 6

Industry Growth and Company Growth

US shipments of prefabricated housing (precut, modular housing) declined sharply in 1999–2004 as the abundant availability of low-cost mortgage financing and other factors led individuals to purchase site-built housing. In 1998, however, some forecasts had projected that prefabricated housing would gain market share at the expense of site-built housing. What would have been the probable impact on market share of a typical company in the prefabricated housing industry under the 1998 optimistic forecast and under actual conditions?

Solution:

Increasing industry demand as forecasted in 1998 would have given companies in the prefabricated housing industry the opportunity to grow without taking market share from one another, mitigating the intensity of competition in this industry. Under actual industry circumstances of declining demand and a shrinking market, in contrast, revenue growth for a prefabricated housing company could happen only through market share gains from its competitors.

5.1.5.2 Using an Industry Life-Cycle Model   In general, new industries tend to be more competitive (with lots of players entering and exiting) than mature industries, which often have stable competitive environments and players that are more interested in protecting what they have than in gaining lots of market share. However, as industries move from maturity to decline, competitive pressures may increase again as industry participants perceive a zero-sum environment and fight over pieces of an ever-shrinking pie.

An important point for the analyst to think about is whether a company is "acting its age" relative to where its industry sits in the life cycle. Companies in growth industries should be building customer loyalty as they introduce consumers to new products or services, building scale, and reinvesting heavily in their operations to capitalize on increasing demand. They are probably not focusing strongly on internal efficiency. These companies are rather like young adults, who are reinvesting their human and financial capital with the goal of becoming more successful in life. Growth companies typically reinvest their cash flows in new products and product platforms rather than returning cash flows to shareholders because these companies still have many opportunities to deploy their capital to make positive returns. Although this analogy to the human life cycle is a helpful way to think about the model, the analyst should also be aware that the analogy is not exact in detail. Long-established companies sometimes find a way to accelerate growth through innovation or by expansion into new markets. Humans cannot really move back to the days of youth. So, a more precise formulation may be "acting its stage" rather than acting its age.

Companies in mature industries are likely to be pursuing replacement demand rather than new buyers and are probably focused on extending successful product lines rather than introducing revolutionary new products. They are also probably focusing on cost rationalization and efficiency gains rather than on taking lots of market share. Importantly, these companies have fewer growth opportunities than in the previous stage, and thus more limited avenues for profitably reinvesting capital, but they often have strong cash flows. Given their strong cash flows and relatively limited reinvestment opportunities, such companies should be, according to a common perspective, returning capital to shareholders via share repurchases or dividends. These companies are rather like middle-aged adults who are harvesting the fruits of their success earlier in life.

What can be a concern is a middle-aged company acting like a young, growth company and pouring capital into projects with low ROIC prospects in an effort to pursue size for its own sake. Many companies have a difficult time managing the transition from growth to maturity, and their returns on capital—and shareholder returns—may suffer until management decides to allocate capital in a manner more appropriate to the company's life-cycle stage.

For example, three large US retailers—Walmart, Home Depot, and McDonalds—all went through the transition to maturity in the first decade of the 21st century. At various times between 2002 and 2005, these companies realized that their size and industry dominance meant that the days of double-digit growth that was driven largely by new store (restaurant) openings were a thing of the past. All three reallocated capital away from opening new stores to other areas—namely, increased inventory efficiency (Home

Depot), improving the customer experience (McDonalds), and increased dividends and share repurchases (all three). As a result, returns on capital for each improved, as did shareholder returns.

5.1.5.3 Limitations of Industry Life-Cycle Analysis   Although models can provide a useful framework for thinking about an industry, the evolution of an industry does not always follow a predictable pattern. Various external factors may significantly affect the shape of the pattern, causing some stages to be longer or shorter than expected and, in certain cases, causing some stages to be skipped altogether.

Technological changes may cause an industry to experience an abrupt shift from growth to decline, thus skipping the shakeout and mature stages. For example, transistors replaced vacuum tubes in the 1960s at a time when the vacuum tube industry was still in its growth stage; word processors replaced typewriters in the 1980s; and today the movie rental industry is experiencing rapid change as consumers increasingly turn to on-demand services such as downloading movies from the internet or through their cable providers.

Regulatory changes can also have a profound impact on the structure of an industry. A prime example is the deregulation of the US telecommunications industry in the 1990s, which transformed a monopolistic industry into an intensely competitive one. AT&T was broken into regional service providers, and many new long distance telephone service entrants, such as Sprint, emerged. The result was a wider range of product and service offerings and lower consumer prices. Changes in government reimbursement rates for health care products and services may (and have) affected the profitability of companies in the health care industry globally.

Social changes also have the ability to affect the profile of an industry. The casual dining industry has benefited over the past 30 years from the increase in the number of dual-income families, who often have more income but less time to cook meals to eat at home.

Demographics also play an important role. As the Baby Boom generation ages, for instance, industry demand for health care services is likely to increase.

Thus, life-cycle models tend to be most useful for analyzing industries during periods of relative stability. They are less practical when the industry may be experiencing rapid change because of external or other special circumstances.

Another limiting factor of models is that not all companies in an industry experience similar performances. The key objective for the analyst is to identify the potential winners while avoiding potential losers. Highly profitable companies can exist in competitive industries with below-average profitability—and vice versa. For example, Nokia has historically been able to use its scale to generate levels of profitability that are well above average despite operating in a highly competitive industry. In contrast, despite the historically above-average growth and profitability of the software industry, countless examples exist of software companies that failed to ever generate a profit and eventually went out of business.

EXAMPLE 7

Industry Life Cycle

1   An industry experiencing slow growth and high prices is best characterized as being in the:

   A   mature stage.

   B   shakeout stage.

   C   embryonic stage.

2 Which of the following statements about the industry life-cycle model is *least* accurate?

  A The model is more appropriately used during a period of rapid change than during a period of relative stability.

  B External factors may cause some stages of the model to be longer or shorter than expected, and in certain cases, a stage may be skipped entirely.

  C Not all companies in an industry will experience similar performance, and very profitable companies can exist in an industry with below-average profitability.

Solution to 1:

C is correct. Both slow growth and high prices are associated with the embryonic stage. High price is not a characteristic of the mature or shakeout stages.

Solution to 2:

A is correct. The statement is the least accurate. The model is best used during a period of relative stability rather than during a period of rapid change.

5.1.6 *Price Competition*

A highly useful tool for analyzing an industry is attempting to think like a customer of the industry. Whatever factor most influences customer purchase decisions is likely to also be the focus of competitive rivalry in the industry. In general, industries for which price is a large factor in customer purchase decisions tend to be more competitive than industries in which customers value other attributes more highly.

Although this depiction may sound like the description of a commodity industry versus a non-commodity industry, it is, in fact, a bit more subtle. Commercial aircraft and passenger cars are certainly more differentiated than lumps of coal or gallons of gasoline, but price nonetheless weighs heavily in the purchase decisions of buyers of aircraft and cars, because fairly good substitutes are easily available. If Airbus charges too much for an A320, an airline can buy a Boeing 737.[14] If BMW's price for a four-door luxury sedan rises too high, customers can switch to a Mercedes or other luxury brand with similar features. Similar switching can be expected as a result of a unilateral price increase in the case of most industries in the "Weak Pricing Power" column of Exhibit 4.

Contrast these industries with asset management, one of a handful of industries that is both fragmented and characterized by strong pricing power. Despite the well-documented impact of fees on future investment returns, the vast majority of asset management customers do not make decisions on the basis of price. Instead, asset management customers focus on historical returns, which allow this highly fragmented industry to maintain strong pricing power. Granted, the index fund arena is very price competitive, because any index fund is a perfect substitute for another fund tracking the same benchmark. But the active management segment of the industry has generally been able to price its products in an implicitly cooperative fashion that enables most players to generate consistently high returns on capital, presumably because price is not uppermost in the mind of a prospective mutual fund investor.

---

14 A small amount of "path dependence" characterizes the airline industry, in that an airline with a large fleet of a particular Airbus model will be marginally more likely to stick with that model for a new purchase than it will be to buy a Boeing, but the aircraft manufacturers' ability to exploit this likelihood is minimal.

Returning to a more capital-intensive industry, consider heavy-equipment manu-facturers, such as Caterpillar, Deere, and Komatsu. A large wheel loader or combine harvester requires a large capital outlay, so price certainly plays a part in the buyers' decisions. However, other factors are important enough to customers to allow these companies a small amount of pricing power. Construction equipment is typically used as a complement to other gear on a large project, which means that downtime for repairs increases costs because, for example, hourly laborers must wait for a bulldozer to be fixed. Broken equipment is also expensive for agricultural users, who may have only a few days in which to harvest a season's crop. Because of the importance to users of their products' reliability and their large service networks—which are important "differentiators" or factors bestowing a competitive advantage—Caterpillar, Komatsu, and Deere have historically been able to price their equipment at levels that have generated solid returns on invested capital.

5.1.7 Industry Comparison

To illustrate how these elements might be applied, Exhibit 7 uses the factors discussed in this reading to examine three industries.

Exhibit 7 Elements of a Strategic Analysis for Three Industries

	Branded Pharmaceuticals	Oil Services	Confections/Candy
Major Companies	Pfizer, Novartis, Merck, GlaxoSmithKline	Schlumberger, Baker Hughes, Halliburton	Cadbury, Hershey, Mars/Wrigley, Nestle
Barriers to Entry/Success	*Very High*: Substantial financial and intellectual capital required to compete effectively. A potential new entrant would need to create a sizable R&D operation, a global distribution network, and large-scale manufacturing capacity.	*Medium*: Technological expertise is required, but high level of innovation allows niche companies to enter the industry and compete in specific areas.	*Very High*: Low financial or technological hurdles, but new players would lack the established brands that drive consumer purchase decisions.
Level of Concentration	*Concentrated*: A small number of companies control the bulk of the global market for branded drugs. Recent mergers have increased level of concentration.	*Fragmented*: Although only a small number of companies provide a full range of services, many smaller players compete effectively in specific areas. Service arms of national oil companies may control significant market share in their own countries, and some product lines are concentrated in the mature US market.	*Very Concentrated*: Top four companies have a large proportion of global market share. Recent mergers have increased level of concentration.
Impact of Industry Capacity	*NA*: Pharmaceutical pricing is primarily determined by patent protection and regulatory issues, including government approvals of drugs and of manufacturing facilities. Manufacturing capacity is of little importance.	*Medium/High*: Demand can fluctuate quickly depending on commodity prices, and industry players often find themselves with too few (or too many) employees on the payroll.	*NA*: Pricing is driven primarily by brand strength. Manufacturing capacity has little effect.

(continued)

Exhibit 7   (Continued)

	Branded Pharmaceuticals	Oil Services	Confections/Candy
Industry Stability	*Stable*: The branded pharmaceutical market is dominated by major companies and consolidation via mega-mergers. Market shares shift quickly, however, as new drugs are approved and gain acceptance or lose patent protection.	*Unstable*: Market shares may shift frequently depending on technology offerings and demand levels.	*Very Stable*: Market shares change glacially.
Life Cycle	*Mature*: Overall demand does not change greatly from year to year.	*Mature*: Demand does fluctuate with energy prices, but normalized revenue growth is only mid-single digits.	*Very Mature*: Growth is driven by population trends and pricing.
Price Competition	*Low/Medium*: In the United States, price is a minimal factor because of consumer- and provider-driven, de-regulated health care system. Price is a larger part of the decision process in single-payer systems, where efficacy hurdles are higher.	*High*: Price is a major factor in purchasers' decisions. Some companies have modest pricing power because of a wide range of services or best-in-class technology, but primary customers (major oil companies) can usually substitute with in-house services if prices are too high. Also, innovation tends to diffuse quickly throughout the industry.	*Low*: A lack of private-label competition keeps pricing stable among established players, and brand/familiarity plays a much larger role in consumer purchase decisions than price.
Demographic Influences	*Positive*: Populations of developed markets are aging, which slightly increases demand.	*NA*	*NA*
Government & Regulatory Influences	*Very High*: All drugs must be approved for sale by national safety regulators. Patent regimes may differ among countries. Also, health care is heavily regulated in most countries.	*Medium*: Regulatory frameworks can affect energy demand at the margin. Also, governments play an important role in allocating exploration opportunities to E&P companies, which can indirectly affect the amount of work flowing down to service companies.	*Low*: Industry is not regulated, but childhood obesity concerns in developed markets are a low-level potential threat. Also, high-growth emerging markets may block entry of established players into their markets, possibly limiting growth.
Social Influences	*NA*	*NA*	*NA*
Technological Influences	*Medium/High*: Biologic (large-molecule) drugs are pushing new therapeutic boundaries, and many large pharmaceutical companies have a relatively small presence in biotech.	*Medium/High*: Industry is reasonably innovative, and players must re-invest in R&D to remain competitive. Temporary competitive advantages are possible via commercialization of new processes or exploitation of accumulated expertise.	*Very Low*: Innovation does not play a major role in the industry.

	Branded Pharmaceuticals	**Oil Services**	**Confections/Candy**
Growth vs. Defensive vs. Cyclical	*Defensive*: Demand for most health care services does not fluctuate with the economic cycle, but demand is not strong enough to be considered "growth."	*Cyclical*: Demand is highly variable and depends on oil prices, exploration budgets, and the economic cycle.	*Defensive*: Demand for candy and gum is extremely stable.

Exhibit 7   (Continued)

Note: "*NA*" in this exhibit stands for "not applicable."

Example 8 reviews some of the information presented in Exhibit 7.

EXAMPLE 8

External Influences

1   Which of the following industries is *most* affected by government regulation?

   A   Oil services.

   B   Pharmaceuticals.

   C   Confections and candy.

2   Which of the following industries is *least* affected by technological innovation?

   A   Oil services.

   B   Pharmaceuticals.

   C   Confections and candy.

3   Which of the following statements about industry characteristics is *least* accurate?

   A   Manufacturing capacity has little effect on pricing in the confections/candy industry.

   B   The branded pharmaceutical industry is considered to be defensive rather than a growth industry.

   C   With respect to the worldwide market, the oil services industry has a high level of concentration with a limited number of service providers.

Solution to 1:

B is correct. Exhibit 7 states that the pharmaceutical industry has high amount of government and regulatory influences.

Solution to 2:

C is correct. Exhibit 7 states that innovation does not play a large role in the candy industry.

Solution to 3:

C is correct; it is a false statement. From a worldwide perspective, the industry is considered fragmented. Although a small number of companies provide the full range of services, competition by many smaller players occurs in niche areas. In addition, national oil service companies control significant market share in their home countries.

5.2 External Influences on Industry Growth, Profitability, and Risk

External factors affecting an industry's growth include macroeconomic, technological, demographic, governmental, and social influences.

5.2.1 Macroeconomic Influences

Trends in overall economic activity generally have significant effects on the demand for an industry's products or services. These trends can be cyclical (i.e., related to the changes in economic activity caused by the business cycle) or structural (i.e., related to enduring changes in the composition or magnitude of economic activity). Among the economic variables that usually affect an industry's revenues and profits are the following:

- gross domestic product or the measure of the value of goods and services produced by an economy, either in current or constant currency (inflation-adjusted) terms;

- interest rates, which represent the cost of debt to consumers and businesses and are important ingredients in financial institutions' revenues and costs;

- the availability of credit, which affects business and consumer spending and financial solvency; and

- inflation, which reflects the changes in prices of goods and services and influences costs, interest rates, and consumer and business confidence.

5.2.2 Technological Influences

New technologies create new or improved products that can radically change an industry and can also change how other industries that use the products conduct their operations.

The computer hardware industry provides one of the best examples of how technological change can affect industries. The 1958 invention of the microchip (also known as an "integrated circuit," which is effectively a computer etched on a sliver of silicon) enabled the computer hardware industry to eventually create a new market of personal computing for the general public and radically extended the use of computers in business, government, and educational institutions.

Moore's law states that the number of transistors that can be inexpensively placed on an integrated circuit doubles approximately every two years. Several other measures of digital technology have improved at exponential rates related to Moore's law, including the size, cost, density and speed of components. As a result of these trends, the computer hardware industry encroached upon and, in time, came to dominate the fields of hardware for word processing and many forms of electronic communication and home entertainment. The computing industry's integrated circuit innovation increased economies of scale and erected large barriers to new entrants because the capital costs of innovation and production became very high. Intel capitalized on both factors which allowed it to garner an industry market leadership position and to become the dominant supplier of the PC industry's highest value component (the microprocessor). Thus, Intel became dominant because of its cost advantage, brand power, and access to capital.

Along the way, the computer hardware industry was supported and greatly assisted by the complementary industries of computer software and telecommunications (particularly in regard to development of the internet); also important were other industries—entertainment (television, movies, games), retailing, and the print media. Ever more powerful integrated circuits and advances in wireless technology, as well as the convergence of media, which the internet and new wireless technology have facilitated, continue to reshape the uses and the roles of PC hardware in business and personal life. In the middle of the 20th century, few people in the world would have imagined they would ever have any use for a home computer. Today, the estimate is that about 1.6 billion people, or almost a quarter of the world's population, have access to connected computing. For the United States, the estimate is at least 76 percent of the population; it is much less in emerging and underdeveloped countries. More than 4 billion mobile cellular telephone subscriptions exist in the world today,[15] and the advances of mobile telephony appear poised to increase this figure dramatically in the years ahead as mobile phone and computer hardware technologies merge to provide new hand-held computing and communication capabilities.

Another example of the effects of technology on an industry is the impact of digital imaging technology on the photographic film industry. Digital imaging uses an electronic image sensor to record an image as electronic data rather than as chemical changes on film. This difference allows a much greater degree of image processing and transmission than in film photography. Since their invention in 1981, digital cameras have become extremely popular and now widely outsell traditional film cameras (although many professional photographers continue to use film for esthetic reasons for certain applications). Digital cameras include such features as video and audio recording. The effects of this major change in photographic technology have caused film and camera manufacturers—including Kodak, Fujifilm, Nikon Corporation, and Pentax Imaging Company—to completely restructure and redesign their products to adapt to the new technology's appeal to consumers.

5.2.3 *Demographic Influences*

Changes in population size, in the distributions of age and gender, and in other demographic characteristics may have significant effects on economic growth and on the amounts and types of goods and services consumed.

The effects of demographics on industries are well exemplified by the impact of the post–World War II Baby Boom in North America on demand for goods and services. Born between 1946 and 1964, this bulge of 76 million people in the North American population has influenced the composition of numerous products and services it needs in its passage from the cradle through childhood, adolescence, early adulthood, middle age, and into retirement. The teenage pop culture of the late 1950s and 1960s and all the products (records, movies, clothes, and fashions associated with it), the surge in demand for housing in the 1970s and 1980s, and the increasing demand for retirement-oriented investment products in the 1990s and early 2000s are all examples of the range of industries affected by this demographic bulge working its way through age categories of the population.

Another example of the effects of demographics on industries is the impact of an aging population in Japan, which has one of the highest percentages of elderly residents (21 percent over the age of 65) and a very low birth rate. Japan's ministry of health estimates that by 2055, the percentage of the population over 65 will rise to

---

15 See www.itu.int/newsroom/press_releases/2009/39.html.

40 percent and the total population will fall by 25 percent. These demographic changes are expected by some observers to have negative effects on the overall economy because, essentially, they imply a declining workforce. However, some sectors of the economy stand to benefit from these trends—for example, the health care industry.

EXAMPLE 9

The Post-World War II Baby Boom and Its Effects on the US Housing Industry

In the United States, Canada, and Australia, the end of World War II marked the beginning of a sustained period of elevated birth rates per thousand in the population. This rise reflected the relief from the hardships of the Great Depression of the 1930s and WWII, increased levels of immigration (immigrants tend to be younger and hence more fertile than average) and a protracted period of postwar economic prosperity. The rate of births in the United States rose from 18.7 per thousand in 1935 and 20.4 per thousand in 1945 to 24.1 per thousand in 1950 and a peak of more than 25.0 per thousand in 1955–1957. Twenty years later, when the babies born during the period 1946–1964 entered adulthood, the housing industry experienced a surge in demand that led to a period of high sales of new homes. The rate of new housing starts in this period rose from 20.1 per thousand of population in 1966 to a peak of 35.3 per thousand in 1972 and remained elevated, except during the economic recession of 1974–1975, until the end of the 1970s.

Another demographic effect on the housing industry arising from the post-WWII Baby Boom came from the children of the Baby Boom generation (the so-called Echo Boomers). The Echo Boomers started to enter their most fertile years in the late 1970s and caused an increase in the number of births per thousand from a post-WWII low of 14.8 in 1975 to a peak of 16.7 in 1990. The Echo Boomers did not have as large an effect on housing demand 20 years later as their parents had had, but there was still a significant increase in new housing starts from 13.7 per thousand in 1995 to a high of 18.8 per thousand in 2005; easily available mortgage financing contributed to the increase.

5.2.4 Governmental Influences

Governmental influence on industries' revenues and profits is pervasive and important. In setting tax rates and rules for corporations and individuals, governments affect profits and incomes, which in turn, affect corporate and personal spending. Governments are also major purchasers of goods and services from a range of industries.

Example 10 illustrates the sudden shifts in wealth that can occur when governments step in to support or quash a securities market innovation. In the example, an **income trust** refers to a type of equity ownership vehicle established as a trust issuing ownership shares known as units. Income trusts became extremely popular among income-oriented investors in Canada in the late 1990s and early 2000s because under then-current regulation, such trusts could avoid taxation on income distributed to unit-holders (investors)—that is, avoid double taxation (once at the corporate level and once at the investor level). As Example 10 describes, the tax advantage that regulations permitted was eventually removed.

The Effects of Tax Increases on Income Trusts in Canada

On 31 October 2006, in an effort to halt the rapid growth of income trust structures in the Canadian stock market, Canada's Minister of Finance James Flaherty announced that these tax-exempt flow-through entities would in the future be taxable on the income, with exemptions only for passive rent-collecting real estate investment trusts. A five year hiatus was established for existing trusts to adapt. He stated that the government needed to clamp down on trusts because too many companies were converting to the high-yield securities, primarily to save taxes. The S&P/TSX Capped Income Trust Index declined 12 percent on the day after the announcement, wiping out C$24 billion in market value.

Often, governments exert their influence indirectly by empowering other regulatory or self-regulatory organizations (e.g., stock exchanges, medical associations, utility rate setters, and other regulatory commissions) to govern the affairs of an industry. By setting the terms of entry into various sectors, such as financial services and health care, and the rules that companies and individuals must adhere to in these fields, governments control the supply, quality, and nature of many products and services and the public's access to them. For example, in the financial industry, the acceptance of savings deposits from and the issuance of securities to the investing public are usually tightly controlled by governments and their agencies. This control is imposed through rules designed to protect investors from fraudulent operators and to ensure that investors receive adequate disclosure about the nature and risks of their investments. Another example is that medical patients in most developed countries are treated by doctors who are trained according to standards set by medical associations acting as self-regulatory organizations empowered under government laws. In addition, the medications that patients receive must be approved by government agencies. In a somewhat different vein, users of tobacco products purchase items for which the marketing and sales taxes are heavily controlled by governments in most developed countries and for which warnings to consumers about the dangers of smoking are mandated by governments. In the case of industries that supply branches of government, such as the military, public works, and law enforcement departments, government contracts directly affect the revenues and profits of the suppliers.

The Effects of Government Purchases on the Aerospace Industry

The aerospace, construction, and firearms industries are prime examples of industries for which governments are major customers and whose revenues and profits are significantly—in some cases, predominantly—affected by their sales to governments. An example is the European Aeronautic Defence and Space Company (EADS), a global leader in aerospace, defense, and related services with head offices in Paris and Ottobrunn, Germany. In 2008, EADS generated revenues of €43.3 billion and employed an international workforce of about 118,000. EADS includes Airbus, a leading manufacturer of commercial aircraft; Airbus Military, providing tanker, transport, and mission aircraft; Eurocopter, the world's largest helicopter supplier; and EADS Astrium, the European leader in space programs, including Ariane and Galileo. Its Defence & Security Division is a provider of comprehensive systems solutions and makes EADS the major

> partner in the Eurofighter consortium and a stakeholder in missile systems provider MBDA. On 3 March 2008, EADS shares rose 9.2 percent after the US Air Force chose its Airbus A330 over Boeing's 767 for an airborne refueling plane contract worth as much as US$35 billion.

5.2.5 Social Influences

Societal changes involving how people work, spend their money, enjoy their leisure time, and conduct other aspects of their lives can have significant effects on the sales of various industries.

Tobacco consumption in the United Kingdom provides a good example of the effects of social influences on an industry. Although the role of government in curbing tobacco advertising, legislating health warnings on the purchases of tobacco products, and banning smoking in public places (such as restaurants, bars, public houses, and transportation vehicles) probably has been the most powerful apparent instrument of changes in tobacco consumption, the forces underlying that change have really been social in nature—namely, increasing consciousness on the part of the population of the damage to the health of tobacco users and those in their vicinity from smoking, the increasing cost to individuals and governments of the chronic illnesses caused by tobacco consumption, and the accompanying shift in public perception of smokers from socially correct to socially incorrect—even inconsiderate or reckless. As a result of these changes in society's views of smoking, cigarette consumption in the United Kingdom declined from 102.5 billion cigarettes in 1990 to less than 65.0 billion in 2009, placing downward pressure on tobacco companies' unit sales.

EXAMPLE 12

The Effects on Various Industries of More Women Entering the Workforce

In 1870, women accounted for only 15 percent of the workforce in the United States outside the home. By 1950, after two world wars and the Great Depression, this figure had risen to 30 percent (it had been even higher temporarily during WWII because of high levels of war-mandated production) and by 2008, to 48 percent. Based on economic reasoning, identify four industries that should have benefitted from the social change that saw women shift from their most frequent historical roles in Western society as full-time homemakers to becoming more frequently full-time participants in the workforce.

Solution:

Industries include the following:

1　The restaurant business. The restaurant business stands to benefit from an increased demand given that women, because of their work responsibilities, may not have the time and energy to prepare meals. Restaurant industry growth was actually high in this period: From accounting for only 25 percent of every food dollar in the United States in 1950, the restaurant industry today consumes more than 44 percent of every food dollar, with 45 percent of current industry revenues arising from a category of restaurant that did not exist in 1950, namely, fast food.

2　Manufacturers of work clothing for women.

3　Home and child care services.

4   Automobile manufacturers. Extra vehicles became necessary to transport two members of the family to work, for instance, and children to school or day care.

5   Housing for the aging. With increasing workforce participation by women, aged family members requiring care or supervision became increasingly unable to rely on non-working female family members to provide care in their homes.

EXAMPLE 13

The Airline Industry: A Case Study of Many Influences

The global airline industry exemplifies many of the concepts and influences we have discussed.

Life-Cycle Stage

The industry can be described as having some mature characteristics because average annual growth in global passenger traffic has remained relatively stable at 4.5 percent in the 2000s (compared with 4.7 percent in the 1990s). Some market segments in the industry, however, are still in their growth phase—notably, the markets of the Middle East and Asia, which are expected to grow at 6.5 percent compared with projected North American growth of 3.2 percent over the next 20 years.

Sensitivity to Business Cycle

The airline industry is a cyclical industry; global economic activity produces swings in revenues and, especially, profitability, because of the industry's high fixed costs and operating leverage. In 2009, for example, global passenger traffic is expected to have declined by approximately 8 percent and airlines are expected to report significant net losses—close to US$9.0 billion, which is down from a global industry profit of US$12.9 billion in 2007. The industry tends to respond early to upward and downward moves in economic cycles; depending on the region, air travel changes at 1.5 times to 2.0 times GDP growth. It is highly regulated, with governments and airport authorities playing a large role in allocating routes and airport slots. Government agencies and the International Airline Transport Association set rules for aircraft and flight safety. Airline customers tend to have low brand loyalty (except at the extremes of high and low prices and service); leisure travelers focus mainly on price, and business travelers focus mostly on schedules and service. Product and service differentiation at particular price points is low because aircraft, cabin configuration, and catering tend to be quite similar in most cases. For leisure travelers, the price competition is intense and is led by low-cost discount carriers, including Southwest Airlines in the United States, Ryanair in Europe, and Air Asia in Asia. For business travelers, the major scheduled airlines and a few service-quality specialists, such as Singapore Airlines, are the main contenders. Fuel costs (typically more than 25 percent of total costs and highly volatile) and labor costs (around 10 percent of total costs) have been the focus of management cost-reduction efforts. The airline industry is highly unionized, and labor strife has frequently been a source of costly disruptions to the industry. Technology has always played a major role in the airline industry, from its origins with small propeller-driven planes through the advent of the jet age to the drive for greater fuel efficiency since the oil price increases of the 1970s. Technology also poses a threat to the growth of business air travel in the form of improved telecommunications—notably, videoconferencing and webcasting. Arguably, the airline industry has been a great force in shaping demography by permitting difficult-to-access geographical areas to be settled with large populations. At the same time, large numbers of post-WWII Baby Boomers have been a factor in generating the growth in demand for air travel in the past half-century. In recent years, social issues have started to play a role in the airline industry; carbon emissions, for example, have come under scrutiny by environmentalists and governments.

6   COMPANY ANALYSIS

Company analysis includes an analysis of the company's financial position, products and/or services, and **competitive strategy** (its plans for responding to the threats and opportunities presented by the external environment). Company analysis takes place after the analyst has gained an understanding of a company's external environment—the macroeconomic, demographic, governmental, technological, and social forces influencing the industry's competitive structure. The analyst should seek to determine whether the strategy is primarily defensive or offensive in its nature and how the company intends to implement the strategy.

Porter identifies two chief competitive strategies: a low-cost strategy (cost leadership) and a product/service differentiation strategy.

In a low-cost strategy, companies strive to become the low-cost producers and to gain market share by offering their products and services at lower prices than their competition while still making a profit margin sufficient to generate a superior rate of return based on the higher revenues achieved. Low-cost strategies may be pursued defensively to protect market positions and returns or offensively to gain market share and increase returns. Pricing also can be defensive (when the competitive environment is one of low rivalry) or aggressive (when rivalry is intense). In the case of intense rivalry, pricing may even become predatory—that is, aimed at rapidly driving competitors out of business at the expense of near-term profitability. The hope in such a strategy is that having achieved a larger market share, the company can later increase prices to generate higher returns than before. For example, the predatory strategy has been alleged by some analysts to have been followed by major airlines trying to protect lucrative routes from discount airlines. Although laws concerning anti-competitive practices often prohibit predatory pricing to gain market share, in most cases, it is difficult to accurately ascribe the costs of products or services with sufficient precision to demonstrate that predatory pricing (as opposed to intense but fair price competition) is occurring. Companies seeking to follow low-cost strategies must have tight cost controls, efficient operating and reporting systems, and appropriate managerial incentives. In addition, they must commit themselves to painstaking scrutiny of production systems and their labor forces and to low-cost designs and product distribution. They must be able to invest in productivity-improving capital equipment and to finance that investment at a low cost of capital.

In differentiation strategies, companies attempt to establish themselves as the suppliers or producers of products and services that are unique either in quality, type, or means of distribution. To be successful, their price premiums must be above their costs of differentiation and the differentiation must be appealing to customers and sustainable over time. Corporate managers who successfully pursue differentiation strategies tend to have strong market research teams to identify and match customer needs with product development and marketing. Such a strategy puts a premium on employing creative and inventive people.

6.1 Elements That Should be Covered in a Company Analysis

A thorough company analysis, particularly as presented in a research report, should

- provide an overview of the company (corporate profile), including a basic understanding of its businesses, investment activities, corporate governance, and perceived strengths and weaknesses;
- explain relevant industry characteristics;
- analyze the demand for the company's products and services;
- analyze the supply of products and services, which includes an analysis of costs;
- explain the company's pricing environment; and
- present and interpret relevant financial ratios, including comparisons over time and comparisons with competitors.

Company analysis often includes forecasting the company's financial statements, particularly when the purpose of the analysis is to use a discounted cash flow method to value the company's common equity.

Exhibit 8 provides a checklist of points to cover in a company analysis. The list may need to be adapted to serve the needs of a particular company analysis and is not exhaustive.

Exhibit 8	A Checklist for Company Analysis

Corporate Profile

- Identity of company's major products and services, current position in industry, and history
- Composition of sales
- Product life-cycle stages/experience curve effects[16]
- Research & development activities
- Past and planned capital expenditures
- Board structure, composition, electoral system, anti-takeover provisions, and other corporate governance issues
- Management strengths, weaknesses, compensation, turnover, and corporate culture
- Benefits, retirement plans, and their influence on shareholder value
- Labor relations
- Insider ownership levels and changes
- Legal actions and the company's state of preparedness
- Other special strengths or weaknesses

Industry Characteristics

- Stage in its life cycle
- Business-cycle sensitivity or economic characteristics

(continued)

---

16 A *product life cycle* relates to stages in the sales of a product. *Experience curve effects* refer to the tendency for the cost of producing a good or service to decline with cumulative output.

Exhibit 8   (Continued)

- Typical product life cycles in the industry (short and marked by technological obsolescence or long, such as pharmaceuticals protected by patents)
- Brand loyalty, customer switching costs, and intensity of competition
- Entry and exit barriers
- Industry supplier considerations (concentration of sources, ability to switch suppliers or enter suppliers' business)
- Number of companies in the industry and whether it is, as determined by market shares, fragmented or concentrated
- Opportunity to differentiate product/service and relative product/service price, cost, and quality advantages/disadvantages
- Technologies used
- Government regulation
- State and history of labor relations
- Other industry problems/opportunities

Analysis of Demand for Products/Services

- Sources of demand
- Product differentiation
- Past record, sensitivities, and correlations with social, demographic, economic, and other variables
- Outlook—short, medium, and long term, including new product and business opportunities

Analysis of Supply of Products/Services

- Sources (concentration, competition, and substitutes)
- Industry capacity outlook—short, medium, and long term
- Company's capacity and cost structure
- Import/export considerations
- Proprietary products or trademarks

Analysis of Pricing

- Past relationships among demand, supply, and prices
- Significance of raw material and labor costs and the outlook for their cost and availability
- Outlook for selling prices, demand, and profitability based on current and anticipated future trends

Financial Ratios and Measures

(in multi-year spreadsheets with historical and forecast data)

  I. **Activity ratios**, measuring how efficiently a company performs such functions as the collection of receivables and inventory management:
  - Days of sales outstanding (DSO)
  - Days of inventory on hand (DOH)

Exhibit 8   (Continued)

- Days of payables outstanding (DPO)

II. Liquidity ratios, measuring a company's ability to meet its short-term obligations:

- Current ratio
- Quick ratio
- Cash ratio
- Cash conversion cycle (DOH + DSO – DPO)

III. Solvency ratios, measuring a company's ability to meet its debt obligations. (In the following, "net debt" is the amount of interest-bearing liabilities after subtracting cash and cash equivalents.)

- Net debt to EBITDA (earnings before interest, taxes, depreciation, and amortization)
- Net debt to capital
- Debt to assets
- Debt to capital (at book and market values)
- Financial leverage ratio (Average total assets/Average total equity)
- Cash flow to debt
- Interest coverage ratio
- Off-balance-sheet liabilities and contingent liabilities
- Non-arm's-length financial dealings

IV. Profitability ratios, measuring a company's ability to generate profitable sales from its resources (assets).

- Gross profit margin
- Operating profit margin
- Pretax profit margin
- Net profit margin
- Return on invested capital or ROIC (Net operating profits after tax/ Average invested capital)
- Return on assets or ROA (Net income/ Average total assets)
- Return on equity or ROE (Net income/Average total equity)

V. Financial Statistics and Related Considerations, quantities and facts about a company's finances that an analyst should understand.

- Growth rate of net sales
- Growth rate of gross profit
- EBITDA
- Net income
- Operating cash flow
- EPS
- Operating cash flow per share
- Operating cash flow in relation to maintenance and total capital expenditures
- Expected rate of return on retained cash flow
- Debt maturities and ability of company to refinance and/or repay debt

(continued)

Exhibit 8   (Continued)

- Dividend payout ratio (Common dividends/Net income available to common shareholders)
- Off-balance-sheet liabilities and contingent liabilities
- Non-arm's-length financial dealings

To evaluate a company's performance, the key measures presented in Exhibit 8 should be compared over time and between companies (particularly peer companies). The following formula can be used to analyze how and why a company's ROE differs from that of other companies or its own ROE in other periods by tracing the differences to changes in its profit margin, the productivity of its assets, or its financial leverage:

$$\text{ROE} = \left(\text{Net profit margin: Net earnings/Net sales}\right)$$
$$\times \left(\text{Asset turnover: Net sales/Average total assets}\right)$$
$$\times \left(\text{Financial leverage: Average total assets/Average common equity}\right)$$

The financial statements of a company over time provide numerous insights into the effects of industry conditions on its performance and the success or failure of its strategies. They also provide a framework for forecasting the company's operating performance when given the analyst's assumptions for numerous variables in the future. The financial ratios listed in Exhibit 8 are applicable to a wide range of companies and industries, but other statistics and ratios are often also used.

6.2 Spreadsheet Modeling

Spreadsheet modeling of financial statements to analyze and forecast revenues, operating and net income, and cash flows has become one of the most widely used tools in company analysis. Although spreadsheet models are a valuable tool for understanding past financial performance and forecasting future performance, the complexity of such models can at times be a problem. Because modeling requires the analyst to predict and input numerous items in financial statements, there is a risk of errors—either in assumptions made or in formulas in the model—which can compound, leading to erroneous forecasts. Yet, those forecasts may seem precise because of the sheer complexity of the model. The result is often a false sense of understanding and security on the part of those who rely on the models. To guard against this, before or after a model is completed, a "reality check" of the model is useful.

Such testing for reasonableness can be done by, first, asking what the few most important changes in income statement items are likely to be from last year to this year and the next year and, second, attempting to quantify the effects of these significant changes or "swing factors" on the bottom line. If an analyst cannot summarize in a few points what factors are realistically expected to change income from year to year and is not convinced that these assumptions are correct, then he or she does not really understand the output of the computer modeling efforts. In general, financial models should be in a format that matches the company's reporting of its financial results or supplementary disclosures or that can be accurately derived from these reports. Otherwise, there will be no natural reality check when the company issues its financial results and the analyst will not be able to compare his or her estimates with actual reported results.

SUMMARY

In this reading, we have provided an overview of industry analysis and illustrated approaches that are widely used by analysts to examine an industry.

- Company analysis and industry analysis are closely interrelated. Company and industry analysis together can provide insight into sources of industry revenue growth and competitors' market shares and thus the future of an individual company's top-line growth and bottom-line profitability.

- Industry analysis is useful for:
  - understanding a company's business and business environment;
  - identifying active equity investment opportunities;
  - formulating an industry or sector rotation strategy; and
  - portfolio performance attribution.

- The three main approaches to classifying companies are:
  - products and/or services supplied;
  - business-cycle sensitivities; and
  - statistical similarities.

- Commercial industry classification systems include:
  - Global Industry Classification Standard;
  - Russell Global Sectors; and
  - Industry Classification Benchmark.

- Governmental industry classification systems include:
  - International Standard Industrial Classification of All Economic Activities;
  - Statistical Classification of Economic Activities in the European Community;
  - Australian and New Zealand Standard Industrial Classification; and
  - North American Industry Classification System.

- A limitation of current classification systems is that the narrowest classification unit assigned to a company generally cannot be assumed to constitute its peer group for the purposes of detailed fundamental comparisons or valuation.

- A peer group is a group of companies engaged in similar business activities whose economics and valuation are influenced by closely related factors.

- Steps in constructing a preliminary list of peer companies:
  - Examine commercial classification systems if available. These systems often provide a useful starting point for identifying companies operating in the same industry.
  - Review the subject company's annual report for a discussion of the competitive environment. Companies frequently cite specific competitors.
  - Review competitors' annual reports to identify other potential comparables.
  - Review industry trade publications to identify additional peer companies.
  - Confirm that each comparable or peer company derives a significant portion of its revenue and operating profit from a similar business activity as the subject company.

- Not all industries are created equal. Some are highly competitive, with many companies struggling to earn returns in excess of their cost of capital, and other industries have attractive characteristics that enable a majority of industry participants to generate healthy profits.

- Differing competitive environments are determined by the structural attributes of the industry. For this important reason, industry analysis is a vital complement to company analysis. The analyst needs to understand the context in which a company operates to fully understand the opportunities and threats that a company faces.

- The framework for strategic analysis known as "Porter's five forces" can provide a useful starting point. Porter maintains that the profitability of companies in an industry is determined by five forces: 1) The influence or threat of new entrants, which in turn is determined by economies of scale, brand loyalty, absolute cost advantages, customer switching costs, and government regulation; 2) the influence or threat of substitute products; 3) the bargaining power of customers, which is a function of switching costs among customers and the ability of customers to produce their own product; 4) the bargaining power of suppliers, which is a function of the feasibility of product substitution, the concentration of the buyer and supplier groups, and switching costs and entry costs in each case; and 5) the intensity of rivalry among established companies, which in turn is a function of industry competitive structure, demand conditions, cost conditions, and the height of exit barriers.

- The concept of barriers to entry refers to the ease with which new competitors can challenge incumbents and can be an important factor in determining the competitive environment of an industry. If new competitors can easily enter the industry, the industry is likely to be highly competitive because incumbents that attempt to raise prices will be undercut by newcomers. As a result, industries with low barriers to entry tend to have low pricing power. Conversely, if incumbents are protected by barriers to entry, they may enjoy a more benign competitive environment that gives them greater pricing power over their customers because they do not have to worry about being undercut by upstarts.

- Industry concentration is often, although not always, a sign that an industry may have pricing power and rational competition. Industry fragmentation is a much stronger signal, however, that the industry is competitive and pricing power is limited.

- The effect of industry capacity on pricing is clear: Tight capacity gives participants more pricing power because demand for products or services exceeds supply; overcapacity leads to price cutting and a highly competitive environment as excess supply chases demand. The analyst should think about not only current capacity conditions but also future changes in capacity levels—how long it takes for supply and demand to come into balance and what effect that process has on industry pricing power and returns.

- Examining the market share stability of an industry over time is similar to thinking about barriers to entry and the frequency with which new players enter an industry. Stable market shares typically indicate less competitive industries, whereas unstable market shares often indicate highly competitive industries with limited pricing power.

- An industry's position in its life cycle often has a large impact on its competitive dynamics, so it is important to keep this positioning in mind when performing strategic analysis of an industry. Industries, like individual companies, tend to evolve over time and usually experience significant changes in the rate of growth and levels of profitability along the way. Just as an investment in an individual company requires careful monitoring, industry analysis is a continuous process that must be repeated over time to identify changes that may be occurring.

- A useful framework for analyzing the evolution of an industry is an industry life-cycle model, which identifies the sequential stages that an industry typically goes through. The five stages of an industry life cycle according to the Hill and Jones model are:
  - embryonic;
  - growth;
  - shakeout;
  - mature; and
  - decline.

- Price competition and thinking like a customer are important factors that are often overlooked when analyzing an industry. Whatever factors most influence customer purchasing decisions are also likely to be the focus of competitive rivalry in the industry. Broadly, industries for which price is a large factor in customer purchase decisions tend to be more competitive than industries in which customers value other attributes more highly.

- External influences on industry growth, profitability, and risk include:
  - technology;
  - demographics;
  - government; and
  - social factors.

- Company analysis takes place after the analyst has gained an understanding of the company's external environment and includes answering questions about how the company will respond to the threats and opportunities presented by the external environment. This intended response is the individual company's competitive strategy. The analyst should seek to determine whether the strategy is primarily defensive or offensive in its nature and how the company intends to implement it.

- Porter identifies two chief competitive strategies:
  - A low-cost strategy (cost leadership) is one in which companies strive to become the low-cost producers and to gain market share by offering their products and services at lower prices than their competition while still making a profit margin sufficient to generate a superior rate of return based on the higher revenues achieved.
  - A product/service differentiation strategy is one in which companies attempt to establish themselves as the suppliers or producers of products and services that are unique either in quality, type, or means of distribution. To be successful, the companies' price premiums must be above their costs of differentiation and the differentiation must be appealing to customers and sustainable over time.

- A checklist for company analysis includes a thorough investigation of:
  - corporate profile;
  - industry characteristics;
  - demand for products/services;
  - supply of products/services;
  - pricing; and

- financial ratios.

■ Spreadsheet modeling of financial statements to analyze and forecast revenues, operating and net income, and cash flows has become one of the most widely used tools in company analysis. Spreadsheet modeling can be used to quantify the effects of the changes in certain swing factors on the various financial statements. The analyst should be aware that the output of the model will depend significantly on the assumptions that are made.

REFERENCES

Cavaglia, Stefano, Jeffrey Diermeier, Vadim Moroz, and Sonia De Zordo. 2004. "Investing in Global Equities." *Journal of Portfolio Management*, vol. 30, no. 3:88–94.

Hill, Charles, and Gareth Jones. 2008. "External Analysis: The Identification of Opportunities and Threats." *Strategic Management: An Integrated Approach*. Boston, MA: Houghton Mifflin Co.

McGahan, Anita M., and Michael E. Porter. 1997. "How Much Does Industry Matter, Really?" *Strategic Management Journal*, vol. 18, no. No. S1:15–30.

Porter, Michael E. 2008. "The Five Competitive Forces That Shape Strategy." *Harvard Business Review*, vol. 86, no. 1:78–93.

PRACTICE PROBLEMS

1 Which of the following is *least likely* to involve industry analysis?

   A Sector rotation strategy.

   B Top-down fundamental investing.

   C Tactical asset allocation strategy.

2 A sector rotation strategy involves investing in a sector by:

   A making regular investments in it.

   B investing in a pre-selected group of sectors on a rotating basis.

   C timing investment to take advantage of business-cycle conditions.

3 Which of the following information about a company would *most likely* depend on an industry analysis? The company's:

   A dividend policy.

   B competitive environment.

   C trends in corporate expenses.

4 Which industry classification system uses a three-tier classification system?

   A Russell Global Sectors.

   B Industry Classification Benchmark.

   C Global Industry Classification Standard.

5 In which sector would a manufacturer of personal care products be classified?

   A Health care.

   B Consumer staples.

   C Consumer discretionary.

6 Which of the following statements about commercial and government industry classification systems is *most* accurate?

   A Many commercial classification systems include private for-profit companies.

   B Both commercial and government classification systems exclude not-for-profit companies.

   C Commercial classification systems are generally updated more frequently than government classification systems.

7 Which of the following is *not* a limitation of the cyclical/non-cyclical descriptive approach to classifying companies?

   A A cyclical company may have a growth component in it.

   B Business-cycle sensitivity is a discrete phenomenon rather than a continuous spectrum.

   C A global company can experience economic expansion in one part of the world while experiencing recession in another part.

8 A company that is sensitive to the business cycle would *most likely*:

   A not have growth opportunities.

   B experience below-average fluctuation in demand.

   C sell products that the customer can purchase at a later date if necessary.

9 Which of the following factors would *most likely* be a limitation of applying business-cycle analysis to global industry analysis?

   A Some industries are relatively insensitive to the business cycle.

   B Correlations of security returns between different world markets are relatively low.

   C One region or country of the world may experience recession while another region experiences expansion.

10 Which of the following statements about peer groups is *most* accurate?

   A Constructing a peer group for a company follows a standardized process.

   B Commercial industry classification systems often provide a starting point for constructing a peer group.

   C A peer group is generally composed of all the companies in the most narrowly defined category used by the commercial industry classification system.

11 With regard to forming a company's peer group, which of the following statements is *not* correct?

   A Comments from the management of the company about competitors are generally not used when selecting the peer group.

   B The higher the proportion of revenue and operating profit of the peer company derived from business activities similar to the subject company, the more meaningful the comparison.

   C Comparing the company's performance measures with those for a potential peer-group company is of limited value when the companies are exposed to different stages of the business cycle.

12 When selecting companies for inclusion in a peer group, a company operating in three different business segments would:

   A be in only one peer group.

   B possibly be in more than one peer group.

   C not be included in any peer group.

13 An industry that *most likely* has both high barriers to entry and high barriers to exit is the:

   A restaurant industry.

   B advertising industry.

   C automobile industry.

14 Which factor is *most likely* associated with stable market share?

   A Low switching costs.

   B Low barriers to entry.

   C Slow pace of product innovation.

15 Which of the following companies *most likely* has the greatest ability to quickly increase its capacity?

   A Restaurant.

   B Steel producer.

   C Legal services provider.

16 A population that is rapidly aging would *most likely* cause the growth rate of the industry producing eye glasses and contact lenses to:

   A decrease.

   B increase.

C   not change.

17 If over a long period of time a country's average level of educational accomplishment increases, this development would *most likely* lead to the country's amount of income spent on consumer discretionary goods to:

A   decrease.

B   increase.

C   not change.

18 If the technology for an industry involves high fixed capital investment, then one way to seek higher profit growth is by pursuing:

A   economies of scale.

B   diseconomies of scale.

C   removal of features that differentiate the product or service provided.

19 Which of the following life-cycle phases is typically characterized by high prices?

A   Mature.

B   Growth.

C   Embryonic.

20 In which of the following life-cycle phases are price wars *most likely* to be absent?

A   Mature.

B   Decline.

C   Growth.

21 When graphically depicting the life-cycle model for an industry as a curve, the variables on the axes are:

A   price and time.

B   demand and time.

C   demand and stage of the life cycle.

22 Which of the following is *most likely* a characteristic of a concentrated industry?

A   Infrequent, tacit coordination.

B   Difficulty in monitoring other industry members.

C   Industry members attempting to avoid competition on price.

23 Which of the following industry characteristics is generally *least likely* to produce high returns on capital?

A   High barriers to entry

B   High degree of concentration

C   Short lead time to build new plants

24 An industry with high barriers to entry and weak pricing power *most likely* has:

A   high barriers to exit.

B   stable market shares.

C   significant numbers of issued patents.

25 Economic value is created for an industry's shareholders when the industry earns a return:

A   below the cost of capital.

B   equal to the cost of capital.

C   above the cost of capital.

26 Which of the following is *not* one of Porter's five forces?

A Intensity of rivalry.

B Bargaining power of suppliers.

C Threat of government intervention.

27 Which of the following industries is *most likely* to be characterized as concentrated with strong pricing power?

A Asset management.

B Alcoholic beverages.

C Household and personal products.

28 Which of the following industries is *most likely* to be considered to have the lowest barriers to entry?

A Oil services.

B Confections and candy.

C Branded pharmaceuticals.

29 With respect to competitive strategy, a company with a successful cost leadership strategy is *most likely* characterized by:

A a low cost of capital.

B reduced market share.

C the ability to offer products at higher prices than competitors.

30 When conducting a company analysis, the analysis of demand for a company's product is *least likely* to consider the:

A company's cost structure.

B motivations of the customer base.

C product's differentiating characteristics.

31 Which of the following statements about company analysis is *most* accurate?

A The complexity of spreadsheet modeling ensures precise forecasts of financial statements.

B The interpretation of financial ratios should focus on comparing the company's results over time but not with competitors.

C The corporate profile would include a description of the company's business, investment activities, governance, and strengths and weaknesses.

SOLUTIONS

1. C is correct. Tactical asset allocation involves timing investments in asset classes and does not make use of industry analysis.

2. C is correct. A sector rotation strategy is conducted by investors wishing to time investment in industries through an analysis of fundamentals and/or business-cycle conditions.

3. B is correct. Determination of a company's competitive environment depends on understanding its industry.

4. A is correct. The Russell system uses three tiers, whereas the other two systems are based on four tiers or levels.

5. B is correct. Personal care products are classified as consumer staples in the "Description of Representative Sectors."

6. C is correct. Commercial systems are generally updated more frequently than government systems, and include only publicly traded for-profit companies.

7. B is correct. Business-cycle sensitivity falls on a continuum and is not a discrete "either–or" phenomenon.

8. C is correct. Customers' flexibility as to when they purchase the product makes the product more sensitive to the business cycle.

9. C is correct. Varying conditions of recession or expansion around the world would affect the comparisons of companies with sales in different regions of the world.

10. B is correct. Constructing a peer group is a subjective process, and a logical starting point is to begin with a commercially available classification system. This system will identify a group of companies that may have properties comparable to the business activity of interest.

11. A is correct because it is a false statement. Reviewing the annual report to find management's discussion about the competitive environment and specific competitors is a suggested step in the process of constructing a peer group.

12. B is correct. The company could be in more than one peer group depending on the demand drivers for the business segments, although the multiple business segments may make it difficult to classify the company.

13. C is correct. For the automobile industry, the high capital requirements and other elements mentioned in the reading provide high barriers to entry, and recognition that auto factories are generally only of use for manufacturing cars implies a high barrier to exit.

14. C is correct. A slow pace of product innovation often means that customers prefer to stay with suppliers they know, implying stable market shares.

15. C is correct. Capacity increases in providing legal services would not involve several factors that would be important to the other two industries, including the need for substantial fixed capital investments or, in the case of a restaurant, outfitting rental or purchased space. These requirements would tend to slow down, respectively, steel production and restaurant expansion.

16. B is correct. Vision typically deteriorates at advanced ages. An increased number of older adults implies more eyewear products will be purchased.

17. B is correct. As their educational level increases, workers are able to perform more skilled tasks, earn higher wages, and as a result, have more income left for discretionary expenditures.

18 A is correct. Seeking economies of scale would tend to reduce per-unit costs and increase profit.

19 C is correct. The embryonic stage is characterized by slow growth and high prices.

20 C is correct. The growth phase is not likely to experience price wars because expanding industry demand provides companies the opportunity to grow even without increasing market share. When industry growth is stagnant, companies may only be able to grow by increasing market share, e.g., by engaging in price competition.

21 B is correct. The industry life-cycle model shows how demand evolves through time as an industry passes from the embryonic stage through the stage of decline.

22 C is correct. The relatively few members of the industry generally try to avoid price competition.

23 C is correct. With short lead times, industry capacity can be rapidly increased to satisfy demand, but it may also lead to overcapacity and lower profits.

24 A is correct. An industry that has high barriers to entry generally requires substantial physical capital and/or financial investment. With weak pricing power in the industry, finding a buyer for excess capacity (i.e., to exit the industry) may be difficult.

25 C is correct. Economic profit is earned and value created for shareholders when the company earns returns above the company's cost of capital.

26 C is correct. Although the threat of government intervention may be considered an element of some of Porter's five forces, it is not one of the listed forces.

27 B is correct. As displayed in Exhibit 4, the alcoholic beverage industry is concentrated and possesses strong pricing power.

28 A is correct. The oil services industry has medium barriers to entry because a company with a high level of technological innovation could obtain a niche market in a specific area of expertise.

29 A is correct. Companies with low cost strategies must be able to invest in productivity-improving equipment and finance that investment at a low cost of capital. Market share and pricing depend on whether the strategy is pursued defensively or offensively.

30 A is correct. The cost structure is an appropriate element when analyzing the supply of the product, but analysis of demand relies on the product's differentiating characteristics and the customers' needs and wants.

31 C is correct. The corporate profile would provide an understanding of these elements.

READING

50

Equity Valuation: Concepts and Basic Tools

by John J. Nagorniak, CFA, and Stephen E. Wilcox, CFA

LEARNING OUTCOMES

Mastery	The candidate should be able to:
☐	a. evaluate whether a security, given its current market price and a value estimate, is overvalued, fairly valued, or undervalued by the market;
☐	b. describe major categories of equity valuation models;
☐	c. explain the rationale for using present value models to value equity and describe the dividend discount and free-cash-flow-to-equity models;
☐	d. calculate the intrinsic value of a non-callable, non-convertible preferred stock;
☐	e. calculate and interpret the intrinsic value of an equity security based on the Gordon (constant) growth dividend discount model or a two-stage dividend discount model, as appropriate;
☐	f. identify companies for which the constant growth or a multistage dividend discount model is appropriate;
☐	g. explain the rationale for using price multiples to value equity and distinguish between multiples based on comparables versus multiples based on fundamentals;
☐	h. calculate and interpret the following multiples: price to earnings, price to an estimate of operating cash flow, price to sales, and price to book value;
☐	i. describe enterprise value multiples and their use in estimating equity value;
☐	j. describe asset-based valuation models and their use in estimating equity value;
☐	k. explain advantages and disadvantages of each category of valuation model.

1 INTRODUCTION

Analysts gather and process information to make investment decisions, including buy and sell recommendations. What information is gathered and how it is processed depend on the analyst and the purpose of the analysis. Technical analysis uses such information as stock price and trading volume as the basis for investment decisions. Fundamental analysis uses information about the economy, industry, and company as the basis for investment decisions. Examples of fundamentals are unemployment rates, gross domestic product (GDP) growth, industry growth, and quality of and growth in company earnings. Whereas technical analysts use information to predict price movements and base investment decisions on the direction of predicted change in prices, fundamental analysts use information to estimate the value of a security and to compare the estimated value to the market price and then base investment decisions on that comparison.

This reading introduces equity valuation models used to estimate the **intrinsic value** (synonym: **fundamental value**) of a security; intrinsic value is based on an analysis of investment fundamentals and characteristics. The fundamentals to be considered depend on the analyst's approach to valuation. In a top-down approach, an analyst examines the economic environment, identifies sectors that are expected to prosper in that environment, and analyzes securities of companies from previously identified attractive sectors. In a bottom-up approach, an analyst typically follows an industry or industries and forecasts fundamentals for the companies in those industries in order to determine valuation. Whatever the approach, an analyst who estimates the intrinsic value of an equity security is implicitly questioning the accuracy of the market price as an estimate of value. Valuation is particularly important in active equity portfolio management, which aims to improve on the return–risk trade-off of a portfolio's benchmark by identifying mispriced securities.

This reading is organized as follows. Section 2 discusses the implications of differences between estimated value and market price. Section 3 introduces three major categories of valuation model. Section 4 presents an overview of present value models with a focus on the dividend discount model. Section 5 describes and examines the use of multiples in valuation. Section 6 explains asset-based valuation and demonstrates how these models can be used to estimate value. Section 7 states conclusions and summarizes the reading.

2 ESTIMATED VALUE AND MARKET PRICE

By comparing estimates of value and market price, an analyst can arrive at one of three conclusions: The security is *undervalued*, *overvalued*, or *fairly valued* in the marketplace. For example, if the market price of an asset is $10 and the analyst estimates intrinsic value at $10, a logical conclusion is that the security is fairly valued. If the security is selling for $20, the security would be considered overvalued. If the security is selling for $5, the security would be considered undervalued. Basically, by estimating value, the analyst is assuming that the market price is not necessarily the best estimate of intrinsic value. If the estimated value exceeds the market price, the analyst infers the security is *undervalued*. If the estimated value equals the market price, the analyst infers the security is *fairly valued*. If the estimated value is less than the market price, the analyst infers the security is *overvalued*.

In practice, the conclusion is not so straightforward. Analysts must cope with uncertainties related to model appropriateness and the correct value of inputs. An analyst's final conclusion depends not only on the comparison of the estimated value and the market price but also on the analyst's confidence in the estimated value (i.e., in the model selected and the inputs used in it). One can envision a spectrum running from relatively high confidence in the valuation model *and* the inputs to relatively low confidence in the valuation model *and/or* the inputs. When confidence is relatively low, the analyst might demand a substantial divergence between his or her own value estimate and the market price before acting on an apparent mispricing. For instance, if the estimate of intrinsic value is $10 and the market price is $10.05, the analyst might reasonably conclude that the security is fairly valued and that the 1/2 of 1 percent market price difference from the estimated value is within the analyst's confidence interval.

Confidence in the convergence of the market price to the intrinsic value over the investment time horizon relevant to the objectives of the portfolio must also be taken into account before an analyst acts on an apparent mispricing or makes a buy, sell, or hold recommendation: The ability to benefit from identifying a mispriced security depends on the market price converging to the estimated intrinsic value.

In seeking to identify mispricing and attractive investments, analysts are treating market prices with skepticism, but they are also treating market prices with respect. For example, an analyst who finds that many securities examined appear to be overvalued will typically recheck models and inputs before acting on a conclusion of overvaluation. Analysts also often recognize and factor into recommendations that different market segments—such as securities closely followed by analysts versus securities relatively neglected by analysts—may differ in how common or persistent mispricing is. Mispricing may be more likely in securities neglected by analysts.

EXAMPLE 1

Valuation and Analyst Response

1   An analyst finds that all the securities analyzed have estimated values higher than their market prices. The securities all appear to be:

   A   overvalued.

   B   undervalued.

   C   fairly valued.

2   An analyst finds that nearly all companies in a market segment have common shares which are trading at market prices above the analyst's estimate of the shares' values. This market segment is widely followed by analysts. Which of the following statements describes the analyst's *most appropriate* first action?

   A   Issue a sell recommendation for each share issue.

   B   Issue a buy recommendation for each share issue.

   C   Reexamine the models and inputs used for the valuations.

3   An analyst, using a number of models and a range of inputs, estimates a security's value to be between ¥250 and ¥270. The security is trading at ¥265. The security appears to be:

   A   overvalued.

   B   undervalued.

   C   fairly valued.

Solution to 1:

B is correct. The estimated intrinsic value for each security is greater than the market price. The securities all appear to be undervalued in the market. Note, however, that the analyst may wish to reexamine the model and inputs to check that the conclusion is valid.

Solution to 2:

C is correct. It seems improbable that all the share issues analyzed are overvalued, as indicated by market prices in excess of estimated value—particularly because the market segment is widely followed by analysts. Thus, the analyst will not issue a sell recommendation for each issue. The analyst will *most appropriately* reexamine the models and inputs prior to issuing any recommendations. A buy recommendation is not an appropriate response to an overvalued security.

Solution to 3:

C is correct. The security's market price of ¥265 is within the range estimated by the analyst. The security appears to be fairly valued.

Analysts often use a variety of models and inputs to achieve greater confidence in their estimates of intrinsic value. The use of more than one model and a range of inputs also helps the analyst understand the sensitivity of value estimates to different models and inputs.

3   MAJOR CATEGORIES OF EQUITY VALUATION MODELS

Three major categories of equity valuation models are as follows:

- **Present value models** (synonym: **discounted cash flow models**). These models estimate the intrinsic value of a security as the present value of the future benefits expected to be received from the security. In present value models, benefits are often defined in terms of cash expected to be distributed to shareholders (**dividend discount models**) or in terms of cash flows available to be distributed to shareholders after meeting capital expenditure and working capital needs (**free-cash-flow-to-equity models**). Many models fall within this category, ranging from the relatively simple to the very complex. In Section 4, we discuss in detail two of the simpler models, the Gordon (constant) growth model and the two-stage dividend discount models.

- **Multiplier models** (synonym: **market multiple models**). These models are based chiefly on share price multiples or enterprise value multiples. The former model estimates intrinsic value of a common share from a price multiple for some fundamental variable, such as revenues, earnings, cash flows, or book value. Examples of the multiples include price to earnings (P/E, share price divided by earnings per share) and price to sales (P/S, share price divided by sales per share). The fundamental variable may be stated on a forward basis (e.g., forecasted EPS for the next year) or a trailing basis (e.g., EPS for the past year), as long as the usage is consistent across companies being examined. Price multiples are also used to compare relative values. The use of the ratio of share price to EPS—that is, the P/E multiple—to judge relative value is an example of this approach to equity valuation.

Enterprise value (EV) multiples have the form (Enterprise value)/(Value of a fundamental variable). Two possible choices for the denominator are earnings before interest, taxes, depreciation, and amortization (EBITDA) and total revenue. Enterprise value, the numerator, is a measure of a company's total market value from which cash and short-term investments have been subtracted (because an acquirer could use those assets to pay for acquiring the company). An estimate of common share value can be calculated indirectly from the EV multiple; the value of liabilities and preferred shares can be subtracted from the EV to arrive at the value of common equity.

- **Asset-based valuation models**. These models estimate intrinsic value of a common share from the estimated value of the assets of a corporation minus the estimated value of its liabilities and preferred shares. The estimated market value of the assets is often determined by making adjustments to the **book value** (synonym: **carrying value**) of assets and liabilities. The theory underlying the asset-based approach is that the value of a business is equal to the sum of the value of the business's assets.

As already mentioned, many analysts use more than one type of model to estimate value. Analysts recognize that each model is a simplification of the real world and that there are uncertainties related to model appropriateness and the inputs to the models. The choice of model(s) will depend on the availability of information to input into the model(s) and the analyst's confidence in the information and in the appropriateness of the model(s).

EXAMPLE 2

Categories of Equity Valuation Models

1 An analyst is estimating the intrinsic value of a new company. The analyst has one year of financial statements for the company and has calculated the average values of a variety of price multiples for the industry in which the company operates. The analyst plans to use at least one model from each of the three categories of valuation models. The analyst is *least likely* to rely on the estimate(s) from the:

   A multiplier model(s).

   B present value model(s).

   C asset-based valuation model(s).

2 Based on a company's EPS of €1.35, an analyst estimates the intrinsic value of a security to be €16.60. Which type of model is the analyst *most likely* to be using to estimate intrinsic value?

   A Multiplier model.

   B Present value model.

   C Asset-based valuation model.

Solution to 1:

B is correct. Because the company has only one year of data available, the analyst is *least likely* to be confident in the inputs for a present value model. The values on the balance sheet, even before adjustment, are likely to be close to market values because the assets are all relatively new. The multiplier models are based on average multiples from the industry.

Solution to 2:

A is correct. The analyst is using a multiplier model based on the P/E multiple. The P/E multiple used was 16.60/1.35 = 12.3.

As you begin the study of specific equity valuation models in the next section, you must bear in mind that any model of value is, by necessity, a simplification of the real world. Never forget this simple fact! You may encounter models much more complicated than the ones discussed here, but even those models will be simplifications of reality.

4 PRESENT VALUE MODELS: THE DIVIDEND DISCOUNT MODEL

Present value models follow a fundamental tenet of economics stating that individuals defer consumption—that is, they invest—for the future benefits expected. Individuals and companies make an investment because they expect a rate of return over the investment period. Logically, the value of an investment should be equal to the present value of the expected future benefits. For common shares, an analyst can equate benefits to the cash flows to be generated by the investment. The simplest present value model of equity valuation is the dividend discount model (DDM), which specifies cash flows from a common stock investment to be dividends.[1] If the issuing company is assumed to be a going concern, the intrinsic value of a share is the present value of expected future dividends. If a constant required rate of return is also assumed, then the DDM expression for the intrinsic value of a share is Equation 1:

$$V_0 = \sum_{t=1}^{\infty} \frac{D_t}{(1+r)^t} \qquad (1)$$

where

V_0 = value of a share of stock today, at $t = 0$
D_t = expected dividend in year t, assumed to be paid at the end of the year
r = required rate of return on the stock

At the shareholder level, cash received from a common stock investment includes any dividends received and the proceeds when shares are sold. If an investor intends to buy and hold a share for one year, the value of the share today is the present value of two cash flows—namely, the expected dividend *plus* the expected selling price in one year:

$$V_0 = \frac{D_1 + P_1}{(1+r)^1} = \frac{D_1}{(1+r)^1} + \frac{P_1}{(1+r)^1} \qquad (2)$$

where P_1 = the expected price per share at $t = 1$.

To estimate the expected selling price, P_1, the analyst could estimate the price another investor with a one-year holding period would pay for the share in one year. If V_0 is based on D_1 and P_1, it follows that P_1 could be estimated from D_2 and P_2:

$$P_1 = \frac{D_2 + P_2}{(1+r)}$$

Substituting the right side of this equation for P_1 in Equation 2 results in V_0 estimated as

$$V_0 = \frac{D_1}{(1+r)} + \frac{D_2 + P_2}{(1+r)^2} = \frac{D_1}{(1+r)} + \frac{D_2}{(1+r)^2} + \frac{P_2}{(1+r)^2}$$

Repeating this process, we find the value for n holding periods is the present value of the expected dividends for the n periods plus the present value of the expected price in n periods:

$$V_0 = \frac{D_1}{(1+r)^1} + \cdots + \frac{D_n}{(1+r)^n} + \frac{P_n}{(1+r)^n}$$

Using summation notation to represent the present value of the n expected dividends, we arrive at the general expression for an n-period holding period or investment horizon:

$$V_0 = \sum_{t=1}^{n}\frac{D_t}{(1+r)^t} + \frac{P_n}{(1+r)^n} \tag{3}$$

The expected value of a share at the end of the investment horizon—in effect, the expected selling price—is often referred to as the **terminal stock value** (or **terminal value**).

EXAMPLE 3

Estimating Share Value for a Three-Year Investment Horizon

For the next three years, the annual dividends of a stock are expected to be €2.00, €2.10, and €2.20. The stock price is expected to be €20.00 at the end of three years. If the required rate of return on the shares is 10 percent, what is the estimated value of a share?

Solution:

The present values of the expected future cash flows can be written as follows:

$$V_0 = \frac{2.00}{(1.10)^1} + \frac{2.10}{(1.10)^2} + \frac{2.20}{(1.10)^3} + \frac{20.00}{(1.10)^3}$$

Calculating and summing these present values gives an estimated share value of $V_0 = 1.818 + 1.736 + 1.653 + 15.026 = €20.23$.

The three dividends have a total present value of €5.207, and the terminal stock value has a present value of €15.026, for a total estimated value of €20.23.

Extending the holding period into the indefinite future, we can say that a stock's estimated value is the present value of all expected future dividends as shown in Equation 1.

Consideration of an indefinite future is valid because businesses established as corporations are generally set up to operate indefinitely. This general form of the DDM applies even in the case in which the investor has a finite investment horizon. For that investor, stock value today depends *directly* on the dividends the investor expects to receive before the stock is sold and depends *indirectly* on the expected dividends for periods subsequent to that sale, because those expected future dividends determine the expected selling price. Thus, the general expression given by Equation 1 holds irrespective of the investor's holding period.

In practice, many analysts prefer to use a free-cash-flow-to-equity (FCFE) valuation model. These analysts assume that dividend-paying *capacity* should be reflected in the cash flow estimates rather than *expected dividends*. FCFE is a measure of dividend-paying capacity. Analysts may also use FCFE valuation models for a non-dividend-paying stock. To use a DDM, the analyst needs to predict the timing and amount of the first dividend and all the dividends or dividend growth thereafter. Making these predictions for non-dividend-paying stock accurately is typically difficult, so in such cases, analysts often resort to FCFE models.

The calculation of FCFE starts with the calculation of cash flow from operations (CFO). CFO is simply defined as net income plus non-cash expenses minus investment in working capital. FCFE is a measure of cash flow generated in a period that is available for distribution to common shareholders. What does "available for distribution" mean? The entire CFO is *not* available for distribution; the portion of the CFO needed for fixed capital investment (FCInv) during the period to maintain the value of the company as a going concern is *not* viewed as available for distribution to common shareholders. Net amounts borrowed (borrowings minus repayments) are considered to be available for distribution to common shareholders. Thus, FCFE can be expressed as

FCFE = CFO − FCInv + Net borrowing   (4)

The information needed to calculate historical FCFE is available from a company's statement of cash flows and financial disclosures. Frequently, under the assumption that management is acting in the interest of maintaining the value of the company as a going concern, reported capital expenditure is taken to represent FCInv. Analysts must make projections of financials to forecast future FCFE. Valuation obtained by using FCFE involves discounting expected future FCFE by the required rate of return on equity; the expression parallels Equation 1:

$$V_0 = \sum_{t=1}^{\infty} \frac{\text{FCFE}_t}{(1+r)^t}$$

EXAMPLE 4

Present Value Models

1 An investor expects a share to pay dividends of $3.00 and $3.15 at the end of Years 1 and 2, respectively. At the end of the second year, the investor expects the shares to trade at $40.00. The required rate of return on the shares is 8 percent. If the investor's forecasts are accurate and the market price of the shares is currently $30, the *most likely* conclusion is that the shares are:

   A overvalued.

   B undervalued.

   C fairly valued.

2 Two investors with different holding periods but the same expectations and required rate of return for a company are estimating the intrinsic value of a common share of the company. The investor with the shorter holding period will *most likely* estimate a:

   A lower intrinsic value.

   B higher intrinsic value.

   C similar intrinsic value.

3 An equity valuation model that focuses on expected dividends rather than the capacity to pay dividends is the:

A dividend discount model.

B free cash flow to equity model.

C cash flow return on investment model.

Solution to 1:

B is correct.

$$V_0 = \frac{3.00}{(1.08)^1} + \frac{3.15}{(1.08)^2} + \frac{40.00}{(1.08)^2} = 39.77$$

The value estimate of $39.77 exceeds the market price of $30, so the conclusion is that the shares are undervalued.

Solution to 2:

C is correct. The intrinsic value of a security is independent of the investor's holding period.

Solution to 3:

A is correct. Dividend discount models focus on expected dividends.

How is the required rate of return for use in present value models estimated? To estimate the required rate of return on a share, analysts frequently use the capital asset pricing model (CAPM):

Required rate of return on share i =

Current expected risk − free rate of return

+ Beta$_i$ [Market (equity) risk premium] (5)

Equation 5 states that the required rate of return on a share is the sum of the current expected risk-free rate plus a risk premium that equals the product of the stock's beta (a measure of non-diversifiable risk) and the market risk premium (the expected return of the market in excess of the risk-free return, where in practice, the "market" is often represented by a broad stock market index). However, even if analysts agree that the CAPM is an appropriate model, their inputs into the CAPM may differ. Thus, there is no uniquely correct answer to the question: What is the required rate of return?

Other common methods for estimating the required rate of return for the stock of a company include adding a risk premium that is based on economic judgments, rather than the CAPM, to an appropriate risk-free rate (usually a government bond) and adding a risk premium to the yield on the company's bonds. Good business and economic judgment is paramount in estimating the required rate of return. In many investment firms, required rates of return are determined by firm policy.

4.1 Preferred Stock Valuation

General dividend discount models are relatively easy to apply to preferred shares. In its simplest form, **preferred stock** is a form of equity (generally, non-voting) that has priority over common stock in the receipt of dividends and on the issuer's assets in the event of a company's liquidation. It may have a stated maturity date at which time payment of the stock's par (face) value is made or it may be perpetual with no maturity date; additionally, it may be callable or convertible.

For a non-callable, non-convertible perpetual preferred share paying a level dividend D and assuming a constant required rate of return over time, Equation 1 reduces to the formula for the present value of a perpetuity. Its value is:

$$V_0 = \frac{D_0}{r} \qquad\qquad (6)$$

For example, a \$100 par value non-callable perpetual preferred stock offers an annual dividend of \$5.50. If its required rate of return is 6 percent, the value estimate would be \$5.50/0.06 = \$91.67.

For a non-callable, non-convertible preferred stock with maturity at time n, the estimated intrinsic value can be estimated by using Equation 3 but using the preferred stock's par value, F, instead of P_n:

$$V_0 = \sum_{t=1}^{n} \frac{D_t}{(1+r)^t} + \frac{F}{(1+r)^n} \qquad\qquad (7)$$

When Equation 7 is used, the most precise approach is to use values for n, r, and D that reflect the payment schedule of the dividends. This method is similar to the practice of fixed-income analysts in valuing a bond. For example, a non-convertible preferred stock with a par value of £20.00, maturity in six years, a nominal required rate of return of 8.20 percent, and semiannual dividends of £2.00 would be valued by using an n of 12, an r of 4.10 percent, a D of £2.00, and an F of £20.00. The result would be an estimated value of £31.01. Assuming payments are annual rather than semiannual (i.e., assuming that $n = 6$, $r = 8.20$ percent, and $D = £4.00$) would result in an estimated value of £30.84.

Preferred stock issues are frequently callable (redeemable) by the issuer at some point prior to maturity, often at par value or at prices in excess of par value that decline to par value as the maturity date approaches. Such call options tend to reduce the value of a preferred issue to an investor because the option to redeem will be exercised by the issuer when it is in the issuer's favor and ignored when it is not. For example, if an issuer can redeem shares at par value that would otherwise trade (on the basis of dividends, maturity, and required rate of return) above par value, the issuer has motivation to redeem the shares.

Preferred stock issues can also include a retraction option that enables the holder of the preferred stock to sell the shares back to the issuer prior to maturity on prespecified terms. Essentially, the holder of the shares has a put option. Such put options tend to increase the value of a preferred issue to an investor because the option to retract will be exercised by the investor when it is in the investor's favor and ignored when it is not. Although the precise valuation of issues with such embedded options is beyond the scope of this reading, Example 5 includes a case in which Equation 7 can be used to approximate the value of a callable, retractable preferred share.

EXAMPLE 5

Preferred Share Valuation: Two Cases

Case 1: Non-callable, Non-convertible, Perpetual Preferred Shares

The following facts concerning the Union Electric Company 4.75 percent perpetual preferred shares (CUSIP identifier: 906548821) are as follows:

- Issuer: Union Electric Co. (owned by Ameren)
- Par value: US\$100
- Dividend: US\$4.75 per year

- Maturity: perpetual
- Embedded options: none
- Credit rating: Moody's Investors Service/Standard & Poor's Ba1/BB
- Required rate of return on Ba1/BB rated preferred shares as of valuation date: 7.5 percent.

A   Estimate the intrinsic value of this preferred share.

B   Explain whether the intrinsic value of this issue would be higher or lower if the issue were callable (with all other facts remaining unchanged).

Solution to 1A:

Basing the discount rate on the required rate of return on Ba1/BB rated preferred shares of 7.5 percent gives an intrinsic value estimate of US$4.75/0.075 = US$63.33.

Solution to 1B:

The intrinsic value would be lower if the issue were callable. The option to redeem or call the issue is valuable to the issuer because the call will be exercised when doing so is in the issuer's interest. The intrinsic value of the shares to the investor will typically be lower if the issue is callable. In this case, because the intrinsic value without the call is much less than the par value, the issuer would be unlikely to redeem the issue if it were callable; thus, callability would reduce intrinsic value, but only slightly.

Case 2: Retractable Term Preferred Shares

Retractable term preferred shares are a type of preferred share that has been issued by Canadian companies. This type of issue specifies a "retraction date" when the preferred shareholders have the option to sell back their shares to the issuer at par value (i.e., the shares are "retractable" or "putable" at that date).[2] At predetermined dates prior to the retraction date, the issuer has the option to redeem the preferred issue at predetermined prices (which are always at or above par value).

An example of a retractable term preferred share currently outstanding is YPG (Yellow Pages) Holdings, series 2, 5 percent first preferreds (TSX: YPG. PR.B). YPG Holdings is Canada's leading local commercial search provider and largest telephone directory publisher. The issue is in Canadian dollars. The shares have a $25 par value and pay a quarterly dividend of $0.3125 [= (5 percent × $25)/4]. As of 29 December 2008, shares were priced at $12.01 and carried ratings from Dominion Bond Rating Service (DBRS) and Standard & Poor's of Pfd-3H and P3, respectively. Thus, the shares are viewed by DBRS as having "adequate" credit quality, qualified by "H," which means relatively high quality within that group. The shares are redeemable at the option of YPG Holdings in June 2009 at $26.75, with redemption prices eventually declining to par value at later dates. The retraction date is 30 June 2017, or eight and half years (34 quarters) from the date (31 December 2008) the shares were being valued. Similarly rated preferred issues had an estimated nominal required rate of return of 15.5 percent (3.875 percent per quarter). Because the issue's market price is

---

2 "Retraction" refers to this option, which is a put option. The terminology is not completely settled: The type of share being called "retractable term preferred" is also known as "hard retractable preferred," with "hard" referring to payment in cash rather than common shares at the retraction date. See the 2009 ScotiaMcLeod report http://www.ritceyteam.com/pdf/guide_to_preferred_shares.pdf.

so far below the prices at which YPG could redeem or call the issue, redemption is considered to be unlikely and the redemption option is assumed here to have minimal value for an investor.

A   Assume that the issue will be retracted in June 2017; the holders of the shares will put the shares to the company in June 2017. Based on the information given, estimate the intrinsic value of a share.

Solution to 2A:

An intrinsic value estimate of a share of this preferred issue is $12.71:

$$
V_0 = \left[\frac{\$0.3125}{(1 + 0.03875)} + \frac{\$0.3125}{(1 + 0.03875)^2} + \ldots + \frac{\$0.3125}{(1 + 0.03875)^{34}} \right]
$$
$$
+ \frac{\$25}{(1 + 0.03875)^{34}} \approx \$12.71
$$

4.2 The Gordon Growth Model

A rather obvious problem when one is trying to implement Equation 1 for common equity is that it requires the analyst to estimate an infinite series of expected dividends. To simplify this process, analysts frequently make assumptions about how dividends will grow or change over time. The Gordon (constant) growth model (Gordon, 1962) is a simple and well-recognized DDM. The model assumes dividends grow indefinitely at a constant rate.

Because of its assumption of a constant growth rate, the Gordon growth model is particularly appropriate for valuing the equity of dividend-paying companies that are relatively insensitive to the business cycle and in a mature growth phase. Examples might include an electric utility serving a slowly growing area or a producer of a staple food product (e.g., bread). A history of increasing the dividend at a stable growth rate is another practical criterion if the analyst believes that pattern will hold in the future.

With a constant growth assumption, Equation 1 can be written as Equation 8, where g is the constant growth rate:

$$
V_0 = \sum_{t=1}^{\infty} \frac{D_0 (1 + g)^t}{(1 + r)^t} = D_0 \left[\frac{(1 + g)}{(1 + r)} + \frac{(1 + g)^2}{(1 + r)^2} + \ldots + \frac{(1 + g)^{\infty}}{(1 + r)^{\infty}} \right] \tag{8}
$$

If required return r is assumed to be strictly greater than growth rate g, then the square-bracketed term in Equation 8 is an infinite geometric series and sums to $[(1 + g)/(r - g)]$. Substituting into Equation 8 produces the Gordon growth model as presented in Equation 9:

$$
V_0 = \frac{D_0 (1 + g)}{r - g} = \frac{D_1}{r - g} \tag{9}
$$

For an illustration of the expression, suppose the current (most recent) annual dividend on a share is €5.00 and dividends are expected to grow at 4 percent per year. The required rate of return on equity is 8 percent. The Gordon growth model estimate of intrinsic value is, therefore, €5.00(1.04)/(0.08 − 0.04) = €5.20/0.04 = €130 per share. Note that the numerator is D_1 not D_0. (Using the wrong numerator is a common error.)

The Gordon growth model estimates intrinsic value as the present value of a growing perpetuity. If the growth rate, g, is assumed to be zero, Equation 8 reduces to the expression for the present value of a perpetuity, given earlier as Equation 6.

In estimating a long-term growth rate, analysts use a variety of methods, including assessing the growth in dividends or earnings over time, using the industry median growth rate, and using the relationship shown in Equation 10 to estimate the sustainable growth rate:

$$g = b \times ROE \tag{10}$$

where

> g = dividend growth rate
> b = earnings retention rate = (1 – Dividend payout ratio)

ROE = return on equity

Example 6 illustrates the application of the Gordon growth model to the shares of an integrated petroleum company. The analyst believes it will not continue to grow at the relatively fast growth rate of its past but will moderate to a lower and stable growth rate in the future. The example asks how much the dividend growth assumption adds to the intrinsic value estimate. The question is relevant to valuation because if the amount is high on a percentage basis, a large part of the value of the share depends on the realization of the growth estimate. One can answer the question by subtracting from the intrinsic value estimate determined by Equation 9 the value determined by Equation 6, which assumes no dividend growth.[3]

EXAMPLE 6

Applying the Gordon Growth Model

Total S.A. (Euronext Paris: FP), one of France's largest corporations and the world's fifth largest publicly traded integrated petroleum company, operates in more than 130 countries. Total engages in all aspects of the petroleum industry, produces base chemicals and specialty chemicals for the industrial and consumer markets, and has interests in the coal mining and power generation sectors. To meet growing energy needs on a long-term basis, Total considers sustainability when making decisions. Selected financial information for Total appears in Exhibit 1.

Exhibit 1	Selected Financial Information for Total S.A.				
Year	**2008**	**2007**	**2006**	**2005**	**2004**
EPS	€6.20	€5.37	€5.44	€5.08	€3.76
DPS	€2.28	€2.07	€1.87	€1.62	€1.35
Payout ratio	37%	39%	34%	32%	36%
ROE	32%	31%	33%	35%	33%
Share price					
(Paris Bourse)	€38.910	€56.830	€54.650	€52.367	€39.657

Note: DPS stands for "dividends per share."
Source: Company website: www.total.com.

---

3 A related concept, the present value of growth opportunities (PVGO), is discussed in more advanced readings.

The analyst estimates the growth rate to be approximately 14 percent based on the dividend growth rate over the period 2004 to 2008 [$1.35(1 + g)^4 = 2.28$, so $g = 14\%$]. To verify that the estimated growth rate of 14 percent is feasible in the future, the analyst also uses the average of Total's retention rate and ROE for the previous five years ($g \approx 0.64 \times 33\% \approx 21\%$) to estimate the sustainable growth rate.

Using a number of approaches, including adding a risk premium to a long-term French government bond and using the CAPM, the analyst estimates a required return of 19 percent. The most recent dividend of €2.28 is used for D_0.

1   Use the Gordon growth model to estimate Total's intrinsic value.

2   How much does the dividend growth assumption add to the intrinsic value estimate?

3   Based on the estimated intrinsic value, is a share of Total undervalued, overvalued, or fairly valued?

4   What is the intrinsic value if the growth rate estimate is lowered to 13 percent?

5   What is the intrinsic value if the growth rate estimate is lowered to 13 percent and the required rate of return estimate is increased to 20 percent?

Solution to 1:

$$V_0 = \frac{€2.28(1 + 0.14)}{0.19 - 0.14} = €51.98$$

Solution to 2:

$$€51.98 - \frac{€2.28}{0.19} = €39.98$$

Solution to 3:

A share of Total appears to be undervalued. The analyst, before making a recommendation, might consider how realistic the estimated inputs are and check the sensitivity of the estimated value to changes in the inputs.

Solution to 4:

$$V_0 = \frac{€2.28(1 + 0.13)}{0.19 - 0.13} = €42.94$$

Solution to 5:

$$V_0 = \frac{€2.28(1 + 0.13)}{0.20 - 0.13} = €36.81$$

The Gordon growth model estimate of intrinsic value is extremely sensitive to the choice of required rate of return r and growth rate g. It is likely that the growth rate assumption and the required return assumption used initially were too high. Worldwide economic growth is typically in the low single digits, making it highly unlikely that Total's dividend can grow at 14 percent into perpetuity. Exhibit 2 presents a further sensitivity analysis of Total's intrinsic value to the required return and growth estimates.

Exhibit 2	Sensitivity Analysis of the Intrinsic-Value Estimate for Total S.A.				
	g = 2%	g = 5%	g = 8%	g = 11%	g = 14%
r = 7%	€46.512	€119.700	—	—	—
r = 10%	€29.070	€47.880	€123.120	—	—
r = 13%	€21.142	€29.925	€49.248	€126.540	—
r = 16%	€16.611	€21.764	€30.780	€50.616	€129.960
r = 19%	€13.680	€17.100	€22.385	€31.635	€51.984

Note that no value is shown when the growth rate exceeds the required rate of return. The Gordon growth model assumes that the growth rate cannot be greater than the required rate of return.

The assumptions of the Gordon model are as follows:

- Dividends are the correct metric to use for valuation purposes.
- The dividend growth rate is forever: It is perpetual and never changes.
- The required rate of return is also constant over time.
- The dividend growth rate is strictly less than the required rate of return.

An analyst might be dissatisfied with these assumptions for many reasons. The equities being examined might not currently pay a dividend. The Gordon assumptions might be too simplistic to reflect the characteristics of the companies being evaluated. Some alternatives to using the Gordon model are as follows:

- Use a more robust DDM that allows for varying patterns of growth.
- Use a cash flow measure other than dividends for valuation purposes.
- Use some other approach (such as a multiplier method) to valuation.

Applying a DDM is difficult if the company being analyzed is not currently paying a dividend. A company may not be paying a dividend if 1) the investment opportunities the company has are all so attractive that the retention and reinvestment of funds is preferable, from a return perspective, to the distribution of a dividend to shareholders or 2) the company is in such shaky financial condition that it cannot afford to pay a dividend. An analyst might still use a DDM to value such companies by assuming that dividends will begin at some future point in time. The analyst might further assume that constant growth occurs after that date and use the Gordon growth model for valuation. Extrapolating from no current dividend, however, generally yields highly uncertain forecasts. Analysts typically choose to use one or more of the alternatives instead of or as a supplement to the Gordon growth model.

EXAMPLE 7

Gordon Growth Model in the Case of No Current Dividend

A company does not currently pay a dividend but is expected to begin to do so in five years (at $t = 5$). The first dividend is expected to be $4.00 and to be received five years from today. That dividend is expected to grow at 6 percent into perpetuity. The required return is 10 percent. What is the estimated current intrinsic value?

Solution:

The analyst can value the share in two pieces:

1 The analyst uses the Gordon growth model to estimate the value at $t = 5$; in the model, the year-ahead dividend is \$4(1.06). Then the analyst finds the present value of this value as of $t = 0$.

2 The analyst finds the present value of the \$4 dividend not "counted" in the estimate in Piece 1 (which values dividends from $t = 6$ onward). Note that the statement of the problem implies that D_0, D_1, D_2, D_3, and D_4 are zero.

Piece 1: The value of this piece is \$65.818:

$$V_n = \frac{D_n(1 + g)}{r - g} = \frac{D_{n+1}}{r - g}$$

$$V_5 = \frac{\$4(1 + 0.06)}{0.10 - 0.06} = \frac{\$4.24}{0.04} = \$106$$

$$V_0 = \frac{\$106}{(1 + 0.10)^5} = \$65.818$$

Piece 2: The value of this piece is \$2.484:

$$V_0 = \frac{\$4}{(1 + 0.10)^5} = \$2.484$$

The sum of the two pieces is \$65.818 + \$2.484 = \$68.30.

Alternatively, the analyst could value the share at $t = 4$, the point at which dividends are expected to be paid in the following year and from which point they are expected to grow at a constant rate.

$$V_4 = \frac{\$4.00}{0.10 - 0.06} = \frac{\$4.00}{0.04} = \$100$$

$$V_0 = \frac{\$100}{(1 + 0.10)^4} = \$68.30$$

The next section addresses the application of the DDM with more flexible assumptions as to the dividend growth rate.

4.3 Multistage Dividend Discount Models

Multistage growth models are often used to model rapidly growing companies. The *two-stage DDM* assumes that at some point the company will begin to pay dividends that grow at a constant rate, but prior to that time the company will pay dividends that are growing at a higher rate than can be sustained in the long run. That is, the company is assumed to experience an initial, finite period of high growth, perhaps prior to the entry of competitors, followed by an infinite period of sustainable growth. The two-stage DDM thus makes use of two growth rates: a high growth rate for an initial, finite period followed by a lower, sustainable growth rate into perpetuity. The Gordon growth model is used to estimate a terminal value at time n that reflects the present value at time n of the dividends received during the sustainable growth period.

Equation 11 will be used here as the starting point for a two-stage valuation model. The two-stage valuation model is similar to Example 7 except that instead of assuming zero dividends for the initial period, the analyst assumes that dividends will exhibit a high rate of growth during the initial period. Equation 11 values the dividends over the short-term period of high growth and the terminal value at the end of the period of high growth. The short-term growth rate, g_S, lasts for n years. The intrinsic value per share in year n, V_n, represents the year n value of the dividends received during the sustainable growth period or the terminal value at time n. V_n can be estimated by using the Gordon growth model as shown in Equation 12, where g_L is the long-term or sustainable growth rate. The dividend in year $n+1$, D_{n+1}, can be determined by using Equation 13:

$$V_0 = \sum_{t=1}^{n} \frac{D_0(1 + g_S)^t}{(1 + r)^t} + \frac{V_n}{(1 + r)^n} \qquad (11)$$

$$V_n = \frac{D_{n+1}}{r - g_L} \qquad (12)$$

$$D_{n+1} = D_0(1 + g_S)^n(1 + g_L) \qquad (13)$$

EXAMPLE 8

Applying the Two-Stage Dividend Discount Model

The current dividend, D_0, is $5.00. Growth is expected to be 10 percent a year for three years and then 5 percent thereafter. The required rate of return is 15 percent. Estimate the intrinsic value.

Solution:

$D_1 = \$5.00(1 + 0.10) = \$5.50$

$D_2 = \$5.00(1 + 0.10)^2 = \$6.05$

$D_3 = \$5.00(1 + 0.10)^3 = \$6.655$

$D_4 = \$5.00(1 + 0.10)^3(1 + 0.05) = \$6.98775$

$V_3 = \dfrac{\$6.98775}{0.15 - 0.05} = \$69.8775$

$V_0 = \dfrac{\$5.50}{(1 + 0.15)} + \dfrac{\$6.05}{(1 + 0.15)^2} + \dfrac{\$6.655}{(1 + 0.15)^3} + \dfrac{\$69.8775}{(1 + 0.15)^3} \approx \$59.68$

The DDM can be extended to as many stages as deemed appropriate. For most publicly traded companies (that is, companies beyond the start-up stage), practitioners assume growth will ultimately fall into three stages:[4] 1) growth, 2) transition, and 3) maturity. This assumption supports the use of a *three-stage DDM*, which makes use of three growth rates: a high growth rate for an initial finite period, followed by a lower growth rate for a finite second period, followed by a lower, sustainable growth rate into perpetuity.

One can make the case that a three-stage DDM would be most appropriate for a fairly young company, one that is just entering the growth phase. The two-stage DDM would be appropriate to estimate the value of an older company that has already moved through its growth phase and is currently in the transition phase (a period with a higher growth rate than the sustainable growth rate) prior to moving to the maturity phase (the period with a lower, sustainable growth rate).

---

4 Sharpe, Alexander, and Bailey (1999).

However, the choice of a two-stage DDM need not rely solely on the age of a company. Long-established companies sometimes manage to restart above-average growth through, for example, innovation, expansion to new markets, or acquisitions. Or a company's long-run growth rate may be interrupted by a period of subnormal performance. If growth is expected to moderate (in the first case) or improve (in the second case) toward some long-term growth rate, a two-stage DDM may be appropriate. Thus, we chose a two-stage DDM to value Brown-Forman in Example 9.

EXAMPLE 9

Two-Stage Dividend Discount Model: Brown-Forman

Brown-Forman Corporation (NYSE: BFB) is a diversified producer of wines and spirits. It was founded in 1870 by George Garvin Brown in Louisville, Kentucky, USA. His original brand, Old Forester Kentucky Straight Bourbon Whisky, was America's first bottled bourbon. Brown-Forman, one of the largest American-owned spirits and wine companies and among the top 10 largest global spirits companies, sells its brands in more than 135 countries and has offices in cities across the globe. In all, Brown-Forman has more than 35 brands in its portfolio of wines and spirits.

The 30 January 2009 *Value Line* report on Brown-Forman appears in Exhibit 3. Brown-Forman has increased its dividends every year except 2000, when the dividend remained at US$0.50 as it was in 1999. On the left side of the report, in the section titled "Annual Rates," dividend growth is shown as 7.5 percent for the past 10 years, 11 percent for the past 5 years, and estimated 5 percent for 2005–2007 to 2011–2013. After a period of growth through acquisition and merger, the pattern suggests that Brown-Forman may be transitioning to a mature growth phase.

The two-stage DDM is arguably a good choice for valuing Brown Forman because the company appears to be transitioning from a high-growth phase (note the 11 percent dividend growth for the past 5 years) to a lower-growth phase (note the forecast of 5 percent dividend growth to 2011–2013). The analyst discussion refers to the company facing "short-term obstacles" and states that the company's "capital appreciation potential for the 3- to 5-year time frame is well below average."

The CAPM can be used to estimate the required return, r, for Brown-Forman. The *Value Line* report (in the upper left corner) estimates beta to be 0.70. Using the yield of about 3.1 percent on 10-year US Treasury notes as a proxy for the risk-free rate and assuming an equity risk premium of 5.0 percent, we find the estimate for r would be 6.6 percent [3.1% + 0.70(5.0%)].

To estimate the intrinsic value at the end of 2008, we use the 2008 dividend of US$1.08 from the *Value Line* report. The dividend is assumed to grow at a rate of 6.5 percent for two years and then 4.0 percent thereafter. The growth rate assumption for the first stage is consistent with the *Value Line* forecast for 2008 to 2009 growth. The assumption of a 4.0 percent perpetual growth rate produces a five-year growth rate assumption near 5 percent,[5] which is consistent with the *Value Line* forecast of 5 percent growth to 2011–2013. Thus:

$$D_{2009} = US\$1.08(1 + 0.065) = US\$1.1502$$

$$D_{2010} = US\$1.08(1 + 0.065)^2 = US\$1.224963$$

---

[5] The exact geometric average annual growth rate can be determined as $[(1+0.065)(1+0.065)(1+0.04)(1+0.04)(1.04)]^{1/5} - 1 = 0.049929 \approx 5.0\%$.

$$D_{2011} = US\$1.08(1 + 0.065)^2 (1 + 0.04) = US\$1.273962$$

$$V_{2010} = \frac{US\$1.273962}{0.066 - 0.04} = US\$48.99854$$

$$V_{2008} = \frac{US\$1.1502}{(1 + 0.066)} + \frac{US\$1.224963}{(1 + 0.066)^2} + \frac{US\$48.99854}{(1 + 0.066)^2} \approx US\$45.28$$

Given a recent price of US\$47.88, as noted at the top of the *Value Line* report, the intrinsic-value estimate of US\$45.28 suggests that Brown-Forman is modestly overvalued.

Exhibit 3　*Value Line* Report on Brown-Forman

BROWN-FORMAN 'B' NYSE-BFB

RECENT PRICE	47.88	P/E RATIO	15.9 (Trailing: 16.6 / Median: 20.0)	RELATIVE P/E RATIO	1.43	DIV'D YLD	2.4%	VALUE LINE

TIMELINESS **2** Raised 6/13/08
SAFETY **1** Raised 5/21/93
TECHNICAL **3** Lowered 1/2/09
BETA .70 (1.00 = Market)

2011-13 PROJECTIONS

	Price	Gain	Ann'l Total Return
High	75	(+55%)	14%
Low	60	(+25%)	8%

Insider Decisions

	M	A	M	J	J	A	S	O	N
to Buy	0	0	1	0	0	0	0	0	0
Options	5	1	0	3	0	0	0	0	0
to Sell	2	1	0	3	0	0	0	0	0

Institutional Decisions

	1Q2008	2Q2008	3Q2008
to Buy	104	120	102
to Sell	136	124	144
Hld's(000)	71761	69673	66806

Percent shares traded 12 / 8 / 4

LEGENDS
16.0 x "Cash Flow" p sh
.... Relative Price Strength
2-for-1 split 1/04
5-for-4 split 10/06
Options: Yes
Shaded area: prior recession
Latest recession began 12/07

Target Price Range 2011 | 2012 | 2013

% TOT. RETURN 12/08

	THIS STOCK	VL ARITH. INDEX
1 yr.	-11.3	-37.4
3 yr.	-1.9	-26.7
5 yr.	50.7	-8.2

| High | 22.2 | 30.8 | 30.9 | 27.7 | 28.8 | 32.2 | 38.0 | 40.1 | 57.9 | 66.0 | 63.9 | 63.0 |
| Low | 16.8 | 20.7 | 22.0 | 16.8 | 23.1 | 23.5 | 24.1 | 34.2 | 37.3 | 52.2 | 50.5 | 40.5 |

1992	1993	1994	1995	1996	1997	1998	1999	2000	2001	2002	2003	2004	2005	2006	2007	2008	2009	© VALUE LINE PUB., INC. 11-13	
6.84	8.12	8.23	8.95	9.18	9.68	10.30	10.88	11.24	11.46	13.60	14.56	15.17	12.91	14.40	17.13	*18.20*	*19.25*	Sales per sh A	22.95
.97	1.13	1.11	1.19	1.26	1.36	1.49	1.62	1.74	1.66	1.98	2.11	2.35	2.63	2.82	3.26	*3.40*	*3.55*	"Cash Flow" per sh	4.50
.75	.76	.86	.92	.98	1.07	1.17	1.27	1.36	1.33	1.46	1.74	1.97	2.32	2.52	2.85	*3.00*	*3.10*	Earnings per sh B	3.95
.34	.37	.39	.41	.42	.44	.46	.50	.50	.53	.56	.60	.68	.81	.90	.97	*1.08*	*1.15*	Div'ds Decl'd per sh C■	1.20
.16	.16	.30	.34	.32	.26	.27	.45	.56	.42	.79	.37	.32	.34	.38	.27	*.30*	*.35*	Cap'l Spending per sh	.50
3.90	2.62	3.10	3.61	4.16	4.67	5.32	6.08	6.94	7.67	5.55	7.14	8.60	10.21	10.21	11.44	*13.25*	*15.00*	Book Value per sh D	21.05
206.66	172.49	172.49	172.49	172.49	172.49	172.49	172.49	171.15	170.87	151.42	151.99	152.36	153.08	154.05	150.74	*151.00*	*150.00*	Common Shs Outst'g E	145.00
14.5	14.6	13.9	16.0	17.3	19.5	22.2	18.8	17.4	19.7	15.3	19.9	19.7	22.5	22.3	19.7	*Bold figures are*		Avg Ann'l P/E Ratio	17.0
.88	.86	.91	1.07	1.08	1.12	1.15	1.07	1.13	1.01	1.07	1.13	1.04	1.20	1.20	1.05	*Value Line*		Relative P/E Ratio	1.13
3.2%	3.3%	3.3%	2.8%	2.5%	2.1%	1.8%	2.1%	2.1%	2.0%	2.0%	1.7%	1.8%	1.6%	1.6%	1.7%	*estimates*		Avg Ann'l Div'd Yield	2.0%

CAPITAL STRUCTURE as of 10/31/08
Total Debt $1199 mill. Due in 5 Yrs $1199 mill.
LT Debt $412 mill.   LT Interest $25 mill.
(20% of Cap'l)
Leases, Uncapitalized Annual rentals $19 mill.
Pension Assets-4/07 $397 mill.
Obligations $451 mill.
Pfd Stock None
Common Stock 150,886,120 shs. (incl.
56,609,413 Cl. 'A' voting shs.)
as of 11/30/08
adjusted for 5x4 stock split effective 10/28/08
MARKET CAP: $7.2 billion (Large Cap)

	1776	1877	1924	1958	2060	2213	2312	1976	2218	2582	*2750*	*2885*	Sales ($mill) A	3325
	21.2%	21.8%	22.8%	20.8%	20.8%	21.4%	22.2%	28.3%	28.3%	28.5%	*28.0%*	*28.0%*	Operating Margin	30.0%
	55.0	62.0	64.0	55.0	55.0	56.0	58.0	44.0	44.0	52.0	*55.0*	*60.0*	Depreciation ($mill)	75.0
	202	218	233	228	245	265.3	300	358	390	440	*455*	*470*	Net Profit ($mill)	575
	36.5%	36.4%	36.3%	34.5%	34.3%	34.1%	32.0%	30.5%	32.2%	31.7%	*32.0%*	*33.0%*	Income Tax Rate	35.0%
	11.4%	11.6%	12.1%	11.6%	11.9%	12.0%	13.0%	18.1%	17.6%	17.0%	*16.5%*	*16.3%*	Net Profit Margin	17.3%
	482	498	456	534	520	714	679	1041	288	472	*750*	*1000*	Working Cap'l ($mill)	1825
	53.0	41.0	40.0	40.0	629	630	352	351	422	417	*400*	*375*	Long-Term Debt ($mill)	300
	917	1048	1187	1311	840	1085	1310	1563	1573	1725	*2000*	*2250*	Shr. Equity ($mill)	3050
	21.0%	20.2%	19.1%	16.9%	16.7%	16.1%	18.7%	19.2%	20.4%	21.7%	*19.5%*	*18.5%*	Return on Total Cap'l	17.5%
	22.0%	20.8%	19.6%	17.4%	29.2%	24.5%	22.9%	22.9%	24.8%	25.5%	*22.8%*	*20.8%*	Return on Shr. Equity	19.0%
	13.4%	12.9%	12.3%	10.2%	17.4%	15.5%	14.4%	14.7%	15.7%	16.3%	*14.5%*	*14.0%*	Retained to Com Eq	13.0%
	39%	38%	37%	41%	40%	37%	37%	36%	37%	36%	*36%*	*35%*	All Div'ds to Net Prof	31%

CURRENT POSITION

(SMILL.)	2006	2007	10/31/08
Cash Assets	369	119	327
Receivables	404	453	534
Inventory (LIFO)	694	685	683
Other	168	199	229
Current Assets	1635	1456	1773
Accts Payable	361	380	371
Debt Due	755	589	787
Other	231	15	8
Current Liab.	1347	984	1166

ANNUAL RATES

of change (per sh)	Past 10 Yrs.	Past 5 Yrs.	Est'd '05-'07 to '11-'13
Sales	5.0%	4.0%	7.5%
"Cash Flow"	8.5%	10.0%	7.5%
Earnings	10.0%	13.0%	7.5%
Dividends	7.5%	11.0%	5.0%
Book Value	10.0%	9.5%	12.0%

QUARTERLY SALES ($ mill.) A

Fiscal Year Begins	Jul.31	Oct.31	Jan.31	Apr.30	Full Fiscal Year
2005	450	551	504	471	1976
2006	505	582	582	549	2218
2007	587	716	672	607	2582
2008	614	738	750	648	2750
2009	650	770	785	680	2885

EARNINGS PER SHARE A B

Fiscal Year Begins	Jul.31	Oct.31	Jan.31	Apr.30	Full Fiscal Year
2005	.53	.70	.64	.45	2.32
2006	.61	.74	.72	.45	2.52
2007	.62	.83	.75	.65	2.85
2008	.69	.94	.77	.60	3.00
2009	.71	.96	.80	.63	3.10

QUARTERLY DIVIDENDS PAID C

Cal-endar	Mar.31	Jun.30	Sep.30	Dec.31	Full Year
2005	.196	.196	.196	.196	.784
2006	.224	.224	.224	.224	.896
2007	.242	.242	.242	.242	.968
2008	.272	.272	.272	.272	1.088
2009	.287				

BUSINESS: Brown-Forman is engaged in the production and marketing of distilled spirits and wines. Major brands include *Jack Daniel's, Southern Comfort, Finlandia, Canadian Mist, Bolla,* and *Korbel.* In the U.S., sells spirits either through wholesale distributors or directly to state governments in those states that control alcohol sales. Sold Hartmann luggage business, 5/07; Lenox tableware division, 9/05; minority stake in Glenmorangie PLC, 11/04. Non-U.S. sales represent 52% of total revenue. Has 4,466 employees. Off. & dir. own about 40% of 'A' and 15% of 'B' shares. (6/08 Proxy). Chairman: Owsley Brown II. CEO: Paul Varga. Incorporated: DE. Address: P.O. Box 1080, Louisville, KY 40201-1080. Telephone: 502-585-1100. Internet: www.brown-forman.com.

Brown-Forman stock is holding its own. The issue is marginally up since our October report, despite the recessionary environment. The company may likely finish its fiscal year on a good note (year ends April 30, 2009). We expect both the top and bottom lines to advance in the mid-single-digit range. However, our forecast for the next fiscal year is not as rosy, anticipating flatish earnings growth and a 5% increase in sales. Like many other beverage companies, BFB may face some short-term headwinds such as declining volume levels and consumer cutbacks.
Short-term obstacles may pressure operating margins a bit. Increased input and fuel costs, along with excise taxes, will likely contribute to slight margin erosion this year. The company has also slightly increased its advertising spending, in an effort to sustain and build consumer interest. The *Jack Daniel's* line is notable in this regard, since interest remains healthy in both domestic and foreign markets. We are optimistic that Brown-Forman can weather the headwinds, especially since many individuals still opt to consume its products in good times and bad.

The company possesses a strong balance sheet. At the end of its fiscal second quarter it had over $300 million in cash, thereby giving it much flexibility. While there are no tentative acquisitions on the burner at the moment, the company is utilizing this excess cash in other ways. In fact, it recently announced a share repurchase program of up to $250 million. BFB also recently increased its dividend payment to shareholders by almost 6%.
Brown-Forman is seeking to reorganize its portfolio. It recently sold two of its wine brands, *Bolla* and *Fontana Candida,* to another organization, Gruppo Italiano Vini, for an undisclosed sum of money. We believe this was a positive move, as it allows BFB the ability to focus and invest in its core brands.
Momentum investors may want to consider this stock since the issue remains a timely selection for year ahead performance. However, it does not warrant much long-term appeal as its capital appreciation potential for the 3- to 5-year time frame is well below average.
Nira Maharaj　　*January 30, 2009*

(A) After excise taxes and discounts related to promotional programs from '94 forward. Fiscal yr. ends Apr. 30th of foll. yr. (B) Primary earnings through '96, dil. thereafter. Excls. net non-

rec. gain (loss): '04, 6¢; '05, 9¢; '06, 8¢ '08 (10¢). Next earnings report due early March. (C) Div'ds historically paid early Jan., Apr., July, and Oct. Special one time dividend $1.65

dist. 5/10/07.■ Div'd reinvestment plan avail. (D) Includes intangibles. In '07: $1387.0 million, $11.50/sh. (E) In millions. Adj for splits.

Company's Financial Strength	A+
Stock's Price Stability	95
Price Growth Persistence	85
Earnings Predictability	100

To subscribe call 1-800-833-0046.

MULTIPLIER MODELS

5

The term **price multiple** refers to a ratio that compares the share price with some sort of monetary flow or value to allow evaluation of the relative worth of a company's stock. Some practitioners use price ratios as a screening mechanism. If the ratio falls below a specified value, the shares are identified as candidates for purchase, and if the ratio exceeds a specified value, the shares are identified as candidates for sale. Many practitioners use ratios when examining a group or sector of stocks and consider the shares for which the ratio is relatively low to be attractively valued securities.

Price multiples that are used by security analysts include the following:

- Price-to-earnings ratio (P/E). This measure is the ratio of the stock price to earnings per share. P/E is arguably the price multiple most frequently cited by the media and used by analysts and investors (Block 1999). The seminal works of McWilliams (1966), Miller and Widmann (1966), Nicholson (1968), Dreman (1977), and Basu (1977) presented evidence of a return advantage to low-P/E stocks.

- Price-to-book ratio (P/B). The ratio of the stock price to book value per share. Considerable evidence suggests that P/B multiples are inversely related to future rates of return (Fama and French 1995).

- Price-to-sales ratio (P/S). This measure is the ratio of stock price to sales per share. O'Shaughnessy (2005) provided evidence that a low P/S multiple is the most useful multiple for predicting future returns.

- Price-to-cash-flow ratio (P/CF). This measure is the ratio of stock price to some per-share measure of cash flow. The measures of cash flow include free cash flow (FCF) and operating cash flow (OCF).

A common criticism of all of these multiples is that they do not consider the future. This criticism is true if the multiple is calculated from trailing or current values of the divisor. Practitioners seek to counter this criticism by a variety of techniques, including forecasting fundamental values (the divisors) one or more years into the future. The resulting forward (leading or prospective) price multiples may differ markedly from the trailing price multiples. In the absence of an explicit forecast of fundamental values, the analyst is making an implicit forecast of the future when implementing such models. The choice of price multiple—trailing or forward—should be used consistently for companies being compared.

Besides the traditional price multiples used in valuation, just presented, analysts need to know how to calculate and interpret other ratios. Such ratios include those used to analyze business performance and financial condition based on data reported in financial statements. In addition, many industries have specialized measures of business performance that analysts covering those industries should be familiar with. In analyzing cable television companies, for example, the ratio of total market value of the company to the total number of subscribers is commonly used. Another common measure is revenue per subscriber. In the oil industry, a commonly cited ratio is proved reserves per common share. Industry-specific or sector-specific ratios such as these can be used to understand the key business variables in an industry or sector as well as to highlight attractively valued securities.

5.1 Relationships among Price Multiples, Present Value Models, and Fundamentals

Price multiples are frequently used independently of present value models. One price multiple valuation approach, the method of comparables, does not involve cash flow forecasts or discounting to present value. A price multiple is often related to fundamentals through a discounted cash flow model, however, such as the Gordon growth model. Understanding such connections can deepen the analyst's appreciation of the factors that affect the value of a multiple and often can help explain reasons for differences in multiples that do not involve mispricing. The expressions that are developed can be interpreted as the *justified value* of a multiple—that is, the value justified by (based on) fundamentals or a set of cash flow predictions. These expressions are an alternative way of presenting intrinsic-value estimates.

As an example, using the Gordon growth model identified previously in Equation 9 and assuming that price equals intrinsic value ($P_0 = V_0$), we can restate Equation 9 as follows:

$$P_0 = \frac{D_1}{r - g} \tag{9.1}$$

To arrive at the model for the justified forward P/E given in Equation 14, we divide both sides of Equation 9.1 by a forecast for next year's earnings, E_1. In Equation 14, the dividend payout ratio, p, is the ratio of dividends to earnings:

$$\frac{P_0}{E_1} = \frac{D_1/E_1}{r - g} = \frac{p}{r - g} \tag{14}$$

Equation 14 indicates that the P/E is inversely related to the required rate of return and positively related to the growth rate; that is, as the required rate of return increases, the P/E declines, and as the growth rate increases, the P/E increases. The P/E and the payout ratio appear to be positively related. This relationship may not be true, however, because a higher payout ratio may imply a slower growth rate as a result of the company retaining a lower proportion of earnings for reinvestment. This phenomenon is referred to as the dividend displacement of earnings.

EXAMPLE 10

Value Estimate Based on Fundamentals

Petroleo Brasileiro SA, commonly known as Petrobras (BOVESPA: PETR), was once labeled "the most expensive oil company" by Bloomberg.com. Data for Petrobras and the oil industry, including the trailing twelve-month (TTM) P/E and payout ratios, appear below.

	Petrobras	Industry
P/E ratio (TTM)	11.77	7.23
Payout ratio (TTM) (%)	24.40	21.66
EPS 5-year growth rate (%)	26.35	15.46
EPS (MRQ) vs. Qtr. 1 yr. ago (% change)	−41.44	−127.53

Note: MRQ stands for "most recent quarter."
Source: Reuters.

Explain how the information shown supports a higher P/E for Petrobras than for the industry.

Solution:

The data support a higher P/E for Petrobras because its payout ratio and five-year EPS growth rate exceed those of the industry. Equation 14 implies a positive relationship between the payout ratio and the P/E multiple. A higher payout ratio supports a higher P/E. Furthermore, to the extent that higher EPS growth implies a high growth rate in dividends, the high EPS growth rate supports a high P/E. Although the Petrobras quarterly EPS have declined relative to EPS of a year ago, the decline is less than that of the industry.

EXAMPLE 11

Determining Justified Forward P/E

Heinrich Gladisch, CFA, is estimating the justified forward P/E for Nestlé (SIX: NESN), one of the world's leading nutrition and health companies. Gladisch notes that sales for 2008 were SFr109.9 billion (US$101.6 billion) and that net income was SFr18.0 billion (US$16.6 billion). He organizes the data for EPS, dividends per share, and the dividend payout ratio for the years 2004–2008 in the following table:

	2004	2005	2006	2007	2008
Earnings per share	SFr1.70	SFr2.08	SFr2.39	SFr2.78	SFr4.87
Year over year % change		22.4%	14.9%	16.3%	75.2%
Dividend per share	SFr0.80	SFr0.90	SFr1.04	SFr1.22	SFr1.40
Year over year % change		12.5%	15.6%	17.3%	14.8%
Dividend payout ratio	47.1%	43.3%	43.5%	43.9%	28.7%

Gladisch calculates that ROE averaged slightly more than 19 percent in the period 2004–2007 but jumped to about 35 percent in 2008. In 2008, however, Nestlé's reported net income included a large nonrecurring component. The company reported 2008 "underlying earnings," which it defined as net income "from continuing operations before impairments, restructuring costs, results on disposals and significant one-off items," to be SFr2.82. Predicting increasing pressure on Nestlé's profit margins from lower-priced goods, particularly in developed markets, Gladisch estimates a long-run ROE of 16 percent.

Gladisch decides that the dividend payout ratios of the 2004–2007 period—averaging 44.5 percent—are more representative of Nestlé's future payout ratio than is the low 2008 dividend payout ratio. The dividend payout ratio in 2008 was lower because management apparently based the 2008 dividend on the components of net income that were expected to continue into the future. Basing a dividend on net income including non-recurring items creates the potential need to reduce dividends in the future. Rounding up the 2004–2007 average, Gladisch settles on an estimate of 45 percent for the dividend payout ratio for use in calculating a justified forward P/E using Equation 14.

Gladisch's firm estimates that the required rate of return for Nestlé's shares is 12 percent per year. Gladisch also finds the following data in UBS and Credit Suisse analyst reports dated, respectively, 9 December 2009 and 16 October 2009:

	2009E	2010E
UBS forecast:		
EPS	SFr2.86	SFr3.10
Year over year % change	−41.3%	8.39%
P/E (based on a price of SFr48.82)	17.1	15.6
Credit Suisse forecast:		
EPS	SFr2.82	SFr3.05
Year over year % change	−42.1%	8.16%
P/E (based on a price of SFr47.88)	16.9	15.6

1. Based only on information and estimates developed by Gladisch and his firm, estimate Nestlé's justified forward P/E.

2. Compare and contrast the justified forward P/E estimate from Question 1 to the estimates from UBS and Credit Suisse.

Solution to 1:

The estimate of the justified forward P/E is 14.1. The dividend growth rate can be estimated by using Equation 10 as $(1 - \text{Dividend payout ratio}) \times \text{ROE} = (1 - 0.45) \times 0.16 = 0.088$, or 8.8 percent. Therefore,

$$\frac{P_0}{E_1} = \frac{p}{r - g} = \frac{0.45}{0.12 - 0.088} = 14.1$$

Solution to 2:

The estimated justified forward P/E of 14.1 is lower than the 2009 P/E estimates of 17.1 by UBS and 16.9 by Credit Suisse. Using a required rate of return of 11.5 percent rather than 12 percent results in a justified forward P/E estimate of $16.7 = 0.45/(0.115 - 0.088)$. Using an ROE of 19 percent (the average ROE of the 2004–2007 period) rather than 16 percent results in a justified forward P/E estimate of $30.0 = 0.45/[0.12 - (0.55)(0.19)] = 0.45/(0.12 - 0.105)$. The justified forward P/E is very sensitive to changes in the inputs.

Justified forward P/E estimates can be sensitive to small changes in assumptions. Therefore, analysts can benefit from carrying out a sensitivity analysis, as shown in Exhibit 4, which is based on Example 11. Exhibit 4 shows how the justified forward P/E varies with changes in the estimates for the dividend payout ratio (columns) and return on equity. The dividend growth rate (rows) changes because of changes in the retention rate (1 − Payout rate) and ROE. Recall g = ROE times retention rate.

Exhibit 4   Estimates for Nestlé's Justified Forward P/E (Required Rate of Return = 12 Percent)

Constant Dividend Growth Rate (%)	Dividend Payout Ratio				
	40.0%	42.5%	45.0%	47.5%	50.0%
7.0	8.0	8.5	9.0	9.5	10.0
7.5	8.9	9.4	10.0	10.6	11.1
8.0	10.0	10.6	11.3	11.9	12.5
8.5	11.4	12.1	12.9	13.6	14.3

Exhibit 4	(Continued)

Constant Dividend Growth Rate (%)	Dividend Payout Ratio				
	40.0%	42.5%	45.0%	47.5%	50.0%
9.0	13.3	14.2	15.0	15.8	16.7
9.5	16.0	17.0	18.0	19.0	20.0
10.0	20.0	21.3	22.5	23.8	25.0
10.5	26.7	28.3	30.0	31.7	33.3

5.2 The Method of Comparables

The method of comparables is the most widely used approach for analysts reporting valuation judgments on the basis of price multiples. This method essentially compares relative values estimated using multiples or the relative values of multiples. The economic rationale underlying the method of comparables is the **law of one price**: Identical assets should sell for the same price. The methodology involves using a price multiple to evaluate whether an asset is fairly valued, undervalued, or overvalued in relation to a benchmark value of the multiple. Choices for the benchmark multiple include the multiple of a closely matched individual stock or the average or median value of the multiple for the stock's industry. Some analysts perform trend or time-series analyses and use past or average values of a price multiple as a benchmark.

Identifying individual companies or even an industry as the "comparable" may present a challenge. Many large corporations operate in several lines of business, so the scale and scope of their operations can vary significantly. When identifying comparables (sometimes referred to as "comps"), the analyst should be careful to identify companies that are most similar according to a number of dimensions. These dimensions include (but are not limited to) overall size, product lines, and growth rate. The type of analysis shown in Section 5.1 relating multiples to fundamentals is a productive way to identify the fundamental variables that should be taken into account in identifying comparables.

EXAMPLE 12

Method of Comparables (1)

As noted previously, P/E is a price multiple frequently used by analysts. Using P/E in the method of comparables can be problematic, however, as a result of business cycle effects on EPS. An alternative valuation tool that is useful during periods of economic slowdown or extraordinary growth is the P/S multiple. Although sales will decline during a recession and increase during a period of economic growth, the change in sales will be less than the change in earnings in percentage terms because earnings are heavily influenced by fixed operating and financing costs (operating and financial leverage).

The following data provide the P/S for most of the major automobile manufacturers in early 2009 (from the *Value Line* stock screener):

Company	P/S
General Motors	0.01
Ford Motor	0.14
Daimler	0.27

(continued)

Company	P/S
Nissan Motor	0.32
Honda Motor	0.49
Toyota Motor	0.66

Which stock appears to be undervalued when compared with the others?

Solution:

The P/S analysis suggests that General Motors shares offer the best value. When the information shown was published, however, General Motors was on the brink of bankruptcy and had submitted several business plans to the US government that included plant closings and elimination of the Pontiac brand. An analyst must be alert for potential explanations of apparently low or high multiples when performing comparables analysis, rather than just assuming a relative mispricing.

EXAMPLE 13

Method of Comparables (2)

Incorporated in the Netherlands, the European Aeronautic Defense and Space Company, or EADS (Euronext Paris: EAD) is a dominant aerospace company in Europe. Its largest subsidiary, Airbus S.A.S., is an aircraft manufacturing company with bases in several European countries. The majority of EADS' profits arise from Airbus operations. Airbus and its primary competitor, Boeing (NYSE: BA), control most of the commercial airplane industry.

Comparisons are frequently made between EADS and Boeing. As noted in Exhibit 5, the companies are about equal in size as measured by total revenues in 2008. Converting total revenues from euros to US dollars using the average daily exchange rate for 2008 of US$1.4726/€ results in a value of $64,242 million for EADS' total revenues. Thus, total revenues for EADS are only 5.5 percent higher than those for Boeing.

The companies do differ, however, in several important areas. EADS derives a greater share of its revenue from commercial aircraft production than does Boeing. Also, the book value of shareholders' equity was negative for Boeing at year-end 2008. Finally, the order backlog for EADS is much higher than that for Boeing. Converting the EADS order backlog from euros to US dollars using the year-end rate for 2008 of $1.3919/€ results in a value of $557,105 million for EADS' order backlog. Thus, the order backlog for EADS is 72.0 percent higher than the backlog for Boeing.[6]

Exhibit 5	Data for EADS and Boeing	
	EADS	**Boeing**
Total revenues (millions)	€43,625	$60,909
12-month revenue growth	10.6%	−8.3%

---

6 Exchange rate data are available from FRED (Federal Reserve Economic Data) at http://research.stlouisfed.org/fred2/.

Exhibit 5   (Continued)

	EADS	Boeing
Percent of revenues from commercial aircraft	69.3%	46.4%
Debt ratio (Total liabilities/Equity)	85.4%	102.4%
Order backlog	€400,248	$323,860
Share price, 31/Dec/08	€12.03	$42.67
EPS (basic)	€1.95	$3.68
DPS	€0.20	$1.62
Dividend payout ratio	10.3%	44.0%
P/E ratio	6.2	11.6

Sources: Company websites: www.eads.com and www.boeing.com.

What data shown in Exhibit 5 support a higher P/E for Boeing than for EADS?

Solution:

Recall from Equation 14 and the discussion that followed it that P/E is directly related to the payout ratio and the dividend growth rate. The P/E is inversely related to the required rate of return. The only data presented in Exhibit 5 that support a higher P/E for Boeing is that company's higher dividend payout ratio (44.0 percent versus 10.3 percent for EADS).

The following implicitly supports a higher P/E for EADS: EADS has higher 12-month revenue growth and a higher backlog of orders, suggesting that it will have a higher future growth rate. Boeing also has a higher debt ratio, which implies greater financial risk and a higher required return.

EXAMPLE 14

Method of Comparables (3)

Canon Inc. (TSE: 7751) is a leading worldwide manufacturer of business machines, cameras, and optical products. Canon was founded in 1937 as a camera manufacturer and is incorporated in Tokyo. The corporate philosophy of Canon is *kyosei* or "living and working together for the common good." The following data can be used to determine a P/E for Canon over the time period 2004–2008. Analyze the P/E of Canon over time and discuss the valuation of Canon.

Year	Price (a)	EPS (b)	P/E (a) ÷ (b)
2004	¥5,546	¥387.8	14.3
2005	¥6,883	¥432.9	15.9
2006	¥6,703	¥342.0	19.6

(continued)

Year	Price (a)	EPS (b)	P/E (a) ÷ (b)
2007	¥5,211	¥377.6	13.8
2008	¥2,782	¥246.2	11.3

Sources: EPS and P/E data are from Canon's website: www.canon.com. P/E is based on share price data from the Tokyo Stock Exchange.

Solution:

Trend analysis of Canon's P/E reveals a peak of 19.6 in 2006. The 2008 P/E of 11.3 is the lowest of the five years reported. This finding suggests that Canon's share price may be underpriced as of year-end 2008. A bullish case for Canon's stock can be made if an analyst believes that P/E will return to its historical average (15.0 over this five-year period) or be higher. Such a bullish prediction requires that an increase in P/E not be offset by a decrease in EPS.

5.3 Illustration of a Valuation Based on Price Multiples

Telefónica S.A. (LSE: TDE), a world leader in the telecommunication sector, provides communication, information, and entertainment products and services in Europe, Africa, and Latin America. It has operated in its home country of Spain since 1924, but as of 2008, more than 60 percent of its business was outside its home market.

Deutsche Telekom AG (FWB: DTE) provides network access, communication services, and value-added services via fixed and mobile networks. It generates more than half of its revenues outside its home country, Germany.

Exhibit 6 provides comparable data for these two communication giants for 2006–2008.

Exhibit 6   Data for Telefónica and Deutsche Telekom

	Telefónica			Deutsche Telekom		
	2008	**2007**	**2006**	**2008**	**2007**	**2006**
(1) Total assets (€ billions)	99.9	105.9	109.0	123.1	120.7	130.2
Asset growth	−5.7%	−2.8%	—	2.0%	−7.3%	—
(2) Net revenues (€ billions)	57.9	56.4	52.9	61.7	62.5	61.3
Revenue growth	2.7%	6.6%	—	−1.3%	2.0%	—
(3) Net cash flow from operating activities (€ billions)	16.4	15.6	15.4	15.4	13.7	14.2
Cash flow growth	5.1%	1.3%	—	12.4%	−3.5%	—
(4) Book value of common shareholders' equity (€ billions)	19.6	22.9	20.0	43.1	45.2	49.7
Debt ratio: $1 - [(4) \div (1)]$	80.4%	78.4%	81.7%	65.0%	62.6%	61.8%
(5) Net profit (€ billions)	7.8	9.1	6.6	1.5	0.6	3.2
Earnings growth	−14.3%	37.9%	—	150.0%	−81.3%	—
(6) Weighted average number of shares outstanding (millions)	4,646	4,759	4,779	4,340	4,339	4,353
(7) Price per share (€)	15.85	22.22	16.22	10.75	15.02	13.84

Exhibit 6   (Continued)

	Telefónica			Deutsche Telekom		
	2008	**2007**	**2006**	**2008**	**2007**	**2006**
Price-to-revenue ratio (P/R):						
(7) ÷ [(2) ÷ (6)]	1.3	1.9	1.5	0.8	1.0	1.0
P/CF:						
(7) ÷ [(3) ÷ (6)]	4.5	6.8	5.0	3.0	4.8	4.2
P/B:						
(7) ÷ [(4) ÷ (6)]	3.8	4.6	3.9	1.1	1.4	1.2
P/E:						
(7) ÷ [(5) ÷ (6)]	9.4	11.6	11.7	31.1	108.6	18.8

Sources: Company websites: www.telefonica.es and www.deutschetelekom.com.

Time-series analysis of all price multiples in Exhibit 6 suggests that both companies are currently attractively valued. For example, the 2008 price-to-revenue ratio (P/R) of 1.3 for Telefónica is below the 2006–2008 average for this ratio of approximately 1.6. The 2008 P/CF of 3.0 for Deutsche Telekom is below the 2006–2008 average for this ratio of approximately 4.0.

A comparative analysis produces somewhat mixed results. The 2008 values for Deutsche Telekom for the P/R, P/CF, P/B multiples are lower than those for Telefónica. This result suggests that Deutsche Telekom is attractively valued when compared with Telefónica. The 2008 P/E for Telefónica, however, is much lower than for Deutsche Telekom.

An analyst investigating these contradictory results would look for information not reported in Exhibit 6. For example, the earnings before interest, taxes, depreciation, and amortization (EBITDA) for Telefónica was €22.9 billion in 2008. The EBITDA value for Deutsche Telekom was €18.0 billion in 2008. The 2008 price-to-EBITDA ratio for Telefónica is [(15.85 × 4,646)/22,900] or [15.85/(22,900/4,646)] = 3.2, whereas the 2008 price-to-EBITDA ratio for Deutsche Telekom is 2.6. Thus, the higher P/E for Deutsche Telekom may be explained by higher depreciation charges, higher interest costs, and/or a greater tax burden.

In summary, the major advantage of using price multiples is that they allow for relative comparisons, both cross-sectional (versus the market or another comparable) and in time series. The approach can be especially beneficial for analysts who are assigned to a particular industry or sector and need to identify the expected best per-forming stocks within that sector. Price multiples are popular with investors because the multiples can be calculated easily and many multiples are readily available from financial websites and newspapers.

Caution is necessary. A stock may be relatively undervalued when compared with its benchmarks but overvalued when compared with an estimate of intrinsic value as determined by one of the discounted cash flow methodologies. Furthermore, differences in reporting rules among different markets and in chosen accounting methods can result in revenues, earnings, book values, and cash flows that are not easily comparable. These differences can, in turn, result in multiples that are not easily comparable. Finally, the multiples for cyclical companies may be highly influenced by current economic conditions.

5.4 Enterprise Value

An alternative to estimating the value of equity is to estimate the value of the enterprise. Enterprise value is most frequently determined as market capitalization plus market value of preferred stock plus market value of debt minus cash and investments (cash equivalents and short-term investments). Enterprise value is often viewed as the cost of a takeover: In the event of a buyout, the acquiring company assumes the acquired company's debt but also receives its cash. Enterprise value is most useful when comparing companies with significant differences in capital structure.

Enterprise value (EV) multiples are widely used in Europe, with EV/EBITDA arguably the most common. EBITDA is a proxy for operating cash flow because it excludes depreciation and amortization. EBITDA may include other non-cash expenses, however, and non-cash revenues. EBITDA can be viewed as a source of funds to pay interest, dividends, and taxes. Because EBITDA is calculated prior to payment to any of the company's financial stakeholders, using it to estimate enterprise value is logically appropriate.

Using enterprise value instead of market capitalization to determine a multiple can be useful to analysts. Even where the P/E is problematic because of negative earnings, the EV/EBITDA multiple can generally be computed because EBITDA is usually positive. An alternative to using EBITDA in EV multiples is to use operating income.

In practice, analysts may have difficulty accurately assessing enterprise value if they do not have access to market quotations for the company's debt. When current market quotations are not available, bond values may be estimated from current quotations for bonds with similar maturity, sector, and credit characteristics. Substituting the book value of debt for the market value of debt provides only a rough estimate of the debt's market value. This is because market interest rates change and investors' perception of the issuer's credit risk may have changed since the debt was issued.

EXAMPLE 15

Estimating the Market Value of Debt and Enterprise Value

Cameco Corporation (NYSE: CCJ) is one of the world's largest uranium producers; it accounts for 15 percent of world production from its mines in Canada and the United States. Cameco estimates it has about 226,796,185 kilograms of proven and probable reserves and holds premier land positions in the world's most promising areas for new uranium discoveries in Canada and Australia. Cameco is also a leading provider of processing services required to produce fuel for nuclear power plants. It generates 1,000 megawatts of electricity through a partnership in North America's largest nuclear generating station located in Ontario, Canada.

For simplicity of exposition in this example, we will present share counts in thousands and all dollar amounts in thousands of Canadian dollars. In 2008, Cameco had 350,130 shares outstanding. Its 2008 year-end share price was $20.99. Therefore, Cameco's 2008 year-end market capitalization was $7,349,229.

In its 2008 Annual Report (available at www.cameco.com), Cameco reported total debt and other liabilities of $2,716,475. The company presented the following schedule for long-term debt payments:

Year	Payment
2009	$10,175
2010	453,288
2011	13,272

Year	Payment
2012	317,452
2013	16,325
Thereafter	412,645
Total	$1,223,157

Cameco's longest maturity debt matures in 2018. We will assume that the $412,645 to be paid "thereafter" will be paid in equal amounts of $82,529 over the 2014 to 2018 time period. A yield curve for zero-coupon Canadian government securities was available from the Bank of Canada. The yield-curve data and assumed risk premiums in Exhibit 7 were used to estimate the market value of Cameco's long-term debt:

Exhibit 7   Estimated Market Value

Year	Yield on Zero-Coupon Government Security (%)	Assumed Risk Premium (%)	Discount Rate (%)	Book Value	Market Value
2009	0.89	0.50	1.39	$10,175	$10,036
2010	1.11	1.00	2.11	$453,288	$434,748
2011	1.39	1.50	2.89	$13,272	$12,185
2012	1.65	2.00	3.65	$317,452	$275,043
2013	1.88	2.50	4.38	$16,325	$13,175
2014	2.10	3.00	5.10	$82,529	$61,234
2015	2.30	3.50	5.80	$82,529	$55,617
2016	2.50	4.00	6.50	$82,529	$49,867
2017	2.71	4.50	7.21	$82,529	$44,105
2018	2.92	5.00	7.92	$82,529	$38,511
				$1,223,157	$994,521

Note from Exhibit 7 that the book value of long-term debt is $1,223,157 and its estimated market value is $994,521. The book value of total debt and liabilities of $2,716,475 minus the book value of long-term debt of $1,223,157 is $1,493,318. If we assume that the market value of that remaining debt is equal to its book value of $1,493,318, an estimate of the market value of total debt and liabilities is that amount plus the estimated market value of long-term debt of $994,521 or $2,487,839.

At the end of 2008, Cameco had cash and equivalents of $269,176. Enterprise value can be estimated as the $7,349,229 market value of stock plus the $2,487,839 market value of debt minus the $269,176 cash and equivalents, or $9,567,892. Cameco's 2008 EBITDA was $1,078,606; an estimate of EV/EBITDA is, therefore, $9,567,892 divided by $1,078,606, or 8.9.

EXAMPLE 16

EV/Operating Income

Exhibit 8 presents data for nine major mining companies. Based on the information in Exhibit 8, which two mining companies seem to be the *most* undervalued?

Exhibit 8   Data for Nine Major Mining Companies

Company	Ticker Symbol	EV (C$ millions)	Operating Income (OI) (C$ millions)	EV/OI
BHP Billiton	BHP	197,112.00	9,794.00	20.1
Rio Tinto	RIO	65,049.60	7,905.00	8.2
Anglo American	AAL	48,927.30	6,208.00	7.9
Barrick Gold	ABX	35,288.00	1,779.00	19.8
Goldcorp	G	28,278.00	616.66	45.9
Newmont Mining	NEM	22,040.80	1,385.00	15.9
AngloGold Ashanti	AU	19,918.30	−362.00	−55.0
Alcoa	AA	17,570.40	4,166.00	4.2
Freeport-McMoRan Copper & Gold	FCX	11,168.40	2,868.75	3.9

Source: www.miningnerds.com

Solution:

Alcoa and Freeport-McMoRan Copper & Gold have the lowest EV/OI and thus appear to be the *most* undervalued or favorably priced on the basis of the EV/OI. Note the negative ratio for AngloGold Ashanti. Negative ratios are difficult to interpret, so other means are used to evaluate companies with negative ratios.

6   ASSET-BASED VALUATION

An asset-based valuation of a company uses estimates of the market or fair value of the company's assets and liabilities. Thus, asset-based valuations work well for companies that do not have a high proportion of intangible or "off the books" assets and that do have a high proportion of current assets and current liabilities. The analyst may be able to value these companies' assets and liabilities in a reasonable fashion by starting with balance sheet items. For most companies, however, balance sheet values are different from market (fair) values, and the market (fair) values can be difficult to determine.

Asset-based valuation models are frequently used together with multiplier models to value private companies. As public companies increase reporting or disclosure of fair values, asset-based valuation may be increasingly used to supplement present value and multiplier models of valuation. Important facts that the practitioner should realize are as follows:

■ Companies with assets that do not have easily determinable market (fair) values—such as those with significant property, plant, and equipment—are very difficult to analyze using asset valuation methods.

- Asset and liability fair values can be very different from the values at which they are carried on the balance sheet of a company.

- Some assets that are "intangible" are shown on the books of the company. Other intangible assets, such as the value from synergies or the value of a good business reputation, may not be shown on the books. Because asset-based valuation may not consider some intangibles, it can give a "floor" value for a situation involving a significant amount of intangibles. When a company has significant intangibles, the analyst should prefer a forward-looking cash flow valuation.

- Asset values may be more difficult to estimate in a hyper-inflationary environment.

We begin by discussing asset-based valuation for hypothetical nonpublic companies and then move on to a public company example. Analysts should consider the difficulties and rewards of using asset-based valuation for companies that are suited to this measure. Owners of small privately held businesses are familiar with valuations arrived at by valuing the assets of the company and then subtracting any relevant liabilities.

EXAMPLE 17

An Asset-Based Valuation of a Family-Owned Laundry

A family owns a laundry and the real estate on which the laundry stands. The real estate is collateral for an outstanding loan of $100,000. How can asset-based valuation be used to value this business?

Solution:

The analyst should get at least two market appraisals for the real estate (building and land) and estimate the cost to extinguish the $100,000 loan. This information would provide estimated values for everything except the laundry as a going concern. That is, the analyst has market values for the building and land and the loan but needs to value the laundry business. The analyst can value the assets of the laundry: the equipment and inventory. The equipment can be valued at depreciated value, inflation-adjusted depreciated value, or replacement cost. Replacement cost in this case means the amount that would have to be spent to buy equivalent used machines. This amount is the market value of the used machines. The analyst will recognize that any intangible value of the laundry (prime location, clever marketing, etc.) is being excluded, which will result in an inaccurate asset-based valuation.

Example 17 shows some of the subtleties present in applying asset-based valuation to determine company value. It also shows how asset-based valuation does not deal with intangibles. Example 18 emphasizes this point.

EXAMPLE 18

An Asset-Based Valuation of a Restaurant

The business being valued is a restaurant that serves breakfast and lunch. The owner/proprietor wants to sell the business and retire. The restaurant space is rented, not owned. This particular restaurant is hugely popular because of the proprietor's cooking skills and secret recipes. How can the analyst value this business?

Solution:

Because of the intangibles, setting a value on this business is challenging. A multiple of income or revenue might be considered. But even those approaches overlook the fact that the proprietor may not be selling his secret recipes and, furthermore, does not intend to continue cooking. Some (or all) of the intangible assets may vanish when the business is sold. Asset-based valuation for this restaurant would begin with estimating the value of the restaurant equipment and inventory and subtracting the value of any liabilities. This approach will provide only a good baseline, however, for a minimum valuation.

For public companies, the assets will typically be so extensive that a piece-by-piece analysis will be impossible, and the transition from book value to market value is a nontrivial task. The asset-based valuation approach is most applicable when the market value of the corporate assets is readily determinable and the intangible assets, which are typically difficult to value, are a relatively small proportion of corporate assets. Asset-based valuation has also been applied to financial companies, natural resource companies, and formerly going-concerns that are being liquidated. Even for other types of companies, however, asset-based valuation of tangible assets may provide a baseline for a minimal valuation.

EXAMPLE 19

An Asset-Based Valuation of an Airline

Consider the value of an airline company that has few routes, high labor and other operating costs, has stopped paying dividends, and is losing millions of dollars each year. Using most valuation approaches, the company will have a negative value. Why might an asset-based valuation approach be appropriate for use by one of the company's competitors that is considering acquisition of this airline?

Solution:

The airline's routes, landing rights, leases of airport facilities, and ground equipment and airplanes may have substantial value to a competitor. An asset-based approach to valuing this company would value the company's assets separately and aside from the money-losing business in which they are presently being utilized.

Analysts recognizing the uncertainties related to model appropriateness and the inputs to the models frequently use more than one model or type of model in valuation to increase their confidence in their estimates of intrinsic value. The choice of models will depend on the availability of information to put into the models. Example 20 illustrates the use of three valuation methods.

EXAMPLE 20

A Simple Example of the Use of Three Major Equity Valuation Models

Company data for dividend per share (DPS), earnings per share (EPS), share price, and price-to-earnings ratio (P/E) for the most recent five years are presented in Exhibit 9. In addition, estimates (indicated by an "E" after the amount) of DPS and EPS for the next five years are shown. The valuation date is at the end of Year 5. The company has 1,000 shares outstanding.

Exhibit 9	Company DPS, EPS, Share Price, and P/E Data			
Year	DPS	EPS	Share Price	TTM P/E
10	$3.10E	$5.20E	—	—
9	$2.91E	$4.85E	—	—
8	$2.79E	$4.65E	—	—
7	$2.65E	$4.37E	—	—
6	$2.55E	$4.30E	—	—
5	$2.43	$4.00	$50.80	12.7
4	$2.32	$3.90	$51.48	13.2
3	$2.19	$3.65	$59.86	16.4
2	$2.14	$3.60	$54.72	15.2
1	$2.00	$3.30	$46.20	14.0

The company's balance sheet at the end of Year 5 is given in Exhibit 10.

Exhibit 10	Balance Sheet as of End of Year 5
Cash	$ 5,000
Accounts receivable	15,000
Inventories	30,000
Net fixed assets	50,000
Total assets	$100,000
Accounts payable	$ 3,000
Notes payable	17,000
Term loans	25,000
Common shareholders' equity	55,000
Total liabilities and equity	$100,000

1 Using a Gordon growth model, estimate intrinsic value. Use a discount rate of 10 percent and an estimate of growth based on growth in dividends over the next five years.

2 Using a multiplier approach, estimate intrinsic value. Assume that a reasonable estimate of P/E is the average trailing twelve-month (TTM) P/E ratio over Years 1 through 4.

3 Using an asset-based valuation approach, estimate value per share from adjusted book values. Assume that the market values of accounts receivable and inventories are as reported, the market value of net fixed assets is 110 percent of reported book value, and the reported book values of liabilities reflect their market values.

Solution to 1:

$$D_5 (1 + g)^5 = D_{10} \quad 2.43(1 + g)^5 = 3.10$$

$$g \approx 5.0\%$$

Estimate of value = V_5 = 2.55/ (0.10 − 0.05) = $51.00

Solution to 2:

Average P/E = (14.0 + 15.2 + 16.4 + 13.2)/4 = 14.7

Estimate of value = $4.00 × 14.7 = $58.80

Solution to 3:

Market value of assets = 5,000 + 15,000 + 30,000 + 1.1(50,000) = $105,000

Market value of liabilities = $3,000 + 17,000 + 25,000 = $45,000

Adjusted book value = $105,000 − 45,000 = $60,000

Estimated value (adjusted book value per share) = $60,000 ÷ 1,000 shares = $60.00

Given the current share price of $50.80, the multiplier and the asset-based valuation approaches indicate that the stock is undervalued. Given the intrinsic value estimated using the Gordon growth model, the analyst is likely to conclude that the stock is fairly priced. The analyst might examine the assumptions in the multiplier and the asset-based valuation approaches to determine why their estimated values differ from the estimated value provided by the Gordon growth model and the market price.

SUMMARY

The equity valuation models used to estimate intrinsic value—present value models, multiplier models, and asset-based valuation—are widely used and serve an important purpose. The valuation models presented here are a foundation on which to base analysis and research but must be applied wisely. Valuation is not simply a numerical analysis. The choice of model and the derivation of inputs require skill and judgment.

When valuing a company or group of companies, the analyst wants to choose a valuation model that is appropriate for the information available to be used as inputs. The available data will, in most instances, restrict the choice of model and influence the way it is used. Complex models exist that may improve on the simple valuation models described in this reading; but before using those models and assuming that complexity increases accuracy, the analyst would do well to consider the "law of parsimony:" A model should be kept as simple as possible in light of the available inputs. Valuation is a fallible discipline, and any method will result in an inaccurate forecast at some time. The goal is to minimize the inaccuracy of the forecast.

Among the points made in this reading are the following:

- An analyst estimating intrinsic value is implicitly questioning the market's estimate of value.

- If the estimated value exceeds the market price, the analyst infers the security is *undervalued*. If the estimated value equals the market price, the analyst infers the security is *fairly valued*. If the estimated value is less than the market price, the analyst infers the security is *overvalued*. Because of the uncertainties involved in valuation, an analyst may require that value estimates differ markedly from market price before concluding that a misvaluation exists.

- Analysts often use more than one valuation model because of concerns about the applicability of any particular model and the variability in estimates that result from changes in inputs.

- Three major categories of equity valuation models are present value, multiplier, and asset-based valuation models.

- Present value models estimate value as the present value of expected future benefits.

- Multiplier models estimate intrinsic value based on a multiple of some fundamental variable.

- Asset-based valuation models estimate value based on the estimated value of assets and liabilities.

- The choice of model will depend upon the availability of information to input into the model and the analyst's confidence in both the information and the appropriateness of the model.

- In the dividend discount model, value is estimated as the present value of expected future dividends.

- In the free cash flow to equity model, value is estimated as the present value of expected future free cash flow to equity.

- The Gordon growth model, a simple DDM, estimates value as $D_1/(r - g)$.

- The two stage dividend discount model estimates value as the sum of the present values of dividends over a short-term period of high growth and the present value of the terminal value at the end of the period of high growth. The terminal value is estimated using the Gordon growth model.

- The choice of dividend model is based upon the patterns assumed with respect to future dividends.

- Multiplier models typically use multiples of the form: P/ measure of fundamental variable or EV/ measure of fundamental variable.

- Multiples can be based upon fundamentals or comparables.

- Asset-based valuations models estimate value of equity as the value of the assets less the value of liabilities.

REFERENCES

Basu, S. 1977. "Investment Performance of Common Stocks in Relation to Their Price-Earnings Ratios: A Test of the Efficient Market Hypothesis." *Journal of Finance*, vol. 32, no. 3:663–682.

Block, S. 1999. "A Study of Financial Analysts: Practice and Theory." *Financial Analysts Journal*, vol. 55, no. 4:86–95.

Dreman, D. 1977. *Psychology of the Stock Market*. New York: AMACOM.

Fama, E., and K. French. 1995. "Size and Book-to-Market Factors in Earnings and Returns." *Journal of Finance*, vol. 50, no. 1:131–155.

McWilliams, J. 1966. "Prices, Earnings and P-E Ratios." *Financial Analysts Journal*, vol. 22, no. 3:137.

Miller, P., and E. Widmann. 1966. "Price Performance Outlook for High & Low P/E Stocks." *1966 Stock & Bond Issue, Commercial & Financial Chronicle*: 26–28.

Nicholson, S. 1968. "Price Ratios in Relation to Investment Results." *Financial Analysts Journal*, vol. 24, no. 1:105–109.

O'Shaughnessy, J. 2005. *What Works on Wall Street*. New York: McGraw-Hill.

Sharpe, W., G. Alexander, and J. Bailey. 1999. *Investments*. New Jersey: Prentice Hall, Inc.

PRACTICE PROBLEMS

1 An analyst estimates the intrinsic value of a stock to be in the range of €17.85 to €21.45. The current market price of the stock is €24.35. This stock is *most likely*:

   A overvalued.

   B undervalued.

   C fairly valued.

2 An analyst determines the intrinsic value of an equity security to be equal to $55. If the current price is $47, the equity is *most likely*:

   A undervalued.

   B fairly valued.

   C overvalued.

3 In asset-based valuation models, the intrinsic value of a common share of stock is based on the:

   A estimated market value of the company's assets.

   B estimated market value of the company's assets plus liabilities.

   C estimated market value of the company's assets minus liabilities.

4 Which of the following is *most likely* used in a present value model?

   A Enterprise value.

   B Price to free cash flow.

   C Free cash flow to equity.

5 Book value is *least likely* to be considered when using:

   A a multiplier model.

   B an asset-based valuation model.

   C a present value model.

6 An analyst is attempting to calculate the intrinsic value of a company and has gathered the following company data: EBITDA, total market value, and market value of cash and short-term investments, liabilities, and preferred shares. The analyst is *least likely* to use:

   A a multiplier model.

   B a discounted cash flow model.

   C an asset-based valuation model.

7 An analyst who bases the calculation of intrinsic value on dividend-paying capacity rather than expected dividends will *most likely* use the:

   A dividend discount model.

   B free cash flow to equity model.

   C cash flow from operations model.

8 An investor expects to purchase shares of common stock today and sell them after two years. The investor has estimated dividends for the next two years, D_1 and D_2, and the selling price of the stock two years from now, P_2. According to the dividend discount model, the intrinsic value of the stock today is the present value of:

   A next year's dividend, D_1.

B future expected dividends, D_1 and D_2.

C future expected dividends and price—D_1, D_2 and P_2.

9 In the free cash flow to equity (FCFE) model, the intrinsic value of a share of stock is calculated as:

A the present value of future expected FCFE.

B the present value of future expected FCFE plus net borrowing.

C the present value of future expected FCFE minus fixed capital investment.

10 With respect to present value models, which of the following statements is *most accurate*?

A Present value models can be used only if a stock pays a dividend.

B Present value models can be used only if a stock pays a dividend or is expected to pay a dividend.

C Present value models can be used for stocks that currently pay a dividend, are expected to pay a dividend, or are not expected to pay a dividend.

11 A Canadian life insurance company has an issue of 4.80 percent, $25 par value, perpetual, non-convertible, non-callable preferred shares outstanding. The required rate of return on similar issues is 4.49 percent. The intrinsic value of a preferred share is *closest to*:

A $25.00.

B $26.75.

C $28.50.

12 Two analysts estimating the value of a non-convertible, non-callable, perpetual preferred stock with a constant dividend arrive at different estimated values. The *most likely* reason for the difference is that the analysts used different:

A time horizons.

B required rates of return.

C estimated dividend growth rates.

13 The Beasley Corporation has just paid a dividend of $1.75 per share. If the required rate of return is 12.3 percent per year and dividends are expected to grow indefinitely at a constant rate of 9.2 percent per year, the intrinsic value of Beasley Corporation stock is *closest* to:

A $15.54.

B $56.45.

C $61.65.

14 An investor is considering the purchase of a common stock with a $2.00 annual dividend. The dividend is expected to grow at a rate of 4 percent annually. If the investor's required rate of return is 7 percent, the intrinsic value of the stock is *closest* to:

A $50.00.

B $66.67.

C $69.33.

15 An analyst gathers or estimates the following information about a stock:

Current price per share	€22.56
Current annual dividend per share	€1.60
Annual dividend growth rate for Years 1–4	9.00%
Annual dividend growth rate for Years 5+	4.00%
Required rate of return	12%

Based on a dividend discount model, the stock is *most likely*:

A undervalued.

B fairly valued.

C overvalued.

16 An analyst is attempting to value shares of the Dominion Company. The company has just paid a dividend of $0.58 per share. Dividends are expected to grow by 20 percent next year and 15 percent the year after that. From the third year onward, dividends are expected to grow at 5.6 percent per year indefinitely. If the required rate of return is 8.3 percent, the intrinsic value of the stock is *closest* to:

A $26.00.

B $27.00.

C $28.00.

17 Hideki Corporation has just paid a dividend of ¥450 per share. Annual dividends are expected to grow at the rate of 4 percent per year over the next four years. At the end of four years, shares of Hideki Corporation are expected to sell for ¥9000. If the required rate of return is 12 percent, the intrinsic value of a share of Hideki Corporation is *closest* to:

A ¥5,850.

B ¥7,220.

C ¥7,670.

18 The Gordon growth model can be used to value dividend-paying companies that are:

A expected to grow very fast.

B in a mature phase of growth.

C very sensitive to the business cycle.

19 The best model to use when valuing a young dividend-paying company that is just entering the growth phase is *most likely* the:

A Gordon growth model.

B two-stage dividend discount model.

C three-stage dividend discount model.

20 An equity analyst has been asked to estimate the intrinsic value of the common stock of Omega Corporation, a leading manufacturer of automobile seats. Omega is in a mature industry, and both its earnings and dividends are expected to grow at a rate of 3 percent annually. Which of the following is *most likely* to be the best model for determining the intrinsic value of an Omega share?

A Gordon growth model.

B Free cash flow to equity model.

C Multistage dividend discount model.

21 A price earnings ratio that is derived from the Gordon growth model is inversely related to the:

A growth rate.

B dividend payout ratio.

C required rate of return.

22 The primary difference between P/E multiples based on comparables and P/E multiples based on fundamentals is that fundamentals-based P/Es take into account:

A future expectations.

B the law of one price.

C historical information.

23 An analyst makes the following statement: "Use of P/E and other multiples for analysis is not effective because the multiples are based on historical data and because not all companies have positive accounting earnings." The analyst's statement is *most likely*:

A inaccurate with respect to both historical data and earnings.

B accurate with respect to historical data and inaccurate with respect to earnings.

C inaccurate with respect to historical data and accurate with respect to earnings.

24 An analyst has prepared a table of the average trailing twelve-month price-to-earning (P/E), price-to-cash flow (P/CF), and price-to-sales (P/S) for the Tanaka Corporation for the years 2005 to 2008.

Year	P/E	P/CF	P/S
2005	4.9	5.4	1.2
2006	6.1	8.6	1.5
2007	8.3	7.3	1.9
2008	9.2	7.9	2.3

As of the date of the valuation in 2009, the trailing twelve-month P/E, P/CF, and P/S are, respectively, 9.2, 8.0, and 2.5. Based on the information provided, the analyst may reasonably conclude that Tanaka shares are *most likely*:

A overvalued.

B undervalued.

C fairly valued.

25 An analyst has gathered the following information for the Oudin Corporation:

   Expected earnings per share = €5.70

   Expected dividends per share = €2.70

   Dividends are expected to grow at 2.75 percent per year indefinitely

   The required rate of return is 8.35 percent

Based on the information provided, the price/earnings multiple for Oudin is *closest* to:

A 5.7.

B 8.5.

C 9.4.

26 An analyst gathers the following information about two companies:

	Alpha Corp.	Delta Co.
Current price per share	$57.32	$18.93
Last year's EPS	$3.82	$1.35
Current year's estimated EPS	$4.75	$1.40

Which of the following statements is *most accurate*?

A   Delta has the higher trailing P/E multiple and lower current estimated P/E multiple.

B   Alpha has the higher trailing P/E multiple and lower current estimated P/E multiple.

C   Alpha has the higher trailing P/E multiple and higher current estimated P/E multiple.

27   An analyst gathers the following information about similar companies in the banking sector:

	First Bank	Prime Bank	Pioneer Trust
P/B	1.10	0.60	0.60
P/E	8.40	11.10	8.30

Which of the companies is *most likely* to be undervalued?

A   First Bank.

B   Prime Bank.

C   Pioneer Trust.

28   The market value of equity for a company can be calculated as enterprise value:

A   minus market value of debt, preferred stock, and short-term investments.

B   plus market value of debt and preferred stock minus short-term investments.

C   minus market value of debt and preferred stock plus short-term investments.

29   Which of the following statements regarding the calculation of the enterprise value multiple is *most likely* correct?

A   Operating income may be used instead of EBITDA.

B   EBITDA may not be used if company earnings are negative.

C   Book value of debt may be used instead of market value of debt.

30   An analyst has determined that the appropriate EV/EBITDA for Rainbow Company is 10.2. The analyst has also collected the following forecasted information for Rainbow Company:

EBITDA = $22,000,000

Market value of debt = $56,000,000

Cash = $1,500,000

The value of equity for Rainbow Company is *closest* to:

A $169 million.

B $224 million.

C $281 million.

31   Enterprise value is most often determined as market capitalization of common equity and preferred stock minus the value of cash equivalents plus the:

A   book value of debt.

B   market value of debt.

C   market value of long-term debt.

32 Asset-based valuation models are best suited to companies where the capital structure does not have a high proportion of:

A   debt.

B   intangible assets.

C   current assets and liabilities.

33 Which of the following is *most likely* a reason for using asset-based valuation?

A   The analyst is valuing a privately held company.

B   The company has a relatively high level of intangible assets.

C   The market values of assets and liabilities are different from the balance sheet values.

34 A disadvantage of the EV method for valuing equity is that the following information may be difficult to obtain:

A   Operating income.

B   Market value of debt.

C   Market value of equity.

35 Which type of equity valuation model is *most likely* to be preferable when one is comparing similar companies?

A   A multiplier model.

B   A present value model.

C   An asset-based valuation model.

36 Which of the following is *most likely* considered a weakness of present value models?

A   Present value models cannot be used for companies that do not pay dividends.

B   Small changes in model assumptions and inputs can result in large changes in the computed intrinsic value of the security.

C   The value of the security depends on the investor's holding period; thus, comparing valuations of different companies for different investors is difficult.

SOLUTIONS

1 A is correct. The current market price of the stock exceeds the upper bound of the analyst's estimate of the intrinsic value of the stock.

2 A is correct. The market price is less than the estimated intrinsic, or fundamental, value.

3 C is correct. Asset-based valuation models calculate the intrinsic value of equity by subtracting liabilities from the market value of assets.

4 C is correct. It is a form of present value, or discounted cash flow, model. Both EV and FCFE are forms of multiplier models.

5 C is correct. Multiplier valuation models (in the form of P/B) and asset-based valuation models (in the form of adjustments to book value) use book value, whereas present value models typically discount future expected cash flows.

6 B is correct. To use a discounted cash flow model, the analyst will require FCFE or dividend data. In addition, the analyst will need data to calculate an appropriate discount rate.

7 B is correct. The FCFE model assumes that dividend-paying capacity is reflected in FCFE.

8 C is correct. According to the dividend discount model, the intrinsic value of a stock today is the present value of all future dividends. In this case, the intrinsic value is the present value of D_1, D_2, and P_2. Note that P_2 is the present value at Period 2 of all future dividends from Period 3 to infinity.

9 A is correct. In the FCFE model, the intrinsic value of stock is calculated by discounting expected future FCFE to present value. No further adjustments are required.

10 C is correct. Dividend discount models can be used for a stock that pays a current dividend or a stock that is expected to pay a dividend. FCFE can be used for both of those stocks and for stocks that do not, or are not expected to, pay dividends in the near future. Both of these models are forms of present value models.

11 B is correct. The expected annual dividend is 4.80% × $25 = $1.20. The value of a preferred share is $1.20/0.0449 = $26.73.

12 B is correct. The required rate of return, r, can vary widely depending on the inputs and is not unique. A preferred stock with a constant dividend would not have a growth rate to estimate, and the investor's time horizon would have no effect on the calculation of intrinsic value.

13 C is correct. $P_0 = D_1/(r - g) = 1.75(1.092)/(0.123 - 0.092) = \$61.65$.

14 C is correct. According to the Gordon growth model, $V_0 = D_1/(r - g)$. In this case, $D_1 = \$2.00 \times 1.04 = \$2.08$, so $V_0 = \$2.08/(0.07 - 0.04) = \$69.3333 = \$69.33$.

15 A is correct. The current price of €22.56 is less than the intrinsic value (V_0) of €24.64; therefore, the stock appears to be currently undervalued. According to the two-stage dividend discount model:

$$V_0 = \sum_{t=1}^{n} \frac{D_0(1 + g_S)^t}{(1 + r)^t} + \frac{V_n}{(1 + r)^n} \text{ and } V_n = \frac{D_{n+1}}{r - g_L}$$

$$D_{n+1} = D_0(1 + g_S)^n(1 + g_L)$$

$$D_1 = €1.60 \times 1.09 = €1.744$$

$$D_2 = €1.60 \times (1.09)^2 = €1.901$$

$$D_3 = €1.60 \times (1.09)^3 = €2.072$$

$$D_4 = €1.60 \times (1.09)^4 = €2.259$$

$$D_5 = [€1.60 \times (1.09)^4](1.04) = €2.349$$

$$V_4 = €2.349/(0.12 - 0.04) = €29.363$$

$$V_0 = \frac{1.744}{(1.12)^1} + \frac{1.901}{(1.12)^2} + \frac{2.072}{(1.12)^3} + \frac{2.259}{(1.12)^4} + \frac{29.363}{(1.12)^4}$$

$$= 1.557 + 1.515 + 1.475 + 1.436 + 18.661$$

$$= €24.64 \text{ (which is greater than the current price of €22.56).}$$

16 C is correct.

$$V_0 = \frac{D_1}{(1+r)} + \frac{D_2}{(1+r)^2} + \frac{P_2}{(1+r)^2}$$

$$= \frac{0.70}{(1.083)} + \frac{0.80}{(1.083)^2} + \frac{31.29}{(1.083)^2}$$

$$= \$28.01$$

Note that $D_1 = 0.58(1.20) = 0.70$, $D_2 = 0.58(1.20)(1.15) = 0.80$, and $P_2 = D_3/(k - g) = 0.80(1.056)/(0.083 - 0.056) = 31.29$

17 B is correct.

$$V_0 = \frac{D_1}{(1+r)} + \frac{D_2}{(1+r)^2} + \frac{D_3}{(1+r)^3} + \frac{D_4}{(1+r)^4} + \frac{P_4}{(1+r)^4}$$

$$= \frac{468}{(1.12)} + \frac{486.72}{(1.12)^2} + \frac{506.19}{(1.12)^3} + \frac{526.44}{(1.12)^4} + \frac{9000}{(1.12)^4}$$

$$= ¥7,220$$

18 B is correct. The Gordon growth model (also known as the constant growth model) can be used to value dividend-paying companies in a mature phase of growth. A stable dividend growth rate is often a plausible assumption for such companies.

19 C is correct. The Gordon growth model is best suited to valuing mature companies. The two-stage model is best for companies that are transitioning from a growth stage to a mature stage. The three-stage model is appropriate for young companies just entering the growth phase.

20 A is correct. The company is a mature company with a steadily growing dividend rate. The two-stage (or multistage) model is unnecessary because the dividend growth rate is expected to remain stable. Although an FCFE model could be used, that model is more often chosen for companies that currently pay no dividends.

21 C is correct. The justified forward P/E is calculated as follows:

$$\frac{P_0}{E_1} = \frac{\dfrac{D_1}{E_1}}{r - g}$$

P/E is inversely related to the required rate of return, r, and directly related to the growth rate, g, and the dividend payout ratio, D/E.

22 A is correct. Multiples based on comparables are grounded in the law of one price and take into account historical multiple values. In contrast, P/E multiples based on fundamentals can be based on the Gordon growth model, which takes into account future expected dividends.

23 A is correct. The statement is inaccurate in both respects. Although multiples can be calculated from historical data, forecasted values can be used as well. For companies without accounting earnings, several other multiples can be used. These multiples are often specific to a company's industry or sector and include price-to-sales and price-to-cash flow.

24 A is correct. Tanaka shares are most likely overvalued. As the table below shows, all the 2009 multiples are currently above their 2005–2008 averages.

Year	P/E	P/CF	P/R
2005	4.9	5.4	1.2
2006	6.1	8.6	1.5
2007	8.3	7.3	1.9
2008	9.2	7.9	2.3
Average	7.1	7.3	1.7

25 B is correct.

$$\frac{P_0}{E_1} = \frac{\dfrac{D_1}{E_1}}{r - g} = \frac{\dfrac{2.7}{5.7}}{0.0835 - 0.0275} = 8.5$$

26 B is correct. P/E = Current price/EPS, and Estimated P/E = Current price/Estimated EPS.

Alpha P/E = \$57.32/\$3.82 = 15.01

Alpha estimated P/E = \$57.32/4.75 = 12.07

Delta P/E = \$18.93/\$1.35 = 14.02

Delta estimated P/E = \$18.93/\$1.40 = 13.52

27 C is correct. Relative to the others, Pioneer Trust has the lowest P/E multiple and the P/B multiple is tied for the lowest with Prime Bank. Given the law of one price, similar companies should trade at similar P/B and P/E levels. Thus, based on the information presented, Pioneer is most likely to be undervalued.

28 C is correct. Enterprise value is calculated as the market value of equity plus the market value of debt and preferred stock minus short-term investments. Therefore, the market value of equity is enterprise value minus the market value of debt and preferred stock plus short-term investments.

29 A is correct. Operating income may be used in place of EBITDA when calculating the enterprise value multiple. EBITDA may be used when company earnings are negative because EBITDA is usually positive. The book value of debt cannot be used in place of market value of debt.

30 A is correct.

EV = 10.2 × 22,000,000 = \$224,400,000

Equity value = EV − Debt + Cash
            = 224,400,000 − 56,000,000 + 1,500,000

= $169,900,000

31 B is correct. The market value of debt must be calculated and taken out of the enterprise value. Enterprise value, sometimes known as the cost of a takeover, is the cost of the purchase of the company, which would include the assumption of the company's debts at market value.

32 B is correct. Intangible assets are hard to value. Therefore, asset-based valuation models work best for companies that do not have a high proportion of intangible assets.

33 A is correct. Asset-based valuations are most often used when an analyst is valuing private enterprises. Both B and C are considerations in asset-based valuations but are more likely to be reasons to avoid that valuation model rather than reasons to use it.

34 B is correct. According to the reading, analysts may have not have access to market quotations for company debt.

35 A is correct. Although all models can be used to compare various companies, multiplier models have the advantage of reducing varying fundamental data points into a format that allows direct comparisons. As long as the analyst applies the data in a consistent manner for all the companies, this approach provides useful comparative data.

36 B is correct. Very small changes in inputs, such as required rate of return or dividend growth rate, can result in large changes to the valuation model output. Some present value models, such as FCFE models, can be used to value companies without dividends. Also, the intrinsic value of a security is independent of the investor's holding period.

Fixed Income

TOPIC LEVEL LEARNING OUTCOME

The candidate should be able to describe fixed-income securities and their markets, yield measures, risk factors, and valuation measures and drivers. The candidate should also be able to calculate yields and values of fixed-income securities.

15

Fixed Income

Basic Concepts

This study session presents the fundamentals of fixed-income investments. Fixed income is one of the largest segments of global financial markets. The first reading introduces elements that define and characterize fixed-income securities. The second reading describes the primary issuers, sectors, and types of bonds. The third reading introduces calculation and interpretation of prices, yields, and spreads for fixed-income securities; market conventions for price/yield calculations and quotations; and spot rates, forward rates, and alternative definitions of a yield curve. The fourth reading focuses on securitization and describes types, characteristics, and risks of asset-backed securities.

READING ASSIGNMENTS

Reading 51	Fixed-Income Securities: Defining Elements by Moorad Choudhry, PhD, and Stephen E. Wilcox, PhD, CFA
Reading 52	Fixed-Income Markets: Issuance, Trading, and Funding by Moorad Choudhry, PhD, Steven V. Mann, PhD, and Lavone F. Whitmer, CFA
Reading 53	Introduction to Fixed-Income Valuation by James F. Adams, PhD, CFA, and Donald J. Smith, PhD
Reading 54	Introduction to Asset-Backed Securities by Frank J. Fabozzi, CFA

Fixed-Income Securities: Defining Elements

by Moorad Choudhry, PhD, and Stephen E. Wilcox, PhD, CFA

LEARNING OUTCOMES

Mastery	The candidate should be able to:
☐	**a.** describe the basic features of a fixed-income security;
☐	**b.** describe functions of a bond indenture;
☐	**c.** compare affirmative and negative covenants and identify examples of each;
☐	**d.** describe how legal, regulatory, and tax considerations affect the issuance and trading of fixed-income securities;
☐	**e.** describe how cash flows of fixed-income securities are structured;
☐	**f.** describe contingency provisions affecting the timing and/or nature of cash flows of fixed-income securities and identify whether such provisions benefit the borrower or the lender.

INTRODUCTION

1

Judged by total market value, fixed-income securities constitute the most prevalent means of raising capital globally. A fixed-income security is an instrument that allows governments, companies, and other types of issuers to borrow money from investors. Any borrowing of money is debt. The promised payments on fixed-income securities are, in general, contractual (legal) obligations of the issuer to the investor. For companies, fixed-income securities contrast to common shares in not having ownership rights. Payment of interest and repayment of principal (amount borrowed) are a prior claim on the company's earnings and assets compared with the claim of common shareholders. Thus, a company's fixed-income securities have, in theory, lower risk than that company's common shares.

In portfolio management, fixed-income securities fulfill several important roles. They are a prime means by which investors—individual and institutional—can prepare to fund, with some degree of safety, known future obligations such as tuition payments or pension obligations. The correlations of fixed-income securities with common shares vary, but adding fixed-income securities to portfolios including common shares is usually an effective way of obtaining diversification benefits.

Among the questions this reading addresses are the following:

- What set of features define a fixed-income security, and how do these features determine the scheduled cash flows?

- What are the legal, regulatory, and tax considerations associated with a fixed-income security, and why are these considerations important for investors?

- What are the common structures regarding the payment of interest and repayment of principal?

- What types of provisions may affect the disposal or redemption of fixed-income securities?

Embarking on the study of fixed-income securities, please note that the terms "fixed-income securities," "debt securities," and "bonds" are often used interchangeably by experts and non-experts alike. We will also follow this convention, and where any nuance of meaning is intended, it will be made clear.[1]

The remainder of this reading is organized as follows. Section 2 describes, in broad terms, what an investor needs to know when investing in fixed-income securities. Section 3 covers both the nature of the contract between the issuer and the bondholders as well as the legal, regulatory, and tax framework within which this contract exists. Section 4 presents the principal and interest payment structures that characterize fixed-income securities. Section 5 discusses the contingency provisions that affect the timing and/or nature of a bond's cash flows. The final section provides a conclusion and summary of the reading.

2　OVERVIEW OF A FIXED-INCOME SECURITY

There are three important elements that an investor needs to know about when investing in a fixed-income security:

- The bond's features, including the issuer, maturity, par value, coupon rate and frequency, and currency denomination. These features determine the bond's scheduled cash flows and, therefore, are key determinants of the investor's expected and actual return.

- The legal, regulatory, and tax considerations that apply to the contractual agreement between the issuer and the bondholders.

- The contingency provisions that may affect the bond's scheduled cash flows. These contingency provisions are options; they give the issuer or the bondholders certain rights affecting the bond's disposal or redemption.

This section describes a bond's basic features and introduces yield measures. The legal, regulatory, and tax considerations and contingency provisions are discussed in Sections 3 and 5, respectively.

---

1 Note that the term "fixed income" is not to be understood literally: Some fixed-income securities have interest payments that change over time. Some experts include preference shares as a type of fixed-income security, but none view them as a type of bond. Finally, in some contexts, bonds refer to the longer-maturity form of debt securities in contrast to money market securities.

2.1 Basic Features of a Bond

All bonds, whether they are "traditional" bonds (i.e., non-securitized bonds) or securitized bonds, are characterized by the same basic features. **Securitized bonds** are created from a process called securitization, which involves moving assets into a special legal entity. This special legal entity then uses the assets as guarantees to back (secure) a bond issue, leading to the creation of securitized bonds. Assets that are typically used to create securitized bonds include residential and commercial mortgages, automobile loans, student loans, and credit card debt, among others.

2.1.1 *Issuer*

Many entities issue bonds: private individuals, such as the musician David Bowie; national governments, such as Singapore or Italy; and companies, such as BP, General Electric, or Tata Group.

Bond issuers are classified into categories based on the similarities of these issuers and their characteristics. Major types of issuers include the following:

- Supranational organizations, such as the World Bank or the European Investment Bank;

- Sovereign (national) governments, such as the United States or Japan;

- Non-sovereign (local) governments, such as the state of Minnesota in the United States, the region of Catalonia in Spain, or the city of Edmonton in Canada;

- Quasi-government entities (i.e., agencies that are owned or sponsored by governments), such as postal services in many countries—for example, Correios in Brazil, La Poste in France, or Pos in Indonesia; and

- Companies (i.e., corporate issuers). Market participants often distinguish between financial issuers (e.g., banks and insurance companies) and non-financial issuers.

Bondholders are exposed to credit risk—that is, the risk of loss resulting from the issuer failing to make full and timely payments of interest and/or repayments of principal. Credit risk is inherent to all debt investments. Bond markets are sometimes classified into sectors based on the issuer's creditworthiness as judged by credit rating agencies. One major distinction is between investment-grade and non-investment-grade (also called high-yield or speculative) bonds.[2] Although a variety of considerations enter into distinguishing the two sectors, the promised payments of investment-grade bonds are perceived as less risky than those of non-investment-grade bonds because of profitability and liquidity considerations. Some regulated financial intermediaries, such as banks and life insurance companies, may face explicit or implicit limitations of holdings of non-investment-grade bonds. The investment policy statements of some investors may also include constraints or limits on such holdings. From the issuer's perspective, an investment-grade credit rating generally allows easier access to bond markets, especially in conditions of limited credit, and at lower interest rates than does a non-investment-grade credit rating.[3]

---

2 The three largest credit rating agencies are Moody's Investors Service, Standard & Poor's, and Fitch Ratings. Bonds rated Baa3 or higher by Moody's and BBB– or higher by Standard & Poor's and Fitch are considered investment grade.

3 Several other distinctions among credit ratings are made. They are discussed in depth in the reading on fundamentals of credit analysis.

2.1.2 Maturity

The maturity date of a bond refers to the date when the issuer is obligated to redeem the bond by paying the outstanding principal amount. The **tenor**, also known as the term to maturity, is the time remaining until the bond's maturity date. The tenor is an important consideration in the analysis of a bond. It indicates the period over which the bondholder can expect to receive the coupon payments and the length of time until the principal is repaid in full.

Maturities typically range from overnight to 30 years or longer. Fixed-income securities with maturities at issuance (original maturity) of one year or less are known as **money market securities**. Issuers of money market securities include governments and companies. Commercial paper and certificates of deposit are examples of money market securities. Fixed-income securities with original maturities that are longer than one year are called **capital market securities**. Although very rare, **perpetual bonds**, such as the consols issued by the sovereign government in the United Kingdom, have no stated maturity date.

2.1.3 Par Value

The **principal amount**, **principal value**, or simply **principal** of a bond is the amount that the issuer agrees to repay the bondholders on the maturity date. This amount is also referred to as the par value, or simply par, face value, nominal value, redemption value, or maturity value. Bonds can have any par value.

In practice, bond prices are quoted as a percentage of their par value. For example, assume that a bond's par value is $1,000. A quote of 95 means that the bond price is $950 (95% × $1,000). When the bond is priced at 100% of par, the bond is said to be trading at par. If the bond's price is below 100% of par, such as in the previous example, the bond is trading at a discount. Alternatively, if the bond's price is above 100% of par, the bond is trading at a premium.

2.1.4 Coupon Rate and Frequency

The coupon rate or nominal rate of a bond is the interest rate that the issuer agrees to pay each year until the maturity date. The annual amount of interest payments made is called the coupon. A bond's coupon is determined by multiplying its coupon rate by its par value. For example, a bond with a coupon rate of 6% and a par value of $1,000 will pay annual interest of $60 (6% × $1,000).

Coupon payments may be made annually, such as those for German government bonds or Bunds. Many bonds, such as government and corporate bonds issued in the United States or government gilts issued in the United Kingdom, pay interest semi-annually. Some bonds make quarterly or monthly interest payments. The acronyms QUIBS (quarterly interest bonds) and QUIDS (quarterly income debt securities) are used by Morgan Stanley and Goldman Sachs, respectively, for bonds that make quarterly interest payments. Many mortgage-backed securities pay interest monthly to match the cash flows of the mortgages backing these bonds. If a bond has a coupon rate of 6% and a par value of $1,000, the periodic interest payments will be $60 if coupon payments are made annually, $30 if they are made semi-annually, $15 if they are made quarterly, and $5 if they are made monthly.

A **plain vanilla bond** or **conventional bond** pays a fixed rate of interest. In this case, the coupon payment does not change during the bond's life. However, there are bonds that pay a floating rate of interest; such bonds are called **floating-rate notes** (FRNs) or **floaters**. The coupon rate of a FRN includes two components: a reference rate plus a spread. The spread, also called margin, is typically constant and expressed in basis points (bps). A **basis point** is equal to 0.01%; put another way, there are 100 basis points in 1%. The spread is set when the bond is issued based on the issuer's creditworthiness at issuance: The higher the issuer's credit quality, the lower the spread. The reference rate, however, resets periodically. Thus, as the reference rate changes, the coupon rate and coupon payment change accordingly.

A widely used reference rate is the London interbank offered rate (Libor). Libor is a collective name for a set of rates covering different currencies for different maturities ranging from overnight to one year. Other reference rates include the Euro interbank offered rate (Euribor), the Hong Kong interbank offered rate (Hibor), or the Singapore interbank offered rate (Sibor) for issues denominated in euros, Hong Kong dollars, and Singapore dollars, respectively. Euribor, Hibor, and Sibor are, like Libor, sets of rates for different maturities up to one year.

For example, assume that the coupon rate of a FRN that makes semi-annual interest payments in June and December is expressed as the six-month Libor + 150 bps. Suppose that in December 20X0, the six-month Libor is 3.25%. The interest rate that will apply to the payment due in June 20X1 will be 4.75% (3.25% + 1.50%). Now suppose that in June 20X1, the six-month Libor has decreased to 3.15%. The interest rate that will apply to the payment due in December 20X1 will decrease to 4.65% (3.15% + 1.50%). More details about FRNs are provided in Section 4.2.1.

All bonds, whether they pay a fixed or floating rate of interest, make periodic coupon payments except for **zero-coupon bonds**. Such bonds do not pay interest, hence their name. Instead, they are issued at a discount to par value and redeemed at par; they are sometimes referred to as **pure discount bonds**. The interest earned on a zero-coupon bond is implied and equal to the difference between the par value and the purchase price. For example, if the par value is $1,000 and the purchase price is $950, the implied interest is $50.

2.1.5 *Currency Denomination*

Bonds can be issued in any currency, although a large number of bond issues are made in either euros or US dollars. The currency of issue may affect a bond's attractiveness. If the currency is not liquid or freely traded, or if the currency is very volatile relative to major currencies, investments in that currency will not appeal to many investors. For this reason, borrowers in developing countries often elect to issue bonds in a currency other than their local currency, such as in euros or US dollars, because doing so makes it easier to place the bond with international investors. Issuers may also choose to issue in a foreign currency if they are expecting cash flows in the foreign currency because the interest payments and principal repayments can act as a natural hedge, reducing currency risk. If a bond is aimed solely at a country's domestic investors, it is more likely that the borrower will issue in the local currency.

Dual-currency bonds make coupon payments in one currency and pay the par value at maturity in another currency. For example, assume that a Japanese company needs to finance a long-term project in the United States that will take several years to become profitable. The Japanese company could issue a yen/US dollar dual-currency bond. The coupon payments in yens can be made from the cash flows generated in Japan, and the principal can be repaid in US dollars using the cash flows generated in the United States once the project becomes profitable.

Currency option bonds can be viewed as a combination of a single-currency bond plus a foreign currency option. They give bondholders the right to choose the currency in which they want to receive interest payments and principal repayments. Bondholders can select one of two currencies for each payment.

Exhibit 1 brings all the basic features of a bond together and illustrates how these features determine the cash flow pattern for a plain vanilla bond. The bond is a five-year Japanese government bond (JGB) with a coupon rate of 0.4% and a par value of ¥10,000. Interest payments are made semi-annually. The bond is priced at par when it is issued and is redeemed at par.

Exhibit 1   Cash Flows for a Plain Vanilla Bond

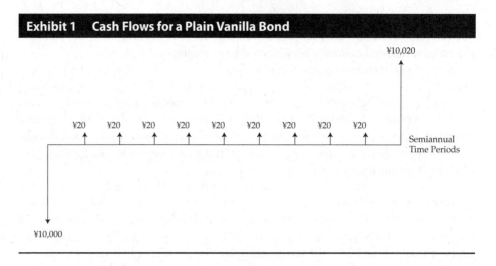

The downward-pointing arrow in Exhibit 1 represents the cash flow paid by the bond investor (received by the issuer) on the day of the bond issue—that is, ¥10,000. The upward-pointing arrows are the cash flows received by the bondholder (paid by the issuer) during the bond's life. As interest is paid semi-annually, the coupon payment is ¥20 [(0.004 × ¥10,000) ÷ 2] every six months for five years—that is, 10 coupon payments of ¥20. The last payment is equal to ¥10,020 because it includes both the last coupon payment and the payment of the par value.

EXAMPLE 1

1   An example of sovereign bond is a bond issued by:

  A   the World Bank.

  B   the city of New York.

  C   the federal German government.

2   The risk of loss resulting from the issuer failing to make full and timely payment of interest is called:

  A   credit risk.

  B   systemic risk.

  C   interest rate risk.

3   A money market security *most likely* matures in:

  A   one year or less.

  B   between one and 10 years.

  C   over 10 years.

4   If the bond's price is higher than its par value, the bond is trading at:

  A   par.

  B   a discount.

  C   a premium.

5   A bond has a par value of £100 and a coupon rate of 5%. Coupon payments are made semi-annually. The periodic interest payment is:

  A   £2.50, paid twice a year.

  B   £5.00, paid once a year.

  C   £5.00, paid twice a year.

6 The coupon rate of a floating-rate note that makes payments in June and December is expressed as six-month Libor + 25 bps. Assuming that the six-month Libor is 3.00% at the end of June 20XX and 3.50% at the end of December 20XX, the interest rate that applies to the payment due in December 20XX is:

A 3.25%.

B 3.50%.

C 3.75%.

7 The type of bond that allows bondholders to choose the currency in which they receive each interest payment and principal repayment is a:

A pure discount bond.

B dual-currency bond.

C currency option bond.

Solution to 1:

C is correct. A sovereign bond is a bond issued by a national government, such as the federal German government. A is incorrect because a bond issued by the World Bank is a supranational bond. B is incorrect because a bond issued by a local government, such as the city of New York, is a non-sovereign bond.

Solution to 2:

A is correct. Credit risk is the risk of loss resulting from the issuer failing to make full and timely payments of interest and/or repayments of principal. B is incorrect because systemic risk is the risk of failure of the financial system. C is incorrect because interest rate risk is the risk that a change in market interest rate affects a bond's value. Systemic risk and interest rate risk are defined in Sections 5.3 and 4.2.1, respectively.

Solution to 3:

A is correct. The primary difference between a money market security and a capital market security is the maturity at issuance. Money market securities mature in one year or less, whereas capital market securities mature in more than one year.

Solution to 4:

C is correct. If a bond's price is higher than its par value, the bond is trading at a premium. A is incorrect because a bond is trading at par if its price is equal to its par value. B is incorrect because a bond is trading at a discount if its price is lower than its par value.

Solution to 5:

A is correct. The annual coupon payment is 5% × £100 = £5.00. The coupon payments are made semi-annually, so £2.50 paid twice a year.

Solution to 6:

A is correct. The interest rate that applies to the payment due in December 20XX is the six-month Libor at the end of June 20XX plus 25 bps. Thus, it is 3.25% (3.00% + 0.25%).

Solution to 7:

C is correct. A currency option bond gives bondholders the right to choose the currency in which they want to receive each interest payment and principal repayment. A is incorrect because a pure discount bond is issued at a discount to par value and redeemed at par. B is incorrect because a dual-currency bond makes coupon payments in one currency and pays the par value at maturity in another currency.

2.2 Yield Measures

There are several yield measures commonly used by market participants. The **current yield** or **running yield** is equal to the bond's annual coupon divided by the bond's price, expressed as a percentage. For example, if a bond has a coupon rate of 6%, a par value of $1,000, and a price of $1,010, the current yield is 5.94% ($60 ÷ $1,010). The current yield is a measure of income that is analogous to the dividend yield for a common share.

The most commonly referenced yield measure is known as the **yield to maturity**, also called the **yield to redemption** or **redemption yield**. The yield to maturity is the internal rate of return on a bond's expected cash flows—that is, the discount rate that equates the present value of the bond's expected cash flows until maturity with the bond's price. The yield to maturity can be considered an estimate of the bond's expected return; it reflects the annual return that an investor will earn on a bond if this investor purchases the bond today and holds it until maturity. There is an inverse relationship between the bond's price and its yield to maturity, all else being equal. That is, the higher the bond's yield to maturity, the lower its price. Alternatively, the higher the bond's price, the lower its yield to maturity. Thus, investors anticipating a lower interest rate environment (in which investors demand a lower yield-to-maturity on the bond) hope to earn a positive return from price appreciation. The reading on understanding risk and return of fixed-income securities covers these fundamentals and more.

3

LEGAL, REGULATORY, AND TAX CONSIDERATIONS

A **bond** is a contractual agreement between the issuer and the bondholders. As such, it is subject to legal considerations. Investors in fixed-income securities must also be aware of the regulatory and tax considerations associated with the bonds in which they invest or want to invest.

3.1 Bond Indenture

The **trust deed** is the legal contract that describes the form of the bond, the obligations of the issuer, and the rights of the bondholders. Market participants frequently call this legal contract the bond **indenture**, particularly in the United States and Canada. The indenture is written in the name of the issuer and references the features of the bond issue, such as the principal value for each bond, the interest rate or coupon rate to be paid, the dates when the interest payments will be made, the maturity date when the bonds will be repaid, and whether the bond issue comes with any contingency provisions. The indenture also includes information regarding the funding sources for the interest payment and principal repayments, and it specifies any collaterals, credit enhancements, or covenants. **Collaterals** are assets or financial guarantees underlying the debt obligation above and beyond the issuer's promise to pay. **Credit enhancements** are provisions that may be used to reduce the credit risk of the bond issue. **Covenants** are clauses that specify the rights of the bondholders and any actions that the issuer is obligated to perform or prohibited from performing.

Because it would be impractical for the issuer to enter into a direct agreement with each of many bondholders, the indenture is usually held by a trustee. The trustee is typically a financial institution with trust powers, such as the trust department of a bank or a trust company. It is appointed by the issuer, but it acts in a fiduciary capacity with the bondholders. The trustee's role is to monitor that the issuer complies with the obligations specified in the indenture and to take action on behalf of the bond-holders when necessary. The trustee's duties tend to be administrative and usually include maintaining required documentation and records; holding beneficial title to, safeguarding, and appraising collateral (if any); invoicing the issuer for interest payments and principal repayments; and holding funds until they are paid, although the actual mechanics of cash flow movements from the issuers to the trustee are typically handled by the principal paying agent. In the event of default, the discretionary powers of the trustee increase considerably. The trustee is responsible for calling meetings of bondholders to discuss the actions to take. The trustee can also bring legal action against the issuer on behalf of the bondholders.

For a plain vanilla bond, the indenture is often a standard template that is updated for the specific terms and conditions of a particular bond issue. For exotic bonds, the document is tailored and can often be several hundred pages.

When assessing the risk–reward profile of a bond issue, investors should be informed by the content of the indenture. They should pay special attention to their rights in the event of default. In addition to identifying the basic bond features described earlier, investors should carefully review the following areas:

- the legal identity of the bond issuer and its legal form;
- the source of repayment proceeds;
- the asset or collateral backing (if any);
- the credit enhancements (if any); and
- the covenants (if any).

We consider each of these areas in the following sections.

3.1.1 *Legal Identity of the Bond Issuer and its Legal Form*

The legal obligation to make the contractual payments is assigned to the bond issuer. The issuer is identified in the indenture by its legal name. For a sovereign bond, the legal issuer is usually the office responsible for managing the national budget, such as HM Treasury (Her Majesty's Treasury) in the United Kingdom. The legal issuer may be different from the body that administers the bond issue process. Using the UK example, the legal obligation to repay gilts lies with HM Treasury, but the bonds are issued by the UK Debt Management Office, an executive agency of HM Treasury.

For corporate bonds, the issuer is usually the corporate legal entity—for example, Wal-Mart Stores Inc., Samsung Electronics Co. Ltd., or Volkswagen AG. However, bonds are sometimes issued by a subsidiary of a parent legal entity. In this case, investors should look at the credit quality of the subsidiary, unless the indenture specifies that the bond liabilities are guaranteed by the parent. When they are rated, subsidiaries often carry a credit rating that is lower than their parent, but this is not always the case. For example, in May 2012, Santander UK plc was rated higher by Moody's than its Spanish parent, Banco Santander.

Bonds are sometimes issued by a holding company, which is the parent legal entity for a group of companies, rather than by one of the operating companies in the group. This issue is important for investors to consider because a holding company may be rated differently from its operating companies and investors may lack recourse to assets held by those companies. If the bonds are issued by a holding company that has fewer (or no) assets to call on should it default, investors face a higher level of credit risk than if the bonds were issued by one of the operating companies in the group.

For securitized bonds, the legal obligation to repay the bondholders often lies with a separate legal entity that was created by the financial institution in charge of the securitization process. The financial institution is known as the sponsor or originator. The legal entity is most frequently referred to as a special purpose entity (SPE) in the United States and a special purpose vehicle (SPV) in Europe, and it is also sometimes called a special purpose company (SPC). The legal form for an SPV may be a limited partnership, a limited liability company, or a trust. Typically, SPVs are thinly capitalized, have no independent management or employees, and have no purpose other than the transactions for which they were created.

Through the securitization process, the sponsor transfers the assets to the SPV to carry out some specific transaction or series of transactions. One of the key reasons for forming an SPV is bankruptcy remoteness. The transfer of assets by the sponsor is considered a legal sale; once the assets have been securitized, the sponsor no longer has ownership rights. Any party making claims following the bankruptcy of the sponsor would be unable to recover the assets or their proceeds. As a result, the SPV's ability to pay interest and repay the principal should remain intact even if the sponsor were to fail—hence the reason why the SPV is also called a bankruptcy-remote vehicle.

3.1.2 *Source of Repayment Proceeds*

The indenture usually describes how the issuer intends to service the debt (make interest payments) and repay the principal. Generally, the source of repayment for bonds issued by supranational organizations is either the repayment of previous loans made by the organization or the paid-in capital from its members. National governments may also act as guarantors for certain bond issues. If additional sources of repayment are needed, the supranational organization can typically call on its members to provide funds.

Sovereign bonds are backed by the "full faith and credit" of the national government and thus by that government's ability to raise tax revenues and print money. Sovereign bonds denominated in local currency are generally considered the safest of all investments because governments have the power to raise taxes to make interest payments and principal repayments. Thus, it is highly probable that interest and principal will be paid fully and on time. As a consequence, the yields on sovereign bonds are typically lower than those for other local issuers.

There are three major sources for repayment of non-sovereign government debt issues, and bonds are usually classified according to these sources. The first source is through the general taxing authority of the issuer. The second source is from the cash flows of the project the bond issue is financing. The third source is from special taxes or fees established specifically for the purpose of funding the payment of interest and repayment of principal.

The source of payment for corporate bonds is the issuer's ability to generate cash flows, primarily through its operations. These cash flows depend on the issuer's financial strength and integrity. Because they carry a higher level of credit risk, corporate bonds typically offer a higher yield than sovereign bonds.

Securitizations typically rely on the cash flows generated by one or more underlying financial assets that serve as the primary source for the contractual payments to bondholders rather than on the claims-paying ability of an operating entity. A wide range of financial assets have been securitized, including residential and commercial mortgages, automobile loans, student loans, credit card receivables, equipment loans and leases, and business trade receivables. Unlike corporate bonds, most securitized bonds are amortized, meaning that the principal amount borrowed is paid back gradually over the specified term of the loan rather than in one lump sum at the maturity of the loan.

3.1.3 *Asset or Collateral Backing*

Collateral backing is a way to alleviate credit risk. Investors should review where they rank compared with other creditors in the event of default and analyze the quality of the collateral backing the bond issue.

3.1.3.1 Seniority Ranking   **Secured bonds** are backed by assets or financial guarantees pledged to ensure debt repayment in the case of default. In contrast, unsecured bonds have no collateral; bondholders have only a general claim on the issuer's assets and cash flows. Thus, unsecured bonds are paid after secured bonds in the event of default. By lowering credit risk, collateral backing increases the bond issue's credit quality and decreases its yield.

A bond's collateral backing might not specify an identifiable asset but instead may be described as the "general plant and infrastructure" of the issuer. In such cases, investors rely on seniority ranking, the systematic way in which lenders are repaid in case of bankruptcy or liquidation. What matters to investors is where they rank compared with other creditors rather than whether there is an asset of sufficient quality and value in place to cover their claims. Senior debt is debt that has a priority claim over subordinated debt or junior debt. Financial institutions issue a large volume of both senior unsecured and subordinated bonds globally; it is not uncommon to see large as well as smaller banks issue such bonds. For example, in 2012, banks as diverse as Royal Bank of Scotland in the United Kingdom and Prime Bank in Bangladesh issued senior unsecured bonds to institutional investors.

Debentures are a type of bond that can be secured or unsecured. In many jurisdictions, debentures are unsecured bonds, with no collateral backing assigned to the bondholders. In contrast, bonds known as "debentures" in the United Kingdom and in other Commonwealth countries, such as India, are usually backed by an asset or pool of assets assigned as collateral support for the bond obligations and segregated from the claims of other creditors. Thus, it is important for investors to review the indenture to determine whether a debenture is secured or unsecured. If the debenture is secured, debenture holders rank above unsecured creditors of the company; they have a specific asset or pool of assets that the trustee can call on to realize the debt in the event of default.

3.1.3.2 Types of Collateral Backing   There is a wide range of bonds that are secured by some form of collateral. Some companies issue collateral trust bonds and equipment trust certificates. **Collateral trust bonds** are secured by securities such as common shares, other bonds, or other financial assets. These securities are pledged by the issuer and typically held by the trustee. **Equipment trust certificates** are bonds secured by specific types of equipment or physical assets, such as aircraft, railroad cars, shipping containers, or oil rigs. They are most commonly issued to take advantage of the tax benefits of leasing. For example, suppose an airline finances the purchase of new aircraft with equipment trust certificates. The legal title to the aircraft is held by the trustee, which issues equipment trust certificates to investors in the amount of the aircraft purchase price. The trustee leases the aircraft to the airline and collects lease payments from the airline to pay the interest on the certificates. When the certificates mature, the trustee sells the aircraft to the airline, uses the proceeds to retire the principal, and cancels the lease.

One of the most common forms of collateral for securitized bonds is mortgaged property. **Mortgage-backed securities** (MBS) are debt obligations that represent claims to the cash flows from pools of mortgage loans, most commonly on residential property. Mortgage loans are purchased from banks, mortgage companies, and other originators and then assembled into pools by a governmental, quasi-governmental, or private entity.

Financial institutions, particularly in Europe, issue covered bonds. A **covered bond** is a debt obligation backed by a segregated pool of assets called a "cover pool". Covered bonds are similar to securitized bonds but offer bondholders additional protection if the financial institution defaults. A financial institution that sponsors securitized bonds transfers the assets backing the bonds to a SPV. If the financial institution defaults, investors who hold bonds in the financial institution have no recourse against the SPV and its pool of assets because the SPV is a bankruptcy-remote vehicle; the only recourse they have is against the financial institution itself. In contrast, in the case of covered bonds, the pool of assets remains on the financial institution's balance sheet. In the event of default, bondholders have recourse against both the financial institution and the cover pool. Thus, the cover pool serves as collateral. If the assets that are included in the cover pool become non-performing (i.e., the assets are not generating the promised cash flows), the issuer must replace them with performing assets. Therefore, covered bonds usually carry lower credit risks and offer lower yields than otherwise similar securitized bonds.

3.1.4 *Credit Enhancement*

Credit enhancement refers to a variety of provisions that can be used to reduce the credit risk of a bond issue and is very often used in securitized bonds. Credit enhancement provides additional collateral, insurance, and/or a third-party guarantee that the issuer will meet its obligations. Thus, it reduces credit risk, which increases the issue's credit quality and decreases the bond's yield.

There are two primary types of credit enhancement: internal and external. Internal credit enhancement relies on structural features regarding the priority of payment or the value of the collateral. External credit enhancement refers to guarantees received from a third party, often called a guarantor. We describe each type in the following sections.

3.1.4.1 Internal Credit Enhancement   Subordination refers to the ordering of claim priorities for ownership or interest in an asset, and it is the most popular internal credit enhancement technique. The cash flows generated by the assets are allocated with different priority to classes of different seniority. The subordinated or junior tranches function as credit protection for the more senior tranches, in the sense that the class of highest seniority has the first claim on available cash flows. This type of protection is commonly referred to as a waterfall structure because in the event of default, the proceeds from liquidating assets will first be used to repay the most senior creditors. Thus, if the issuer defaults, losses are allocated from the bottom up (from the most junior to the most senior tranche). The most senior tranche is typically unaffected unless losses exceed the amount of the subordinated tranches, which is why the most senior tranche is usually rated Aaa/AAA.

Overcollateralization refers to the process of posting more collateral than is needed to obtain or secure financing. For example, in the case of MBS, the principal amount of an issue may be $100 million while the principal value of the mortgages underlying the issue may equal $120 million. One major problem associated with overcollateralization is the valuation of the collateral. For example, one of the most significant contributors to the 2007–2009 credit crisis was a valuation problem with the residential housing assets backing MBS. Many properties were originally valued in excess of the worth of the issued securities. But as property prices fell and homeowners started to default on their mortgages, the credit quality of many MBS declined sharply. The result was a rapid rise in yields and panic among investors in these securities.

Excess spread, sometimes called excess interest cash flow, is the difference between the cash flow received from the assets used to secure the issue and the interest paid to investors. The excess spread is sometimes deposited into a reserve account and serves as a first line of protection against losses. In a process called turboing, the excess spread is used to retire principal, with senior issues having the first claim on these funds.

3.1.4.2 External Credit Enhancement One form of an external credit enhancement is a **surety bond** or a bank guarantee. Surety bonds and bank guarantees are very similar in nature because they both reimburse investors for any losses incurred if the issuer defaults. However, there is usually a maximum amount that is guaranteed, called the penal sum. The major difference between a surety bond and a bank guarantee is that the former is issued by a rated and regulated insurance company, whereas the latter is issued by a bank.

A **letter of credit** from a financial institution is another form of an external credit enhancement for a bond issue. The financial institution provides the issuer with a credit line to reimburse any cash flow shortfalls from the assets backing the issue. Letters of credit are becoming less common forms of credit enhancement as a result of the rating agencies downgrading the long-term debt of several banks that were providers of letters of credit.

Surety bonds, bank guarantees, and letters of credit expose the investor to third-party (or counterparty) risk, the possibility that a guarantor cannot meet its obligations. A cash collateral account mitigates this concern because the issuer immediately borrows the credit-enhancement amount and then invests that amount, usually in highly rated short-term commercial paper. Because this is an actual deposit of cash rather than a pledge of cash, a downgrade of the cash collateral account provider will not necessarily result in a downgrade of the bond issue backed by that provider.

3.1.5 Covenants

Bond covenants are legally enforceable rules that borrowers and lenders agree on at the time of a new bond issue. An indenture will frequently include affirmative (or positive) and negative covenants. Affirmative covenants enumerate what issuers are required to do, whereas negative covenants enumerate what issuers are prohibited from doing.

Affirmative covenants are typically administrative in nature. For example, frequently used affirmative covenants include what the issuer will do with the proceeds from the bond issue and the promise of making the contractual payments. The issuer may also promise to comply with all laws and regulations, maintain its current lines of business, insure and maintain its assets, and pay taxes as they come due. These types of covenants typically do not impose additional costs to the issuer and do not materially constrain the issuer's discretion regarding how to operate its business.

In contrast, negative covenants are frequently costly and do materially constrain the issuer's potential business decisions. The purpose of negative covenants is to protect bondholders from such problems as the dilution of their claims, asset withdrawals or substitutions, and suboptimal investments by the issuer. Examples of negative covenants include the following:

- *Restrictions on debt* regulate the issue of additional debt. Maximum acceptable debt usage ratios (sometimes called leverage ratios or gearing ratios) and minimum acceptable interest coverage ratios are frequently specified, permitting new debt to be issued only when justified by the issuer's financial condition.

- *Negative pledges* prevent the issuance of debt that would be senior to or rank in priority ahead of the existing bondholders' debt.

- *Restrictions on prior claims* protect unsecured bondholders by preventing the issuer from using assets that are not collateralized (called unencumbered assets) to become collateralized.

- *Restrictions on distributions to shareholders* restrict dividends and other payments to shareholders such as share buy-backs (repurchases). The restriction typically operates by reference to the borrower's profitability; that is, the covenant sets a base date, usually at or near the time of the issue, and permits dividends and share buy-backs only to the extent of a set percentage of earnings or cumulative earnings after that date.

- *Restrictions on asset disposals* set a limit on the amount of assets that can be disposed by the issuer during the bond's life. The limit on cumulative disposals is typically set as a percentage of a company's gross assets. The usual intent is to protect bondholder claims by preventing a break-up of the company.

- *Restrictions on investments* constrain risky investments by blocking speculative investments. The issuer is essentially forced to devote its capital to its going-concern business. A companion covenant may require the issuer to stay in its present line of business.

- *Restrictions on mergers and acquisitions* prevent these actions unless the company is the surviving company or unless the acquirer delivers a supplemental indenture to the trustee expressly assuming the old bonds and terms of the old indenture. These requirements effectively prevent a company from avoiding its obligations to bondholders by selling out to another company.

These are only a few examples of negative covenants. The common characteristic of all negative covenants is ensuring that the issuer will not take any actions that would significantly reduce its ability to make interest payments and repay the principal. Bondholders, however, rarely wish to be too specific about how an issuer should run its business because doing so would imply a degree of control that bondholders legally want to avoid. In addition, very restrictive covenants may not be in the bondholders' best interest if they force the issuer to default when default is avoidable. For example, strict restrictions on debt may prevent the issuer from raising new funds that are necessary to meet its contractual obligations; strict restrictions on asset disposals may prohibit the issuer from selling assets or business units and obtaining the necessary liquidity to make interest payments or principal repayments; and strict restrictions on mergers and acquisitions may prevent the issuer from being taken over by a stronger company that would be able to honor the issuer's contractual obligations.

EXAMPLE 2

1 The term *most likely* used to refer to the legal contract under which a bond is issued is:

   A indenture.

   B debenture.

   C letter of credit.

2 The individual or entity that *most likely* assumes the role of trustee for a bond issue is:

   A a financial institution appointed by the issuer.

   B the treasurer or chief financial officer of the issuer.

   C a financial institution appointed by a regulatory authority.

3 The individual or entity *most likely* responsible for the timely payment of interest and repayment of principal to bondholders is the:

   A trustee.

   B primary or lead bank of the issuer.

    C treasurer or chief financial officer of the issuer.

4 The major advantage of issuing bonds through a special purpose vehicle is:

    A bankruptcy remoteness.

    B beneficial tax treatments.

    C greater liquidity and lower issuing costs.

5 The category of bond *most likely* repaid from the repayment of previous loans made by the issuer is:

    A sovereign bonds.

    B supranational bonds.

    C non-sovereign bonds.

6 The type of collateral used to secure collateral trust bonds is *most likely*:

    A securities.

    B mortgages.

    C physical assets.

7 The external credit enhancement that has the *least* amount of third-party risk is a:

    A surety bond.

    B letter of credit.

    C cash collateral account.

8 An example of an affirmative covenant is the requirement:

    A that dividends will not exceed 60% of earnings.

    B to insure and perform periodic maintenance on financed assets.

    C that the debt-to-equity ratio will not exceed 0.4 and times interest earned will not fall below 8.0.

9 An example of a covenant that protects bondholders against the dilution of their claims is a restriction on:

    A debt.

    B investments.

    C mergers and acquisitions.

Solution to 1:

A is correct. The contract between a bond issuer and the bondholders is very often called an indenture or deed trust. The indenture documents the terms of the issue, including the principal amount, the coupon rate, and the payments schedule. It also provides information about the funding sources for the contractual payments and specifies whether there are any collateral, credit enhancement, or covenants. B is incorrect because a debenture is a type of bond. C is incorrect because a letter of credit is an external credit enhancement.

Solution to 2:

A is correct. The issuer chooses a financial institution with trust powers, such as the trust department of a bank or a trust company, to act as a trustee for the bond issue.

Solution to 3:

A is correct. Although the issuer is ultimately the source of the contractual payments, it is the trustee that ensures timely payments. Doing so is accomplished by invoicing the issuer for interest payments and principal repayments and holding the funds until they are paid.

Solution to 4:

A is correct. A SPV is a bankruptcy-remote vehicle. Bankruptcy remoteness is achieved by transferring the assets from the sponsor to the SPV. Once this transfer is completed, the sponsor no longer has ownership rights. If the sponsor defaults, no claims can be made to recover the assets that were transferred or the proceeds from the transfer to the SPV.

Solution to 5:

B is correct. The source of payment for bonds issued by supranational organizations is either the repayment of previous loans made by the organization or the paid-in capital of its member states. A is incorrect because national governments rely on their taxing authority and money creation to repay their debt. C is incorrect because non-sovereign bonds are typically repaid from the issuer's taxing authority or the cash flows of the project being financed.

Solution to 6:

A is correct. Collateral trust bonds are secured by securities, such as common shares, other bonds, or other financial assets. B is incorrect because mortgage-backed securities are secured by mortgages. C is incorrect because equipment trust certificates are backed by physical assets such as aircraft, railroad cars, shipping containers, or oil rigs.

Solution to 7:

C is correct. The third-party (or counterparty) risk for a surety bond and a letter of credit arises from both being future promises to pay. In contrast, a cash collateral account allows the issuer to immediately borrow the credit-enhancement amount and then invest it.

Solution to 8:

B is correct. Affirmative covenants indicate what the issuer "must do" and are administrative in nature. A covenant requiring the issuer to insure and perform periodic maintenance on financed assets is an example of affirmative covenant. A and C are incorrect because they are negative covenants; they indicate what the issuer cannot do.

Solution to 9:

A is correct. A restriction on debt typically takes the form of a maximum acceptable debt usage ratio or a minimum acceptable interest coverage ratio. Thus, it limits the issuer's ability to issue new debt that would dilute the bondholders' claims. B and C are incorrect because they are covenants that restrict the issuer's business activities by preventing the company from making investments or being taken over, respectively.

3.2 Legal and Regulatory Considerations

Fixed-income securities are subject to different legal and regulatory requirements depending on where they are issued and traded, as well as who holds them. Unfortunately, there are no unified legal and regulatory requirements that apply globally.

An important consideration for investors is where the bonds are issued and traded because it affects the laws and regulation that apply. The global bond markets consist of national bond markets and the Eurobond market. A national bond market includes all the bonds that are issued and traded in a specific country, and denominated in the currency of that country. Bonds issued by entities that are incorporated in that country are called domestic bonds, whereas bonds issued by entities that are incorporated in another country are called foreign bonds. If Ford Motor Company issues bonds denominated in US dollars in the United States, these bonds will be classified as domestic. If Volkswagen Group or Toyota Motor Corporation (or their German or Japanese subsidiaries) issue bonds denominated in US dollars in the United States, these bonds will be classified as foreign. Foreign bonds very often receive nicknames. For example, foreign bonds are called "kangaroo bonds" in Australia, "maple bonds" in Canada, "panda bonds" in China, "Samurai bonds" in Japan, "kimchi bonds" in South Korea, "matrioshka bonds" in Russia, "matador bonds" in Spain, "bulldog bonds" in the United Kingdom, and "Yankee bonds" in the United States. National regulators may make distinctions both between and among resident and non-resident issuers, and they may have different requirements regarding the issuance process, the level of disclosures, or the restrictions imposed on the bond issuer and/or the investors who can purchase the bonds.

Governments and companies have issued foreign bonds in London since the 19th century, and foreign bond issues expanded in such countries as the United States, Japan, and Switzerland during the 1980s. But the 1960s saw the emergence of another bond market: the Eurobond market. The Eurobond market was created primarily to bypass the legal, regulatory, and tax constraints imposed on bond issuers and investors, particularly in the United States. Bonds issued and traded on the Eurobond market are called **Eurobonds**, and they are named after the currency in which they are denominated. For example, Eurodollar and Euroyen bonds are denominated in US dollars and Japanese yens, respectively. Bonds that are denominated in euros are called euro-denominated Eurobonds.

Eurobonds are typically less regulated than domestic and foreign bonds because they are issued outside the jurisdiction of any single country. They are usually unsecured bonds and can be denominated in any currency, including the issuer's domestic currency.[4] They are underwritten by an international syndicate—that is, a group of financial institutions from different jurisdictions. Most Eurobonds are **bearer bonds**, meaning that the trustee does not keep records of who owns the bonds; only the clearing system knows who the bond owners are. In contrast, most domestic and foreign bonds are **registered bonds** for which ownership is recorded by either name or serial number. Some investors may prefer bearer bonds to registered bonds, possibly for tax reasons.

A reference is sometimes made to global bonds. A global bond is issued simultaneously in the Eurobond market and in at least one domestic bond market. Issuing bonds in several markets at the same time ensures that there is sufficient demand for large bond issues, and that the bonds can be purchased by all investors, no matter where these investors are located. For example, the World Bank is a regular issuer of global bonds. Many market participants refer to foreign bonds, Eurobonds, and global bonds as international bonds as opposed to domestic bonds.

The differences among domestic bonds, foreign bonds, Eurobonds, and global bonds matter to investors because these bonds are subject to different legal, regulatory, and as described in Section 3.3, tax requirements. They are also characterized by differences in the frequency of interest payments and the way the interest payment is

---

4 Eurobonds denominated in US dollars cannot be sold to US investors at the time of issue because they are not registered with the US Securities and Exchange Commission (SEC). Most Eurobonds are sold to investors in Europe, the Middle East, and Asia Pacific.

calculated, which affect the bond's cash flows and thus its price. Note, however, that the currency in which a bond is denominated has a stronger effect on its price than where the bond is issued or traded. This is because market interest rates have a strong influence on a bond's price, and the market interest rates that affect a bond are those associated with the currency in which the bond is denominated.

As the emergence and growth of the Eurobond market illustrates, legal and regulatory considerations affect the dynamics of the global fixed-income markets. Exhibit 2 compares the amount of domestic and international debt outstanding for the 15 countries that were the largest domestic debt issuers at the end of December 2011. The reported amounts are based on the residence of the issuer.

Exhibit 2	**Domestic and International Debt Securities by Residence of Issuer at the End of December 2011**	
Issuers	**Domestic Debt Securities (US$ billions)**	**International Debt Securities (US$ billions)**
All issuers	**69,912.7**	**28,475.4**
United States	26,333.1	6,822.0
Japan	14,952.5	180.6
China	3,344.8	28.3
France	3,307.6	1,977.0
Italy	3,077.7	1,135.0
Germany	2,534.2	2,120.6
United Kingdom	1,743.8	3,671.4
Canada	1,547.7	710.9
Brazil	1,488.8	137.4
Spain	1,448.7	1,499.5
South Korea	1,149.0	154.6
Australia	1,023.4	586.4
Netherlands	955.5	2,019.7
Denmark	714.6	142.6
India	596.1	26.1

Source: Based on data from the Bank of International Settlements, Tables 11 and 16A, available at www.bis.org/statistics/secstats.htm, (accessed 6 September 2012).

EXAMPLE 3

1 An example of a domestic bond is a bond issued by:

   A LG Group from South Korea, denominated in British pounds, and sold in the United Kingdom.

   B the UK Debt Management Office, denominated in British pounds, and sold in the United Kingdom.

   C Wal-Mart from the United States, denominated in US dollars, and sold in various countries in North America, Europe, the Middle East, and Asia Pacific.

2 A bond issued by Sony in Japan, denominated in US dollars but not registered with the SEC, and sold to an institutional investor in the Middle East, is *most likely* an example of a:

A Eurobond.

B global bond.

C foreign bond.

Solution to 1:

B is correct. A domestic bond is issued by a local issuer, denominated in local currency, and sold in the domestic market. Gilts are British pound–denominated bonds issued by the UK Debt Management Office in the United Kingdom. Thus, they are UK domestic bonds. A is incorrect because a bond issued by LG Group from South Korea, denominated in British pounds, and sold in the United Kingdom, is an example of a foreign bond (bulldog bond). C is incorrect because a bond issued by Wal-Mart from the United States, denominated in US dollars, and sold in various countries in North America, Europe, the Middle East, and Asia Pacific is most likely an example of a global bond, particularly if it is also sold in the Eurobond market.

Solution to 2:

A is correct. A Eurobond is a bond that is issued internationally, outside the jurisdiction of any single country. Thus, a bond issued by Sony from Japan, denominated in US dollars but not registered with the SEC, is an example of a Eurobond. B is incorrect because global bonds are bonds that are issued simultaneously in the Eurobond market and in at least one domestic bond market. C is incorrect because if Sony's bond issue were a foreign bond (Yankee bond), it would be registered with the SEC.

3.3 Tax Considerations

Generally speaking, the income portion of a bond investment is taxed at the ordinary income tax rate, which is typically the same tax rate that an individual would pay on wage or salary income. Tax-exempt securities are the exception to this rule. For example, interest income received by holders of municipal bonds issued in the United States is often exempt from federal income tax and from the income tax of the state in which the bonds are issued. The tax status of bond income may also depend on where the bond is issued and traded. For example, some domestic bonds pay their interest net of income tax. Other bonds, including some Eurobonds, make gross interest payments.

In addition to earnings from interest, a bond investment may also generate a capital gain or loss. If a bond is sold before its maturity date, the price is likely to have changed compared with the purchase price. This change will generate a capital gain if the bond price has increased or a capital loss if the bond price has decreased. From the stand point of taxes, a capital gain or loss is usually treated differently from taxable income. In addition, in some countries, there is a different tax rate for long-term and short-term capital gains. For example, capital gains that are recognized more than 12 months after the original purchase date may be taxed at a long-term capital gains tax rate, whereas capital gains that are recognized within 12 months of purchasing the investment may be taxed as a short-term capital gain. Very often, the tax rate for long-term capital gains is lower than the tax rate for short-term capital gains, and the tax rate for short-term capital gains is equal to the ordinary income tax rate, although there are exceptions. Not all countries, however, implement a capital gains tax. Furthermore, differences in national and local legislation often result in a very diverse set of aggregate country capital gains tax rates.

For bonds issued at a discount, an additional tax consideration is related to the tax status of the original issue discount. The original issue discount is the difference between the par value and the original issue price. In some countries, such as the United States, a prorated portion of the discount must be included in interest income every tax year. This is not the case in other countries, such as Japan. Exhibit 3 illustrates the potential importance of this tax consideration.

Exhibit 3

Original Issue Discount Tax Provision

Assume a hypothetical country, Zinland, where the local currency is the zini (Z). The market interest rate in Zinland is 10%, and both interest income and capital gains are taxed. Companies A and B issue 20-year bonds with a par value of Z1,000. Company A issues a coupon bond with an annual coupon rate of 10%. Investors buy Company A's bonds for Z1,000. Every year, they receive and pay tax on their Z100 annual interest payments. When Company A's bonds mature, bondholders receive the par value of Z1,000. Company B issues a zero-coupon bond at a discount. Investors buy Company B's bonds for Z148.64. They do not receive any cash flows until Company B pays the par value of Z1,000 when the bonds mature.

Company A's bonds and Company B's bonds are economically identical in the sense that they have the same maturity (20 years) and the same yield to maturity (10%). Company A's bonds make periodic payments, however, whereas Company B's bonds defer payment until maturity. Investors in Company A's bonds must include the annual interest payments in taxable income. When they receive their original Z1,000 investment back at maturity, they face no capital gain or loss. Without an original issue discount tax provision, investors in Company B's bonds do not have any taxable income until the bonds mature. When they receive the par value at maturity, they face a capital gain on the original issue discount—that is, on Z851.36 (Z1,000 − Z148.64). The purpose of an original issue discount tax provision is to tax investors in Company B's bonds the same way as investors in Company A's bonds. Thus, a prorated portion of the Z851.36 original issue discount is included in taxable income every tax year until maturity. This allows investors in Company B's bonds to increase their cost basis in the bonds so that at maturity, they face no capital gain or loss.

Some jurisdictions also have tax provisions for bonds bought at a premium. They may allow investors to deduct a prorated portion of the amount paid in excess of the bond's par value from their taxable income every tax year until maturity. For example, if an investor pays $1,005 for a bond that has a par value of $1,000 and matures five years later, she can deduct $1 from her taxable income every tax year for five years. But the deduction may not be required; the investor may have the choice either to deduct a prorated portion of the premium each year or to deduct nothing and declare a capital loss when the bond is redeemed at maturity.

EXAMPLE 4

1   The coupon payment is *most likely* to be taxed as:

   A   ordinary income.

   B   short-term capital gain.

C   long-term capital gain.

2   Assume that a company issues bonds in the hypothetical country of Zinland, where the local currency is the zini (Z). There is an original issue discount tax provision in Zinland's tax code. The company issues a 10-year zero-coupon bond with a par value of Z1,000 and sells it for Z800. An investor who buys the zero-coupon bond at issuance and holds it until maturity *most likely*:

A   has to include Z20 in his taxable income every tax year for 10 years and has to declare a capital gain of Z200 at maturity.

B   has to include Z20 in his taxable income every tax year for 10 years and does not have to declare a capital gain at maturity.

C   does not have to include anything in his taxable income every tax year for 10 years but has to declare a capital gain of Z200 at maturity.

Solution to 1:

A is correct. Interest income is typically taxed at the ordinary income tax rate, which may be the same tax rate that individuals pay on wage and salary income.

Solution to 2:

B is correct. The original issue discount tax provision requires the investor to include a prorated portion of the original issue discount in his taxable income every tax year until maturity. The original issue discount is the difference between the par value and the original issue price—that is, Z1,000 − Z800 = Z200. The bond's maturity is 10 years. Thus, the prorated portion that must be included each year is Z200 ÷ 10 = Z20. The original issue discount tax provision allows the investor to increase his cost basis in the bond so that when the bond matures, the investor faces no capital gain or loss.

STRUCTURE OF A BOND'S CASH FLOWS

4

The most common payment structure by far is that of a plain vanilla bond, as depicted in Exhibit 1. These bonds make periodic, fixed coupon payments and a lump-sum payment of principal at maturity. But there are other structures regarding both the principal repayment and the interest payments. This section discusses the major schedules observed in the global fixed-income markets. Schedules for principal repayments and interest payments are typically similar for a particular type of bond, such as 10-year US Treasury bonds. However, payment schedules vary considerably between types of bonds, such as government bonds versus corporate bonds.

4.1 Principal Repayment Structures

How the amount borrowed is repaid is an important consideration for investors because it affects the level of credit risk they face from holding the bonds. Any provision that periodically retires some of the principal amount outstanding is a way to reduce credit risk.

4.1.1 *Bullet, Fully Amortized, and Partially Amortized Bonds*

The payment structure of a plain vanilla bond has been used for nearly every government bond ever issued as well as for the majority of corporate bonds. Such a bond is also known as a bullet bond because the entire payment of principal occurs at maturity.

In contrast, an **amortizing bond** has a payment schedule that calls for periodic payments of interest and repayments of principal. A bond that is fully amortized is characterized by a fixed periodic payment schedule that reduces the bond's outstanding principal amount to zero by the maturity date. A partially amortized bond also makes fixed periodic payments until maturity, but only a portion of the principal is repaid by the maturity date. Thus, a **balloon payment** is required at maturity to retire the bond's outstanding principal amount.

Exhibit 4 illustrates the differences in the payment schedules for a bullet bond, a fully amortized bond, and a partially amortized bond. For the three bonds, the principal amount is $1,000, the maturity is five years, the coupon rate is 6%, and interest payments are made annually. The market interest rate used to discount the bonds' expected cash flows until maturity is assumed to be constant at 6%. The bonds are issued and redeemed at par. For the partially amortized bond, the balloon payment is $200 at maturity.[5]

Exhibit 4 Example of Payment Schedules for Bullet, Fully Amortized, and Partially Amortized Bonds

Bullet Bond

Year	Investor Cash Flows	Interest Payment	Principal Repayment	Outstanding Principal at the End of the Year
0	−$1,000.00			$1,000.00
1	60.00	$60.00	$0.00	1,000.00
2	60.00	60.00	0.00	1,000.00
3	60.00	60.00	0.00	1,000.00
4	60.00	60.00	0.00	1,000.00
5	1,060.00	60.00	1,000.00	0.00

Fully Amortized Bond

Year	Investor Cash Flows	Interest Payment	Principal Repayment	Outstanding Principal at the End of the Year
0	−$1,000.00			
1	237.40	$60.00	$177.40	$822.60
2	237.40	49.36	188.04	634.56
3	237.40	38.07	199.32	435.24
4	237.40	26.11	211.28	223.96
5	237.40	13.44	223.96	0.00

Partially Amortized Bond

Year	Investor Cash Flows	Interest Payment	Principal Repayment	Outstanding Principal at the End of the Year
0	−$1,000.00			
1	201.92	$60.00	$141.92	$858.08
2	201.92	51.48	150.43	707.65
3	201.92	42.46	159.46	548.19

---

5 The examples in this reading were created in Microsoft Excel. Numbers may differ from the results obtained using a calculator because of rounding.

| Exhibit 4 | (Continued) | | | |

Partially Amortized Bond

Year	Investor Cash Flows	Interest Payment	Principal Repayment	Outstanding Principal at the End of the Year
4	201.92	32.89	169.03	379.17
5	401.92	22.75	379.17	0.00

Investors pay $1,000 now to purchase any of the three bonds. For the bullet bond, they receive the coupon payment of $60 (6% × $1,000) every year for five years. The last payment is $1,060 because it includes both the last coupon payment and the principal amount.

For the fully amortized bond, the annual payment, which includes both the coupon payment and the principal repayment, is constant. Thus, this annual payment can be viewed as an annuity. This annuity lasts for five years; its present value, discounted at the market interest rate of 6%, is equal to the bond price of $1,000. Therefore, the annual payment is $237.40. The first year, the interest part of the payment is $60 (6% × $1,000), which implies that the principal repayment part is $177.40 ($237.40 − $60). This repayment leaves an outstanding principal amount, which becomes the basis for the calculation of the interest the following year, of $822.60 ($1,000 − $177.40). The second year, the interest part of the payment is $49.36 (6% × $822.60), the principal repayment part is $188.04 ($237.40 − $49.36), and the outstanding principal amount is $634.56 ($822.60 − $188.04). The fifth year, the outstanding principal amount is fully repaid. Note that the annual payment is constant but, over time, the interest payment decreases and the principal repayment increases.

The partially amortized bond can be viewed as the combination of two elements: a five-year annuity plus the balloon payment at maturity. The sum of the present values of these two elements is equal to the bond price of $1,000. As for the fully amortized bond, the discount rate is the market interest rate of 6%, making the constant amount for the annuity $201.92. This amount represents the annual payment for the first four years. For Years 1 through 4, the split between interest and principal is done the same way as for the fully amortized bond. The interest part of the payment is equal to 6% multiplied by the outstanding principal at the end of the previous year; the principal repayment part is equal to $201.92 minus the interest part of the payment for the year; and the outstanding principal amount at the end of the year is equal to the outstanding principal amount at the end of the previous year minus the principal repayment for the year. In Year 5, investors receive $401.92; this amount is calculated either as the sum of the interest payment ($22.75) and the outstanding principal amount ($379.17) or as the constant amount of the annuity ($201.92) plus the balloon payment ($200). As for the fully amortized bond, the interest payment decreases and the principal repayment increases over time. Because the principal amount is not fully amortized, interest payments are higher for the partially amortized bond than for the fully amortized bond, except the first year when they are equal.

Exhibit 4 does not address the complexity of the repayment structure for some bonds, such as many securitized bonds. For example, mortgage-backed securities face prepayment risk, which is the possible early repayment of mortgage principal. Borrowers usually have the right to prepay mortgages, which typically occurs when a current homeowner purchases a new home or when homeowners refinance their mortgages because market interest rates have fallen.

EXAMPLE 5

1 The structure that requires the largest repayment of principal at maturity is that of a:

   A bullet bond.

   B fully amortized bond.

   C partially amortized bond.

2 A plain vanilla bond has a maturity of 10 years, a par value of £100, and a coupon rate of 9%. Interest payments are made annually. The market interest rate is assumed to be constant at 9%. The bond is issued and redeemed at par. The principal repayment the first year is *closest* to:

   A £0.00.

   B £6.58.

   C £10.00.

3 Relative to a fully amortized bond, the coupon payments of an otherwise similar partially amortized bond are:

   A lower or equal.

   B equal.

   C higher or equal.

Solution to 1:

A is correct. The entire repayment of principal occurs at maturity for a bullet (or plain vanilla) bond, whereas it occurs over time for fully and partially amortized bonds. Thus, the largest repayment of principal at maturity is that of a bullet bond.

Solution to 2:

A is correct. A plain vanilla (or bullet) bond does not make any principal repayment until the maturity date. B is incorrect because £6.58 would be the principal repayment for a fully amortized bond.

Solution to 3:

C is correct. Except at maturity, the principal repayments are lower for a partially amortized bond than for an otherwise similar fully amortized bond. Consequently, the principal amounts outstanding and, therefore, the amounts of interest payments are higher for a partially amortized bond than for a fully amortized bond, all else equal. The only exception is the first interest payment, which is the same for both repayment structures. This is because no principal repayment has been made by the time the first coupon is paid.

4.1.2 Sinking Fund Arrangements

A **sinking fund arrangement** is another approach that can be used to achieve the same goal of periodically retiring the bond's principal outstanding. The term sinking fund refers to an issuer's plans to set aside funds over time to retire the bond. Originally, a sinking fund was a specified cash reserve that was segregated from the rest of the issuer's business for the purpose of repaying the principal. More generally today, a sinking fund arrangement specifies the portion of the bond's principal outstanding, perhaps 5%, that must be repaid each year throughout the bond's life or after a specified date. This repayment occurs whether or not an actual segregated cash reserve has been created.

Typically, the issuer will forward repayment proceeds to the bond's trustee. The trustee will then either redeem bonds to this value or select by lottery the serial numbers of bonds to be paid off. The bonds for repayment may be listed in business newspapers, such as the *Wall Street Journal* or the *Financial Times*.

As well as the standard version described above, another type of sinking fund arrangement operates by redeeming a steadily increasing amount of the bond's notional principal (total amount) each year. Any remaining principal is then redeemed at maturity. It is common to find utility and energy companies in the United States, the United Kingdom, and the Commonwealth countries that issue bonds with sinking fund arrangements that incorporate such a provision.

Another common variation is for the bond issue to include a call provision, which gives the issuer the option to repurchase the bonds before maturity—callable bonds are discussed in Section 5.1. The issuer can usually repurchase the bonds at the market price, at par, or at a specified sinking fund price, whichever is the lowest. To allocate the burden of the call provision fairly among bondholders, the bonds to be retired are selected at random based on serial number. Usually, the issuer can repurchase only a small portion of the bond issue. Some indentures, however, allow issuers to use a doubling option to repurchase double the required number of bonds.

The benefit of a sinking fund arrangement is that it ensures that a formal plan is in place for retiring the debt. For an investor, a sinking fund arrangement reduces the risk the issuer will default when the principal is due, thereby reducing the credit risk of the bond issue. But investors experience potential disadvantages with sinking fund arrangements. First, investors face reinvestment risk, the risk associated with having to reinvest cash flows at an interest rate that may be lower than the current yield to maturity. If the serial number of an investor's bonds is selected, the bonds will be repaid and the investor will have to reinvest the proceeds. If market interest rates have fallen since the investor purchased the bonds, he or she probably will not be able to purchase a bond offering the same return. Another potential disadvantage for investors occurs if the issuer has the option to repurchase bonds at below market prices. For example, an issuer could exercise a call option to buy back bonds at par on bonds priced above par. In this case, investors would suffer a loss.

Exhibit 5 illustrates an example of a sinking fund arrangement.

Exhibit 5

Example of a Sinking Fund Arrangement

The notional principal of the bond issue is £200 million. The sinking fund arrangement calls for 5% of the outstanding principal amount to be retired in Years 10 through 19, with the outstanding balance paid off at maturity in 20 years.

Year	Outstanding Principal at the Beginning of the Year (£ millions)	Sinking Fund Payment (£ millions)	Outstanding Principal at the End of the Year (£ millions)	Final Principal Repayment (£ millions)
0			200.00	
1 to 9	200.00	0.00	200.00	
10	200.00	10.00	190.00	
11	190.00	9.50	180.50	
12	180.50	9.03	171.48	
13	171.48	8.57	162.90	

(continued)

	Exhibit 5 **(Continued)**			
Year	**Outstanding Principal at the Beginning of the Year (£ millions)**	**Sinking Fund Payment (£ millions)**	**Outstanding Principal at the End of the Year (£ millions)**	**Final Principal Repayment (£ millions)**
14	162.90	8.15	154.76	
15	154.76	7.74	147.02	
16	147.02	7.35	139.67	
17	139.67	6.98	132.68	
18	132.68	6.63	126.05	
19	126.05	6.30	119.75	
20	119.75			119.75

There is no repayment of the principal during the first nine years. Starting the 10th year, the sinking fund arrangement calls for 5% of the outstanding principal amount to be retired each year. In Year 10, £10 million (5% × £200 million) are paid off, which leaves an outstanding principal balance of £190 million. In Year 11, the principal amount repaid is £9.50 million (5% × £190 million). The final repayment of the remaining balance (£119.75 million) is a balloon payment at maturity.

4.2 Coupon Payment Structures

A coupon is the interest payment that the bond issuer makes to the bondholder. A conventional bond pays a fixed periodic coupon over a specified time to maturity. Most frequently, the coupon is paid semi-annually for sovereign and corporate bonds; this is the case in the United States, the United Kingdom, and Commonwealth countries such as Bangladesh, India, and New Zealand. Eurobonds usually pay an annual coupon, although some Eurobonds make quarterly coupon payments. The norm for bonds issued in the eurozone is for an annual coupon, although there are exceptions.

Fixed-rate coupons are not the only coupon payment structure, however. A wide range of coupon types is offered in the global fixed-income markets. This variety exists to meet the differing needs of both issuers and investors.

4.2.1 *Floating-Rate Notes*

Floating-rate notes do not have a fixed coupon; instead, their coupon rate is linked to an external reference rate, such as Libor. Thus, a FRN's interest rate will fluctuate periodically during the bond's life, following the changes in the reference rate. As a consequence, the FRN's cash flows are not known with certainty. Large issuers of FRNs include government-sponsored enterprises (GSEs), such as the Federal Home Loan Banks (FHLB), the Federal National Mortgage Association ("Fannie Mae"), and the Federal Home Loan Mortgage Corporation ("Freddie Mac") in the United States, as well as banks and financial institutions in Europe and Asia Pacific. It is rare for national governments to issue FRNs because investors in sovereign bonds generally prefer fixed-coupon bonds.

Almost all FRNs have quarterly coupons, although counter examples do exist. FRNs usually pay a fixed spread over the specified reference rate. A typical coupon rate may be the three-month US dollar Libor + 20 bps (i.e., Libor + 0.20%) for a US dollar-denominated bond or the three-month Euribor + 20 bps for a euro-denominated FRN. Occasionally the spread is not fixed; in this case, the bond is known as a **variable-rate note**.

Contrary to plain vanilla, fixed-rate securities that decline in value in a rising interest rate environment, FRNs are less affected when interest rates increase because their coupon rates vary with market interest rates and are reset at regular, short-term intervals. Thus, FRNs have little interest rate risk—that is, the risk that a change in market interest rate affects a bond's value. FRNs are frequently favored by investors who expect that interest rates will rise. That said, investors still face credit risk when investing in FRNs. If an issuer's credit risk does not change from one coupon reset date to the next, the FRN's price generally will stay close to the par value. However, if there is a change in the issuer's credit quality that affects the perceived credit risk associated with the bond, the price of the FRN will deviate from its par value. A higher level of credit risk will lead to a lower price and a higher yield.

Additional features observed in FRNs may include a floor or a cap. A floor (floored FRN) prevents the coupon from falling below a specified minimum rate. This feature benefits the bondholders, who are guaranteed that the interest rate will not fall below the specified rate during a time of falling interest rates. In contrast, a cap (capped FRN) prevents the coupon from rising above a specified maximum rate. This feature benefits the issuer, because it sets a limit to the interest rate paid on the debt during a time of rising interest rates. It is also possible to have a collared FRN, which includes both a cap and a floor.

An inverse or reverse FRN, or simply an inverse floater, is a bond whose coupon rate has an inverse relationship to the reference rate. The basic structure is the same as an ordinary FRN except for the direction in which the coupon rate is adjusted. When interest rates fall, the coupon rate on an ordinary FRN decreases; in contrast, the coupon rate on a reverse FRN increases. Thus, inverse FRNs are typically favored by investors who expect interest rates to decline.

4.2.2 *Step-Up Coupon Bonds*

The coupon of a **step-up coupon bond**, which may be fixed or floating, increases by specified margins at specified dates. An example of a bond with a step-up coupon is the FRN that was issued by the British bank Holding Bank of Scotland (HBOS) in 2005. This FRN had a 20-year maturity, and the coupon was linked to the three-month Libor plus an initial spread of 50 bps. The spread was scheduled to increase to 250 bps over Libor in 2015 for the bond's tenor.

Bonds with step-up coupons offer bondholders some protection against rising interest rates, and they may be an important feature for callable bonds. When interest rates increase, there is a higher likelihood that the issuer will not call the bonds, particularly if the bonds have a fixed rate of interest. The step-up coupon allows bondholders to receive a higher coupon, in line with the higher market interest rates. Alternatively, when interest rates decrease or remain stable, the step-up feature acts as an incentive for the issuer to call the bond before the spread increases and the interest expense rises. Thus, at issuance, most investors viewed the bond issued by HBOS as a 10-year investment, given that they expected the issuer to redeem it after 10 years to avoid paying the higher coupon.

Redeeming the bond when the spread increases is not automatic, however; the issuer may choose to keep the bond despite its increasing cost. This may happen if refinancing the bond is necessary and alternatives are less advantageous for this issuer. For example, a financial crisis may make it difficult for the issuer to refinance. Alternatively, the issuer's credit quality may have deteriorated, which would lead to a higher spread, potentially making the coupon rate on the new bond more expensive than that on the existing bond despite the stepped-up coupon. Although the issuer does not have to call the bond before the spread increases, there is an implicit expectation from investors that it will. Failure to do so may be viewed negatively by market participants and reduce investors' appetite for that particular issuer's bonds in the future.

4.2.3 Credit-Linked Coupon Bonds

A **credit-linked coupon bond** has a coupon that changes when the bond's credit rating changes. An example of a bond with a credit-linked coupon is one of British Telecom's bonds maturing in 2020. It has a coupon rate of 9%, but the coupon will increase by 50 bps for every credit rating downgrade below the bond's credit rating at the time of issuance and will decrease by 50 bps for every credit rating upgrade above the bond's credit rating at the time of issuance.

Bonds with credit-linked coupons are attractive to investors who are concerned about the future creditworthiness of the issuer. They may also provide some general protection against a poor economy because credit ratings tend to decline the most during recessions. A potential problem associated with these bonds is that increases in the coupon payments resulting from a downgrade may ultimately result in further deteriorations of the credit rating or even contribute to the issuer's default.

4.2.4 Payment-in-Kind Coupon Bonds

A payment-in-kind (PIK) coupon bond typically allows the issuer to pay interest in the form of additional amounts of the bond issue rather than as a cash payment. Such bonds are favored by issuers who are concerned that the issuer may face potential cash flow problems in the future. They are used, for example, in financing companies that have a high debt burden, such as companies going through a leveraged buyout (a form of acquisition in which the financing consists primarily of debt). Because investors are aware of the additional credit risk associated with these bonds, they usually demand a higher yield for holding bonds with PIK coupons.

Other forms of PIK arrangements can also be found, such as paying the bondholders with common shares worth the amount of coupon due. With a PIK toggle note, the borrower has the option, for each interest period, to pay interest in cash, to make the interest payment in kind, or some mix of the two. Cash payments or payments in kind are frequently at the discretion of the borrower, but whether the payment is made in cash or in kind can be determined by an earnings or cash flow trigger identified in the indenture.

4.2.5 Deferred Coupon Bonds

A **deferred coupon bond**, sometimes called a **split coupon bond**, pays no coupons for its first few years but then pays a higher coupon than it otherwise normally would for the remainder of its life. Issuers of deferred coupon bonds are usually seeking ways to conserve cash in the years immediately following the bond issue, which may indicate poorer credit quality. Deferred coupon bonds are also common in project financing when the assets being developed do not generate any income during the development phase. A deferred coupon bond allows the issuer to delay interest payments until the project is completed and the cash flows generated by the assets being financed can be used to service the debt.

One of the main advantages of investing in a deferred coupon bond is that these bonds are typically priced at significant discounts to par. Investors may also find the deferred coupon structure to be very helpful in managing taxes. If taxes due on the interest income can be delayed, investors may be able to minimize taxes. This tax advantage, however, depends on the jurisdiction concerned and how its tax rules apply to deferred coupon payments.

A zero-coupon bond can be thought of as an extreme form of deferred coupon bond. These securities pay no interest to the investor and thus are issued at a deep discount to par value. At maturity, the bondholder receives the par value of the bond as payment. Effectively, a zero-coupon bond defers all interest payments until maturity.

4.2.6 *Index-Linked Bonds*

An **index-linked bond** has its coupon payments and/or principal repayment linked to a specified index. In theory, a bond can be indexed to any published variable, including an index reflecting prices, earnings, economic output, commodities, or foreign currencies. **Inflation-linked bonds** are an example of index-linked bonds. They offer investors protection against inflation by linking a bond's coupon payments and/or the principal repayment to an index of consumer prices such as the U.K Retail Price Index (RPI) or the US Consumer Price Index (CPI). The advantage of using the RPI or CPI is that these indices are well-known, transparent, and published regularly.

Governments are large issuers of inflation-linked bonds, also called **linkers**. The United Kingdom was one of the first developed countries to issue inflation-linked bonds in 1981, offering gilts linked to the UK RPI, its main measure of the rate of inflation. In 1997, the US Treasury began introducing Treasury inflation-indexed securities (TIIS) or Treasury inflation-protected securities (TIPS) linked to the US CPI. Inflation-linked bonds are now more frequently being offered by corporate issuers, including both financial and non-financial companies.

A bond's stated coupon rate represents the nominal interest rate received by the bondholders. But inflation reduces the actual value of the interest received. The interest rate that bondholders actually receive, net of inflation, is the real interest rate; it is approximately equal to the nominal interest rate minus the rate of inflation. By increasing the coupon payments and/or the principal repayment in line with increases in the price index, inflation-linked bonds reduce inflation risk. An example of an inflation-linked bond is the 1.25% UK Treasury index-linked gilt maturing in 2017: Bondholders receive a real interest rate of 1.25%, and the actual interest payments are adjusted in line with changes in the UK RPI.

Exhibit 6 shows the national governments that issue the largest amounts of inflation-linked bonds. These sovereign issuers can be grouped into three categories. Countries such as Brazil, Chile, and Colombia have issued inflation-linked bonds because they were experiencing extremely high rates of inflation when borrowing, and offering inflation-linked bonds was their only available alternative to raise funds. The second category includes the United Kingdom, Australia, and Sweden. These countries have issued inflation-linked bonds in an effort to add credibility to the government's commitment to disinflationary policies and also to capitalize on the demand from investors still concerned about inflation risk. The third category, which includes the United States, Canada, Germany, and France, consists of national governments that are most concerned about the social welfare benefits associated with inflation-linked securities. Theoretically, inflation-linked bonds provide investors the benefit of a long-term asset with a fixed real return that is free from inflation risk.

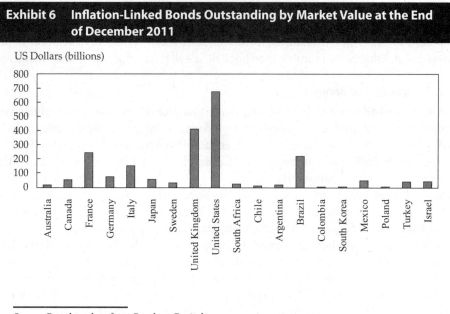

Exhibit 6   Inflation-Linked Bonds Outstanding by Market Value at the End of December 2011

Source: Based on data from Barclays Capital.

Different methods have been used for linking the cash flows of an index-linked bond to a specified index; the link can be made via the interest payments, the principal repayment, or both. The following examples describe how the link between the cash flows and the index is established, using inflation-linked bonds as an illustration.

- Zero-coupon-indexed bonds pay no coupon, so the inflation adjustment is made via the principal repayment only: The principal amount to be repaid at maturity increases in line with increases in the price index during the bond's life. This type of bond has been issued in Sweden.

- Interest-indexed bonds pay a fixed nominal principal amount at maturity but an index-linked coupon during the bond's life. Thus, the inflation adjustment applies to the interest payments only. This type of bond was briefly issued by the Australian government in the late 1980s, but it never became a significant part of the inflation-linked bond market.

- **Capital-indexed bonds** pay a fixed coupon rate but it is applied to a principal amount that increases in line with increases in the index during the bond's life. Thus, both the interest payments and the principal repayment are adjusted for inflation. Such bonds have been issued by governments in Australia, Canada, New Zealand, the United Kingdom, and the United States.

- Indexed-annuity bonds are fully amortized bonds, in contrast to interest-indexed and capital-indexed bonds that are non-amortizing coupon bonds. The annuity payment, which includes both payment of interest and repayment of the principal, increases in line with inflation during the bond's life. Indexed-annuity bonds linked to a price index have been issued by local governments in Australia, but not by the national government.

Exhibit 7 illustrates the different methods used for inflation-linked bonds.

Exhibit 7

Examples of Inflation-Linked Bonds

Assume a hypothetical country, Lemuria, where the currency is the lemming (L). The country issued 20-year bonds linked to the domestic Consumer Price Index (CPI). The bonds have a par value of L1,000. Lemuria's economy has been free of inflation until the most recent six months, when the CPI increased by 5%.

Suppose that the bonds are zero-coupon-indexed bonds. There will never be any coupon payments. Following the 5% increase in the CPI, the principal amount to be repaid increases to L1,050 [L1,000 × (1 + 0.05)] and will continue increasing in line with inflation until maturity.

Now, suppose that the bonds are coupon bonds that make semi-annual interest payments based on an annual coupon rate of 4%. If the bonds are interest-indexed bonds, the principal amount at maturity will remain L1,000 regardless of the CPI level during the bond's life and at maturity. The coupon payments, however, will be adjusted for inflation. Prior to the increase in inflation, the semi-annual coupon payment was L20 [(0.04 × L1,000) ÷ 2]. Following the 5% increase in the CPI, the semi-annual coupon payment increases to L21 [L20 × (1 + 0.05)]. Future coupon payments will also be adjusted for inflation.

If the bonds are capital-indexed bonds, the annual coupon rate remains 4%, but the principal amount is adjusted for inflation and the coupon payment is based on the inflation-adjusted principal amount. Following the 5% increase in the CPI, the inflation-adjusted principal amount increases to L1,050 [L1,000 × (1 + 0.05)], and the new semi-annual coupon payment is L21 [(0.04 × L1,050) ÷ 2]. The principal amount will continue increasing in line with increases in the CPI until maturity, and so will the coupon payments.

If the bonds are indexed-annuity bonds, they are fully amortized. Prior to the increase in inflation, the semi-annual payment was L36.56—the annuity payment based on a principal amount of L1,000 paid back in 40 semi-annual payments with an annual discount rate of 4%. Following the 5% increase in the CPI, the annuity payment increases to L38.38 [L36.56 × (1 + 0.05)]. Future annuity payments will also be adjusted for inflation in a similar manner.

Financial institutions also issue index-linked bonds that are connected to a stock market index. An **equity-linked note** (ELN) is a fixed-income security that differs from a conventional bond in that the final payment is based on the return of an equity index. A typical ELN is principal protected, which means that the investor is guaranteed to receive at maturity a percentage of the original amount invested in the ELN, usually 100%. The guarantee, however, is only as good as the financial institution from which the investor purchased the ELN. If the issuer defaults, ELNs may end up worthless even if the return of the equity index to which the bond was linked was positive. ELNs can be thought of as a zero-coupon bond with a return profile linked to the value of the equity index. If the equity index increases in value from its level when the ELN was issued, the investor receives a positive return.

EXAMPLE 6

1 Floating-rate notes *most likely* pay:

A annual coupons.

B quarterly coupons.

C semi-annual coupons.

2 A zero-coupon bond can *best* be considered a:

   A step-up bond.

   B credit-linked bond.

   C deferred coupon bond.

3 The bonds that do **not** offer protection to the investor against increases in market interest rates are:

   A step-up bonds.

   B floating rate notes.

   C inverse floating rate notes.

4 The US Treasury offers Treasury Inflation-Protected Securities (TIPS). The principal of TIPS increases with inflation and decreases with deflation based on changes in the US Consumer Price Index. When TIPS mature, an investor is paid the original principal or inflation-adjusted principal, whichever is greater. TIPS pay interest twice a year based on a fixed real coupon rate that is applied to the inflation-adjusted principal. TIPS are *most likely*:

   A capital-indexed bonds.

   B interest-indexed bonds.

   C indexed-annuity bonds.

5 Assume a hypothetical country, Lemuria, where the national government has issued 20-year capital-indexed bonds linked to the domestic Consumer Price Index (CPI). Lemuria's economy has been free of inflation until the most recent six months, when the CPI increased. Following the increase in inflation:

   A the principal amount remains unchanged but the coupon rate increases.

   B the coupon rate remains unchanged but the principal amount increases.

   C the coupon payment remains unchanged but the principal amount increases.

Solution to 1:

B is correct. Most FRNs pay interest quarterly and are tied to a three-month reference rate such as Libor.

Solution to 2:

C is correct. Because interest is effectively deferred until maturity, a zero-coupon bond can be thought of as a deferred coupon bond. A and B are incorrect because both step-up bonds and credit-linked bonds pay regular coupons. For a step-up bond, the coupon increases by specified margins at specified dates. For a credit-linked bond, the coupon changes when the bond's credit rating changes.

Solution to 3:

C is correct. The coupon rate on an inverse FRN has an inverse relationship to the reference rate. Thus, an inverse FRN does not offer protection to the investor when market interest rates increase but when they decrease. A and B are incorrect because step-up bonds and FRNs both offer protection against increases in market interest rates.

Solution to 4:

A is correct. TIPS have a fixed coupon rate, and the principal is adjusted based on changes in the CPI. Thus, TIPS are an example of capital-indexed bonds. B is incorrect because with an interest-index bond, it is the principal repayment at maturity that is fixed and the coupon that is linked to an index. C is incorrect because indexed-annuity bonds are fully amortized bonds, not bullet bonds. The annuity payment (interest payment and principal repayment) is adjusted based on changes in an index.

Solution to 5:

B is correct. Following an increase in inflation, the coupon rate of a capital-indexed bond remains unchanged, but the principal amount is adjusted upward for inflation. Thus, the coupon payment, which is equal to the fixed coupon rate multiplied by the inflation-adjusted principal amount, increases.

BONDS WITH CONTINGENCY PROVISIONS

5

A contingency refers to some future event or circumstance that is possible but not certain. A **contingency provision** is a clause in a legal document that allows for some action if the event or circumstance does occur. For bonds, the term **embedded option** refers to various contingency provisions found in the indenture. These contingency provisions provide the issuer or the bondholders the right, but not the obligation, to take some action. These rights are called "options." These options are not independent of the bond and cannot be traded separately—hence the term "embedded." Some common types of bonds with embedded options include callable bonds, putable bonds, and convertible bonds. The options embedded in these bonds grant either the issuer or the bondholders certain rights affecting the disposal or redemption of the bond.

5.1 Callable Bonds

The most widely used embedded option is the call provision. A **callable bond** gives the issuer the right to redeem all or part of the bond before the specified maturity date. The primary reason why issuers choose to issue callable bonds rather than non-callable bonds is to protect themselves against a decline in interest rates. This decline can come either from market interest rates falling or from the issuer's credit quality improving. If market interest rates fall or credit quality improves, the issuer of a callable bond has the right to replace an old, expensive bond issue with a new, cheaper bond issue. In other words, the issuer can benefit from a decline in interest rates by being able to refinance its debt at a lower interest rate. For example, assume that the market interest rate was 6% at the time of issuance and that a company issued a bond with a coupon rate of 7%—the market interest rate plus a spread of 100 bps. Now assume that the market interest rate has fallen to 4% and that the company's creditworthiness has not changed; it can still issue at the market interest rate plus 100 bps. If the original bond is callable, the company can redeem it and replace it with a new bond paying 5% annually. If the original bond is non-callable, the company must carry on paying 7% annually and cannot benefit from the decline in market interest rates.

As illustrated in this example, callable bonds are advantageous to the issuer of the security. Put another way, the call option has value to the *issuer*. Callable bonds present investors with a higher level of reinvestment risk than non-callable bonds; that is, if the bonds are called, bondholders have to reinvest funds in a lower interest rate environment. For this reason, callable bonds have to offer a higher yield and sell at a lower price than otherwise similar non-callable bonds. The higher yield and lower price compensate the bondholders for the value of the call option to the issuer.

Callable bonds have a long tradition and are commonly issued by corporate issuers. Although first issued in the US market, they are now frequently issued in every major bond market and in a variety of forms.

The details about the call provision are specified in the indenture. These details include the call price, which represents the price paid to bondholders when the bond is called. The call premium is the amount over par paid by the issuer if the bond is called. There may be restrictions on when the bond can be called, or the bond may have different call prices depending on when it is called. The call schedule specifies the dates and prices at which a bond may be called. Some callable bonds are issued with a call protection period, also called lockout period, cushion, or deferment period. The call protection period prohibits the issuer from calling a bond early in its life and is often added as an incentive for investors to buy the bond. The earliest time that a bond might be called is known as the call date.

Make-whole calls first appeared in the US corporate bond market in the mid-1990s and have become more commonplace ever since. A typical make-whole call requires the issuer to make a lump-sum payment to the bondholders based on the present value of the future coupon payments and principal repayment not paid because of the bond being redeemed early. The discount rate used is usually some pre-determined spread over the yield to maturity of an appropriate sovereign bond. The typical result is a redemption value that is significantly greater than the bond's current market price. A make-up call provision is less detrimental to bondholders than a regular call provision because it allows them to be compensated if the issuer calls the bond. Issuers, however, rarely invoke this provision because redeeming a bond that includes a make-whole provision before the maturity date is costly. Issuers tend to include a make-whole provision as a "sweetener" to make the bond issue more attractive to potential buyers and allow them to pay a lower coupon rate.

Available exercise styles on callable bonds include the following:

- American call, sometimes referred to as continuously callable, for which the issuer has the right to call a bond at any time starting on the first call date.

- European call, for which the issuer has the right to call a bond only once on the call date.

- **Bermuda-style** call, for which the issuer has the right to call bonds on specified dates following the call protection period. These dates frequently correspond to coupon payment dates.

EXAMPLE 7

Assume a hypothetical 30-year bond is issued on 15 August 2012 at a price of 98.195 (as a percentage of par). Each bond has a par value of $1,000. The bond is callable in whole or in part every 15 August from 2022 at the option of the issuer. The call prices are shown below.

Year	Call Price	Year	Call Price
2022	103.870	2028	101.548
2023	103.485	2029	101.161
2024	103.000	2030	100.774
2025	102.709	2031	100.387

Year	Call Price	Year	Call Price
2026	102.322	2032 and thereafter	100.000
2027	101.955		

1 The call protection period is:

   A 10 years.

   B 11 years.

   C 20 years.

2 The call premium (per bond) in 2026 is *closest* to:

   A $2.32.

   B $23.22.

   C $45.14.

3 The call provision is *most likely*:

   A a Bermuda call.

   B a European call.

   C an American call.

Solution to 1:

A is correct. The bonds were issued in 2012 and are first callable in 2022. The call protection period is 2022 − 2012 = 10 years.

Solution to 2:

B is correct. The call prices are stated as a percentage of par. The call price in 2026 is $1,023.22 (102.322% × $1,000). The call premium is the amount paid above par by the issuer. The call premium in 2026 is $23.22 ($1,023.22 − $1,000).

Solution to 3:

A is correct. The bond is callable every 15 August from 2022—that is, on specified dates following the call protection period. Thus, the embedded option is a Bermuda call.

5.2 Putable Bonds

A put provision gives the bondholders the right to sell the bond back to the issuer at a pre-determined price on specified dates. **Putable bonds** are beneficial for the bondholder by guaranteeing a pre-specified selling price at the redemption dates. If interest rates rise after the issue date, thus depressing the bond's price, the bondholders can put the bond back to the issuer and get cash. This cash can be reinvested in bonds that offer higher yields, in line with the higher market interest rates.

Because a put provision has value to the *bondholders*, the price of a putable bond will be higher than the price of an otherwise similar bond issued without the put provision. Similarly, the yield on a bond with a put provision will be lower than the yield on an otherwise similar non-putable bond. The lower yield compensates the issuer for the value of the put option to the investor.

The indenture lists the redemption dates and the prices applicable to the sale of the bond back to the issuer. The selling price is usually the par value of the bond. Depending on the terms set out in the indenture, putable bonds may allow buyers to force a sellback only once or multiple times during the bond's life. Putable bonds that incorporate a single sellback opportunity are referred to as one-time put bonds, whereas those that allow these sellback opportunities more frequently are known as multiple put bonds. Multiple put bonds offer more flexibility for investors, so they are generally more expensive than one-time put bonds. Available exercise styles on putable bonds are similar to those on callable bonds. An American put gives the bondholder the right to sell the bond back to the issuer at any time starting on the first put date. In contrast, the bondholder can put the bond back to the issuer only once on the put date in the case of a European put and only on specified dates in the case of a Bermuda put.

Typically, putable bonds incorporate one- to five-year put provisions. Their increasing popularity has often been motivated by investors wanting to protect themselves against major declines in bond prices. One benefit of this rising popularity has been an improvement in liquidity in some markets, because the put protection attracts more conservative classes of investors. The global financial crisis that started in 2008 showed that these securities can often exacerbate liquidity problems, however, because they provide a first claim on the issuer's assets. The put provision gives bondholders the opportunity to convert their claim into cash before other creditors.

5.3 Convertible Bonds

A **convertible bond** is a hybrid security with both debt and equity features. It gives the bondholder the right to exchange the bond for a specified number of common shares in the issuing company. Thus, a convertible bond can be viewed as the combination of a straight bond (option-free bond) plus an embedded equity call option. Convertible bonds can also include additional provisions, the most common being a call provision.

From the investor's perspective, a convertible bond offers several advantages relative to a non-convertible bond. First, it gives the bondholder the ability to convert into equity in case of share price appreciation, and thus participate in the equity upside. At the same time, the bondholder receives downside protection; if the share price does not appreciate, the convertible bond offers the comfort of regular coupon payments and the promise of principal repayment at maturity. Even if the share price and thus the value of the equity call option decline, the price of a convertible bond cannot fall below the price of the straight bond. Consequently, the value of the straight bond acts as a floor for the price of the convertible bond.

Because the conversion provision is valuable to *bondholders*, the price of a convertible bond is higher than the price of an otherwise similar bond without the conversion provision. Similarly, the yield on a convertible bond is lower than the yield on an otherwise similar non-convertible bond. However, most convertible bonds offer investors a yield advantage; the coupon rate on the convertible bond is typically higher than the dividend yield on the underlying common share.

From the issuer's perspective, convertible bonds offer two main advantages. The first is reduced interest expense. Issuers are usually able to offer below-market coupon rates because of investors' attraction to the conversion feature. The second advantage is the elimination of debt if the conversion option is exercised. But the conversion option is dilutive to existing shareholders.

Key terms regarding the conversion provision include the following:

■ The **conversion price** is the price per share at which the convertible bond can be converted into shares.

■ The **conversion ratio** is the number of common shares that each bond can be converted into. The indenture sometimes does not stipulate the conversion ratio but only mentions the conversion price. The conversion ratio is equal to the par value divided by the conversion price. For example, if the par value is 1,000€ and the conversion price is 20€, the conversion ratio is 1,000€ ÷ 20€ = 50:1, or 50 common shares per bond.

- The **conversion value**, sometimes called the parity value, is the current share price multiplied by the conversion ratio. For example, if the current share price is 33€ and the conversion ratio is 30:1, the conversion value is 33€ × 30 = 990€.

- The conversion premium is the difference between the convertible bond's price and its conversion value. For example, if the convertible bond's price is 1,020€ and the conversion value is 990€, the conversion premium is 1,020€ − 990€ = 30€.

- Conversion parity occurs if the conversion value is equal to the convertible bond's price. Using the previous two examples, if the current share price is 34€ instead of 33€, then both the convertible bond's price and the conversion value are equal to 1,020€ (i.e., a conversion premium equal to 0). This condition is referred to as parity. If the common share is selling for less than 34€, the condition is below parity. In contrast, if the common share is selling for more than 34€, the condition is above parity.

Generally, convertible bonds have maturities of five to 10 years. First-time or younger issuers are usually able to issue convertible bonds of up to three years in maturity only. Although it is common for convertible bonds to reach conversion parity before maturity, bondholders rarely exercise the conversion option before that time. Early conversion would eliminate the yield advantage of continuing to hold the convertible bond; investors would typically receive in dividends less than they would receive in coupon payments. For this reason, it is common to find convertible bonds that are also callable by the issuer on a set of specified dates. If the convertible bond includes a call provision and the conversion value is above the current share price, the issuer may force the bondholders to convert their bonds into common shares before maturity. For this reason, callable convertible bonds have to offer a higher yield and sell at a lower price than otherwise similar non-callable convertible bonds. Some indentures specify that the bonds can be called only if the share price exceeds a specified price, giving investors more predictability about the share price at which the issuer may force conversion.

Although somewhat similar in purpose to a conversion option, a **warrant** is actually not an embedded option but rather an "attached" option. A warrant entitles the holder to buy the underlying stock of the issuing company at a fixed exercise price until the expiration date. Warrants are considered yield enhancements; they are frequently attached to bond issues as a "sweetener." Warrants are actively traded in some financial markets, such as the Deutsche Börse and the Hong Kong Stock Exchange.

Several European banks have been issuing a type of convertible bond called contingent convertible bonds. **Contingent convertible bonds**, nicknamed "CoCos," are bonds with contingent write-down provisions. Two main features distinguish bonds with contingent write-down provisions from the traditional convertible bonds just described. A traditional convertible bond is convertible at the option of the bondholder, and conversion occurs on the upside—that is, if the issuer's share price increases. In contrast, bonds with contingent write-down provisions are convertible on the downside. In the case of CoCos, conversion is automatic if a specified event occurs—for example, if the bank's core Tier 1 capital ratio (a measure of the bank's proportion of core equity capital available to absorb losses) falls below the minimum requirement set by the regulators. Thus, in the event that the bank experiences losses that reduce its equity capital below the minimum requirement, CoCos are a way to reduce the bank's likelihood of default and, therefore, systemic risk—that is, the risk of failure of the financial system. When the bank's core Tier 1 capital falls below the minimum requirement, the CoCos immediately convert into equity, automatically recapitalizing the bank, lightening the debt burden, and reducing the risk of default.

Because the conversion is not at the option of the bondholders but automatic, CoCos force bondholders to take losses. For this reason, CoCos must offer a higher yield than otherwise similar bonds.

Exhibit 8 shows the relative importance of plain vanilla (straight fixed-rate), floating-rate, and equity-related bonds to the total amount of international bonds outstanding. It indicates that the majority of bond issues are plain vanilla bonds.

Exhibit 8	Outstanding Bonds and Notes by Type of Interest Payment and Conversion Features at the End of March 2012	
Type of Bond	**Amount (US$ billions)**	**Weight**
Straight fixed-rate issues	20,369.9	71.2%
Floating-rate issues	7,749.6	27.1%
Equity-related issues		
Convertibles	491.9	1.7%
Warrants	2.3	0.0%
Total	28,613.7	100.0%

Source: Based on data from the Bank of International Settlements, Table 13B, available at www.bis.org/statistics/secstats.htm, (accessed 7 September 2012).

EXAMPLE 8

1 Which of the following is **not** an example of an embedded option?

A Warrant

B Call provision

C Conversion provision

2 The type of bonds with an embedded option that would *most likely* sell at a lower price than an otherwise similar bond without the embedded option is a:

A putable bond.

B callable bond.

C convertible bond.

3 The additional risk inherent to a callable bond is *best* described as:

A credit risk.

B interest rate risk.

C reinvestment risk.

4 The put provision of a putable bond:

A limits the risk to the issuer.

B limits the risk to the bondholder.

C does not materially affect the risk of either the issuer or the bondholder.

5 Assume that a convertible bond issued in South Korea has a par value of ₩1,000,000 and is currently priced at ₩1,100,000. The underlying share price is ₩40,000 and the conversion ratio is 25:1. The conversion condition for this bond is:

A parity.

B above parity.

C below parity.

Solution to 1:

A is correct. A warrant is a separate, tradable security that entitles the holder to buy the underlying common share of the issuing company. B and C are incorrect because the call provision and the conversion provision are embedded options.

Solution to 2:

B is correct. The call provision is an option that benefits the issuer. Because of this, callable bonds sell at lower prices and higher yields relative to otherwise similar non-callable bonds. A and C are incorrect because the put provision and the conversion provision are options that benefit the investor. Thus, putable bonds and convertible bonds sell at higher prices and lower yields relative to otherwise similar bonds that lack those provisions.

Solution to 3:

C is correct. Reinvestment risk refers to the effect that lower interest rates have on available rates of return when reinvesting the cash flows received from an earlier investment. Because bonds are typically called following a decline in market interest rates, reinvestment risk is particularly relevant for the holder of a callable bond. A is incorrect because credit risk refers to the risk of loss resulting from the issuer failing to make full and timely payments of interest and/or repayments of principal. B is incorrect because interest rate risk is the risk that a change in market interest rate affects a bond's value. Credit risk and interest rate risk are not inherent to callable bonds.

Solution to 4:

B is correct. A putable bond limits the risk to the bondholder by guaranteeing a pre-specified selling price at the redemption dates.

Solution to 5:

C is correct. The conversion value of the bond is ₩40,000 × 25 = ₩1,000,000. The price of the convertible bond is ₩1,100,000. Thus, the conversion value of the bond is less than the bond's price, and this condition is referred to as below parity.

CONCLUSION AND SUMMARY

6

This reading provides an introduction to the salient features of fixed-income securities while noting how these features vary among different types of securities. Important points include the following:

■ The three important elements that an investor needs to know when investing in a fixed-income security are (1) the bond's features, which determine its scheduled cash flows and thus the bondholder's expected and actual return; (2) the legal, regulatory, and tax considerations that apply to the contractual agreement between the issuer and the bondholders; and (3) the contingency provisions that may affect the bond's scheduled cash flows.

- The basic features of a bond include the issuer, maturity, par value (or principal), coupon rate and frequency, and currency denomination.

- Issuers of bonds include supranational organizations, sovereign governments, non-sovereign governments, quasi-government entities, and corporate issuers.

- Bondholders are exposed to credit risk and may use bond credit ratings to assess the credit quality of a bond.

- A bond's principal is the amount the issuer agrees to pay the bondholder when the bond matures.

- The coupon rate is the interest rate that the issuer agrees to pay to the bondholder each year. The coupon rate can be a fixed rate or a floating rate. Bonds may offer annual, semi-annual, quarterly, or monthly coupon payments depending on the type of bond and where the bond is issued.

- Bonds can be issued in any currency. Bonds such as dual-currency bonds and currency option bonds are connected to two currencies.

- The yield to maturity is the discount rate that equates the present value of the bond's future cash flows until maturity to its price. Yield to maturity can be considered an estimate of the market's expectation for the bond's return.

- A plain vanilla bond has a known cash flow pattern. It has a fixed maturity date and pays a fixed rate of interest over the bond's life.

- The bond indenture or trust deed is the legal contract that describes the form of the bond, the issuer's obligations, and the investor's rights. The indenture is usually held by a financial institution called a trustee, which performs various duties specified in the indenture.

- The issuer is identified in the indenture by its legal name and is obligated to make timely payments of interest and repayment of principal.

- For securitized bonds, the legal obligation to repay bondholders often lies with a separate legal entity—that is, a bankruptcy-remote vehicle that uses the assets as guarantees to back a bond issue.

- How the issuer intends to service the debt and repay the principal should be described in the indenture. The source of repayment proceeds varies depending on the type of bond.

- Collateral backing is a way to alleviate credit risk. Secured bonds are backed by assets or financial guarantees pledged to ensure debt payment. Examples of collateral-backed bonds include collateral trust bonds, equipment trust certificates, mortgage-backed securities, and covered bonds.

- Credit enhancement can be internal or external. Examples of internal credit enhancement include subordination, overcollateralization, and excess spread. A surety bond, a bank guarantee, a letter of credit, and a cash collateral account are examples of external credit enhancement.

- Bond covenants are legally enforceable rules that borrowers and lenders agree on at the time of a new bond issue. Affirmative covenants enumerate what issuers are required to do, whereas negative covenants enumerate what issuers are prohibited from doing.

- An important consideration for investors is where the bonds are issued and traded, because it affects the laws, regulation, and tax status that apply. Bonds issued in a particular country in local currency are domestic bonds if they are issued by entities incorporated in the country and foreign bonds if they are issued by entities incorporated in another country. Eurobonds are issued internationally, outside the jurisdiction of any single country and are subject to a lower level of listing, disclosure, and regulatory requirements than domestic or foreign bonds. Global bonds are issued in the Eurobond market and at least one domestic market at the same time.

■ Although some bonds may offer special tax advantages, as a general rule, interest is taxed at the ordinary income tax rate. Some countries also implement a capital gains tax. There may be specific tax provisions for bonds issued at a discount or bought at a premium.

■ An amortizing bond is a bond whose payment schedule requires periodic payment of interest and repayment of principal. This differs from a bullet bond, whose entire payment of principal occurs at maturity. The amortizing bond's outstanding principal amount is reduced to zero by the maturity date for a fully amortized bond, but a balloon payment is required at maturity to retire the bond's outstanding principal amount for a partially amortized bond.

■ Sinking fund agreements provide another approach to the periodic retirement of principal, in which an amount of the bond's principal outstanding amount is usually repaid each year throughout the bond's life or after a specified date.

■ A floating-rate note or floater is a bond whose coupon is set based on some reference rate plus a spread. FRNs can be floored, capped, or collared. An inverse FRN is a bond whose coupon has an inverse relationship to the reference rate.

■ Other coupon payment structures include bonds with step-up coupons, which pay coupons that increase by specified amounts on specified dates; bonds with credit-linked coupons, which change when the issuer's credit rating changes; bonds with payment-in-kind coupons that allow the issuer to pay coupons with additional amounts of the bond issue rather than in cash; and bonds with deferred coupons, which pay no coupons in the early years following the issue but higher coupons thereafter.

■ The payment structures for index-linked bonds vary considerably among countries. A common index-linked bond is an inflation-linked bond or linker whose coupon payments and/or principal repayments are linked to a price index. Index-linked payment structures include zero-coupon-indexed bonds, interest-indexed bonds, capital-indexed bonds, and indexed-annuity bonds.

■ Common types of bonds with embedded options include callable bonds, putable bonds, and convertible bonds. These options are "embedded" in the sense that there are provisions provided in the indenture that grant either the issuer or the bondholder certain rights affecting the disposal or redemption of the bond. They are not separately traded securities.

■ Callable bonds give the issuer the right to buy bonds back prior to maturity, thereby raising the reinvestment risk for the bondholder. For this reason, callable bonds have to offer a higher yield and sell at a lower price than otherwise similar non-callable bonds to compensate the bondholders for the value of the call option to the issuer.

■ Putable bonds give the bondholder the right to sell bonds back to the issuer prior to maturity. Putable bonds offer a lower yield and sell at a higher price than otherwise similar non-putable bonds to compensate the issuer for the value of the put option to the bondholders.

■ A convertible bond gives the bondholder the right to convert the bond into common shares of the issuing company. Because this option favors the bondholder, convertible bonds offer a lower yield and sell at a higher price than otherwise similar non-convertible bonds.

PRACTICE PROBLEMS

1   A 10-year bond was issued four years ago. The bond is denominated in US dollars, offers a coupon rate of 10% with interest paid semi-annually, and is currently priced at 102% of par. The bond's:

   A   tenor is six years.

   B   nominal rate is 5%.

   C   redemption value is 102% of the par value.

2   A sovereign bond has a maturity of 15 years. The bond is *best* described as a:

   A   perpetual bond.

   B   pure discount bond.

   C   capital market security.

3   A company has issued a floating-rate note with a coupon rate equal to the three-month Libor + 65 basis points. Interest payments are made quarterly on 31 March, 30 June, 30 September, and 31 December. On 31 March and 30 June, the three-month Libor is 1.55% and 1.35%, respectively. The coupon rate for the interest payment made on 30 June is:

   A   2.00%.

   B   2.10%.

   C   2.20%.

4   The legal contract that describes the form of the bond, the obligations of the issuer, and the rights of the bondholders can be *best* described as a bond's:

   A   covenant.

   B   indenture.

   C   debenture.

5   Which of the following is a type of external credit enhancement?

   A   Covenants

   B   A surety bond

   C   Overcollaterization

6   An affirmative covenant is *most likely* to stipulate:

   A   limits on the issuer's leverage ratio.

   B   how the proceeds of the bond issue will be used.

   C   the maximum percentage of the issuer's gross assets that can be sold.

7   Which of the following *best* describes a negative bond covenant? The issuer is:

   A   required to pay taxes as they come due.

   B   prohibited from investing in risky projects.

   C   required to maintain its current lines of business.

8   A South African company issues bonds denominated in pound sterling that are sold to investors in the United Kingdom. These bonds can be *best* described as:

   A   Eurobonds.

   B   global bonds.

   C   foreign bonds.

This question set was developed by Lee M. Dunham, CFA (Omaha, NE, USA), and Elbie Louw, CFA, CIPM (Pretoria, South Africa). Copyright © 2013 CFA Institute.

9 Relative to domestic and foreign bonds, Eurobonds are *most likely* to be:

   A bearer bonds.

   B registered bonds.

   C subject to greater regulation.

10 An investor in a country with an original issue discount tax provision purchases a 20-year zero-coupon bond at a deep discount to par value. The investor plans to hold the bond until the maturity date. The investor will *most likely* report:

   A a capital gain at maturity.

   B a tax deduction in the year the bond is purchased.

   C taxable income from the bond every year until maturity.

11 A bond that is characterized by a fixed periodic payment schedule that reduces the bond's outstanding principal amount to zero by the maturity date is *best* described as a:

   A bullet bond.

   B plain vanilla bond.

   C fully amortized bond.

12 If interest rates are expected to increase, the coupon payment structure *most likely* to benefit the issuer is a:

   A step-up coupon.

   B inflation-linked coupon.

   C cap in a floating-rate note.

13 Investors who believe that interest rates will rise *most likely* prefer to invest in:

   A inverse floaters.

   B fixed-rate bonds.

   C floating-rate notes.

14 A 10-year, capital-indexed bond linked to the Consumer Price Index (CPI) is issued with a coupon rate of 6% and a par value of 1,000. The bond pays interest semi-annually. During the first six months after the bond's issuance, the CPI increases by 2%. On the first coupon payment date, the bond's:

   A coupon rate increases to 8%.

   B coupon payment is equal to 40.

   C principal amount increases to 1,020.

15 The provision that provides bondholders the right to sell the bond back to the issuer at a predetermined price prior to the bond's maturity date is referred to as:

   A a put provision.

   B a make-whole call provision.

   C an original issue discount provision.

16 Which of the following provisions is a benefit to the issuer?

   A Put provision

   B Call provision

   C Conversion provision

17 Relative to an otherwise similar option-free bond, a:

   A putable bond will trade at a higher price.

   B callable bond will trade at a higher price.

   C convertible bond will trade at a lower price.

SOLUTIONS

1 A is correct. The tenor of the bond is the time remaining until the bond's maturity date. Although the bond had a maturity of 10 years at issuance (original maturity), it was issued four years ago. Thus, there are six years remaining until the maturity date.

B is incorrect because the nominal rate is the coupon rate, i.e., the interest rate that the issuer agrees to pay each year until the maturity date. Although interest is paid semi-annually, the nominal rate is 10%, not 5%. C is incorrect because it is the bond's price, not its redemption value (also called principal amount, principal value, par value, face value, nominal value, or maturity value), that is equal to 102% of the par value.

2 C is correct. A capital market security has an original maturity longer than one year.

A is incorrect because a perpetual bond does not have a stated maturity date. Thus, the sovereign bond, which has a maturity of 15 years, cannot be a perpetual bond. B is incorrect because a pure discount bond is a bond issued at a discount to par value and redeemed at par. Some sovereign bonds (e.g., Treasury bills) are pure discount bonds, but others are not.

3 C is correct. The coupon rate that applies to the interest payment due on 30 June is based on the three-month Libor rate prevailing on 31 March. Thus, the coupon rate is 1.55% + 0.65% = 2.20%.

4 B is correct. The indenture, also referred to as trust deed, is the legal contract that describes the form of the bond, the obligations of the issuer, and the rights of the bondholders.

A is incorrect because covenants are only one element of a bond's indenture. Covenants are clauses that specify the rights of the bondholders and any actions that the issuer is obligated to perform or prohibited from performing. C is incorrect because a debenture is a type of bond. In many jurisdictions, debentures are unsecured bonds.

5 B is correct. A surety bond is an external credit enhancement, i.e., a guarantee received from a third party. If the issuer defaults, the guarantor who provided the surety bond will reimburse investors for any losses, usually up to a maximum amount called the penal sum.

A is incorrect because covenants are legally enforceable rules that borrowers and lenders agree upon when the bond is issued. C is incorrect because overcollateralization is an internal, not external, credit enhancement. Collateral is a guarantee underlying the debt above and beyond the issuer's promise to pay, and overcollateralization refers to the process of posting more collateral than is needed to obtain or secure financing. Collateral, such as assets or securities pledged to ensure debt payments, is not provided by a third party. Thus, overcollateralization is not an external credit enhancement.

6 B is correct. Affirmative (or positive) covenants enumerate what issuers are required to do and are typically administrative in nature. A common affirmative covenant describes what the issuer intends to do with the proceeds from the bond issue.

A and C are incorrect because imposing a limit on the issuer's leverage ratio or on the percentage of the issuer's gross assets that can be sold are negative covenants. Negative covenants prevent the issuer from taking actions that could reduce its ability to make interest payments and repay the principal.

7 B is correct. Prohibiting the issuer from investing in risky projects restricts the issuer's potential business decisions. These restrictions are referred to as negative bond covenants.

A and C are incorrect because paying taxes as they come due and maintaining the current lines of business are positive covenants.

8 C is correct. Bonds sold in a country and denominated in that country's currency by an entity from another country are referred to as foreign bonds.

A is incorrect because Eurobonds are bonds issued outside the jurisdiction of any single country. B is incorrect because global bonds are bonds issued in the Eurobond market and at least one domestic country simultaneously.

9 A is correct. Eurobonds are typically issued as bearer bonds, i.e., bonds for which the trustee does not keep records of ownership. In contrast, domestic and foreign bonds are typically registered bonds for which ownership is recorded by either name or serial number.

B is incorrect because Eurobonds are typically issued as bearer bonds, not registered bonds. C is incorrect because Eurobonds are typically subject to lower, not greater, regulation than domestic and foreign bonds.

10 C is correct. The original issue discount tax provision requires the investor to include a prorated portion of the original issue discount in his taxable income every tax year until maturity. The original issue discount is equal to the difference between the bond's par value and its original issue price.

A is incorrect because the original issue discount tax provision allows the investor to increase his cost basis in the bond so that when the bond matures, he faces no capital gain or loss. B is incorrect because the original issue discount tax provision does not require any tax deduction in the year the bond is purchased or afterwards.

11 C is correct. A fully amortized bond calls for equal cash payments by the bond's issuer prior to maturity. Each fixed payment includes both an interest payment component and a principal repayment component such that the bond's outstanding principal amount is reduced to zero by the maturity date.

A and B are incorrect because a bullet bond or plain vanilla bond only make interest payments prior to maturity. The entire principal repayment occurs at maturity.

12 C is correct. A cap in a floating-rate note (capped FRN) prevents the coupon rate from increasing above a specified maximum rate. This feature benefits the issuer in a rising interest rate environment because it sets a limit to the interest rate paid on the debt.

A is incorrect because a bond with a step-up coupon is one in which the coupon, which may be fixed or floating, increases by specified margins at specified dates. This feature benefits the bondholders, not the issuer, in a rising interest rate environment because it allows bondholders to receive a higher coupon in line with the higher market interest rates. B is incorrect because inflation-linked bonds have their coupon payments and/or principal repayment linked to an index of consumer prices. If interest rates increase as a result of inflation, this feature is a benefit for the bondholders, not the issuer.

13 C is correct. In contrast to fixed-rate bonds that decline in value in a rising interest rate environment, floating-rate notes (FRNs) are less affected when interest rates increase because their coupon rates vary with market interest rates and are reset at regular, short-term intervals. Consequently, FRNs are favored by investors who believe that interest rates will rise.

A is incorrect because an inverse floater is a bond whose coupon rate has an inverse relationship to the reference rate, so when interest rates rise, the coupon rate on an inverse floater decreases. Thus, inverse floaters are favored by investors who believe that interest rates will decline, not rise. B is incorrect because fixed rate-bonds decline in value in a rising interest rate environment. Consequently, investors who expect interest rates to rise will likely avoid investing in fixed-rate bonds.

14 C is correct. Capital-indexed bonds pay a fixed coupon rate that is applied to a principal amount that increases in line with increases in the index during the bond's life. If the consumer price index increases by 2%, the coupon rate remains unchanged at 6%, but the principal amount increases by 2% and the coupon payment is based on the inflation-adjusted principal amount. On the first coupon payment date, the inflation-adjusted principal amount is 1,000 × (1 + 0.02) = 1,020 and the semi-annual coupon payment is equal to (0.06 × 1,020) ÷ 2 = 30.60.

15 A is correct. A put provision provides bondholders the right to sell the bond back to the issuer at a predetermined price prior to the bond's maturity date.

B is incorrect because a make-whole call provision is a form of call provision; i.e., a provision that provides the issuer the right to redeem all or part of the bond before its maturity date. A make-whole call provision requires the issuer to make a lump sum payment to the bondholders based on the present value of the future coupon payments and principal repayments not paid because of the bond being redeemed early by the issuer. C is incorrect because an original issue discount provision is a tax provision relating to bonds issued at a discount to par value. The original issue discount tax provision typically requires the bondholders to include a prorated portion of the original issue discount (i.e., the difference between the par value and the original issue price) in their taxable income every tax year until the bond's maturity date.

16 B is correct. A call provision (callable bond) gives the issuer the right to redeem all or part of the bond before the specified maturity date. If market interest rates decline or the issuer's credit quality improves, the issuer of a callable bond can redeem it and replace it by a cheaper bond. Thus, the call provision is beneficial to the issuer.

A is incorrect because a put provision (putable bond) is beneficial to the bondholders. If interest rates rise, thus lowering the bond's price, the bondholders have the right to sell the bond back to the issuer at a predetermined price on specified dates. C is incorrect because a conversion provision (convertible bond) is beneficial to the bondholders. If the issuing company's share price increases, the bondholders have the right to exchange the bond for a specified number of common shares in the issuing company.

17 A is correct. A put feature is beneficial to the bondholders. Thus, the price of a putable bond will typically be higher than the price of an otherwise similar non-putable bond.

B is incorrect because a call feature is beneficial to the issuer. Thus, the price of a callable bond will typically be lower, not higher, than the price of an otherwise similar non-callable bond. C is incorrect because a conversion feature is beneficial to the bondholders. Thus, the price of a convertible bond will typically be higher, not lower, than the price of an otherwise similar non-convertible bond.

Fixed-Income Markets: Issuance, Trading, and Funding

by Moorad Choudhry, PhD, Steven V. Mann, PhD, and Lavone F. Whitmer, CFA

LEARNING OUTCOMES

Mastery	The candidate should be able to:
☐	a. describe classifications of global fixed-income markets;
☐	b. describe the use of interbank offered rates as reference rates in floating-rate debt;
☐	c. describe mechanisms available for issuing bonds in primary markets;
☐	d. describe secondary markets for bonds;
☐	e. describe securities issued by sovereign governments, non-sovereign governments, government agencies, and supranational entities;
☐	f. describe types of debt issued by corporations;
☐	g. describe short-term funding alternatives available to banks;
☐	h. describe repurchase agreements (repos) and their importance to investors who borrow short term.

INTRODUCTION

1

Global fixed-income markets represent the largest subset of financial markets in terms of number of issuances and market capitalization. These markets bring borrowers and lenders together to allocate capital globally to its highest and most efficient uses. Fixed-income markets include not only publicly traded securities, such as commercial paper, notes, and bonds, but also securitized and non-securitized loans. At the end of

2010, the total amount of debt and equity outstanding was about \$212 trillion globally.[1] The global fixed-income market represented approximately 75% of this total; simply put, global debt markets are three times larger than global equity markets.

Understanding how fixed-income markets are structured and how they operate is important for debt issuers and investors. Debt issuers have financing needs that must be met. For example, a government may need to finance an infrastructure project, a new hospital, or a new school. A company may require funds to expand its business. Financial institutions also have funding needs, and they are among the largest issuers of fixed-income securities. Fixed income is an important asset class for both individual and institutional investors. Thus, investors need to understand the characteristics of fixed-income securities including how these securities are issued and traded.

Among the questions this reading addresses are the following:

- What are the key bond market sectors?

- How are bonds sold in primary markets and traded in secondary markets?

- What types of bonds are issued by governments, government-related entities, financial companies, and non-financial companies?

- What additional sources of funds are available to banks?

The remainder of this reading is organized as follows. Section 2 presents an overview of global fixed-income markets and how these markets are classified, including some descriptive statistics on the size of the different bond market sectors. Section 2 also identifies the major issuers of and investors in fixed-income securities and presents fixed-income indices. Section 3 discusses how fixed-income securities are issued in primary markets, and how these securities are then traded in secondary markets. Sections 4 to 6 examine different bond market sectors and present sovereign government bonds; non-sovereign government, quasi-government, and supranational bonds; and corporate debt. Section 7 discusses the additional short-term funding alternatives available to banks, including repurchase agreements. Section 8 concludes and summarizes the reading.

2 OVERVIEW OF GLOBAL FIXED-INCOME MARKETS

Although there is no standard classification of fixed-income markets, many investors and market participants use criteria to structure fixed-income markets and identify bond market sectors. This section starts by describing the most widely used ways of classifying fixed-income markets.

2.1 Classification of Fixed-Income Markets

Common criteria used to classify fixed-income markets include the type of issuer; the bonds' credit quality, maturity, currency denomination, and type of coupon; and where the bonds are issued and traded.

---

1 Charles Roxburgh, Susan Lund, and John Piotowski, "Mapping Global Capital Markets," McKinsey & Company (2011). The \$212 trillion amount is based on a sample of 79 countries and includes the market capitalization of stock markets; the principal amount outstanding of bonds issued by governments, financial, and non-financial companies; securitized debt instruments; and the book value of the loans held on the balance sheets of banks and other financial institutions.

2.1.1 *Classification by Type of Issuer*

One way of classifying fixed-income markets is by type of issuer, which usually leads to the identification of three bond market sectors: the government and government-related sector, the corporate sector, and the structured finance sector. The government and government-related sector includes the bonds issued by supranational (international) organizations, such as the World Bank; sovereign (national) governments; non-sovereign (local) governments, such as provinces, regions, states, or cities; and quasi-government entities that are either owned or sponsored by governments, such as rail services or utilities in many countries. The corporate sector refers to the bonds issued by financial and non-financial companies. The structured finance sector, also known as the securitized sector, includes bonds created from the process of securitization, which transforms private transactions between borrowers and lenders into securities traded in public markets. The government, government-related, and corporate sectors and the securities associated with these sectors are discussed in depth in Sections 4 to 7. The securitized sector will be covered in a separate reading.

Exhibit 1 presents data on global capital markets at the end of December 2010. As mentioned in the introduction, the combined sectors of the global debt markets are three times larger than the global equity markets. Exhibit 1 also indicates that the largest issuers of bonds are governments and financial institutions. However, the last column shows that in the aftermath of the global financial crisis that started in 2008, the amount of bonds issued by governments increased, whereas the amount of bonds issued by financial institutions decreased. In addition, the last two columns of Exhibit 1 show that the sector that grew the fastest between 1990 and 2009 was the securitized sector, but it was also the sector that shrank the most after 2008. The last row is a reminder that although the focus of many market participants and this reading is on publicly traded securities, bank loans remain an important component of global capital markets. In many countries, bank loans are the primary source of capital, particularly for small and medium-size companies.

Exhibit 1	Global Debt and Equity Outstanding by Sector at the End of December 2010			
Sector	Amount (US$ trillions)	Weight	Compound Annual Growth Rate 1990–2009	Annual Growth Rate 2009–2010
Stock markets	$54	26%	7.2%	5.6%
Bonds issued by governments	41	19	7.8	11.9
Bonds issued by financial companies	42	20	9.5	−3.3
Bonds issued by nonfinancial companies	10	5	6.7	9.7
Securitized debt instruments	15	7	12.7	−5.6
Bank loans	49	23	4.1	5.9

Notes: Data include 79 countries. The amounts reflect the market capitalization of stock markets; the principal amount outstanding of bonds issued by governments, financial, and non-financial companies; securitized debt instruments; and the book value of the loans held on the balance sheets of banks and other financial institutions.

Source: Data from Exhibit E1 in Charles Roxburgh, Susan Lund, and John Piotowski, "Mapping Global Capital Markets," McKinsey & Company (2011):4.

Exhibit 2 shows the amounts of debt and equity outstanding and the total capital as a percentage of GDP for various countries and economic areas at the end of December 2010. It indicates that financial markets relative to GDP are much smaller in emerging countries than in developed countries. Debt and equity capital represent more than 400% of GDP in the United States, Japan, and Western Europe, versus less than 200% in Central and Eastern Europe (CEE), the Commonwealth of Independent States (CIS), Latin America, and the Middle East and Africa. India and China are in between, mainly because of the growth of their financial markets since the mid-1990s.

Exhibit 2	Global Debt and Equity Outstanding for Various Countries and Economic Areas at the End of December 2010 (US$ trillions)						
Economic Area	Bank Loans	Securitized Debt Instruments	Bonds Issued by Nonfinancial Companies	Bonds Issued by Financial Companies	Bonds Issued by Governments	Stock Markets	Total Capital as a Percentage of GDP
United States	$44	$77	$31	$116	$75	$119	462%
Japan	106	10	18	31	220	72	457
Western Europe	110	15	19	115	72	69	400
Other Developed	91	29	20	47	49	152	388
China	127	2	10	16	28	97	280
India	60	4	1	7	44	93	209
Middle East and Africa	66	2	5	6	15	96	190
Other Asia	54	1	10	7	34	62	168
Latin America	27	3	3	20	38	57	148
CEE and CIS	62	0	2	6	24	48	142

Note: CEE and CIS stand for Central and Eastern Europe and Commonwealth of Independent States, respectively.
Source: Data are from Exhibit E2 in Charles Roxburgh, Susan Lund, and John Piotowski, "Mapping Global Capital Markets," McKinsey & Company (2011):8.

2.1.2 *Classification by Credit Quality*

Investors who hold bonds are exposed to credit risk, which is the risk of loss resulting from the issuer failing to make full and timely payments of interest and/or principal. Bond markets can be classified based on the issuer's creditworthiness as judged by the credit rating agencies. Ratings of Baa3 or above by Moody's Investors Service or BBB– or above by Standard & Poor's (S&P) and Fitch Ratings are considered investment grade. In contrast, ratings below these levels are referred to as non-investment grade, high yield, speculative, or "junk." An important point to understand is that credit ratings are not static; they will change if the probability of default for an issuer changes.

One of the reasons why the distinction between investment-grade and high-yield bond markets matters is because institutional investors may be prohibited from investing in, or restricted in their exposure to, lower-quality or lower-rated securities. Prohibition or restriction in high-yield bond holdings generally arise because of a more restrictive risk–reward profile that forms part of the investor's investment objectives and constraints. For example, regulated banks and life insurance companies are usually limited to investing in very highly rated securities. In contrast, the sovereign wealth funds of both Qatar and Kuwait have no formal restrictions on what type of assets they can hold or on the percentage split between bond market sectors. Globally, investment-grade bond markets tend to be more liquid than high-yield bond markets.

2.1.3 *Classification by Maturity*

Fixed-income securities can also be classified by the original maturity of the bonds when they are issued. Securities that are issued with a maturity at issuance (original maturity) ranging from overnight to one year are money market securities. Some of these securities are issued by sovereign governments, such as Treasury bills. The corporate sector also issues fixed-income securities with short maturities. Examples include commercial paper and negotiable certificates of deposit, which are discussed in Sections 6.2 and 7.2.3, respectively. In contrast, capital market securities are securities that are issued with an original maturity longer than one year.

2.1.4 *Classification by Currency Denomination*

One of the critical ways to distinguish among fixed-income securities is by currency denomination. The currency denomination of the bond's cash flows influences which country's interest rates affect a bond's price. For example, if a bond is denominated in yen, its price will be primarily driven by the credit quality of the issuer and by Japanese interest rates.

Exhibit 3 presents data on the currency denomination of international bonds, which are bonds issued by entities outside their country of origin, either in their domestic currency or in a foreign currency. It shows that approximately 79% of international bonds are denominated either in Euros or in US dollars.

Exhibit 3	Amounts of International Bonds Outstanding by Currency Denomination at the End of December 2011	
Currency	**Amount (US$ billions)**	**Weight**
Euro (EUR)	$9,665.9	46.0%
US Dollar (USD)	6,900.8	32.9
British Pound Sterling (GBP)	2,052.3	9.8
Japanese Yen (JPY)	762.0	3.6
Swiss Franc (CHF)	393.4	1.9
Australian Dollar (AUD)	317.2	1.5
Canadian Dollar (CAD)	313.1	1.5
Swedish Krona (SEK)	103.0	0.5
Norwegian Krone (NOK)	86.4	0.4
Hong Kong Dollar (HKD)	63.5	0.3
Yuan Renminbi (CNY)	38.9	0.2
Other Currencies	305.0	1.5
Total	**21,001.5**	**100.0%**

Source: Based on data from Bank of International Settlements, Tables 13A and 13B, available at www.bis.org/statistics/secstats.htm (accessed 12 December 2012).

2.1.5 *Classification by Type of Coupon*

Another way of classifying fixed-income markets is by type of coupon. Some bonds pay a fixed rate of interest; others, called floating-rate bonds, floating-rate notes (FRNs) or floaters, pay a rate of interest that adjusts to market interest rates at regular, short-term intervals (e.g., quarterly).

2.1.5.1 Demand and Supply of Fixed-Rate vs. Floating-Rate Debt

Balance sheet risk management considerations explain much of the demand and supply of floating-rate debt. For instance, the funding of banks—that is, the money banks raise to make loans to companies and individuals—is often short term and issued at rates that change or reset frequently. When there is a mismatch between the interest paid on the liabilities (money the bank borrowed) and the interest received on the assets (money the bank lent or invested), banks are exposed to interest rate risk—that is, the risk associated with a change in interest rate. In an effort to limit the volatility of their net worth resulting from interest rate risk, banks that issue floating-rate debt often prefer to make floating-rate loans and invest in floating-rate bonds or in other adjustable-rate assets. In addition to institutions with short-term funding needs, demand for floating-rate bonds comes from investors who believe that interest rates will rise. In that case, investors will benefit from holding floating-rate investments compared with fixed-rate ones.

On the supply side, issuance of floating-rate debt comes from institutions needing to finance short-term loans, such as consumer finance companies. Corporate borrowers also view floating-rate bonds as an alternative to using bank liquidity facilities (e.g., lines of credit), particularly when they are a lower cost option, and as an alternative to borrowing long-term at fixed rates when they expect interest rates will fall.

2.1.5.2 Reference Rates

The coupon rate of a floating rate bond is typically expressed as a reference rate plus a spread or margin. The spread is usually set when the bond is issued and remains constant until maturity. It is primarily a function of the issuer's credit risk at issuance: the lower the issuer's credit quality (the higher its credit risk), the higher the spread. The reference rate, however, resets periodically. Therefore, the coupon rate adjusts to the level of market interest rates each time the reference rate is reset. The choice of the reference rate is critical because the reference rate is the primary driver of a bond's coupon rate. Thus, the issuer's cost of financing and the investor's return from investing in the bonds depend on the reference rate.

Different reference rates are used depending on where the bonds are issued and their currency denomination. The **London interbank offered rate** (Libor) is the reference rate for a lot of floating-rate bonds, in particular those issued in the Eurobond market. For example, a typical coupon rate for a floater denominated in British sterling that pays coupons semi-annually is the sterling six-month Libor plus a spread. The coupon rate that is paid at the end of a six-month period is set based on the sterling six-month Libor at the beginning of the period, and it remains constant throughout the six months. Every six months, the coupon rate is reset in line with the sterling six-month Libor. For floating-rate bonds denominated in US dollars, the reference rate is usually the US dollar Libor—the US dollar three-month Libor if the coupons are paid quarterly or the US dollar 12-month Libor if the coupons are paid annually.

As illustrated in these examples, "Libor" is a collective name for multiple rates. Libor rates reflect the rates at which a select set of banks believe they could borrow unsecured funds from other banks in the London interbank money market for different currencies and different borrowing periods ranging from overnight to one year—the **interbank money market** or **interbank market** is the market of loans and deposits between banks for maturities up to one year. The sidebar describes how the Libor rates are determined and identifies some of the issues associated with Libor.

Administration of Libor

As of the time of this writing in late 2012, the process by which Libor rates are set is in transition. Historically, Libor rates were set by the British Bankers' Association (BBA). Every business day, a select group of 18 banks would submit to the BBA the rates at which they believed they could borrow from other banks in the London interbank market for 10 currencies and 15 borrowing periods.[2] The submitted rates would be ranked from highest to lowest, and the upper and lower four submissions would be discarded. The arithmetic mean of the remaining 10 rates became the Libor rates for a particular combination of currency and maturity. The 150 Libor rates would then be communicated to market participants for use as reference rates in many different types of debt, including floating-rate bonds.

One of the advantages of Libor has been its prevalence of use. The shortcoming of Libor as historically set was that Libor rates were not based on readily observable market rates but on banks' own estimates of their borrowing rates. Because the rates at which a bank can borrow money are an indication of its credit risk, banks had an incentive to understate their reported borrowing rates. A scandal emerged in 2012 as it was recognized that, at times, Libor rates drifted away from the underlying reality. How the Libor rates are set will certainly evolve going forward. In September 2012, the Financial Services Authority (FSA), a UK regulator, announced that the BBA would be relieved of oversight of Libor. It is also possible that over time, market rates may emerge as an alternative way of setting Libor and other reference rates.

Although there are Libor rates for currencies such as the euro and the yen, alternative interbank offered rates may be used for floating-rate debt issued in these currencies, such as the Euro interbank offered rate (Euribor) and the Tokyo interbank offered rate (Tibor), respectively. Similar sets of interbank offered rates exist in other markets, for instance, the Singapore interbank offered rate (Sibor), the Hong Kong interbank offered rate (Hibor), the Mumbai interbank offered rate (Mibor), or the Korea interbank offered rate (Koribor) for floating-rate debt issued in Singapore dollar, Hong Kong dollar, Indian rupee, or the Korean won, respectively. All these different interbank offered rates are sets of rates for borrowing periods of various maturities of up to one year. The processes to determine them are similar, except that the sets of banks and organizations fixing the daily rates are different.

The use of these interbank offered rates extends beyond setting coupon rates for floating-rate debt. These rates are also used as reference rates for other debt instruments including mortgages, derivatives such as interest rate and currency swaps, and many other financial contracts and products. As of November 2012, it is estimated that nearly $300 trillion of financial instruments are tied to Libor.

2.1.6 Classification by Geography

A distinction is very often made between the domestic bond, foreign bond, and Eurobond markets. Bonds issued in a specific country, denominated in the currency of that country, and sold in that country are classified as domestic bonds if they are issued by an issuer domiciled in that country and foreign bonds if they are issued by an issuer domiciled in another country. Domestic and foreign bonds are subject to the legal, regulatory, and tax requirements that apply in that particular country. In

---

2 The question asked is, "At what rate could you borrow funds, were you to do so by asking for and then accepting interbank offers in a reasonable market size just prior to 11am?" Since Libor was established in 1986, the number of currencies has increased from three to 10, and the number of periods has also increased from 12 to 15, resulting in 150 rates as of 2012. But the number of rates is likely to go down in 2013 with the elimination of some of the currencies and maturities.

contrast, a Eurobond is issued internationally, outside the jurisdiction of the country in whose currency the bond is denominated. The Eurobond market is characterized by less reporting, regulatory and tax constraints than domestic and foreign bond markets. These fewer constraints explain why approximately 80% of entities that issue bonds outside their country of origin choose to do so in the Eurobond market rather than in a foreign bond market. In addition, Eurobonds are attractive for issuers because it gives them the ability to reach out to more investors globally. Access to a wider pool of investors often allows issuers to raise more capital and usually at a lower cost.

Exhibit 4 presents data on the residence of issuers and a breakdown of the amount of bonds outstanding between the government, financial, and non-financial sectors. It shows that 59% of issuers are located in the United States and Japan, and that the residents of 10 countries account for 90% of the global bond markets. Exhibit 4 also indicates that the split between the three sectors varies among countries. For example, the government sector represents 74% of the amount of bonds outstanding in Japan, but non-financial corporate issuers only account for 7% of the $15.7 trillion of bonds outstanding. In contrast, the corporate sector is the largest sector in countries such as the Netherlands, Spain, the United Kingdom, or the United States, although the majority of bonds are issued by financial rather than non-financial companies.

Exhibit 4 Amount of Bonds Outstanding by Residence of Issuer and Type of Issuer at the End of December 2011 (US$ billions)

Country	All Issuers		Government		Financial		Non-Financial	
	Amount	Global Weight	Amount	Sector Weight	Amount	Sector Weight	Amount	Sector Weight
United States	$33,582	40%	$12,954	39%	$14,938	44%	$5,690	17%
Japan	15,700	19	11,552	74	3,111	20	1,038	7
United Kingdom	5,275	6	2,040	39	2,537	48	699	13
Germany	4,383	5	2,079	47	2,175	50	129	3
France	4,382	5	1,910	44	1,947	44	525	12
Italy	3,686	4	2,078	56	1,492	40	116	3
Spain	2,307	3	871	38	1,416	61	19	1
Netherlands	2,246	3	401	18	1,730	77	116	5
Canada	1,899	2	1,178	62	399	21	322	17
Australia	1,847	2	479	26	1,186	64	182	10
Rest of the world	8,748	10	3,184	36	4,830	55	734	8
Total	$84,055	100%	$38,726	46%	$35,761	43%	$9,570	11%

Source: Based on data from Bank of International Settlements, Tables 13A and 13B, available from www.bis.org/statistics/secstats.htm (accessed 12 December 2012).

Investors make a distinction between countries with established capital markets (developed markets) and countries where the capital markets are in earlier stages of development (emerging markets). For emerging bond markets, a further distinction is made between bonds issued in local currency and bonds issued in a foreign currency, such as the euro or the US dollar.

Emerging bond markets are much smaller than developed bond markets, which is the reason why they do not appear in Exhibit 4. But as demand from local and international investors has increased, issuance and trading of emerging market bonds have risen in volume and value. International investors' interest in emerging market bonds has been triggered by a desire to diversify risk across several jurisdictions in the belief that investment returns across markets are not closely correlated. In addition, emerging market bonds usually offer higher yields (return) than developed market bonds because of the higher perceived risk. Emerging countries typically lag developed countries in the areas of political stability, property rights, and contract enforcement, which often leads to a higher credit risk and higher yields. Many emerging countries, however, are less indebted than their developed counterparts and benefit from higher growth prospects, which appeals to many investors.

2.1.7 Other Classifications of Fixed-Income Markets

There are various other ways of classifying fixed-income markets. Investors or market participants may classify fixed-income markets based on some specific characteristics associated with the fixed-income securities. Specific market sectors that are of interest to some investors are inflation-linked bonds and, in some jurisdictions, tax-exempt bonds. Issuance of either type of bond tends to be limited to certain types of issuers. Inflation-linked bonds or linkers are typically issued by governments, government-related entities, and corporate issuers that have an investment-grade rating. They offer investors protection against inflation by linking the coupon payment and/or the principal repayment to an index of consumer prices.

Tax-exempt bonds can only be issued in those jurisdictions that recognize such tax exemption. In the United States for example, there is an income tax exemption for some of the bonds issued by governments or by some non-profit organizations. In particular, local governments can issue **municipal bonds** (or **munis**) that are tax exempt (they can also issue taxable municipal bonds, although tax-exempt munis are more frequently issued than taxable munis). Tax-exempt municipal bonds are of interest to investors who are subject to income tax because the interest income on these bonds is typically exempt from federal income tax and from income tax of the state where the bonds are issued, subject to certain restrictions. The coupon rate on a tax-exempt municipal bond is lower than that on an otherwise similar taxable bond to reflect the implied income tax rate. Investors are willing to accept a lower coupon rate on a tax-exempt municipal bond compared with an otherwise similar taxable bond because the income received from municipal bonds is not taxable. Tax-exempt bonds also exist in other jurisdictions. For example, the National Highways Authority of India (NHAI) issues tax-exempt bonds. In countries that implement a capital gains tax, there may be tax exemptions for some types of bonds. In the United Kingdom for example, government gilts are not subject to capital gains tax.

EXAMPLE 1

1 Which of the following is *most likely* an issuer of bonds?

   A Hedge fund

   B Pension fund

   C Local government

2 A bond issued by a city would *most likely* be classified as a:

   A supranational bond.

   B quasi-government bond.

   C non-sovereign government bond.

3 A fixed-income security issued with a maturity at issuance of nine months is *most likely* classified as a:

   A securitized investment.

   B capital market security.

C money market security.

4 The price of a bond issued in the United States by a British company and denominated in US dollars is *most likely* to:

A change as US interest rates change.

B change as British interest rates change.

C be unaffected by changes in US and British interest rates.

5 Interbank offered rates are *best* described as the rates at which major banks can:

A issue short-term debt.

B borrow unsecured funds from other major banks.

C borrow from other major banks against some form of collateral.

6 A company issues floating-rate bonds. The coupon rate is expressed as the three-month Libor plus a spread. The coupon payments are *most likely* to increase as:

A Libor increases.

B the spread increases.

C the company's credit quality decreases.

Solution to 1:

C is correct. Major issuers of bonds include sovereign (national) governments, non-sovereign (local) governments, quasi-government agencies, supranational organizations, and financial and non-financial companies. A and B are incorrect because hedge funds and pension funds are typically investors in, not issuers of, bonds.

Solution to 2:

C is correct. Non-sovereign (local) government bond issuers include provinces, regions, states, and cities. A is incorrect because supranational bonds are issued by international organizations. B is incorrect because quasi-government bonds are issued by agencies that are either owned or sponsored by governments.

Solution to 3:

C is correct. Money market securities are issued with a maturity at issuance (original maturity) ranging from overnight to one year. A is incorrect because securitization does not relate to a bond's maturity but to the process that transforms private transactions between borrowers and lenders into securities traded in public markets. B is incorrect because capital market securities are issued with an original maturity longer than one year.

Solution to 4:

A is correct. The currency denomination of a bond's cash flows influences which country's interest rates affect a bond's price. The price of a bond issued by a British company and denominated in US dollars will be affected by US interest rates.

Solution to 5:

B is correct. Interbank offered rates represent a set of interest rates at which major banks believe they could borrow unsecured funds from other major banks in the interbank money market for different currencies and different borrowing periods ranging from overnight to one year.

Solution to 6:

A is correct. The coupon payments of a floating-rate bond that is tied to the three-month Libor will reset every three months, based on changes in Libor. Thus, as Libor increases, so will the coupon payments. B is incorrect because the spread on a floating-rate bond is typically constant; it is set when the bond is issued and does not change afterward. C is incorrect because the issuer's credit quality affects the spread and thus the coupon rate that serves as the basis for the calculation of the coupon payments, but only when the spread is set—that is, at issuance.

2.2 Fixed-Income Indices

A fixed-income index is a multi-purpose tool used by investors and investment managers to describe a given bond market or sector, as well as to evaluate the performance of investments and investment managers. Most fixed-income indices are constructed as portfolios of securities that reflect a particular bond market or sector. The index construction—that is, the security selection and the index weighting—varies among indices.[3] Index weighting may be based on price or value (market capitalization).

There are literally dozens of fixed-income indices globally, capturing different aspects of the fixed-income markets discussed earlier. One of the most popular set of indices is the Barclays Capital Global Aggregate Bond Index, which represents a broad-based measure of the global investment-grade fixed-rate bond market. It has an index history beginning on 1 January 1990 and contains three important components: the US Aggregate Bond Index (formerly Lehman Aggregate Bond Index), the Pan-European Aggregate Bond Index, and the Asian-Pacific Aggregate Bond Index. These indices reflect the investment-grade sectors of the US, European, and Asian-Pacific bond markets, respectively.

With respect to emerging markets, one of the most widely followed indices is the J.P. Morgan Emerging Market Bond Index (EMBI) Global, which includes US dollar-denominated Brady bonds (bonds issued primarily by Latin American countries in the late 1980s under a debt restructuring plan aimed at converting bank loans into tradable securities), Eurobonds and loans issued by sovereign and quasi-sovereign entities in several emerging markets.

Another popular set of indices is the FTSE Global Bond Index Series, which has been set up to provide coverage of different classes of securities related to the government and corporate bond markets. It includes indices of global government bonds, euro-denominated government bonds from emerging markets, sterling- and euro-denominated investment-grade corporate bonds, and covered bonds from Germany and other European Union issuers. Covered bonds are debt obligations issued by banks and backed (secured) by a segregated pool of assets.

Many other fixed-income indices are available to investors and investment managers to measure and report performance.

2.3 Investors in Fixed-Income Securities

The overview of fixed-income markets has so far focused on the supply side. Before discussing bond issuers in greater detail, it is important to say a few words about the demand side because demand for a particular type of bond or issuer may affect supply. After all, market prices are the result of the interaction between demand and supply; neither one can be considered in isolation. For example, an increase in demand

---

3 Fixed-income indices are discussed in greater details in the reading on security market indices.

for inflation-linked bonds as a result of investors' desire to protect the value of their portfolios against inflation risk may lead governments to issue a greater quantity of this type of bond. By issuing relatively more inflation-linked bonds for which there is demand, a government not only manages to sell its bond issue and get the funds required, but it may also benefit from a lower cost of financing.

There are different types of investors in fixed-income securities. Major categories of bond investors include central banks, institutional investors, and retail investors. The first two typically invest directly in fixed-income securities. In contrast, retail investors often invest indirectly through fixed-income mutual funds or exchange-traded funds (ETFs).

Central banks use open market operations to implement monetary policy. **Open market operations** refer to the purchase or sale of bonds, usually sovereign bonds issued by the national government. By purchasing (selling) domestic bonds, central banks increase (decrease) the monetary base in the economy. Central banks may also purchase and sell bonds denominated in foreign currencies as part of their efforts to manage the relative value of the domestic currency and their country's foreign reserves.

Institutional investors, including pension funds, some hedge funds, charitable foundations and endowments, insurance companies, and banks, represent the largest groups of investors in fixed-income securities. Another major group of investors is sovereign wealth funds, which are state-owned investment funds that tend to have very long investment horizons and aim to preserve or create wealth for future generations.

Finally, retail investors often invest heavily in fixed-income securities because of the attractiveness of relatively stable prices and steady income production.

Fixed-income markets are dominated by institutional investors in part because of the high informational barriers to entry. Fixed-income securities are far more diverse than equity securities because of the variety of types of issuers and securities. In addition, unlike common shares that are primarily issued and traded in organized markets, the issuance and trading of bonds very often occurs over the counter. Thus, fixed-income securities are more difficult to understand and access than equity securities. For these reasons, institutional investors tend to invest directly in bonds, whereas most retail investors prefer to use investment vehicles, such as mutual funds and ETFs.

EXAMPLE 2

1   Open market operations describe the process used by central banks to buy and sell bonds to:

   A   implement fiscal policy.

   B   control the monetary base.

   C   issue and repay government debt.

2   Retail investors *most likely*:

   A   do not invest in fixed income.

   B   invest in fixed income directly by buying and selling securities.

   C   invest in fixed income indirectly through mutual funds or exchange-traded funds.

Solution to 1:

B is correct. Open market operations refer to the purchase or sale of bonds, usually sovereign bonds issued by the national government. By purchasing (selling) bonds, central banks increase (decrease) the monetary base in the economy, thus controlling the money supply. A is incorrect because open market operations help facilitate monetary policy, not fiscal policy (which is the taxing and spending by the national government). C is incorrect because although Treasury departments and some central banks may facilitate the issuance and repayment of government debt, open market operations specifically refer to the implementation of monetary policy.

Solution to 2:

C is correct. Retail investors typically invest heavily in fixed-income securities because of the attractiveness of relatively stable prices and steady income production. However, because most retail investors lack the expertise to value fixed-income securities and are not large enough investors to buy and sell them directly, they usually invest in fixed income indirectly through mutual funds and exchange-traded funds.

PRIMARY AND SECONDARY BOND MARKETS

3

Primary bond markets are markets in which issuers first sell bonds to investors to raise capital. In contrast, **secondary bond markets** are markets in which existing bonds are subsequently traded among investors. As with all financial markets, primary and secondary bond markets are regulated within the framework of the overall financial system. An established independent regulatory authority is usually responsible for overseeing both the structure of the markets and the credentials of market participants.

3.1 Primary Bond Markets

Issuances in primary bond markets are frequent. Exhibit 5 presents data on net bond issuances (i.e., the difference between new bond issuances and bond repayments). It shows that during the year 2011, the amount of new bond issuances exceeded the amount of bond repayments by $3.8 trillion globally, a growth of approximately 4%. In all the largest bond markets, there were more new bond issuances than bond repayments in value.

Exhibit 5	Amounts of Bonds Outstanding at the End of December 2011 and Amounts of Net Bond Issuances in 2011 by Residence of the Issuer (US$ billions)	
Country	**Amount of Bonds Outstanding**	**Net Bond Issuances**
United States	$33,582	$559.7
Japan	15,700	457.5
United Kingdom	5,275	77.2
Germany	4,383	25.5
France	4,382	322.1
Italy	3,686	197.6
Spain	2,307	64.2
Netherlands	2,246	65.2
Canada	1,899	111.7
Australia	1,847	100.8

(continued)

	Amount of Bonds	
Country	**Outstanding**	**Net Bond Issuances**
Rest of the world	8,748	1,796.2
Total	**$84,055**	**$3,777.7**

Source: Based on data from Bank of International Settlements, Tables 14A, 14B, and 16A, available at www.bis.org/statistics/secstats.htm (accessed 30 October 2012).

In the remainder of this section, we discuss the process for issuing bonds in primary markets. Different bond issuing mechanisms are used depending on the type of issuer and the type of bond issued. A bond issue can be sold via a **public offering** (or **public offer**), in which any member of the public may buy the bonds, or via a **private placement**, in which only a selected group of investors may buy the bonds.

3.1.1 Public Offerings

Investment banks play a critical role in bond issuance by assisting the issuer in accessing the primary market and by providing an array of financial services. The most common bond issuing mechanisms are underwritten offerings, best effort offerings, and auctions. In an **underwritten offering**, also called a **firm commitment offering**, the investment bank guarantees the sale of the bond issue at an offering price that is negotiated with the issuer. Thus, the investment bank, called the **underwriter**, takes the risk associated with selling the bonds. In contrast, in a **best effort offering**, the investment bank only serves as a broker. It only tries to sell the bond issue at the negotiated offering price if it is able to for a commission. Thus, the investment bank has less risk and correspondingly less incentive to sell the bonds in a best effort offering than in an underwritten offering. An **auction** is a bond issuing mechanism that involves bidding.

3.1.1.1 Underwritten Offerings   Underwritten offerings are typical bond issuing mechanisms for corporate bonds, some local government bonds (such as municipal bonds in the United States), and some securitized instruments (such as mortgage-backed securities). The underwriting process typically includes six phases.

The underwriting process starts with the determination of the funding needs. Often with the help of an adviser or advisers, the issuer must determine how much money must be raised, the type of bond offering, and whether the bond issue should be underwritten.

Once the issuer has decided that the bond issue should be underwritten, it must select the underwriter, which is typically an investment bank. The underwriter of a bond issue takes the risk of buying the newly issued bonds from the issuer, and then resells them to investors or to dealers who then sell them to investors. The difference between the purchase price of the new bond issue and the reselling price to investors is the underwriter's revenue. A relatively small-size bond issue may be underwritten by a single investment bank. It is more common for larger bond issues, however, to be underwritten by a group, or syndicate, of investment banks. In this case, the bond issue is referred to as a **syndicated offering**. There is a lead underwriter that invites other investment banks to join the syndicate and that coordinates the effort. The syndicate is collectively responsible for determining the pricing of the bond issue and for placing (selling) the bonds with investors.

The third phase of an underwritten offering is to structure the transaction. Before the bond issue is announced, the issuer and the lead underwriter discuss the terms of the bond issue, such as the bond's notional principal (total amount), the coupon rate, and the expected offering price. The underwriter or the syndicate typically organize the necessary regulatory filings and prepare the offering circular or prospectus that provides information about the terms of the bond issue. The issuer must also choose a trustee, which is typically a trust company or the trust department of a bank, to oversee the master bond agreement. The bond offering is formally launched the day the transaction is announced, usually in the form of a press release. The announcement specifies the new bond issue's terms and conditions, including the bond's features, such as the maturity date, the currency denomination, and the expected coupon range, as well as the expected offering price. The issuer also releases the offering circular or prospectus. The final terms may differ from these terms as a result of changes in market conditions between the announcement day and the pricing day.

The success of the bond issue depends on the underwriter or syndicate's discernment in assessing market conditions and in pricing the bond issue accordingly. The pricing of the bond issue is, therefore, an important phase of an underwritten offering. Ideally, the bond issue should be priced so that the amount of bonds available is equal to the demand for the bonds by investors. If the offering price is set too high, the offering will be undersubscribed—that is, there will be insufficient demand for the bond issue. As a consequence, the underwriter or syndicate will fail to sell the entire bond issue. Alternatively, if the offering price is set too low, the offering will be oversubscribed. Underwriters may aim at a small oversubscription because it reduces the risk of being unable to sell the entire bond issue. But a large oversubscription would be detrimental for the issuer, who would end up raising less capital than if the bond issue had been priced at a higher level and in line with demand for the bonds by investors.

Between the announcement of a bond issue and the end of the subscription period, the underwriter or syndicate must gauge what the demand for the bond issue is and at what price the bond should be offered to ensure that the entire bond issue is placed without running the risk of a large oversubscription. There are different ways for underwriters to do so. The bond issue is usually marketed to potential investors. This may be by an indirect approach, such as an advertisement in a newspaper, a commonly used approach for bond issued by household names, or through direct marketing and road shows, aimed at institutional investors such as pension funds and insurance companies. The underwriter or syndicate may also approach large institutional investors and discuss with them the kind of bond issues they are willing to buy. These buyers are known as the "anchor." For some, but not all, bond issues, the grey market is another way for underwriters to gauge investor's interest. The **grey market**, also called "when issued" market, is a forward market for bonds about to be issued. Trading in the grey market helps underwriters determine what the final offering price should be.

The pricing day is the last day when investors can commit to buy the bond issue, and it is also the day when the final terms of the bond issue are agreed on. The following day, called the "offering day," the underwriting agreement that includes the bond issue's final terms is signed. The underwriting process enters the issuing phase. The underwriter or the syndicate purchases the entire bond issue from the issuer, delivers the proceeds, and starts reselling the bonds through its sales network.

The underwriting process comes to an end about 14 days later, on the closing day, when the bonds are delivered to investors. Investors no longer receive a paper settlement; instead, the bond itself is represented by a global note that is typically held by the paying agent.

3.1.1.2 Shelf Registration   A **shelf registration** allows certain authorized issuers to offer additional bonds to the general public without having to prepare a new and separate offering circular for each bond issue. Rather, the issuer prepares a single, all-encompassing offering circular that describes a range of future bond issuances, all under the same document. This master prospectus may be in place for years before it is replaced or updated, and it may be used to cover multiple bond issuances in the meantime. For example, the British retailer Tesco did a shelf registration in 2010 for a series of issues under a universal aggregate $10 billion of bonds. The company could have elected to issue the entire size at once. Instead, it has issued smaller notional amounts at different intervals since 2010.

Under a shelf registration, each individual offering is prefaced with a short issue announcement document. This document must confirm that there has been no change to material elements of the issuer's business, or otherwise describe any changes to the issuer's financial condition since the master prospectus was filed. Because shelf issuances are subject to a lower level of scrutiny compared with standard public offerings, they are only an option for well-established issuers that have convinced the regulatory authorities of their financial strength. Additionally, certain jurisdictions may only allow shelf registrations to be purchased by "qualified" institutional investors—that is, institutional investors that meet a set of criteria set forth by the regulators.

3.1.1.3 Auctions   An auction is a method that involves bidding. It is helpful in providing price discovery (i.e., it facilitates supply and demand in determining prices) and in allocating securities. In many countries, most sovereign bonds are sold to the public via a public auction. For example, in 2011, the United States conducted 269 public auctions and issued approximately $7.5 trillion of new securities such as Treasury bills, notes, bonds, and Treasury Inflation-Protected Securities (TIPS). The public auction process used in the United States is a single-price auction through which all the winning bidders pay the same price and receive the same coupon rate for the bonds. In contrast, the public auction process used in Canada and Germany is a multiple-price auction process, which generates multiple prices and coupon rates for the same bond issue.

The US sovereign bond market is one of the largest and most liquid bond markets globally, so we will illustrate the US single-price auction process. This process includes three phases: announcement, bidding and issuance. First, the US Treasury announces the auction and provides information about the bond issue, such as the amount of securities being offered, the auction date, the issue date, the maturity date, bidding close times, and other pertinent information.

After the auction announcement is made, dealers, institutional investors, and individual investors may enter competitive or non-competitive bids. With competitive bids, a bidder specifies the rate (yield) that is considered acceptable; if the rate determined at auction is lower than the rate specified in the competitive bid, the investor will not be offered any securities. In contrast, with non-competitive bids, a bidder agrees to accept the rate determined at auction; non-competitive bidders always receive their securities. At the close of the auction, the US Treasury accepts all non-competitive bids and competitive bids in ascending order of their rates (lowest to highest) until the amount of bids is equal to the amount the issuer requires. All bidders receive the same rate, based on the highest accepted bid. This single-price auction process encourages aggressive bidding and potentially results in a lower cost of funds (i.e., lower coupon rate) for the U.S Treasury because all the winning bidders pay the same price.

On the issue day, the U.S Treasury delivers the securities to the winning bidders and collects the proceeds from investors. After the auction process is complete, the securities are traded in secondary markets like other securities.

Exhibit 6 shows the results of a US Treasury public auction.

Exhibit 6	Results of a US Treasury Public Auction on 16 October 2012
Term and Type of Security	28-Day Bill
CUSIP Number	9127955L1
High rate[a]	0.125%
Allotted at high	21.85%
Price	99.990278
Investment rate[b]	0.127%
Median rate[c]	0.115%
Low rate[d]	0.100%
Issue date	18 October 2012
Maturity date	15 November 2012

	Tendered	Accepted
Competitive	$160,243,967,000	$39,676,092,000
Non-competitive	224,607,300	224,607,300
FIMA (non-competitive)	100,000,000	100,000,000
Subtotal[e]	$160,568,574,300	$40,000,699,300[f]
SOMA	$0	$0
Total	$160,568,574,300	$40,000,699,300

	Tendered	Accepted
Primary Dealer[g]	$137,250,000,000	$26,834,200,000
Direct Bidder[h]	13,450,000,000	4,079,425,000
Indirect Bidder[i]	9,543,967,000	8,762,467,000
Total Competitive	$160,243,967,000	$39,676,092,000

[a] All tenders at lower rates were accepted in full.
[b] Equivalent coupon-issue yield.
[c] 50% of the amount of accepted competitive tenders was tendered at or below that rate.
[d] 5% of the amount of accepted competitive tenders was tendered at or below that rate.
[e] Bid-to-cover ratio: $160,568,574,300/$40,000,699,300 = 4.01.
[f] Awards to combined Treasury Direct systems = $134,591,900.
[g] Primary dealers as submitters bidding for their own house accounts.
[h] Non-primary dealer submitters bidding for their own house accounts.
[i] Customers placing competitive bids through a direct submitter, including Foreign and International Monetary Authorities placing bids through the Federal reserve Bank of New York.
Note: FIMA stands for Foreign and International Monetary Authority and reflects the non-competitive bids made by investors from foreign countries. SOMA stands for System Open Market Account and reflects the Federal Reserve's open market operations.
Source: Based on information from www.treasurydirect.gov.

The rate determined at auction was 0.125%. T-bills are pure discount bonds; they are issued at a discount to par value and redeemed at par. Investors paid 99.990278% of par—that is, approximately $999.90. The US Treasury received bids for $160.6 billion, but only raised $40.0 billion. All the non-competitive bids ($324.6 million) were accepted, but only a quarter ($39.7 of the $160.2 billion) of competitive bids was accepted. Note that half the competitive bids were submitted with a rate lower than 0.115%. All bidders, however, received the rate of 0.125%.

Exhibit 6 also identifies the types of bidders. Most US Treasury securities are bought at auction by primary dealers. **Primary dealers** are financial institutions that are authorized to deal in new issues of US Treasury securities. They have established business relationships with the Federal Reserve Bank of New York (New York Fed), which implements US monetary policy. Primary dealers serve primarily as trading counterparties of the New York Fed and are required to participate meaningfully in open market operations and in all auctions of US Treasury securities. They also provide the New York Fed with market information. Institutional investors and central banks are the largest investors in US Treasury securities; only a very small amount of these bonds is purchased directly by individual investors.

3.1.2 *Private Placements*

A private placement is typically a non-underwritten, unregistered offering of bonds that are sold only to an investor or a small group of investors. Typical investors in privately placed bonds are large institutional investors. A private placement can be accomplished directly between the issuer and the investor(s) or through an investment bank. Because privately placed bonds are unregistered and may be restricted securities that can only be purchased by some types of investors, there is usually no active secondary market to trade them. However, trading may be possible under certain conditions. For example, restricted securities issued under Rule 144A in the United Sates cannot be sold to the public, but they can be traded among qualified institutional investors. Even if trading is possible, privately placed bonds typically exhibit lower liquidity than publicly issued bonds. Insurance companies and pension funds are major buyers of privately placed bonds because they do not need every security in their portfolio to be liquid and they often value the additional yield offered by these bonds.

Private placements sometimes represent a step in the company's financing evolution between **syndicated loans** (loans from a group of lenders to a single borrower further discussed in Section 6.1) and public offerings. Privately placed bonds are often issued in small aggregate amounts, at times by unknown issuers. Many investors may not be willing to undertake the credit analysis that is required for a new name, in particular if the offering amount is small. Unlike in a public offering in which the bonds are often sold to investors on a take-it-or-leave-it basis, investors in a private placement can influence the structure of the bond issue, including such considerations as asset and collateral backing, credit enhancements, and covenants. It is common for privately placed bonds to have more customized and restrictive covenants than publicly issued ones. In addition to being able to negotiate the terms of the bonds and align them with their needs, investors in private placements are rewarded by getting the bonds, which is not always the case in public offerings in which investors cannot know for sure when the issue will become available and how many securities they will be allocated.

Private placements are also offered by regular bond issuers, in particular for smaller amounts of capital raised in major currencies, such as US dollars, euros, or sterling. Private placements are usually more flexible than public offerings and allow regular issuers to tailor the bond issue to their own needs.

3.2 Secondary Bond Markets

Secondary markets, also called the "aftermarket," are where existing securities are traded among investors. Securities can be traded directly from investor to investor, or through a broker or dealer to facilitate the transaction. The major participants in secondary bond markets globally are large institutional investors and central banks. The presence of retail investors in secondary bonds markets is limited, unlike in secondary equity markets.

The key to understanding how secondary bond markets are structured and function is to understand liquidity. Liquidity refers to the ability to trade (buy or sell) securities quickly and easily at prices close to their fair market value. Liquidity involves much more than "how quickly one can turn a bond into cash." This statement implicitly assumes a long position, but some market participants need to buy quickly when covering a short position. The other aspect of liquidity that is often ignored is that speed of trading alone does not constitute a liquid market. One can always buy something quickly by offering a very high price or sell something quickly by accepting a very low price. In a liquid market, trading takes place quickly at prices close to the security's fair market value.

There are two main ways for secondary markets to be structured: as an organized exchange or as an over-the-counter market. An **organized exchange** provides a place where buyers and sellers can meet to arrange their trades. Although buy or sell orders may come from anywhere, the transaction must take place at the exchange according to the rules imposed by the exchange. In contrast, with **over-the-counter (OTC) markets**, buy and sell orders initiated from various locations are matched through a communications network. Thus, OTC markets need electronic trading platforms over which users submit buy and sell orders. Bloomberg Fixed Income Electronic Trading platform is an example of such a platform through which dealers stand ready to trade in multiple bond markets globally. Although there is some trading of government bonds and very active corporate bonds on many stock exchanges around the world, the vast majority of bonds are traded in OTC markets.

The liquidity demands of fixed-income investors have evolved since the early 1990s. The type of investors who would buy and hold a bond to maturity that once dominated the fixed-income markets has been supplanted by institutional investors who trade actively. The dynamics of global fixed-income markets reflect this change in the relative demand for liquidity.

We will illustrate how secondary markets work by using the example of Eurobonds. The most important Eurobond trading center by volume is in London, although a large number of market participants are also based in Brussels, Frankfurt, Zurich, and Singapore. Liquidity is supplied by Eurobond market makers, of which approximately 35 are registered with the International Capital Market Association (ICMA). ICMA is an association of banks and other financial institutions that provides a regulatory framework for international bond markets and that is behind much of the established uniform practices that are observed by all market participants in the Eurobond market.

The level of commitment to the different sectors of the market varies among market makers. The **bid–offer spread** or **bid–ask spread**, which reflects the prices at which dealers will buy from a customer (bid) and sell to a customer (offer or ask), is very often used as an indicator of liquidity. It can be as low as 5 bps for very liquid bond issues, such as issues of the World Bank, to no price quoted for illiquid issues. A reasonable spread is of the order of 10–12 bps, whereas an illiquid spread may be in excess of 50 bps. When there is no bid or offer price, the issue is completely illiquid for trading purposes.

Settlement is the process that occurs after the trade is made. The bonds are passed to the buyer and payment is received by the seller. Secondary market settlement for government and quasi-government bonds typically takes place on a $T + 1$ basis—that is, the day after the transaction date—whereas corporate bonds usually settle on a $T + 3$ basis. Cash settlement, in which trading and settlement occur the same day, is standard for some government and quasi-government bonds and for many money market trades. Trades clear within either or both of the two main clearing systems, Euroclear and Clearstream. Settlement occurs by means of a simultaneous exchange of bonds for cash on the books of the clearing system. An electronic bridge connecting Euroclear and Clearstream allows transfer of bonds from one system to the other, so it is not necessary to have accounts at both systems. Both systems operate on a paperless, computerized book-entry basis, although a bond issue is still represented by a physical document, the global note mentioned earlier. All participants in either system will have their own internal account set up, and they may also act as agent for buyers or sellers who do not possess an account.

EXAMPLE 3

1 Which of the following *best* describes a primary market for bonds? A market:

  A in which bonds are issued for the first time to raise capital.

  B that has a specific location where the trading of bonds takes place.

  C in which existing bonds are traded among individuals and institutions.

2 US Treasury bonds are typically sold to the public via a(n):

  A auction.

  B primary dealer.

  C secondary bond market.

3 In a single-price bond auction, an investor who places a competitive bid and specifies a rate that is above the rate determined at auction will *most likely*:

  A not receive any bonds.

  B receive the bonds at the rate determined at auction.

  C receive the bonds at the rate specified in the investor's competitive bid.

4 A bond purchased in a secondary market is *most likely* purchased from:

  A the bond's issuer.

  B the bond's lead underwriter.

  C another investor in the bond.

5 Corporate bonds will *most likely* settle on the:

  A trade date.

  B trade date plus one day.

  C trade date plus three days.

Solution to 1:

A is correct. Primary bond markets are markets in which bonds are issued for the first time to raise capital. B is incorrect because having a specific location where the trading of bonds takes place is not a requirement for a primary bond market. C is incorrect because a market in which existing bonds are traded among individuals and institutions is the definition of a secondary, not primary, market.

Solution to 2:

A is correct. US Treasury bonds are typically sold to the public via an auction. B is incorrect because primary dealers are often bidders in the auction; they are financial institutions that are active in trading US Treasury bonds. C is incorrect because any bond issue coming directly to the market is considered to be in the primary, not the secondary, market.

SOVEREIGN BONDS

4

National governments issue bonds primarily for fiscal reasons—to fund spending when tax revenues are insufficient to cover expenditures. To meet their spending goals, national governments issue bonds in various types and amounts. This section discusses bonds issued by national governments, often referred to as **sovereign bonds** or **sovereigns**.

4.1 Characteristics of Sovereign Bonds

Sovereign bonds denominated in local currency have different names in different countries. For example, they are named US Treasuries in the United States, Japanese government bonds (JGBs) in Japan, gilts in the United Kingdom, Bunds in Germany, and obligations assimilables du Trésor (OATs) in France. Some investors or market participants may refer to sovereign bonds as Treasury securities or Treasuries for short, on the principle that the national Treasury department is often in charge of managing a national government's funding needs.

Names may also vary depending on the original maturity of the sovereign bond. For example, US government bonds are named Treasury bills (T-bills) when the original maturity is one year or shorter, Treasury notes (T-notes) when the original maturity is longer than one year and up to 10 years, and Treasury bonds (T-bonds) when the original maturity is longer than 10 years; in Spain, the sovereigns issued by Tesoro Público are named letras del Tesoro, bonos del Estado, and obligaciones del Estado depending on the sovereign's original maturity, one year or shorter, longer than one year and up to five years, or longer than five years, respectively. Although very rare, some bonds, such as the consols in the United Kingdom, have no stated maturity date.

The majority of the trading in secondary markets is of sovereign securities that were most recently issued. These securities are called **on-the-run**. The latest sovereign bond issue for a given maturity is also referred to as a **benchmark issue** because it serves as a benchmark against which to compare bonds that have the same features (i.e., maturity, coupon type and frequency, and currency denomination) but that are issued by another type of issuer (e.g., non-sovereign, corporate). As a general rule, as sovereign securities age, they trade less frequently.

One salient difference between money market securities, such as T-bills, and capital market securities, such as T-notes and T-bonds, is the interest provision. As illustrated in Exhibit 6, T-bills are pure discount bonds; they are issued at a discount to par value and redeemed at par. The difference between the par value and the issue price is the interest paid on the borrowing. In contrast, capital market securities are typically coupon (or coupon-bearing) bonds; these securities make regular coupon payments and repay the par value at maturity. Bunds pay coupons annually, whereas US Treasuries, JGBs, gilts, and OATs make semi-annual coupon payments.

4.2 Credit Quality of Sovereign Bonds

Sovereign bonds are usually unsecured obligations of the sovereign issuer—that is, they are not backed by collateral but by the taxing authority of the national government. When a national government runs a budget surplus, excess tax revenues over expenditures is the primary source of funds for making interest payments and repaying the principal. In contrast, when a country runs a budget deficit, the source of the funds used for the payment of interest and repayment of principal comes from rolling over existing debt into new debt (refinancing).

Highly rated sovereign bonds denominated in local currency are virtually free of credit risk. Credit rating agencies assign ratings to sovereign bonds, and these ratings are called "sovereign ratings." The highest rating (i.e., highest credit quality and lowest credit risk) is AAA by S&P and Fitch and Aaa by Moody's. As of late 2012, only a handful of sovereign issuers were rated at this (theoretically) risk-free level by the three credit rating agencies, including Germany, Singapore, Switzerland, the Netherlands, and the United Kingdom. The global financial crisis that started in 2008 resulted in many national governments reaching potentially unsustainable levels of debt, with the pace of spending far exceeding tax revenues. Many of these national governments suffered downgrades from the AAA/Aaa level, including Ireland in 2009, Spain in 2010, and the United States, which was downgraded by S&P in 2011.

Credit rating agencies make a distinction between bonds issued in the sovereign's local currency and bonds issued in a foreign currency. In theory, a government can make interest payments and repay the principal by generating cash flows from its unlimited power (in the short run at least) to tax its citizens. A national government also has the ability to print its own currency, whereas it is restricted in being able to pay in a foreign currency only what it earns in exports or can exchange in financial markets. Thus, it is common to observe a higher credit rating for sovereign bonds issued in local currency than for those issued in a foreign currency. But there are limits to a government's ability to reduce the debt burden. As the sovereign debt crisis that followed the global financial crisis has shown, taxing citizens can only go so far in paying down debt before the taxation becomes an economic burden. Additionally, printing money only serves to weaken a country's currency relative to other currencies over time.

The national government of a country that has a strong domestic savings base has the luxury of being able to issue bonds in its local currency and sell them to domestic investors. If the local currency is liquid and freely traded, the sovereign issuer may also attract foreign investors who may want to hold that sovereign issuer's bonds and have exposure to that country's local currency. A national government may also issue in a foreign currency when there is demand for the sovereign issuer's bonds, but not necessarily in the sovereign's local currency. For example, demand from overseas investors has caused national governments such as Switzerland and Sweden to issue sovereign bonds in US dollars and euros. Emerging market countries may also have to issue in major currencies because international investors may be willing to accept the credit risk but not the foreign exchange (currency) risk associated with emerging market bonds. When a sovereign issuer raises debt in a foreign currency, it usually swaps the proceeds into its local currency.

4.3 Types of Sovereign Bonds

National governments issue different types of bonds, some of them paying a fixed rate of interest and others paying a floating rate, including inflation-linked bonds.

4.3.1 Fixed-Rate Bonds

Fixed-rate bonds (i.e., bonds that pay a fixed rate of interest) are by far the most common type of sovereign bond. National governments routinely issue two types of fixed-rate bonds: zero-coupon bonds (or pure discount bonds) and coupon bonds. A zero-coupon bond does not pay interest. Instead, it is issued at a discount to par value and redeemed at par at maturity. Coupon bonds are issued with a stated rate of interest and make interest payments periodically, such as semi-annually or annually. They have a terminal cash flow equal to the final interest payment plus the par value. As mentioned earlier, most sovereign bonds with an original maturity of one year or less are zero-coupon bonds, whereas bonds with an original maturity longer than one year are typically issued as coupon bonds.

4.3.2 Floating-Rate Bonds

The price of a bond changes in the opposite direction from the change in interest rates, a relationship that is fully explained in the reading on understanding the risk and return of fixed-income securities. Thus, investors who hold fixed-rate bonds are exposed to interest rate risk: As interest rates increase, bond prices decrease, which lowers the value of their portfolio. In response to public demand for less interest rate risk, some national governments around the world issue bonds with a floating rate of interest that resets periodically based on changes in the level of a reference rate such as Libor. Although interest rate risk still exists on floating-rate bonds, it is far less pronounced than that on fixed-rate bonds.

Examples of countries where the national government issues floating-rate bonds include Germany, Spain, and Belgium in developed markets and Brazil, Turkey, Mexico, Indonesia, and Poland in emerging markets. The largest sovereign issuers, such as the United States, Japan, and the United Kingdom, have never issued bonds whose coupon rate is tied to a reference rate. However, as of the time of this writing, the United States is contemplating adding such bonds to its range of debt offerings.

4.3.3 Inflation-Linked Bonds

Fixed-income investors are exposed to inflation risk. The cash flows of fixed-rate bonds are fixed by contract. If a particular country experiences an inflationary episode, the purchasing power of the fixed cash flows is eroded over time. Thus, to respond to the demand for less inflation risk, many national governments issue inflation-linked bonds or linkers, whose cash flows are adjusted for inflation. First issuers of inflation-linked bonds were the governments of Argentina, Brazil, and Israel. The United States introduced inflation-linked securities in January 1997, calling them Treasury Inflation-Protected Securities (TIPS). Other countries where the national government has issued inflation-linked bonds include the United Kingdom, Sweden, Australia, and Canada in developed markets and Brazil, South Africa, and Chile in emerging markets.

As explained in the reading on fixed-income securities, the index to which the coupon payments and/or principal repayments are linked is typically an index of consumer prices. Inflation-linked bonds can be structured a variety of ways: The inflation adjustment can be made via the coupon payments, the principal repayment, or both. In the United States, the index used is the Consumer Price Index for All Urban Consumers (CPI-U). In the United Kingdom, it is the Retail Price Index (RPI) (All Items). In France, there are two inflation-linked bonds with two different indices: the French consumer price index (CPI) (excluding tobacco) and the Eurozone's Harmonized Index of Consumer Prices (HICP) (excluding tobacco). Although linking the cash flow payments to a consumer price index reduces inflation risk, it does not necessarily eliminate the effect of inflation completely because the consumer price index may be an imperfect proxy for inflation.

EXAMPLE 4

1 Sovereign bonds with a maturity at issuance shorter than one year are *most likely*:

   A floating-rate bonds.

   B zero-coupon bonds.

   C coupon-bearing bonds.

2 Floating-rate bonds are issued by national governments as the *best* way to reduce:

   A credit risk.

   B inflation risk.

   C interest rate risk.

3 Sovereign bonds whose coupon payments and/or principal repayments are adjusted by a consumer price index are *most likely* known as:

   A linkers.

   B floaters.

   C consols.

Solution to 1:

B is correct. Most bonds issued by national governments with a maturity at issuance (original maturity) shorter than one year are zero-coupon bonds. A and C are incorrect because floating-rate bonds and coupon-bearing bonds are typically types of sovereign bonds with maturities longer than one year.

Solution to 2:

C is correct. The coupon rates of floating-rate bonds are reset periodically based on changes in the level of a reference rate such as Libor, which reduces interest rate risk. A is incorrect because credit risk, although low for sovereign bonds, cannot be reduced by linking the coupon rate to a reference rate. B is incorrect because although inflation risk is lower for floating-rate bonds than for fixed-rate bonds, floating-rate bonds are not as good as inflation-linked bonds to reduce inflation risk.

Solution to 3:

A is correct because sovereign bonds whose coupon payments and/or principal repayment are adjusted by a consumer price index are known as inflation-linked bonds or linkers. B is incorrect because floaters describe floating-rate bonds that have a coupon rate tied to a reference rate such as Libor. C is incorrect because consols are sovereign bonds with no stated maturity date issued by the UK government.

NON-SOVEREIGN GOVERNMENT, QUASI-GOVERNMENT, AND SUPRANATIONAL BONDS

5

This section covers the bonds issued by local governments and by government-related entities.

5.1 Non-Sovereign Bonds

Levels of government below the national level such as provinces, regions, states, and cities issue bonds called **non-sovereign government bonds** or **non-sovereign bonds**. These bonds are typically issued to finance public projects, such as schools, motorways, hospitals, bridges, and airports. The sources for paying interest and repaying the principal include the taxing authority of the local government, the cash flows of the project the bond issue is financing, or special taxes and fees established specifically for the purpose of making interest payments and principal repayments. Non-sovereign bonds are not necessarily guaranteed by the national government.

As mentioned in Section 2.1.7, bonds issued by state and local governments in the United States are known as municipal bonds, and they often offer income tax exemptions. In the United Kingdom, non-sovereign bonds are known as local authority bonds. Other non-sovereign bonds include those issued by state authorities such as the 16 *Lander* in Germany.

Credit ratings for non-sovereign bonds vary widely because of the differences in credit and collateral quality. Because default rates of non-sovereign bonds are historically low, they very often receive high credit ratings. However, non-sovereign bonds usually trade at a higher yield and lower price than sovereign bonds with similar characteristics. The additional yield depends on the credit quality and the liquidity of the bond issue: The higher the non-sovereign bond's credit quality and liquidity, the lower the additional yield.

5.2 Quasi-Government Bonds

National governments establish organizations that perform various functions for them. These organizations often have both public and private sector characteristics, but they are not actual governmental entities. They are referred to as quasi-government entities, although they take different names in different countries. These quasi-government entities often issue bonds to fund specific financing needs. These bonds are known as **quasi-government bonds** or **agency bonds**.

Examples of quasi-government entities include government-sponsored enterprises (GSEs) in the United States, such as the Federal National Mortgage Association ("Fannie Mae"), the Federal Home Loan Mortgage Corporation ("Freddie Mac"), and the Federal Home Loan Bank (FHLB). GSEs were among the largest issuers of bonds before the global financial crisis that started in 2008. Other examples of quasi-government entities that issue bonds include Hydro Quebec in Canada or the Japan Bank for International Cooperation (JBIC). In the case of JBIC's bonds, timely payments of interest and repayment of principal are guaranteed by the Japanese government. Most quasi-government bonds, however, do not offer an explicit guarantee by the national government, although investors often perceive an implicit guarantee.

Because a quasi-government entity typically does not have direct taxing authority, bonds are repaid from the cash flows generated by the entity or from the project the bond issue is financing. Quasi-government bonds may be backed by collateral, but this is not always the case. Quasi-government bonds are usually rated very high by the credit rating agencies because historical default rates are extremely low. Bonds that are guaranteed by the national government receive the highest ratings and trade at a lower yield and higher price than otherwise similar bonds that are not backed by the sovereign government's guarantee.

5.3 Supranational Bonds

A form of often highly rated bonds is issued by supranational agencies, also referred to as multilateral agencies. The most well-known supranational agencies are the International Bank for Reconstruction and Development (the World Bank), the International Monetary Fund (IMF), the European Investment Bank (EIB), the Asian Development Bank (ADB), and the African Development Bank (AFDB). Bonds issued by supranational agencies are called **supranational bonds**.

Supranational bonds are typically plain vanilla bonds, although floating-rate bonds and callable bonds are sometimes issued. Highly rated supranational agencies, such as the World Bank, frequently issue large-size bond issues that are often used as benchmarks issues when there is no liquid sovereign bond available.

EXAMPLE 5

1 Relative to sovereign bonds, non-sovereign bonds with similar characteristics *most likely* trade at a yield that is:
   A lower.
   B the same.
   C higher.
2 Bonds issued by a governmental agency are *most likely*:
   A repaid from the cash flows generated by the agency.
   B guaranteed by the national government that sponsored the agency.
   C backed by the taxing power of the national government that sponsored the agency.

Solution to 1:

C is correct. Non-sovereign bonds usually trade at a higher yield and lower price than sovereign bonds with similar characteristics. The higher yield is because of the higher credit risk associated with non-sovereign issuers relative to sovereign issuers, although default rates of local governments are historically low and their credit quality is usually high. The higher yield may also be a consequence of non-sovereign bonds being less liquid than sovereign bonds with similar characteristics.

Solution to 2:

A is correct. Most bonds issued by a governmental agency are repaid from the cash flows generated by the agency or from the project the bond issue is financing. B and C are incorrect because although some bonds issued by governmental agencies are guaranteed by the national government or are backed by the taxing power of the national government that sponsored the agency, bonds are most likely repaid first from the cash flows generated by the agency.

CORPORATE DEBT

6

Companies differ from governments and government-related entities in that their primary goal is profit; they must be profitable to stay in existence. Thus, profitability is an important consideration when companies make decisions, including financing decisions. Companies routinely raise debt as part of their overall capital structure, both to fund short-term spending needs (e.g., working capital) as well as long-term capital investments. We have so far focused on publicly issued debt, but loans from banks and other financial institutions are a significant part of the debt raised by companies. For example, it is estimated that European companies traditionally meet 70% of their borrowing needs from banks and only 30% from financial markets.[4] However, as banks have been deleveraging and reducing the amount of loans to companies following the global financial crisis that started in 2008, companies, in particular those with high credit quality, have turned to financial markets to issue bonds. They have been taking advantage of the low interest rate environment and the increased appetite of investors for corporate bonds.

6.1 Bank Loans and Syndicated Loans

A **bilateral loan** is a loan from a single lender to a single borrower. Companies routinely use bilateral loans from their banks, and these bank loans are governed by the bank loan documents. Bank loans are the primary source of debt financing for small and medium-size companies as well as for large companies in countries where bond markets are either under-developed or where most bond issuances are from government, government-related entities, and financial institutions. Access to bank loans depends not only on the characteristics and financial health of the company, but also on market conditions and bank capital availability.

A syndicated loan is a loan from a group of lenders, called the "syndicate," to a single borrower. A syndicated loan is a hybrid between relational lending and publicly traded debt. Syndicated loans are primarily originated by banks, and the loans are extended to companies but also to governments and government-related entities. The coordinator, or lead bank, originates the loan, forms the syndicate, and processes the payments. In addition to banks, a variety of lenders participate in the syndicate, such as pension funds, insurance companies, and hedge funds. Syndicated loans are a way for these institutional investors to participate in corporate lending while diversifying the credit risk among a group of lenders.

In recent years, a secondary market in syndicated loans has developed. These loans are often packaged and securitized, and the securitized instruments are then sold in secondary markets to investors. These securitized instruments are discussed in depth in a subsequent reading.

Most bilateral and syndicated loans are floating-rate loans, and the interest rate is based on a reference rate plus a spread. The reference rate may be Libor, a sovereign rate (e.g., the T-bill rate), or the prime lending rate, also called the "prime rate." The prime rate formerly reflected the interest rate at which banks lent to their most creditworthy customers, but it now tends to be driven by the overnight rate at which banks lend to each other. Bank loans can be customized to the borrower's needs. They can have different maturities, as well as different interest payment and principal repayment structures. The frequency of interest payments varies among bank loans. Some loans are bullet loans, in which the entire payment of principal occurs at maturity, and others are amortizing loans, in which the principal is repaid over time.

---

4 Neil O'Hara, "In or Out of MTNs?" *FTSE Global Markets*, no. 65 (October 2012):32–34.

For highly rated companies, both bilateral and syndicated loans can be more expensive than bonds issued in financial markets. Thus, companies often turn to money and capital markets to raise funds, which allows them to diversify their sources of financing.

6.2 Commercial Paper

Commercial paper is a short-term, unsecured promissory note issued in the public market or via a private placement that represents a debt obligation of the issuer. Commercial paper was first issued in the United States more than a century ago. It later appeared in the United Kingdom, in other European countries, and then in the rest of the world.

6.2.1 Characteristics of Commercial Paper

Commercial paper is a valuable source of flexible, readily available, and relatively low-cost short-term financing. It is a source of funding for working capital and seasonal demands for cash. It is also a source of **bridge financing**—that is, interim financing that provides funds until permanent financing can be arranged. Suppose a company wants to build a new distribution center in southeast China and wants to finance this investment with an issuance of long-term bonds. The market conditions for issuing long-term bonds may currently be volatile, which would translate into a higher cost of borrowing. Rather than issuing long-term bonds immediately, the company may opt to raise funds with commercial paper and wait for a more favorable environment in which to sell long-term bonds.

The largest issuers of commercial paper are financial institutions, but some non-financial companies are also regular issuers of commercial paper. Although the focus of this section is on corporate borrowers, sovereign governments and supranational agencies routinely issue commercial paper as well.

The maturity of commercial paper can range from overnight to one year, but a typical issue matures in less than three months.

6.2.2 Credit Quality of Commercial Paper

Traditionally, only the largest, most stable companies issued commercial paper. Although only the strongest, highest-rated companies issue low-cost commercial paper, issuers from across the risk spectrum can issue commercial paper with higher yields than higher-rated companies. Thus, investors in commercial paper are exposed to various levels of credit risk depending on the issuer's creditworthiness. Many investors perform their own credit analysis, but most investors also assess a commercial paper's credit quality by using the ratings provided by the credit rating agencies. Exhibit 7 presents the range of commercial paper ratings from the main credit rating agencies. Commercial paper rated adequate or above (shaded area of Exhibit 7) is called "prime paper," and it is typically considered investment grade by investors.

Exhibit 7	Commercial Paper Ratings		
Credit Quality	**Moody's**	**S&P**	**Fitch**
Superior	P1	A1+/A1	F1+/F1
Satisfactory	P2	A2	F2
Adequate	P3	A3	F3
Speculative	NP	B/C	F4
Defaulted	NP	D	F5

In most cases, maturing commercial paper is paid with the proceeds of new issuances of commercial paper, a practice referred to as "rolling over the paper." This practice creates a risk that the issuer will be unable to issue new paper at maturity, referred to as rollover risk. As a safeguard against rollover risk, the credit rating agencies require that commercial paper issuers secure **backup lines of credit** from banks. The purpose of the backup lines of credit is to ensure that the issuer will have access to sufficient liquidity to repay maturing commercial paper if rolling over the paper is not a viable option. This is why backup lines of credit are sometimes called "liquidity enhancement" or "backup liquidity lines." Issuers of commercial paper may be unable to roll over the paper as a result of either market-wide or company-specific events. For example, financial markets could be in the midst of a financial crisis that would make it difficult to roll over the paper. A company could also be experiencing some sort of financial distress such that it could only issue new commercial paper at significantly higher rates. In this case, the company could draw on its credit lines instead of rolling over its paper. Most commercial paper issuers maintain 100% backing, although some large, high credit quality issues carry less than 100% backing. Backup lines of credit typically contain a "material adverse change" provision that allows the bank to cancel the backup line of credit if the financial condition of the issuer deteriorates substantially.

Historically, defaults on commercial paper have been relatively rare, primarily because commercial paper has a short maturity. Each time existing paper matures, investors have the opportunity to assess the issuer's financial position, and they can refuse to buy the new paper if they estimate that the issuer's credit risk is too high. Thus, the commercial paper market is quicker in withdrawing financing when an issuer's credit quality deteriorates than markets for longer-term securities. This reduces the exposure of the commercial paper market to defaults. In addition, corporate managers realize that defaulting on commercial paper would prevent any future issuance of this valuable financing alternative.

The combination of short-dated maturity, relatively low credit risk, and a large number of issuers makes commercial paper attractive to a diverse range of institutional investors, including money market mutual funds, bank liquidity desks, local authorities, and institutional investors that have liquidity constraints. Most commercial paper investors hold their position to maturity. The result is little secondary market trading except for the largest issues. Investors who wish to sell commercial paper prior to maturity can either sell the paper back to the dealer, to another investor, or in some cases, directly back to the issuer.

The yield on commercial paper is higher than that on short-term sovereign bonds of the same maturity for two main reasons. First, commercial paper is exposed to credit risk unlike most highly rated sovereign bonds. Second, commercial paper markets are generally less liquid than short-term sovereign bond markets. Thus, investors require higher yields to compensate for the lower liquidity. In the United States, the yield on commercial paper also tends to be higher than that on short-term municipal bonds for tax reasons. Income generated by investments in commercial paper is subject to income taxes, whereas income from many municipal bonds is tax exempt. Thus, to attract taxable investors, bonds that are subject to income taxes must offer higher yields than those that are tax exempt.

6.2.3 *US Commercial Paper vs. Eurocommercial Paper*

The US commercial paper (USCP) market is the largest commercial paper market in the world, although there are other active commercial paper markets in other countries. Commercial paper issued in the international market is known as Eurocommercial paper (ECP). Although ECP is a similar instrument to USCP, there are some differences between the two. These differences are shown in Exhibit 8.

Exhibit 8	USCP vs. ECP	
Feature	**US Commercial Paper**	**Eurocommercial Paper**
Currency	US dollar	Any currency
Maturity	Overnight to 270 days[a]	Overnight to 364 days
Interest	Discount basis	Interest-bearing basis
Settlement	$T + 0$ (trade date)	$T + 2$ (trade date plus two days)
Negotiable	Can be sold to another party	Can be sold to another party

[a] In the United States, securities with an original maturity in excess of 270 days must be registered with the Securities and Exchange Commission (SEC). To avoid the time and expense associated with a SEC registration, issuers of US commercial paper rarely offer maturities longer than 270 days.

An important difference between USCP and ECP is related to the interest provision. USCP is typically issued on a discount basis—that is, USCP is issued at a discount to par value and pays full par value at maturity. The difference between the par value and the issue price is the interest paid on the borrowing. In contrast, ECP is usually issued at, and trades on, an interest-bearing or yield basis. In other words, the rate quoted on a trade of ECP is the actual interest rate earned on the investment, and the interest payment is made in addition to the par value at maturity. The distinction between the discount and the interest-bearing basis is illustrated in Exhibit 9. Some aspects of the calculation, such as the day count convention, are discussed in the introduction to fixed-income valuation reading.

Exhibit 9	

Interest Calculation: Discount vs. Interest-Bearing Basis

A US bank and a German industrial company both issue $50 million of 180-day, 5% commercial paper. The US bank issues its commercial paper domestically, and the German industrial company issues Eurocommercial paper.

US bank:

Issues $50,000,000 180-day USCP.

Interest is $1,250,000 [$50,000,000 × 0.05 × (180/360)]

Interest on USCP is on a discount basis. Proceeds received are $48,750,000 [$50,000,000 – $1,250,000].

At maturity, the bank repays the par value of $50,000,000.

German industrial company:

Issues $50,000,000 180-day ECP.

Interest is $1,250,000 [$50,000,000 × 0.05 × (180/360)].

Interest on ECP is on an interest-bearing basis. Proceeds received are the par value of $50,000,000.

At maturity, the company repays $51,250,000 [$50,000,000 + $1,250,000].

The amount of interest is the same for both companies. In the case of USCP, investors receive the interest by getting a discount on the par value when the commercial paper is issued. In the case of ECP, investors receive the interest by getting an additional payment (or add-on) to the par value when the commercial paper is repaid. However, note that the investors' return is not the same. Investors earn 2.56% on their 180-day investment in USCP ($1,250,000 ÷ $48,750,000) versus 2.50% on their 180-day investment in ECP ($1,250,000 ÷ $50,000,000).

Typical transaction sizes in ECP are also much smaller than in USCP, and it is difficult to place longer-term ECP with investors. The ECP market also exhibits less liquidity than the USCP market.

6.3 Corporate Notes and Bonds

Companies are active participants in global capital markets and regularly issue corporate notes and bonds. These securities can be placed directly with specific investors via private placements or sold in public securities markets. This section discusses various characteristics of corporate notes and bonds.

6.3.1 *Maturities*

There is no universally accepted taxonomy as to what constitutes short-, medium-, and long-term maturities. For our purposes, short term refers to original maturities of five years or less; intermediate term to original maturities longer than five years and up to 12 years; and long term to original maturities longer than 12 years. Those securities with maturities between 1 and 12 years are often considered notes, whereas securities with maturities greater than 12 years are considered bonds. It is not uncommon, however, to refer to bonds for all securities, irrespective of their original maturity.

In practice, most corporate bonds range in term to maturity between 1 and 30 years. In Europe, however, there are also bond issues with maturities of 40 and 50 years. In addition, during the 1990s a number of corporate bonds were issued in the United States with maturities of 100 years; these bonds are called "century bonds." The first century bond was issued by the Walt Disney Company in 1993 as part of its medium-term note program.

Medium-term note (MTN) is a misnomer. As the century bond example above illustrates, MTNs can have very long maturities. From the perspective of the issuer, the initial purpose of MTNs was to fill the funding gap between commercial paper and long-term bonds. It is for this reason that they are referred to as "medium term." The MTN market can be broken into three segments: short-term securities that carry floating or fixed rates, medium- to long-term securities that primarily bear a fixed rate of interest, and structured notes. MTNs have the unique characteristic of being securities that are offered continuously to investors by an agent of the issuer. This feature gives the borrower maximum flexibility for issuing securities on a continuous basis. Financial institutions are the primary issuers of MTNs, in particular short-term ones. Life insurance companies, pension funds, and banks are among the largest buyers of MTNs because they can customize the bond issue to their needs and stipulate the amount and characteristics of the securities they want to purchase. These investors are often willing to accept less liquidity than they would get with a comparable publicly issued bond because the yield is slightly higher. But the cost savings in registration and underwriting often makes MTNs a lower cost option for the issuer.

6.3.2 *Coupon Payment Structures*

Corporate notes and bonds have a range of coupon payment structures. Financial and non-financial companies issue conventional coupon bonds that pay a fixed periodic coupon during the bond's life. They also issue bonds for which the periodic coupon payments adjust to changes in market conditions and/or changes to the issuer's credit quality. Such bonds typically offer investors the opportunity to reduce their exposure to a particular type of risk. For example, FRNs, whose coupon payments adjust to changes in the level of market interest rates, are a way to limit interest rate risk; some of the inflation-linked bonds whose coupon payments adjust to changes in the level of a consumer price index offer a protection against inflation risk; credit-linked coupon bonds, whose coupon payments adjust to changes in the issuer's credit quality, are a way to reduce credit risk. Whether the periodic coupon is fixed or not, coupon payments can be made quarterly, semi-annually, or annually depending on the type of bond and where the bonds are issued and traded.

Other coupon payment structures exist. Zero-coupon bonds pay no coupon. Deferred coupon bonds pay no coupon initially, but then offer a higher coupon. Payment-in-kind (PIK) coupon bonds make periodic coupon payments, but not necessarily in cash; the issuer may pay interest in the form of securities, such as bonds or common shares. These types of coupon payment structures give issuers more flexibility regarding the servicing of their debt.

6.3.3 Principal Repayment Structures

Corporate note or bond issues have either a serial or a term maturity structure. With a **serial maturity structure**, the maturity dates are spread out during the bond's life; a stated number of bonds mature and are paid off each year before final maturity. With a **term maturity structure**, the bond's notional principal is paid off in a lump sum at maturity. Because there is no regular repayment of the principal outstanding throughout the bond's life, a term maturity structure carries more credit risk than a serial maturity structure.

A sinking fund arrangement is a way to reduce credit risk by making the issuer set aside funds over time to retire the bond issue. For example, a corporate bond issue may require a specified percentage of the bond's outstanding principal amount to be retired each year. The issuer may satisfy this requirement in one of two ways. The most common approach is for the issuer to make a random call for the specified percentage of bonds that must be retired and to pay the bondholders whose bonds are called the sinking fund price, which is typically par. Alternatively, the issuer can deliver bonds to the trustee with a total amount equal to the amount that must be retired. To do so, the issuer may purchase the bonds in the open market. The sinking fund arrangement on a term maturity structure accomplishes the same goal as the serial maturity structure—that is, both result in a portion of the bond issue being paid off each year. With a serial maturity structure, however, the bondholders know which bonds will mature and will thus be paid off each year. In contrast, the bonds retired annually with a sinking fund arrangement are designated by a random drawing.

6.3.4 Asset or Collateral Backing

Unlike most highly rated sovereign bonds, all corporate debt is exposed to varying degrees of credit risk. Thus, corporate debt is structured with this risk in mind. An important consideration for investors is seniority ranking—that is, the systematic way in which lenders are repaid if the issuer defaults. In the case of secured debt, there is some form of collateral pledged to ensure payment of the debt. In contrast, in the case of unsecured debt, claims are settled by the general assets of the company in accordance with the priority of payments that applies either legally or contractually and as described in the bond indenture. Within each category of debt (secured and unsecured), there are finer gradations of rankings, which are discussed in depth in the reading on fundamentals of credit analysis.

There is a wide range of bonds that are secured by some form of collateral. Companies that need to finance equipment or physical assets may issue equipment trust certificates. Corporate issuers also sell collateral trust bonds that are secured by securities, such as common shares, bonds, or other financial assets. Banks, particularly in Europe, may issue covered bonds, which are a debt obligation that is secured by a segregated pool of assets. Mortgage-backed securities and other asset-backed securities are also secured forms of debt.

Companies can and do default on their debt. Debt secured by collateral may still experience losses, but investors in secured debt usually fare better than in unsecured debt in bankruptcy proceedings. Investors who face a higher level of credit risk typically require a higher yield than investors exposed to very little credit risk.

6.3.5 *Contingency Provisions*

Contingency provisions are clauses in the indenture that provide the issuer or the bondholders rights that affect the disposal or redemption of the bond. The three commonly used contingency provisions are call, put, and conversion provisions.

Callable bonds give issuers the ability to retire debt prior to maturity. The most compelling reason for them to do so is to take advantage of lower borrowing rates. By calling the bonds before their maturity date, the issuer can substitute a new, lower cost bond issue for an older, higher cost one. In addition, companies may also retire debt to eliminate restrictive covenants or to alter their capital structure to improve flexibility. Because the call provision is a valuable option for the issuer, investors demand compensation ex ante (before investing in the bond). Thus, other things equal, investors require a higher yield (and thus pay a lower price) for a callable bond than for an otherwise similar non-callable bond.

Companies also issue putable bonds, which give the bondholders the right to sell the bond back to the issuer at a predetermined price on specified dates before maturity. Most putable bonds pay a fixed rate of interest, although some bonds may have step-up coupons that increase by specified margins at specified dates. Because the put provision is a valuable option for the bondholders, putable bonds offer a lower yield (and thus have a higher price) than otherwise similar non-putable bonds. The main corporate issuers of putable bonds are investment-grade companies. Putable bonds may offer them a cheaper way of raising capital, in particular if the company estimates that the benefit of a lower coupon outweighs the risk associated with the put provision.

A convertible bond is a hybrid security that lies on a continuum between debt and equity. It consists of a long position in an option-free bond and a conversion option that gives the bondholder the right to convert the bond into a specified number of shares of the issuer's common shares. From the point of view of the issuer, convertible bonds make it possible to raise funds that may not be possible without the incentive associated with the conversion option. The more common issuers of convertibles bonds are newer companies that have not established a presence in debt capital markets but who are able to present a more attractive package to institutional investors by including an equity upside potential. Established issuers of bonds may also prefer to issue convertible bonds because they are usually sold at a lower coupon rate than otherwise similar non-convertible bonds as a result of investors' attraction to the conversion provision. However, there is a potential equity dilution effect if the bonds are converted. From the investor's point of view, convertible bonds represent a means of accessing the equity upside potential of the issuer but at a lower risk–reward profile because there is the floor of the coupon payments in the meantime.

6.3.6 *Issuance, Trading, and Settlement*

In the era before electronic settlement, there were some differences in the processes of issuing and settling corporate bonds depending on where the securities were registered. This is no longer the case; the processes of issuing and settling bonds are now essentially the same globally. New corporate bond issues are usually sold to investors by investment banks acting as underwriters in the case of underwritten offerings or brokers in the case of best effort offerings. They are then settled via the local settlement system. These local systems typically possess a "bridge" to the two Eurobond systems, Euroclear and Clearstream. As for Eurobonds from the corporate sector, they are all issued, traded, and settled in the same way, irrespective of the issuer and its local jurisdiction.

Most bond prices are quoted in basis points. The vast majority of corporate bonds are traded over the counter through dealers who "make a market" in bonds and sell from their inventory. Dealers do not typically charge a commission or a transaction fee. Instead, they earn a profit from the bid–offer spread.

For corporate bonds, settlement differences exist primarily between new bond issues and the secondary trading of bonds. The issuing phase for an underwritten offering usually takes several days. Thus, settlement takes longer for new bond issued than for the secondary trading of bonds, for which settlement is typically on a $T + 3$ basis, although it can extend to $T + 7$ in some jurisdictions.

EXAMPLE 6

1 A loan made by a group of banks to a private company is *most likely*:

   A a bilateral loan.

   B a syndicated loan.

   C a private placement.

2 Which of the following statements relating to commercial paper is *most accurate*? Companies issue commercial paper:

   A only for funding working capital.

   B only as an interim source of financing.

   C both for funding working capital and as an interim source of funding.

3 Maturities of Eurocommercial paper range from:

   A overnight to three months.

   B overnight to one year.

   C three months to one year.

4 A bond issue that has a stated number of bonds that mature and are paid off each year before final maturity *most likely* has a:

   A term maturity.

   B serial maturity.

   C sinking fund arrangement.

Solution to 1:

B is correct. A loan from a group of lenders to a single borrower is a syndicated loan. A is incorrect because a bilateral loan is a loan from a single lender to a single borrower. C is incorrect because a private placement involves placing the debt issued by a borrower directly with a lender or a group of lenders. The fact that the borrower is a private company is irrelevant.

Solution to 2:

C is correct. Companies use commercial paper as a source of funding working capital and seasonal demand for cash, as well as an interim source of financing until permanent financing can be arranged.

Solution to 3:

B is correct. Eurocommercial paper ranges in maturity from overnight to 364 days.

Solution to 4:

B is correct. With a serial maturity structure, a stated number of bonds mature and are paid off each year before final maturity. A is incorrect because a bond issue with a term maturity structure is paid off in one lump sum at maturity. C is incorrect because a sinking fund arrangement, like a serial maturity structure, results in a portion of the bond issue being paid off every year. However, with a serial maturity structure, the bonds are paid off because the maturity dates are spread out during the life of the bond and the bonds that are retired are maturing; the bondholders know in advance which bonds will be retired. In contrast, the bonds retired annually with a sinking fund arrangement are designated by a random drawing.

SHORT-TERM FUNDING ALTERNATIVES AVAILABLE TO BANKS

7

Funding refers to the amount of money or resources necessary to finance some specific project or enterprise. Accordingly, funding markets are markets in which debt issuers borrow to meet their financial needs. Companies have a range of funding alternatives, including bank loans, commercial paper, notes, and bonds. Financial institutions such as banks have larger financing needs than non-financial companies because of the nature of their operations. This section discusses the additional funding alternatives that are available to them. The majority of these funding alternatives have short maturities.

Banks, such as deposit-taking (or depositary) institutions, typically have access to funds obtained from the retail market—that is, deposit accounts from their customers. However, it is quite common for banks to originate more loans than they have retail deposits. Thus, whenever the amount of retail deposits is insufficient to meet their financial needs, banks also need to raise funds from the wholesale market. Wholesale funds include central bank funds, interbank deposits, and certificates of deposit. In addition to filling the gaps between loans and deposits, banks raise wholesale funds to minimize their funding cost. At the margin, wholesale funds may be less expensive (in terms of interest expense) than deposit funding. Finally, financial institutions may raise wholesale funds as a balance sheet risk management tool to reduce interest rate risk, as discussed in Section 2.1.5.1.

7.1 Retail Deposits

One of the primary sources of funding for deposit-taking banks is their retail deposit base, which includes funds from both individual and commercial depositors. There are several types of retail deposit accounts. Demand deposits, also known as checking accounts, are available to customers "on demand." Depositors have immediate access to the funds in their deposit accounts and use the funds as a form of payment for transactions. Because the funds are available immediately, deposit accounts typically pay no interest. Savings accounts, in contrast, pay interest and allow depositors to accumulate wealth in a very liquid form. But savings accounts do not offer the same transactional convenience as demand deposits. Money market accounts were originally designed to compete with money market mutual funds. They offer money market rates of return and depositors can access funds at short or no notice. Thus, money market accounts are, for depositors, an intermediate between demand deposit and savings accounts.

7.2 Short-Term Wholesale Funds

Wholesale funds available for banks include central bank funds, interbank funds, and certificates of deposit.

7.2.1 Central Bank Funds

Many countries require deposit-taking banks to place a reserve balance with the national central bank. The reserve funds help to ensure sufficient liquidity should depositors require withdrawal of funds. When a bank cannot obtain short-term funding, most countries allow that bank to borrow from the central bank. In aggregate, the reserve funds act as a liquidity buffer providing comfort to depositors and investors that the central bank can act as lender of last resort.

Treatment of interest on reserve funds varies among countries, from a low interest payment, to no interest payment, to charges for keeping reserve funds. Additionally, there is an opportunity cost to the banks for holding reserves with the central bank in that these funds cannot be invested with higher interest or loaned out to consumers or commercial enterprises. Some banks have an excess over the minimum required funds to be held in reserve. At the same time, other banks are running short of required reserves. This imbalance is solved through the **central bank funds market**, which allows banks that have a surplus of funds to loan money to banks that need funds for maturities of up to one year. These funds are known as central bank funds and are called "overnight funds" when the maturity is one day and "term funds" when the maturity ranges from two days to one year. The interest rates at which central bank funds are bought (i.e., borrowed) and sold (i.e., lent) are short-term interest rates determined by the markets but influenced by the central bank's open market operations. These rates are termed the **central bank funds rates**.

In the United States, the central bank is the Federal Reserve (Fed). The central bank funds and funds rate are called Fed funds and Fed funds rates, respectively. Other short-term interest rates, such as the yields on Treasury bills, are highly correlated with the Fed funds rate. The most widely followed rate is known as the Fed funds effective rate, which is the volume-weighted average of rates for Fed fund trades arranged throughout the day by the major New York City brokers. Fed funds are traded between banks and other financial institutions globally and may be transacted directly or through money market brokers.

7.2.2 Interbank Funds

The interbank market is the market of loans and deposits between banks. The term to maturity of an interbank loan or deposit ranges from overnight to one year. The rate on an interbank loan or deposit can be quoted relative to a reference rate, such as an interbank offered rate or as a fixed interest rate. An interbank deposit is unsecured, so banks placing deposits with another bank need to have an interbank line of credit in place for that institution. Usually, a large bank will make a two-way price, indicating the rate at which it will lend funds and the rate at which it will borrow funds for a specific maturity, on demand. Interest on the deposit is payable at maturity. Much interbank dealing takes place on the Reuters electronic dealing system, so that the transaction is done without either party speaking to the other.

Because the market is unsecured, it is essentially based on confidence in the banking system. At times of stress, such as in the aftermath of the Lehman Brothers' bankruptcy in 2008, the market is prone to "dry up" as banks withdraw from funding other banks.

7.2.3 Large-Denomination Negotiable Certificates of Deposit

A **certificate of deposit** (CD) is an instrument that represents a specified amount of funds on deposit for a specified maturity and interest rate. CDs are an important source of funds for financial institutions. A CD may take one of two forms: non-negotiable or negotiable. If the CD is non-negotiable, the deposit plus the interest are paid to the initial depositor at maturity. A withdrawal penalty is imposed if the depositor withdraws funds prior to the maturity date.

Alternatively, a negotiable CD allows any depositor (initial or subsequent) to sell the CD in the open market prior to the maturity date. Negotiable CDs were introduced in the United States in the early 1960s when various types of deposits were constrained by interest rate ceilings. At the time, bank deposits were not an attractive investment because investors earned a below-market interest rate unless they were prepared to commit their capital for an extended period of time. The introduction of negotiable CDs enabled bank customers to buy a three-month or longer negotiable instrument yielding a market interest rate and to recover their investment by selling it in the market. This innovation helped banks increase the amount of funds raised in the money markets. It also fostered competition among deposit-taking institutions.

There are two types of negotiable CDs: large-denomination CDs and small-denomination CDs. Thresholds between small- and large-denomination CDs vary among countries. For example, in the United States, large-denomination CDs are usually issued in denominations of $1 million or more. Small-denomination CDs are a retail-oriented product, and they are of secondary importance as a funding alternative. Large-denomination CDs, in contrast, are an important source of wholesale funds and are typically traded among institutional investors.

Like other money market securities, CDs are available in domestic bond markets as well as in the Eurobond market. Most CDs have maturities shorter than one year and pay interest at maturity. CDs with longer maturities are called "term CDs."

Yields on CDs are driven primarily by the credit risk of the issuing bank and to a lesser extent by the term to maturity. The spread attributable to credit risk will vary with economic conditions and confidence in the banking system in general and in the issuing bank in particular. As with all debt instruments, spreads widen during times of financial turmoil as a result of an increase in risk aversion.

7.3 Repurchase and Reverse Repurchase Agreements

Repurchase agreements are another important source of funding not only for banks but also for other market participants. A **repurchase agreement** or **repo** is the sale of a security with a simultaneous agreement by the seller to buy the same security back from the purchaser at an agreed-on price and future date.[5] In practical terms, a repurchase agreement can be viewed as a collateralized loan in which the security sold and subsequently repurchased represents the collateral posted. One party is borrowing money and providing collateral for the loan at an interest rate that is typically lower than on an otherwise similar bank loan. The other party is lending money while accepting a security as collateral for the loan.

Repurchase agreements are a common source of money market funding for dealer firms in many countries. An active market in repurchase agreements underpins every liquid bond market. Financial and non-financial companies participate actively in the market as both sellers and buyers of collateral depending on their circumstances. Central banks are also active users of repurchase agreements in their daily open market operations; they either lend to the market to increase the supply of funds or withdraw surplus funds from the market.

---

5 Repurchase agreements can be structured such that the transaction is terminable on demand.

7.3.1 *Structure of Repurchase and Reverse Repurchase Agreements*

Suppose a government securities dealer purchases a 2.25% UK gilt that matures in three years. The dealer wants to fund the position overnight through the end of the next business day. The dealer could finance the transaction with its own funds, which is what other market participants, such as insurance companies or pension funds, may do in similar circumstances. But a securities dealer typically uses leverage (debt) to fund the position. Rather than borrowing from a bank, the dealer uses a repurchase agreement to obtain financing by using the gilt as collateral for the loan.

A repurchase agreement may be constructed as follows: The dealer sells the 2.25% UK gilt that matures in three years to a counterparty for cash today. At the same time, the dealer makes a promise to buy the same gilt the next business day for an agreed-on price. The price at which the dealer repurchases the gilt is known as the **repurchase price**. The date when the gilt is repurchased, the next business day in this example, is called the **repurchase date**. When the term of a repurchase agreement is one day, it is called an "overnight repo." When the agreement is for more than one day, it is called a "term repo." An agreement lasting until the final maturity date is known as a "repo to maturity."

As in any borrowing or lending transaction, the interest rate of the loan must be negotiated in the agreement. The interest rate on a repurchase agreement is called the **repo rate**. Several factors affect the repo rate:

- The *risk* associated with the collateral. Repo rates are typically lower for highly rated collaterals, such as highly rated sovereign bonds. They increase with the level of credit risk associated with the collateral underlying the transaction.

- The *term* of the repurchase agreement. Repo rates generally increase with maturity because long-term rates are typically higher than short-term rates in normal circumstances.

- The *delivery requirement* for the collateral. Repo rates are usually lower when delivery to the lender is required.

- The *supply and demand conditions* of the collateral. The more scarce a specific piece of collateral, the lower the repo rate against it because the borrower has a security that lenders of cash want for specific reasons, perhaps because the underlying issue is in great demand. The demand for such collateral means that it considered to be "on special." Collateral that is not special is known as "general collateral." The party that has a need for collateral that is on special is typically required to lend funds at a below-market repo rate to obtain the collateral.

- The *interest rates of alternative financing* in the money market.

The interest on a repurchase agreement is paid on the repurchase date—that is, at the termination of the agreement. Note that any coupon paid by the security during the repurchase agreement belongs to the seller of the security (i.e., the borrower of cash).

When a repurchase agreement is viewed through the lens of the cash lending counterparty, the transaction is referred to as a **reverse repurchase agreement** or **reverse repo**. In the above example, the counterparty agrees to buy the 2.25% UK gilt that matures in three years and promises to sell it back the next business day at the agreed-on price. The counterparty is making a collateralized loan to the dealer. Reverse repurchase agreements are very often used to borrow securities to cover short positions.

The question of whether a particular transaction is labeled a repurchase agreement or a reverse repurchase agreement depends on one's point of view. Standard practice is to view the transaction from the dealer's perspective. If the dealer is borrowing cash from a counterparty and providing securities as collateral, the transaction is termed a repurchase agreement. If the dealer is borrowing securities and lending cash to the counterparty, the transaction is termed a reverse repurchase agreement.

7.3.2 *Credit Risk Associated with Repurchase Agreements*

Each market participant in a repurchase agreement is exposed to the risk that the counterparty defaults, regardless of the collateral exchanged. Credit risk is present even if the collateral is a highly rated sovereign bond. Suppose that a dealer (i.e., the borrower of cash) defaults and is not in a position to repurchase the collateral on the specified repurchase date. The lender of funds takes possession of the collateral and retains any income owed to the borrower. The risk is that the price of the collateral has fallen following the inception of the repurchase agreement, causing the market value of the collateral to be lower than the unpaid repurchase price. Conversely, suppose the investor (i.e., the lender of cash) defaults and is unable to deliver the collateral on the repurchase date. The risk is that the price of the collateral has risen since the inception of the repurchase agreement, resulting in the dealer now holding an amount of cash lower than the market value of the collateral. In this case, the investor is liable for any excess of the price paid by the dealer for replacement of the securities over the repurchase price.

Although both parties to a repurchase agreement are subject to credit risk, the agreement is structured as if the lender of funds is the most vulnerable party. Specifically, the amount lent is lower than the collateral's market value. The difference between the market value of the security used as collateral and the value of the loan is known as the **repo margin**, although the term **haircut** is more commonly used, particularly in the United States. The repo margin allows for some worsening in market value, and thus provides the cash lender a margin of safety if the collateral's market value declines. Repo margins vary by transaction and are negotiated bilaterally between the counterparties. The level of margin is a function of the following factors:

- The *length* of the repurchase agreement. The longer the repurchase agreement, the higher the repo margin.
- The *quality* of the collateral. The higher the quality of the collateral, the lower the repo margin.
- The *credit quality* of the counterparty. The higher the creditworthiness of the counterparty, the lower the repo margin.
- The *supply and demand conditions* of the collateral. Repo margins are lower if the collateral is in short supply or if there is a high demand for it.

EXAMPLE 7

1. Which of the following are **not** considered wholesale funds?
   - **A** Interbank funds
   - **B** Central bank funds
   - **C** Repurchase agreements

2. For a deposit-taking bank, holding reserves with the national central bank is:
   - **A** a requirement.
   - **B** an opportunity cost.
   - **C** an opportunity to receive interest on excess funds.

3. A large-denomination negotiable certificate of deposit *most likely*:
   - **A** is traded in the open market.
   - **B** is purchased by retail investors.
   - **C** has a penalty for early withdrawal of funds.

4 From the dealer's viewpoint, a repurchase agreement is *best* described as a type of:

    A collateralized short-term lending.

    B collateralized short-term borrowing.

    C uncollateralized short-term borrowing.

5 The interest on a repurchase agreement is known as the:

    A repo rate.

    B repo yield.

    C repo margin.

6 The level of repo margin is higher:

    A the higher the quality of the collateral.

    B the higher the credit quality of the counterparty.

    C the longer the length of the repurchase agreement.

Solution to 1:

C is correct. Wholesale funds refer to the funds that financial institutions lend to and borrow from each other. They include central bank funds, interbank funds, and certificates of deposit. Although repurchase agreements are an important source of funding for banks, they are not considered wholesale funds.

Solution to 2:

B is correct. Funds held in reserve with the national central bank are an opportunity cost because they cannot be invested with higher interest or loaned out to consumers or commercial enterprises. A is incorrect because although many countries require deposit-taking banks to place a reserve balance with the national central bank, this is not always the case. C is incorrect because some central banks pay no interest on reserve funds, and sometimes even charge for keeping reserve funds.

Solution to 3:

A is correct. Large-denomination negotiable certificates of deposit (CDs) can be traded in the open market. B is incorrect because it is small-denomination, not large-denomination, negotiable CDs that are primarily purchased by retail investors. C is incorrect because it is non-negotiable, not negotiable, CDs that have a penalty for early withdrawal of funds.

Solution to 4:

B is correct. In a repurchase agreement, a security is sold with a simultaneous agreement by the seller to buy the same security back from the purchaser later at a higher price. Thus, a repurchase agreement is similar to a collateralized short-term borrowing in which the security sold and subsequently repurchased represents the collateral posted. A is incorrect because collateralized short-term lending is a description of a reverse repurchase agreement. C is incorrect because a repurchase agreement involves collateral. Thus, it is a collateralized, not uncollateralized, short-term borrowing.

Solution to 5:

A is correct. The repo rate is the interest rate on a repurchase agreement. B is incorrect because the interest on a repurchase agreement is known as the repo rate, not repo yield. C is incorrect because the repo margin refers to the difference between the market value of the security used as collateral and the value of the loan.

CONCLUSION AND SUMMARY

8

Debt financing is an important source of funds for governments, government-related entities, financial institutions, and non-financial companies. Well-functioning fixed-income markets help ensure that capital is allocated efficiently to its highest and best use globally. Important points include the following:

■ The most widely used ways of classifying fixed-income markets include the type of issuer; the bonds' credit quality, maturity, currency denomination, and type of coupon; and where the bonds are issued and traded.

■ Based on the type of issuer, the three major bond market sectors are the government and government-related sector, the corporate sector, and the structured finance sector. The major issuers of bonds globally are governments and financial institutions.

■ Investors make a distinction between investment-grade and high-yield bond markets based on the issuer's credit quality.

■ Money markets are where securities with original maturities ranging from overnight to one year are issued and traded, whereas capital markets are where securities with original maturities longer than one year are issued and traded.

■ The majority of bonds are denominated in either euros or US dollars.

■ Investors make a distinction between bonds that pay a fixed rate versus a floating rate of interest. The coupon rate of floating-rate bonds is expressed as a reference rate plus a spread. Interbank offered rates, such as Libor, are the most commonly used reference rates for floating-rate debt and other financial instruments.

■ Interbank offered rates are sets of rates that reflect the rates at which banks believe they could borrow unsecured funds from other banks in the interbank market for different currencies and different maturities.

■ Based on where the bonds are issued and traded, a distinction is made between domestic and international bond markets. The latter includes the Eurobond market, which falls outside the jurisdiction of any single country and is characterized by less reporting, regulatory and tax constraints. Investors also make a distinction between developed and emerging bond markets.

■ Fixed-income indices are used by investors and investment managers to describe bond markets or sectors and to evaluate performance of investments and investment managers.

■ The largest investors in bonds include central banks; institutional investors, such as pension funds, some hedge funds, charitable foundations and endowments, insurance companies, and banks; and retail investors.

■ Primary markets are markets in which issuers first sell bonds to investors to raise capital. Secondary markets are markets in which existing bonds are subsequently traded among investors.

- There are two mechanisms for issuing a bond in primary markets: a public offering, in which any member of the public may buy the bonds, or a private placement, in which only an investor or small group of investors may buy the bonds either directly from the issuer or through an investment bank.

- Public bond issuing mechanisms include underwritten offerings, best effort offerings, shelf registrations, and auctions.

- When an investment bank underwrites a bond issue, it buys the entire issue and takes the risk of reselling it to investors or dealers. In contrast, in a best efforts offering, the investment bank serves only as a broker and sells the bond issue only if it is able to do so. Underwritten and best effort offerings are frequently used in the issuance of corporate bonds.

- The underwriting process typically includes six phases: the determination of the funding needs, the selection of the underwriter, the structuring and announcement of the bond offering, pricing, issuance, and closing.

- A shelf registration is a method for issuing securities in which the issuer files a single document with regulators that describes a range of future issuances.

- An auction is a public offering method that involves bidding, and that is helpful in providing price discovery and in allocating securities. It is frequently used in the issuance of sovereign bonds.

- Most bonds are traded in over-the-counter (OTC) markets, and institutional investors are the major buyers and sellers of bonds in secondary markets.

- Sovereign bonds are issued by national governments primarily for fiscal reasons. They take different names and forms depending on where they are issued, their maturities, and their coupon types. Most sovereign bonds are fixed-rate bonds, although some national governments also issue floating-rate bonds and inflation-linked bonds.

- Local governments, quasi-government entities, and supranational agencies issue bonds, which are named non-sovereign, quasi-government, and supranational bonds, respectively.

- Companies raise debt in the form of bilateral loans, syndicated loans, commercial paper, notes, and bonds.

- Commercial paper is a short-term unsecured security that is used by companies as a source of short-term and bridge financing. Investors in commercial paper are exposed to credit risk, although defaults are rare. Many issuers roll over their commercial paper on a regular basis.

- Corporate bonds and notes take different forms depending on the maturities, coupon payment, and principal repayment structures. Important considerations also include collateral backing and contingency provisions.

- Medium-term notes are securities that are offered continuously to investors by an agent of the issuer. They can have short-term or long-term maturities.

- Financial institutions have access to additional sources of funds, such as retail deposits, central bank funds, interbank funds, large-denomination negotiable certificates of deposit, and repurchase agreements.

- A repurchase agreement is similar to a collateralized loan. It involves the sale of a security (the collateral) with a simultaneous agreement by the seller (the borrower) to buy the same security back from the purchaser (the lender) at an agreed-on price in the future. Repurchase agreements are a common source of funding for dealer firms and are also used to borrow securities to implement short positions.

PRACTICE PROBLEMS

1   In most countries, the bond market sector with the smallest amount of bonds outstanding is *most likely* the:

   A   government sector.

   B   financial corporate sector.

   C   non-financial corporate sector.

2   The distinction between investment grade debt and non-investment grade debt is *best* described by differences in:

   A   tax status.

   B   credit quality.

   C   maturity dates.

3   A bond issued internationally, outside the jurisdiction of the country in whose currency the bond is denominated, is *best* described as a:

   A   Eurobond.

   B   foreign bond.

   C   municipal bond.

4   Compared with developed markets bonds, emerging markets bonds *most likely*:

   A   offer lower yields.

   B   exhibit higher risk.

   C   benefit from lower growth prospects.

5   With respect to floating-rate bonds, a reference rate such as the London inter-bank offered rate (Libor) is *most likely* used to determine the bond's:

   A   spread.

   B   coupon rate.

   C   frequency of coupon payments.

6   Which of the following statements is *most accurate*? An interbank offered rate:

   A   is a single reference rate.

   B   applies to borrowing periods of up to 10 years.

   C   is used as a reference rate for interest rate swaps.

7   An investment bank that underwrites a bond issue *most likely*:

   A   buys and resells the newly issued bonds to investors or dealers.

   B   acts as a broker and receives a commission for selling the bonds to investors.

   C   incurs less risk associated with selling the bonds than in a best efforts offering.

8   In major developed bond markets, newly issued sovereign bonds are *most* often sold to the public via a(n):

   A   auction.

   B   private placement.

   C   best efforts offering.

This question set was developed by Michael Whitehurst, CFA (San Diego, CA, USA). Copyright © 2013 by CFA Institute.

9 A mechanism by which an issuer may be able to offer additional bonds to the general public without preparing a new and separate offering circular *best* describes:

A the grey market.

B a shelf registration.

C a private placement.

10 Which of the following statements related to secondary bond markets is *most accurate*?

A Newly issued corporate bonds are issued in secondary bond markets.

B Secondary bond markets are where bonds are traded between investors.

C The major participants in secondary bond markets globally are retail investors.

11 A bond market in which a communications network matches buy and sell orders initiated from various locations is *best* described as an:

A organized exchange.

B open market operation.

C over-the-counter market.

12 A liquid secondary bond market allows an investor to sell a bond at:

A the desired price.

B a price at least equal to the purchase price.

C a price close to the bond's fair market value.

13 Sovereign bonds are *best* described as:

A bonds issued by local governments.

B secured obligations of a national government.

C bonds backed by the taxing authority of a national government.

14 Agency bonds are issued by:

A local governments.

B national governments.

C quasi-government entities.

15 The type of bond issued by a multilateral agency such as the International Monetary Fund (IMF) is *best* described as a:

A sovereign bond.

B supranational bond.

C quasi-government bond.

16 Which of the following statements relating to commercial paper is *most accurate*?

A There is no secondary market for trading commercial paper.

B Only the strongest, highly rated companies issue commercial paper.

C Commercial paper is a source of interim financing for long-term projects.

17 Eurocommerical paper is *most likely*:

A negotiable.

B denominated in euro.

C issued on a discount basis.

18 When issuing debt, a company may use a sinking fund arrangement as a means of reducing:

   A   credit risk.

   B   inflation risk.

   C   interest rate risk.

19 Which of the following is a source of wholesale funds for banks?

   A   Demand deposits

   B   Money market accounts

   C   Negotiable certificates of deposit

20 A characteristic of negotiable certificates of deposit is:

   A   they are mostly available in small denominations.

   B   they can be sold in the open market prior to maturity.

   C   a penalty is imposed if the depositor withdraws funds prior to maturity.

21 A repurchase agreement is *most* comparable to a(n):

   A   interbank deposit.

   B   collateralized loan.

   C   negotiable certificate of deposit.

22 The repo margin on a repurchase agreement is *most likely* to be lower when:

   A   the underlying collateral is in short supply.

   B   the maturity of the repurchase agreement is long.

   C   the credit risk associated with the underlying collateral is high.

SOLUTIONS

1 C is correct. In most countries, the largest issuers of bonds are the national and local governments as well as financial institutions. Thus, the bond market sector with the smallest amount of bonds outstanding is the non-financial corporate sector.

2 B is correct. The distinction between investment grade and non-investment grade debt relates to differences in credit quality, not tax status or maturity dates. Debt markets are classified based on the issuer's creditworthiness as judged by the credit ratings agencies. Ratings of Baa3 or above by Moody's Investors Service or BBB– or above by Standard & Poor's and Fitch Ratings are considered investment grade, whereas ratings below these levels are referred to as non-investment grade (also called high yield, speculative, or junk).

3 A is correct. Eurobonds are issued internationally, outside the jurisdiction of any single country. B is incorrect because foreign bonds are considered international bonds, but they are issued in a specific country, in the currency of that country, by an issuer domiciled in another country. C is incorrect because municipal bonds are US domestic bonds issued by a state or local government.

4 B is correct. Many emerging countries lag developed countries in the areas of political stability, property rights, and contract enforcement. Consequently, emerging market bonds usually exhibit higher risk than developed markets bonds. A is incorrect because emerging markets bonds typically offer higher (not lower) yields than developed markets bonds to compensate investors for the higher risk. C is incorrect because emerging markets bonds usually benefit from higher (not lower) growth prospects than developed markets bonds.

5 B is correct. The coupon rate of a floating-rate bond is expressed as a reference rate plus a spread. Different reference rates are used depending on where the bond is issued and its currency denomination, but one of the most widely used set of reference rates is Libor. A and C are incorrect because a bond's spread and frequency of coupon payments are typically set when the bond is issued and do not change during the bond's life.

6 C is correct. Interbank offered rates are used as reference rates not only for floating-rate bonds, but also for other debt instruments including mortgages, derivatives such as interest rate and currency swaps, and many other financial contracts and products. A and B are incorrect because an interbank offered rate such as Libor or Euribor is a set of reference rates (not a single reference rate) for different borrowing periods of up to one year (not 10 years).

7 A is correct. In an underwritten offering (also called firm commitment offering), the investment bank (called the underwriter) guarantees the sale of the bond issue at an offering price that is negotiated with the issuer. Thus, the underwriter takes the risk of buying the newly issued bonds from the issuer, and then reselling them to investors or to dealers who then sell them to investors. B and C are incorrect because the bond issuing mechanism where an investment bank acts as a broker and receives a commission for selling the bonds to investors, and incurs less risk associated with selling the bonds, is a best efforts offering (not an underwritten offering).

8 A is correct. In major developed bond markets, newly issued sovereign bonds are sold to the public via an auction. B and C are incorrect because sovereign bonds are rarely issued via private placements or best effort offerings.

9 B is correct. A shelf registration allows certain authorized issuers to offer additional bonds to the general public without having to prepare a new and separate offering circular. The issuer can offer multiple bond issuances under the same master prospectus, and only has to prepare a short document when additional bonds are issued. A is incorrect because the grey market is a forward market for bonds about to be issued. C is incorrect because a private placement is a non-underwritten, unregistered offering of bonds that are not sold to the general public but directly to an investor or a small group of investors.

10 B is correct. Secondary bond markets are where bonds are traded between investors. A is incorrect because newly issued bonds (whether from corporate issuers or other types of issuers) are issued in primary (not secondary) bond markets. C is incorrect because the major participants in secondary bond markets globally are large institutional investors and central banks (not retail investors).

11 C is correct. In over-the-counter (OTC) markets, buy and sell orders are initiated from various locations and then matched through a communications network. Most bonds are traded in OTC markets. A is incorrect because on organized exchanges, buy and sell orders may come from anywhere, but the transactions must take place at the exchange according to the rules imposed by the exchange. B is incorrect because open market operations refer to central bank activities in secondary bond markets. Central banks buy and sell bonds, usually sovereign bonds issued by the national government, as a means to implement monetary policy.

12 C is correct. Liquidity in secondary bond markets refers to the ability to buy or sell bonds quickly at prices close to their fair market value. A and B are incorrect because a liquid secondary bond market does not guarantee that a bond will sell at the price sought by the investor, or that the investor will not face a loss on his or her investment.

13 C is correct. Sovereign bonds are usually unsecured obligations of the national government issuing the bonds; they are not backed by collateral, but by the taxing authority of the national government. A is incorrect because bonds issued by local governments are non-sovereign (not sovereign) bonds. B is incorrect because sovereign bonds are typically unsecured (not secured) obligations of a national government.

14 C is correct. Agency bonds are issued by quasi-government entities. These entities are agencies and organizations usually established by national governments to perform various functions for them. A and B are incorrect because local and national governments issue non-sovereign and sovereign bonds, respectively.

15 B is correct. The IMF is a multilateral agency that issues supranational bonds. A and C are incorrect because sovereign bonds and quasi-government bonds are issued by national governments and by entities that perform various functions for national governments, respectively.

16 C is correct. Companies use commercial paper not only as a source of funding working capital and seasonal demand for cash, but also as a source of interim financing for long-term projects until permanent financing can be arranged. A is incorrect because there is a secondary market for trading commercial paper, although trading is limited except for the largest issues. B is incorrect because commercial paper is issued by companies across the risk spectrum, although only the strongest, highly rated companies issue *low-cost* commercial paper.

17 A is correct. Commercial paper, whether US commercial paper or Eurocommercial paper, is negotiable—that is, investors can buy and sell commercial paper on secondary markets. B is incorrect because Eurocommercial paper can be denominated in any currency. C is incorrect because Eurocommercial paper is more frequently issued on an interest-bearing (or yield) basis than on a discount basis.

18 A is correct. A sinking fund arrangement is a way to reduce credit risk by making the issuer set aside funds over time to retire the bond issue. B and C are incorrect because a sinking fund arrangement has no effect on inflation risk or interest rate risk.

19 C is correct. Wholesale funds available for banks include central bank funds, interbank funds, and negotiable certificates of deposit. A and B are incorrect because demand deposits (also known as checking accounts) and money market accounts are retail deposits (not wholesale funds).

20 B is correct. A negotiable certificate of deposit (CD) allows any depositor (initial or subsequent) to sell the CD in the open market prior to maturity. A is incorrect because negotiable CDs are mostly available in large (not small) denominations. Large-denomination negotiable CDs are an important source of wholesale funds for banks, whereas small-denomination CDs are not. C is incorrect because a penalty is imposed if the depositor withdraws funds prior to maturity for non-negotiable (instead of negotiable) CDs.

21 B is correct. A repurchase agreement (repo) can be viewed as a collateralized loan where the security sold and subsequently repurchased represents the collateral posted. A and C are incorrect because interbank deposits and negotiable certificates of deposit are unsecured deposits—that is, there is no collateral backing the deposit.

22 A is correct. The repo margin (the difference between the market value of the underlying collateral and the value of the loan) is a function of the supply and demand conditions of the collateral. The repo margin is typically lower if the underlying collateral is in short supply or if there is a high demand for it. B and C are incorrect because the repo margin is usually higher (not lower) when the maturity of the repurchase agreement is long and when the credit risk associated with the underlying collateral is high.

Introduction to Fixed-Income Valuation

by James F. Adams, PhD, CFA, and Donald J. Smith, PhD

LEARNING OUTCOMES

Mastery	The candidate should be able to:
☐	**a.** calculate a bond's price given a market discount rate;
☐	**b.** identify the relationships among a bond's price, coupon rate, maturity, and market discount rate (yield-to-maturity);
☐	**c.** define spot rates and calculate the price of a bond using spot rates;
☐	**d.** describe and calculate the flat price, accrued interest, and the full price of a bond;
☐	**e.** describe matrix pricing;
☐	**f.** calculate and interpret yield measures for fixed-rate bonds, floating-rate notes, and money market instruments;
☐	**g.** define and compare the spot curve, yield curve on coupon bonds, par curve, and forward curve;
☐	**h.** define forward rates and calculate spot rates from forward rates, forward rates from spot rates, and the price of a bond using forward rates;
☐	**i.** compare, calculate, and interpret yield spread measures.

INTRODUCTION

1

Globally, the fixed-income market is a key source of financing for businesses and governments. In fact, the total market value outstanding of corporate and government bonds is significantly larger than that of equity securities. Similarly, the fixed-income market, which is also called the debt market or bond market, represents a significant investing opportunity for institutions as well as individuals. Pension funds, mutual funds, insurance companies, and sovereign wealth funds, among others, are major fixed-income investors. Retirees who desire a relatively stable income stream often hold fixed-income securities. Clearly, understanding how to value fixed-income securities is important to investors, issuers, and financial analysts. This reading focuses on the valuation of traditional (option-free) fixed-rate bonds, although other debt securities, such as floating-rate notes and money market instruments, are also covered.

Section 2 describes and illustrates basic bond valuation, which includes pricing a bond using a market discount rate for each of the future cash flows and pricing a bond using a series of spot rates. Valuation using spot rates allows for each future cash flow to be discounted at a rate associated with its timing. This valuation methodology for future cash flows has applications well beyond the fixed-income market. Relationships among a bond's price, coupon rate, maturity, and market discount rate (yield-to-maturity) are also described and illustrated.

Section 3 describes how bond prices and yields are quoted and calculated in practice. When bonds are actively traded, investors can observe the price and calculate various yield measures. However, these yield measures differ by the type of bond. In practice, different measures are used for fixed-rate bonds, floating-rate notes, and money market instruments. When a bond is not actively traded, matrix pricing is often used to estimate the value based on comparable securities.

Section 4 addresses the maturity or term structure of interest rates. This discussion involves an analysis of yield curves, which illustrates the relationship between yields-to-maturity and times-to-maturity on bonds with otherwise similar characteristics. Various types of yield curves are described.

Section 5 focuses on yield spreads over benchmark interest rates. When investors want relatively higher yields, they have to be prepared to bear more risk. Yield spreads are measures of how much additional yield over the benchmark security (usually a government bond) investors expect for bearing additional risk. A summary of key points and practice problems conclude the reading.

2   BOND PRICES AND THE TIME VALUE OF MONEY

Bond pricing is an application of discounted cash flow analysis. The complexity of the pricing depends on the particular bond's features and rate (or rates) used to do the discounting. This section starts with using a single discount factor for all future cash flows and concludes with the most general approach to bond valuation. The general approach to bond valuation is to use a series of spot rates that correspond to the timing of the future cash flows.

2.1 Bond Pricing with a Market Discount Rate

On a traditional (option-free) fixed-rate bond, the promised future cash flows are a series of coupon interest payments and repayment of the full principal at maturity. The coupon payments are on regularly scheduled dates, for example, an annual payment bond might pay interest on 15 June of each year for five years. The final coupon typically is paid together with the full principal on the maturity date. The price of the bond at issuance is the present value of the promised cash flows. The **market discount rate** is used in the time-value-of-money calculation to obtain the present value. The market discount rate is the rate of return required by investors given the risk of the investment in the bond. It is also called the **required yield**, or the **required rate of return**.

For example, suppose the coupon rate on a bond is 4% and the payment is made once a year. If the time-to-maturity is five years and the market discount rate is 6%, the price of the bond is 91.575 per 100 of **par value**. The par value is the amount of principal on the bond.

$$\frac{4}{(1.06)^1} + \frac{4}{(1.06)^2} + \frac{4}{(1.06)^3} + \frac{4}{(1.06)^4} + \frac{104}{(1.06)^5} =$$
$$3.774 + 3.560 + 3.358 + 3.168 + 77.715 = 91.575$$

The final cash flow of 104 is the redemption of principal (100) plus the coupon payment for that date (4). The price of the bond is the sum of the present values of the five cash flows. The price per 100 of par value may be interpreted as the percentage of par value. If the par value is USD100,000, the coupon payments are USD4,000 each year and the price of the bond is USD91,575. Its price is 91.575% of par value. This bond is described as trading at a **discount** because the price is below par value.

Suppose that another five-year bond has a coupon rate of 8% paid annually. If the market discount rate is again 6%, the price of the bond is 108.425.

$$\frac{8}{(1.06)^1} + \frac{8}{(1.06)^2} + \frac{8}{(1.06)^3} + \frac{8}{(1.06)^4} + \frac{108}{(1.06)^5} =$$
$$7.547 + 7.120 + 6.717 + 6.337 + 80.704 = 108.425$$

This bond is trading at a **premium** because its price is above par value.

If another five-year bond pays a 6% annual coupon and the market discount rate still is 6%, the bond would trade at par value.

$$\frac{6}{(1.06)^1} + \frac{6}{(1.06)^2} + \frac{6}{(1.06)^3} + \frac{6}{(1.06)^4} + \frac{106}{(1.06)^5} =$$
$$5.660 + 5.340 + 5.038 + 4.753 + 79.209 = 100.000$$

The coupon rate indicates the amount the issuer promises to pay the bondholders each year in interest. The market discount rate reflects the amount investors need to receive in interest each year in order to pay full par value for the bond. Therefore, assuming that these three bonds have the same risk, which is consistent with them having the same market discount rate, the 4% bond offers a "deficient" coupon rate. The amount of the discount below par value is the present value of the deficiency, which is 2% of par value each year. The present value of the deficiency, discounted using the market discount rate, is –8.425.

$$\frac{-2}{(1.06)^1} + \frac{-2}{(1.06)^2} + \frac{-2}{(1.06)^3} + \frac{-2}{(1.06)^4} + \frac{-2}{(1.06)^5} = -8.425$$

The price of the 4% coupon bond is 91.575 (= 100 – 8.425). In the same manner, the 8% bond offers an "excessive" coupon rate given the risk because investors require only 6%. The amount of the premium is the present value of the excess cash flows, which is +8.425. The price of the 8% bond is 108.425 (= 100 + 8.425).

These examples demonstrate that the price of a fixed-rate bond, relative to par value, depends on the relationship of the coupon rate to the market discount rate. Here is a summary of the relationships:

■ When the coupon rate is less than the market discount rate, the bond is priced at a discount below par value.

■ When the coupon rate is greater than the market discount rate, the bond is priced at a premium above par value.

■ When the coupon rate is equal to the market discount rate, the bond is priced at par value.

At this point, it is assumed that the bond is priced on a coupon payment date. If the bond is between coupon payment dates, the price paid will include accrued interest, which is interest that has been earned but not yet paid. Accrued interest is discussed in detail in Section 3.1.

Equation 1 is a general formula for calculating a bond price given the market discount rate:

$$PV = \frac{PMT}{\left(1 + r\right)^1} + \frac{PMT}{\left(1 + r\right)^2} + \cdots + \frac{PMT + FV}{\left(1 + r\right)^N} \qquad (1)$$

where

PV = present value, or the price of the bond
PMT = coupon payment per period
FV = future value paid at maturity, or the par value of the bond
r = market discount rate, or required rate of return per period
N = number of evenly spaced periods to maturity

The examples so far have been for an annual payment bond, which is the convention for most European bonds. Asian and North American bonds generally make semiannual payments, and the stated rate is the annual coupon rate. Suppose the coupon rate on a bond is stated to be 8% and the payments are made twice a year (semiannually) on 15 June and 15 December. For each 100 in par value (FV = 100), the coupon payment per period is 4 (PMT = 4). If there are three years to maturity, there are six evenly spaced semiannual periods (N = 6). If the market discount rate is 3% per semiannual period (r = 0.03), the price of the bond is 105.417 per 100 of par value.

$$\frac{4}{\left(1.03\right)^1} + \frac{4}{\left(1.03\right)^2} + \frac{4}{\left(1.03\right)^3} + \frac{4}{\left(1.03\right)^4} + \frac{4}{\left(1.03\right)^5} + \frac{104}{\left(1.03\right)^6} = 105.417$$

If the actual par value of the bond investment is in Singapore dollars—for instance, SGD 100,000—the price is SGD 105,417. This bond is trading at a premium above par value because the coupon rate of 4% *per period* is greater than the market discount rate of 3% *per period*. Usually, those interest rates are annualized by multiplying the rate per period by the number of periods in a year. Therefore, an equivalent statement is that the bond is priced at a premium because its stated *annual* coupon rate of 8% is greater than the stated *annual* market discount rate of 6%. Interest rates, unless stated otherwise, are typically quoted as annual rates.

EXAMPLE 1

Bonds Trading at a Discount, at a Premium, and at Par

Identify whether each of the following bonds is trading at a discount, at par value, or at a premium. Calculate the prices of the bonds per 100 in par value using Equation 1. If the coupon rate is deficient or excessive compared with the market discount rate, calculate the amount of the deficiency or excess per 100 of par value.

Bond	Coupon Payment per Period	Number of Periods to Maturity	Market Discount Rate per Period
A	2	6	3%
B	6	4	4%
C	5	5	5%
D	0	10	2%

Solutions:

Bond A

$$\frac{2}{(1.03)^1} + \frac{2}{(1.03)^2} + \frac{2}{(1.03)^3} + \frac{2}{(1.03)^4} + \frac{2}{(1.03)^5} + \frac{102}{(1.03)^6} = 94.583$$

Bond A is trading at a discount. Its price is below par value because the coupon rate per period (2%) is less than the required yield per period (3%). The deficiency per period is the coupon rate minus the market discount rate, times the par value: $(0.02 - 0.03) \times 100 = -1$. The present value of deficiency is -5.417, discounted using the required yield (market discount rate) per period.

$$\frac{-1}{(1.03)^1} + \frac{-1}{(1.03)^2} + \frac{-1}{(1.03)^3} + \frac{-1}{(1.03)^4} + \frac{-1}{(1.03)^5} + \frac{-1}{(1.03)^6} = -5.417$$

The amount of the deficiency can be used to calculate the price of the bond; the price is 94.583 (= 100 − 5.417).

Bond B

$$\frac{6}{(1.04)^1} + \frac{6}{(1.04)^2} + \frac{6}{(1.04)^3} + \frac{106}{(1.04)^4} = 107.260$$

Bond B is trading at a premium because the coupon rate per period (6%) is greater than the market discount rate per period (4%). The excess per period is the coupon rate minus market discount rate, times the par value: $(0.06 - 0.04) \times 100 = +2$. The present value of excess is $+7.260$, discounted using the required yield per period.

$$\frac{2}{(1.04)^1} + \frac{2}{(1.04)^2} + \frac{2}{(1.04)^3} + \frac{2}{(1.04)^4} = 7.260$$

The price of the bond is 107.260 (= 100 + 7.260).

Bond C

$$\frac{5}{(1.05)^1} + \frac{5}{(1.05)^2} + \frac{5}{(1.05)^3} + \frac{5}{(1.05)^4} + \frac{105}{(1.05)^5} = 100.000$$

Bond C is trading at par value because the coupon rate is equal to the market discount rate. The coupon payments are neither excessive nor deficient given the risk of the bond.

Bond D

$$\frac{100}{(1.02)^{10}} = 82.035$$

Bond D is a zero-coupon bond, which always will trade at a discount below par value (as long as the required yield is greater than zero). The deficiency in the coupon payments is -2 per period: $(0 - 0.02) \times 100 = -2$.

$$\frac{-2}{(1.02)^1} + \frac{-2}{(1.02)^2} + \frac{-2}{(1.02)^3} + \frac{-2}{(1.02)^4} + \frac{-2}{(1.02)^5} +$$

$$\frac{-2}{(1.02)^6} + \frac{-2}{(1.02)^7} + \frac{-2}{(1.02)^8} + \frac{-2}{(1.02)^9} + \frac{-2}{(1.02)^{10}} = -17.965$$

The price of the bond is 82.035 (= 100 − 17.965).

2.2 Yield-to-Maturity

If the market price of a bond is known, Equation 1 can be used to calculate its **yield to maturity** (sometimes called the redemption yield or yield-to-redemption). The yield-to-maturity is the internal rate of return on the cash flows—the uniform interest rate such that when the future cash flows are discounted at that rate, the sum of the present values equals the price of the bond. It is the *implied* market discount rate.

The yield-to-maturity is the rate of return on the bond to an investor given three critical assumptions:

1 The investor holds the bond to maturity.

2 The issuer makes all of the coupon and principal payments in the full amount on the scheduled dates. Therefore, the yield-to-maturity is the *promised* yield—the yield assuming the issuer does not default on any of the payments.

3 The investor is able to reinvest coupon payments at that same yield. This is a characteristic of an internal rate of return.

For example, suppose that a four-year, 5% annual coupon payment bond is priced at 105 per 100 of par value. The yield-to-maturity is the solution for the rate, r, in this equation:

$$105 = \frac{5}{(1+r)^1} + \frac{5}{(1+r)^2} + \frac{5}{(1+r)^3} + \frac{105}{(1+r)^4}$$

Solving by trial-and-error search, or using the time-value-of-money keys on a financial calculator, obtains the result that $r = 0.03634$. The bond trades at a premium because its coupon rate (5%) is greater than the yield that is required by investors (3.634%).

Yields-to-maturity do not depend on the actual amount of par value in a fixed-income portfolio. For example, suppose a Japanese institutional investor owns a three-year, 2.5% semiannual payment bond having a par value of JPY100 million. The bond currently is priced at JPY98,175,677. The yield per semiannual period can be obtained by solving this equation for r:

$$98.175677 = \frac{1.25}{(1+r)^1} + \frac{1.25}{(1+r)^2} + \frac{1.25}{(1+r)^3} + \frac{1.25}{(1+r)^4} + \frac{1.25}{(1+r)^5} + \frac{101.25}{(1+r)^6}$$

The yield per semiannual period turns out to be 1.571% ($r = 0.01571$), which can be annualized to be 3.142% ($0.01571 \times 2 = 0.03142$). In general, a three-year, 2.5% semiannual bond for *any* amount of par value has an annualized yield-to-maturity of 3.142% if it is priced at 98.175677% of par value.

EXAMPLE 2

Yields-to-Maturity for a Premium, Discount, and Zero-Coupon Bond

Calculate the yields-to-maturity for the following bonds. The prices are stated per 100 of par value.

Bond	Coupon Payment per Period	Number of Periods to Maturity	Price
A	3.5	4	103.75
B	2.25	6	96.50
C	0	60	22.375

Solutions:

Bond A

$$103.75 = \frac{3.5}{(1+r)^1} + \frac{3.5}{(1+r)^2} + \frac{3.5}{(1+r)^3} + \frac{103.5}{(1+r)^4}, \quad r = 0.02503$$

Bond A is trading at a premium, so its yield-to-maturity per period (2.503%) must be lower than its coupon rate per period (3.5%).

Bond B

$$96.50 = \frac{2.25}{(1+r)^1} + \frac{2.25}{(1+r)^2} + \frac{2.25}{(1+r)^3} + \frac{2.25}{(1+r)^4} +$$

$$\frac{2.25}{(1+r)^5} + \frac{102.25}{(1+r)^6}, \quad r = 0.02894$$

Bond B is trading at a discount, so the yield-to-maturity per period (2.894%) must be higher than the coupon rate per period (2.25%).

Bond C

$$22.375 = \frac{100}{(1+r)^{60}}, \quad r = 0.02527$$

Bond C is a zero-coupon bond trading at a significant discount below par value. Its yield-to-maturity is 2.527% per period.

2.3 Relationships between the Bond Price and Bond Characteristics

The price of a fixed-rate bond will change whenever the market discount rate changes. Four relationships about the change in the bond price given the market discount rate are

1   The bond price is inversely related to the market discount rate. When the market discount rate increases, the bond price decreases (the inverse effect).

2   For the same coupon rate and time-to-maturity, the percentage price change is greater (in absolute value, meaning without regard to the sign of the change) when the market discount rate goes down than when it goes up (the convexity effect).

3   For the same time-to-maturity, a lower-coupon bond has a greater percentage price change than a higher-coupon bond when their market discount rates change by the same amount (the coupon effect).

4   Generally, for the same coupon rate, a longer-term bond has a greater percentage price change than a shorter-term bond when their market discount rates change by the same amount (the maturity effect).

Exhibit 1 illustrates these relationships using nine annual coupon payment bonds. The bonds have different coupon rates and times-to-maturity but otherwise are the same in terms of risk. The coupon rates are 10%, 20%, and 30% for bonds having 10, 20, and 30 years to maturity. At first, the bonds are all priced at a market discount rate of 20%. Equation 1 is used to determine the prices. Then the market discount rate is decreased by 1 percentage point, from 20% to 19%, and next, it is increased from 20% to 21%.

				Discount Rates Go Down		Discount Rates Go Up	
Bond	**Coupon Rate**	**Maturity**	**Price at 20%**	**Price at 19%**	**% Change**	**Price at 21%**	**% Change**
A	10.00%	10	58.075	60.950	4.95%	55.405	−4.60%
B	20.00%	10	100.000	104.339	4.34%	95.946	−4.05%
C	30.00%	10	141.925	147.728	4.09%	136.487	−3.83%
D	10.00%	20	51.304	54.092	5.43%	48.776	−4.93%
E	20.00%	20	100.000	105.101	5.10%	95.343	−4.66%
F	30.00%	20	148.696	156.109	4.99%	141.910	−4.56%
G	10.00%	30	50.211	52.888	5.33%	47.791	−4.82%
H	20.00%	30	100.000	105.235	5.23%	95.254	−4.75%
I	30.00%	30	149.789	157.581	5.20%	142.716	−4.72%

Exhibit 1   Relationships between Bond Prices and Bond Characteristics

The first relationship is that the bond price and the market discount rate move inversely. All bond prices in Exhibit 1 go up when the rates go down from 20% to 19%, and all prices go down when the rates go up from 20% to 21%. This happens because of the fixed cash flows on a fixed-rate bond. The numerators in Equation 1 do not change when the market discount rate in the denominators rises or falls. Therefore, the price (PV) moves inversely with the market discount rate (r).

The second relationship reflects the convexity effect. In Exhibit 1, the percentage price changes are calculated using this equation:

$$\% \text{ Change} = \frac{\text{New price} - \text{Old price}}{\text{Old price}}$$

For example, when the market discount rate falls on Bond A, the price rises from 58.075 to 60.950. The percentage price increase is 4.95%.

$$\% \text{ Change} = \frac{60.950 - 58.075}{58.075} = 0.0495$$

For each bond, the percentage price increases are greater in *absolute value* than the percentage price decreases. This implies that the relationship between bond prices and the market discount rate is not linear; instead, it is curved. It is described as being "convex." The convexity effect is shown in Exhibit 2 for a 10%, 10-year bond.

Exhibit 2   The Convex Relationship between the Market Discount Rate and the Price of a 10-Year, 10% Annual Coupon Payment Bond

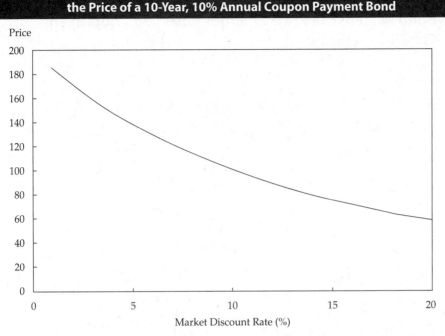

The third relationship is the coupon effect. Consider Bonds A, B, and C, which have 10 years to maturity. For both the decrease and increase in the yield-to-maturity, Bond A has a larger percentage price change than Bond B, and Bond B has a larger change than C. The same pattern holds for the 20-year and 30-year bonds. Therefore, lower-coupon bonds have more price volatility than higher-coupon bonds, other things being equal.

The fourth relationship is the maturity effect. Compare the results for Bonds A and D, for Bonds B and E, and for Bonds C and F. The 20-year bonds have greater percentage price changes than the 10-year bonds for either an increase or a decrease in the market discount rate. In general, longer-term bonds have more price volatility than shorter-term bonds, other things being equal.

There are exceptions to the maturity effect. That is why the word "generally" appears in the statement of the relationship at the beginning of this section. Compare the results in Exhibit 1 for Bonds D and G, for Bonds E and H, and for Bonds F and I. For the higher-coupon bonds trading at a premium, Bonds F and I, the usual property holds—the 30-year bonds have greater percentage price changes than the 20-year bonds. The same pattern holds for Bonds E and H, which are priced initially at par value. The exception is illustrated in the results for Bonds D and G, which are priced at a discount because the coupon rate is lower than the market discount rate. The 20-year, 10% bond has a greater percentage price change than the 30-year, 10% bond. Exceptions to the maturity effect are rare in practice. They occur only for low-coupon (but not zero-coupon), long-term bonds trading at a discount. The maturity effect always holds on zero-coupon bonds, as it does for bonds priced at par value or at a premium above par value.

One final point to note in Exhibit 1 is that Bonds B, E, and H, which have coupon rates of 20%, all trade at par value when the market discount rate is 20%. A bond having a coupon rate equal to the market discount rate is priced at par value on a coupon payment date, regardless of the number of years to maturity.

Bond Percentage Price Changes Based on Coupon and Time-to-Maturity

An investor is considering the following six annual coupon payment government bonds:

Bond	Coupon Rate	Time-to-Maturity	Yield-to-Maturity
A	0%	2 years	5.00%
B	5%	2 years	5.00%
C	8%	2 years	5.00%
D	0%	4 years	5.00%
E	5%	4 years	5.00%
F	8%	4 years	5.00%

1 Based on the relationships between bond prices and bond characteristics, which bond will go up in price the *most* on a percentage basis if all yields go down from 5.00% to 4.90%?

2 Based on the relationships between the bond prices and bond characteristics, which bond will go down in price the *least* on a percentage basis if all yields go up from 5.00% to 5.10%?

Solution to 1:

Bond D will go up in price the most on a percentage basis because it has the lowest coupon rate (the coupon effect) and the longer time-to-maturity (the maturity effect). There is no exception to the maturity effect in these bonds because there are no low-coupon bonds trading at a discount.

Solution to 2:

Bond C will go down in price the least on a percentage basis because it has the highest coupon rate (the coupon effect) and the shorter time-to-maturity (the maturity effect). There is no exception to the maturity effect because Bonds C and F are priced at a premium above par value.

Exhibit 2 demonstrates the impact on a bond price assuming the time-to-maturity does not change. It shows an *instantaneous* change in the market discount rate from one moment to the next.

But bond prices change as time passes even if the market discount rate remains the same. As time passes, the bondholder comes closer to receiving the par value at maturity. The **constant-yield price trajectory** illustrates the change in the price of a fixed-income bond over time. This trajectory shows the "pull to par" effect on the price of a bond trading at a premium or a discount to par value. If the issuer does not default, the price of a bond approaches par value as its time-to-maturity approaches zero.

Exhibit 3 shows the constant-yield price trajectories for 4% and 12% annual coupon payment, 10-year bonds. Both bonds have a market discount rate of 8%. The 4% bond's initial price is 73.160 per 100 of par value. The price increases each year and approaches par value as the maturity date nears. The 12% bond's initial price is 126.840, and it decreases each year, approaching par value as the maturity date nears. Both prices are "pulled to par."

Exhibit 3	Constant-Yield Price Trajectories for 4% and 12% Annual Coupon Payment, 10-Year Bonds at a Market Discount Rate of 8%

Discount Bond	73.160	75.012	77.013	79.175	81.508	84.029	86.751	89.692	92.867	96.296	100.00
Premium Bond	126.84	124.98	122.98	120.82	118.49	115.97	113.24	110.30	107.13	103.70	100.00

2.4 Pricing Bonds with Spot Rates

When a fixed-rate bond is priced using the market discount rate, the same discount rate is used for each cash flow. A more fundamental approach to calculate the price of a bond is to use a sequence of market discount rates that correspond to the cash flow dates. These market discount rates are called **spot rates**. Spot rates are yields-to-maturity on zero-coupon bonds maturing at the date of each cash flow. Sometimes these are called "zero rates." Bond price (or value) determined using the spot rates is sometimes referred to as the bond's "no-arbitrage value." If a bond's price differs from its no-arbitrage value, an arbitrage opportunity exists in the absence of transaction costs.

Suppose that the one-year spot rate is 2%, the two-year spot rate is 3%, and the three-year spot rate is 4%. Then, the price of a three-year bond that makes a 5% annual coupon payment is 102.960.

$$\frac{5}{(1.02)^1} + \frac{5}{(1.03)^2} + \frac{105}{(1.04)^3} =$$
$$4.902 + 4.713 + 93.345 = 102.960$$

This three-year bond is priced at a premium above par value, so its yield-to-maturity must be less than 5%. Using Equation 1, the yield-to-maturity is 3.935%.

$$102.960 = \frac{5}{(1+r)^1} + \frac{5}{(1+r)^2} + \frac{105}{(1+r)^3}, \quad r = 0.03935$$

When the coupon and principal cash flows are discounted using the yield-to-maturity, the same price is obtained.

$$\frac{5}{(1.03935)^1} + \frac{5}{(1.03935)^2} + \frac{105}{(1.03935)^3} =$$
$$4.811 + 4.629 + 93.520 = 102.960$$

Notice that the present values of the individual cash flows discounted using spot rates differ from those using the yield-to-maturity. The present value of the first coupon payment is 4.902 when discounted at 2%, but it is 4.811 when discounted at 3.935%. The present value of the final cash flow, which includes the redemption of principal, is 93.345 at 4% and 93.520 at 3.935%. Nevertheless, the sum of the present values using either approach is 102.960.

Equation 2 is a general formula for calculating a bond price given the sequence of spot rates:

$$PV = \frac{PMT}{(1 + Z_1)^1} + \frac{PMT}{(1 + Z_2)^2} + \cdots + \frac{PMT + FV}{(1 + Z_N)^N} \tag{2}$$

where

Z_1 = spot rate, or the zero-coupon yield, or zero rate, for Period 1

Z_2 = spot rate, or the zero-coupon yield, or zero rate, for Period 2

Z_N = spot rate, or the zero-coupon yield, or zero rate, for Period N

EXAMPLE 4

Bond Prices and Yields-to-Maturity Based on Spot Rates

Calculate the price (per 100 of par value) and the yield-to-maturity for a four-year, 3% annual coupon payment bond given the following two sequences of spot rates.

Time-to-Maturity	Spot Rates A	Spot Rates B
1 year	0.39%	4.08%
2 years	1.40%	4.01%
3 years	2.50%	3.70%
4 years	3.60%	3.50%

Solution:

Spot Rates A

$$\frac{3}{(1.0039)^1} + \frac{3}{(1.0140)^2} + \frac{3}{(1.0250)^3} + \frac{103}{(1.0360)^4} =$$
$$2.988 + 2.918 + 2.786 + 89.412 = 98.104$$

Given spot rates A, the four-year, 3% bond is priced at 98.104.

$$98.104 = \frac{3}{(1 + r)^1} + \frac{3}{(1 + r)^2} + \frac{3}{(1 + r)^3} + \frac{103}{(1 + r)^4}, \quad r = 0.03516$$

The yield-to-maturity is 3.516%.

Spot Rates B

$$\frac{3}{(1.0408)^1} + \frac{3}{(1.0401)^2} + \frac{3}{(1.0370)^3} + \frac{103}{(1.0350)^4} =$$
$$2.882 + 2.773 + 2.690 + 89.759 = 98.104$$

$$98.104 = \frac{3}{(1+r)^1} + \frac{3}{(1+r)^2} + \frac{3}{(1+r)^3} + \frac{103}{(1+r)^4}, \quad r = 0.03516$$

Given spot rates B, the four-year, 3% bond is again priced at 98.104 to yield 3.516%.

This example demonstrates that two very different sequences of spot rates can result in the same bond price and yield-to-maturity. Spot rates A are increasing for longer maturities, whereas spot rates B are decreasing.

PRICES AND YIELDS: CONVENTIONS FOR QUOTES AND CALCULATIONS

3

When investors purchase shares, they pay the quoted price. For bonds, however, there can be a difference between the quoted price and the price paid. This section explains why this difference occurs and how to calculate the quoted price and the price that will be paid. It also describes how prices are estimated for bonds that are not actively traded, and demonstrates how yield measures are calculated for fixed-rate bonds, floating-rate notes, and money market instruments.

3.1 Flat Price, Accrued Interest, and the Full Price

When a bond is between coupon payment dates, its price has two parts: the **flat price** (PV^{Flat}) and the **accrued interest** (AI). The sum of the parts is the **full price** (PV^{Full}), which also is called the invoice or "dirty" price. The flat price, which is the full price minus the accrued interest, is also called the quoted or "clean" price.

$$PV^{Full} = PV^{Flat} + AI \tag{3}$$

The flat price usually is quoted by bond dealers. If a trade takes place, the accrued interest is added to the flat price to obtain the full price paid by the buyer and received by the seller on the **settlement date**. The settlement date is when the bond buyer makes cash payment and the seller delivers the security.

The reason for using the flat price for quotation is to avoid misleading investors about the market price trend for the bond. If the full price were to be quoted by dealers, investors would see the price rise day after day even if the yield-to-maturity did not change. That is because the amount of accrued interest increases each day. Then, after the coupon payment is made, the quoted price would drop dramatically. Using the flat price for quotation avoids that misrepresentation. It is the flat price that is "pulled to par" along the constant-yield price trajectory shown in Exhibit 3.

Accrued interest is the proportional share of the next coupon payment. Assume that the coupon period has "T" days between payment dates and that "t" days have gone by since the last payment. The accrued interest is calculated using Equation 4:

$$AI = \frac{t}{T} \times PMT \tag{4}$$

where

t = number of days from the last coupon payment to the settlement date

T = number of days in the coupon period

t/T = fraction of the coupon period that has gone by since the last payment

PMT = coupon payment per period

Notice that the accrued interest part of the full price does not depend on the yield-to-maturity. Therefore, it is the flat price that is affected by a market discount rate change.

There are different conventions used in bond markets to count days. The two most common day-count conventions are actual/actual and 30/360. For the actual/actual method, the actual number of days is used, including weekends, holidays, and leap days. For example, a semiannual payment bond pays interest on 15 May and 15 November of each year. The accrued interest for settlement on 27 June would be the actual number of days between 15 May and 27 June (t = 43 days) divided by the actual number of days between 15 May and 15 November (T = 184 days), times the coupon payment. If the stated coupon rate is 4.375%, the accrued interest is 0.511209 per 100 of par value.

$$AI = \frac{43}{184} \times \frac{4.375}{2} = 0.511209$$

Day-count conventions vary from market to market. However, actual/actual is most common for government bonds.

The 30/360 day-count convention often is used on corporate bonds. It *assumes* that each month has 30 days and that a full year has 360 days. Therefore, for this method, there are assumed to be 42 days between 15 May and 27 June: 15 days between 15 May and 30 May and 27 days between 1 June and 27 June. There are assumed to be 180 days in the six-month period between 15 May and 15 November. The accrued interest on a 4.375% semiannual payment corporate bond is 0.510417 per 100 of par value.

$$AI = \frac{42}{180} \times \frac{4.375}{2} = 0.510417$$

The full price of a fixed-rate bond between coupon payments given the market discount rate per period (r) can be calculated with Equation 5:

$$PV^{Full} = \frac{PMT}{(1+r)^{1-t/T}} + \frac{PMT}{(1+r)^{2-t/T}} + \cdots + \frac{PMT + FV}{(1+r)^{N-t/T}} \qquad \text{(5)}$$

This is very similar to Equation 1. The difference is that the next coupon payment (PMT) is discounted for the remainder of the coupon period, which is $1 - t/T$. The second coupon payment is discounted for that fraction plus another full period, $2 - t/T$.

Equation 5 is simplified by multiplying the numerator and denominator by the expression $(1 + r)^{t/T}$. The result is Equation 6:

$$PV^{Full} = \left[\frac{PMT}{(1+r)^1} + \frac{PMT}{(1+r)^2} + \cdots + \frac{PMT + FV}{(1+r)^N} \right] \times (1+r)^{t/T} \qquad \text{(6)}$$
$$= PV \times (1+r)^{t/T}$$

An advantage to Equation 6 is that PV, the expression in the brackets, is easily obtained using the time-value-of-money keys on a financial calculator because there are N evenly spaced periods. PV here is identical to Equation 1 and is not the same as PV^{Flat}.

For example, consider a 5% semiannual coupon payment government bond that matures on 15 February 2024. Accrued interest on this bond uses the actual/actual day-count convention. The coupon payments are made on 15 February and 15 August of each year. The bond is to be priced for settlement on 14 May 2015. That date is 88 days into the 181-day period. There are actually 88 days from the last coupon on 15 February to 14 May and 181 days between 15 February and the next coupon on 15 August. The annual yield-to-maturity is stated to be 4.80%. That corresponds to a market discount rate of 2.40% per semiannual period. As of the beginning of the coupon period on 15 February 2015, there would be 18 evenly spaced semiannual periods until maturity. The first step is to solve for PV using Equation 1, whereby PMT = 2.5, N = 18, FV = 100, and r = 0.0240.

$$PV = \frac{2.5}{(1.0240)^1} + \frac{2.5}{(1.0240)^2} + \cdots + \frac{102.5}{(1.0240)^{18}} = 101.447790$$

The price of the bond would be 101.447790 per 100 of par value if its yield-to-maturity is 2.40% per period on the last coupon payment date. This is not the actual price for the bond on that date. It is a "what-if" price using the required yield that corresponds to the settlement date of 14 May 2015.

Equation 6 can be used to get the full price for the bond.

$$PV^{Full} = 101.447790 \times (1.0240)^{88/181} = 102.624323$$

The full price is 102.624323 per 100 of par value. The accrued interest is 1.215470 per 100 of par value.

$$AI = \frac{88}{181} \times 2.5 = 1.215470$$

The flat price is 101.408853 per 100 of par value.[1]

$$PV^{Flat} = PV^{Full} - AI = 102.624323 - 1.215470 = 101.408853$$

EXAMPLE 5

Calculating the Full Price, Accrued Interest, and Flat Price for a Bond

A 6% German corporate bond is priced for settlement on 18 June 2015. The bond makes semiannual coupon payments on 19 March and 19 September of each year and matures on 19 September 2026. The corporate bond uses the 30/360 day-count convention for accrued interest. Calculate the full price, the accrued interest, and the flat price per EUR100 of par value for three stated annual yields-to-maturity: (A) 5.80%, (B) 6.00%, and (C) 6.20%.

Solution:

Given the 30/360 day-count convention assumption, there are 89 days between the last coupon on 19 March 2015 and the settlement date on 18 June 2015 (11 days between 19 March and 30 March, plus 60 days for the full months of April and May, plus 18 days in June). Therefore, the fraction of the coupon period that has gone by is assumed to be 89/180. At the beginning of the period, there are 11.5 years (and 23 semiannual periods) to maturity.

(A) *Stated annual yield-to-maturity of 5.80%, or 2.90% per semiannual period:*

The price at the beginning of the period is 101.661589 per 100 of par value.

$$PV = \frac{3}{(1.0290)^1} + \frac{3}{(1.0290)^2} + \cdots + \frac{103}{(1.0290)^{23}} = 101.661589$$

The full price on 18 June is EUR103.108770.

$$PV^{Full} = 101.661589 \times (1.0290)^{89/180} = 103.108770$$

The accrued interest is EUR1.483333, and the flat price is EUR101.625437.

---

1 Microsoft Excel users can obtain the flat price using the PRICE financial function: PRICE ("5/14/2015," "2/15/2024," 0.05, 0.0480, 100, 2, 1). The inputs are the settlement date, maturity date, annual coupon rate as a decimal, annual yield-to-maturity as a decimal, par value, number of periods in the year, and the code for the day-count (0 for 30/360, 1 for actual/actual).

$$AI = \frac{89}{180} \times 3 = 1.4833333$$

$$PV^{Flat} = 103.108770 - 1.483333 = 101.625437$$

(B) *Stated annual yield-to-maturity of 6.00%, or 3.00% per semiannual period:*

The price at the beginning of the period is par value, as expected, because the coupon rate and the market discount rate are equal.

$$PV = \frac{3}{(1.0300)^1} + \frac{3}{(1.0300)^2} + \cdots + \frac{103}{(1.0300)^{23}} = 100.000000$$

The full price on 18 June is EUR101.472251.

$$PV^{Full} = 100.000000 \times (1.0300)^{89/180} = 101.472251$$

The accrued interest is EUR1.483333, and the flat price is EUR99.988918.

$$AI = \frac{89}{180} \times 3 = 1.4833333$$

$$PV^{Flat} = 101.472251 - 1.483333 = 99.988918$$

The flat price of the bond is a little below par value, even though the coupon rate and the yield-to-maturity are equal, because the accrued interest does not take into account the time value of money. The accrued interest is the interest earned by the owner of the bond for the time between the last coupon payment and the settlement date, 1.483333 per 100 of par value. However, that interest income is not received until the next coupon date. In theory, the accrued interest should be the *present value* of 1.483333. In practice, however, accounting and financial reporting need to consider issues of practicality and materiality. For those reasons, the calculation of accrued interest in practice neglects the time value of money. Therefore, compared to theory, the reported accrued interest is a little "too high" and the flat price is a little "too low." The full price, however, is correct because it is the sum of the present values of the future cash flows, discounted using the market discount rate.

(C) *Stated annual yield-to-maturity of 6.20%, or 3.10% per semiannual period:*

The price at the beginning of the period is 98.372607 per 100 of par value.

$$PV = \frac{3}{(1.0310)^1} + \frac{3}{(1.0310)^2} + \cdots + \frac{103}{(1.0310)^{23}} = 98.372607$$

The full price on 18 June is EUR99.868805.

$$PV^{Full} = 98.372607 \times (1.0310)^{89/180} = 99.868805$$

The accrued interest is EUR1.483333, and the flat price is EUR98.385472.

$$AI = \frac{89}{180} \times 3 = 1.4833333$$

$$PV^{Flat} = 99.868805 - 1.483333 = 98.385472$$

The accrued interest is the same in each case because it does not depend on the yield-to-maturity. The differences in the flat prices indicate the differences in the rate of return that is required by investors.

3.2 Matrix Pricing

Some fixed-rate bonds are not actively traded. Therefore, there is no market price available to calculate the rate of return required by investors. The same problem occurs for bonds that are not yet issued. In these situations, it is common to estimate the market discount rate and price based on the quoted or flat prices of more frequently traded comparable bonds. These comparable bonds have similar times-to-maturity, coupon rates, and credit quality. This estimation process is called **matrix pricing**.

For example, suppose that an analyst needs to value a three-year, 4% semiannual coupon payment corporate bond, Bond X. Assume that Bond X is not actively traded and that there are no recent transactions reported for this particular security. However, there are quoted prices for four corporate bonds that have very similar credit quality:

- Bond A: two-year, 3% semiannual coupon payment bond trading at a price of 98.500

- Bond B: two-year, 5% semiannual coupon payment bond trading at a price of 102.250

- Bond C: five-year, 2% semiannual coupon payment bond trading at a price of 90.250

- Bond D: five-year, 4% semiannual coupon payment bond trading at a price of 99.125

The bonds are displayed in a matrix according to the coupon rate and the time-to-maturity. This matrix is shown in Exhibit 4.

Exhibit 4	Matrix Pricing Example			
	2% Coupon	3% Coupon	4% Coupon	5% Coupon
Two Years		98.500		102.250
		3.786%		3.821%
Three Years			Bond X	
Four Years				
Five Years	90.250		99.125	
	4.181%		4.196%	

In Exhibit 4, below each bond price is the yield-to-maturity. It is stated as the yield per semiannual period times two. For example, the yield-to-maturity on the two-year, 3% semiannual coupon payment corporate bond is 3.786%.

$$98.500 = \frac{1.5}{(1+r)^1} + \frac{1.5}{(1+r)^2} + \frac{1.5}{(1+r)^3} + \frac{101.5}{(1+r)^4}, \quad r = 0.01893, \quad \times 2 = 0.03786$$

Next, the analyst calculates the average yield for each year: 3.8035% for the two-year bonds and 4.1885% for the five-year bonds.

$$\frac{0.03786 + 0.03821}{2} = 0.038035$$

$$\frac{0.04181 + 0.04196}{2} = 0.041885$$

The estimated three-year market discount rate can be obtained with linear interpolation. The interpolated yield is 3.9318%.

$$0.038035 + \left(\frac{3-2}{5-2}\right) \times (0.041885 - 0.038035) = 0.039318$$

Using 3.9318% as the estimated three-year annual market discount rate, the three-year, 4% semiannual coupon payment corporate bond has an estimated price of 100.191 per 100 of par value.

$$\frac{2}{(1.019659)^1} + \frac{2}{(1.019659)^2} + \frac{2}{(1.019659)^3} + \frac{2}{(1.019659)^4} + \frac{2}{(1.019659)^5} +$$

$$\frac{102}{(1.019659)^6} = 100.191$$

Notice that 3.9318% is the stated annual rate. It is divided by two to get the yield per semiannual period: (0.039318/2 = 0.019659).

Matrix pricing also is used in underwriting new bonds to get an estimate of the **required yield spread** over the **benchmark rate**. The benchmark rate typically is the yield-to-maturity on a government bond having the same, or close to the same, time-to-maturity. The spread is the difference between the yield-to-maturity on the new bond and the benchmark rate. The yield spread is the additional compensation required by investors for the difference in the credit risk, liquidity risk, and tax status of the bond relative to the government bond. This spread is sometimes called the **spread over the benchmark**. Yield spreads are often stated in terms of basis points (bps), where one **basis point** equals one-hundredth of a percentage point. For example, if a yield-to-maturity is 2.25% and the benchmark rate is 1.50%, the yield spread is 0.75%, or 75 bps. Yield spreads are covered in more detail later in this reading.

Suppose that a corporation is about to issue a five-year bond. The corporate issuer currently has a four-year, 3% annual coupon payment debt liability on its books. The price of that bond is 102.400 per 100 of par value. This is the full price, which is the same as the flat price because the accrued interest is zero. This implies that the coupon payment has just been made and there are four full years to maturity. The four-year rate of return required by investors for this bond is 2.36%.

$$102.400 = \frac{3}{(1+r)^1} + \frac{3}{(1+r)^2} + \frac{3}{(1+r)^3} + \frac{103}{(1+r)^4}, \quad r = 0.0236$$

Suppose that there are no four-year government bonds to calculate the yield spread on this security. However, there are three-year and five-year government bonds that have yields-to-maturity of 0.75% and 1.45%, respectively. The average of the two yields-to-maturity is 1.10%, which is the estimated yield for the four-year government bond. Therefore, the estimated yield spread is 126 bps over the implied benchmark rate (0.0236 − 0.0110 = 0.0126).

There usually is a different yield spread for each maturity and for each credit rating. The term structure of "risk-free" rates, which is discussed further in Section 4, is the relationship between yields-to-maturity on "risk-free" bonds and times-to-maturity. The quotation marks around "risk-free" indicate that no bond is truly without risk. The primary component of the yield spread for many bonds is compensation for credit risk, not for time-to-maturity, and as a result, the yield spreads reflect the **term structure of credit spreads**. The term structure of credit spreads is the relationship between the spreads over the "risk-free" (or benchmark) rates and times-to-maturity. These term structures are covered in more detail in later readings.

The issuer now has an estimate of the four-year yield spread, 126 bps. This spread is a reference point for estimating the five-year spread for the newly issued bond. Suppose that the term structure of credit spreads for bonds of the corporate issuer's quality indicates that five-year spreads are about 25 bps higher than four-year spreads. Therefore, the estimated five-year required yield spread is 151 bps (0.0126 + 0.0025 =

0.0151). Given the yield-to-maturity of 1.45% on the five-year government bond, the expected market discount rate for the newly issued bond is 2.96% (0.0145 + 0.0151 = 0.0296). The corporation might set the coupon rate to be 3% and expect that the bond can be sold for a small premium above par value.

EXAMPLE 6

Using Matrix Pricing to Estimate Bond Price

An analyst needs to assign a value to an illiquid four-year, 4.5% annual coupon payment corporate bond. The analyst identifies two corporate bonds that have similar credit quality: One is a three-year, 5.50% annual coupon payment bond priced at 107.500 per 100 of par value, and the other is a five-year, 4.50% annual coupon payment bond priced at 104.750 per 100 of par value. Using matrix pricing, the estimated price of the illiquid bond per 100 of par value is *closest* to:

A 103.895.

B 104.991.

C 106.125.

Solution:

B is correct. The first step is to determine the yields-to-maturity on the observed bonds. The required yield on the three-year, 5.50% bond priced at 107.500 is 2.856%.

$$107.500 = \frac{5.50}{(1+r)^1} + \frac{5.50}{(1+r)^2} + \frac{105.50}{(1+r)^3}, \quad r = 0.02856$$

The required yield on the five-year, 4.50% bond priced at 104.750 is 3.449%.

$$104.750 = \frac{4.50}{(1+r)^1} + \frac{4.50}{(1+r)^2} + \frac{4.50}{(1+r)^3} + \frac{4.50}{(1+r)^4} + \frac{104.50}{(1+r)^5}, \quad r = 0.03449$$

The estimated market discount rate for a four-year bond having the same credit quality is the average of two required yields:

$$\frac{0.02856 + 0.03449}{2} = 0.031525$$

Given an estimated yield-to-maturity of 3.1525%, the estimated price of the illiquid four-year, 4.50% annual coupon payment corporate bond is 104.991 per 100 of par value.

$$\frac{4.50}{(1.031525)^1} + \frac{4.50}{(1.031525)^2} + \frac{4.50}{(1.031525)^3} + \frac{104.50}{(1.031525)^4} = 104.991$$

3.3 Yield Measures for Fixed-Rate Bonds

There are many ways to measure the rate of return on a fixed-rate bond investment. Consider a five-year, zero-coupon government bond. The purchase price today is 80. The investor receives 100 at redemption in five years. One possible yield measure is 25%—the gain of 20 divided by the amount invested, 80. However, investors want a yield measure that is *standardized* to allow for comparison between bonds that have different times-to-maturity. Therefore, yield measures typically are *annualized*. A possible annual rate for this zero-coupon bond is 5% per year—25% divided by five years. But for bonds maturing in more than one year, investors want an *annualized and compounded* yield-to-maturity. Money market rates on instruments maturing in one year or less typically are *annualized but not compounded*. They are stated on a simple interest basis. This concept is covered later in this reading.

In general, an annualized and compounded yield on a fixed-rate bond depends on the assumed number of periods in the year, which is called the **periodicity** of the annual rate. Typically, the periodicity matches the frequency of coupon payments. A bond that pays semiannual coupons has a stated annual yield-to-maturity for a periodicity of two—the rate per semiannual period times two. A bond that pays quarterly coupons has a stated annual yield for a periodicity of four—the rate per quarter times four. It is always important to know the periodicity of a stated annual rate.

The periodicity of the annual market discount rate for a zero-coupon bond is *arbitrary* because there are no coupon payments. For semiannual compounding, the annual yield-to-maturity on the five-year, zero-coupon bond priced at 80 per 100 of par value is stated to be 4.5130%. This annual rate has a periodicity of two.

$$80 = \frac{100}{(1 + r)^{10}}, \quad r = 0.022565, \quad \times 2 = 0.045130$$

For quarterly compounding, the annual yield-to-maturity is stated to be 4.4880%. This annual rate has a periodicity of four.

$$80 = \frac{100}{(1 + r)^{20}}, \quad r = 0.011220, \quad \times 4 = 0.044880$$

For monthly compounding, the annual yield-to-maturity is stated to be 4.4712%. This annual rate has a periodicity of 12.

$$80 = \frac{100}{(1 + r)^{60}}, \quad r = 0.003726, \quad \times 12 = 0.044712$$

For annual compounding, the yield-to-maturity is stated to be 4.5640%. This annual rate has a periodicity of one.

$$80 = \frac{100}{(1 + r)^{5}}, \quad r = 0.045640, \quad \times 1 = 0.045640$$

This is known as an **effective annual rate**. An effective annual rate has a periodicity of one because there is just one compounding period in the year.

In this zero-coupon bond example, 2.2565% compounded two times a year, 1.1220% compounded four times a year, and 0.3726% compounded twelve times a year are all equivalent to an effective annual rate of 4.5640%. The compounded total return is the same for each expression for the annual rate. They differ in terms of the number of compounding periods per year—that is, in terms of the *periodicity* of the annual rate. For a given pair of cash flows, the stated annual rate and the periodicity are inversely related.

The most common periodicity for USD-denominated bond yields is two because most bonds in the USD market make semiannual coupon payments. An annual rate having a periodicity of two is known as a **semiannual bond basis yield**, or **semiannual bond equivalent yield**. Therefore, a semiannual bond basis yield is the yield per semiannual period times two. It is important to remember that "semiannual bond basis yield" and "yield per semiannual period" have different meanings. For example, if a bond yield is 2% per semiannual period, its annual yield is 4% when stated on a semiannual bond basis.

An important tool used in fixed-income analysis is to convert an annual yield from one periodicity to another. These are called periodicity, or compounding, conversions. A general formula to convert an annual percentage rate for *m* periods per year, denoted APR_m, to an annual percentage rate for *n* periods per year, APR_n, is Equation 7.

$$\left(1 + \frac{APR_m}{m}\right)^m = \left(1 + \frac{APR_n}{n}\right)^n \tag{7}$$

For example, suppose that a three-year, 5% semiannual coupon payment corporate bond is priced at 104 per 100 of par value. Its yield-to-maturity is 3.582%, quoted on a semiannual bond basis for a periodicity of two: $0.01791 \times 2 = 0.03582$.

$$104 = \frac{2.5}{(1+r)^1} + \frac{2.5}{(1+r)^2} + \frac{2.5}{(1+r)^3} + \frac{2.5}{(1+r)^4} + \frac{2.5}{(1+r)^5} + \frac{102.5}{(1+r)^6}, \quad r = 0.01791$$

To compare this bond with others, an analyst converts this annualized yield-to-maturity to quarterly and monthly compounding. That entails using Equation 7 to convert from a periodicity of $m = 2$ to periodicities of $n = 4$ and $n = 12$.

$$\left(1 + \frac{0.03582}{2}\right)^2 = \left(1 + \frac{APR_4}{4}\right)^4, \quad APR_4 = 0.03566$$

$$\left(1 + \frac{0.03582}{2}\right)^2 = \left(1 + \frac{APR_{12}}{12}\right)^{12}, \quad APR_{12} = 0.03556$$

An annual yield-to-maturity of 3.582% for semiannual compounding provides the same rate of return as annual yields of 3.566% and 3.556% for quarterly and monthly compounding, respectively. A general rule for these periodicity conversions is *compounding more frequently at a lower annual rate corresponds to compounding less frequently at a higher annual rate*. This rule can be used to check periodicity conversion calculations.

EXAMPLE 7

Yield Conversion Based on Periodicity

A five-year, 4.50% semiannual coupon payment government bond is priced at 98 per 100 of par value. Calculate the annual yield-to-maturity stated on a semiannual bond basis, rounded to the nearest basis point. Convert that annual yield to:

A an annual rate that can be used for direct comparison with otherwise comparable bonds that make *quarterly* coupon payments and

B an annual rate that can be used for direct comparison with otherwise comparable bonds that make *annual* coupon payments.

Solution:

The stated annual yield-to-maturity on a semiannual bond basis is 4.96% ($0.0248 \times 2 = 0.0496$).

$$98 = \frac{2.25}{(1+r)^1} + \frac{2.25}{(1+r)^2} + \frac{2.25}{(1+r)^3} + \frac{2.25}{(1+r)^4} + \frac{2.25}{(1+r)^5} + \frac{2.25}{(1+r)^6} +$$

$$\frac{2.25}{(1+r)^7} + \frac{2.25}{(1+r)^8} + \frac{2.25}{(1+r)^9} + \frac{102.25}{(1+r)^{10}}, \quad r = 0.0248$$

A Convert 4.96% from a periodicity of two to a periodicity of four:

$$\left(1 + \frac{0.0496}{2}\right)^2 = \left(1 + \frac{APR_4}{4}\right)^4, \quad APR_4 = 0.0493$$

The annual percentage rate of 4.96% for compounding semiannually compares with 4.93% for compounding quarterly. That makes sense because increasing the frequency of compounding lowers the annual rate.

B Convert 4.96% from a periodicity of two to a periodicity of one:

$$\left(1 + \frac{0.0496}{2}\right)^2 = \left(1 + \frac{APR_1}{1}\right)^1, \quad APR_1 = 0.0502$$

The annual rate of 4.96% for compounding semiannually compares with an effective annual rate of 5.02%. Converting from more frequent to less frequent compounding entails raising the annual percentage rate.

An important concern for quoting and calculating bond yields-to-maturity is the actual timing of the cash flows. Consider a 6% semiannual payment corporate bond that matures on 15 March 2022. Suppose that for settlement on 23 January 2014, the bond is priced at 98.5 per 100 of par value to yield 6.236% quoted on a semiannual bond basis. Its coupon payments are scheduled for 15 March and 15 September of each year. The yield calculation implicitly assumes that the payments are made on those dates. It neglects the reality that 15 March 2015 is a Sunday and 15 September 2018 is a Saturday. In fact, the coupon payments will be made to investors on the following Monday.

Yield measures that neglect weekends and holidays are quoted on what is called **street convention**. The street convention yield-to-maturity is the internal rate of return on the cash flows assuming the payments are made on the scheduled dates. This assumption simplifies bond price and yield calculations and commonly is used in practice. Sometimes the **true yield** is also quoted. The true yield-to-maturity is the internal rate of return on the cash flows using the actual calendar of weekends and bank holidays. The true yield is never higher than the street convention yield because weekends and holidays delay the time to payment. The difference is typically small, no more than a basis point or two. Therefore, the true yield is not commonly used in practice. Sometimes, a **government equivalent yield** is quoted for a corporate bond. A government equivalent yield restates a yield-to-maturity based on 30/360 day-count to one based on actual/actual. The government equivalent yield on a corporate bond can be used to obtain the spread over the government yield. Doing so keeps the yields stated on the same day-count convention basis.

Another yield measure that is commonly quoted for fixed-income bonds is the **current yield**, also called the income or interest yield. The current yield is the sum of the coupon payments received over the year divided by the flat price. For example, a 10-year, 2% semiannual coupon payment bond is priced at 95 per 100 of par value. Its current yield is 2.105%.

$$\frac{2}{95} = 0.02105$$

The current yield is a crude measure of the rate of return to an investor because it neglects the frequency of coupon payments in the numerator and any accrued interest in the denominator. It focuses only on interest income. In addition to collecting and reinvesting coupon payments, the investor has a gain if the bond is purchased at a discount and is redeemed at par value. The investor has a loss if the bond is purchased at a premium and is redeemed at par value. Sometimes the **simple yield** on a bond is quoted. It is the sum of the coupon payments plus the straight-line amortized share of the gain or loss, divided by the flat price. Simple yields are used mostly to quote Japanese government bonds, known as "JGBs."

EXAMPLE 8

Comparing Yields for Different Periodicities

An analyst observes these reported statistics for two bonds.

	Bond A	Bond B
Annual Coupon Rate	8.00%	12.00%
Coupon Payment Frequency	Semiannually	Quarterly
Years to Maturity	5 Years	5 Years
Price (per 100 of par value)	90	105
Current Yield	8.889%	11.429%
Yield-to-Maturity	10.630%	10.696%

1   Confirm the calculation of the two yield measures for the two bonds.

2   The analyst believes that Bond B has a little more risk than Bond A. How much additional compensation, in terms of a higher yield-to-maturity, does a buyer of Bond B receive for bearing this risk compared with Bond A?

Solution to 1:

Current Yield for Bond A

$$\frac{8}{90} = 0.08889$$

Yield-to-Maturity for Bond A

$$90 = \frac{4}{(1 + r)^1} + \frac{4}{(1 + r)^2} + \cdots + \frac{104}{(1 + r)^{10}}, \quad r = 0.05315, \quad \times 2 = 0.10630$$

Current Yield for Bond B

$$\frac{12}{105} = 0.11429$$

Yield-to-Maturity for Bond B

$$105 = \frac{3}{(1 + r)^1} + \frac{3}{(1 + r)^2} + \cdots + \frac{103}{(1 + r)^{20}}, \quad r = 0.02674, \quad \times 4 = 0.10696$$

Solution to 2:

The yield-to-maturity on Bond A of 10.630% is an annual rate for compounding semiannually. The yield-to-maturity on Bond B of 10.696% is an annual rate for compounding quarterly. The difference in the yields is *not* 6.6 bps (0.10696 – 0.10630 = 0.00066). It is essential to compare the yields for the same periodicity to make a statement about relative value.

10.630% for a periodicity of two converts to 10.492% for a periodicity of four:

$$\left(1 + \frac{0.10630}{2}\right)^2 = \left(1 + \frac{APR_4}{4}\right)^4, \quad APR_4 = 0.10492$$

10.696% for a periodicity of four converts to 10.839% for a periodicity of two:

$$\left(1 + \frac{0.10696}{4}\right)^4 = \left(1 + \frac{APR_2}{2}\right)^2, \quad APR_2 = 0.10839$$

The additional compensation for the greater risk in Bond B is 20.9 bps (0.10839 − 0.10630 = 0.00209) when the yields are stated on a semiannual bond basis. The additional compensation is 20.4 bps (0.10696 − 0.10492 = 0.00204) when both are annualized for quarterly compounding.

If a fixed-rate bond contains an **embedded option**, other yield measures are used. An embedded option is part of the security and cannot be removed and sold separately. For example, a **callable bond** contains an embedded call option that gives the issuer the right to buy the bond back from the investor at specified prices on pre-determined dates. The preset dates usually coincide with coupon payment dates after a **call protection** period. A call protection period is the time during which the issuer of the bond is not allowed to exercise the call option.

Suppose that a seven-year, 8% annual coupon payment bond is first callable in four years. That gives the investor four years of protection against the bond being called. After the call protection period, the issuer might exercise the call option if interest rates decrease or the issuer's credit quality improves. Those circumstances allow the issuer to refinance the debt at a lower cost of funds. The preset prices that the issuer pays if the bond is called often are at a premium above par. For example, the "call schedule" for this bond might be that it is first callable at 102 (per 100 of par value) on the coupon payment date in four years, callable at 101 in five years, and at par value on coupon payment dates thereafter.

The yield-to-maturity on this seven-year, 8% callable bond is just one of several traditional yield measures for the investment. Others are yield-to-first-call, yield-to-second-call, and so on. If the current price for the bond is 105 per 100 of par value, the yield-to-first-call in four years is 6.975%.

$$105 = \frac{8}{(1+r)^1} + \frac{8}{(1+r)^2} + \frac{8}{(1+r)^3} + \frac{8+102}{(1+r)^4}, \quad r = 0.06975$$

The yield-to-second-call in five years is 6.956%.

$$105 = \frac{8}{(1+r)^1} + \frac{8}{(1+r)^2} + \frac{8}{(1+r)^3} + \frac{8}{(1+r)^4} + \frac{8+101}{(1+r)^5}, \quad r = 0.06956$$

The yield-to-third-call is 6.953%.

$$105 = \frac{8}{(1+r)^1} + \frac{8}{(1+r)^2} + \frac{8}{(1+r)^3} + \frac{8}{(1+r)^4} + \frac{8}{(1+r)^5} + \frac{8+100}{(1+r)^6}, \quad r = 0.06953$$

Finally, the yield-to-maturity is 7.070%.

$$105 = \frac{8}{(1+r)^1} + \frac{8}{(1+r)^2} + \frac{8}{(1+r)^3} + \frac{8}{(1+r)^4} + \frac{8}{(1+r)^5} + \frac{8}{(1+r)^6} +$$
$$\frac{8+100}{(1+r)^7}, \quad r = 0.07070$$

Each calculation is based on Equation 1, whereby the call price (or par value) is used for *FV*. The lowest of the sequence of yields-to-call and the yield-to-maturity is known as the **yield-to-worst**. In this case, it is the yield-to-third-call of 6.953%. The intent of this yield measure is to provide to the investor the most conservative assumption for the rate of return.

The yield-to-worst is a commonly cited yield measure for fixed-rate callable bonds used by bond dealers and investors. However, a more precise approach is to use an option pricing model and an assumption about future interest rate volatility to value the embedded call option. The value of the embedded call option is added to the flat price of the bond to get the **option-adjusted price**. The investor bears the call risk (the bond issuer has the option to call), so the embedded call option reduces the value of the bond from the investor's perspective. The investor pays a lower price for the callable bond than if it were option-free. If the bond were non-callable, its price would be higher. The option-adjusted price is used to calculate the **option-adjusted yield**. The option-adjusted yield is the required market discount rate whereby the price is adjusted for the value of the embedded option. The value of the call option is the price of the option-free bond minus the price of the callable bond.

3.4 Yield Measures for Floating-Rate Notes

Floating-rate notes are very different from a fixed-rate bond. The interest payments on a floating-rate note, which often is called a floater or an FRN, are not fixed. Instead, they vary from period to period depending on the current level of a reference interest rate. The interest payments could go up or down; that is why they "float." The intent of an FRN is to offer the investor a security that has less market price risk than a fixed-rate bond when market interest rates fluctuate. In principle, a floater has a stable price even in a period of volatile interest rates. With a traditional fixed-income security, interest rate volatility affects the price because the future cash flows are constant. With a floating-rate note, interest rate volatility affects future interest payments.

The reference rate on a floating-rate note usually is a short-term money market rate, such as three-month Libor (the London Interbank Offered Rate). The principal on the floater typically is non-amortizing and is redeemed in full at maturity. The reference rate is determined at the beginning of the period, and the interest payment is made at the end of the period. This payment structure called "in arrears." The most common day-count conventions for calculating accrued interest on floaters are actual/360 and actual/365.

Although there are many varieties of FRNs, only the most common and traditional floaters are covered here. On these floaters, a specified yield spread is added to, or subtracted from, the reference rate. For example, the floater might reset its interest rate quarterly at three-month Libor plus 0.50%. This specified yield spread over the reference rate is called the **quoted margin** on the FRN. The role of the quoted margin is to compensate the investor for the difference in the credit risk of the issuer and that implied by the reference rate. For example, a company with a stronger credit rating than that of the banks included in Libor may be able to obtain a "sub-Libor" cost of borrowed funds, which results in a negative quoted margin. An AAA rated company might be able to issue an FRN that pays three-month Libor minus 0.25%.

The **required margin** is the yield spread over, or under, the reference rate such that the FRN is priced at par value on a rate reset date. Suppose that a traditional floater is issued at par value and pays three-month Libor plus 0.50%. The quoted margin is 50 bps. If there is no change in the credit risk of the issuer, the required margin remains at 50 bps. On each quarterly reset date, the floater will be priced at par value. Between coupon dates, its flat price will be at a premium or discount to par value if Libor goes down or up. However, if the required margin continues to be the same as the quoted margin, the flat price is "pulled to par" as the next reset date nears. At the reset date, any change in Libor is included in the interest payment for the next period.

Changes in the required margin usually come from changes in the issuer's credit risk. Changes in liquidity or tax status also could affect the required margin. Suppose that on a reset date, the required margin goes up to 75 bps because of a downgrade in the issuer's credit rating. A floater having a quoted margin of 50 bps now pays its investors a "deficient" interest payment. This FRN will be priced at a discount below par value. The amount of the discount is the present value of the deficient future cash flows. That annuity is 25 bps per period for the remaining life of the bond. It is the difference between the required and quoted margins. If the required margin goes down from 50 bps to 40 bps, the FRN will be priced at a premium. The amount of the premium is the present value of the 10 bp annuity for the "excess" interest payment each period.

Fixed-rate and floating-rate bonds are essentially the same with respect to changes in credit risk. With fixed-rate bonds, the premium or discount arises from a difference in the fixed coupon rate and the required yield-to-maturity. With floating-rate bonds, the premium or discount arises from a difference in the fixed quoted margin and the required margin. However, fixed-rate and floating-rate bonds are very different with respect to changes in benchmark interest rates.

The valuation of a floating-rate note needs a pricing model. Equation 8 is a simplified FRN pricing model. Following market practice, the required margin is called the **discount margin**.

$$
PV = \frac{\dfrac{(\text{Index} + QM) \times FV}{m}}{\left(1 + \dfrac{\text{Index} + DM}{m}\right)^{1}} + \frac{\dfrac{(\text{Index} + QM) \times FV}{m}}{\left(1 + \dfrac{\text{Index} + DM}{m}\right)^{2}} + \cdots +
$$

$$
\frac{\dfrac{(\text{Index} + QM) \times FV}{m} + FV}{\left(1 + \dfrac{\text{Index} + DM}{m}\right)^{N}} \tag{8}
$$

where

PV = present value, or the price of the floating-rate note

Index = reference rate, stated as an annual percentage rate

QM = quoted margin, stated as an annual percentage rate

FV = future value paid at maturity, or the par value of the bond

m = periodicity of the floating-rate note, the number of payment periods per year

DM = discount margin, the required margin stated as an annual percentage rate

N = number of evenly spaced periods to maturity

This equation is similar to Equation 1, which is the basic pricing formula for a fixed-rate bond given the market discount rate. In Equation 1, *PMT* is the coupon payment *per period*. Here, *annual* rates are used. The first interest payment is the annual rate for the period (Index + *QM*) times the par value (*FV*) and divided by the number of periods in the year (*m*). In Equation 1, the market discount rate per period (*r*) is used to discount the cash flows. Here, the discount rate per period is the reference rate plus the discount margin (Index + *DM*) divided by the periodicity (*m*).

This is a simplified FRN pricing model for several reasons. First, *PV* is for a rate reset date when there are *N* evenly spaced periods to maturity. There is no accrued interest so that the flat price is the full price. Second, the model assumes a 30/360 day-count convention so that the periodicity is an integer. Third, and most important, the same reference rate (Index) is used for all payment periods in both the numerators and denominators. More complex FRN pricing models use projected future rates for Index in the numerators and spot rates in the denominators. Therefore, the calculation for *DM* depends on the simplifying assumptions in the pricing model.

Suppose that a two-year FRN pays six-month Libor plus 0.50%. Currently, six-month Libor is 1.25%. In Equation 8, Index = 0.0125, *QM* = 0.0050, and *m* = 2. The numerators in Equation 8, ignoring the repayment of principal, are 0.875.

$$\frac{(\text{Index} + QM) \times FV}{m} = \frac{(0.0125 + 0.0050) \times 100}{2} = 0.875$$

Suppose that the yield spread required by investors is 40 bps over the reference rate, $DM = 0.0040$. The assumed discount rate per period is 0.825%.

$$\frac{\text{Index} + DM}{m} = \frac{0.0125 + 0.0040}{2} = 0.00825$$

Using Equation 8 for $N = 4$, the FRN is priced at 100.196 per 100 of par value.

$$\frac{0.875}{(1 + 0.00825)^1} + \frac{0.875}{(1 + 0.00825)^2} + \frac{0.875}{(1 + 0.00825)^3} + \frac{0.875 + 100}{(1 + 0.00825)^4} = 100.196$$

This floater is priced at a premium above par value because the quoted margin is greater than the discount margin.

A similar calculation is to estimate the discount margin given the market price of the floating-rate note. Suppose that a five-year FRN pays three-month Libor plus 0.75% on a quarterly basis. Currently, three-month Libor is 1.10%. The price of the floater is 95.50 per 100 of par value, a discount below par value because of a downgrade in the issuer's credit rating.

$$\frac{(\text{Index} + QM) \times FV}{m} = \frac{(0.0110 + 0.0075) \times 100}{4} = 0.4625$$

In Equation 8, use $PV = 95.50$ and $N = 20$.

$$95.50 = \frac{0.4625}{\left(1 + \dfrac{0.0110 + DM}{4}\right)^1} + \frac{0.4625}{\left(1 + \dfrac{0.0110 + DM}{4}\right)^2} + \cdots + \frac{0.4625 + 100}{\left(1 + \dfrac{0.0110 + DM}{4}\right)^{20}}$$

This has the same format as Equation 1, which can be used to solve for the market discount rate per period, $r = 0.7045\%$.

$$95.50 = \frac{0.4625}{(1 + r)^1} + \frac{0.4625}{(1 + r)^2} + \cdots + \frac{0.4625 + 100}{(1 + r)^{20}}, \quad r = 0.007045$$

This can be used to solve for $DM = 1.718\%$.

$$0.007045 = \frac{0.0110 + DM}{4}, \quad DM = 0.01718$$

If this FRN was issued at par value, investors required at that time a spread of only 75 bps over three-month Libor. Now, after the credit downgrade, investors require an *estimated* discount margin of 171.8 bps. The floater trades at a discount because the quoted margin remains fixed at 75 bps. The calculated discount margin is an estimate because it is based on a simplified FRN pricing model.

EXAMPLE 9

Calculating the Discount Margin for a Floating-Rate Note

A four-year French floating-rate note pays three-month Euribor (Euro Interbank Offered Rate, an index produced by the European Banking Federation) plus 1.25%. The floater is priced at 98 per 100 of par value. Calculate the discount margin for the floater assuming that three-month Euribor is constant at 2%. Assume the 30/360 day-count convention and evenly spaced periods.

Solution:

By assumption, the interest payment each period is 0.8125 per 100 of par value.

$$\frac{(\text{Index} + QM) \times FV}{m} = \frac{(0.0200 + 0.0125) \times 100}{4} = 0.8125$$

The discount margin can be estimated by solving for DM in this equation.

$$98 = \frac{0.8125}{\left(1 + \dfrac{0.0200 + DM}{4}\right)^1} + \frac{0.8125}{\left(1 + \dfrac{0.0200 + DM}{4}\right)^2} + \cdots +$$

$$\frac{0.8125 + 100}{\left(1 + \dfrac{0.0200 + DM}{4}\right)^{16}}$$

The solution for the discount rate per period is 0.9478%.

$$98 = \frac{0.8125}{(1 + r)^1} + \frac{0.8125}{(1 + r)^2} + \cdots + \frac{0.8125 + 100}{(1 + r)^{16}}, \quad r = 0.009478$$

Therefore, $DM = 1.791\%$.

$$0.009478 = \frac{0.0200 + DM}{4}, \quad DM = 0.01791$$

The quoted margin is 125 bps over the Euribor reference rate. Using the simplified FRN pricing model, it is estimated that investors require a 179.1 bp spread for the floater to be priced at par value.

3.5 Yield Measures for Money Market Instruments

Money market instruments are short-term debt securities. They range in time-to-maturity from overnight sale and repurchase agreements (repos) to one-year bank certificates of deposit. Money market instruments also include commercial paper, government issues of less than one year, bankers' acceptances, and time deposits based on such indices as Libor and Euribor. Money market mutual funds are a major investor in such securities. These mutual funds can invest only in certain eligible money market securities.

There are several important differences in yield measures between the money market and the bond market:

1   Bond yields-to-maturity are annualized and compounded. Yield measures in the money market are annualized but not compounded. Instead, the rate of return on a money market instrument is stated on a simple interest basis.

2   Bond yields-to-maturity can be calculated using standard time-value-of-money analysis and with formulas programmed into a financial calculator. Money market instruments often are quoted using nonstandard interest rates and require different pricing equations than those used for bonds.

3   Bond yields-to-maturity usually are stated for a common periodicity for all times-to-maturity. Money market instruments having different times-to-maturity have different periodicities for the annual rate.

In general, quoted money market rates are either **discount rates** or **add-on rates**. Although market conventions vary around the world, commercial paper, Treasury bills (a US government security issued with a maturity of one year or less), and bankers' acceptances often are quoted on a discount rate basis. Bank certificates of deposit, repos, and such indices as Libor and Euribor are quoted on an add-on rate basis. It is important to understand that "discount rate" has a unique meaning in the money market. In general, discount rate means "interest rate used to calculate a present value"—for instance, "market discount rate" as used in this reading. In the money market, however, discount rate is a specific type of quoted rate. Some examples will clarify this point.

Equation 9 is the pricing formula for money market instruments quoted on a discount *rate* basis.

$$PV = FV \times \left(1 - \frac{\text{Days}}{\text{Year}} \times DR\right)$$

(9)

where

PV = present value, or the price of the money market instrument

FV = future value paid at maturity, or the face value of the money market instrument

Days = number of days between settlement and maturity

Year = number of days in the year

DR = discount rate, stated as an annual percentage rate

Suppose that a 91-day US Treasury bill (T-bill) with a face value of USD10 million is quoted at a discount rate of 2.25% for an assumed 360-day year. Enter FV = 10,000,000, Days = 91, Year = 360, and DR = 0.0225. The price of the T-bill is USD9,943,125.

$$PV = 10,000,000 \times \left(1 - \frac{91}{360} \times 0.0225\right) = 9,943,125$$

The unique characteristics of a money market discount rate can be examined with Equation 10, which transforms Equation 9 algebraically to isolate the DR term.

$$DR = \left(\frac{\text{Year}}{\text{Days}}\right) \times \left(\frac{FV - PV}{FV}\right)$$

(10)

The first term, Year/Days, is the periodicity of the annual rate. The second term reveals the odd character of a money market discount rate. The numerator, $FV - PV$, is the interest earned on the T-bill, USD56,875 (= 10,000,000 − 9,943,125), over the 91 days to maturity. However, the denominator is FV, not PV. In theory, an interest rate is the amount earned divided by the investment amount (PV)—not divided by the total return at maturity, which includes the earnings (FV). Therefore, by design, a money market discount rate *understates* the rate of return to the investor, and it *understates* the cost of borrowed funds to the issuer. That is because PV is less than FV (as long as DR is greater than zero).

Equation 11 is the pricing formula for money market instruments quoted on an add-on rate basis.

$$PV = \frac{FV}{\left(1 + \frac{\text{Days}}{\text{Year}} \times AOR\right)}$$

(11)

where

PV = present value, principal amount, or the price of the money market instrument

FV = future value, or the redemption amount paid at maturity including interest

Days = number of days between settlement and maturity

Year = number of days in the year

AOR = add-on rate, stated as an annual percentage rate

Suppose that a Canadian pension fund buys a 180-day banker's acceptance (BA) with a quoted add-on rate of 4.38% for a 365-day year. If the initial principal amount is CAD10 million, the redemption amount due at maturity is found by re-arranging Equation 11 and entering $PV = 10,000,000$, Days = 180, Year = 365, and $AOR = 0.0438$.

$$FV = 10,000,000 + \left(10,000,000 \times \frac{180}{365} \times 0.0438\right) = 10,216,000$$

At maturity, the pension fund receives CAD10,216,000, the principal of CAD10 million plus interest of CAD216,000. The interest is calculated as the principal times the fraction of the year times the annual add-on rate. It is added to the principal to determine the redemption amount.

Suppose that after 45 days, the pension fund sells the BA to a dealer. At that time, the quoted add-on rate for a 135-day BA is 4.17%. The sale price for the BA can be calculated using Equation 11 for $FV = 10,216,000$, Days = 135, Year = 365, and $AOR = 0.0417$. The sale price is CAD10,060,829.

$$PV = \frac{10,216,000}{\left(1 + \frac{135}{365} \times 0.0417\right)} = 10,060,829$$

The characteristics of an add-on rate can be examined with Equation 12, which transforms Equation 11 algebraically to isolate the AOR term.

$$AOR = \left(\frac{\text{Year}}{\text{Days}}\right) \times \left(\frac{FV - PV}{PV}\right) \tag{12}$$

This equation indicates that an add-on rate is a reasonable yield measure for a money market investment. The first term, Year/Days, is the periodicity of the annual rate. The second term is the interest earned, $FV - PV$, divided by PV, the amount invested.

The pension fund's rate of return on its 45-day investment in the banker's acceptance can be calculated with Equation 12. Enter Year = 365, Days = 45, $FV = 10,060,829$, and $PV = 10,000,000$. Notice that FV here is the sale price, not the redemption amount.

$$AOR = \left(\frac{365}{45}\right) \times \left(\frac{10,060,829 - 10,000,000}{10,000,000}\right) = 0.04934$$

The rate of return, stated on a 365-day add-on rate basis, is 4.934%. This result is an annual rate for a periodicity of 8.11 (= 365/45). Implicitly, this assumes that the investment can be replicated 8.11 times over the year.

Investment analysis is made difficult for money market securities because (1) some instruments are quoted on a discount rate basis and others on an add-on rate basis and (2) some are quoted for a 360-day year and others for a 365-day year. Another difference is that the "amount" of a money market instrument quoted on a discount rate basis typically is the face value paid at maturity. However, the "amount" when quoted on an add-on rate basis usually is the principal, the price at issuance. To make money market investment decisions, it is essential to compare instruments on a common basis. An example illustrates this point.

Suppose that an investor is comparing two money market instruments: (A) 90-day commercial paper quoted at a discount rate of 5.76% for a 360-day year and (B) 90-day bank time deposit quoted at an add-on rate of 5.90% for a 365-day year. Which offers the higher expected rate of return assuming that the credit risks are the same? The price of the commercial paper is 98.560 per 100 of face value, calculated using Equation 9 and entering $FV = 100$, Days = 90, Year = 360, and $DR = 0.0576$.

$$PV = 100 \times \left(1 - \frac{90}{360} \times 0.0576\right) = 98.560$$

Next, use Equation 12 to solve for the *AOR* for a 365-day year, whereby *Year* = 365, *Days* = 90, *FV* = 100, and *PV* = 98.560.

$$AOR = \left(\frac{365}{90}\right) \times \left(\frac{100 - 98.560}{98.560}\right) = 0.05925$$

The 90-day commercial paper discount rate of 5.76% converts to an add-on rate for a 365-day year of 5.925%. This converted rate is called a **bond equivalent yield**, or sometimes just an "investment yield." A bond equivalent yield is a money market rate stated on a 365-day add-on rate basis. If the risks are the same, the commercial paper offers 2.5 bps more in annual return than the bank time deposit.

EXAMPLE 10

Comparing Money Market Instruments Based on Bond Equivalent Yields

Suppose that a money market investor observes quoted rates on the following four 180-day money market instruments:

Money Market Instrument	Quotation Basis	Assumed Number of Days in the Year	Quoted Rate
A	Discount Rate	360	4.33%
B	Discount Rate	365	4.36%
C	Add-On Rate	360	4.35%
D	Add-On Rate	365	4.45%

Calculate the bond equivalent yield for each instrument. Which instrument offers the investor the highest rate of return if the credit risk is the same?

Solution:

A Use Equation 9 to get the price per 100 of par value, where *FV* = 100, *Days* = 180, Year = 360, and *DR* = 0.0433.

$$PV = 100 \times \left(1 - \frac{180}{360} \times 0.0433\right) = 97.835$$

Use Equation 12 to get the bond equivalent yield, where Year = 365, Days = 180, *FV* = 100, and *PV* = 97.835.

$$AOR = \left(\frac{365}{180}\right) \times \left(\frac{100 - 97.835}{97.835}\right) = 0.04487$$

The bond equivalent yield for Bond A is 4.487%.

B Use Equation 9 to get the price per 100 of face value, where *FV* = 100, Days = 180, Year = 365, and *DR* = 0.0436.

$$PV = 100 \times \left(1 - \frac{180}{365} \times 0.0436\right) = 97.850$$

Use Equation 12 to get the bond equivalent yield, where Year = 365, Days = 180, *FV* = 100, and *PV* = 97.850.

$$AOR = \left(\frac{365}{180}\right) \times \left(\frac{100 - 97.850}{97.850}\right) = 0.04456$$

The bond equivalent yield for Bond B is 4.456%.

C   First, determine the redemption amount per 100 of principal ($PV = 100$), where Days = 180, Year = 360, and $AOR = 0.0435$.

$$FV = 100 + \left(100 \times \frac{180}{360} \times 0.0435\right) = 102.175$$

Use Equation 12 to get the bond equivalent yield, where Year = 365, Days = 180, $FV = 102.175$, and $PV = 100$.

$$AOR = \left(\frac{365}{180}\right) \times \left(\frac{102.175 - 100}{100}\right) = 0.04410$$

The bond equivalent yield for Bond C is 4.410%.

Another way to get the bond equivalent yield for Bond C is to observe that the AOR of 4.35% for a 360-day year can be obtained using Equation 12 for Year = 360, Days = 180, $FV = 102.175$, and $PV = 100$.

$$AOR = \left(\frac{360}{180}\right) \times \left(\frac{102.175 - 100}{100}\right) = 0.0435$$

Therefore, an add-on rate for a 360-day year only needs to be multiplied by the factor of 365/360 to get the 365-day year bond equivalent yield.

$$\frac{365}{360} \times 0.0435 = 0.04410$$

D   The quoted rate for Bond D of 4.45% is a bond equivalent yield, which is defined as an add-on rate for a 365-day year.

If the risk of these money market instruments is the same, Bond A offers the highest rate of return on a bond equivalent yield basis, 4.487%.

The third difference between yield measures in the money market and the bond market is the periodicity of the annual rate. Because bond yields-to-maturity are computed using interest rate compounding, there is a well-defined periodicity. For instance, bond yields-to-maturity for semiannual compounding are annualized for a periodicity of two. Money market rates are computed using simple interest without compounding. In the money market, the periodicity is the number of days in the year divided by the number of days to maturity. Therefore, money market rates for different times-to-maturity have different periodicities.

Suppose that an analyst prefers to convert money market rates to a semiannual bond basis so that the rates are directly comparable to yields on bonds that make semiannual coupon payments. The quoted rate for a 90-day money market instrument is 10%, quoted as a bond equivalent yield, which means its periodicity is 365/90. Using Equation 7, the conversion is from $m = 365/90$ to $n = 2$ for $APR_{365/90} = 0.10$.

$$\left(1 + \frac{0.10}{365/90}\right)^{365/90} = \left(1 + \frac{APR_2}{2}\right)^2, \quad APR_2 = 0.10127$$

Therefore, 10% for a periodicity of 365/90 corresponds to 10.127% for a periodicity of two. The difference is significant—12.7 bps. In general, the difference depends on the level of the annual percentage rate. When interest rates are lower, the difference between the annual rates for any two periodicities is reduced.

THE MATURITY STRUCTURE OF INTEREST RATES

There are many reasons why the yields-to-maturity on any two bonds are different. Suppose that the yield-to-maturity is higher on Bond X than on Bond Y. The following are some possible reasons for the difference between the yields:

- Currency—Bond X could be denominated in a currency with a higher expected rate of inflation than the currency in which Bond Y is denominated.

- Credit risk—Bond X could have a non-investment-grade rating of BB, and Bond Y could have an investment-grade rating of AA.

- Liquidity—Bond X could be illiquid, and Bond Y could be actively traded.

- Tax Status—Interest income on Bond X could be taxable, whereas interest income on Bond Y could be exempt from taxation.

- Periodicity—Bond X could make a single annual coupon payment, and its yield-to-maturity could be quoted for a periodicity of one. Bond Y could make monthly coupon payments, and its yield-to-maturity could be annualized for a periodicity of 12.

Obviously, another reason is that Bond X and Bond Y could have different times-to-maturity. This factor explaining the differences in yields is called the **maturity structure**, or **term structure**, of interest rates. It involves the analysis of yield curves, which are relationships between yields-to-maturity and times-to-maturity. There are different types of yield curves, depending on the characteristics of the underlying bonds.

In theory, maturity structure should be analyzed for bonds that have the same properties other than time-to-maturity. The bonds should be denominated in the same currency and have the same credit risk, liquidity, and tax status. Their annual rates should be quoted for the same periodicity. Also, they should have the same coupon rate so that they each have the same degree of coupon reinvestment risk. In practice, maturity structure is analyzed for bonds for which these strong assumptions rarely hold.

The ideal dataset would be yields-to-maturity on a series of *zero-coupon* government bonds for a full range of maturities. This dataset is the government bond **spot curve**, sometimes called the zero or "strip" curve (because the coupon payments are "stripped" off of the bonds). The spot, zero, or strip curve is a sequence of yields-to-maturity on zero-coupon bonds. Often, these government spot rates are interpreted as the "risk-free" yields; in this context, "risk-free" refers only to default risk. There still could be a significant amount of inflation risk to the investor, as well as liquidity risk.

A government bond spot curve is illustrated in Exhibit 5 for maturities ranging from 1 to 30 years. The annual yields are stated on a semiannual bond basis, which facilitates comparison to coupon-bearing bonds that make semiannual payments.

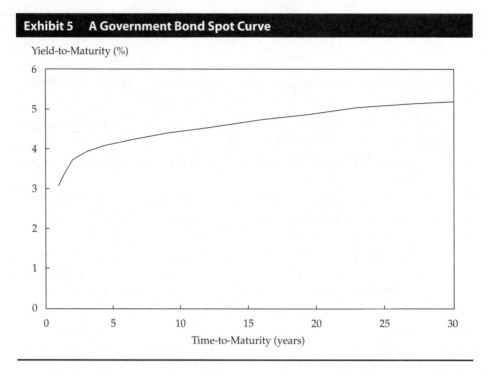

Exhibit 5   A Government Bond Spot Curve

Yield-to-Maturity (%)

Time-to-Maturity (years)

This spot curve is upward sloping and flattens for longer times-to-maturity. Longer-term government bonds usually have higher yields than shorter-term bonds. This pattern is typical under normal market conditions. Sometimes, a spot curve is downward sloping in that shorter-term yields are higher than longer-term yields. This downward sloping spot curve is called an inverted yield curve. The theories that attempt to explain the shape of the yield curve and its implications for future financial market conditions are covered in later readings.

This hypothetical spot curve is ideal for analyzing maturity structure because it best meets the "other things being equal" assumption. These government bonds presumably have the same currency, credit risk, liquidity, and tax status. Most importantly, they have no coupon reinvestment risk because there are no coupons to reinvest. However, most actively traded government and corporate bonds make coupon payments. Therefore, analysis of maturity structure usually is based on price data on government bonds that make coupon payments. These coupon bonds might not have the same liquidity and tax status. Older ("seasoned") bonds tend to be less liquid than newly issued debt because they are owned by "buy-and-hold" institutional and retail investors. Governments issue new debt for regular times-to-maturity—for instance, 5-year and 10-year bonds. The current 6-year bond could be a 10-year bond that was issued four years ago. Also, as interest rates fluctuate, older bonds are priced at a discount or premium to par value, which can lead to tax differences. In some countries, capital gains have different tax treatment than capital losses and interest income.

Analysts usually use only the most recently issued and actively traded government bonds to build a yield curve. These bonds have similar liquidity, and because they are priced closer to par value, they have fewer tax effects. A problem is that there are limited data for the full range of maturities. Therefore, it is necessary to *interpolate* between observed yields. Exhibit 6 illustrates a yield curve for a government that issues 2-year, 3-year, 5-year, 7-year, 10-year, and 30-year bonds that make semiannual coupon payments. Straight-line interpolation is used between those points on the yield curve for coupon bonds.

Exhibit 6   A Government Bond Yield Curve

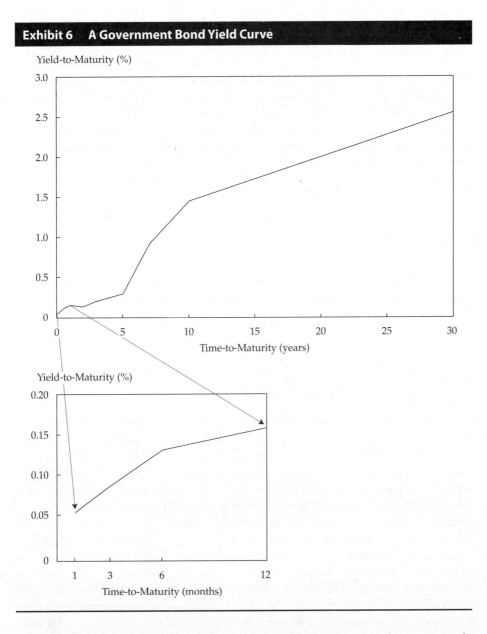

Exhibit 6 also includes yields for short-term government securities having 1 month, 3 months, 6 months, and 12 months to maturity. Although these money market instruments might have been issued and traded on a discount rate basis, they typically are reported as bond equivalent yields. It is important for the analyst to know whether they have been converted to the same periodicity as the longer-term government bonds. If not, the observed yield curve can be misleading because the number of periods in the year is not the same.

In addition to the yield curve on coupon bonds and the spot curve on zero-coupon bonds, maturity structure can be assessed using a **par curve**. A par curve is a sequence of yields-to-maturity such that each bond is priced at par value. The bonds, of course, are assumed to have the same currency, credit risk, liquidity, tax status, and annual yields stated for the same periodicity. Between coupon payment dates, the flat price (not the full price) is assumed to be equal to par value.

The par curve is obtained from a spot curve. On a coupon payment date, the following equation can be used to calculate a par rate given the sequence of spot rates.

$$100 = \frac{PMT}{(1 + z_1)^1} + \frac{PMT}{(1 + z_2)^2} + \cdots + \frac{PMT + 100}{(1 + z_N)^N} \qquad (13)$$

This equation is very similar to Equation 2 whereby $PV = FV = 100$. The problem is to solve for PMT algebraically. Then, $PMT/100$ is equal to the par rate *per period*.

An example illustrates the calculation of the par curve given a spot curve. Suppose the spot rates on government bonds are 5.263% for one year, 5.616% for two years, 6.359% for three years, and 7.008% for four years. These are effective annual rates. The one-year par rate is 5.263%.

$$100 = \frac{PMT + 100}{(1.05263)^1}, \quad PMT = 5.263$$

The two-year par rate is 5.606%.

$$100 = \frac{PMT}{(1.05263)^1} + \frac{PMT + 100}{(1.05616)^2}, \quad PMT = 5.606$$

The three-year and four-year par rates are 6.306% and 6.899%, respectively.

$$100 = \frac{PMT}{(1.05263)^1} + \frac{PMT}{(1.05616)^2} + \frac{PMT + 100}{(1.06359)^3}, \quad PMT = 6.306$$

$$100 = \frac{PMT}{(1.05263)^1} + \frac{PMT}{(1.05616)^2} + \frac{PMT}{(1.06359)^3} + \frac{PMT + 100}{(1.07008)^4}, \quad PMT = 6.899$$

The fixed-income securities covered so far have been **cash market securities**. Money market securities often are settled on a "same day," or "cash settlement," basis. Other securities have a difference between the trade date and the settlement date. For instance, if a government bond trades on a $T + 1$ basis, there is a one-day difference between the trade date and the settlement date. If a corporate bond trades on a $T + 3$ basis, the seller delivers the bond and the buyer makes payment in three business days. Cash markets are also called spot markets, which can be confusing because spot rate can have two meanings. It can mean the "rate on a bond traded in the spot, or cash, market." It can also mean "yield on a zero-coupon bond," which is the meaning of spot rate used in this reading.

A **forward market** is for future delivery, beyond the usual settlement time period in the cash market. Agreement to the terms for the transaction is on the trade date, but delivery of the security and payment for it is deferred to a future date. A **forward rate** is the interest rate on a bond or money market instrument traded in a forward market. For example, suppose that in the cash market, a five-year zero-coupon bond is priced at 81 per 100 of par value. Its yield-to-maturity is 4.2592%, stated on a semiannual bond basis.

$$81 = \frac{100}{(1 + r)^{10}}, \quad r = 0.021296, \quad \times 2 = 0.042592$$

Suppose that a dealer agrees to deliver a five-year bond two years into the future for a price of 75 per 100 of par value. The credit risk, liquidity, and tax status of this bond traded in the forward market are the same as the one in the cash market. The forward rate is 5.8372%.

$$75 = \frac{100}{(1 + r)^{10}}, \quad r = 0.029186, \quad \times 2 = 0.058372$$

The notation for forward rates is important to understand. Although finance textbook authors use varying notation, the most common market practice is to name this forward rate the "2y5y". This is pronounced "the two-year into five-year rate," or simply "the 2's, 5's." The idea is that the first number (two years) refers to the length of the forward period in years from today and the second number (five years) refers to the **tenor** of the underlying bond. The tenor is the time-to-maturity for a bond (or a derivative contract). Therefore, 5.8372% is the "2y5y" forward rate for the zero-coupon bond—the five-year yield two years into the future. Note that the bond that will be a five-year zero in two years currently has seven years to maturity. In the money market, the forward rate usually refers to months. For instance, an analyst might inquire about the "1m6m" forward rate on Euribor, which is the rate on six-month Euribor one month into the future.

Implied forward rates (also known as forward yields) are calculated from spot rates. An implied forward rate is a break-even reinvestment rate. It links the return on an investment in a shorter-term zero-coupon bond to the return on an investment in a longer-term zero-coupon bond. Suppose that the shorter-term bond matures in A periods and the longer-term bond matures in B periods. The yields-to-maturity per period on these bonds are denoted z_A and z_B. The first is an A-period zero-coupon bond trading in the cash market. The second is a B-period zero-coupon cash market bond. The implied forward rate between period A and period B is denoted $IFR_{A,B-A}$. It is a forward rate on a security that starts in period A and ends in period B. Its tenor is $B - A$ periods.

Equation 14 is a general formula for the relationship between the two spot rates and the implied forward rate.

$$(1 + z_A)^A \times (1 + IFR_{A,B-A})^{B-A} = (1 + z_B)B \qquad \textbf{(14)}$$

Suppose that the yields-to-maturity on three-year and four-year zero-coupon bonds are 3.65% and 4.18%, respectively, stated on a semiannual bond basis. An analyst would like to know the "3y1y" implied forward rate, which is the implied one-year forward yield three years into the future. Therefore, $A = 6$ (periods), $B = 8$ (periods), $B - A = 2$ (periods), $z_6 = 0.0365/2$ (per period), and $z_8 = 0.0418/2$ (per period).

$$\left(1 + \frac{0.0365}{2}\right)^6 \times \left(1 + IFR_{6,2}\right)^2 = \left(1 + \frac{0.0418}{2}\right)^8, \quad IFR_{6,2} = 0.02889,$$
$$\times 2 = 0.05778$$

The "3y1y" implied forward yield is 5.778%, annualized for a periodicity of two.

Equation 14 can be used to construct a **forward curve**. A forward curve is a series of forward rates, each having the same time frame. These forward rates might be observed on transactions in the derivatives market. Often, the forward rates are implied from transactions in the cash market. Exhibit 7 displays the forward curve that is calculated from the government bond spot curve shown in Exhibit 5. These are one-year forward rates stated on a semiannual bond basis.

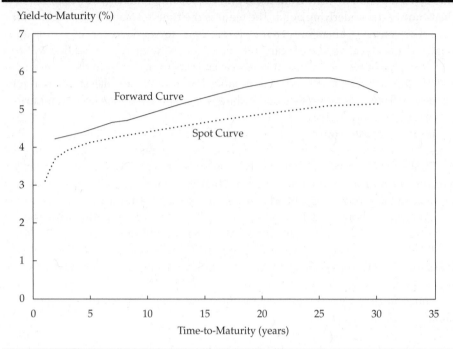

Exhibit 7   A Government Bond Spot Curve and Forward Curve

Yield-to-Maturity (%)

Time-to-Maturity (years)

A forward rate can be interpreted as an incremental, or marginal, return for extending the time-to-maturity for an additional time period. Suppose an investor has a four-year investment horizon and is choosing between buying a three-year zero-coupon bond that is priced to yield 3.65% and a four-year zero that is priced to yield 4.18%. The incremental, or marginal, return for the fourth year is 5.778%, the "3y1y" implied forward rate. If the investor's view on future bond yields is that the one-year yield in three years is likely to be less than 5.778%, the investor might prefer to buy the four-year bond. However, if the investor's view is that the one-year yield will be more than the implied forward rate, the investor might prefer the three-year bond and the opportunity to reinvest at the expected higher rate. That explains why an implied forward rate is the *breakeven reinvestment rate*. Implied forward rates are very useful to investors as well as bond issuers in making maturity decisions.

EXAMPLE 11

Computing Forward Rates

Suppose that an investor observes these prices and yields-to-maturity on zero-coupon government bonds:

Maturity	Price	Yield-to-Maturity
1 year	97.50	2.548%
2 years	94.25	2.983%
3 years	91.75	2.891%

The prices are per 100 of par value. The yields-to-maturity are stated on a semiannual bond basis.

1 Compute the "1y1y" and "2y1y" implied forward rates, stated on a semiannual bond basis.

2 The investor has a three-year investment horizon and is choosing between (1) buying the two-year zero and reinvesting in another one-year zero in two years and (2) buying and holding to maturity the three-year zero. The investor decides to buy the two-year bond. Based on this decision, which of the following is the minimum yield-to-maturity the investor expects on one-year zeros two years from now?

A 2.548%

B 2.707%

C 2.983%

Solution to 1:

The "1y1y" implied forward rate is 3.419%. In Equation 14, A = 2 (periods), B = 4 (periods), B − A = 2 (periods), z_2 = 0.02548/2 (per period), and z_4 = 0.02983/2 (per period).

$$\left(1 + \frac{0.02548}{2}\right)^2 \times \left(1 + IFR_{2,2}\right)^2 = \left(1 + \frac{0.02983}{2}\right)^4, \quad IFR_{2,2} = 0.017095,$$

$$\times 2 = 0.03419$$

The "2y1y" implied forward rate is 2.707%. In Equation 14, A = 4 (periods), B = 6 (periods), B − A = 2 (periods), z_4 = 0.02983/2 (per period), and z_6 = 0.02891/2 (per period).

$$\left(1 + \frac{0.02983}{2}\right)^4 \times \left(1 + IFR_{4,2}\right)^2 = \left(1 + \frac{0.02891}{2}\right)^6, \quad IFR_{4,2} = 0.013536,$$

$$\times 2 = 0.02707$$

Solution to 2:

B is correct. The investor's view is that the one-year yield in two years will be greater than or equal to 2.707%.

The "2y1y" implied forward rate of 2.707% is the breakeven reinvestment rate. If the investor expects the one-year rate in two years to be less than that, the investor would prefer to buy the three-year zero. If the investor expects the one-year rate in two years to be greater than 2.707%, the investor might prefer to buy the two-year zero and reinvest the cash flow.

The forward curve has many applications in fixed-income analysis. Forward rates are used to make maturity choice decisions. They are used to identify arbitrage opportunities between transactions in the cash market for bonds and in derivatives markets. Forward rates are important in the valuation of derivatives, especially interest rate swaps and options. Those applications for the forward curve are covered in other readings.

Forward rates can be used to value a fixed-income security in the same manner as spot rates because they are interconnected. The spot curve can be calculated from the forward curve, and the forward curve can be calculated from the spot curve. Either curve can be used to value a fixed-rate bond. An example will illustrate this process.

Suppose the current forward curve for one-year rates is the following:

Time Period	Forward Rate
0y1y	1.88%
1y1y	2.77%
2y1y	3.54%
3y1y	4.12%

These are annual rates stated for a periodicity of one. They are effective annual rates. The first rate, the "0y1y," is the one-year spot rate. The others are one-year forward rates. Given these rates, the spot curve can be calculated as the *geometric average* of the forward rates.

The two-year implied spot rate is 2.3240%.

$$(1.0188 \times 1.0277) = (1 + z_2)^2, z_2 = 0.023240$$

The following are the equations for the three-year and four-year implied spot rates.

$$(1.0188 \times 1.0277 \times 1.0354) = (1 + z_3)^3, z_3 = 0.027278$$

$$(1.0188 \times 1.0277 \times 1.0354 \times 1.0412) = (1 + z_4)^4, z_4 = 0.030741$$

The three-year implied spot rate is 2.7278%, and the four-year spot rate is 3.0741%.

Suppose that an analyst needs to value a four-year, 3.75% annual coupon payment bond that has the same risks as the bonds used to obtain the forward curve. Using the implied spot rates, the value of the bond is 102.637 per 100 of par value.

$$\frac{3.75}{(1.0188)^1} + \frac{3.75}{(1.023240)^2} + \frac{3.75}{(1.027278)^3} + \frac{103.75}{(1.030741)^4} = 102.637$$

The bond also can be valued using the forward curve.

$$\frac{3.75}{(1.0188)} + \frac{3.75}{(1.0188 \times 1.0277)} + \frac{3.75}{(1.0188 \times 1.0277 \times 1.0354)}$$
$$+ \frac{103.75}{(1.0188 \times 1.0277 \times 1.0354 \times 1.0412)} = 102.637$$

5　YIELD SPREADS

A yield spread, in general, is the difference in yield between different fixed income securities. This section describes a number of yield spread measures.

5.1　Yield Spreads over Benchmark Rates

In fixed-income security analysis, it is important to understand *why* bond prices and yields-to-maturity change. To do this, it is useful to separate a yield-to-maturity into two components: the **benchmark** and the **spread**. The benchmark yield for a fixed-income security with a given time-to-maturity is the base rate, often a government bond yield. The spread is the difference between the yield-to-maturity and the benchmark.

The reason for this separation is to distinguish between macroeconomic and microeconomic factors that affect the bond price and, therefore, its yield-to-maturity. The benchmark captures the macroeconomic factors: the expected rate of inflation in the currency in which the bond is denominated, general economic growth and the business cycle, foreign exchange rates, and the impact of monetary and fiscal policy. Changes in those factors impact all bonds in the market, and the effect is seen mostly in changes in the benchmark yield. The spread captures the microeconomic factors specific to the bond issuer and the bond itself: credit risk of the issuer and changes in the quality rating on the bond, liquidity and trading in comparable securities, and the tax status of the bond. It should be noted, however, that general yield spreads across issuers can widen and narrow with changes in macroeconomic factors.

Exhibit 8 illustrates the building blocks of the yield-to-maturity, starting with the benchmark and the spread. The benchmark is often called the risk-free rate of return. Also, the benchmark can be broken down into the expected real rate and the expected inflation rate in the economy. The yield spread is called the risk premium over the "risk-free" rate of return. The risk premium provides the investor with compensation for the credit and liquidity risks, and possibly the tax impact of holding a specific bond.

Exhibit 8   Yield-to-Maturity Building Blocks

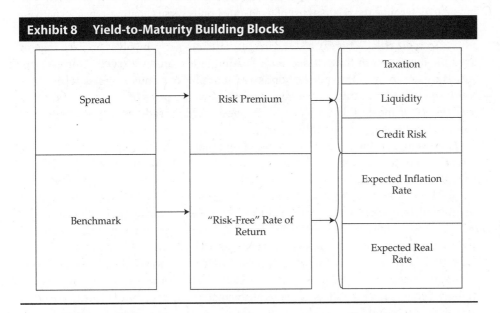

The benchmark varies across financial markets. Fixed-rate bonds often use a government benchmark security with the same time-to-maturity as, or the closest time-to-maturity to, the specified bond. This benchmark is usually the most recently issued government bond and is called the **on-the-run** security. The on-the-run government bond is the most actively traded security and has a coupon rate closest to the current market discount rate for that maturity. That implies that it is priced close to par value. Seasoned government bonds are called **off-the-run**. On-the-run bonds typically trade at slightly lower yields-to-maturity than off-the-run bonds having the same or similar times-to-maturity because of differences in demand for the securities and, sometimes, differences in the cost of financing the government security in the repo market.

A frequently used benchmark for floating-rate notes is Libor. As a composite interbank rate, it is not a risk-free rate. The yield spread over a specific benchmark is referred to as the **benchmark spread** and is usually measured in basis points. If no benchmark exists for a specific bond's tenor or a bond has an unusual maturity, interpolation is used to derive an implied benchmark. Also, bonds with very long tenors are priced over the longest available benchmark bond. For example, 100-year bonds (often called "century bonds") in the United States are priced over the 30-year US Treasury benchmark rate.

In the United Kingdom, the United States, and Japan, the benchmark rate for fixed-rate bonds is a government bond yield. The yield spread in basis points over an actual or interpolated government bond is known as the **G-spread**. The spread over a government bond is the return for bearing greater credit, liquidity, and other risks relative to the sovereign bond. Euro-denominated corporate bonds are priced over a EUR interest rate swap benchmark. For example, a newly issued five-year EUR bond might be priced at a rate of "mid-swaps" plus 150 bps, where "mid-swaps" is the average of the bid and offered swap rates. The yield spread is over a five-year EUR swap rate rather than a government benchmark. Note that the government bond yield or swap rate used as the benchmark for a specific corporate bond will change over time as the remaining time-to-maturity changes.

The yield spread of a specific bond over the standard swap rate in that currency of the same tenor is known as the **I-spread** or **interpolated spread** to the swap curve. This yield spread over Libor allows comparison of bonds with differing credit and liquidity risks against an interbank lending benchmark. Issuers often use the Libor spread to determine the relative cost of fixed-rate bonds versus floating-rate alternatives, such as an FRN or commercial paper. Investors use the Libor spread as a measure of a bond's credit risk. Whereas a standard interest rate swap involves an exchange of fixed for floating cash flows based on a floating index, an **asset swap** converts the periodic fixed coupon of a specific bond to a Libor plus or minus a spread. If the bond is priced close to par, this conversion approximates the price of a bond's credit risk over the Libor index. Exhibit 9 illustrates these yield spreads using the Bloomberg Fixed Income Relative Value (FIRV) page.

This example is for the 5.70% IBM bond that matures on 14 September 2017. The spreads are in the top-left corner of the page. The bond's flat price was 120.878 per 100 of par value on 1 May 2012, and its yield-to-maturity was 1.618%. On that date, the yield spread over a particular Treasury benchmark was 85 bps. Its G-spread over an interpolated government bond yield was 77 bps. These two spreads typically differ by a few basis points, especially if the benchmark is on-the-run and has a somewhat different maturity date. The bond's I-spread was 50 bps. That Libor spread is smaller than the G-spread because five-year Treasury yields were lower than five-year Libor swap rates at that time. The use of these spreads in investor strategies will be covered in more detail in later readings. In general, an analyst will track these spreads relative to their averages and historical highs and lows in an attempt to identify relative value.

5.2 Yield Spreads over the Benchmark Yield Curve

A yield curve shows the relationship between yields-to-maturity and times-to-maturity for securities with the same risk profile. For example, the government bond yield curve is the relationship between the yields of on-the-run government bonds and their times-to-maturity. The swap yield curve shows the relationship between fixed Libor swap rates and their times-to-maturity.

Each of these yield curves represents the term structure of benchmark interest rates, whether for "risk-free" government yields or "risky" fixed swap rates. Benchmark yield curves tend to be upward-sloping because investors typically demand a premium for holding longer-term securities. In general, investors face greater price risk for a given change in yield for longer-term bonds. This topic is covered further in the reading "Understanding Fixed-Income Risk and Return." The term structure of interest rates is dynamic, with short-term rates driven by central bank policy and longer-term rates affected by long-term growth and inflation expectations.

Isolating credit risk over varying times-to-maturity gives rise to a term structure of credit spreads that is distinct for each borrower. The G-spread and I-spread each use the same discount rate for each cash flow. Another approach is to calculate a constant yield spread over a government (or interest rate swap) spot curve instead. This spread is known as the **zero volatility spread (Z-spread)** of a bond over the benchmark rate. In Exhibit 9, the Z-spread for the IBM bond was reported to be 52 bps.

The Z-spread over the benchmark spot curve can be calculated with Equation 15:

$$PV = \frac{PMT}{\left(1 + z_1 + Z\right)^1} + \frac{PMT}{\left(1 + z_2 + Z\right)^2} + \cdots + \frac{PMT + FV}{\left(1 + z_N + Z\right)^N} \qquad \textbf{(15)}$$

The benchmark spot rates—z_1, z_2, ..., z_N—are derived from the government yield curve (or from fixed rates on interest rate swaps). Z is the Z-spread per period and is the same for all time periods. In Equation 15, N is an integer, so the calculation is on a coupon date when the accrued interest is zero. Sometimes, the Z-spread is

Exhibit 9 Bloomberg FIRV Page for the 5.70% IBM Bond

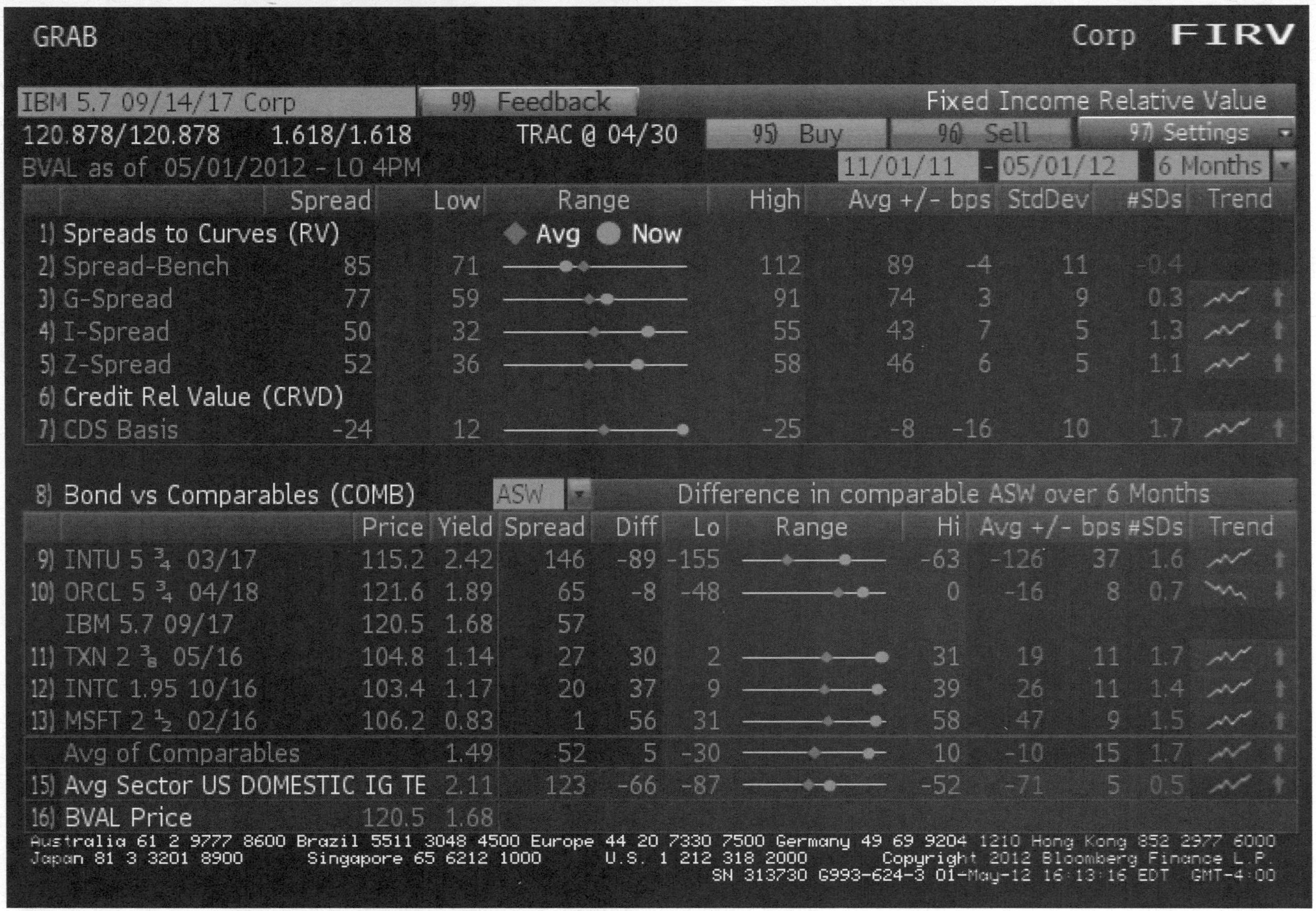
GRAB
Corp FIRV
IBM 5.7 09/14/17 Corp
99) Feedback
Fixed Income Relative Value
120.878/120.878 1.618/1.618 TRAC @ 04/30
95) Buy 96) Sell 97) Settings
BVAL as of 05/01/2012 - LO 4PM
11/01/11 - 05/01/12 6 Months
Spread Low Range High Avg +/- bps StdDev #SDs Trend
1) Spreads to Curves (RV) Avg Now
2) Spread-Bench 85 71 112 89 -4 11 -0.4
3) G-Spread 77 59 91 74 3 9 0.3
4) I-Spread 50 32 55 43 7 5 1.3
5) Z-Spread 52 36 58 46 6 5 1.1
6) Credit Rel Value (CRVD)
7) CDS Basis -24 12 -25 -8 -16 10 1.7
8) Bond vs Comparables (COMB) ASW Difference in comparable ASW over 6 Months
Price Yield Spread Diff Lo Range Hi Avg +/- bps #SDs Trend
9) INTU 5 3/4 03/17 115.2 2.42 146 -89 -155 -63 -126 37 1.6
10) ORCL 5 3/4 04/18 121.6 1.89 65 -8 -48 0 -16 8 0.7
IBM 5.7 09/17 120.5 1.68 57
11) TXN 2 3/8 05/16 104.8 1.14 27 30 2 31 19 11 1.7
12) INTC 1.95 10/16 103.4 1.17 20 37 9 39 26 11 1.4
13) MSFT 2 1/2 02/16 106.2 0.83 1 56 31 58 47 9 1.5
Avg of Comparables 1.49 52 5 -30 10 -10 15 1.7
15) Avg Sector US DOMESTIC IG TE 2.11 123 -66 -87 -52 -71 5 0.5
16) BVAL Price 120.5 1.68
Australia 61 2 9777 8600 Brazil 5511 3048 4500 Europe 44 20 7330 7500 Germany 49 69 9204 1210 Hong Kong 852 2977 6000
Japan 81 3 3201 8900 Singapore 65 6212 1000 U.S. 1 212 318 2000 Copyright 2012 Bloomberg Finance L.P.
SN 313730 G993-624-3 01-May-12 16:13:16 EDT GMT-4:00

called the static spread because it is constant (and has zero volatility). In practice, the Z-spread is usually calculated in a spreadsheet using a goal seek function or similar solver function.

The Z-spread is also used to calculate the **option-adjusted spread** (OAS) on a callable bond. The OAS, like the option-adjusted yield, is based on an option-pricing model and an assumption about future interest rate volatility. Then, the value of the embedded call option, which is stated in basis points per year, is subtracted from the yield spread. In particular, it is subtracted from the Z-spread:

OAS = Z-spread − Option value (in basis points per year)

This important topic is covered in later readings.

EXAMPLE 12

The G-Spread and the Z-Spread

A 6% annual coupon corporate bond with two years remaining to maturity is trading at a price of 100.125. The two-year, 4% annual payment government benchmark bond is trading at a price of 100.750. The one-year and two-year government spot rates are 2.10% and 3.635%, respectively, stated as effective annual rates.

1   Calculate the G-spread, the spread between the yields-to-maturity on the corporate bond and the government bond having the same maturity.

2   Demonstrate that the Z-spread is 234.22 bps.

Solution to 1:

The yield-to-maturity for the corporate bond is 5.932%.

$$100.125 = \frac{6}{(1+r)^1} + \frac{106}{(1+r)^2}, \quad r = 0.05932$$

The yield-to-maturity for the government benchmark bond is 3.605%.

$$100.750 = \frac{4}{(1+r)^1} + \frac{104}{(1+r)^2}, \quad r = 0.03605$$

The G-spread is 232.7 bps: 0.05932 − 0.03605 = 0.02327.

Solution to 2:

Solve for the value of the corporate bond using $z_1 = 0.0210$, $z_2 = 0.03635$, and $Z = 0.023422$:

$$\frac{6}{(1+0.0210+0.023422)^1} + \frac{106}{(1+0.03635+0.023422)^2}$$

$$= \frac{6}{(1.044422)^1} + \frac{106}{(1.059772)^2} = 100.125$$

SUMMARY

This reading covers the principles and techniques that are used in the valuation of fixed-rate bonds, as well as floating-rate notes and money market instruments. These building blocks are used extensively in fixed-income analysis. The following are the main points made in the reading:

- The market discount rate is the rate of return required by investors given the risk of the investment in the bond.

- A bond is priced at a premium above par value when the coupon rate is greater than the market discount rate.

- A bond is priced at a discount below par value when the coupon rate is less than the market discount rate.

- The amount of any premium or discount is the present value of the "excess" or "deficiency" in the coupon payments relative to the yield-to-maturity.

- The yield-to-maturity, the internal rate of return on the cash flows, is the implied market discount rate given the price of the bond.

- A bond price moves inversely with its market discount rate.

- The relationship between a bond price and its market discount rate is convex.

- The price of a lower-coupon bond is more volatile than the price of a higher-coupon bond, other things being equal.

- Generally, the price of a longer-term bond is more volatile than the price of shorter-term bond, other things being equal. An exception to this phenomenon can occur on low-coupon (but not zero-coupon) bonds that are priced at a discount to par value.

- Assuming no default, premium and discount bond prices are "pulled to par" as maturity nears.

- A spot rate is the yield-to-maturity on a zero-coupon bond.

- A yield-to-maturity can be approximated as a weighted average of the underlying spot rates.

- Between coupon dates, the full (or invoice, or "dirty") price of a bond is split between the flat (or quoted, or "clean") price and the accrued interest.

- Flat prices are quoted to not misrepresent the daily increase in the full price as a result of interest accruals.

- Accrued interest is calculated as a proportional share of the next coupon payment using either the actual/actual or 30/360 methods to count days.

- Matrix pricing is used to value illiquid bonds by using prices and yields on comparable securities having the same or similar credit risk, coupon rate, and maturity.

- The periodicity of an annual interest rate is the number of periods in the year.

- A yield quoted on a semiannual bond basis is an annual rate for a periodicity of two. It is the yield per semiannual period times two.

- The general rule for periodicity conversions is that compounding more frequently at a lower annual rate corresponds to compounding less frequently at a higher annual rate.

- Street convention yields assume payments are made on scheduled dates, neglecting weekends and holidays.

- The current yield is the annual coupon payment divided by the flat price, thereby neglecting as a measure of the investor's rate of return the time value of money, any accrued interest, and the gain from buying at a discount and the loss from buying at a premium.

- The simple yield is like the current yield but includes the straight-line amortization of the discount or premium.

- The yield-to-worst on a callable bond is the lowest of the yield-to-first-call, yield-to-second-call, and so on, calculated using the call price for the future value and the call date for the number of periods.

- The option-adjusted yield on a callable bond is the yield-to-maturity after adding the theoretical value of the call option to the price.

- A floating-rate note (floater, or FRN) maintains a more stable price than a fixed-rate note because interest payments adjust for changes in market interest rates.

- The quoted margin on a floater is typically the specified yield spread over or under the reference rate, which often is Libor.

- The discount margin on a floater is the spread required by investors, and to which the quoted margin must be set, for the FRN to trade at par value on a rate reset date.

- Money market instruments, having one year or less time-to-maturity, are quoted on a discount rate or add-on rate basis.

- Money market discount rates understate the investor's rate of return (and the borrower's cost of funds) because the interest income is divided by the face value or the total amount redeemed at maturity, and not by the amount of the investment.

- Money market instruments need to be converted to a common basis for analysis.

- A money market bond equivalent yield is an add-on rate for a 365-day year.

- The periodicity of a money market instrument is the number of days in the year divided by the number of days to maturity. Therefore, money market instruments with different times-to-maturity have annual rates for different periodicities.

- In theory, the maturity structure, or term structure, of interest rates is the relationship between yields-to-maturity and times-to-maturity on bonds having the same currency, credit risk, liquidity, tax status, and periodicity.

- A spot curve is a series of yields-to-maturity on zero-coupon bonds.

- A frequently used yield curve is a series of yields-to-maturity on coupon bonds.

- A par curve is a series of yields-to-maturity assuming the bonds are priced at par value.

- In a cash market, the delivery of the security and cash payment is made on a settlement date within a customary time period after the trade date—for example, "T + 3."

- In a forward market, the delivery of the security and cash payment is made on a predetermined future date.

- A forward rate is the interest rate on a bond or money market instrument traded in a forward market.

- An implied forward rate (or forward yield) is the breakeven reinvestment rate linking the return on an investment in a shorter-term zero-coupon bond to the return on an investment in a longer-term zero-coupon bond.

- An implied forward curve can be calculated from the spot curve.

- Implied spot rates can be calculated as geometric averages of forward rates.

- A fixed-income bond can be valued using a market discount rate, a series of spot rates, or a series of forward rates.

- A bond yield-to-maturity can be separated into a benchmark and a spread.

- Changes in benchmark rates capture macroeconomic factors that affect all bonds in the market—inflation, economic growth, foreign exchange rates, and monetary and fiscal policy.

- Changes in spreads typically capture microeconomic factors that affect the particular bond—credit risk, liquidity, and tax effects.

- Benchmark rates are usually yields-to-maturity on government bonds or fixed rates on interest rate swaps.

- A G-spread is the spread over or under a government bond rate, and an I-spread is the spread over or under an interest rate swap rate.

- A G-spread or an I-spread can be based on a specific benchmark rate or on a rate interpolated from the benchmark yield curve.

- A Z-spread (zero-volatility spread) is based on the entire benchmark spot curve. It is the constant spread that is added to each spot rate such that the present value of the cash flows matches the price of the bond.

- An option-adjusted spread (OAS) on a callable bond is the Z-spread minus the theoretical value of the embedded call option.

PRACTICE PROBLEMS

1 A portfolio manager is considering the purchase of a bond with a 5.5% coupon rate that pays interest annually and matures in three years. If the required rate of return on the bond is 5%, the price of the bond per 100 of par value is *closest* to:

    A   98.65.

    B   101.36.

    C   106.43.

2 A bond with two years remaining until maturity offers a 3% coupon rate with interest paid annually. At a market discount rate of 4%, the price of this bond per 100 of par value is *closest* to:

    A   95.34.

    B   98.00.

    C   98.11.

3 An investor who owns a bond with a 9% coupon rate that pays interest semiannually and matures in three years is considering its sale. If the required rate of return on the bond is 11%, the price of the bond per 100 of par value is *closest* to:

    A   95.00.

    B   95.11.

    C   105.15.

4 A bond offers an annual coupon rate of 4%, with interest paid semiannually. The bond matures in two years. At a market discount rate of 6%, the price of this bond per 100 of par value is *closest* to:

    A   93.07.

    B   96.28.

    C   96.33.

5 A bond offers an annual coupon rate of 5%, with interest paid semiannually. The bond matures in seven years. At a market discount rate of 3%, the price of this bond per 100 of par value is *closest* to:

    A   106.60.

    B   112.54.

    C   143.90.

6 A zero-coupon bond matures in 15 years. At a market discount rate of 4.5% per year and assuming annual compounding, the price of the bond per 100 of par value is *closest* to:

    A   51.30.

    B   51.67.

    C   71.62.

7 Consider the following two bonds that pay interest annually:

This question set was created by Mark Bhasin, CFA (New York, NY), Ryan C. Fuhrmann, CFA (Carmel, IN), Louis Lemos, CFA (Louisville, KY), Susan Ryan, CFA (East Hartland, CT), and Michael Whitehurst, CFA (San Diego, CA). Copyright © 2013 by CFA Institute.

Bond	Coupon Rate	Time-to-Maturity
A	5%	2 years
B	3%	2 years

At a market discount rate of 4%, the price difference between Bond A and Bond B per 100 of par value is *closest* to:

A 3.70.

B 3.77.

C 4.00.

The following information relates to Questions 8 and 9

Bond	Price	Coupon Rate	Time-to-Maturity
A	101.886	5%	2 years
B	100.000	6%	2 years
C	97.327	5%	3 years

8 Which bond offers the lowest yield-to-maturity?

  A Bond A

  B Bond B

  C Bond C

9 Which bond will *most likely* experience the smallest percent change in price if the market discount rates for all three bonds increase by 100 basis points?

  A Bond A

  B Bond B

  C Bond C

10 Suppose a bond's price is expected to increase by 5% if its market discount rate decreases by 100 basis points. If the bond's market discount rate increases by 100 basis points, the bond price is *most likely* to change by:

  A 5%.

  B less than 5%.

  C more than 5%.

The following information relates to Questions 11 and 12

Bond	Coupon Rate	Maturity (years)
A	6%	10
B	6%	5
C	8%	5

All three bonds are currently trading at par value.

11 Relative to Bond C, for a 200 basis point decrease in the required rate of return, Bond B will *most likely* exhibit a(n):

A equal percentage price change.

B greater percentage price change.

C smaller percentage price change.

12 Which bond will *most likely* experience the greatest percentage change in price if the market discount rates for all three bonds increase by 100 basis points?

A Bond A

B Bond B

C Bond C

13 An investor considers the purchase of a 2-year bond with a 5% coupon rate, with interest paid annually. Assuming the sequence of spot rates shown below, the price of the bond is *closest* to:

Time-to-Maturity	Spot Rates
1 year	3%
2 years	4%

A 101.93.

B 102.85.

C 105.81.

14 A 3-year bond offers a 10% coupon rate with interest paid annually. Assuming the following sequence of spot rates, the price of the bond is *closest* to:

Time-to-Maturity	Spot Rates
1 year	8.0%
2 years	9.0%
3 years	9.5%

A 96.98.

B 101.46.

C 102.95.

The following information relates to Questions 15–17

Bond	Coupon Rate	Time-to-Maturity	Time-to-Maturity	Spot Rates
X	8%	3 years	1 year	8%
Y	7%	3 years	2 years	9%
Z	6%	3 years	3 years	10%

All three bonds pay interest annually.

15 Based upon the given sequence of spot rates, the price of Bond X is *closest* to:

A 95.02.

B 95.28.

C 97.63.

16 Based upon the given sequence of spot rates, the price of Bond Y is *closest* to:

A 87.50.

B 92.54.

C 92.76.

17 Based upon the given sequence of spot rates, the yield-to-maturity of Bond Z is *closest* to:

A 9.00%.

B 9.92%.

C 11.93%

---

18 Bond dealers *most* often quote the:

A flat price.

B full price.

C full price plus accrued interest.

The following information relates to Questions 19–21

Bond G, described in the exhibit below, is sold for settlement on 16 June 2014.

Annual Coupon	5%
Coupon Payment Frequency	Semiannual
Interest Payment Dates	10 April and 10 October
Maturity Date	10 October 2016
Day Count Convention	30/360
Annual Yield-to-Maturity	4%

19 The full price that Bond G will settle at on 16 June 2014 is *closest* to:

A 102.36.

B 103.10.

C   103.65.

20 The accrued interest per 100 of par value for Bond G on the settlement date of 16 June 2014 is *closest* to:

A   0.46.

B   0.73.

C   0.92.

21 The flat price for Bond G on the settlement date of 16 June 2014 is *closest* to:

A   102.18.

B   103.10.

C   104.02.

---

22 Matrix pricing allows investors to estimate market discount rates and prices for bonds:

A   with different coupon rates.

B   that are not actively traded.

C   with different credit quality.

23 When underwriting new corporate bonds, matrix pricing is used to get an estimate of the:

A   required yield spread over the benchmark rate.

B   market discount rate of other comparable corporate bonds.

C   yield-to-maturity on a government bond having a similar time-to-maturity.

24 A bond with 20 years remaining until maturity is currently trading for 111 per 100 of par value. The bond offers a 5% coupon rate with interest paid semiannually. The bond's annual yield-to-maturity is *closest* to:

A   2.09%.

B   4.18%.

C   4.50%.

25 The annual yield-to-maturity, stated for with a periodicity of 12, for a 4-year, zero-coupon bond priced at 75 per 100 of par value is *closest* to:

A   6.25%.

B   7.21%.

C   7.46%.

26 A 5-year, 5% semiannual coupon payment corporate bond is priced at 104.967 per 100 of par value. The bond's yield-to-maturity, quoted on a semiannual bond basis, is 3.897%. An analyst has been asked to convert to a monthly periodicity. Under this conversion, the yield-to-maturity is *closest to*:

A   3.87%.

B   4.95%.

C   7.67%.

The following information relates to Questions 27–30

A bond with 5 years remaining until maturity is currently trading for 101 per 100 of par value. The bond offers a 6% coupon rate with interest paid semiannually. The bond is first callable in 3 years, and is callable after that date on coupon dates according to the following schedule:

End of Year	Call Price
3	102
4	101
5	100

27 The bond's annual yield-to-maturity is *closest* to:

A 2.88%.

B 5.77%.

C 5.94%.

28 The bond's annual yield-to-first-call is *closest* to:

A 3.12%.

B 6.11%.

C 6.25%.

29 The bond's annual yield-to-second-call is *closest* to:

A 2.97%.

B 5.72%.

C 5.94%.

30 The bond's yield-to-worst is *closest* to:

A 2.88%.

B 5.77%.

C 6.25%.

31 A two-year floating-rate note pays 6-month Libor plus 80 basis points. The floater is priced at 97 per 100 of par value. Current 6-month Libor is 1.00%. Assume a 30/360 day-count convention and evenly spaced periods. The discount margin for the floater in basis points (bps) is *closest* to:

A 180 bps.

B 236 bps.

C 420 bps.

32 An analyst evaluates the following information relating to floating rate notes (FRNs) issued at par value that have 3-month Libor as a reference rate:

Floating Rate Note	Quoted Margin	Discount Margin
X	0.40%	0.32%
Y	0.45%	0.45%
Z	0.55%	0.72%

Based only on the information provided, the FRN that will be priced at a premium on the next reset date is:

A   FRN X.

B   FRN Y.

C   FRN Z.

33 A 365-day year bank certificate of deposit has an initial principal amount of USD 96.5 million and a redemption amount due at maturity of USD 100 million. The number of days between settlement and maturity is 350. The bond equivalent yield is *closest* to:

A   3.48%.

B   3.65%.

C   3.78%.

34 The bond equivalent yield of a 180-day banker's acceptance quoted at a discount rate of 4.25% for a 360-day year is *closest* to:

A   4.31%.

B   4.34%.

C   4.40%.

35 Which of the following statements describing a par curve is *incorrect*?

A   A par curve is obtained from a spot curve.

B   All bonds on a par curve are assumed to have different credit risk.

C   A par curve is a sequence of yields-to-maturity such that each bond is priced at par value.

36 A yield curve constructed from a sequence of yields-to-maturity on zero-coupon bonds is the:

A   par curve.

B   spot curve.

C   forward curve.

37 The rate, interpreted to be the incremental return for extending the time-to-maturity of an investment for an additional time period, is the:

A   add-on rate.

B   forward rate.

C   yield-to-maturity.

The following information relates to Questions 38 and 39

Time Period	Forward Rate
"0y1y"	0.80%
"1y1y"	1.12%
"2y1y"	3.94%
"3y1y"	3.28%
"4y1y"	3.14%

All rates are annual rates stated for a periodicity of one (effective annual rates).

38 The 3-year implied spot rate is *closest* to:

A   1.18%.

B   1.94%.

C   2.28%.

39 The value per 100 of par value of a two-year, 3.5% coupon bond, with interest payments paid annually, is *closest* to:

A   101.58.

B   105.01.

C   105.82.

---

40 The spread component of a specific bond's yield-to-maturity is *least likely* impacted by changes in:

A   its tax status.

B   its quality rating.

C   inflation in its currency of denomination.

41 The yield spread of a specific bond over the standard swap rate in that currency of the same tenor is *best* described as the:

A   I-spread.

B   Z-spread.

C   G-spread.

The following information relates to Question 42

Bond	Coupon Rate	Time-to-Maturity	Price
UK Government Benchmark Bond	2%	3 years	100.25
UK Corporate Bond	5%	3 years	100.65

Both bonds pay interest annually. The current three-year EUR interest rate swap benchmark is 2.12%.

42 The G-spread in basis points (bps) on the UK corporate bond is *closest* to:

A   264 bps.

B   285 bps.

C   300 bps.

---

43 A corporate bond offers a 5% coupon rate and has exactly 3 years remaining to maturity. Interest is paid annually. The following rates are from the benchmark spot curve:

Time-to-Maturity	Spot Rate
1 year	4.86%
2 years	4.95%
3 years	5.65%

The bond is currently trading at a Z-spread of 234 basis points. The value of the bond is *closest to*:

A   92.38.

B   98.35.

C   106.56.

44   An option-adjusted spread (OAS) on a callable bond is the Z-spread:

A   over the benchmark spot curve.

B   minus the standard swap rate in that currency of the same tenor.

C   minus the value of the embedded call option expressed in basis points per year.

SOLUTIONS

1 B is correct. The bond price is closest to 101.36. The price is determined in the following manner:

$$PV = \frac{PMT}{(1+r)^1} + \frac{PMT}{(1+r)^2} + \frac{PMT + FV}{(1+r)^3}$$

where:

PV = present value, or the price of the bond
PMT = coupon payment per period
FV = future value paid at maturity, or the par value of the bond
r = market discount rate, or required rate of return per period

$$PV = \frac{5.5}{(1+0.05)^1} + \frac{5.5}{(1+0.05)^2} + \frac{5.5+100}{(1+0.05)^3}$$

$PV = 5.24 + 4.99 + 91.13 = 101.36$

2 C is correct. The bond price is closest to 98.11. The formula for calculating the price of this bond is:

$$PV = \frac{PMT}{(1+r)^1} + \frac{PMT + FV}{(1+r)^2}$$

where:

PV = present value, or the price of the bond
PMT = coupon payment per period
FV = future value paid at maturity, or the par value of the bond
r = market discount rate, or required rate of return per period

$$PV = \frac{3}{(1+0.04)^1} + \frac{3+100}{(1+0.04)^2} = 2.88 + 95.23 = 98.11$$

3 A is correct. The bond price is closest to 95.00. The bond has six semiannual periods. Half of the annual coupon is paid in each period with the required rate of return also being halved. The price is determined in the following manner:

$$PV = \frac{PMT}{(1+r)^1} + \frac{PMT}{(1+r)^2} + \frac{PMT}{(1+r)^3} + \frac{PMT}{(1+r)^4} + \frac{PMT}{(1+r)^5} + \frac{PMT + FV}{(1+r)^6}$$

where:

PV = present value, or the price of the bond
PMT = coupon payment per period
FV = future value paid at maturity, or the par value of the bond
r = market discount rate, or required rate of return per period

$$PV = \frac{4.5}{(1+0.055)^1} + \frac{4.5}{(1+0.055)^2} + \frac{4.5}{(1+0.055)^3} + \frac{4.5}{(1+0.055)^4} + \frac{4.5}{(1+0.055)^5} + \frac{4.5+100}{(1+0.055)^6}$$

$$PV = 4.27 + 4.04 + 3.83 + 3.63 + 3.44 + 75.79 = 95.00$$

4 B is correct. The bond price is closest to 96.28. The formula for calculating this bond price is:

$$PV = \frac{PMT}{(1+r)^1} + \frac{PMT}{(1+r)^2} + \frac{PMT}{(1+r)^3} + \frac{PMT+FV}{(1+r)^4}$$

where:

PV = present value, or the price of the bond
PMT = coupon payment per period
FV = future value paid at maturity, or the par value of the bond
r = market discount rate, or required rate of return per period

$$PV = \frac{2}{(1+0.03)^1} + \frac{2}{(1+0.03)^2} + \frac{2}{(1+0.03)^3} + \frac{2+100}{(1+0.03)^4}$$

$$PV = 1.94 + 1.89 + 1.83 + 90.62 = 96.28$$

5 B is correct. The bond price is closest to 112.54. The formula for calculating this bond price is:

$$PV = \frac{PMT}{(1+r)^1} + \frac{PMT}{(1+r)^2} + \frac{PMT}{(1+r)^3} + \cdots + \frac{PMT+FV}{(1+r)^{14}}$$

where:

PV = present value, or the price of the bond
PMT = coupon payment per period
FV = future value paid at maturity, or the par value of the bond
r = market discount rate, or required rate of return per period

$$PV = \frac{2.5}{(1+0.015)^1} + \frac{2.5}{(1+0.015)^2} + \frac{2.5}{(1+0.015)^3} + \cdots + \frac{2.5}{(1+0.015)^{13}} + \frac{2.5+100}{(1+0.015)^{14}}$$

$$PV = 2.46 + 2.43 + 2.39 + \ldots + 2.06 + 83.21 = 112.54$$

6 B is correct. The price of the zero-coupon bond is closest to 51.67. The price is determined in the following manner:

$$PV = \frac{100}{(1+r)^N}$$

where:

PV = present value, or the price of the bond
r = market discount rate, or required rate of return per period
N = number of evenly spaced periods to maturity

$$PV = \frac{100}{(1+0.045)^{15}}$$

$PV = 51.67$

7 B is correct. The price difference between Bonds A and B is closest to 3.77. One method for calculating the price difference between two bonds with an identical term to maturity is to use the following formula:

$$PV = \frac{PMT}{(1+r)^1} + \frac{PMT}{(1+r)^2}$$

where:

PV = price difference
PMT = coupon difference per period
r = market discount rate, or required rate of return per period

In this case the coupon difference is (5% − 3%), or 2%.

$$PV = \frac{2}{(1+0.04)^1} + \frac{2}{(1+0.04)^2} = 1.92 + 1.85 = 3.77$$

8 A is correct. Bond A offers the lowest yield-to-maturity. When a bond is priced at a premium above par value the yield-to-maturity (YTM), or market discount rate is less than the coupon rate. Bond A is priced at a premium, so its YTM is below its 5% coupon rate. Bond B is priced at par value so its YTM is equal to its 6% coupon rate. Bond C is priced at a discount below par value, so its YTM is above its 5% coupon rate.

9 B is correct. Bond B will most likely experience the smallest percent change in price if market discount rates increase by 100 basis points. A higher-coupon bond has a smaller percentage price change than a lower-coupon bond when their market discount rates change by the same amount (the coupon effect). Also, a shorter-term bond generally has a smaller percentage price change than a longer-term bond when their market discount rates change by the same amount (the maturity effect). Bond B will experience a smaller percent change in price than Bond A because of the coupon effect. Bond B will also experience a smaller percent change in price than Bond C because of the coupon effect and the maturity effect.

10 B is correct. The bond price is most likely to change by less than 5%. The relationship between bond prices and market discount rate is not linear. The percentage price change is greater in absolute value when the market discount rate goes down than when it goes up by the same amount (the convexity effect). If a 100 basis point decrease in the market discount rate will cause the price of the bond to increase by 5%, then a 100 basis point increase in the market discount rate will cause the price of the bond to decline by an amount less than 5%.

11 B is correct. Generally, for two bonds with the same time-to-maturity, a lower coupon bond will experience a greater percentage price change than a higher coupon bond when their market discount rates change by the same amount. Bond B and Bond C have the same time-to-maturity (5 years); however, Bond B offers a lower coupon rate. Therefore, Bond B will likely experience a greater percentage change in price in comparison to Bond C.

12 A is correct. Bond A will likely experience the greatest percent change in price due to the coupon effect and the maturity effect. For two bonds with the same time-to-maturity, a lower-coupon bond has a greater percentage price change than a higher-coupon bond when their market discount rates change by the same amount. Generally, for the same coupon rate, a longer-term bond has a greater percentage price change than a shorter-term bond when their market discount rates change by the same amount. Relative to Bond C, Bond A and Bond B both offer the same lower coupon rate of 6%; however, Bond A has a longer time-to-maturity than Bond B. Therefore, Bond A will likely experience the greater percentage change in price if the market discount rates for all three bonds increase by 100 basis points.

13 A is correct. The bond price is closest to 101.93. The price is determined in the following manner:

$$PV = \frac{PMT}{(1+Z_1)^1} + \frac{PMT+FV}{(1+Z_2)^2}$$

where:

PV = present value, or the price of the bond
PMT = coupon payment per period
FV = future value paid at maturity, or the par value of the bond
Z_1 = spot rate, or the zero-coupon yield, for Period 1
Z_2 = spot rate, or the zero-coupon yield, for Period 2

$$PV = \frac{5}{(1+0.03)^1} + \frac{5+100}{(1+0.04)^2}$$

$PV = 4.85 + 97.08 = 101.93$

14 B is correct. The bond price is closest to 101.46. The price is determined in the following manner:

$$PV = \frac{PMT}{(1+Z_1)^1} + \frac{PMT}{(1+Z_2)^2} + \frac{PMT+FV}{(1+Z_3)^3}$$

where:

PV = present value, or the price of the bond
PMT = coupon payment per period
FV = future value paid at maturity, or the par value of the bond
Z_1 = spot rate, or the zero-coupon yield, or zero rate, for period 1
Z_2 = spot rate, or the zero-coupon yield, or zero rate, for period 2
Z_3 = spot rate, or the zero-coupon yield, or zero rate, for period 3

$$PV = \frac{10}{(1+0.08)^1} + \frac{10}{(1+0.09)^2} + \frac{10+100}{(1+0.095)^3}$$

$PV = 9.26 + 8.42 + 83.78 = 101.46$

15 B is correct. The bond price is closest to 95.28. The formula for calculating this bond price is:

$$PV = \frac{PMT}{(1+Z_1)^1} + \frac{PMT}{(1+Z_2)^2} + \frac{PMT+FV}{(1+Z_3)^3}$$

where:

PV = present value, or the price of the bond
PMT = coupon payment per period

FV = future value paid at maturity, or the par value of the bond

Z_1 = spot rate, or the zero-coupon yield, or zero rate, for period 1

Z_2 = spot rate, or the zero-coupon yield, or zero rate, for period 2

Z_3 = spot rate, or the zero-coupon yield, or zero rate, for period 3

$$PV = \frac{8}{(1 + 0.08)^1} + \frac{8}{(1 + 0.09)^2} + \frac{8 + 100}{(1 + 0.10)^3}$$

$$PV = 7.41 + 6.73 + 81.14 = 95.28$$

16 C is correct. The bond price is closest to 92.76. The formula for calculating this bond price is:

$$PV = \frac{PMT}{(1 + Z_1)^1} + \frac{PMT}{(1 + Z_2)^2} + \frac{PMT + FV}{(1 + Z_3)^3}$$

where:

PV = present value, or the price of the bond

PMT = coupon payment per period

FV = future value paid at maturity, or the par value of the bond

Z_1 = spot rate, or the zero-coupon yield, or zero rate, for period 1

Z_2 = spot rate, or the zero-coupon yield, or zero rate, for period 2

Z_3 = spot rate, or the zero-coupon yield, or zero rate, for period 3

$$PV = \frac{7}{(1 + 0.08)^1} + \frac{7}{(1 + 0.09)^2} + \frac{7 + 100}{(1 + 0.10)^3}$$

$$PV = 6.48 + 5.89 + 80.39 = 92.76$$

17 B is correct. The yield-to-maturity is closest to 9.92%. The formula for calculating the price of Bond Z is:

$$PV = \frac{PMT}{(1 + Z_1)^1} + \frac{PMT}{(1 + Z_2)^2} + \frac{PMT + FV}{(1 + Z_3)^3}$$

where:

PV = present value, or the price of the bond

PMT = coupon payment per period

FV = future value paid at maturity, or the par value of the period 1

Z_1 = spot rate, or the zero-coupon yield, or zero rate Period 2

Z_2 = spot rate, or the zero-coupon yield, or zero for period 3

Z_3 = spot rate, or the zero-coupon yield, or

$$PV = \frac{6}{(1 + 0.08)^1} + \frac{6}{(1 + 0.09)^2} + \frac{6 + 1}{}$$

$$PV = 5.56 + 5.05 + 79.64 = \text{o-maturity can be calculated as:}$$

Using this price, the $\frac{\overline{T} + FV}{(1 + r)^3}$

$$PV = \frac{PMT}{(1}$$

$$PV = 100 \times (1 - 0.02125)$$

$$PV = 100 \times 0.97875$$

$$PV = 97.875$$

The bond equivalent yield (AOR) is calculated as:

$$AOR = \left(\frac{\text{Year}}{\text{Days}}\right) \times \left(\frac{FV - PV}{PV}\right)$$

where:

   PV = present value, principal amount, or the price of the money market
        instrument

   FV = future value, or the redemption amount paid at maturity including
        interest

Days = number of days between settlement and maturity

 Year = number of days in the year

AOR = add-on rate (bond equivalent yield), stated as an annual percentage rate

$$AOR = \left(\frac{365}{180}\right) \times \left(\frac{100 - PV}{PV}\right)$$

$$AOR = \left(\frac{365}{180}\right) \times \left(\frac{100 - 97.875}{97.875}\right)$$

$$AOR = 2.02778 \times 0.02171$$

$$AOR = 0.04402, \text{ or approximately } 4.40\%$$

Note that the PV is calculated using an assumed 360-day year and the AOR (bond equivalent yield) is calculated using a 365-day year.

35 B is correct. All bonds on a par curve are assumed to have similar, not different, credit risk. Par curves are obtained from spot curves and all bonds used to derive the par curve are assumed to have the same credit risk, as well as the same periodicity, currency, liquidity, tax status, and annual yields. A par curve is a sequence of yields-to-maturity such that each bond is priced at par value.

36 B is correct. The spot curve, also known as the strip or zero curve, is the yield curve constructed from a sequence of yields-to-maturities on zero-coupon bonds. The par curve is a sequence of yields-to-maturity such that each bond is priced at par value. The forward curve is constructed using a series of forward rates, each having the same timeframe.

37 B is correct. The forward rate can be interpreted to be the incremental or marginal return for extending the time-to-maturity of an investment for an additional time period. The add-on rate (bond equivalent yield) is a rate quoted for money market instruments such as bank certificates of deposit and indices such as Libor and Euribor. Yield-to-maturity is the internal rate of return on the bond's cash flows—the uniform interest rate such that when the bond's future cash flows are discounted at that rate, the sum of the present values equals the price of the bond. It is the implied market discount rate.

38 B is correct. The 3 year implied spot rate is closest to 1.94%. It is calculated as the geometric average of the one-year forward rates:

$$(1.0080 \times 1.0112 \times 1.0394) = (1 + z_3)^3$$

$$1.05945 = (1 + z_3)^3$$

$$[1.05945]^{1/3} = [(1 + z_3)^3]^{1/3}$$

$$1.01944 = 1 + z_3$$

$$1.01944 - 1 = z_3$$

$$0.01944 = z_3, z_3 = 1.944\% \text{ or approximately } 1.94\%$$

39 B is correct. The value per 100 of par value is closest to105.01. Using the forward curve, the bond price is calculated as follows:

$$\frac{3.5}{1.0080} + \frac{103.5}{(1.0080 \times 1.0112)} = 3.47 + 101.54 = 105.01$$

40 C is correct. The spread component of a specific bond's yield-to-maturity is least likely impacted by changes in inflation of its currency of denomination. The effect of changes in macroeconomic factors, such as the expected rate of inflation in the currency of denomination, is seen mostly in changes in the benchmark yield. The spread or risk premium component is impacted by microeconomic factors specific to the bond and bond issuer including tax status and quality rating.

41 A is correct. The I-spread, or interpolated spread, is the yield spread of a specific bond over the standard swap rate in that currency of the same tenor. The yield spread in basis points over an actual or interpolated government bond is known as the G-spread. The Z-spread (zero-volatility spread) is the constant spread such that is added to each spot rate such that the present value of the cash flows matches the price of the bond.

42 B is correct. The G-spread is closest to 285 bps. The benchmark rate for UK fixed-rate bonds is the UK government benchmark bond. The Euro interest rate spread benchmark is used to calculate the G-spread for Euro-denominated corporate bonds, not UK bonds. The G-spread is calculated as follows:

Yield-to-maturity on the UK corporate bond:

$$100.65 = \frac{5}{(1+r)^1} + \frac{5}{(1+r)^2} + \frac{105}{(1+r)^3}, r = 0.04762 \text{ or } 476 \text{ bps}$$

Yield-to-maturity on the UK government benchmark bond:

$$100.25 = \frac{2}{(1+r)^1} + \frac{2}{(1+r)^2} + \frac{102}{(1+r)^3}, r = 0.01913 \text{ or } 191 \text{ bps}$$

The G-spread is 476 − 191 = 285 bps.

43 A is correct. The value of the bond is closest to 92.38. The calculation is:

$$PV = \frac{PMT}{(1+z_1+Z)^1} + \frac{PMT}{(1+z_2+Z)^2} + \frac{PMT+FV}{(1+z_3+Z)^3}$$

$$= \frac{5}{(1+0.0486+0.0234)^1} + \frac{5}{(1+0.0495+0.0234)^2} + \frac{105}{(1+0.0565+0.0234)^3}$$

$$= \frac{5}{1.0720} + \frac{5}{1.15111} + \frac{105}{1.25936} = 4.66 + 4.34 + 83.38 = 92.38$$

44 C is correct. The option value in basis points per year is subtracted from the Z-spread to calculate the option-adjusted spread (OAS). The Z-spread is the constant yield spread over the benchmark spot curve. The I-spread is the yield spread of a specific bond over the standard swap rate in that currency of the same tenor.

Introduction to Asset-Backed Securities

by Frank J. Fabozzi, CFA

LEARNING OUTCOMES

Mastery	The candidate should be able to:
☐	**a.** explain benefits of securitization for economies and financial markets;
☐	**b.** describe the securitization process, including the parties to the process, the roles they play, and the legal structures involved;
☐	**c.** describe types and characteristics of residential mortgage loans that are typically securitized;
☐	**d.** describe types and characteristics of residential mortgage-backed securities, and explain the cash flows and credit risk for each type;
☐	**e.** explain the motivation for creating securitized structures with multiple tranches (e.g., collateralized mortgage obligations), and the characteristics and risks of securitized structures;
☐	**f.** describe the characteristics and risks of commercial mortgage-backed securities;
☐	**g.** describe types and characteristics of non-mortgage asset-backed securities, including the cash flows and credit risk of each type;
☐	**h.** describe collateralized debt obligations, including their cash flows and credit risk.

INTRODUCTION

1

Previous readings examined the risk characteristics of various basic fixed-income instruments and the relationships among maturity, coupon, and interest rate changes. This reading introduces an additional level of complexity—that of fixed-income instruments created through a process known as **securitization**. This process involves moving assets from the owner of the assets into a special legal entity. In addition to bonds issued by governments and companies, the fixed-income market includes securities that are backed, or collateralized, by a pool (collection) of assets, such as loans and receivables. These fixed-income securities are referred to generically as **asset-backed securities** (ABS). The special legal entity then uses the assets as collateral, and the assets' cash flows are used to pay the interest and repay the principal owed to the holders of the asset-backed bonds. Assets that are typically used to create asset backed bonds are called **securitized assets** and include, among others, residential mortgage loans, commercial mortgage loans, automobile loans, student loans, bank loans, and credit card debt. Advances and innovations in securitization have led to bonds collateralized by all kinds of income-yielding assets.

This reading discusses the benefits of securitization, describes the securitization process, and explains the investment characteristics of securitized instruments. The terminology regarding securitized securities varies by jurisdiction, however, so the use of terms will be clarified in this reading. A **mortgage-backed security** (MBS) is, by definition, an asset-backed security, but a distinction is often made between MBS and ABS backed by non-mortgage assets. Throughout this reading, the term "mortgage-backed securities," or MBS, refers to securities backed by high-quality real estate mortgages and the term "asset-backed securities," or ABS, refers to securities backed by other types of assets.

Much of the discussion and many examples in the reading refer to the United States primarily because the securitization market in the United States is the largest in the world. Moreover, it is considerably larger than those in other countries.

To underline the importance of securitization from a macroeconomic perspective, Section 2 begins with a discussion of the benefits of securitization for economies and financial markets. The reading then turns in Section 3 to the securitization process; the text identifies all of the parties to the process and points out the key role of the special legal entity in making the creation of asset-backed bonds for companies and other fund-raising entities worthwhile. Sections 4–6 explain bonds backed by mortgage loans for real estate property. The various types of residential mortgage loan designs around the world are described in Section 4. The focus of Section 5 is on residential MBS (RMBS), whereas Section 6 is devoted to commercial MBS (CMBS). Section 7 discusses the two major types of non-mortgage loans that are typically securitized throughout the world: automobile loan receivable ABS and credit card receivable ABS. Finally, an asset-backed product called a collateralized debt obligation (CDO) is covered in Section 8. Section 9 concludes the reading with a summary.

2 BENEFITS OF SECURITIZATION FOR ECONOMIES AND FINANCIAL MARKETS

Securitization is a process in which relatively simple debt obligations, such as loans or bonds, are repackaged into more complex structures that involve the participation of several new entities. The securitization of pools of loans into multiple securities provides an economy with a number of benefits.[1]

Traditionally, most financing of mortgages and other types of financial assets has been through financial institutions such as commercial banks. For investors to participate in such financing, they must hold some combination of deposits, debt, or common equity issued by banks. This creates an additional layer (the bank) between the borrowers and the ultimate investors. In addition, the process makes it difficult for ultimate investors to specialize in exposure to particular types of assets they might desire to hold. By being constrained to hold bank deposits and securities, ultimate investors are also affected by economic risks undertaken in other sections of bank portfolios.

---

1 For a more detailed discussion, see Fabozzi and Kothari (2008).

Securitization solves a number of these problems. It lowers or removes the wall between ultimate investors and originating borrowers. It allows ultimate investors to achieve better legal claims on underlying mortgages and portfolios of receivables and allows them to tailor interest rate and credit risks to suit their needs. Because of disintermediation (lessening the role of intermediaries), the costs paid by borrowers can be effectively lowered while the risk-adjusted returns to ultimate investors can be enhanced. At the same time, banks can improve their profitability by increasing loan origination more than they would be able to do if they could engage only in those activities they could finance themselves (with their own deposits, debt, and equity). That is, securitization allows banks to increase the amount of funds available to lend, which ultimately benefits governments and companies that need to borrow. Indeed, securitization works because it benefits borrowers, investors, and banks (and/or other financial intermediaries). The asset-backed bonds are sold in the public market. So, effectively, securitization allows banks to originate (create) loans, package (pool) the loans to use as collateral for the asset-backed bonds, and sell those asset-backed bonds to the public.

Securitization also allows for the creation of tradable securities with better liquidity than the original loans on the bank's balance sheet. In making loans and receivables tradable, securitization makes financial markets more efficient and improves liquidity for the underlying financial claims. Thus, securitization reduces liquidity risk in the financial system. In fact, an adviser to the People's Bank of China gave this very reason for its plans to launch a pilot securitization program in March 2012 that would permit certain Chinese commercial lenders to securitize such assets as car loans. The adviser stated that securitization could help banks in China transform illiquid assets on their books into liquid assets.[2] The process by which liquidity improves will become clear when securitization is described in more detail in Section 3.

An additional benefit is that securitization enables innovations in investment products, which allow investors to access asset classes matching their risk, return, and maturity profiles that are otherwise not directly available. For example, a pension fund with a long-term horizon can gain direct access to long-term housing loans by investing in RMBS without having to invest in bank bonds or stocks. Although few institutional or individual investors are willing to purchase real estate loans, automobile loans, or credit card receivables directly, they would be willing to invest in a security backed by such loans or receivables that had characteristics similar to a standard bond, particularly if doing so will not require the specialized resources needed to originate, monitor, and collect the payments from the underlying loans.

For these reasons, securitization is as necessary to an economy as are security exchanges. Sovereign governments throughout the world have embraced securitization. For example, the Italian government has used securitization since the late 1990s for privatizing public assets. In emerging market countries, securitization is widely used. For example, companies and banks in South America with high credit ratings have used securitization to sell receivables on exports, such as oil at favorable financing costs.

Although securitization brings many benefits to economies, it is not without risks. These risks are widely attributed to have precipitated the turmoil in financial markets during 2007–2009. Many of these risks are described in this reading.

---

2 "China Revives Giant Securitization Program" (2012), p. 6.

EXAMPLE 1

Securitization and the Financial Stability Board

The following appeared in the July 2011 publication by the Joint Forum titled "Report on Securitization Incentives" and published by the Bank for International Settlements:

> Re-establishing sustainable securitization markets has been high on the agenda of the Group of Twenty (G-20), the Financial Stability Board (FSB, an international body established to coordinate and promote implementation of the work of financial authorities and standard setting bodies), and other international organizations and national governments since the onset of the crisis.
>
> The FSB's November 20, 2010, report to the G-20 leaders noted, in particular, that "Re-establishing securitization on a sound basis remains a priority in order to support provision of credit to the real economy and improve banks' access to funding in many jurisdictions."

Explain what is meant by the quotation in the FSB's November 20 report.

Solution:

Funding via securitization is a means by which non-bank entities can provide investment funds to various sectors of the economy without those sectors relying exclusively on banks. Securitization allows banks to originate, monitor, and collect loans beyond what they could do if limited to their own deposits and capital. Thus, securitization allows the non-bank and bank sectors to provide credit to the real economy more cheaply and efficiently than would otherwise be available only from banks.

---

3   THE SECURITIZATION PROCESS

When assets are securitized, several legal and regulatory conditions must be satisfied, which necessitates the introduction of new parties into the process to facilitate the transaction. In this section, the securitization process is described and the parties to a securitization are introduced by way of a hypothetical securitization transaction.

3.1 An Example of a Securitization Transaction

Consider the case of Mediquip, a manufacturer of medical equipment that ranges in cost from US$50,000 to US$300,000. Some of this equipment is sold for cash. The majority of Mediquip's sales, however, are made through loans granted by the company to its customers. These loans, which represent an asset to Mediquip, have maturities of five years and carry a fixed interest rate. The loans are fully amortizing with monthly payments; that is, the borrowers will make equal payments each month consisting of principal and interest. The total principal paid from the 60 loan payments (12 months × 5 years) is such that the amount borrowed will be fully repaid (fully amortized) at the end of the term.

Mediquip's credit department makes the decision about whether to extend credit to customers and services the loans that are made. Servicing involves collecting payments from borrowers, notifying borrowers who may be delinquent, and if necessary, recovering and disposing of the medical equipment if the borrower does not make loan repayments by a specified time. The medical equipment serves as collateral for the loan made to customers. Recall that collateral are assets or financial guarantees underlying a debt obligation above and beyond the borrower's promise to pay. If one of its customers defaults, Mediquip can seize the medical equipment and sell it to try to recoup the remaining principal on the loan. Although the servicer of such loans need not be the originator of the loans, the assumption in this example is that Mediquip will be the servicer.

The following is an illustration of how these loans can be used in a securitization. Assume that Mediquip has US$200 million of loans. This amount is shown on Mediquip's balance sheet as an asset. Assume also that Mediquip wants to raise US$200 million in cash, which just happens to be the amount of the loans. Because he is aware of the potentially lower costs of securitization, Mediquip's treasurer decides to raise the funds via a securitization rather than by issuing corporate bonds for US$200 million. To do so, Mediquip will set up a legal entity often called a **special purpose vehicle** (SPV) but sometimes also called a special purpose entity (SPE) or special purpose company (SPC). The critical role of this legal entity will soon become clear. In our example, the SPV that is set up is called Medical Equipment Trust (MET).

The securitization transaction is diagramed in Exhibit 1. The top of Exhibit 1 reflects Mediquip's business model as described above. As shows on the right-hand side, Mediquip sells to MET US$200 million of the loans and receives from MET US$200 million cash—in this example, the costs associated with the securitization process are ignored. As illustrated at the bottom of Exhibit 1, MET obtains the US$200 million from investors by selling securities that are backed by the US$200 million of loans. These securities are the asset-backed securities mentioned earlier.

Exhibit 1   Securitization Transaction for Mediquip

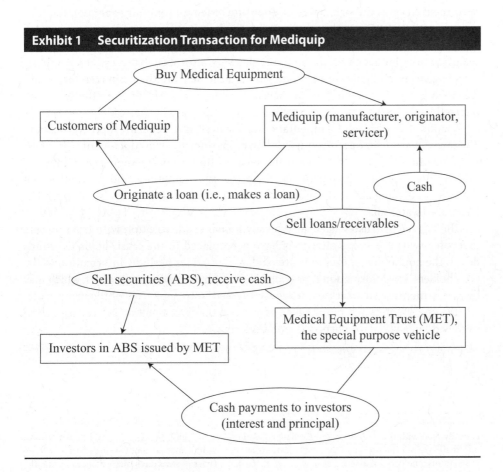

The securitization process requires the publication of a prospectus, a document that contains information about the securitization transaction.[3] In our example, MET (the SPV) would be called either the "issuer" or the "trust." Mediquip, the seller of the collateral to MET, would be called the "seller" or "depositor." The prospectus might then state, "The securities represent obligations of the issuer only and do not represent obligations of, or interests in, Mediquip or any of its affiliates." Notice that the term "collateral: in this statement is used differently from how it was earlier described. Here, collateral means the pool of securitized assets from which the cash flows will be generated.

The payments that are received from the collateral are distributed to pay servicing fees, other administrative fees and, as illustrated at the bottom of Exhibit 1, to make cash payments (interest and principal) to the security holders; that is, the investors who bought the ABS. The prospectus sets forth in considerable detail the priority and amount of payments to be made to the servicer, administrators, and the security holders. Because ABS usually include different bond classes or tranches,[4] the prospectus must specify the priority and amount of payments in the event that the cash flows generated by the pool of securitized assets is insufficient to make all cash payments to security holders. The structure adopted in a securitization transaction is commonly referred to as the **waterfall** because of the cascading flow of payments between bond classes.

3.2 Parties and Their Role to a Securitization Transaction

Thus far, three parties to a securitization have been noted: the seller of the collateral (also referred to as the originator or depositor; Mediquip in our example), the SPV (sometimes referred to in the prospectus as the issuer or trust; MET in our example), and the servicer (here, Mediquip is the servicer). Other parties are also involved in a securitization: independent accountants, lawyers/attorneys, trustees, underwriters, rating agencies, and guarantors. The seller and the SPV are the main counterparties. All the other parties, including the servicer when it is different from the seller, are referred to as third parties to the transaction.

A good deal of legal documentation is involved in a securitization transaction. The lawyers/attorneys are responsible for preparing the legal documents. The first is the purchase agreement between the seller of the assets (Mediquip) and the SPV (MET). The purchase agreement sets forth the representations and warranties that the seller is making about the assets sold. The second legal document sets forth the structure's waterfall.

The trustee or trustee agent is typically a financial institution with trust powers that safeguards the assets after they have been placed in the trust, holds the funds due to the bondholders until they are paid, and provides periodic information to the bondholders. The information is provided in the form of remittance reports, which may be issued monthly, quarterly, or whenever agreed to by the terms of the prospectus.

The underwriters and rating agencies perform the same function in a securitization as they do in a standard corporate bond offering.

---

3 To be more precise, in the United States, a "base prospectus" and a "supplementary prospectus" are typically filed with the Securities and Exchange Commission. The base prospectus provides definitions, information about the parties to the securitization, and certain information about securities to be offered in the future: the types of assets that may be securitized, the types of structures that will be used, and the types of credit enhancement (the last two are discussed in Section 5.3). The supplementary prospectus provides the details of a specific securitization.

4 In a securitization, the terms "bond class" and "tranche" are used interchangeably. The latter means "slice" in French.

Finally, a securitization may have an entity that guarantees part of the obligations issued by the SPV. These entities are called "guarantors." Because of their important role for securitized instruments, guarantors are discussed thoroughly in Section 5.3.2 about external credit enhancement.

EXAMPLE 2

A Securitization by Harley-Davidson

Harley-Davidson, Inc. manufactures and markets motorcycles. The following information is taken from a filing with the US Securities and Exchange Commission for a securitization related to the purchase of Harley-Davidson motorcycles:

> Issuer: Harley-Davidson Motorcycle Trust 2005-2
>
> US$487,000,000 3.79% Harley-Davidson Motorcycle Contract Backed Notes, Class A-1
>
> US $251,180,000 4.07% Harley-Davidson Motorcycle Contract Backed Notes, Class A-2
>
> US$ 36,820,000 4.27% Harley-Davidson Motorcycle Contract Backed Notes, Class B
>
> Seller and Servicer: Harley-Davidson Credit Corp.
>
> Contracts: The assets underlying the notes are fixed-rate, simple interest, conditional sales contracts, promissory notes, and security agreements relating to the purchase of new or used motorcycles.

With this information, identify the collateral and the parties to this securitization.

Solution:

In a securitization, a pool of debt obligations is used as collateral for the securities issued. In this securitization, the debt obligations that have been securitized are the "contracts" described in the information set above. These contracts are basically loans provided to purchasers of motorcycles manufactured by Harley-Davidson, Inc. and designated subsidiaries. The loans go by different names, such as conditional sales agreements, promissory notes, and security agreements. The loans carry a fixed interest rate.

The issuer or trust of the three bond classes is Harley-Davidson Motorcycle Trust 2005-2. Although not directly stated in the information set, Harley-Davidson Motorcycle Trust 2005-2 is also the SPV. This SPV purchases the contracts from Harley-Davidson Credit Corp., the seller or depositor. We might have expected the contracts to have been purchased from Harley-Davidson, Inc., but it is Harley-Davidson Credit Corp. that originates the loans and is, therefore, the seller of the loans, as noted in the information set. The loans also have to be serviced, and as indicated in the information set, Harley-Davidson Credit Corp. is also the servicer of the contracts.

3.3 Bonds Issued

A simple transaction may involve the sale of only one bond class, such as the class with a par value of US$200 million as in the Mediquip and MET example. Let us call this class Bond Class A. Suppose MET issues 200,000 certificates for Bond Class A with a par value of US$1,000 per certificate. Thus, each certificate holder is entitled to 1/200,000 of the payments from the collateral after payment of fees and expenses.

A structure may be more complicated. For example, there may be rules for distribution of principal and interest other than on a pro rata basis to the various bond classes. For instance, suppose MET issued the following four bond classes, with a total par value of US$200 million: A1 (US$80 million), A2 (US$60 million), A3 (US$40 million), and A4 (US$20 million). In such a structure, rules will be established for the distribution of interest and principal to the four bond classes. Some bond classes may receive payments earlier than others.

The motivation for the creation of different structures is the redistribution of a type of risk, called prepayment risk, among bond classes. **Prepayment risk** is the uncertainty that the cash flows will be different from the scheduled cash flows as set forth in the loan agreement due to the borrowers' ability to alter payments, usually to take advantage of interest rate movements. For example, borrowers tend to pay off part or all of their loans when interest rate decline, refinancing at a lower interest rate if necessary. The creation of bond classes is referred to as **time tranching** and is further discussed in Section 5.2.

Another common structure in a securitization transaction is **subordination**. In such a structure, there is more than one bond class, and the bond classes differ as to how they will share any losses resulting from defaults of the borrowers whose loans are in the pool of loans. The bond classes are classified as senior bond classes or subordinated bond classes, and the structure is called a senior/subordinated structure. Losses are realized by the subordinate bond classes before any losses are realized by the senior bond classes. For example, suppose MET issued US$180 million par value of Bond Class A (the senior bond class) and US$20 million par value of Bond Class B (the subordinate bond class). In this structure, Bond Class B will absorb losses up to US$ 20 million. Thus, as long as defaults by borrowers do not exceed US$20 million, Bond Class A will be repaid fully its US$180 million. The purpose of this structure is to redistribute the credit risk associated with the collateral. This is referred to as **credit tranching**; that is, a set of bond classes is created to allow investors a choice in the amount of credit risk that they prefer to bear. As explained in Section 5.3.1, the senior/subordinated structure is a form of credit enhancement.

More than one subordinated bond class may be created. Suppose MET issued the following structure:

Bond Class	Par Value ($ millions)
A (senior)	180
B (subordinated)	14
C (subordinated)	6
Total	200

In this structure, Bond Class A is the senior bond class whereas both Bond Class B and Bond Class C are subordinated bond classes from the perspective of Bond Class A. The rules for the distribution of losses are as follows. All losses on the collateral are absorbed by Bond Class C before any losses are realized by Bond Class B and then Bond Class A. Consequently, if the losses on the collateral do not exceed US$6 million, no losses will be realized by Bond Class A and Bond Class B. If the losses exceed US$6 million, Bond Class B must absorb the loss up to an additional US$14 million (its par value). For example, if the total loss on the collateral is US$16 million, Bond Class C loses its entire par value ($6 million) and Bond Class B realizes a loss of US$10 million of its US$14 million par value. Bond Class A does not realize any loss in this scenario. Clearly, Bond Class A realizes a loss only if the loss from the collateral exceeds US$20 million.

It is possible, and quite common, to have structures with both time tranching and credit tranching.

EXAMPLE 3

Bond Classes and Tranching

Return to the Harley-Davidson securitization described in Example 2. How many bond classes are there in the securitization transaction? If the A-1 Notes are senior to the A-2 Notes, which are, in turn, senior to the B Notes, does the transaction have time and/or credit tranching?

Solution:

There are three bond classes or tranches in the securitization transaction: Class A-1, Class A-2, and Class B. Each bond class has a fixed but different interest rate. The transaction has credit tranching because the three bond classes display a senior/subordinated structure: The A-1 bond class is senior to the A-2 bond class, and both are senior to the subordinated bond class, B. From the description, the structure does not seem to involve time tranching because all bond classes receive interest payments and principal repayments as the payments are made by borrowers.

3.4 Key Role of the Special Purpose Vehicle

As a special legal entity, the SPV plays a pivotal role in the securitization process. In fact, the establishment of a legal structure that plays the same role as the SPV in terms of protecting the rights of creditors investing in asset-backed bonds is a prerequisite in any country that wants to allow securitization. Indeed, without a provision in a country's legal system for the equivalent of an SPV, the benefits of using securitization by an entity seeking to raise funds would not exist. Let's explain why using our example involving Mediquip and MET.

Assume Mediquip is a company that has a credit rating obtained from a credit-rating agency, such as Standard & Poor's, Moody's Investors Service, or Fitch Ratings. A credit rating reflects the opinion of a credit-rating agency about the creditworthiness of an entity and/or the debt securities it issues. Suppose the credit rating assigned to Mediquip is BB (or, double B). Such a credit rating means that Mediquip is just below what is referred to as an investment-grade credit rating.

Suppose again that Mediquip's treasurer wants to raise US$200 million and is contemplating doing so by issuing a five-year corporate bond rather than securitizing the loans. The treasurer is, of course, concerned about the interest rate the company will have to pay and would like the lowest possible interest rate available relative to some benchmark interest rate. The difference between the interest rate that the issuer has to pay on the five-year corporate bond and the benchmark interest rate is the spread. The spread reflects the compensation investors require to buy the corporate bond, which is riskier than bonds issued at the benchmark interest rate. The major factor affecting the spread is the company's credit rating, hence the reason the spread is called a "credit spread."

Another factor that will influence the credit spread is whether the bond is backed by collateral (that is, backed by assets or financial guarantees). A corporate bond that has collateral is often referred to as a secured bond. The collateral usually reduces the credit spread, making the credit spread of a secured bond lower than that of an otherwise identical unsecured corporate bond. In our example, Mediquip's treasurer can use the loans on the medical equipment as collateral for the secured corporate bond offering. So, if Mediquip, with a credit rating of BB, issues a five-year corporate bond to raise US$200 million, the credit spread will reflect its credit rating primarily and the collateral slightly. We will soon see why the collateral affects the credit spread only slightly.

Now suppose that instead of using the loans to its customers as collateral for a secured corporate bond issue, Mediquip's treasurer sells the loan contracts in an arm's length transaction to MET, the SPV. After the sale of the receivables by Mediquip to MET is completed, MET, not Mediquip, legally owns the receivables. As a result, if Mediquip is forced into bankruptcy while the receivables sold are still outstanding, Mediquip's creditors cannot recover the receivables, which are legally owned by MET. The legal implication is that when MET issues bonds that are backed by the cash flows from the pool of loans, investors contemplating the purchase of any bond class evaluate the credit risk associated with collecting the payments due on the receivables independent of Mediquip's credit rating.

Credit ratings are assigned to each of the various bond classes created in the securitization and depend on how the credit-rating agencies evaluate the credit risk based on the collateral (i.e., the loans). So, because of the creation of a SPV, the quality of the collateral, and the capital structure of the SPV, a company can raise funds via securitization in which some of the bond classes have a better credit rating than the company that is seeking to raise funds. As a consequence, in aggregate, the funding cost of issuing an asset-backed bond is less than that of issuing a corporate bond. Lowering funding cost is the key role of the SPV in a securitization.

A fair question is why a securitization can have a lower credit cost than a corporate bond secured by the same collateral as the securitization. The reason is that the SPV is a bankruptcy-remote vehicle. As mentioned above, in a properly structured securitization, the assets belong to the SPV, not to the entity that sold the assets to the SPV in exchange for funds. In many countries, including the United States, when a company is liquidated, creditors receive distributions based on the *absolute priority rule* to the extent that assets are available. The absolute priority rule is the principle that senior creditors are paid in full before subordinated creditors are paid anything. For secured creditors and unsecured creditors, the absolute priority rule guarantees their seniority relative to equity holders.

In liquidations, the absolute priority rule generally holds. In contrast, when a company is reorganized, the strict absolute priority has not always been upheld by the courts. Thus, although investors in the debt of a company may believe they have priority over the equity owners and priority over other classes of debtors, the actual outcome of a reorganization may be far different from the terms stated in the debt agreement; that is, there is no assurance that if the corporate bond has collateral (i.e., backed by assets), the rights of the bondholders will be respected. For this reason, the credit spread for a bond backed by collateral does not decrease dramatically.

In the case of a securitization, the courts (in most jurisdictions) have no discretion to change seniority because the bankruptcy of a company does not affect the SPV. The rules set forth in the securitization's structure about how losses are to be absorbed by each bond class in the capital structure of the securitization are unaffected by the company's bankruptcy. This important decoupling of the credit risk of the entity needing funds from the bond classes issued by the SPV makes it clear that the SPV's legal role is critical.

However, all countries do not have the same legal framework. Impediments have arisen in some countries with respect to the issuance of asset-backed bonds because the concept of trust law is not as well developed globally as it is in the United States.[5] Thus, investors should be aware of the legal considerations that apply in the jurisdictions where they purchase asset-backed bonds.

EXAMPLE 4

The Special Purpose Vehicle and Bankruptcy

Agnelli Industries, a manufacturer of industrial machine tools based in Bergamo, Italy, has €400 million of receivables on its balance sheet that it would like to securitize. The receivables represent payments Agnelli expects to receive for machine tools it has sold to various customers in Europe. Agnelli's corporate bonds have a credit rating below investment grade. Agnelli securitizes the receivables by selling them to the Agnelli Trust (the special purpose vehicle), which then issues the following bonds that all have a maturity of five years:

Bond Class	Par Value (€ millions)
A (senior)	280
B (subordinated)	60
C (subordinated)	60
Total	400

The Class A bonds in the securitization have an investment-grade credit rating.

1 How can a class of an asset-backed bond have an investment-grade rating when Agnelli's corporate bonds do not?

2 Assume that two years after the issuance of the asset-backed bonds, Agnelli Industries files for bankruptcy. What is the effect of the bankruptcy on the holders of the asset-backed bonds?

Solution to 1:

The Class A bonds can have an investment-grade credit rating when Agnelli's corporate bonds do not because the asset-backed bonds are issued by the Agnelli Trust, a SPV that is a separate legal entity from Agnelli Industries. The investors who hold Agnelli Industries bonds and/or stock have no legal claim on the cash flows from the securitized receivables that are the collateral for the asset-backed bonds. Credit-rating agencies evaluate the credit risk of these cash flows independently from those of Agnelli Industries itself. For this reason, the Class A bonds can have a higher credit rating even than Agnelli Industries' corporate bonds.

Solution to 2:

If the securitization transaction is viewed as a true sale, the fact that Agnelli Industries files for bankruptcy does not affect the holders of the asset-backed bonds. These bondholders face credit risk only to the extent that the customers

---

5 In many EU countries, the creditors are protected in the recognition of the securitization transaction as a true sale. The SPV has full legal ownership of the securitized assets, which are de-recognized from the seller's balance sheet. In the event of default of the originator/servicer, the SPV can appoint a substitute company to the service role and continue to pay bondholders from the income stream of the securitized assets without the other creditors of the initial originator/servicer being able to have any recourse or claim to these assets.

> who bought the machine tools do not make the obligatory payments on their loans. As long as the customers continue to make payments, all three bond classes will receive their expected cash flows. These cash flows are completely and legally independent of anything that happens to Agnelli Industries itself.

4   RESIDENTIAL MORTGAGE LOANS

Before describing the various types of residential mortgage-backed securities, this section briefly discusses the fundamental features of the raw product: the residential mortgage loan. The mortgage designs described in this section are those that are typically securitized.

A **mortgage loan**, or simply mortgage, is a loan secured by the collateral of some specified real estate property that obliges the borrower (often someone wishing to buy a home) to make a predetermined series of payments to the lender (often initially a bank or mortgage company). The mortgage gives the lender the right to foreclose on the loan if the borrower defaults—that is, a **foreclosure** allows the lender to take possession of the mortgaged property and then sell it in order to recover funds toward satisfying the debt obligation.

Typically, the amount of the loan advanced to purchase the property is less than the property's purchase price. The borrower makes a down payment, and the amount borrowed is the difference between the property's purchase price and the down payment. When the loan is first taken out, the borrower's equity in the property is equal to the down payment. Over time, as the market value of the property changes, the borrower's equity also changes. It also changes as the borrower makes mortgage payments that include principal repayment.

The ratio of the property's purchase price to the amount of the mortgage is called the **loan-to-value ratio** (LTV). The higher the LTV, the lower the borrower's equity; the lower the LTV, the greater the borrower's equity. From the lender's perspective, the more equity the borrower has (i.e., the lower the LTV), the less likely the borrower is to default. Moreover, the lower the LTV, the more protection the lender has for recovering the amount loaned if the borrower does default and the lender repossesses and sells the property.

Throughout the world, there are a considerable number of mortgage designs. Mortgage design means the specification of (1) the maturity of the loan, (2) how the interest rate is determined, (3) how the principal is to be repaid (i.e., the amortization schedule), (4) whether the borrower has the option to prepay and in this case, whether any prepayment penalties might be imposed, and (5) the rights of the lender in a foreclosure.

A study by Lea (2010) provides an excellent review of mortgage designs in Australia, Canada, Denmark, Ireland, Japan, Germany, the Netherlands, South Korea, Spain, the United Kingdom, and the United States.[6] This section draws on this study to describe the five specifications of a mortgage design.

---

6 Lea (2010, Table 2, p. 17).

4.1 Maturity

In the United States, the typical maturity of a mortgage ranges from 15 to 30 years. For most countries in Europe, a residential mortgage typically has a maturity between 20 and 40 years, but in some countries (e.g., France and Spain), it can be as long as 50 years. Japan is an extreme case; the maturity of a mortgage can be 100 years.[7] Notice that what is called the term of a mortgage means the number of years to maturity.

4.2 Interest Rate Determination

The interest rate on a mortgage loan is called the **mortgage rate** or **contract rate**. How the mortgage rate is determined varies considerably among countries. The four basic ways that the mortgage rate can be specified are as follows:

- *Fixed rate*: The mortgage rate remains the same during the life of the mortgage. The United States and France have a high proportion of this type of interest rate determination, as did Denmark until recently. Although fixed-rate mortgage loans are not the dominant form in Germany, they do exist there.

- *Adjustable or variable rate:* The mortgage rate is reset periodically (daily, weekly, monthly, or annually). The determination of the new mortgage rate for an adjustable-rate mortgage (ARM) at the reset date may be based on some reference rate or index (in which case, it is called an indexed-referenced ARM) or a rate determined at the lender's discretion (in which case, it is called a reviewable ARM). Residential mortgage loans in Australia, Ireland, South Korea, Spain, and the United Kingdom are dominated by adjustable-rate loans. In Australia, Ireland, and the United Kingdom, the reviewable mortgage loan is standard. In South Korea and Spain, the rate is tied to an index or reference rate. Canada and the United States have ARMs that are typically tied to an index or reference rate, although this type of ARMs is not the dominant form of interest rate determination. An important feature of an ARM is that it will usually have a maximum interest rate by which the mortgage rate can change at a reset date and a maximum interest rate that the mortgage rate can reach during the mortgage's life.

- *Initial period fixed rate:* The mortgage rate is fixed for some initial period and is then adjusted. The adjustment may call for a new fixed rate or for a variable rate. When the adjustment calls for a fixed rate, the mortgage is referred to as a rollover or renegotiable mortgage. This mortgage design is dominant in Canada, Denmark, Germany, the Netherlands, and Switzerland. When the mortgage starts out with a fixed rate and then becomes an adjustable rate after a specified initial term, the mortgage is referred to as a hybrid mortgage. Hybrid mortgages are popular in the United Kingdom.

- *Convertible*: The mortgage rate is initially either a fixed rate or an adjustable rate. At some point, the borrower has the option to convert the mortgage into a fixed rate or an adjustable rate for the remainder of the mortgage's life. Almost half of the mortgages in Japan are convertible.

---

7 The term of residential mortgages is usually in line with the age of the borrower at the end of the loan maturity period, with the borrower's retirement age being a usual upper limit.

4.3 Amortization Schedule

In most countries, residential mortgages are **amortizing loans**. The amortization of a loan means the gradual reduction of the amount borrowed over time. Assuming no prepayments are made by the borrower, the periodic mortgage payments made by the borrower consist of interest payments and scheduled principal repayments. The scheduled principal repayment is the amount of reduction of the outstanding mortgage balance and is thus referred to as the amortization. As discussed in a previous reading, there are two types of amortizing loans: fully amortizing loans and partially amortizing loans. In a fully amortizing loan, the sum of all the scheduled principal repayments during the mortgage's life is such that when the last mortgage payment is made, the loan is fully repaid. Most residential mortgage loans in the United States are fully amortizing loans. In a partially amortizing loan, the sum of all the scheduled principal repayments is less than the amount borrowed. The last payment that has to be made is then the unpaid mortgage balance, and that last payment is said to be a "balloon" payment.

If no scheduled principal repayment is specified for a certain number of years, the loan is said to be an **interest-only mortgage**. Interest-only mortgages are available in Australia, Denmark, Finland, France, Germany, Greece, Ireland, the Netherlands, Portugal, South Korea, Spain, Switzerland, and the United Kingdom.[8] Interest-only mortgages are also available to a limited extent in the United States. A special type of interest-only mortgage is one in which there are no scheduled principal repayments over the entire life of the loan. In this case, the balloon payment is equal to the original loan amount. These mortgages, referred to as "interest-only lifetime mortgages" or "bullet mortgages," are available in Denmark, the Netherlands, and the United Kingdom.

4.4 Prepayments and Prepayment Penalties

A prepayment is any payment toward the repayment of principal that is in excess of the scheduled principal repayment. A mortgage loan may entitle the borrower to prepay all or part of the outstanding mortgage principal prior to the scheduled due date the principal must be repaid. This contractual provision is referred to as a **prepayment option** or an **early repayment option**. However, the mortgage may stipulate some sort of monetary penalty when a borrower prepays within a certain time period after the mortgage is originated, and this time period may extend for the full life of the loan. Such mortgage designs are referred to as **prepayment penalty mortgages**. Prepayment penalty mortgages are common in Europe. Although the proportion of prepayment penalty mortgages is small in the United States, they do exist.

From the lender's or investor's viewpoint, the effect of allowing prepayments is that the amount and timing of the cash flows from a mortgage loan cannot be known with certainty. This risk was referred to as prepayment risk in Section 3. Prepayment risk affects all mortgage loans that allow prepayment, not just the level-payment, fixed-rate, fully amortized mortgage.

The purpose of the prepayment penalty is to compensate the lender for the difference between the contract rate and the prevailing mortgage rate if the borrower prepays when interest rates decline. Hence, the penalty is effectively a mechanism that provides for yield maintenance for the lender. The method for calculating the penalty varies.

---

8 See Table 7 in Scanlon, Lunde, and Whitehead (2008).

4.5 Rights of the Lender in a Foreclosure

A mortgage can be a recourse loan or a non-recourse loan. When the borrower fails to make the contractual loan payments, the lender can repossess the property and sell it, but the proceeds received from the sale of the property may be insufficient to recoup the losses. In a **recourse loan**, the lender has a claim against the borrower for the shortfall between the amount of the mortgage balance outstanding and the proceeds received from the sale of the property. In a **non-recourse loan**, the lender does not have such a claim, so the lender can look only to the property to recover the outstanding mortgage balance. In the United States, residential mortgages are typically non-recourse loans. Residential mortgages in most European countries are recourse loans.

The recourse/non-recourse feature of a mortgage has implications for projecting the likelihood of defaults by borrowers. In the United States, for example, if the value of the property declines below the amount owed by the borrower, the borrower has an incentive, even if resources are available to continue to make mortgage payments, to default and allow the lender to foreclose on the property. This type of default by a borrower is referred to as a "strategic default." In countries where residential mortgage loans have a recourse provision, a strategic default is less likely because the lender can seek restitution from the borrower's other assets and/or income in an attempt to recover the shortfall. Now that the basics of a residential mortgage have been set out, we can turn our attention to how these mortgages are securitized—that is, transformed into mortgage-backed securities. In the following sections, we focus on the US residential mortgage sector because it is the largest in the world. In addition, many non-US investors hold US mortgage-backed securities in their portfolios.

RESIDENTIAL MORTGAGE-BACKED SECURITIES

5

The bonds created from the securitization of mortgage loans for the purchase of residential properties are residential mortgage-backed securities (RMBS). In countries such as the United States, Canada, Japan, and South Korea, a distinction is often made between securities that are guaranteed by the government or a quasi-government entity, and securities that are not. Quasi-government entities are usually created by governments to perform various functions for them. Examples of quasi-government entities include government-sponsored enterprises (GSEs) such as Fannie Mae (previously the Federal National Mortgage Association) and Freddie Mac (previously the Federal Home Loan Mortgage Corporation) in the United States, and the Japan Bank for International Cooperation (JBIC).

In the United States, securities backed by residential mortgage loans are divided into three sectors: (1) those guaranteed by a federal agency, (2) those guaranteed by either of the two GSEs, and (3) those issued by private entities and that are not guaranteed by a federal agency or a GSE. The first two sectors are referred to as **agency RMBS**, and the third sector, as **non-agency RMBS**.

Agency RMBS include securities issued by the Government National Mortgage Association, popularly referred to as Ginnie Mae. This entity is a federally related institution because it is part of the US Department of Housing and Urban Development. As a result, the RMBS that it guarantees carry the full faith and credit of the US government with respect to timely payment of both interest and principal.

Agency RMBS also include RMBS issued by Fannie Mae and Freddie Mac. These RMBS do *not* carry the full faith and credit of the US government.[9] They differ from non-agency RMBS in two ways. First, for RMBS issued by GSEs, credit risk is reduced by the guarantee of the GSE itself. In contrast, as will be explained in Section 5.3, non-agency RMBS use credit enhancements to reduce credit risk. The second way in which RMBS issued by GSEs and non-agency RMBS differ is that the mortgage loans in the loan pool of RMBS issued by Fannie Mae and Freddie Mac must satisfy specific underwriting standards established by various government agencies. In contrast, no such restrictions apply to the types of mortgage loans that can be used to back a non-agency RMBS.

This section starts with a discussion of agency RMBS, which include mortgage pass-through securities and collateralized mortgage obligations. We then turn to non-agency RMBS.[10]

5.1 Mortgage Pass-Through Securities

A **mortgage pass-through security** is a security created when one or more holders of mortgages form a pool of mortgages and sell shares or participation certificates in the pool. A pool can consist of several thousand or only a few mortgages. When a mortgage is included in a pool of mortgages that is used as collateral for a mortgage pass-through security, the mortgage is said to be securitized.

5.1.1 *Cash Flow Characteristics*

The cash flow of a mortgage pass-through security depends on the cash flow of the underlying pool of mortgages. The cash flow consists of monthly mortgage payments representing interest, the scheduled repayment of principal, and any prepayments. Payments are made to security holders each month. Neither the amount nor the timing of the cash flow from the pool of mortgages, however, is necessarily identical to that of the cash flow passed through to investors. The monthly cash flow for a mortgage pass-through security is less than the monthly cash flow of the underlying pool of mortgages by an amount equal to servicing and other fees.

The servicing fee is the charge related to servicing the mortgage loan. Servicing involves collecting monthly payments, forwarding proceeds to owners of the loan, sending payment notices to borrowers, reminding borrowers when payments are overdue, maintaining records of principal balances, initiating foreclosure proceedings if necessary, and furnishing tax information to borrowers when applicable. The servicing fee is typically a portion of the mortgage rate. The other fees are those charged by the issuer or guarantor of the mortgage pass-through security for guaranteeing the issue.

A mortgage pass-through security's coupon rate is called the **pass-through rate**. The pass-through rate is less than the mortgage rate on the underlying pool of mortgages by an amount equal to the servicing and other fees. The pass-through rate that the investor receives is said to be "net interest" or "net coupon."

Not all of the mortgages that are included in a pool of mortgages that are securitized have the same mortgage rate and the same maturity. Consequently, for each mortgage pass-through security, a **weighted average coupon rate** (WAC) and a **weighted average maturity** (WAM) are determined. The WAC is found by weighting the mortgage rate of each mortgage loan in the pool by the percentage of the mortgage

---

9 In September 2008, both GSEs were placed in conservatorship. In a conservatorship, a judge appoints an entity to take charge of the financial affairs of another entity.

10 A popular bond market index, the Barclays Capital US Aggregate Bond Index, has a sector called the "mortgage sector." In the mortgage sector, Barclays Capital includes only agency RMBS that are mortgage pass-through securities.

outstanding relative to the outstanding amount of all the mortgages in the pool. The WAM is found by weighting the remaining number of months to maturity for each mortgage loan in the pool by the amount of the outstanding mortgage balance.

5.1.2 *Conforming and Non-Conforming Loans*

For a loan to be included in a pool of loans backing an agency RMBS, it must meet specified underwriting standards. These standards set forth the maximum size of the loan, the loan documentation required, the maximum loan-to-value ratio, and whether or not insurance is required. If a loan satisfies the underwriting standards for inclusion as collateral for an agency RMBS, it is called a "conforming mortgage." If a loan fails to satisfy the underwriting standards, it is called a "non-conforming mortgage."

Non-conforming mortgages used as collateral for mortgage pass-through securities are privately issued. These securities are considered non-agency mortgage pass-through securities and are issued by thrift institutions, commercial banks, and private conduits. Private conduits may purchase non-conforming mortgages, pool them, and then sell mortgage pass-through securities whose collateral is the underlying pool of non-conforming mortgages.

5.1.3 *Measures of Prepayment Rate*

In describing prepayments, market participants refer to the prepayment rate or prepayment speed. The two key prepayment rate measures are the single monthly mortality (SMM) rate, a monthly measure, and its corresponding annualized rate, the conditional prepayment rate (CPR).

The SMM for a month is determined as follows:

$$\text{SMM} = \text{Prepayment for month} \div (\text{Beginning mortgage balance for month} - \text{Scheduled principal repayment for month}) \tag{1}$$

When market participants describe the assumed prepayment for a pool of residential mortgage loans, they refer to the annualized SMM, which is the CPR. A CPR of 6%, for example, means that approximately 6% of the outstanding mortgage balance at the beginning of the year is expected to be prepaid by the end of the year.

A key factor in the valuation of a mortgage pass-through security and other products derived from a pool of mortgages is forecasting the future prepayment rate. This task involves prepayment modeling. Prepayment modeling uses characteristics of the mortgage pool and other factors to develop a statistical model for forecasting prepayments.

In the United States, market participants describe prepayment rates in terms of a prepayment pattern or benchmark over the life of a mortgage pool. This pattern is the Public Securities Association (PSA) prepayment benchmark. The PSA prepayment benchmark is expressed as a monthly series of CPRs. The PSA prepayment benchmark assumes that prepayment rates are low for newly originated mortgages and then speed up as the mortgages become seasoned. Slower or faster rates are then referred to as some percentage of PSA. Rather than going into the details of the PSA prepayment benchmark, this discussion will establish some PSA assumptions. What is important to remember is that the benchmark is said to be 100 PSA. A PSA assumption greater than 100 PSA means that prepayments are assumed to be faster than the benchmark. In contrast, a PSA assumption lower than 100 PSA means that prepayments are assumed to be slower than the benchmark.

EXAMPLE 5

Cash Flow Uncertainty

Why is the cash flow for a mortgage pass-through security unknown?

Solution:

The cash flow is unknown because the prepayment rate over the life of the mortgages in the mortgage pool is unknown and can only be projected on the basis of an *assumed* prepayment rate.

5.1.4 *Cash Flow Construction*

Let us see how to construct the monthly cash flow for a hypothetical mortgage pass-through security. We assume that:

- The underlying pool of mortgages has a par value of US$800 million.
- The mortgages are fixed-rate, level-payment, and fully amortizing loans.
- The weighted average of the coupon rate (WAC) for the mortgage loans in the pool is 6%.
- The weighted average of the maturity (WAM) for the mortgage loans in the pool is 357 months.
- The pass-through rate (that is, the coupon rate net of servicing and other fees) is 5.5%.

Exhibit 2 shows the cash flows to bondholders for selected months assuming a prepayment rate of 165 PSA. The SMM in Column 3 and mortgage payments in Column 4 are given. The net interest in Column 5 is the amount available to pay bondholders after servicing and other fees. It is equal to the beginning mortgage balance in Column 1 multiplied by the pass-through rate of 5.5% and then divided by 12. The scheduled principal repayment in Column 6 is the difference between the mortgage payment in Column 4 and the gross interest payment. The gross interest payment is equal to the beginning mortgage balance in Column 2 multiplied by the WAC of 6% and then divided by 12. The prepayment in Column 7 is found by applying Equation 1, using the SMM provided in Column 3, the beginning mortgage balance in Column 1 and the scheduled principal repayment in Column 6.[11] The total principal repayment is the sum of the scheduled principal repayment in Column 6 and the prepayment in Column 7. Subtracting this amount from the beginning mortgage balance for the month gives the beginning mortgage balance for the following month. Finally, the projected cash flow for this mortgage pass-through security is the sum of the net interest in Column 5 and the total principal repayment in Column 8.

---

11 The SMM in Column 3 is rounded, which results in some rounding error in the calculation of the prepayments in Column 7 and, thus, of the total principal repayments and the cash flows in Columns 8 and 9, respectively..

| | Exhibit 2 | Monthly Cash Flow to Bondholders for a US$800 Million Mortgage Pass-Through Security with a WAC of 6.0%, and a WAM of 357 Months and a 5.5% Pass-Through Rate, Assuming 165 PSA | | | | | | | |

(1)	(2)	(3)	(4)	(5)	(6)	(7)	(8)	(9)
Month	Beginning of Month Mortgage Balance	SMM	Mortgage Payment	Net Interest Payment	Scheduled Principal Repayment	Prepayment	Total Principal Repayment	Cash Flow
1	800,000,000	0.00111	4,810,844	3,666,667	810,844	884,472	1,695,316	5,361,982
2	798,304,684	0.00139	4,805,520	3,658,896	813,996	1,104,931	1,918,927	5,577,823
3	796,385,757	0.00167	4,798,862	3,650,101	816,933	1,324,754	2,141,687	5,791,788
⋮								
29	674,744,235	0.00865	4,184,747	3,092,578	811,026	5,829,438	6,640,464	9,733,042
30	668,103,771	0.00865	4,148,550	3,062,142	808,031	5,772,024	6,580,055	9,642,198
⋮								
100	326,937,929	0.00865	2,258,348	1,498,466	623,659	2,822,577	3,446,236	4,944,702
101	323,491,693	0.00865	2,238,814	1,482,670	621,355	2,792,788	3,414,143	4,896,814
⋮								
200	103,307,518	0.00865	947,322	473,493	430,784	889,871	1,320,655	1,794,148
201	101,986,863	0.00865	939,128	467,440	429,193	878,461	1,307,654	1,775,094
⋮								
300	19,963,930	0.00865	397,378	91,501	297,559	170,112	467,670	559,172
301	19,496,260	0.00865	393,941	89,358	296,460	166,076	462,536	551,893
⋮								
356	484,954	0.00865	244,298	2,223	241,873	2,103	243,976	246,199
357	240,978	0.00865	242,185	1,104	240,980	0	240,980	242,084

5.1.5 Weighted Average Life

A standard practice in the bond market is to refer to the maturity of a bond. This practice is not followed for mortgage-backed securities because principal repayments (scheduled principal repayments and prepayments) are made over the life of the security. Although an MBS has a "legal maturity," which is the date when the last scheduled principal payment is due, the legal maturity does not reveal much about the characteristic of the security as it pertains to interest rate risk. For example, a 30-year, option-free, corporate bond and an MBS with a 30-year legal maturity with the same coupon rate are not equivalent in terms of interest rate risk. Of course, duration can be computed for both the corporate bond and the MBS to assess the sensitivity of the bonds to interest rate movements. But a measure widely used by market participants for MBS is the **weighted average life** or simply the **average life** of the MBS. This measure gives investors an indication of how long they can expect to hold the MBS before it is paid off. In other words, the average life of the MBS is the convention-based average time to receipt of all principal repayments (scheduled principal repayments and projected prepayments).

A mortgage pass-through security's average life depends on the prepayment assumption, as illustrated in the following table. The table below provides the average life for various prepayment rates for the mortgage pass-through security used in Exhibit 2. Notice that at the assumed prepayment rate of 165 PSA, the mortgage pass-through security has an average life of 8.6 years but the average life diminishes rapidly as the prepayment rate goes up. So, at a prepayment rate of 600 PSA, the average life of the pass-through security is only 3.2 years.

PSA assumption	100	125	165	250	400	600
Average life (years)	11.2	10.1	8.6	6.4	4.5	3.2

5.1.6 *Contraction Risk and Extension Risk*

An investor who owns mortgage pass-through securities does not know what the future cash flows will be because these future cash flows depend on actual prepayments. As we noted earlier, this risk is called prepayment risk. This prepayment risk has two components: contraction risk and extension risk, both of which largely reflect changes in the general level of interest rates.

Contraction risk is the risk that when interest rates decline, the security will have a shorter maturity than was anticipated at the time of purchase because homeowners refinance at now-available lower interest rates. A security becoming shorter in maturity when interest rates decline has two adverse consequences. First, the proceeds received must now be reinvested at lower interest rates. Second, if the bond is prepayable or callable, its price appreciation is not as great as that of an otherwise identical bond that does not have a prepayment or call option.

In contrast, **extension risk** is the risk that when interest rates rise, fewer prepayments will occur because homeowners are reluctant to give up the benefits of a contractual interest rate that now looks low. As a result, the security becomes longer in maturity than anticipated at the time of purchase. From the investors' perspective, the value of the security has fallen because interest rates are higher whereas the income they receive (and can potentially reinvest) is typically limited to the interest payment and scheduled principal repayments.

EXAMPLE 6

Mortgage Pass-Through Securities and Prepayment Rate

In Exhibit 2, the assumed prepayment rate was 165 PSA. Suppose that, instead, the prepayment rate is faster than 165 PSA. What would happen to the maturity of the mortgage pass-through security? What type of prepayment risk would an investor be exposed to at prepayment rates faster than 165 PSA, and what would be the consequences for the investor?

Solution:

The maturity of the mortgage pass-through security would be less than 357 months and would be said to "contract" compared with the maturity at 165 PSA. The investor would face contraction risk; that is, the investor would receive payments faster than anticipated. An investor who decides to retain the security would face the prospect of having to reinvest those payments at relatively low interest rates. An investor who decides to sell the security would have to do so at a price lower than that of an otherwise identical bond with no prepayment risk.

5.2 Collateralized Mortgage Obligations

As noted in the previous section, prepayment risk is an important consideration when investing in mortgage pass-through securities. Some institutional investors are concerned with extension risk and others with contraction risk. This problem can be mitigated by redistributing the cash flows of mortgage-related products (mortgage pass-through securities or pools of loans) to different bond classes or tranches though a process called "structuring." This process leads to the creation of securities that have different exposures to prepayment risk and thus different risk–return patterns relative to the mortgage-related product from which they were created.

When the cash flows of mortgage-related products are redistributed to various tranches, the resulting securities are called **collateralized mortgage obligations** (CMOs). The mortgage-related products from which the cash flows are obtained are considered the collateral. Note that in contrast to a mortgage pass-through security, the collateral is not a pool of mortgage loans but a mortgage pass-through security. In fact, in actual deals, the collateral is usually a pool of mortgage pass-through securities, hence the reason market participants sometimes use the terms "collateral" and "mortgage pass-through securities" interchangeably.

The creation of a CMO cannot eliminate prepayment risk; it can only distribute the various forms of this risk among various classes of bondholders. The CMO's major financial innovation is that the securities can be created to closely satisfy the asset/liability needs of institutional investors, thereby broadening the appeal of mortgage-backed products.

A wide range of CMO structures exists. The major ones are reviewed in the following subsections.

5.2.1 *Sequential-Pay Tranches*

The first CMO was structured so that each class of bond (the tranches) would be retired sequentially. Such structures are called "sequential-pay CMOs." The rule for the monthly distribution of the principal repayments (scheduled principal repayment plus prepayments) to the tranches in this structure is as follows. First, distribute all principal payments to Tranche 1 until the principal balance for Tranche 1 is zero. After Tranche 1 is paid off, distribute all principal payments to Tranche 2 until the principal balance for Tranche 2 is zero. After Tranche 2 is paid off, then do the same for Tranche 3, and so on.

To illustrate a sequential-pay CMO, let us use a hypothetical transaction called CMO-01. Assume that the collateral for CMO-01 is the mortgage pass-through security described in Section 5.1.4. The total par value of the collateral is US$800 million, the pass-through coupon rate is 5.5%, the WAC is 6%, and the WAM is 357 months. From this US$800 million of collateral, four tranches are created, as shown in Exhibit 3. In this simple structure, the coupon rate is the same for each tranche and also the same as the coupon rate on the collateral. This feature is for simplicity; typically, the coupon rate varies by tranche.[12]

Exhibit 3	CMO-01: Sequential-Pay Structure with Four Tranches	
Tranche	**Par Amount (US$)**	**Coupon Rate (%)**
A	389,000,000	5.5
B	72,000,000	5.5

(continued)

---

12 Keep in mind that the coupon rate for a tranche will be affected by the term structure of interest rates (i.e., basically, the yield curve). Typically, yield increases as maturity increases. A CMO will have tranches with different average lives. Usually, the longer the average life, the higher the coupon rate should be. So, in the hypothetical four-tranche sequential-pay structure shown in Exhibit 3, Tranche A might have a 4.2% coupon rate, Tranche B a 4.8% coupon rate, Tranche C a 5.2% coupon rate, and Tranche D a 5.5% coupon rate. In any event, investors will evaluate each tranche based on its perceived risk and will price it accordingly. Consequently, investors will pay a price for the tranche that reflects the yield they expect to receive given the particular coupon rate. Separately, the difference between the coupon rate paid by the underlying mortgages (5.5%) and the coupon rate paid to each of the tranches that has a coupon rate of less than what is paid by the underlying mortgages is used to create securities called "structured interest-only tranches." A discussion of these tranches is beyond the scope of this reading.

Exhibit 3   (Continued)

Tranche	Par Amount (US$)	Coupon Rate (%)
C	193,000,000	5.5
D	146,000,000	5.5
Total	800,000,000	

Payment rules: *For payment of monthly coupon interest:* Disburse monthly coupon interest to each tranche on the basis of the amount of principal outstanding for each tranche at the beginning of the month. *For disbursement of principal payments:* Disburse principal payments to Tranche A until it is completely paid off. After Tranche A is completely paid off, disburse principal payments to Tranche B until it is completely paid off. After Tranche B is completely paid off, disburse principal payments to Tranche C until it is completely paid off. After Tranche C is completely paid off, disburse principal payments to Tranche D until it is completely paid off.

Remember that a CMO is created by redistributing the cash flows—interest payments and principal repayments—to the various tranches on the basis of a set of payment rules. The payment rules at the bottom of Exhibit 3 describe how the cash flows from the mortgage pass-through security are to be distributed to the four tranches. CMO-01 has separate rules for the distribution of the interest payment and the principal repayment (the principal repayment being the sum of the scheduled principal repayment and the prepayments).

Although the payment rules for the distribution of the principal payments are known, the precise amount of the principal repayment in each month is not. This amount will depend on the cash flow of the collateral, which depends on the actual prepayment rate of the collateral. The assumed PSA rate only allows one to determine the projected, not actual, cash flow to be projected.

Consider what has been accomplished by creating the CMO. Earlier, you saw that, with a prepayment rate of 165 PSA, the mortgage pass-through security's average life was 8.6 years. Exhibit 4 reports the average lives of the collateral and the four tranches when different prepayment rates are assumed. Notice that the four tranches have average lives that are shorter or longer than the collateral, thereby attracting investors who have preferences for different average lives.

Exhibit 4   Average Life for the Collateral and the Four Tranches of CMO-01 for Various Prepayment Rates

Prepayment Rate (PSA)	Average Life (years)				
	Collateral	Tranche A	Tranche B	Tranche C	Tranche D
100	11.2	4.7	10.4	15.1	24.0
125	10.1	4.1	8.9	13.2	22.4
165	8.6	3.4	7.3	10.9	19.8
250	6.4	2.7	5.3	7.9	15.2
400	4.5	2.0	3.8	5.3	10.3
600	3.2	1.6	2.8	3.8	7.0

A major problem that remains is the considerable variability of the average life for the tranches. How this issue can be handled is shown in the next section, but at this point, note that some protection against prepayment risk is provided for each tranche. The protection arises because prioritizing the distribution of principal (i.e., establishing the payment rules for principal) effectively protects the shorter-term tranche (A in this structure) against extension risk. This protection must come from somewhere; it actually comes from the longer-term tranches. Similarly, Tranches C and D provide protection against extension risk for Tranches A and B. At the same time, Tranches C and D benefit because they are provided protection against contraction risk; the protection comes from Tranches A and B. This CMO structure allows investors concerned about extension risk to invest in Tranches A or B and those concerned about contraction risk can invest in Tranches C or D.

5.2.2 *Planned Amortization Class Tranches*

A common structure in CMOs is to include planned amortization class (PAC) tranches, which offer greater predictability of the cash flows as long as the prepayment rate is within a specified band over the collateral's life. The greater predictability of the cash flows for PAC tranches occurs because a principal repayment schedule must be satisfied. PAC bondholders have priority over all other tranches in the CMO structure in receiving principal repayments from the collateral. The greater certainty of the cash flows for the PAC tranches comes at the expense of the non-PAC tranches, called **support tranches** or companion tranches. These tranches absorb the prepayment risk first. Because PAC tranches have limited (but not complete) protection against both extension risk and contraction risk, they are said to provide two-sided prepayment protection.

To illustrate how to create PAC tranches, we will use again the US$800 million mortgage pass-through security from Section 5.1.4 with a coupon rate of 5.5%, a WAC of 6%, and a WAM of 357 months as collateral to create a CMO called CMO-02. The creation of PAC tranches requires the specification of two PSA prepayment rates: a *lower* PSA prepayment assumption and an *upper* PSA prepayment assumption. The lower and upper PSA prepayment assumptions are called the "initial PAC collar" or the "initial PAC band." The PAC collar for a CMO is typically dictated by market conditions. In our example, the lower and upper PSA prepayment assumptions are 100PSA and 250 PSA, respectively, so the initial PAC collar is 100–250 PSA.

Exhibit 5 shows the structure of CMO-02. The structure contains only two tranches: a 5.5% coupon PAC tranche created assuming an initial PAC collar of 100–250 PSA and a support tranche.

Exhibit 5	CMO-02: CMO Structure with One PAC Tranche and One Support Tranche	
Tranche	**Par Amount (US$)**	**Coupon Rate (%)**
P (PAC)	487,600,000	5.5
S (support)	312,400,000	5.5
Total	800,000,000	

Payment rules: *For payment of monthly coupon interest:* Disburse monthly coupon interest to each tranche on the basis of the amount of principal outstanding for each tranche at the beginning of the month. *For disbursement of principal payments:* Disburse principal payments to Tranche P on the basis of its schedule of principal repayments. Tranche P has priority with respect to current and future principal payments to satisfy the schedule. Any excess principal payments in a month over the amount necessary to satisfy the schedule for Tranche P are paid to Tranche S. When Tranche S is completely paid off, all principal payments are to be made to Tranche P regardless of the schedule.

Exhibit 6 reports the average life for the PAC tranche and the support tranche in CMO-02 assuming various *actual* prepayment rates. Notice that between 100 PSA and 250 PSA, the average life for the PAC bond is stable at 7.7 years. At slower or faster

PSA rates, however, the schedule is broken and the average life changes—extending when the prepayment rate is less than 100 PSA and contracting when it is greater than 250 PSA. Even so, there is much less variability for the average life of the PAC tranche compared to the support tranche.

Exhibit 6   Average Life for the PAC Tranche and the Support Tranche in CMO-02 for Various Actual Prepayment Rates and an Initial PAC Collar of 100–250 PSA

	Average Life (Years)	
Prepayment Rate (PSA)	PAC Tranche (P)	Support Tranche (S)
50	10.2	24.9
75	8.6	22.7
100	7.7	20.0
165	7.7	10.7
250	7.7	3.3
400	5.5	1.9
600	4.0	1.4

Most CMO PAC structures have more than one PAC tranches. A sequence of six PAC tranches (i.e., PAC tranches paid off in sequence as specified by a principal schedule) is not uncommon. For example, consider CMO-03 in Exhibit 7. This structure has four PAC tranches (P-A, P-B, P-C, and P-D). The total dollar amount of the PAC and support tranches is the same as for CMO-02 in Exhibit 5. The difference is that instead of one PAC tranche with a schedule, there are four PAC tranches with schedules. The PAC tranches are paid off in sequence.

Exhibit 7   CMO-03: CMO Structure with Sequential PAC Tranches and One Support Tranche

Tranche	Par Amount (US$)	Coupon Rate (%)
P-A	287,600,000	5.5%
P-B	90,000,000	5.5%
P-C	60,000,000	5.5%
P-D	50,000,000	5.5%
S	312,400,000	5.5%
Total	800,000,000	

Payment rules: *For payment of monthly coupon interest:* Disburse monthly coupon interest to each tranche on the basis of the amount of principal outstanding for each tranche at the beginning of the month. *For disbursement of principal payments:* Disburse principal payments to Tranche P-A on the basis of its schedule of principal repayments. Tranche P-A has priority with respect to current and future principal payments to satisfy the schedule. Any excess principal payments in a month over the amount necessary to satisfy the schedule while P-A is outstanding is paid to Tranche S. Once P-A is paid off, disburse principal payments to Tranche P-B on the basis of its schedule of principal repayments. Tranche P-B has priority with respect to current and future principal payments to satisfy the schedule. Any excess principal payments in a month over the amount necessary to satisfy the schedule while P-B is outstanding are paid to Tranche S. The same rule applies for P-C and P-D. When Tranche S is completely paid off, all principal payments are to be made to the outstanding PAC tranches regardless of the schedule.

Remember that the creation of a mortgage-backed security, whether it is a mortgage pass-through or a CMO, cannot make prepayment risk disappear. Where does the reduction of prepayment risk (both extension risk and contraction risk) that a PAC tranche offers investors come from? The answer is that it comes from the support tranches.

5.2.3 Support Tranches

The support tranches defer principal payments to the PAC tranches if the collateral prepayments are slow; support tranches do not receive any principal until the PAC tranches receive their scheduled principal repayment. This rule reduces the extension risk of the PAC tranches. Similarly, the support tranches absorb any principal repayments in excess of the scheduled principal repayments that are made. This rule reduces the contraction risk of the PAC tranches. Thus, the key to the prepayment protection offered by a PAC tranche is the amount of support tranches outstanding. If the support tranches are paid off quickly because of faster-than-expected prepayments, they no longer provide any protection for the PAC tranches.

Support tranches expose investors to the greatest level of prepayment risk. Therefore, investors must be particularly careful in assessing the cash flow characteristics of support tranches in order to reduce the likelihood of adverse portfolio consequences resulting from prepayments.

EXAMPLE 7

Mortgage Pass-Through Securities Compared with CMOs

In a portfolio management meeting, you hear one of your colleagues make the following statement: "Mortgage pass-through securities are not as complicated as collateralized mortgage obligations, which divide the cash flows into different bond classes. The agency CMOs are far more risky than the pass-throughs." How would you respond?

Solution:

The statement is incorrect. There are various types of agency CMOs—such as sequential-pay bond classes, PAC bond classes, and support bond classes. The fact that the cash flows from the collateral are allocated to different bond classes does not make them riskier. Indeed, the purpose of creating different bond classes in a CMO is to provide a risk–return profile that is more suitable to investors that the risk-return profile of the mortgage pass-through securities. For example, a mortgage pass-through security has considerably more variability in average life than does a PAC bond created from that mortgage pass-through security. In contrast, a support bond has greater average-life variability than a mortgage pass-through security has. Therefore, bond classes in a CMO may be more or less risky than a mortgage pass-through security with respect to prepayment risk. A blanket statement about relative riskiness, such as the one made in the meeting, is incorrect.

5.2.4 Floating-Rate Tranches

Often, there is a demand for tranches that have a floating rate. Although the collateral pays a fixed rate, it is possible to create a tranche with a floating rate. This is done by constructing a floater and an inverse floater combination from any of the fixed-rate tranches in a CMO structure. Because the floating-rate tranche pays a higher rate when interest rates go up and the inverse floater pays a lower rate when interest rates go up, they offset each other. Thus, a fixed-rate tranche can be used to satisfy the demand for a floating-rate tranche.

In a similar vein, other types of tranches to satisfy the various needs of investors are possible.

EXAMPLE 8

Selecting a Suitable Tranche

Which tranche in a CMO structure is *most* suitable for the following investors?

1 An investor who is most concerned about contraction risk

2 An investor who would like the investment to have a predictable and stable average life

3 An investor who expects that interest rates will fall

4 An investor who is willing to accept significant prepayment risk if compensated with a relatively high expected return

Solution to 1:

This investor should probably invest in the later-paying tranches in a sequential structure, such as the C or D tranches in the earlier examples. For example, the D tranche receives scheduled principal payments and prepayments last and faces considerable extension risk, but it has the lowest contraction risk. Another suitable bond class would be a PAC tranche with a maturity that has the target maturity sought by the investor. This tranche can be found in a CMO that has sequential PAC tranches, such as in Exhibit 7.

Solution to 2:

The investor should choose a PAC bond. As long as prepayment rates remain within the PAC collar, the life of the bond is predictable and stable.

Solution to 3:

An investor betting on a fall in rates should probably invest in an inverse floating-rate tranche. The inverse floater will pay a coupon rate that is inversely related to prevailing interest rates and hence will benefit this investor the most.

Solution to 4:

This investor should choose a support or companion tranche to a PAC tranche. Because the PAC bond has a stable average life at prepayment rates within the PAC band, all prepayment risk is absorbed by the support tranche for prepayment rates within the band. Even at rates outside the band, prepayment risk is first absorbed by the support tranche. Investors will be compensated for bearing this risk in the sense that, if properly priced, the support tranche will have a higher expected rate of return than the PAC tranche.

5.3 Non-agency Residential Mortgage-Backed Securities

Agency RMBS are those issued by Ginnie Mae, Fannie Mae, and Freddie Mac. A good deal of space in this reading is devoted to those securities because they represent a large sector of the investment-grade bond market and are included in the portfolios of many US as well as non-US investors. RMBS issued by any other entity are non-agency RMBS. Because they are not guaranteed by the government or by a GSE, credit risk is an important consideration when investing in non-agency RMBS.

Prior to the problems that occurred in the mortgage market in mid-2007, market participants typically identified two types of transactions based on the credit quality of the mortgage loans in the pool: prime loans and subprime loans. Generally, for a loan to be considered prime, the borrower must be viewed as having high credit quality; that is, the borrower must have strong employment and credit histories, income sufficient to pay the loan obligation, and substantial equity in the underlying property. When the borrower has lower credit quality or if the loan is not a first lien on the property (that is, a party other than the current potential lender has a prior claim on the underlying property), the loan is treated as subprime.

Non-agency RMBS share many features and structuring techniques with agency CMOs. However, two complementary mechanisms are usually required in structuring non-agency RMBS. First, the cash flows are distributed by rules, such as the waterfall, that dictate the allocation of interest payments and principal repayments to tranches with various degrees of priority/seniority. Second, there are rules for the allocation of realized losses, which specify that subordinated bond classes have lower payment priority than senior classes.

When forecasting the future cash flows of non-agency RMBS, investors must factor in two important components. The first is the assumed default rate for the collateral. The second is the recovery rate, because even though the collateral may default, not all of the outstanding mortgage balance may be lost. The repossession and subsequent sale of the recovered property may provide cash flows that will be available to pay bondholders. That amount is based on the assumed amount that will be recovered.

In order to obtain a favorable credit rating, non-agency RMBS often require one or more credit enhancements. Non-agency RMBS, as well as all the asset-backed bonds discussed in the remainder of this reading, are credit enhanced—that is, support is provided for one or more of the bondholders in the structure. Credit enhancement levels are determined relative to a specific credit rating desired by the issuer for a security. There are two general types of credit enhancement structures: internal and external. Each type is described here.

5.3.1 *Internal Credit Enhancements*

The most common forms of internal credit enhancement are senior/subordinated structures, reserve funds, and overcollateralization.

Section 3.3 provided a description of a senior/subordinated structure for asset-backed bonds. The subordinated bond classes are also referred to as "junior bond classes" or "non-senior bond classes." In this form of internal credit enhancement, the subordinated bond classes in the structure provide credit support for the senior bond classes. The subordination levels (i.e., the amount of credit protection for a bond class) are set at the time of issuance. The subordination levels change over time, however, as voluntary prepayments and defaults occur. To protect investors in non-agency RMBS, a deal is designed to keep the amount of credit enhancement from deteriorating over time. A mechanism called the "shifting interest mechanism" locks out subordinated bond classes from receiving payments for a period of time if the credit enhancement for senior tranches deteriorates because of poor performance of the collateral.

Reserve funds are another form of internal credit enhancement, and come in two forms: a cash reserve fund and an excess spread account. A cash reserve fund is a deposit of cash provided to the SPV from the proceeds of the sale of the loan pool by the entity seeking to raise funds. An excess spread account involves the allocation into an account of any amounts resulting from monthly funds remaining after paying out the interest to the bond classes as well as servicing and other fees. For example, suppose that the interest rate paid by the borrowers in the loan pool is 5.50%. Also assume that servicing and other fees are 0.75% and that the interest rate paid to the bond classes is 4.25%. So, for this example, 5.50% is available to make payments to the bond classes and to cover servicing and other fees. Of that amount, 0.75% is paid for servicing and other fees and 4.75% (5.50% – 0.75%) is available to pay the bond classes. But only 4.25% must be paid out to the bond classes, leaving 0.50% (4.75% – 4.25%). This 0.50%, or 50 basis points (bps), is called the "excess spread." This amount can be placed in a reserve account. Reserve funds from the cash reserve fund or the excess spread account provide credit support because they can be used to pay for possible future losses. If any funds remain in the reserve account after the last bond class in the securitization is paid off, they are returned to the entity that is the residual owner of the SPV.[13]

Overcollateralization in a structure refers to a situation in which the value of the collateral exceeds the amount of the par value of the outstanding bond classes issued by the SPV. For example, if US$400 million par value is issued and if the collateral at issuance has a par value of US$407, the structure has US$7 million in overcollateralization. Over time, the amount of overcollateralization changes as a result of defaults, amortization, and prepayments. Overcollateralization represents a form of internal credit enhancement because it can be used to absorb losses.

5.3.2 *External Credit Enhancements*

External credit enhancement means that credit support in the case of defaults resulting in losses in the pool of loans is provided in the form of a financial guarantee by a third party to the transaction. The most common third-party financial guarantors are monoline insurance companies. A monoline insurance company, also referred to as a monoline insurer, is a private insurance company whose business is restricted to providing guarantees for financial products, such as municipal securities and ABS. Following the financial difficulties and downgrading of the major monoline insurers as a result of the financial crisis that began in the mortgage market in mid-2007, few structures in recent years have used credit enhancement from a monoline insurer.

EXAMPLE 9

Credit Enhancements

Unlike an agency RMBS, a non-agency RMBS requires credit enhancement. Explain why.

Solution:

An agency RMBS issued by Ginnie Mae is backed by the full faith and credit of the US government. Effectively, the US government can be viewed as the credit enhancer or the third-party guarantor of the RMBS. In the case of a RMBS issued by Fannie Mae or Freddie Mac, the GSE is the guarantor and it charges a fee for insuring the issue. In contrast, non-agency RMBS have no third-party guarantor with a high credit rating like that of the US government that can provide protection against losses in the pool. In the absence of such a guarantee, it is difficult for a non-agency RMBS bond class in a securitization to obtain a high, investment-grade rating to make it attractive to conservative investors. Hence, some form of internal or external credit enhancement becomes necessary for non-agency RMBS.

---

13 The residual owner is the sponsor of the SPV in the form of tranches that it retains that pay no interest rate—Mediquip in the example we used in Section 3.

The focus in Section 5 has been on residential MBS. The next section turns to the securitization of commercial real estate.

COMMERCIAL MORTGAGE-BACKED SECURITIES

6

Commercial mortgage-backed securities (CMBS) are backed by a pool of commercial mortgage loans on income-producing property, such as multifamily properties (e.g., apartment buildings), office buildings, industrial properties (including warehouses), shopping centers, hotels, and health care facilities (e.g., senior housing care facilities). The basic building block of the CMBS transaction is a commercial loan that was originated either to finance a commercial purchase or to refinance a prior mortgage obligation.

6.1 Credit Risk

In the United States and other countries where commercial mortgage loans are non-recourse loans, the lender can look only to the income-producing property backing the loan for interest payment and principal repayment. If a default occurs, the lender can use only the proceeds from the sale of the property for repayment and has no recourse to the borrower for any unpaid balance. The lender must view each property individually, and lenders evaluate each property using measures that have been found useful in assessing credit risk. The treatment of CMBS can vary by country.

Two measures that have been found to be key indicators of potential credit performance are the loan-to-value ratio, which was discussed in Section 4, and the debt-to-service-coverage (DSC) ratio. The DSC ratio is the property's annual net operating income (NOI) divided by the debt service (i.e., the annual amount of interest payment and principal repayment). The NOI is defined as the rental income reduced by cash operating expenses and a non-cash replacement reserve reflecting depreciation of the facilities over time. A DSC ratio that exceeds 1.0 indicates that the cash flow from the property is sufficient to cover debt servicing while maintaining facilities in their initial state of repair. The higher the ratio, the more likely it is that the borrower will be able to meet debt-servicing requirements from the property's cash flow.

6.2 Basic CMBS Structure

A credit-rating agency determines the level of credit enhancement necessary to achieve a desired credit rating. For example, if specific DSC and LTV ratios are needed and those ratios cannot be met at the loan level, subordination is used to achieve the desired credit rating.

Interest on principal outstanding is paid to all tranches. Losses arising from loan defaults are charged against the principal balance of the lowest priority CMBS tranche outstanding. This tranche may not be rated by credit-rating agencies; in this case, this unrated tranche is called the "first-loss piece," "residual tranche," or "equity tranche." The total loss charged will include the amount previously advanced and the actual loss incurred in the sale of the loan's underlying property.

Two characteristics that are usually specific to CMBS structures are the presence of a call protection and a balloon maturity provision.

6.2.1 *Call Protection*

A critical investment feature that distinguishes RMBS from CMBS is the call protection available to investors. An investor in a RMBS is exposed to considerable prepayment risk because the borrower has the right to prepay a loan, in whole or in part, before the scheduled principal repayment date. As explained in Section 4.4, a borrower in the United States usually does not pay any penalty for prepayment. The discussion of CMOs highlighted how investors can purchase certain types of tranches (e.g., sequential-pay and PAC tranches) to modify or reduce prepayment risk.

With CMBS, investors have considerable call protection. In fact, it is this protection that results in CMBS trading in the market more like corporate bonds than like RMBS. This call protection comes either at the structure level or at the loan level. Structural call protection is achieved when CMBS are structured to have sequential-pay tranches, by credit rating. A lower-rated tranche cannot be paid down until the higher-rated tranche is completely retired, so the AAA rated bonds must be paid off before the AA rated bonds are, and so on. Principal losses resulting from defaults, however, are affected from the bottom of the structure upward.

At the loan level, four mechanisms offer investors call protection: prepayment lockouts, prepayment penalty points, yield maintenance charges, and defeasance. A prepayment lockout is a contractual agreement that prohibits any prepayments during a specified period of time. Prepayment penalty points are predetermined penalties that a borrower who wants to refinance must pay to do so—a point is equal to 1% of the outstanding loan balance. A yield maintenance charge, also called a "make-whole charge," is a penalty paid by the borrower that makes refinancing solely to get a lower mortgage rate uneconomical for the borrower. In its simplest terms, a yield maintenance charge is designed to make the lender indifferent as to the timing of prepayments.

With defeasance, the borrower provides sufficient funds for the servicer to invest in a portfolio of government securities that replicates the cash flows that would exist in the absence of prepayments. That is, the cash payments that must be met by the borrower are projected on the basis of the terms of the loan. Then, a portfolio of government securities is constructed in such a way that the interest payment and the principal repayment from the portfolio will be sufficient to pay off each obligation when it comes due. The portfolio is constructed so that when the last obligation is paid off, the value of the portfolio is zero (i.e., there are no funds remaining). The cost of assembling such a portfolio is the cost of defeasing the loan that must be repaid by the issuer.[14]

6.2.2 *Balloon Maturity Provisions*

Many commercial loans backing CMBS transactions are balloon loans that require substantial principal repayment at maturity of the loan. If the borrower fails to make the balloon payment, the borrower is in default. The lender may extend the loan over a period of time called the "workout period." In doing so, the lender may modify the original loan terms and charge a higher interest rate, called the "default interest rate," during the workout period.

The risk that a borrower will not be able to make the balloon payment because either the borrower cannot arrange for refinancing or cannot sell the property to generate sufficient funds to pay off the balloon balance is called "balloon risk." Because the term of the loan is extended by the lender during the workout period, balloon risk is a type of extension risk.

---

14 This portfolio strategy for paying off liabilities has been used by municipal bond issuers; the resulting bonds are referred to as "pre-refunded bonds." It is also an investment strategy used by insurance companies to pay off liabilities.

EXAMPLE 10

A Commercial Mortgage-Backed Security

Information about a CMBS issued in April 2013 by Citigroup Commercial Mortgage Trust 2013-GCJ11 is provided in the following table.

Classes of Offered Certificates	Initial Principal (or Notional) Amount	Initial Pass-Through Rate
A-1	$75,176,000	0.754%
A-2	$290,426,000	1.987%
A-3	$150,000,000	2.815%
A-4	$236,220,000	3.093%
A-AB	$92,911,000	2.690%
X-A	$948,816,000	1.937%
A-S	$104,083,000	3.422%
B	$75,423,000	3.732%
C	$42,236,000	

The collateral for this CMBS is a pool of 72 fixed-rate mortgage loans secured by first liens (first claims) on various types of commercial, multifamily, and manufactured housing community properties.

1 What is the meaning of the following statement in the offering?

"If you acquire Class B certificates, then your rights to receive distributions of amounts collected or advanced on or in respect of the mortgage loans will be subordinated to those of the holders of the Class A-1, Class A-2, Class A-3, Class A-4, Class A-AB, Class X-A, and Class A-S certificates. If you acquire Class C certificates, then your rights to receive distributions of amounts collected or advanced on or in respect of the mortgage loans will be subordinated to those of the holders of the Class B certificates and all other classes of offered certificates."

2 The offering states the following provisions. What do these three provisions mean?

"Prepayment Penalty Description" or "Prepayment Provision" means the number of payments from the first due date through and including the maturity date for which a Mortgage Loan is, as applicable, (i) locked out from prepayment, (ii) provides for payment of a prepayment premium or yield maintenance charge in connection with a prepayment, (iii) permits defeasance.

3 Explain the following risk stated in the offering: "the risk that it may be more difficult for the borrower to refinance these loans or to sell the related mortgaged property for purposes of making any balloon payment on the entire balance of such loans and the related additional debt at maturity."

4 The information in the offering states the NOI and DSC ratio. What are these measures and what is their purpose?

Solution to 1:

The term "certificates" here means "bond classes" or "tranches" as these terms have been used throughout this reading. The description of the bond classes in the quotation means that the issue has an internal credit enhancement of the senior/subordinated type. Bond Class B provides protection for all of the bond classes listed above it. Similarly, Bond Class C is considered the equity or residual tranche and provides protection for all other bond classes, including Class B; it is the first-loss piece. Because it is the residual tranche, Class C has no specific pass-through rate in the table. Investors in Class C will price it on the basis of some expected residual rate of return, but they could do better or worse than expected depending on how interest rate movements and default rates affect the performance of the other tranches.

Solution to 2:

The provisions mean that the individual commercial mortgages that are the collateral for the CMBS have prepayment protection. Specifically, the structure has three of the four types of call protection, namely, a prepayment lockout, a yield maintenance charge, and defeasance.

Solution to 3:

This risk is the balloon risk, which is the risk that if the borrower cannot refinance the balloon payment, the bonds may extend in maturity because the lender has to wait to obtain the outstanding principal until the borrower can obtain a loan to refinance the balloon amount.

Solution to 4:

The CMBS has credit risk. The NOI and DSC ratio are two commonly used measures of credit risk for a commercial mortgage.

To this point, this reading has addressed the securitization of real estate property, both residential and commercial. Section 7 discusses the securitization of debt obligations in which the underlying asset is not real estate.

7   NON-MORTGAGE ASSET-BACKED SECURITIES

Numerous types of non-mortgage assets have been used as collateral in securitization. The largest in most countries are auto loan and lease receivables, credit card receivables, personal loans, and commercial loans. What is important to keep in mind is that, regardless of the asset type, ABS share the same type of risk from a credit perspective.

ABS can be categorized based on the way the collateral repays—that is, whether the collateral is amortizing or non-amortizing. Traditional residential mortgage loans and automobile loans are examples of amortizing loans. The cash flows for an amortizing loan include interest payments, scheduled principal repayments and any prepayments, if permissible. If the loan has no schedule for paying down the principal, it is a non-amortizing loan. Because a non-amortizing loan does not involve principal repayments, the prepayment issue does not affect it. A credit card receivable is an example of a non-amortizing loan.

Let us see what happens when an amortizing loan is the collateral. Suppose that 1,000 such loans with a total face value of US$100 million are the collateral. Over time, some of the loans will pay off. The principal received from the scheduled repayment and any prepayments are distributed to the bond classes on the basis of the waterfall. Consequently, over time, the number of loans will drop from 1,000 and the total face value will fall to less than US$100 million.

Now, what happens if the collateral is 1,000 loans that are non-amortizing? Some of these loans will pay off in whole or in part before the maturity of the bond. When those loans are paid off, what happens next depends on whether the loans were paid off during the lockout period or after it. The "lockout period" or "revolving period" is the period during which the principal received is reinvested to acquire additional loans with a principal equal to the total principal received from the cash flow. This can result in more or fewer than 1,000 loans, but the loans will still have a total face value of US$100 million. When the lockout period is over, any principal that is repaid will not be used to reinvest in new loans but instead distributed to the bond classes.

This reading cannot cover all types of non-mortgage assets that have been securitized. It will consider the securitization of the two most popular non-mortgage assets in most countries: auto loan receivables and credit card receivables, the former being an amortizing loan and the latter, a non-amortizing loan.

7.1 Auto Loan Receivable-Backed Securities

Automobile securitization includes deals backed by auto loan and lease receivables. The focus in this section is on the largest type of automobile securitizations, that is, auto loan-backed securities. In some countries, auto loan-backed securities represent the largest or second largest sector of the securitization market.

The cash flows for auto loan-backed securities consist of regularly scheduled monthly loan payments (interest payment and scheduled principal repayments) and any prepayments. For securities backed by auto loans, prepayments result from sales and trade-ins requiring full payoff of the loan, repossession and subsequent resale of vehicles, insurance proceeds received upon loss or destruction of vehicles, payoffs of the loan with cash to save on the interest cost, and refinancing of the loans at a lower interest rate.

All auto loan-backed securities have some form of credit enhancement, often a senior/subordinated so the senior tranches have credit enhancement due to the presence of subordinated tranches. In addition, many auto loan-backed securities come with a reserve account, overcollateralization, and excess interest on the receivables.

To illustrate the typical structure of auto loan-backed securities, let us use the example of Fideicomiso Financiero Autos VI, a loan securitization in Argentina outstanding at the end of 2012. The collateral is a pool of 827 auto loans denominated in Argentine pesos (ARS). The loans were originated by BancoFinansur. The following three securities were in the structure: Class A Floating Rate Debt Securities (ARS22,700,000); Class B Floating Rate Debt Securities (ARS1,970,000), and Certificates (ARS5,988,245). The reference rate for the floating-rate debt securities was BADLAR (Buenos Aires Deposits of Large Amount Rate), the benchmark rate for loans in Argentina. This reference rate is the average rate on 30-day deposits of at least ARS1 million. For Class A, the interest rate was BADLAR plus 450 bps, with a minimum rate of 18% and a maximum rate of 26%; for Class B, it was BADLAR plus 650 bps, with 20% and 28% as the minimum and maximum rates, respectively. This loan securitization has a senior/subordinated structure. Class B and the Certificates provide credit enhancement for Class A, and the Certificates provide credit enhancement for Class B. Further credit enhancement comes from overcollateralization, the presence of excess spread, and reserve funds.

EXAMPLE 11

Example of Auto Loan-Backed Notes

The following information is from the prospectus supplement for US$877,670,000 of automobile receivables-backed notes issued by AmeriCredit Automobile Receivables Trust 2013-4 Issuing Entity:

> The collateral for this securitization is a pool of sub-prime automobile loan contracts secured for new and used automobiles and light-duty trucks and vans.
>
> The issuing entity will issue seven classes of asset-backed notes pursuant to the indenture. The notes are designated as the "*Class A-1 Notes*," the "*Class A-2 Notes*," the "*Class A-3 Notes*," the "*Class B Notes*," the "*Class C Notes*," the "*Class D Notes*," and the "*Class E Notes*." The Class A-1 Notes, the Class A-2 Notes and the Class A-3 Notes are the "*Class A Notes*."
>
> The Class A Notes, the Class B Notes, the Class C Notes, and the Class D Notes are being offered by this prospectus supplement and are sometimes referred to as the *publicly offered notes*. The Class E Notes are not being offered by this prospectus supplement, and will initially be retained by the depositor or an affiliate of the depositor. The Class E Notes are sometimes referred to as the *privately placed notes*.
>
> Each class of notes will have the initial note principal balance, interest rate, and final scheduled distribution date listed in the following table:

	Publicly Offered Notes		
Class	Initial Note Principal Balance (US$)	Interest Rate (%)	Final Scheduled Distribution Date
A-1	168,000,000	0.25	8 August 2014
A-2	279,000,000	0.74	8 November 2016
A-3	192,260,000	0.96	9 April 2018
B	68,870,000	1.66	10 September 2018
C	85,480,000	2.72	9 September 2019
D	84,060,000	3.31	8 October 2019

	Privately Placed Notes		
Class	Initial Note Principal Balance (US$)	Interest Rate (%)	Final Scheduled Distribution Date
E	22,330,000	4.01	8 January 2021

> Interest on each class of notes will accrue during each interest period at the applicable interest rate.
>
> On the closing date, approximately US$18,997,361 will be deposited into the reserve account, which is 2.0% of the expected initial aggregate principal balance of the automobile loan contracts.
>
> The overcollateralization amount represents the amount by which the aggregate principal balance of the automobile loan contracts exceeds the principal balance of the notes. On the closing date, the

> initial amount of overcollateralization will be approximately 5.25% of the aggregate principal balance of the automobile loan contracts as of the cutoff date."

1 What does "sub-prime" imply about the credit quality of the borrowers?

2 What is the purpose of the reserve account?

3 What is the role played by overcollateralization?

4 If in the first two years after issuance there are losses on the loans of US$40 million over and above the protection provided by the reserve account and any overcollateralization, which bond class(es) would realize the losses?

Solution to 1:

A subprime loan is one granted to borrowers with lower credit quality. Like any subprime loans, subprime automobile loans are contracts made to borrowers who have experienced prior credit difficulties or who cannot otherwise document strong credit.

Solution to 2:

The purpose of a reserve account is to provide credit enhancement. More specifically, the reserve account is a form of internal credit enhancement that will protect the bondholders against losses up to 2% of the par value of the entire issue.

Solution to 3:

Overcollateralization means that the aggregate principal balance of the automobile loan contracts exceeds the principal balance of the notes. It represents another form of internal credit enhancement. Overcollateralization can be used to absorb losses from the collateral.

Solution to 4:

The bond class that absorbs the losses first is the Class E Notes. That bond class will absorb losses up to its principal amount of US$22,330,000. That means there is still US$17,670,000 to be absorbed by another bond class, which would be the Class D Notes.

7.2 Credit Card Receivable-Backed Securities

When a purchase is made on a credit card, the issuer of the credit card (the lender) extends credit to the cardholder (the borrower). Credit cards are issued by banks, credit card companies, retailers, and travel and entertainment companies. At the time of purchase, the cardholder is agreeing to repay the amount borrowed (i.e., the cost of the item purchased) plus any applicable finance charges. The amount that the cardholder has agreed to pay the issuer of the credit card is a receivable from the perspective of the issuer of the credit card. Credit card receivables are used as collateral for the issuance of credit card receivable-backed securities.

For a pool of credit card receivables, the cash flows consist of finance charges collected, fees, and principal repayments. Finance charges collected represent the periodic interest the credit card borrower is charged on the unpaid balance after the grace period. Fees include late payment fees and any annual membership fees.

Interest is paid to security holders periodically (e.g., monthly, quarterly, or semi-annually). The interest rate may be fixed or floating—roughly half of the securities are floaters. The floating rate is typically uncapped—that is, it has no upper limit unless the country where the asset-backed bonds are issued has usury rate laws that impose a cap.

As noted earlier, credit card receivable-backed securities are non-amortizing loans. They have lockout periods during which the cash flow that is paid out to security holders is based only on finance charges collected and fees. When the lockout period is over, the principal is no longer reinvested but paid to investors.

Certain provisions in credit card receivable-backed securities require early amortization of the principal if certain events occur. Such provisions are referred to as "early amortization" or "rapid amortization" provisions and are included to safeguard the credit quality of the issue. The only way the principal cash flows can be altered is by the triggering of the early amortization provision.

Consider the GE Capital Credit Card Master Note Trust Series 2013-1 transaction issued in March 2013. The originator of the credit card receivables is GE Capital Retail Bank, and the servicer is GE Capital Corporation. The collateral is an account of several private-label and co-branded credit card issuers, including JCPenney, Lowe's Home Improvement, Sam's Club, Walmart, Gap, and Chevron. The structure of this US$969.085 million transaction is as follows: Class A notes, US$800,000,000; Class B notes, US$100,946,373; and Class C notes, US$68,138,802.Thus, the issue has a senior/subordinate structure. The Class A notes are the senior notes and were rated by Moody's as Aaa and by Fitch as AAA. The Class B notes were rated A2 by Moody's and A+ by Fitch. The Class C notes were rated Baa2 by Moody's and BBB+ by Fitch.

EXAMPLE 12

Credit Card Receivable-Backed vs. Auto Loan-Backed Securities

What are the two main ways in which credit card receivable-backed securities differ from auto loan receivable-backed securities?

Solution:

First, the collateral for credit card receivable-backed securities are non-amortizing loans, whereas the collateral for auto loan-backed securities are loans that fully amortize. Second, for auto loan-backed securities, principal is distributed to the bond classes each month, and as a result, the amount of the outstanding pool balance declines over time. For credit card receivable-backed securities, principal received during the lockout period is used to acquire additional credit card receivables. After the lockout period, principal repayments are used to pay off the outstanding principal.

---

8   COLLATERALIZED DEBT OBLIGATIONS

Collateralized debt obligation (CDO) is a generic term used to describe a security backed by a diversified pool of one or more debt obligations: CDOs backed by corporate and emerging market bonds are collateralized bond obligations (CBOs); CDOs backed by leveraged bank loans are collateralized loan obligations (CLOs); CDOs backed by ABS, RMBS, CMBS, and other CDOs are structured finance CDOs; CDOs backed by a portfolio of credit default swaps for other structured securities are synthetic CDOs.

8.1 Structure of a CDO Transaction

Although a CDO involves the creation of an SPV, it is not an asset-back security. In an ABS, the funds necessary to pay the bond classes come from a pool of loans that must be serviced. In a CDO, however, there is a need for a CDO manager, also called "**collateral manager**," to buy and sell debt obligations for and from the CDO's portfolio of assets (i.e., the collateral) to generate sufficient cash flows to meet the obligations to the CDO bondholders.

The funds to purchase the collateral assets for a CDO are obtained from the issuance of debt obligations. These debt obligations are bond classes or tranches. The bond classes include senior bond classes, mezzanine bond classes (bond classes with credit ratings between senior and subordinated bond classes), and subordinated bond classes (often referred to as the residual or equity class). The motivation for investors to invest in senior or mezzanine bond classes is to earn a potentially higher yield than on a comparably rated corporate bond by gaining exposure to debt products that they may not otherwise be able to purchase. Equity class investors have the potential to earn an equity-type return, thereby offsetting the increased risk from investing in the subordinated class. The key to whether or not a CDO is economical is whether a structure can be created that offers a competitive return for the subordinated tranche.

The basic economics of the CDO is that the funds are raised by the sale of the bond classes and the CDO manager invests those funds in assets. The CDO manager seeks to earn a rate of return higher than the aggregate cost of the bond classes. The benefit of the return in excess of what is paid out to the bond classes accrues to the equity holders and to the CDO manager. In other words, this is a leveraged transaction in which the equity investors are using borrowed funds (the bond classes issued) to generate a return above the funding cost.

As with ABS, each class of CDO bonds is structured to provide a specific level of risk for investors. The CDO is constructed so as to impose restrictions on the CDO manager via various tests and limits that must be satisfied for the CDO to meet investors' varying risk appetites while still providing adequate protection for the senior bond class. If the CDO manager fails certain pre-specified tests, a provision is triggered that requires the payoff of the principal to the senior bond class until the tests are satisfied. This process would effectively deleverage the CDO because the cheapest funding source for the CDO, the senior bond class, would be reduced.

The ability of the CDO manager to make the interest payments to the bond classes and pay off the bond classes as they mature depends on the performance of the collateral. The proceeds to meet the obligations to the CDO bond classes can come from one or more of the following sources: interest payments from the collateral assets, maturing of collateral assets, and sale of collateral assets. The cash flows and credit risks of a CDO are best illustrated by an example.

8.2 Illustration of a CDO Transaction

Although various motivations may prompt a sponsor to create a CDO, the following example uses a CDO for which the purpose is to capture what market participants mistakenly label a CDO arbitrage transaction. The term "arbitrage" is not used here in the traditional sense—that is, a risk-free transaction that earns an expected positive net profit but requires no net investment of money. The term is used here in a loose sense to describe a transaction in which the motivation is to capture a spread between the return that could potentially be earned on the portfolio of assets (the collateral) and the funding cost.

To understand the structure of a CDO transaction and its risks, consider the following US$100 million CDO:

Tranche	Par Value (US$)	Coupon Rate[a]
Senior	80,000,000	Libor + 70 bps
Mezzanine	10,000,000	10-year US Treasury rate + 200 bps
Subordinated/equity	10,000,000	—

[a] Libor is the dollar London Interbank Offered Rate, a commonly-used reference rate for floating-rate debt.

Suppose that the collateral consists of bonds that all mature in 10 years and that the coupon rate for every bond is the 10-year US Treasury rate plus 400 bps. Because the collateral pays a fixed rate (the 10-year US Treasury rate plus 400 bps) but the senior tranche requires a floating-rate payment (Libor plus 70 bps), the CDO manager enters into an interest rate swap agreement with another party. An interest rate swap is simply an agreement to periodically exchange interest payments. The payments are calculated based on a notional amount. This amount is not exchanged between the two parties. Rather, it is simply used to determine the amount of interest payment of each party. The notional amount of the swap is the par value amount of the senior tranche, i.e., US$80 million in this example. Suppose that through the interest rate swap, the CDO manager agrees to do the following: (1) pay a fixed rate each year equal to the 10-year US Treasury rate plus 100 bps and (2) receive Libor).

Assume that the 10-year US Treasury rate at the time this CDO is issued is 7%. Now, consider the cash flows for each year. First, let us look at the collateral. Assuming no default, the collateral will pay interest each year equal to the 10-year US Treasury rate of 7% plus 400 bps—that is, 11%. So, the interest will be 11% × US$100,000,000 = US$11,000,000.

Now, let us determine the interest that must be paid to the senior and mezzanine tranches. For the senior tranche, the interest payment will be US$80,000,000 × (Libor + 70 bps). For the mezzanine tranche, the coupon rate is the 10-year US Treasury rate plus 200 bps. So the coupon rate for the first interest payment is 9% and the interest that must be paid to mezzanine tranches is 9% × US$10,000,000 = US$900,000.

Finally, consider the interest rate swap. In this agreement, the CDO manager agreed to pay the swap counterparty the 10-year US Treasury rate plus 100 bps based on a notional amount of US$80 million. So, the amount paid to the swap counterparty is 8% × US$80,000,000 = US$6,400,000 the first year. The amount received from the swap counterparty is Libor based on a notional amount of US$80 million—that is, Libor × US$80,000,000.

All of this information can now be put together. The amounts coming into the CDO are:

Interest from collateral	$11,000,000
Interest from swap counterparty	$80,000,000 × Libor
Total interest received	$11,000,000 + $80,000,000 × Libor

The amounts to be paid to the senior and mezzanine tranches and to the swap counterparty are:

Interest to senior tranche	$80,000,000 × (Libor + 70 bps)
Interest to mezzanine tranche	$900,000
Interest to swap counterparty	$6,400,000
Total interest paid	$7,300,000 + $80,000,000 × (Libor + 70 bps)

Netting the amounts coming in and going out produces the following:

Total interest received	$11,000,000	+ $80,000,000	× Libor
Total interest paid	$7,300,000	+ $80,000,000	× (Libor + 70 bps)
Net interest	$3,700,000	− $80,000,000	× (70 bps)

Because 70 bps times US$80 million is US$560,000, the net interest remaining is US$3,140,000 (US$3,700,000 − US$560,000). From this amount, any fees—including the CDO manager's fees—must be paid. The balance is then the amount available to pay the subordinated/equity tranche. If the fees are US$640,000, then the cash flow available to the subordinated/equity tranche for the year is US$2.5 million ($3,140,000 − $640,000). Because the tranche has a par value of US$10 million and is assumed to be sold at par, the annual return is thus 25%.

Obviously, some simplifying assumptions have been made in this example. For instance, this example assumed that no defaults would occur. Furthermore, it assumed that all of the securities purchased by the CDO manager are non-callable and, therefore, that the coupon rate would not decline because securities were called. Despite these simplifying assumptions, the example does demonstrate the economics of an arbitrage CDO transaction, the need for the use of an interest rate swap, and how the subordinated/equity tranche will realize a return.

Some of the risks follow from the assumptions. In the case of defaults in the collateral for example, there is a risk that the manager will fail to earn a return sufficient to pay off the investors in the senior and mezzanine tranches, resulting in a loss for those classes of bondholders. Investors in the subordinated/equity tranche risk the loss of their entire investment. Even if payments are made to these investors, the return they realize may not be the return expected at the time of purchase.

Moreover, after some period, the CDO manager must begin repaying principal to the senior and mezzanine tranches. The interest rate swap must be structured to take this requirement into account because the entire amount of the senior tranche is not outstanding for the life of the collateral.

EXAMPLE 13

Motivation for Creating a CDO

An arbitrage collateralized debt obligation relies on securitization but is different from a traditional asset-backed security in terms of its motivation. Explain why.

Solution:

As with an ABS, the creation of an arbitrage CDO involves the creation of an SPV and the pooling of debt obligations. The purpose and management of an arbitrage CDO, however, are different from those of an ABS. With an ABS, the cash flows from the collateral are used to pay off the holders of the bond classes without the active management of the collateral—that is, without a manager altering the composition of the debt obligations in the pool that is backing the securitization. In contrast, in an arbitrage CDO, a CDO manager buys and sells debt obligations with the dual purpose of not only paying off the holders of the bond classes but also generating an attractive/competitive return for the subordinated/equity tranche and for the manager.

SUMMARY

- The securitization process involves pooling relatively straight-forward debt obligations, such as loans or bonds, and using the cash flows from the pool of debt obligations to pay off the bond created in the securitization process.

- Securitization has several benefits. It allows investors direct access to liquid investments and payment streams that would be unattainable if all the financing were performed through banks. It enables banks to increase loan origination, monitoring, and collections at economic scales greater than if they used only their own in-house loan portfolios. The end result is lower costs of borrowing for entities raising funds, higher risk-adjusted returns to investors, and greater efficiency and profitability for the banking sector.

- The parties to a securitization include the special purpose vehicle (SPV, also called the trust) that is the issuer of the securities and the seller of the pool of loans (also called the depositor). The SPV is a bankruptcy-remote vehicle that plays a pivotal role in the securitization process.

- The securities issued are called asset-backed securities (ABS) or mortgage-backed securities (MBS) when the assets that are securitized are mortgage loans. A common structure in a securitization is subordination, which leads to the creation of more than one bond class or tranche. Bond classes differ as to how they will share any losses resulting from defaults of the borrowers whose loans are in the collateral (pool of loans). The credit ratings assigned to the various bond classes depends on how the credit-rating agencies evaluate the credit risks of the collateral and any credit enhancements.

- The payments that are received from the collateral are distributed to pay interest and repay principal to the security holders as well as to pay servicing and other fees. The details regarding the priority of payments are set forth in the structure's waterfall.

- The motivation for the creation of different types of structures is to redistribute prepayment risk and credit risk efficiently among different bond classes in the securitization. Prepayment risk is the uncertainty that the actual cash flows will be different from the scheduled cash flows as set forth in the loan agreements because borrowers may alter payments to take advantage of interest rate movements.

- Because of the SPV, the securitization of a company's assets may include some bond classes that have better credit ratings than the company itself or its corporate bonds. Thus, in the aggregate, the company's funding cost is often lower when raising funds through securitization than by issuing corporate bonds.

- A mortgage loan is a loan secured by the collateral of some specified real estate property which obliges the borrower to make a predetermined series of payments to the lender. The cash flow of a mortgage includes (1) interest, (2) scheduled principal payments, and (3) prepayments (any principal repaid in excess of the scheduled principal). The ratio of the property's purchase price to the amount of the mortgage is called the loan-to-value ratio.

- The various mortgage designs throughout the world specify (1) the maturity of the loan, (2) how the interest rate is determined (i.e., fixed rate versus adjustable or variable rate), (3) how the principal is repaid (i.e., whether the loan is amortizing or not and if it is, whether it is fully amortizing or partially amortizing with a balloon payment), (4) whether the borrower has the option to prepay and in this case, whether any prepayment penalties might be imposed, and (5) the rights of the lender in a foreclosure (i.e., whether the loan is a recourse or non-recourse loan).

- In the United States, there are three sectors for securities backed by residential mortgages: (1) those guaranteed by a federal agency (Ginnie Mae) whose securities are backed by the full faith and credit of the US government, (2) those guaranteed by either of the two GSEs (Fannie Mae and Freddie Mac) but not by the US government, and (3) those issued by private entities that are not guaranteed by a federal agency or a GSE. The first two sectors are referred to as agency residential mortgage-backed securities (RMBS), and the third sector as non-agency RMBS.

- A mortgage pass-through security is created when one or more holders of mortgages form a pool of mortgages and sell shares or participation certificates in the pool. The cash flow of a mortgage pass-through security depends on the cash flow of the underlying pool of mortgages and consists of monthly mortgage payments representing interest, the scheduled repayment of principal, and any prepayments, net of servicing and other fees.

- Market participants measure the prepayment rate using two measures: the single monthly mortality (SMM) rate and its corresponding annualized rate, namely, the conditional prepayment rate (CPR). For MBS, the measure widely used by market participants to assess the sensitivity of the securitized bonds to interest rate movements is the weighted average life (WAL) or simply average life of the MBS instead of duration.

- Market participants use the Public Securities Association (PSA) prepayment benchmark to describe prepayment rates. A PSA assumption greater than 100 PSA means that prepayments are assumed to be faster than the benchmark, whereas a PSA assumption lower than 100 PSA means that prepayments are assumed to be slower than the benchmark.

- Prepayment risk includes two components: contraction risk and extension risk. The former is the risk that when interest rates decline, the security will have a shorter maturity than was anticipated at the time of purchase because homeowners refinance at now-available lower interest rates. The latter is the risk that when interest rates rise, fewer prepayments will occur because homeowners are reluctant to give up the benefits of a contractual interest rate that now looks low.

- The creation of a collateralized mortgage obligation (CMO) can help manage prepayment risk by distributing the various forms of prepayment risk among different classes of bondholders. The CMO's major financial innovation is that the securities created more closely satisfy the asset/liability needs of institutional investors, thereby broadening the appeal of mortgage-backed products.

- The most common types of CMO tranches are sequential-pay tranches, planned amortization class (PAC) tranches, support tranches, and floating-rate tranches.

- Non-agency RMBS share many features and structuring techniques with agency CMOs. However, they typically include two complementary mechanisms. First, the cash flows are distributed by rules, such as the waterfall, that dictate the allocation of interest payments and principal repayments to tranches with various degrees of priority/seniority. Second, there are rules for the allocation of realized losses, which specify that subordinated bond classes have lower payment priority than senior classes.

- In order to obtain favorable credit rating, non-agency RMBS and non-mortgage ABS often require one or more credit enhancements. The most common forms of internal credit enhancement are senior/subordinated structures, reserve funds, and overcollateralization. In external credit enhancement, credit support in the case of defaults resulting in losses in the pool of loans is provided in the form of a financial guarantee by a third party to the transaction.

▪ Commercial mortgage-backed securities (CMBS) are securities backed by a pool of commercial mortgage loans on income-producing property.

▪ Two key indicators of the potential credit performance of CMBS are the debt-to-service-coverage ratio and the loan-to-value ratio. The DSC ratio is the property's annual net operating income divided by the debt service.

▪ CMBS have considerable call protection, which allows CMBS to trade in the market more like corporate bonds than like RMBS. This call protection comes in two forms: at the structure level and at the loan level. The creation of sequential-pay tranches is an example of call protection at the structure level. At the loan level, four mechanisms offer investors call protection: prepayment lockouts, prepayment penalty points, yield maintenance charges, and defeasance.

▪ ABS are backed by a wide range of asset types. The most popular non-mortgage ABS are auto loan receivable-backed securities and credit card receivable-backed securities. The collateral is amortizing for auto loan-backed securities and non-amortizing for credit card receivable-backed securities. As with non-agency RMBS, these ABS must offer credit enhancement to be appealing to investors.

▪ A collateralized debt obligation (CDO) is a generic term used to describe a security backed by a diversified pool of one or more debt obligations (e.g., corporate and emerging market bonds, leveraged bank loans, ABS, RMBS, CMBS or CDO).

▪ Like an ABS, a CDO involves the creation of an SPV. But in contrary to an ABS where the funds necessary to pay the bond classes come from a pool of loans that must be serviced, a CDO requires a collateral manager to buy and sell debt obligations for and from the CDO's portfolio of assets to generate sufficient cash flows to meet the obligations of the CDO bondholders and to generate a fair return for the equity holders.

▪ The structure of a CDO includes senior, mezzanine, and subordinated/equity bond classes.

REFERENCES

"China Revives Giant Securitization Program." 2012. *Asset-Backed Alert* (23 March).

Fabozzi, Frank J., and Vinod Kothari. 2008. *Introduction to Securitization*. Hoboken, NJ: John Wiley & Sons: 284–290.

Lea, Michael. 2010. "International Comparison of Mortgage Product Offerings." Special report published jointly by the Research Institute for Housing America and the American Bankers Association (September).

Scanlon, Kathleen, Jens Lunde, and Christine Whitehead. 2008. "Mortgage Product Innovation in Advanced Economies: More Choice, More Risk." *European Journal of Housing Policy*, vol. 8, no. 2 (June):109–131.

PRACTICE PROBLEMS

1 Securitization is beneficial for banks because it:

   A repackages bank loans into simpler structures.

   B increases the funds available for banks to lend.

   C allows banks to maintain ownership of their securitized assets.

2 In a securitization, a special purpose vehicle (SPV) is responsible for the:

   A issuance of the asset-backed securities.

   B collection of payments from the borrowers.

   C recovery of underlying assets for delinquent loans.

3 In a securitization structure, time tranching provides investors with the ability to choose between:

   A extension risk and contraction risk.

   B fully amortizing loans and partially amortizing loans.

   C senior bonds and subordinate bonds.

4 William Marolf obtains a 5 million EUR mortgage loan from Bank Nederlandse. A year later the principal on the loan is 4 million EUR and Marolf defaults on the loan. Bank Nederlandse forecloses, sells the property for 2.5 million EUR, and is entitled to collect the shortfall, 1.5 million EUR, from Marolf. Marolf *most likely* had a:

   A bullet loan.

   B recourse loan.

   C non-recourse loan.

5 Fran Martin obtains a non-recourse mortgage loan for $500,000. One year later, when the outstanding balance of the mortgage is $490,000, Martin cannot make his mortgage payments and defaults on the loan. The lender forecloses on the loan and sells the house for $315,000. What amount is the lender entitled to claim from Martin?

   A $0.

   B $175,000.

   C $185,000.

6 Anne Bogaert reviews the status of her home mortgage schedule for the month of January 2014:

Date	Item	Balance
01 January 2014	Outstanding mortgage loan balance	$500,000
31 January 2014	Total monthly required payment	$10,000
31 January 2014	Interest component of total monthly required payment	$2,500

On 31 January 2014, Boagert makes a payment of $15,000 rather than $10,000. What will be outstanding mortgage loan balance immediately after the payment is made?

   A $485,000

   B $487,500

    C $490,000

7 Which of the following describes a typical feature of a non-agency residential mortgage-backed security (RMBS)?

    A   Senior-subordinate structure in bond classes

    B   A pool of conforming mortgages as collateral

    C   A guarantee by the appropriate government sponsored enterprise (GSE)

8 Maria Nyugen is an analyst for an insurance company that invests in residential mortgage passthrough securities. Nyugen reviews the monthly cash flow of one underlying mortgage pool to determine the cash flow to be passed through to investors:

Total principal paid including prepayment	$1,910,542
Scheduled principal to be paid before prepayment	$910,542
Gross coupon interest paid	$3,562,500
Servicing fees	$337,500
Other fees for guaranteeing the issue	$58,333

Based on Nyugen's table, the total cash flow to be passed through to the investors is *closest* to:

    A $4,473,042.

    B $5,077,209.

    C $5,473,042.

9 In the context of mortgage-backed securities, a conditional prepayment rate (CPR) of 8% means that approximately 8% of an outstanding mortgage pool balance at the beginning of the year will be prepaid:

    A   in the current month.

    B   by the end of the year.

    C   over the life of the mortgages.

10 For a mortgage passthrough security, which of the following risks *most likely* increases as interest rates decline?

    A   Balloon

    B   Extension

    C   Contraction

11 From a lender's perspective, balloon risk can *best* be described as a type of:

    A   extension risk.

    B   contraction risk.

    C   interest rate risk.

12 Credit risk is a factor for commercial mortgage-backed securities because they are backed by mortgage loans that:

    A   are non-recourse.

    B   have limited call protection.

    C   have no prepayment penalty points.

13 Which commercial mortgage-backed security (CMBS) characteristic causes CMBS to trade more like a corporate bond than an agency residential mortgage-backed security (RMBS)?

    A   Call protection

    B   Internal credit enhancement

   C Debt-to-service coverage ratio level

14 An excess spread account incorporated into a securitized structure is designed to limit:

   A credit risk.

   B extension risk.

   C contraction risk.

15 Which of the following *best* describes the cash flow that owners of credit card receivable-backed securities receive during the lockout period?

   A Only principal payments collected

   B Only finance charges and fees collected

   C No cash flow is received as all cash flow collected is reinvested.

SOLUTIONS

1 B is correct. Securitization increases the funds available for banks to lend because they no longer have to hold all the loans they originate on their balance sheet. The securitization process allows banks to remove loans from their balance sheets and issue bonds that are backed by those loans with the participation of several new entities. Securitization repackages relatively simple debt obligations, such as bank loans, into more complex structures. The process of securitization involves moving or selling assets from the owner of the assets—in this case, the banks—into a special legal entity called a special purpose vehicle (SPV).

A is incorrect because securitization is a process in which simple debt obligations, such as bank loans, are repackaged into more complex (not simpler) structures.

C is incorrect because the process of securitization involves moving or selling assets from the owner of the assets, in this case, the banks, into a special legal entity. A special purpose vehicle (SPV) is the legal entity which issues and sells the asset-backed bonds.

2 A is correct. In a securitization, a special purpose vehicle (SPV) is the special legal entity responsible for the issuance of the asset-backed securities. In a prospectus for a securitization, the SPV is referred to as either the "issuer" or the "trust." The originator or depositor sells assets (loans or receivables) to the SPV for cash. The SPV obtains the cash used to pay the originator by selling asset-backed securities that are backed or collateralized by the originator's assets. The servicer is responsible for both the collection of payments from the borrowers and the recovery of underlying assets for delinquent loans.

B is incorrect because the servicer (not the SPV) is responsible for the collection of payments from the borrowers.

C is incorrect because the servicer (not the SPV) is responsible for recovery of the underlying assets from borrowers who are delinquent.

3 A is correct. Time tranching is the process in which a set of bond classes or tranches is created that allow investors a choice in the type of prepayment risk, extension or contraction, that they prefer to bear. Senior and subordinate bond classes are used in credit tranching structures as a form of credit enhancement. Credit tranching structures allow investors to choose the amount of credit risk that they prefer to bear.

B is incorrect because fully and partially amortizing loans are the two types of amortizing loans. Amortization is a loan specification or design and refers to how the principal on a loan is repaid.

C is incorrect because senior and subordinate bond classes are used in credit tranching structures as a means of credit enhancement. Credit tranching structures redistribute the credit risk associated with the underlying collateral and allow investors to choose the amount of credit risk that they prefer to bear.

4 B is correct. Bank Nederlandse has a claim against Marolf for 1.5 million EUR, the shortfall between the amount of the mortgage balance outstanding and the proceeds received from the sale of the property. This indicates that the mortgage loan is a recourse loan. The recourse/non-recourse feature indicates the rights of a lender in foreclosure. If Marolf had a non-recourse loan, the bank would have only been entitled to the proceeds from the sale of the underlying property, or 2.5 million EUR.

A is incorrect because a bullet loan is a special type of interest-only mortgage for which there are no scheduled principal payments over the entire term of the loan. Since the unpaid balance is less than the original mortgage loan, it is unlikely that Marolf has an interest only mortgage.

C is incorrect because Bank Nederlandse has a claim against Marolf for the shortfall between the amount of the mortgage balance outstanding and the proceeds received from the sale of the property. A non-recourse loan limits the rights of a lender in a foreclosure to the proceeds from the sale of the underlying property.

5   A is correct. Because the loan has a non-recourse feature, the lender can only look to the underlying property to recover the outstanding mortgage balance and has no further claim against the borrower. The lender is simply entitled to foreclose on the home and sell it.

B and C are incorrect because the lender would be entitled to claim the shortfall between the mortgage balance outstanding and the proceeds received from the sale of the property only if the loan was of the recourse (not non-recourse) type.

6   B is correct. The difference between the $10,000 monthly mortgage payment and the $2,500 portion of the payment that represents interest equals $7,500, which is the amount of the total required payment applied to reduce the outstanding mortgage balance. In addition, a payment made in excess of the monthly mortgage payment is called a prepayment. The prepayment of $5,000 is a partial pay down of the mortgage balance. The outstanding mortgage balance after the $15,000 payment is the 01/01/2014 mortgage balance of $500,000 – $7,500 – $5,000 = $487,500.

A is incorrect because $485,000 is calculated by subtracting the total mortgage payment of $10,000 plus the prepayment of $5,000 from the outstanding mortgage balance of $500,000. The outstanding mortgage balance should not be reduced by the $2,500 interest component.

C is incorrect because $490,000 is calculated by subtracting only the total required mortgage payment of $10,000 from the outstanding mortgage balance of $500,000, which ignores the interest component of the total required payment.

7   A is correct. Non-agency RMBS are credit enhanced, either internally or externally. The most common forms of internal credit enhancements are senior/subordinate structures, reserve funds, and overcollateralization. Conforming mortgages are used as collateral for agency (not non-agency) mortgage passthrough securities. An agency RMBS, rather than a non-agency RMBS, issued by a GSE (government sponsored enterprise), is guaranteed by the respective GSE.

B is incorrect because non-conforming (not comforming) mortgages are used as collateral for non-agency mortgage passthrough securities. To be included in a pool of loans backing an agency RMBS, it must meet specified underwriting standards. If a loan satisfies the underwriting standards for inclusion as collateral for an agency mortgage-backed security, it is called a conforming mortgage. If a loan fails to satisfy the underwriting standards, it is called a non-conforming loan.

C is incorrect because an agency RMBS, rather than a non-agency RMBS, issued by a GSE (government sponsored enterprise), is guaranteed by the respective GSE. The RMBS issued by GSEs are those issued by Fannie Mae (previously referred to as the Federal National Mortgage Association) and Freddie Mac (previously referred to as the Federal Home Loan Mortgage Corporation).

8 B is correct. The cash flow of the underlying mortgage pool consists of monthly mortgage payments representing interest, the scheduled repayment of principal, and any prepayments. The monthly cash flow for a passthrough security is less than the monthly cash flow of the underlying pool by an amount equal to servicing and other fees. The other fees are those charged by the issuer or guarantor of the passthrough for guaranteeing the issue. The gross interest is calculated using the weighted average coupon (WAC) rate for the mortgage loans in the pool. The total cash flow to be received by the investors is $1,910,542 of total principal plus the $3,562,500 gross coupon interest less servicing and other fees, or $1,910,542 + $3,562,500 − $337,500 − $58,333 = $5,077,029.

A is incorrect because the $4,473,042 is calculated by adding the scheduled principal payments of $910,542 to the gross coupon interest of $3,562,500. The cash flow for a passthrough security is the mortgage cash flow of the underlying mortgage pool which includes the scheduled repayment of principal, any prepayments and gross coupon interest less the amount equal to servicing and other fees.

C is incorrect because $5,473,042 is calculated by adding the total principal of $1,910,542 to the gross interest of $3,562,500. The monthly cash flow for a passthrough is less than the monthly cash flow of the underlying pool by an amount equal to servicing and other fees which total $337,500 + $58,333 = 395,833.

9 B is correct. CPR is an annualized rate which indicates the percentage of the mortgage balance at the beginning of the year which is expected to be prepaid by the end of the year. The single monthly mortality rate (SMM) is a monthly measure of the percentage of the mortgage balance available to prepay for a pool of mortgages that is projected to prepay in the given month. The prepayment rate over the life of mortgages in the mortgage pool could only be computed at the end of the life of the mortgages.

A is incorrect because the single monthly mortality rate (SMM), not the CPR, is the percentage of the outstanding mortgage balance available to prepay for a pool of mortgages at the beginning of the month that is projected to prepay that month.

C is incorrect because the prepayment rate over the life of the mortgages in a mortgage pool could only be computed at the end of the life of the mortgages and therefore can only be projected based on an assumed prepayment rate.

10 C is correct. When interest rates decline, a passthrough security is subject to contraction risk. Contraction risk is the risk that the security will be shorter in maturity than was anticipated when the security was purchased due to higher than expected prepayments (which typically occurs when interest rates decline). Extension risk is the risk that when interest rates rise, there are fewer prepayments and, as a result, the security becomes longer in maturity than anticipated at the time of purchase. Balloon risk (common with commercial mortgage-backed securities), a type of extension risk, is the risk that a borrower will not be able to make the balloon payment when due.

A is incorrect because balloon risk is a type of extension risk. A passthrough security is subject to extension risk when interest rates rise (not decline).

B is incorrect because extension risk is the risk that when interest rates rise (not decline), there are fewer prepayments and, as a result, the security becomes longer in maturity than anticipated at the time of purchase.

11 A is correct. From a lender's perspective, balloon risk refers to the risk that a borrower will not be able to make the balloon payment when due. Since the term of the loan will be extended by the lender during the workout period, balloon risk is a type of extension risk. Extension risk is the undesired lengthening in the expected life of a security.

B is incorrect because balloon risk is a type of extension (not contraction) risk. Contraction risk would be the risk that the security will be shorter in maturity than was anticipated when the security was purchased.

C is incorrect because, from the lender's perpective, balloon risk relates to the undesired lengthening in the expected life of the security (extension risk). A borrower (not the lender) may face interest rate risk if planning to refinance the balloon amount on the balloon payment date. The interest rate on a new loan to refinance the balloon balance on the balloon payment date is unknown, and thus the borrower is exposed to interest rate risk.

12 A is correct. Because commercial mortgage loans are non-recourse loans, the lender can only look to the income-producing property backing the loan for interest and principal repayment. If there is a default, the lender looks to the proceeds from the sale of the property for repayment and has no recourse against the borrower for any unpaid mortgage loan balance. Call protection addresses prepayment risk. Investors have considerable call protection at both the structure and the loan level with CMBS. At the loan level, there are four mechanisms that offer investors call protection: prepayment penalty points, prepayment lockouts, yield maintenance charges, and defeasance.

B is incorrect because call protection addresses prepayment risk. Investors have considerable call protection at both the structure and the loan level with CMBS.

C is incorrect because at the loan level there are four mechanisms that offer investors call protection: prepayment penalty points, prepayment lockouts, yield maintenance and defeasance.

13 A is correct. With CMBS, investors have considerable call protection. An investor in a RMBS is exposed to considerable prepayment risk, but with CMBS, call protection is available to the investor at both the structure and the loan level. The call protection results in CMBS trading in the market more like a corporate bond than a RMBS. Both internal credit enhancement and the debt-to-service coverage (DSC) ratio address credit risk, not prepayment risk. Internal credit enhancements are available for CMBS, but are not needed for an agency RMBS which is issued with a guarantee by its respective GSE. The DSC ratio level is used as a key indicator of the potential credit performance of the property underlying a commercial mortgage loan.

B is incorrect because an internal credit enhancement mechanism such as "subordination" is used to achieve desired rating levels for a CMBS. An agency RMBS is guaranteed by the respective GSE and does not require a credit enhancement mechanism to reduce credit risk. Both credit enhancement and government guarantees address credit risk, not prepayment risk.

C is incorrect because the debt-to-service coverage (DSC) ratio level is used as a key indicator of the potential credit performance of the property underlying a commercial mortgage loan. If certain DSC levels are needed, then an internal credit enhancement mechanism is used to achieve a desired rating level. The loan-to-value ratio is used for residential mortgage loans. Both ratios are indicators of credit performance and do not address prepayment risk.

14 A is correct. Because of credit risk, all structures have some form of credit enhancement. An excess spread account is a form of internal credit enhancement which involves the allocation of any amounts into an account resulting from monthly funds remaining after paying out the interest to the bond classes, servicing fees, and administrative fees. The excess spread is a design feature of the structure. Time tranching (not an excess spread account) addresses prepayment risk (extension or contraction) to allow investors a choice in the type of prepayment risk that they prefer to bear.

B and C are incorrect because an excess spread account is a form of internal credit enhancement. Time tranching addresses prepayment risk (extension or contraction) to allow investors a choice in the type of prepayment risk that they prefer to bear.

15 B is correct. During the lockout period, the cash flow that is paid out to security holders is based only on finance charges collected and fees. After the lockout period, the principal is no longer reinvested but paid to investors.

A and C are incorrect because, during the lockout period, the cash flow paid out to credit card receivable-backed security holders is based only on collected finance charges and fees. After the lockout period, the principal is no longer reinvested but paid to investors.

16

Fixed Income

Analysis of Risk

This study session focuses on the analysis risks associated with fixed-income securities; emphasis is on interest rate and credit risks. The first reading describes the sources of return on fixed-income securities and measures and analysis of interest rate risk. The second reading introduces measures and analysis of credit risk of fixed-income securities.

READING ASSIGNMENTS

Understanding Fixed-Income Risk and Return

by James F. Adams, PhD, CFA, and Donald J. Smith, PhD

LEARNING OUTCOMES

Mastery	The candidate should be able to:
☐	a. calculate and interpret the sources of return from investing in a fixed-rate bond;
☐	b. define, calculate, and interpret Macaulay, modified, and effective durations;
☐	c. explain why effective duration is the most appropriate measure of interest rate risk for bonds with embedded options;
☐	d. define key rate duration and describe the key use of key rate durations in measuring the sensitivity of bonds to changes in the shape of the benchmark yield curve;
☐	e. explain how a bond's maturity, coupon, embedded options, and yield level affect its interest rate risk;
☐	f. calculate the duration of a portfolio and explain the limitations of portfolio duration;
☐	g. calculate and interpret the money duration of a bond and price value of a basis point (PVBP);
☐	h. calculate and interpret approximate convexity and distinguish between approximate and effective convexity;
☐	i. estimate the percentage price change of a bond for a specified change in yield, given the bond's approximate duration and convexity;
☐	j. describe how the term structure of yield volatility affects the interest rate risk of a bond;
☐	k. describe the relationships among a bond's holding period return, its duration, and the investment horizon;
☐	l. explain how changes in credit spread and liquidity affect yield-to-maturity of a bond and how duration and convexity can be used to estimate the price effect of the changes.

1 INTRODUCTION

It is important for analysts to have a well-developed understanding of the risk and return characteristics of fixed-income investments. Beyond the vast worldwide market for publicly and privately issued fixed-rate bonds, many financial assets and liabilities with known future cash flows may be evaluated using the same principles. The starting point for this analysis is the yield-to-maturity, or internal rate of return on future cash flows, which was introduced in the fixed-income valuation reading. The return on a fixed-rate bond is affected by many factors, the most important of which is the receipt of the interest and principal payments in the full amount and on the scheduled dates. Assuming no default, the return is also affected by changes in interest rates that affect coupon reinvestment and the price of the bond if it is sold before it matures. Measures of the price change can be derived from the mathematical relationship used to calculate the price of the bond. The first of these measures (duration) estimates the change in the price for a given change in interest rates. The second measure (convexity) improves on the duration estimate by taking into account the fact that the relationship between price and yield-to-maturity of a fixed-rate bond is not linear.

Section 2 uses numerical examples to demonstrate the sources of return on an investment in a fixed-rate bond, which includes the receipt and reinvestment of coupon interest payments and the redemption of principal if the bond is held to maturity. The other source of return is capital gains (and losses) on the sale of the bond prior to maturity. Section 2 also shows that fixed-income investors holding the same bond can have different exposures to interest rate risk if their investment horizons differ. Discussion of credit risk, although critical to investors, is postponed to Section 5 so that attention can be focused on interest rate risk.

Section 3 provides a thorough review of bond duration and convexity, and shows how the statistics are calculated and used as measures of interest rate risk. Although procedures and formulas exist to calculate duration and convexity, these statistics can be approximated using basic bond-pricing techniques and a financial calculator. Commonly used versions of the statistics are covered, including Macaulay, modified, effective, and key rate durations. The distinction is made between risk measures that are based on changes in the bond's yield-to-maturity (i.e., *yield* duration and convexity) and on benchmark yield curve changes (i.e., *curve* duration and convexity).

Section 4 returns to the issue of the investment horizon. When an investor has a short-term horizon, duration (and convexity) are used to estimate the change in the bond price. In this case, yield volatility matters. In particular, bonds with varying times-to-maturity have different degrees of yield volatility. When an investor has a long-term horizon, the interaction between coupon reinvestment risk and market price risk matters. The relationship among interest rate risk, bond duration, and the investment horizon is explored.

Section 5 discusses how the tools of duration and convexity can be extended to credit and liquidity risks and highlights how these different factors can affect a bond's return and risk.

A summary of key points and practice problems in the CFA Institute multiple-choice format conclude the reading.

2 SOURCES OF RETURN

An investor in a fixed-rate bond has three sources of return: (1) receipt of the promised coupon and principal payments on the scheduled dates, (2) reinvestment of coupon payments, and (3) potential capital gains or losses on the sale of the bond prior to maturity. In this section, it is assumed that the issuer makes the coupon and principal payments as scheduled. This reading focuses primarily on interest rate risk (the risk that interest rates will change), which affects the reinvestment of coupon payments and the market price if the bond is sold prior to maturity. Credit risk is considered in Section 5 of this reading and is the primary subject of the reading "Fundamentals of Credit Analysis."

When a bond is purchased at a premium or a discount, it adds another aspect to the rate of return. Recall from the reading on fixed-income valuation that a discount bond offers the investor a "deficient" coupon rate, or one below the market discount rate. The amortization of the discount in each period brings the return in line with the market discount rate as the bond's carrying value is "pulled to par." For a premium bond, the coupon rate exceeds the market discount rate and the amortization of the premium adjusts the return to match the market discount rate. Through amortization, the bond's carrying value reaches par value at maturity.

A series of examples will demonstrate the effect of a change in interest rates on two investors' realized rate of returns. Interest rates are the rates at which coupon payments are reinvested and the market discount rates at the time of purchase and at the time of sale if the bond is not held to maturity. In Examples 1 and 2, interest rates are unchanged. The two investors, however, have different time horizons for holding the bond. Examples 3 and 4 show the impact of an increase in interest rates on the two investors' total return. Examples 5 and 6 show the impact of a decrease in interest rates. In each of the six examples, an investor initially buys a 10-year, 8% annual coupon payment bond at a price of 85.503075 per 100 of par value. The bond's yield-to-maturity is 10.40%.

$$85.503075 = \frac{8}{(1+r)^1} + \frac{8}{(1+r)^2} + \frac{8}{(1+r)^3} + \frac{8}{(1+r)^4} + \frac{8}{(1+r)^5} +$$
$$\frac{8}{(1+r)^6} + \frac{8}{(1+r)^7} + \frac{8}{(1+r)^8} + \frac{8}{(1+r)^9} + \frac{108}{(1+r)^{10}}, \quad r = 0.1040$$

EXAMPLE 1

A "buy-and-hold" investor purchases a 10-year, 8% annual coupon payment bond at 85.503075 per 100 of par value and holds it until maturity. The investor receives the series of 10 coupon payments of 8 (per 100 of par value) for a total of 80, plus the redemption of principal (100) at maturity. In addition to collecting the coupon interest and the principal, the investor has the opportunity to reinvest the cash flows. If the coupon payments are reinvested at 10.40%, the future value of the coupons on the bond's maturity date is 129.970678 per 100 of par value.

$$\left[8 \times (1.1040)^9\right] + \left[8 \times (1.1040)^8\right] + \left[8 \times (1.1040)^7\right] + \left[8 \times (1.1040)^6\right] +$$
$$\left[8 \times (1.1040)^5\right] + \left[8 \times (1.1040)^4\right] + \left[8 \times (1.1040)^3\right] + \left[8 \times (1.1040)^2\right] +$$
$$\left[8 \times (1.1040)^1\right] + 8 = 129.970678$$

The first coupon payment of 8 is reinvested at 10.40% for nine years until maturity, the second is reinvested for eight years, and so forth. The future value of the annuity is obtained easily on a financial calculator, using 8 for the payment that is received at the end of each of the 10 periods. The amount in excess of the coupons, 49.970678 (= 129.970678 − 80), is the "interest-on-interest" gain from compounding.

The investor's total return is 229.970678, the sum of the reinvested coupons (129.970678) and the redemption of principal at maturity (100). The realized rate of return is 10.40%.

$$85.503075 = \frac{229.970678}{(1+r)^{10}}, \quad r = 0.1040$$

Example 1 demonstrates that the yield-to-maturity at the time of purchase measures the investor's rate of return under three assumptions: (1) The investor holds the bond to maturity, (2) there is no default by the issuer, and (3) the coupon interest payments are reinvested at that same rate of interest.

Example 2 considers another investor who buys the 10-year, 8% annual coupon payment bond and pays the same price. This investor, however, has a four-year investment horizon. Therefore, coupon interest is only reinvested for four years, and the bond is sold immediately after receiving the fourth coupon payment.

EXAMPLE 2

A second investor buys the 10-year, 8% annual coupon payment bond and sells the bond after four years. Assuming that the coupon payments are reinvested at 10.40% for four years, the future value of the reinvested coupons is 37.347111 per 100 of par value.

$$\left[8 \times (1.1040)^3\right] + \left[8 \times (1.1040)^2\right] + \left[8 \times (1.1040)^1\right] + 8 = 37.347111$$

The interest-on-interest gain from compounding is 5.347111 (= 37.347111 − 32). After four years, when the bond is sold, it has six years remaining until maturity. If the yield-to-maturity remains 10.40%, the sale price of the bond is 89.668770.

$$\frac{8}{(1.1040)^1} + \frac{8}{(1.1040)^2} + \frac{8}{(1.1040)^3} + \frac{8}{(1.1040)^4} +$$

$$\frac{8}{(1.1040)^5} + \frac{108}{(1.1040)^6} = 89.668770$$

The total return is 127.015881 (= 37.347111 + 89.668770) and the realized rate of return is 10.40%.

$$85.503075 = \frac{127.015881}{(1+r)^4}, \quad r = 0.1040$$

In Example 2, the investor's **horizon yield** is 10.40%. A horizon yield is the internal rate of return between the total return (the sum of reinvested coupon payments and the sale price or redemption amount) and the purchase price of the bond. The horizon yield on a bond investment is the annualized holding-period rate of return.

Example 2 demonstrates that the realized horizon yield matches the original yield-to-maturity if (1) coupon payments are reinvested at the same interest rate as the original yield-to-maturity, and (2) the bond is sold at a price on the constant-yield price trajectory, which implies that the investor does not have any capital gains or losses when the bond is sold.

Capital gains arise if a bond is sold at a price above its constant-yield price trajectory and capital losses occur if a bond is sold at a price above below its constant-yield price trajectory. This trajectory is based on the yield-to-maturity when the bond is purchased. The trajectory is shown in Exhibit 1 for a 10-year, 8% annual payment bond purchased at a price of 85.503075 per 100 of par value.

Exhibit 1   Constant-Yield Price Trajectory for a 10-Year, 8% Annual Payment Bond

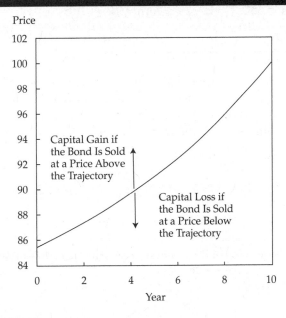

Note: Price is price per 100 of par value

A point on the trajectory represents the **carrying value** of the bond at that time. The carrying value is the purchase price plus the amortized amount of the discount if the bond is purchased at a price below par value. If the bond is purchased at a price above par value, the carrying value is the purchase price minus the amortized amount of the premium.

The amortized amount for each year is the change in the price between two points on the trajectory. The initial price of the bond is 85.503075 per 100 of par value. Its price (the carrying value) after one year is 86.393394, calculated using the original yield-to-maturity of 10.40%. Therefore, the amortized amount for the first year is 0.890319 (= 86.393394 – 85.503075). The bond price in Example 2 increases from 85.503075 to 89.668770, and that increase over the four years is movement *along* the constant-yield price trajectory. At the time the bond is sold, its carrying value is also 89.668770, so there is no capital gain or loss.

Examples 3 and 4 demonstrate the impact on investors' realized horizon yields if interest rates go up by 100 basis points (bps). The market discount rate on the bond increases from 10.40% to 11.40%. Coupon reinvestment rates go up by 100 bps as well.

EXAMPLE 3

The buy-and-hold investor purchases the 10-year, 8% annual payment bond at 85.503075. After the bond is purchased and before the first coupon is received, interest rates go up to 11.40%. The future value of the reinvested coupons at 11.40% for 10 years is 136.380195 per 100 of par value.

$$\left[8 \times (1.1140)^9 \right] + \left[8 \times (1.1140)^8 \right] + \left[8 \times (1.1140)^7 \right] + \left[8 \times (1.1140)^6 \right] +$$

$$\left[8 \times (1.1140)^5 \right] + \left[8 \times (1.1140)^4 \right] + \left[8 \times (1.1140)^3 \right] + \left[8 \times (1.1140)^2 \right] +$$

$$\left[8 \times (1.1140)^1 \right] + 8 = 136.380195$$

The total return is 236.380195 (= 136.380195 + 100). The investor's realized rate of return is 10.70%.

$$85.503075 = \frac{236.380195}{(1 + r)^{10}}, \quad r = 0.1070$$

In Example 3, the buy-and-hold investor benefits from the higher coupon reinvestment rate. The realized horizon yield is 10.70%, 30 bps higher than the outcome in Example 1, when interest rates are unchanged. There is no capital gain or loss because the bond is held until maturity. The carrying value at the maturity date is par value, the same as the redemption amount.

EXAMPLE 4

The second investor buys the 10-year, 8% annual payment bond at 85.503075 and sells it in four years. After the bond is purchased, interest rates go up to 11.40%. The future value of the reinvested coupons at 11.40% after four years is 37.899724 per 100 of par value.

$$\left[8 \times (1.1140)^3 \right] + \left[8 \times (1.1140)^2 \right] + \left[8 \times (1.1140)^1 \right] + 8 = 37.899724$$

The sale price of the bond after four years is 85.780408.

$$\frac{8}{(1.1140)^1} + \frac{8}{(1.1140)^2} + \frac{8}{(1.1140)^3} + \frac{8}{(1.1140)^4} +$$

$$\frac{8}{(1.1140)^5} + \frac{108}{(1.1140)^6} = 85.780408$$

The total return is 123.680132 (= 37.899724 + 85.780408), resulting in a realized four-year horizon yield of 9.67%.

$$85.503075 = \frac{123.680132}{(1 + r)^4}, \quad r = 0.0967$$

In Example 4, the second investor has a lower realized rate of return compared with the investor in Example 2, in which interest rates are unchanged. The future value of reinvested coupon payments goes up by 0.552613 (= 37.899724 − 37.347111) per 100 of par value because of the higher interest rates. But there is a *capital loss* of 3.888362 (= 89.668770 − 85.780408) per 100 of par value. Notice that the capital loss is measured from the bond's carrying value, the point on the constant-yield price trajectory, and not from the original purchase price. The bond is now sold at a price below the constant-yield price trajectory. The reduction in the realized four-year horizon yield from 10.40% to 9.67% is a result of the capital loss being greater than the gain from reinvesting coupons at a higher rate, which reduces the investor's total return.

Examples 5 and 6 complete the series of rate-of-return calculations for the two investors. Interest rates decline by 100 bps. The required yield on the bond falls from 10.40% to 9.40% after the purchase of the bond. The interest rates at which the coupon payments are reinvested fall as well.

EXAMPLE 5

The buy-and-hold investor purchases the 10-year bond at 85.503075 and holds the security until it matures. After the bond is purchased and before the first coupon is received, interest rates go down to 9.40%. The future value of reinvesting the coupon payments at 9.40% for 10 years is 123.888356 per 100 of par value.

$$\left[8 \times (1.0940)^9\right] + \left[8 \times (1.0940)^8\right] + \left[8 \times (1.0940)^7\right] + \left[8 \times (1.0940)^6\right] +$$

$$\left[8 \times (1.0940)^5\right] + \left[8 \times (1.0940)^4\right] + \left[8 \times (1.0940)^3\right] + \left[8 \times (1.0940)^2\right] +$$

$$\left[8 \times (1.0940)^1\right] + 8 = 123.888356$$

The total return is 223.888356, the sum of the future value of reinvested coupons and the redemption of par value. The investor's realized rate of return is 10.10%.

$$85.503075 = \frac{223.888356}{(1+r)^{10}}, \quad r = 0.1010$$

In Example 5, the buy-and-hold investor suffers from the lower coupon reinvestment rates. The realized horizon yield is 10.10%, 30 bps lower than the result in Example 1, when interest rates are unchanged. There is no capital gain or loss because the bond is held until maturity. Examples 1, 3, and 5 indicate that the interest rate risk for a buy-and-hold investor arises entirely from changes in coupon reinvestment rates.

EXAMPLE 6

The second investor buys the 10-year bond at 85.503075 and sells it in four years. After the bond is purchased, interest rates go down to 9.40%. The future value of the reinvested coupons at 9.40% is 36.801397 per 100 of par value.

$$\left[8 \times (1.0940)^3\right] + \left[8 \times (1.0940)^2\right] + \left[8 \times (1.0940)^1\right] + 8 = 36.801397$$

This reduction in future value is offset by the higher sale price of the bond, which is 93.793912 per 100 of par value.

$$\frac{8}{(1.0940)^1} + \frac{8}{(1.0940)^2} + \frac{8}{(1.0940)^3} + \frac{8}{(1.0940)^4} +$$

$$\frac{8}{(1.0940)^5} + \frac{108}{(1.0940)^6} = 93.793912$$

The total return is 130.595309 (= 36.801397 + 93.793912), and the realized yield is 11.17%.

$$85.503075 = \frac{130.595309}{(1+r)^4}, \quad r = 0.1117$$

The investor in Example 6 has a capital gain of 4.125142 (= 93.793912 − 89.668770). The capital gain is measured from the carrying value, the point on the constant-yield price trajectory. That gain offsets the reduction in the future value of reinvested coupons of 0.545714 (= 37.347111 − 36.801397). The total return is higher than that in Example 2, in which the interest rate remains at 10.40%.

In these examples, interest income for the investor is the return associated with the *passage of time*. Therefore, interest income includes the receipt of coupon interest, the reinvestment of those cash flows, and the amortization of the discount from purchase at a price below par value (or the premium from purchase at a price above par value) to bring the return back in line with the market discount rate. A capital gain or loss is the return to the investor associated with the *change in the value* of the security. On the fixed-rate bond, a change in value arises from a change in the yield-to-maturity, which is the implied market discount rate. In practice, the manner in which interest income and capital gains and losses are calculated and reported on financial statements depends on financial and tax accounting rules.

This series of examples illustrates an important point about fixed-rate bonds: The *investment horizon* is at the heart of understanding interest rate risk and return. There are two offsetting types of interest rate risk that affect the bond investor: coupon reinvestment risk and market price risk. The future value of reinvested coupon payments (and in a portfolio, the principal on bonds that mature before the horizon date) *increases* when interest rates go up and *decreases* when rates go down. The sale price on a bond that matures after the horizon date (and thus needs to be sold) *decreases* when interest rates go up and *increases* when rates go down. Coupon reinvestment risk matters more when the investor has a long-term horizon relative to the time-to-maturity of the bond. For instance, a buy-and-hold investor only has coupon reinvestment risk. Market price risk matters more when the investor has a short-term horizon relative to the time-to-maturity. For example, an investor who sells the bond before the first coupon is received has only market price risk. Therefore, two investors holding the same bond (or bond portfolio) can have different exposures to interest rate risk if they have different investment horizons.

EXAMPLE 7

An investor buys a four-year, 10% annual coupon payment bond priced to yield 5.00%. The investor plans to sell the bond in two years once the second coupon payment is received. Calculate the purchase price for the bond and the horizon yield assuming that the coupon reinvestment rate after the bond purchase and the yield-to-maturity at the time of sale are (1) 3.00%, (2) 5.00%, and (3) 7.00%.

Solution:

The purchase price is 117.729753.

$$\frac{10}{(1.0500)^1} + \frac{10}{(1.0500)^2} + \frac{10}{(1.0500)^3} + \frac{110}{(1.0500)^4} = 117.729753$$

1   3.00%: The future value of reinvested coupons is 20.300.

$$(10 \times 1.0300) + 10 = 20.300$$

The sale price of the bond is 113.394288.

$$\frac{10}{(1.0300)^1} + \frac{110}{(1.0300)^2} = 113.394288$$

Total return: 20.300 + 113.394288 = 133.694288.

If interest rates go down from 5.00% to 3.00%, the realized rate of return over the two-year investment horizon is 6.5647%, higher than the original yield-to-maturity of 5.00%.

$$117.729753 = \frac{133.694288}{(1+r)^2}, \quad r = 0.065647$$

2 5.00%: The future value of reinvested coupons is 20.500.

$$(10 \times 1.0500) + 10 = 20.500$$

The sale price of the bond is 109.297052.

$$\frac{10}{(1.0500)^1} + \frac{110}{(1.0500)^2} = 109.297052$$

Total return: 20.500 + 109.297052 = 129.797052.

If interest rates remain 5.00% for reinvested coupons and for the required yield on the bond, the realized rate of return over the two-year investment horizon is equal to the yield-to-maturity of 5.00%.

$$117.729753 = \frac{129.797052}{(1+r)^2}, \quad r = 0.050000$$

3 7.00%: The future value of reinvested coupons is 20.700.

$$(10 \times 1.0700) + 10 = 20.700$$

The bond is sold at 105.424055.

$$\frac{10}{(1.0700)^1} + \frac{110}{(1.0700)^2} = 105.424055$$

Total return: 20.700 + 105.424055 = 126.124055.

$$117.729753 = \frac{126.124055}{(1+r)^2}, \quad r = 0.035037$$

If interest rates go up from 5.00% to 7.00%, the realized rate of return over the two-year investment horizon is 3.5037%, lower than the yield-to-maturity of 5.00%.

INTEREST RATE RISK ON FIXED-RATE BONDS

3

This section covers two commonly used measures of interest rate risk: duration and convexity. It distinguishes between risk measures based on changes in a bond's own yield to maturity (yield duration and convexity) and those that affect the bond based on changes in a benchmark yield curve (curve duration and convexity).

3.1 Macaulay, Modified, and Approximate Duration

The duration of a bond measures the sensitivity of the bond's full price (including accrued interest) to changes in the bond's yield-to-maturity or, more generally, to changes in benchmark interest rates. Duration estimates changes in the bond price assuming that variables other than the yield-to-maturity or benchmark rates are held constant. Most importantly, the time-to-maturity is unchanged. Therefore, duration measures the *instantaneous* (or, at least, same-day) change in the bond price. The accrued interest is the same, so it is the flat price that goes up or down when the full price changes. Duration is a useful measure because it represents the approximate amount of time a bond would have to be held for the market discount rate at purchase to be realized if there is a single change in interest rate. If the bond is held for the duration period, an increase from reinvesting coupons is offset by a decrease in price if interest rates increase and a decrease from reinvesting coupons is offset by an increase in price if interest rates decrease.

There are several types of bond duration. In general, these can be divided into **yield duration** and **curve duration**. Yield duration is the sensitivity of the bond price with respect to the bond's own yield-to-maturity. Curve duration is the sensitivity of the bond price (or more generally, the market value of a financial asset or liability) with respect to a benchmark yield curve. The benchmark yield curve could be the government yield curve on coupon bonds, the spot curve, or the forward curve, but in practice, the government par curve is often used. Yield duration statistics used in fixed-income analysis include Macaulay duration, modified duration, money duration, and the price value of a basis point (PVBP). A curve duration statistic often used is effective duration. Effective duration is covered in Section 3.2.

Macaulay duration is named after Frederick Macaulay, the Canadian economist who first wrote about the statistic in a book published in 1938.[1] Equation 1 is a general formula to calculate the Macaulay duration (MacDur) of a traditional fixed-rate bond.

$$MacDur = \left[\frac{\dfrac{(1 - t/T) \times PMT}{(1 - r)^{1-t/T}} + \dfrac{(2 - t/T) \times PMT}{(1 + r)^{2-t/T}} + \cdots + \dfrac{(N - t/T) \times (PMT + FV)}{(1 + r)^{N-t/T}}}{\dfrac{PMT}{(1 + r)^{1-t/T}} + \dfrac{PMT}{(1 + r)^{2-t/T}} + \cdots + \dfrac{PMT + FV}{(1 + r)^{N-t/T}}} \right] \qquad (1)$$

where

t = the number of days from the last coupon payment to the settlement date

T = the number of days in the coupon period

t/T = the fraction of the coupon period that has gone by since the last payment

PMT = the coupon payment per period

FV = the future value paid at maturity, or the par value of the bond

r = the yield-to-maturity, or the market discount rate, per period

N = the number of evenly spaced periods to maturity as of the beginning of the current period

The denominator in Equation 1 is the full price (PV^{Full}) of the bond including accrued interest. It is the present value of the coupon interest and principal payments, with each cash flow discounted by the same market discount rate, r.

$$PV^{Full} = \frac{PMT}{(1 + r)^{1-t/T}} + \frac{PMT}{(1 + r)^{2-t/T}} + \cdots + \frac{PMT + FV}{(1 + r)^{N-t/T}} \qquad (2)$$

---

1 Frederick R. Macaulay, *Some Theoretical Problems Suggested by the Movements of Interest Rates, Bond Yields and Stock Prices in the United States since 1856* (New York: National Bureau of Economic Research, 1938).

Equation 3 combines Equations 1 and 2 to reveal an important aspect of the Macaulay duration: Macaulay duration is a weighted average of the time to receipt of the bond's promised payments, where the weights are the shares of the full price that correspond to each of the bond's promised future payments.

$$
\text{MacDur} = \left\{ (1 - t/T)\left[\frac{\frac{PMT}{(1+r)^{1-t/T}}}{PV^{Full}}\right] + (2 - t/T)\left[\frac{\frac{PMT}{(1+r)^{2-t/T}}}{PV^{Full}}\right] + \cdots + (N - t/T)\left[\frac{\frac{PMT + FV}{(1+r)^{N-t/T}}}{PV^{Full}}\right] \right\} \tag{3}
$$

The time to receipt of cash flow measured in terms of time periods are $1 - t/T$, $2 - t/T, ..., N - t/T$. The weights are the present values of the cash flows divided by the full price. Therefore, Macaulay duration is measured in terms of time periods. A couple of examples will clarify this calculation.

Consider first the 10-year, 8% annual coupon payment bond used in Examples 1–6. The bond's yield-to-maturity is 10.40%, and its price is 85.503075 per 100 of par value. This bond has 10 evenly spaced periods to maturity. Settlement is on a coupon payment date so that $t/T = 0$. Exhibit 2 illustrates the calculation of the bond's Macaulay duration.

Exhibit 2 Macaulay Duration of a 10-Year, 8% Annual Payment Bond

Period	Cash Flow	Present Value	Weight	Period × Weight
1	8	7.246377	0.08475	0.0847
2	8	6.563747	0.07677	0.1535
3	8	5.945423	0.06953	0.2086
4	8	5.385347	0.06298	0.2519
5	8	4.878032	0.05705	0.2853
6	8	4.418507	0.05168	0.3101
7	8	4.002271	0.04681	0.3277
8	8	3.625245	0.04240	0.3392
9	8	3.283737	0.03840	0.3456
10	108	40.154389	0.46963	4.6963
		85.503075	1.00000	7.0029

The first two columns of Exhibit 2 show the number of periods to the receipt of the cash flow and the amount of the payment per 100 of par value. The third column is the present value of the cash flow. For example, the final payment is 108 (the last coupon payment plus the redemption of principal) and its present value is 40.154389.

$$\frac{108}{(1.1040)^{10}} = 40.154389$$

The sum of the present values is the full price of the bond. The fourth column is the weight, the share of total market value corresponding to each cash flow. The final payment of 108 per 100 of par value is 46.963% of the bond's market value.

$$\frac{40.154389}{85.503075} = 0.46963$$

The sum of the weights is 1.00000. The fifth column is the number of periods to the receipt of the cash flow (the first column) multiplied by the weight (the fourth column). The sum of that column is 7.0029, which is the Macaulay duration of this 10-year, 8% annual coupon payment bond. This statistic is sometimes reported as 7.0029 *years*, although the time frame is not needed in most applications.

Now consider an example *between* coupon payment dates. A 6% semiannual payment corporate bond that matures on 14 February 2022 is purchased for settlement on 11 April 2014. The coupon payments are 3 per 100 of par value, paid on 14 February and 14 August of each year. The yield-to-maturity is 6.00% quoted on a street-convention semiannual bond basis. The full price of this bond comprises the flat price plus accrued interest. The flat price for the bond is 99.990423 per 100 of par value. The accrued interest is calculated using the 30/360 method to count days. This settlement date is 57 days into the 180-day semiannual period, so $t/T = 57/180$. The accrued interest is 0.950000 (= $57/180 \times 3$) per 100 of par value. The full price for the bond is 100.940423 (= 99.990423 + 0.950000). Exhibit 3 shows the calculation of the bond's Macaulay duration.

Exhibit 3	Macaulay Duration of an Eight-Year, 6% Semiannual Payment Bond Priced to Yield 6.00%				
Period	Time to Receipt	Cash Flow	Present Value	Weight	Time × Weight
1	0.6833	3	2.940012	0.02913	0.019903
2	1.6833	3	2.854381	0.02828	0.047601
3	2.6833	3	2.771244	0.02745	0.073669
4	3.6833	3	2.690528	0.02665	0.098178
5	4.6833	3	2.612163	0.02588	0.121197
6	5.6833	3	2.536080	0.02512	0.142791
7	6.6833	3	2.462214	0.02439	0.163025
8	7.6833	3	2.390499	0.02368	0.181959
9	8.6833	3	2.320873	0.02299	0.199652
10	9.6833	3	2.253275	0.02232	0.216159
11	10.6833	3	2.187645	0.02167	0.231536
12	11.6833	3	2.123927	0.02104	0.245834
13	12.6833	3	2.062065	0.02043	0.259102
14	13.6833	3	2.002005	0.01983	0.271389
15	14.6833	3	1.943694	0.01926	0.282740
16	15.6833	103	64.789817	0.64186	10.066535
			100.940423	1.00000	12.621268

There are 16 semiannual periods to maturity between the last coupon payment date of 14 February 2014 and maturity on 14 February 2022. The time to receipt of cash flow in semiannual periods is in the second column: 0.6833 = 1 − 57/180, 1.6833 = 2 − 57/180, etc. The cash flow for each period is in the third column. The annual yield-to-maturity is 6.00%, so the yield per semiannual period is 3.00%. When that yield is used to get the present value of each cash flow, the full price of the bond is 100.940423, the sum of the fourth column. The weights, which are the shares of the full price corresponding to each cash flow, are in the fifth column. The Macaulay duration is the sum of the items in the sixth column, which is the weight multiplied by the time to receipt of each cash flow. The result, 12.621268, is the Macaulay duration on an eight-year, 6% semiannual payment bond for settlement on 11 April 2014 measured in *semiannual periods*. Similar to coupon rates and yields-to-maturity, duration statistics invariably are annualized in practice. Therefore, the Macaulay duration typically is reported as 6.310634 *years* (= 12.621268/2).[2] (Such precision for the duration statistic is not needed in practice. Typically, "6.31 years" is enough. The full precision is shown here to illustrate calculations.)

Another approach to calculating the Macaulay duration is to use a closed-form equation derived using calculus and algebra. Equation 4 is a general closed-form formula for determining the Macaulay duration of a fixed-rate bond, where *c* is the coupon rate per period (*PMT/FV*).[3]

$$\text{MacDur} = \left\{ \frac{1+r}{r} - \frac{1+r+\left[N \times (c-r)\right]}{c \times \left[(1+r)^N - 1\right] + r} \right\} - (t/T) \tag{4}$$

The Macaulay duration of the 10-year, 8% annual payment bond is calculated by entering $r = 0.1040$, $c = 0.0800$, $N = 10$, and $t/T = 0$ into Equation 4.

$$\text{MacDur} = \frac{1+0.1040}{0.1040} - \frac{1+0.1040+\left[10 \times (0.0800-0.1040)\right]}{0.0800 \times \left[(1+0.1040)^{10} - 1\right] + 0.1040} = 7.0029$$

Therefore, the weighted average time to receipt of the interest and principal payments that will result in realization of the initial market discount rate on this 10-year bond is 7.00 years.

The Macaulay duration of the 6% semiannual payment bond maturing on 14 February 2022 is obtained by entering $r = 0.0300$, $c = 0.0300$, $N = 16$, and $t/T = 57/180$ into Equation 4.

$$\text{MacDur} = \left[\frac{1+0.0300}{0.0300} - \frac{1+0.0300+\left[16 \times (0.0300-0.0300)\right]}{0.0300 \times \left[(1+0.0300)^{16} - 1\right] + 0.0300} \right] - (57/180)$$

$$= 12.621268$$

Equation 4 uses the yield-to-maturity *per period*, the coupon rate *per period*, the number of *periods* to maturity, and the fraction of the current *period* that has gone by. Its output is the Macaulay duration in terms of *periods*. It is converted to annual duration by dividing by the number of periods in the year.

The calculation of the **modified duration** (ModDur) statistic of a bond requires a simple adjustment to Macaulay duration. It is the Macaulay duration statistic divided by one plus the yield per period.

$$\text{ModDur} = \frac{\text{MacDur}}{1+r} \tag{5}$$

For example, the modified duration of the 10-year, 8% annual payment bond is 6.3432.

---

2 Microsoft Excel users can obtain the Macaulay duration using the DURATION financial function: DURATION ("4/11/2014," "2/14/2022," 0.06, 0.06, 2, 0). The inputs are the settlement date, maturity date, annual coupon rate as a decimal, annual yield-to-maturity as a decimal, periodicity, and the code for the day count (0 for 30/360, 1 for actual/actual).

3 The step-by-step derivation of this formula is in Donald J. Smith, *Bond Math: The Theory behind the Formulas* (Hoboken, NJ: John Wiley & Sons, 2011).

$$\text{ModDur} = \frac{7.0029}{1.1040} = 6.3432$$

The modified duration of the 6% semiannual payment bond maturing on 14 February 2022 is 12.253658 semiannual periods.

$$\text{ModDur} = \frac{12.621268}{1.0300} = 12.253658$$

The annualized modified duration of the bond is 6.126829 (= 12.253658/2).[4]

Although modified duration might seem to be just a Macaulay duration with minor adjustments, it has an important application in risk measurement: Modified duration provides an estimate of the percentage price change for a bond given a change in its yield-to-maturity.

$$\%\Delta PV^{Full} \approx -\text{AnnModDur} \times \Delta\text{Yield} \tag{6}$$

The percentage price change refers to the full price, including accrued interest. The AnnModDur term in Equation 6 is the *annual* modified duration, and the ΔYield term is the change in the *annual* yield-to-maturity. The $\approx$ sign indicates that this calculation is an estimation. The minus sign indicates that bond prices and yields-to-maturity move inversely.

If the annual yield on the 6% semiannual payment bond that matures on 14 February 2022 jumps by 100 bps, from 6.00% to 7.00%, the estimated loss in value for the bond is 6.1268%.

$$\%\Delta PV^{Full} \approx -6.126829 \times 0.0100 = -0.061268$$

If the yield-to-maturity were to drop by 100 bps to 5.00%, the estimated gain in value is also 6.1268%.

$$\%\Delta PV^{Full} \approx -6.126829 \times -0.0100 = 0.061268$$

Modified duration provides a *linear* estimate of the percentage price change. In terms of absolute value, the change is the same for either an increase or decrease in the yield-to-maturity. Recall from "Introduction to Fixed-Income Valuation" that for a given coupon rate and time-to-maturity, the percentage price change is greater (in absolute value) when the market discount rate goes down than when it goes up. Later in this reading, a "convexity adjustment" to duration is introduced. It improves the accuracy of this estimate, especially when a large change in yield-to-maturity (such as 100 bps) is considered.

The modified duration statistic for a fixed-rate bond is easily obtained if the Macaulay duration is already known. An alternative approach is to *approximate* modified duration directly. Equation 7 is the approximation formula for annual modified duration.

$$\text{ApproxModDur} = \frac{(PV_-) - (PV_+)}{2 \times (\Delta\text{Yield}) \times (PV_0)} \tag{7}$$

The objective of the approximation is to estimate the slope of the line tangent to the price–yield curve. The slope of the tangent and the approximated slope are shown in Exhibit 4.

---

[4] Microsoft Excel users can obtain the modified duration using the MDURATION financial function: MDURATION ("4/11/2014," "2/14/2022," 0.06, 0.06, 2, 0). The inputs are the same as for the Macaulay duration in Footnote 2.

Exhibit 4 Approximate Modified Duration

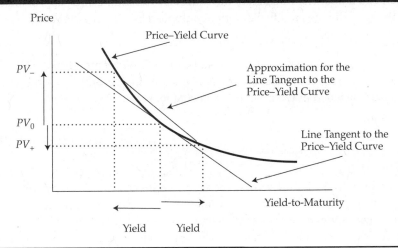

To estimate the slope, the yield-to-maturity is changed up and down by the same amount—the ΔYield. Then the bond prices given the new yields-to-maturity are calculated. The price when the yield is increased is denoted PV_+. The price when the yield-to-maturity is reduced is denoted PV_-. The original price is PV_0. These prices are the full prices, including accrued interest. The slope of the line based on PV_+ and PV_- is the approximation for the slope of the line tangent to the price–yield curve. The following example illustrates the remarkable accuracy of this approximation. In fact, as ΔYield approaches zero, the approximation approaches AnnModDur.

Consider the 6% semiannual coupon payment corporate bond maturing on 14 February 2022. For settlement on 11 April 2014, the full price (PV_0) is 100.940423 given that the yield-to-maturity is 6.00%.

$$PV_0 = \left[\frac{3}{(1.03)^1} + \frac{3}{(1.03)^2} + \cdots + \frac{103}{(1.03)^{16}}\right] \times (1.03)^{57/180} = 100.940423$$

Raise the annual yield-to-maturity by five bps, from 6.00% to 6.05%. This increase corresponds to an increase in the yield-to-maturity per semiannual period of 2.5 bps, from 3.00% to 3.025% per period. The new full price (PV_+) is 100.631781.

$$PV_+ = \left[\frac{3}{(1.03025)^1} + \frac{3}{(1.03025)^2} + \cdots + \frac{103}{(1.03025)^{16}}\right] \times (1.03025)^{57/180} = 100.631781$$

Lower the annual yield-to-maturity by five bps, from 6.00% to 5.95%. This decrease corresponds to a decrease in the yield-to-maturity per semiannual period of 2.5 bps, from 3.00% to 2.975% per period. The new full price (PV_-) is 101.250227.

$$PV_- = \left[\frac{3}{(1.02975)^1} + \frac{3}{(1.02975)^2} + \cdots + \frac{103}{(1.02975)^{16}}\right] \times (1.02975)^{57/180} = 101.250227$$

Enter these results into Equation 7 for the 5 bp change in the annual yield-to-maturity, or ΔYield = 0.0005:

$$\text{ApproxModDur} = \frac{101.250227 - 100.631781}{2 \times 0.0005 \times 100.940423} = 6.126842$$

The "exact" annual modified duration for this bond is 6.126829 and the "approximation" is 6.126842—virtually identical results. Therefore, although duration can be calculated using the approach in Exhibits 2 and 3—basing the calculation on the weighted average time to receipt of each cash flow—or using the closed-form formula as in Equation 4, it can also be estimated quite accurately using the basic bond-pricing equation and a financial calculator. The Macaulay duration can be approximated as well—the approximate modified duration multiplied by one plus the yield per period.

$$\text{ApproxMacDur} = \text{ApproxModDur} \times (1 + r) \tag{8}$$

The approximation formulas produce results for *annualized* modified and Macaulay durations. The frequency of coupon payments and the periodicity of the yield-to-maturity are included in the bond price calculations.

EXAMPLE 8

Assume that the 3.75% US Treasury bond that matures on 15 August 2041 is priced to yield 5.14% for settlement on 15 October 2014. Coupons are paid semiannually on 15 February and 15 August. The yield-to-maturity is stated on a street-convention semiannual bond basis. This settlement date is 61 days into a 184-day coupon period, using the actual/actual day-count convention. Compute the approximate modified duration and the approximate Macaulay duration for this Treasury bond assuming a 5 bp change in the yield-to-maturity.

Solution:

The yield-to-maturity per semiannual period is 0.0257 (= 0.0514/2). The coupon payment per period is 1.875 (= 3.75/2). At the beginning of the period, there are 27 years (54 semiannual periods) to maturity. The fraction of the period that has passed is 61/184. The full price at that yield-to-maturity is 80.501507 per 100 of par value.

$$PV_0 = \left[\frac{1.875}{(1.0257)^1} + \frac{1.875}{(1.0257)^2} + \cdots + \frac{101.875}{(1.0257)^{54}} \right] \times (1.0257)^{61/184} = 80.501507$$

Raise the yield-to-maturity from 5.14% to 5.19%—therefore, from 2.57% to 2.595% per semiannual period, and the price becomes 79.886293 per 100 of par value.

$$PV_+ = \left[\frac{1.875}{(1.02595)^1} + \frac{1.875}{(1.02595)^2} + \cdots + \frac{101.875}{(1.02595)^{54}} \right] \times (1.02595)^{61/184}$$
$$= 79.886293$$

Lower the yield-to-maturity from 5.14% to 5.09%—therefore, from 2.57% to 2.545% per semiannual period, and the price becomes 81.123441 per 100 of par value.

$$PV_- = \left[\frac{1.875}{(1.02545)^1} + \frac{1.875}{(1.02545)^2} + \cdots + \frac{101.875}{(1.02545)^{54}} \right] \times (1.02545)^{61/184}$$
$$= 81.123441$$

The approximate annualized modified duration for the Treasury bond is 15.368.

$$\text{ApproxModDur} = \frac{81.123441 - 79.886293}{2 \times 0.0005 \times 80.501507} = 15.368$$

The approximate annualized Macaulay duration is 15.763.

$$\text{ApproxMacDur} = 15.368 \times 1.0257 = 15.763$$

Therefore, from these statistics, the investor knows that the weighted average time to receipt of interest and principal payments is 15.763 years (the Macaulay duration) and that the estimated loss in the bond's market value is 15.368% (the modified duration) if the market discount rate were to suddenly go up by 1% from 5.14% to 6.14%.

3.2 Effective Duration

Another approach to assess the interest rate risk of a bond is to estimate the percentage change in price given a change in a benchmark yield curve—for example, the government par curve. This estimate, which is very similar to the formula for approximate modified duration, is called the **effective duration**. The effective duration of a bond is the sensitivity of the bond's price to a change in a benchmark yield curve. The formula to calculate effective duration (EffDur) is Equation 9.

$$\text{EffDur} = \frac{(PV_-) - (PV_+)}{2 \times (\Delta\text{Curve}) \times (PV_0)} \tag{9}$$

The difference between approximate modified duration and effective duration is in the denominator. Modified duration is a *yield duration* statistic in that it measures interest rate risk in terms of a change in the bond's own yield-to-maturity (ΔYield). Effective duration is a *curve duration* statistic in that it measures interest rate risk in terms of a parallel shift in the benchmark yield curve (ΔCurve).

Effective duration is essential to the measurement of the interest rate risk of a complex bond, such as a bond that contains an embedded call option. The duration of a callable bond is *not* the sensitivity of the bond price to a change in the yield-to-worst (i.e., the lowest of the yield-to-maturity, yield-to-first-call, yield-to-second-call, and so forth). The problem is that future cash flows are uncertain because they are contingent on future interest rates. The issuer's decision to call the bond depends on the ability to refinance the debt at a lower cost of funds. In brief, a callable bond does not have a well-defined internal rate of return (yield-to-maturity). Therefore, yield duration statistics, such as modified and Macaulay durations, do not apply; effective duration is the appropriate duration measure.

The specific option-pricing models that are used to produce the inputs to effective duration for a callable bond are covered in later readings. However, as an example, suppose that the full price of a callable bond is 101.060489 per 100 of par value. The option-pricing model inputs include (1) the length of the call protection period, (2) the schedule of call prices and call dates, (3) an assumption about credit spreads over benchmark yields (which includes any liquidity spread as well), (4) an assumption about future interest rate volatility, and (5) the level of market interest rates (e.g., the government par curve). The analyst then holds the first four inputs constant and raises and lowers the fifth input. Suppose that when the government par curve is raised and lowered by 25 bps, the new full prices for the callable bond from the model are 99.050120 and 102.890738, respectively. Therefore, $PV_0 = 101.060489$, PV_+ = 99.050120, $PV_- = 102.890738$, and ΔCurve = 0.0025. The effective duration for the callable bond is 7.6006.

$$\text{EffDur} = \frac{102.890738 - 99.050120}{2 \times 0.0025 \times 101.060489} = 7.6006$$

This curve duration measure indicates the bond's sensitivity to the benchmark yield curve—in particular, the government par curve—assuming no change in the credit spread. In practice, a callable bond issuer might be able to exercise the call option and obtain a lower cost of funds if (1) benchmark yields fall and the credit spread over the benchmark is unchanged or (2) benchmark yields are unchanged and the credit spread is reduced (e.g., because of an upgrade in the issuer's rating). A pricing model can be used to determine a "credit duration" statistic—that is, the sensitivity of the bond price to a change in the credit spread. On a traditional fixed-rate bond, modified duration estimates the percentage price change for a change in the benchmark yield and/or the credit spread. For bonds that do not have a well-defined internal rate of return because the future cash flows are not fixed—for instance, callable bonds and floating-rate notes—pricing models are used to produce different statistics for changes in benchmark interest rates and for changes in credit risk.

Another fixed-income security for which yield duration statistics, such as modified and Macaulay durations, are not relevant is a mortgage-backed bond. These securities arise from a residential (or commercial) loan portfolio securitization. The key point for measuring interest rate risk on a mortgage-backed bond is that the cash flows are contingent on homeowners' ability to refinance their debt at a lower rate. In effect, the homeowners have call options on their mortgage loans.

A practical consideration in using effective duration is in setting the change in the benchmark yield curve. With approximate modified duration, accuracy is improved by choosing a smaller yield-to-maturity change. But the pricing models for more-complex securities, such as callable and mortgage-backed bonds, include assumptions about the behavior of the corporate issuers, businesses, or homeowners. Rates typically need to change by a minimum amount to affect the decision to call a bond or refinance a mortgage loan because issuing new debt involves transaction costs. Therefore, estimates of interest rate risk using effective duration are not necessarily improved by choosing a smaller change in benchmark rates. Effective duration has become an important tool in the financial analysis of not only traditional bonds but also financial liabilities. Example 9 demonstrates such an application of effective duration.

EXAMPLE 9

Defined-benefit pension schemes typically pay retirees a monthly amount based on their wage level at the time of retirement. The amount could be fixed in nominal terms or indexed to inflation. These programs are referred to as "defined-benefit pension plans" when US GAAP or IFRS accounting standards are used. In Australia, they are called "superannuation funds."

A British defined-benefit pension scheme seeks to measure the sensitivity of its retirement obligations to market interest rate changes. The pension scheme manager hires an actuarial consultancy to model the present value of its liabilities under three interest rate scenarios: (1) a base rate of 5%, (2) a 100 bp increase in rates, up to 6%, and (3) a 100 bp drop in rates, down to 4%.

The actuarial consultancy uses a complex valuation model that includes assumptions about employee retention, early retirement, wage growth, mortality, and longevity. The following chart shows the results of the analysis.

Interest Rate Assumption	Present Value of Liabilities
4%	GBP973.5 million
5%	GBP926.1 million
6%	GBP871.8 million

Compute the effective duration of the pension scheme's liabilities.

Solution:

PV_0 = 926.1, PV_+ = 871.8, PV_- = 973.5, and $\Delta Curve$ = 0.0100. The effective duration of the pension scheme's liabilities is 5.49.

$$EffDur = \frac{973.5 - 871.8}{2 \times 0.0100 \times 926.1} = 5.49$$

> This effective duration statistic for the pension scheme's liabilities might be used in asset allocation decisions to decide the mix of equity, fixed income, and alternative assets.

Although effective duration is the most appropriate interest rate risk measure for bonds with embedded options, it also is useful with traditional bonds to supplement the information provided by the Macaulay and modified yield durations. Exhibit 5 displays the Bloomberg Yield and Spread (YAS) Analysis page for the 0.625% US Treasury note that matures on 31 May 2017.

Exhibit 5   Bloomberg YAS Page for the 0.625% US Treasury Note

<HELP> for explanation.   Govt **YAS**

T 0 ⅝ 05/31/17 Govt   90) Feedback   Yield and Spread Analysis
99-16+/99-16¾   0.725/0.723   BGN @ 17:00   95) Buy   96) Sell   97) Settings
1) Yield & Spread   2) Yields   3) Pricing   4) Descriptive   5) Graphs   6) Custom

T 0.625 5/31/17 (912828SY7) | Risk
Spread   0 bp vs 5y T 0 ⅝ 05/31/17 | Maturity   OAS
Price   99-16¾   ⇄   99-16¾ 17:01:2 | Mod Duration   4.853   4.882
Yield   0.723368 Wst   0.723368 S/A | Risk   4.831   4.860
Wkout   05/31/2017 @ 100.00   Yld 6 6 | Convexity   0.262   0.264
Settle   06/22/12   06/22/12 | PV   0.01   0.04831   N.A.
                                             | Benchmark Risk   4.831   4.860
                                             | Risk Hedge   1,000 M   1,000 M
                                             | Proceeds Hedge   1,000 M

Spread | Yield Calculations | Invoice
11) G-Spr   0.0 | Street Convention 0.723368 | Face   1,000 M
12) I-Sprd   -26.8 | Equiv 1 /Yr   0.724676 | Principal   995,234.38
13) Basis   78.1 | Mmkt (Act/ 360) | Accrued   (22 Days)   375.68
14) Z-Spr   -26.6 | Current Yield   0.627993 | Total (USD)   995,610.06
15) ASW   -26.0 | True Yield   0.723361 |
16) OAS   0.0 |
TED   27.5
After Tax (Inc 35.00 % CG 15.00 %)   0.490
Issue Price = 99.397. OID Bond with Acquisition Prem.

Australia 61 2 9777 8600 Brazil 5511 3048 4500 Europe 44 20 7330 7500 Germany 49 69 9204 1210 Hong Kong 852 2977 6000
Japan 81 3 3201 8900   Singapore 65 6212 1000   U.S. 1 212 318 2000   Copyright 2012 Bloomberg Finance L.P.
SN 682652 EDT GMT-4:00 H192-1717-0 21-Jun-2012 17:01:45

In Exhibit 5, the quoted (flat) price for the bond is 99 – 16 ¾, which is equal to 99 and 16 ¾ 32nds per 100 of par value for settlement on 22 June 2012. Most bond prices are stated in decimals, but US Treasuries are usually quoted in fractions. As a decimal, the flat price is 99.523438. The accrued interest uses the actual/actual day-count method. That settlement date is 22 days into a 183-day semiannual coupon payment period. The accrued interest is 0.037568 per 100 of par value (= 22/183 × 0.00625/2 × 100). The full price of the bond is 99.561006. The yield-to-maturity of the bond is 0.723368%, stated on a street-convention semiannual bond basis.

The modified duration for the bond is shown in Exhibit 5 to be 4.853, which is the conventional *yield* duration statistic. Its *curve* duration, however, is 4.882, which is the price sensitivity with respect to changes in the US Treasury par curve. On Bloomberg, the effective duration is called the "OAS duration" because it is based on the option-pricing model that is also used to calculate the option-adjusted spread. The small difference arises because the government yield curve is not flat. When the par curve is shifted in the model, the government spot curve is also shifted, although not in the same "parallel" manner. Therefore, the change in the bond price is not exactly the same as it would be if its own yield-to-maturity changed by the same amount as the change in the par curve. In general, the modified duration and effective duration on a traditional option-free bond are not identical. The difference narrows when the yield curve is flatter, the time-to-maturity is shorter, and the bond is priced closer to par value (so that the difference between the coupon rate and the yield-to-maturity is smaller). The modified duration and effective duration on an option-free bond are identical only in the rare circumstance of an absolutely flat yield curve.

Above, the effective duration for a sample callable bond was calculated as:

$$\text{EffDur} = \frac{102.890738 - 99.050120}{2 \times 0.0025 \times 101.060489} = 7.6006$$

This duration measure indicates the bond's sensitivity to the benchmark yield curve assuming that all yields change by the same amount.

3.3 Key Rate Duration

Key rate duration provides further insight into a bond's sensitivity to changes in the benchmark yield curve. A **key rate duration** (or **partial duration**) is a measure of a bond's sensitivity to a change in the benchmark yield curve at a specific maturity segment. In contrast to effective duration, key rate durations help identify "shaping risk" for a bond—that is, a bond's sensitivity to changes in the shape of the benchmark yield curve (e.g., the yield curve becoming steeper or flatter).

The previous illustration of effective duration assumed a parallel shift of 25 bps at all maturities. However, the analyst may want to know how the price of the callable bond is expected to change if benchmark rates at short maturities (say up to 2 years) shifted up by 25 bps but longer maturity benchmark rates remained unchanged. This scenario would represent a flattening of the yield curve, given that the yield curve is upward sloping. Using key rate durations, the expected price change would be approximately equal to minus the key rate duration for the short maturity segment times the 0.0025 interest rate shift at that segment. Of course, for parallel shifts in the benchmark yield curve, key rate durations will indicate the same interest rate sensitivity as effective duration.

3.4 Properties of Bond Duration

The Macaulay and modified yield duration statistics for a traditional fixed-rate bond are functions of the input variables: the coupon rate or payment per period, the yield-to-maturity per period, the number of periods to maturity (as of the beginning of the period), and the fraction of the period that has gone by. The properties of bond duration are obtained by changing one of these variables while holding the others constant. Because duration is the basic measure of interest rate risk on a fixed-rate bond, these properties are important to understand.

The closed-form formula for Macaulay duration, presented as Equation 4 and again here, is useful in demonstrating the characteristics of the bond duration statistic.

$$\text{MacDur} = \left\{ \frac{1+r}{r} - \frac{1+r+\left[N \times (c-r)\right]}{c \times \left[(1+r)^N - 1\right] + r} \right\} - (t/T)$$

The same characteristics hold for modified duration. Consider first the fraction of the period that has gone by (t/T). Macaulay and modified durations depend on the day-count basis used to obtain the yield-to-maturity. The duration of a bond that uses the actual/actual method to count days is slightly different from that of an otherwise comparable bond that uses the 30/360 method. The key point is that for a constant yield-to-maturity (r), the expression in braces is unchanged as time passes during the period. Therefore, the Macaulay duration decreases smoothly as t goes from $t = 0$ to $t = T$, which creates a "saw-tooth" pattern. This pattern for a typical fixed-rate bond is illustrated in Exhibit 6.

Exhibit 6   Macaulay Duration between Coupon Payments with a Constant Yield-to-Maturity

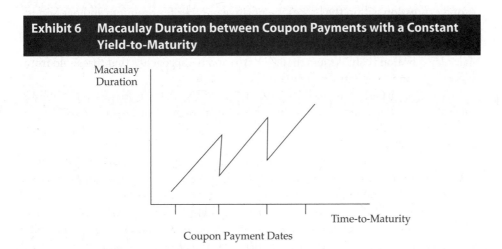

As times passes during the coupon period (moving from right to left in the diagram), the Macaulay duration declines smoothly and then jumps upward after the coupon is paid.

The characteristics of bond duration related to changes in the coupon rate, the yield-to-maturity, and the time-to-maturity are illustrated in Exhibit 7.

Exhibit 7   Properties of the Macaulay Yield Duration

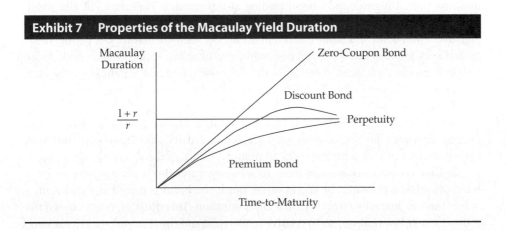

Exhibit 7 shows the graph for coupon payment dates when $t/T = 0$, thus not displaying the saw-tooth pattern between coupon payments. The relationship between the Macaulay duration and the time-to-maturity for a zero-coupon bond is the 45-degree line: MacDur = N when $c = 0$ (and $t/T = 0$). Therefore, the Macaulay duration of a zero-coupon bond is its time-to-maturity.

A **perpetuity** or perpetual bond, which also is called a consol, is a bond that does not mature. There is no principal to redeem. The investor receives a fixed coupon payment forever, unless the bond is callable. Non-callable perpetuities are rare, but they have an interesting Macaulay duration: MacDur = $(1 + r)/r$ as N approaches infinity. In effect, the second expression within the braces approaches zero as the number of periods to maturity increases because N in the numerator is a coefficient but N in the denominator is an exponent and the denominator increases faster than the numerator as N grows larger.

Typical fixed-rate coupon bonds with a stated maturity date are portrayed in Exhibit 7 as the premium and discount bonds. The usual pattern is that longer times-to-maturity correspond to higher Macaulay duration statistics. This pattern always holds for bonds trading at par value or at a premium above par. In Equation 4, the second expression within the braces is a positive number for premium and par bonds. The numerator is positive because the coupon rate (c) is greater than or equal to the yield-to-maturity (r), whereas the denominator is always positive. Therefore, the Macaulay duration is always less than $(1 + r)/r$, and it approaches that threshold from below as the time-to-maturity increases.

The curious result displayed in Exhibit 7 is in the pattern for discount bonds. Generally, the Macaulay duration increases for a longer time-to-maturity. But at some point when the time-to-maturity is high enough, the Macaulay duration exceeds $(1 + r)/r$, reaches a maximum, and then approaches the threshold from above. In Equation 4, such a pattern develops when the number of periods (N) is large and the coupon rate (c) is below the yield-to-maturity (r). Then the numerator of the second expression within the braces can become negative. The implication is that on long-term discount bonds, the interest rate risk can actually be less than on a shorter-term bond, which explains why the word "generally" is needed in describing the maturity effect for the relationship between bond prices and yields-to-maturity. Generally, for the same coupon rate, a longer-term bond has a greater percentage price change than a shorter-term bond when their yields-to-maturity change by the same amount. The exception is when the longer-term bond actually has a lower duration statistic.

Coupon rates and yields-to-maturity are both inversely related to the Macaulay duration. In Exhibit 7, for the same time-to-maturity and yield-to-maturity, the Macaulay duration is higher for a zero-coupon bond than for a low-coupon bond trading at a discount. Also, the low-coupon bond trading at a discount has a higher duration than a high-coupon bond trading at a premium. Therefore, all else being equal, a lower-coupon bond has a higher duration and more interest rate risk than a higher-coupon bond. The same pattern holds for the yield-to-maturity. A higher yield-to-maturity reduces the weighted average of the time to receipt of cash flow. More weight is on the cash flows received in the near term, and less weight is on the cash flows received in the more-distant future periods if those cash flows are discounted at a higher rate.

In summary, the Macaulay and modified duration statistics for a fixed-rate bond depend primarily on the coupon rate, yield-to-maturity, and time-to-maturity. A higher coupon rate or a higher yield-to-maturity reduces the duration measures. A longer time-to-maturity *usually* leads to a higher duration. It *always* does so for a bond priced at a premium or at par value. But if the bond is priced at a discount, a longer time-to-maturity *might* lead to a lower duration. This situation only occurs if the coupon rate is low (but not zero) relative to the yield and the time-to-maturity is long.

EXAMPLE 10

A hedge fund specializes in investments in emerging market sovereign debt. The fund manager believes that the implied default probabilities are too high, which means that the bonds are viewed as "cheap" and the credit spreads are too high. The hedge fund plans to take a position on one of these available bonds.

Bond	Time-to-Maturity	Coupon Rate	Price	Yield-to-Maturity
(A)	10 years	10%	58.075279	20%
(B)	20 years	10%	51.304203	20%
(C)	30 years	10%	50.210636	20%

The coupon payments are annual. The yields-to-maturity are effective annual rates. The prices are per 100 of par value.

1   Compute the approximate modified duration of each of the three bonds using a 1 bp change in the yield-to-maturity and keeping precision to six decimals (because approximate duration statistics are very sensitive to rounding).

2   Which of the three bonds is expected to have the highest percentage price increase if the yield-to-maturity on each decreases by the same amount—for instance, by 10 bps from 20% to 19.90%?

Solution to 1:

Bond A:

$PV_0 = 58.075279$

$PV_+ = 58.047598$

$$\frac{10}{(1.2001)^1} + \frac{10}{(1.2001)^2} + \cdots + \frac{110}{(1.2001)^{10}} = 58.047598$$

$PV_- = 58.102981$

$$\frac{10}{(1.1999)^1} + \frac{10}{(1.1999)^2} + \cdots + \frac{110}{(1.1999)^{10}} = 58.102981$$

The approximate modified duration of Bond A is 4.768.

$$\text{ApproxModDur} = \frac{58.102981 - 58.047598}{2 \times 0.0001 \times 58.075279} = 4.768$$

Bond B:

$PV_0 = 51.304203$

$PV_+ = 51.277694$

$$\frac{10}{(1.2001)^1} + \frac{10}{(1.2001)^2} + \cdots + \frac{110}{(1.2001)^{20}} = 51.277694$$

$PV_- = 51.330737$

$$\frac{10}{(1.1999)^1} + \frac{10}{(1.1999)^2} + \cdots + \frac{110}{(1.1999)^{20}} = 51.330737$$

The approximate modified duration of Bond B is 5.169.

$$\text{ApproxModDur} = \frac{51.330737 - 51.277694}{2 \times 0.0001 \times 51.304203} = 5.169$$

Bond C:

$PV_0 = 50.210636$

$PV_+ = 50.185228$

$$\frac{10}{(1.2001)^1} + \frac{10}{(1.2001)^2} + \cdots + \frac{110}{(1.2001)^{30}} = 50.185228$$

$PV_- = 50.236070$

$$\frac{10}{(1.1999)^1} + \frac{10}{(1.1999)^2} + \cdots + \frac{110}{(1.1999)^{30}} = 50.236070$$

The approximate modified duration of Bond C is 5.063.

$$\text{ApproxModDur} = \frac{50.236070 - 50.185228}{2 \times 0.0001 \times 50.210636} = 5.063$$

Solution to 2:

Despite the significant differences in times-to-maturity (10, 20, and 30 years), the approximate modified durations on the three bonds are fairly similar (4.768, 5.169, and 5.063). Because the yields-to-maturity are so high, the additional time to receipt of interest and principal payments on the 20- and 30-year bonds have low weight. Nevertheless, Bond B, with 20 years to maturity, has the highest modified duration. If the yield-to-maturity on each is decreased by the same amount—for instance, by 10 bps, from 20% to 19.90%—Bond B would be expected to have the highest percentage price increase because it has the highest modified duration. This example illustrates the relationship between the Macaulay duration and the time-to-maturity on discount bonds in Exhibit 7. The 20-year bond has a higher duration than the 30-year bond.

Callable bonds require the use of effective duration because Macaulay and modified yield duration statistics are not relevant. The yield-to-maturity for callable bonds is not well-defined because future cash flows are uncertain. Exhibit 8 illustrates the impact of the change in the benchmark yield curve (ΔCurve) on the price of a callable bond price compared with that on a comparable non-callable bond. The two bonds have the same credit risk, coupon rate, payment frequency, and time-to-maturity. The vertical axis is the bond price. The horizontal axis is a particular benchmark yield—for instance, a point on the par curve for government bonds.

Exhibit 8   Interest Rate Risk Characteristics of a Callable Bond

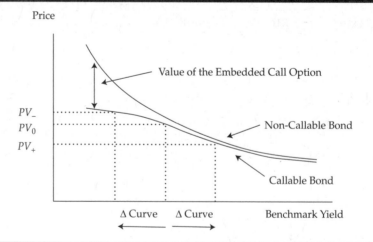

As shown in Exhibit 8, the price of the non-callable bond is always greater than that of the callable bond with otherwise identical features. The difference is the value of the embedded call option. Recall that the call option is an option to the issuer and not the holder of the bond. When interest rates are high compared with the coupon rate, the value of the call option is low. When rates are low, the value of the call option is much greater because the issuer is more likely to exercise the option to refinance the debt at a lower cost of funds. The investor bears the "call risk" because if the bond is called, the investor must reinvest the proceeds at a lower interest rate.

Exhibit 8 shows the inputs for calculating the effective duration of the callable bond. The entire benchmark curve is raised and lowered by the same amount, ΔCurve. The key point is that when benchmark yields are high, the effective durations of the callable and non-callable bonds are very similar. Although the exhibit does not illustrate it, the slopes of the lines tangent to the price–yield curve are about the same in such a situation. But when interest rates are low, the effective duration of the callable bond is lower than that of the otherwise comparable non-callable bond. That is because the callable bond price does not increase as much when benchmark yields fall. The slope of the line tangent to the price–yield curve would be flatter. The presence of the call option limits price appreciation. Therefore, an embedded call option reduces the effective duration of the bond, especially when interest rates are falling and the bond is more likely to be called. The lower effective duration can also be interpreted as a shorter expected life—the weighted average of time to receipt of cash flow is reduced.

Exhibit 9 considers another embedded option—a put option.

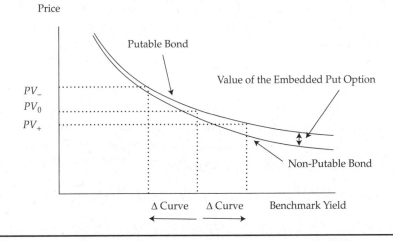

A putable bond allows the investor to sell the bond back to the issuer prior to maturity, usually at par value, which protects the investor from higher benchmark yields or credit spreads that otherwise would drive the bond to a discounted price. Therefore, the price of a putable bond is always higher than that of an otherwise comparable non-putable bond. The price difference is the value of the embedded put option.

An embedded put option reduces the effective duration of the bond, especially when rates are rising. If interest rates are low compared with the coupon rate, the value of the put option is low and the impact of a change in the benchmark yield on the bond's price is very similar to the impact on the price of a non-putable bond. But when benchmark interest rates rise, the put option becomes more valuable to the investor. The ability to sell the bond at par value limits the price depreciation as rates rise. In summary, the presence of an embedded option reduces the sensitivity of the bond price to changes in the benchmark yield curve, assuming no change in credit risk.

3.5 Duration of a Bond Portfolio

Similar to equities, bonds are typically held in a portfolio. There are two ways to calculate the duration of a bond portfolio: (1) the weighted average of time to receipt of the *aggregate* cash flows and (2) the weighted average of the individual bond durations that comprise the portfolio. The first method is the theoretically correct approach, but it is difficult to use in practice. The second method is commonly used by fixed-income portfolio managers, but it has its own limitations. The differences in these two methods to compute portfolio duration can be examined with a numerical example.

Suppose an investor holds the following portfolio of two *zero-coupon* bonds:

Bond	Maturity	Price	Yield	Macaulay Duration	Modified Duration	Par Value	Market Value	Weight
(X)	1 year	98.00	2.0408%	1	0.980	10,000,000	9,800,000	0.50
(Y)	30 years	9.80	8.0503%	30	27.765	100,000,000	9,800,000	0.50

The prices are per 100 of par value. The yields-to-maturity are effective annual rates. The total market value for the portfolio is 19,600,000. The portfolio is evenly weighted in terms of market value between the two bonds.

The first approach views the portfolio as a series of aggregated cash flows. Its **cash flow yield** is 7.8611%. A cash flow yield is the internal rate of return on a series of cash flows, usually used on a complex security such as a mortgage-backed bond (using projected cash flows based on a model of prepayments as a result of refinancing) or a portfolio of fixed-rate bonds. It is the solution for r in the following equation.

$$19,600,000 = \frac{10,000,000}{(1+r)^1} + \frac{0}{(1+r)^2} + \cdots + \frac{0}{(1+r)^{29}} + \frac{100,000,000}{(1+r)^{30}}, \quad r = 0.078611$$

The Macaulay duration of the portfolio in this approach is the weighted average of time to receipt of aggregated cash flow. The cash flow yield is used to obtain the weights. This calculation is similar to Equation 1, and the portfolio duration is 16.2825.

$$MacDur = \left[\frac{\dfrac{1 \times 10,000,000}{(1.078611)^1} + \dfrac{30 \times 100,000,000}{(1.078611)^{30}}}{\dfrac{10,000,000}{(1.078611)^1} + \dfrac{100,000,000}{(1.078611)^{30}}} \right] = 16.2825$$

There are just two future cash flows in the portfolio—the redemption of principal on the two zero-coupon bonds. In more complex portfolios, a series of coupon and principal payments may occur on some dates, with an aggregated cash flow composed of coupon interest on some bonds and principal on those that mature.

The modified duration of the portfolio is the Macaulay duration divided by one plus the cash flow yield per period (here, the periodicity is 1).

$$ModDur = \frac{16.2825}{1.078611} = 15.0958$$

The modified duration for the portfolio is 15.0958. That statistic indicates the percentage change in the market value given a change in the cash flow yield. If the cash flow yield increases or decreases by 100 bps, the market value of the portfolio is expected to increase or decrease by about 15.0958%.

Although this approach is "theoretically correct," it is difficult to use in practice. First, the cash flow yield is not commonly calculated for bond portfolios. Second, the amount and timing of future coupon and principal payments are uncertain if the portfolio contains callable or putable bonds or floating-rate notes. Third, interest rate risk is usually expressed as a change in benchmark interest rates, not as a change in the cash flow yield. Fourth, the change in the cash flow yield is not necessarily the same amount as the change in the yields-to-maturity on the individual bonds. For instance, if the yields-to-maturity on the two zero-coupon bonds in this portfolio both increase or decrease by 10 bps, the cash flow yield increases or decreases by only 9.52 bps.

In practice, the second approach to portfolio duration is commonly used. The Macaulay and modified durations for the portfolio are calculated as the weighted average of the statistics for the individual bonds. The shares of overall portfolio market value are the weights. This weighted average is an approximation of the "theoretically correct" portfolio duration, which is obtained using the first approach. This approximation becomes more accurate when the differences in the yields-to-maturity on the bonds in the portfolio are smaller. When the yield curve is flat, the two approaches produce the same portfolio duration.

Given the equal "50/50" weights in this simple numerical example, this version of portfolio duration is easily computed.

Average Macaulay duration = $(1 \times 0.50) + (30 \times 0.50) = 15.50$

Average modified duration = $(0.980 \times 0.50) + (27.765 \times 0.50) = 14.3725$

Note that $0.980 = 1/1.020404$ and $27.765 = 30/1.080503$. An advantage of the second approach is that callable bonds, putable bonds, and floating-rate notes can be included in the weighted average using the effective durations for these securities.

The main advantage to the second approach is that it is easily used as a measure of interest rate risk. For instance, if the yields-to-maturity on the bonds in the portfolio increase by 100 bps, the estimated drop in the portfolio value is 14.3725%. However, this advantage also indicates a limitation: This measure of portfolio duration implicitly assumes a **parallel shift** in the yield curve. A parallel yield curve shift implies that all rates change by the same amount in the same direction. In reality, interest rate changes frequently result in a steeper or flatter yield curve. Yield volatility is discussed later in this reading.

EXAMPLE 11

An investment fund owns the following portfolio of three fixed-rate government bonds:

	Bond A	Bond B	Bond C
Par value	EUR25,000,000	EUR25,000,000	EUR50,000,000
Coupon rate	9%	11%	8%
Time-to-maturity	6 years	8 years	12 years
Yield-to-maturity	9.10%	9.38%	9.62%
Market value	EUR24,886,343	EUR27,243,887	EUR44,306,787
Macaulay duration	4.761	5.633	7.652

The total market value of the portfolio is EUR96,437,017. Each bond is on a coupon date so that there is no accrued interest. The market values are the full prices given the par value. Coupons are paid semiannually. The yields-to-maturity are stated on a semiannual bond basis, meaning an annual rate for a periodicity of 2. The Macaulay durations are annualized.

1 Calculate the average (annual) modified duration for the portfolio using the shares of market value as the weights.

2 Estimate the percentage loss in the portfolio's market value if the (annual) yield-to-maturity on each bond goes up by 20 bps.

Solution to 1:

The average (annual) modified duration for the portfolio is 6.0495.

$$\left(\frac{4.761}{1 + \frac{0.0910}{2}} \times \frac{24{,}886{,}343}{96{,}437{,}017} \right) + \left(\frac{5.633}{1 + \frac{0.0938}{2}} \times \frac{27{,}243{,}887}{96{,}437{,}017} \right) +$$

$$\left(\frac{7.652}{1 + \frac{0.0962}{2}} \times \frac{44{,}306{,}787}{96{,}437{,}017} \right) = 6.0495$$

Note that the annual modified duration for each bond is the annual Macaulay duration, which is given, divided by one plus the yield-to-maturity per semi-annual period.

Solution to 2:

The estimated decline in market value if each yield rises by 20 bps is 1.21%: $-6.0495 \times 0.0020 = -0.0121$.

3.6 Money Duration of a Bond and the Price Value of a Basis Point

Modified duration is a measure of the *percentage price change* of a bond given a change in its yield-to-maturity. A related statistic is **money duration**. The money duration of a bond is a measure of the *price change* in units of the currency in which the bond is denominated. The money duration can be stated per 100 of par value or in terms of the actual position size of the bond in the portfolio. In the United States, money duration is commonly called "dollar duration."

Money duration (MoneyDur) is calculated as the annual modified duration times the full price (PV^{Full}) of the bond, including accrued interest.

$$\text{MoneyDur} = \text{AnnModDur} \times PV^{Full} \tag{10}$$

The estimated change in the bond price in currency units is calculated using Equation 11, which is very similar to Equation 6. The difference is that for a given change in the annual yield-to-maturity (ΔYield), modified duration estimates the percentage price change and money duration estimates the change in currency units.

$$\Delta PV^{Full} \approx -\text{MoneyDur} \times \Delta \text{Yield} \tag{11}$$

For an example of money duration, consider the 6% semiannual coupon payment bond that matures on 14 February 2022 and is priced to yield 6.00% for settlement on 11 April 2014. The full price of the bond is 100.940423 per 100 of par value, and the annual modified duration is 6.1268. Suppose that a Hong Kong–based life insurance company has a position in the bond for a par value of HKD100,000,000. The market value of the investment is HKD100,940,423. The money duration of this bond is HKD618,441,784 (= 6.1268 × HKD100,940,423). Therefore, if the yield-to-maturity rises by 100 bps—from 6.00% to 7.00%—the expected loss is approximately HKD6,184,418 (= HKD618,441,784 × 0.0100). On a percentage basis, that expected loss is approximately 6.1268%. The "convexity adjustment" introduced in the next section makes these estimates more accurate.

Another version of money duration is the **price value of a basis point** (PVBP) for the bond. The PVBP is an estimate of the change in the full price given a 1 bp change in the yield-to-maturity. The PVBP can be calculated using a formula similar to that for the approximate modified duration. Equation 12 is the formula for the PVBP.

$$PVBP = \frac{(PV_-) - (PV_+)}{2}$$

(12)

PV_- and PV_+ are the full prices calculated by decreasing and increasing the yield-to-maturity by 1 bp. The PVBP is also called the "PV01," standing for the "price value of an 01"or "present value of an 01," where "01" means 1 bp. In the United States, it is commonly called the "DV01," or the "dollar value of a 01." A related statistic, sometimes called a "basis point value" (or BPV), is the money duration times 0.0001 (1 bp).

For a numerical example of the PVBP calculation, consider the 0.625% semiannual coupon payment US Treasury note that matures on 31 May 2017. In Exhibit 5, the PVBP for the Treasury note is shown to be 0.04831. Its yield-to-maturity is 0.723368%, and the settlement date is 22 days into a 183-day period. To confirm this result, calculate the new prices by increasing and decreasing the yield-to-maturity. First, increase the yield by 1 bp (0.01%), from 0.723368% to 0.733368%, to solve for a PV_+ of 99.512707.

$$PV_+ = \left[\frac{0.3125}{\left(1 + \frac{0.00733368}{2}\right)^1} + \cdots + \frac{100.3125}{\left(1 + \frac{0.00733368}{2}\right)^{10}} \right] \times \left(1 + \frac{0.00733368}{2}\right)^{22/183}$$

$$= 99.512707$$

Then, decrease the yield-to-maturity by 1 bp, from 0.723368% to 0.713368%, to solve for a PV_- of 99.609333.

$$PV_- = \left[\frac{0.3125}{\left(1 + \frac{0.00713368}{2}\right)^1} + \cdots + \frac{100.3125}{\left(1 + \frac{0.00713368}{2}\right)^{10}} \right] \times \left(1 + \frac{0.00713368}{2}\right)^{22/183}$$

$$= 99.609333$$

The PVBP is obtained by substituting these results into Equation 12.

$$PVBP = \frac{99.609333 - 99.512707}{2} = 0.04831$$

Another money duration statistic reported on the Bloomberg YAS page is "risk." It is shown to be 4.831. Bloomberg's risk statistic is simply the PVBP (or PV01) times 100.

EXAMPLE 12

A life insurance company holds a USD10 million (par value) position in a 4.50% ArcelorMittal bond that matures on 25 February 2017. The bond is priced (flat) at 98.125 per 100 of par value to yield 5.2617% on a street-convention semiannual bond basis for settlement on 27 June 2014. The total market value of the position, including accrued interest, is USD9,965,000, or 99.650 per 100 of par value. The bond's (annual) Macaulay duration is 2.4988.

1 Calculate the money duration per 100 in par value for the ArcelorMittal bond.

2 Using the money duration, estimate the loss on the position for each 1 bp increase in the yield-to-maturity for that settlement date.

Solution to 1:

The money duration is the annual modified duration times the full price of the bond per 100 of par value.

$$\left(\frac{\dfrac{2.4988}{1+\dfrac{0.052617}{2}}}{}\right) \times \text{USD99.650} = \text{USD242.62}$$

Solution to 2:

For each 1 bp increase in the yield-to-maturity, the loss is estimated to be USD0.024262 per 100 of par value: USD242.62 × 0.0001 = USD0.024262.

Given a position size of USD10 million in par value, the estimated loss per basis-point increase in the yield is USD2,426.20. The money duration is per 100 of par value, so the position size of USD10 million is divided by 100.

$$\text{USD0.024262} \times \frac{\text{USD10,000,000}}{100} = \text{USD2,426.20}$$

3.7 Bond Convexity

Modified duration measures the primary effect on a bond's percentage price change given a change in the yield-to-maturity. A secondary effect is measured by the convexity statistic, which is illustrated in Exhibit 10 for a traditional (option-free) fixed-rate bond.

Exhibit 10   Convexity of a Traditional (Option-Free) Fixed-Rate Bond

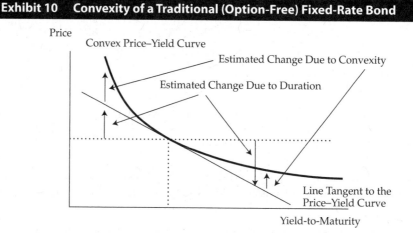

The true relationship between the bond price and the yield-to-maturity is the curved (convex) line shown in Exhibit 10. This curved line shows the actual bond price given its market discount rate. Duration (in particular, money duration) estimates the change in the bond price along the straight line that is tangent to the curved line. For small yield-to-maturity changes, there is little difference between the lines. But for larger changes, the difference becomes significant.

The convexity statistic for the bond is used to improve the estimate of the percentage price change provided by modified duration alone. Equation 13 is the convexity-adjusted estimate of the percentage change in the bond's full price.[5]

---

[5] Readers who have studied calculus will recognize this equation as the first two terms of a Taylor series expansion. The first term, the modified duration, includes the first derivative of the bond price with respect to a change in the yield. The second term, the convexity, includes the second derivative.

$$\%\Delta PV^{Full} \approx$$

$$(-\text{AnnModDur} \times \Delta\text{Yield}) + \left[\frac{1}{2} \times \text{AnnConvexity} \times (\Delta\text{Yield})^2\right] \tag{13}$$

The first bracketed expression, the "first-order" effect, is the same as Equation 6. The (annual) modified duration, AnnModDur, is multiplied by the change in the (annual) yield-to-maturity, ΔYield. The second bracketed expression, the "second-order" effect, is the **convexity adjustment**. The convexity adjustment is the annual convexity statistic, AnnConvexity, times one-half, multiplied by the change in the yield-to-maturity *squared*. This additional term is a positive amount on a traditional (option-free) fixed-rate bond for either an increase or decrease in the yield. In Exhibit 10, this amount adds to the linear estimate provided by the duration alone, which brings the adjusted estimate very close to the actual price on the curved line. But it still is an estimate, so the $\approx$ sign is used.

Similar to the Macaulay and modified durations, the annual convexity statistic can be calculated in several ways. It can be calculated using tables, such as Exhibits 2 and 3. It also is possible to derive a closed-form equation for the convexity of a fixed-rate bond on and between coupon payment dates using calculus and algebra.[6] But like modified duration, convexity can be approximated with accuracy. Equation 14 is the formula for the approximate convexity statistic, ApproxCon.

$$\text{ApproxCon} = \frac{(PV_-) + (PV_+) - \left[2 \times (PV_0)\right]}{(\Delta\text{Yield})^2 \times (PV_0)} \tag{14}$$

This equation uses the same inputs as Equation 7 for ApproxModDur. The new price when the yield-to-maturity is increased is PV_+. The new price when the yield is decreased by the same amount is PV_-. The original price is PV_0. These are the full prices, including accrued interest, for the bond.

The accuracy of this approximation can be demonstrated with the special case of a zero-coupon bond. The absence of coupon payments simplifies the interest rate risk measures. The Macaulay duration of a zero-coupon bond is $N - t/T$ in terms of periods to maturity. The exact convexity statistic of a zero-coupon bond, also in terms of periods, is calculated with Equation 15.

$$\text{Convexity (of a zero-coupon bond)} = \frac{\left[N - (t/T)\right] \times \left[N + 1 - (t/T)\right]}{(1+r)^2} \tag{15}$$

N is the number of periods to maturity as of the beginning of the current period, t/T is the fraction of the period that has gone by, and r is the yield-to-maturity per period.

For an example of this calculation, consider a long-term, zero-coupon US Treasury bond. The bond's Bloomberg YAS page is shown in Exhibit 11.

---

6 The step-by-step derivation for a closed-form equation for convexity on and between coupon payment dates is in Donald J. Smith, *Bond Math: The Theory behind the Formulas* (Hoboken, NJ: John Wiley & Sons, 2011).

Exhibit 11   Bloomberg YAS Page for the Zero-Coupon US Treasury Bond

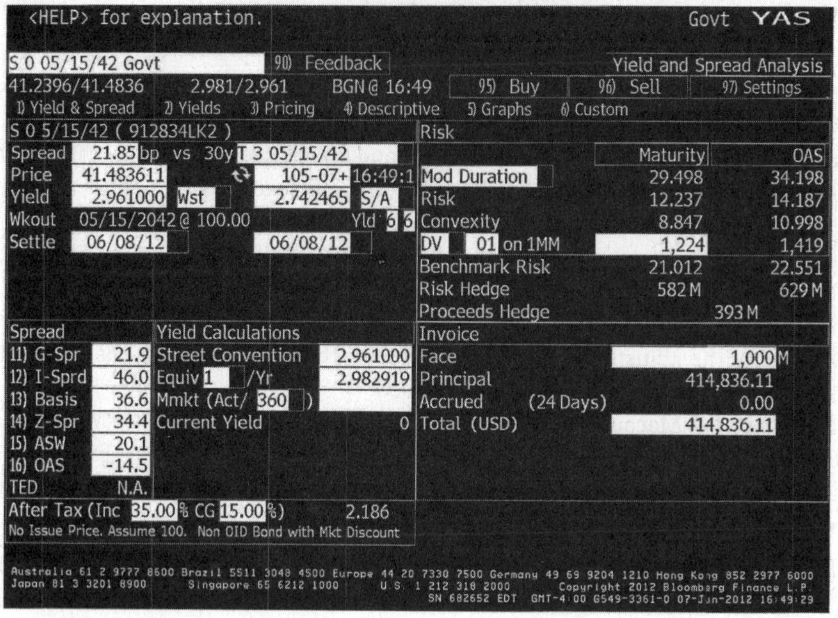

The bond matures on 15 May 2042 and was priced at 41.483611 per 100 of par value for settlement on 8 June 2012. Its yield-to-maturity was 2.961% stated on a street-convention semiannual bond basis. Even though it is a zero-coupon bond, its yield-to-maturity is based on the actual/actual day-count convention. That settlement date was 24 days into a 184-day period. The annual modified duration was 29.498.

For this bond, $N = 60$, $t/T = 24/184$, and $r = 0.02961/2$. Entering these variables into Equation 15 produces a convexity of 3,538.68 in terms of semiannual periods.

$$\frac{\left[60 - (24/184)\right] \times \left[60 + 1 - (24/184)\right]}{\left(1 + \frac{0.02961}{2}\right)^2} = 3{,}538.68$$

As with the other statistics, convexity is annualized in practice and for use in the convexity adjustment in Equation 13. It is divided by the periodicity *squared*. The yield-to-maturity on this zero-coupon bond is stated on a semiannual bond basis, meaning a periodicity of 2. Therefore, the annualized convexity statistic is 884.7.

$$\frac{3{,}538.68}{4} = 884.7$$

For example, suppose that the yield-to-maturity is expected to fall by 10 bps, from 2.961% to 2.861%. Given the (annual) modified duration of 29.498 and (annual) convexity of 884.7, the expected percentage price gain is 2.9940%.

$$\%\Delta PV^{Full} \approx \left[-29.498 \times -0.0010\right] + \left[\frac{1}{2} \times 884.7 \times (-0.0010)^2\right]$$

$$= 0.029498 + 0.000442$$

$$= 0.029940$$

Modified duration alone (under)estimates the gain to be 2.9498%. The convexity adjustment adds 4.42 bps.

The long-term, zero-coupon bond of Exhibit 11 demonstrates the significant difference between *yield* duration and convexity and *curve* duration and convexity, even on an option-free bond. Its modified duration is 29.498, whereas its effective duration is 34.198. Its yield convexity is reported on the Bloomberg page to be 8.847, and its effective convexity is 10.998. (Note that Bloomberg scales the convexity statistics by dividing by 100.) In general, the differences are heightened when the benchmark yield curve is not flat, when the bond has a long time-to-maturity, and the bond is priced at a significant discount or premium.

To obtain the ApproxCon for this long-term, zero-coupon bond, calculate PV_0, PV_+, and PV_- for yields-to-maturity of 2.961%, 2.971%, and 2.951%, respectively. For this exercise, $\Delta \text{Yield} = 0.0001$.

$$PV_0 = \frac{100}{\left(1 + \dfrac{0.02961}{2}\right)^{60}} \times \left(1 + \frac{0.02961}{2}\right)^{24/184} = 41.483617$$

$$PV_+ = \frac{100}{\left(1 + \dfrac{0.02971}{2}\right)^{60}} \times \left(1 + \frac{0.02971}{2}\right)^{24/184} = 41.361431$$

$$PV_- = \frac{100}{\left(1 + \dfrac{0.02951}{2}\right)^{60}} \times \left(1 + \frac{0.02951}{2}\right)^{24/184} = 41.606169$$

The price of the zero-coupon bond is actually 41.483611, not 41.483617. In this calculation, PV_0 is slightly different because the quoted yield-to-maturity is rounded.[7] It is appropriate to use the calculated PV_0 to be consistent with the change in the yield-to-maturity.

Using these results, first calculate ApproxModDur using Equation 7 to confirm that these inputs are correct. In Exhibit 11, modified duration is stated to be 29.498.

$$\text{ApproxModDur} = \frac{41.606169 - 41.361431}{2 \times 0.0001 \times 41.483617} = 29.498$$

Using Equation 14, ApproxCon is 882.3.

$$\text{ApproxCon} = \frac{41.606169 + 41.361431 - (2 \times 41.483617)}{(0.0001)^2 \times 41.483617} = 882.3$$

This result, 882.3, is an approximation for *annualized* convexity. The number of periods in the year is included in the price calculations. This approximation is quite close to the "exact" result using the closed-form equation for the special case of the zero-coupon bond, 884.7. The difference is not likely to be meaningful for practical applications.

Because this is an individual zero-coupon bond, it is easy to calculate the new price if the yield-to-maturity does go down by 10 bps, to 2.861%.

$$\frac{100}{\left(1 + \dfrac{0.02861}{2}\right)^{60}} \times \left(1 + \frac{0.02861}{2}\right)^{24/184} = 42.725841$$

Therefore, the actual percentage price increase is 2.9945%.

$$\frac{42.725841 - 41.483611}{41.483611} = 0.029945$$

---

7 Given the price of 41.483611, the yield-to-maturity is 2.96100046%.

The convexity-adjusted estimation of 2.9940% is very close to the actual change. Using the approximate convexity of 882.3 instead of the exact convexity of 884.7 would not have had a meaningful impact.

$$\%\Delta PV^{Full} \approx \left(-29.458 \times -0.0010\right) + \left[\frac{1}{2} \times 882.3 \times \left(-0.0010\right)^2\right]$$

$$= 0.029458 + 0.000441$$

$$= 0.029899$$

The "exact" convexity adjustment is 4.42 bps. The "approximate" convexity adjustment is 4.41 bps.

EXAMPLE 13

An Italian bank holds a large position in a 7.25% annual coupon payment corporate bond that matures on 4 April 2029. The bond's yield-to-maturity is 7.44% for settlement on 27 June 2014, stated as an effective annual rate. That settlement date is 83 days into the 360-day year using the 30/360 method of counting days.

1 Calculate the full price of the bond per 100 of par value.

2 Calculate the approximate modified duration and approximate convexity using a 1 bp increase and decrease in the yield-to-maturity.

3 Calculate the estimated convexity-adjusted percentage price change resulting from a 100 bp increase in the yield-to-maturity.

4 Compare the estimated percentage price change with the actual change, assuming the yield-to-maturity jumps to 8.44% on that settlement date.

Solutions:

There are 15 years from the beginning of the current period on 4 April 2014 to maturity on 4 April 2029.

1 The full price of the bond is 99.956780 per 100 of par value.

$$PV_0 = \left[\frac{7.25}{\left(1.0744\right)^1} + \cdots + \frac{107.25}{\left(1.0744\right)^{15}}\right] \times \left(1.0744\right)^{83/360} = 99.956780$$

2 $PV_+ = 99.869964$, and $PV_- = 100.043703$.

$$PV_+ = \left[\frac{7.25}{\left(1.0745\right)^1} + \cdots + \frac{107.25}{\left(1.0745\right)^{15}}\right] \times \left(1.0745\right)^{83/360} = 99.869964$$

$$PV_- = \left[\frac{7.25}{\left(1.0743\right)^1} + \cdots + \frac{107.25}{\left(1.0743\right)^{15}}\right] \times \left(1.0743\right)^{83/360} = 100.043703$$

The approximate modified duration is 8.6907.

$$\text{ApproxModDur} = \frac{100.043703 - 99.869964}{2 \times 0.0001 \times 99.956780} = 8.6907$$

The approximate convexity is 107.046.

$$\text{ApproxCon} = \frac{100.043703 + 99.869964 - \left(2 \times 99.956780\right)}{\left(0.0001\right)^2 \times 99.956780} = 107.046$$

3 The convexity-adjusted percentage price drop resulting from a 100 bp increase in the yield-to-maturity is estimated to be 8.1555%. Modified duration alone estimates the percentage drop to be 8.6907%. The convexity adjustment adds 53.52 bps.

$$\%\Delta PV^{Full} \approx (-8.6907 \times 0.0100) + \left[\frac{1}{2} \times 107.046 \times (0.0100)^2\right]$$

$$= -0.086907 + 0.005352$$

$$= -0.081555$$

4 The new full price if the yield-to-maturity goes from 7.44% to 8.44% on that settlement date is 91.780921.

$$PV^{Full} = \left[\frac{7.25}{(1.0844)^1} + \cdots + \frac{107.25}{(1.0844)^{15}}\right] \times (1.0844)^{83/360} = 91.780921$$

$$\%\Delta PV^{Full} = \frac{91.780921 - 99.956780}{99.956780} = -0.081794$$

The actual percentage change in the bond price is −8.1794%. The convexity-adjusted estimate is −8.1555%, whereas the estimated change using modified duration alone is −8.6907%.

The money duration of a bond indicates the first-order effect on the full price of a bond in units of currency given a change in the yield-to-maturity. The **money convexity** statistic (MoneyCon) is the second-order effect. The money convexity of the bond is the annual convexity multiplied by the full price, such that

$$\Delta PV^{Full} \approx -(\text{MoneyDur} \times \Delta\text{Yield}) + \left[\frac{1}{2} \times \text{MoneyCon} \times (\Delta\text{Yield})^2\right] \qquad \textbf{(16)}$$

For a money convexity example, consider again the Hong Kong–based life insurance company that has a HKD100,000,000 position in the 6.00% bond that matures on 14 February 2022. In Section 3.5, using the money duration alone, the estimated loss is HKD6,184,418 if the yield-to-maturity increases by 100 bps. The money duration for the position is HKD618,441,784. That estimation is improved by including the convexity adjustment. In Section 3.1, these inputs are calculated to obtain the approximate modified duration of 6.1268 for a 5 bp change in the yield-to-maturity (ΔYield = 0.0005): PV_0 = 100.940423, PV_+ = 100.631781, and PV_- = 101.250227. Enter these into Equation 14 to calculate the approximate convexity.

$$\text{ApproxCon} = \frac{101.250227 + 100.631781 - (2 \times 100.940423)}{(0.0005)^2 \times 100.940423} = 46.047$$

The money convexity is 46.047 times the market value of the position, HKD100,940,423. The convexity-adjusted loss given a 100 bp jump in the yield-to-maturity is HKD5,952,018.

$$-\left[(6.1268 \times \text{HKD}100,940,423) \times 0.0100\right] +$$

$$\left[\frac{1}{2} \times (46.047 \times \text{HKD}100,940,423) \times (0.0100)^2\right]$$

$$= -\text{HKD}6,184,418 + \text{HKD}232,400$$

$$= -\text{HKD}5,952,018$$

The factors that lead to greater convexity are the same as for duration. A fixed-rate bond with a longer time-to-maturity, a lower coupon rate, and a lower yield-to-maturity has greater convexity than a bond with a shorter time-to-maturity, a higher coupon rate, and a higher yield-to-maturity. Another factor is the dispersion of cash flows, meaning the degree to which payments are spread out over time. If two bonds have the same duration, the one that has the greater dispersion of cash flows has the greater convexity. The positive attributes of greater convexity for an investor are shown in Exhibit 12.

Exhibit 12   The Positive Attributes of Greater Bond Convexity on a Traditional (Option-Free) Bond

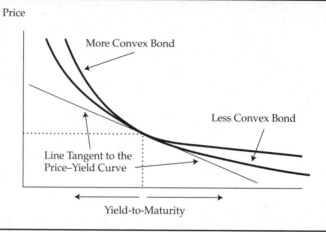

The two bonds in Exhibit 12 are assumed to have the same price, yield-to-maturity, and modified duration. Therefore, they share the same line tangent to their price–yield curves. The benefit of greater convexity occurs when their yields-to-maturity change. For the same decrease in yield-to-maturity, the more convex bond *appreciates more* in price. And for the same increase in yield-to-maturity, the more convex bond *depreciates less* in price. The conclusion is that the more convex bond outperforms the less convex bond in both bull (rising price) and bear (falling price) markets. This conclusion assumes, however, that this positive attribute is not "priced into" the bond. To the extent that it is included, the more convex bond would have a higher price (and lower yield-to-maturity). That does not diminish the value of convexity. It only suggests that the investor has to pay for it. As economists say, "There is no such thing as a free lunch."

EXAMPLE 14

The investment manager for a UK defined-benefit pension scheme is considering two bonds about to be issued by a large life insurance company. The first is a 30-year, 4% semiannual coupon payment bond. The second is a 100-year, 4% semiannual coupon payment "century" bond. Both bonds are expected to trade at par value at issuance.

Calculate the approximate modified duration and approximate convexity for each bond using a 5 bp increase and decrease in the annual yield-to-maturity. Retain accuracy to six decimals per 100 of par value.

Solution:

In the calculations, the yield per semiannual period goes up by 2.5 bps to 2.025% and down by 2.5 bps to 1.975%. The 30-year bond has an approximate modified duration of 17.381 and an approximate convexity of 420.80.

$$PV_+ = \frac{2}{(1.02025)^1} + \cdots + \frac{102}{(1.02025)^{60}} = 99.136214$$

$$PV_- = \frac{2}{(1.01975)^1} + \cdots + \frac{102}{(1.01975)^{60}} = 100.874306$$

$$\text{ApproxModDur} = \frac{100.874306 - 99.136214}{2 \times 0.0005 \times 100} = 17.381$$

$$\text{ApproxCon} = \frac{100.874306 + 99.136214 - (2 \times 100)}{(0.0005)^2 \times 100} = 420.80$$

The 100-year century bond has an approximate modified duration of 24.527 and an approximate convexity of 1,132.88.

$$PV_+ = \frac{2}{(1.02025)^1} + \cdots + \frac{102}{(1.02025)^{200}} = 98.787829$$

$$PV_- = \frac{2}{(1.01975)^1} + \cdots + \frac{102}{(1.01975)^{200}} = 101.240493$$

$$\text{ApproxModDur} = \frac{101.240493 - 98.787829}{2 \times 0.0005 \times 100} = 24.527$$

$$\text{ApproxCon} = \frac{101.240493 + 98.787829 - (2 \times 100)}{(0.0005)^2 \times 100} = 1,132.88$$

The century bond offers a higher modified duration—24.527 compared with 17.381—and a much greater degree of convexity—1,132.88 compared with 420.80.

In the same manner that the primary, or first-order, effect of a shift in the benchmark yield curve is measured by effective duration, the secondary, or second-order, effect is measured by **effective convexity**. The effective convexity of a bond is a *curve convexity* statistic that measures the secondary effect of a change in a benchmark yield curve. A pricing model is used to determine the new prices when the benchmark curve is shifted upward (PV_+) and downward (PV_-) by the same amount (ΔCurve). These changes are made holding other factors constant—for example, the credit spread. Then, Equation 17 is used to calculate the effective convexity (EffCon) given the initial price (PV_0).

$$\text{EffCon} = \frac{\left[(PV_-) + (PV_+)\right] - \left[2 \times (PV_0)\right]}{(\Delta\text{Curve})^2 \times (PV_0)} \qquad \textbf{(17)}$$

This equation is very similar to Equation 14, for approximate *yield* convexity. The difference is that in Equation 14, the denominator includes the change in the yield-to-maturity squared, $(\Delta\text{Yield})^2$. Here, the denominator includes the change in the benchmark yield curve squared, $(\Delta\text{Curve})^2$.

Consider again the callable bond example in Section 3.2. It is assumed that an option-pricing model is used to generate these callable bond prices: $PV_0 = 101.060489$, $PV_+ = 99.050120$, $PV_- = 102.890738$, and ΔCurve = 0.0025. The effective duration for the callable bond is 7.6006.

$$\text{EffDur} = \frac{102.890738 - 99.050120}{2 \times 0.0025 \times 101.060489} = 7.6006$$

Using these inputs in Equation 17, the effective convexity is −285.17.

$$\text{EffCon} = \frac{102.890738 + 99.050120 - (2 \times 101.060489)}{(0.0025)^2 \times 101.060489} = -285.17$$

Negative convexity, which could be called "concavity," is an important feature of callable bonds. Putable bonds, on the other hand, always have positive convexity. As a second-order effect, effective convexity indicates the change in the first-order effect (i.e., effective duration) as the benchmark yield curve is changed. In Exhibit 8, as the benchmark yield goes down, the slope of the line tangent to the curve for the non-callable bond steepens, which indicates positive convexity. But the slope of the line tangent to the callable bond flattens as the benchmark yield goes down. Technically, it reaches an inflection point, which is when the effective convexity shifts from positive to negative.

In summary, when the benchmark yield is high and the value of the embedded call option is low, the callable and the non-callable bonds experience very similar effects from interest rate changes. They both have positive convexity. But as the benchmark yield is reduced, the curves diverge. At some point, the callable bond moves into the range of negative convexity, which indicates that the embedded call option has more value to the issuer and is more likely to be exercised. This situation limits the potential price appreciation of the bond arising from lower interest rates, whether because of a lower benchmark yield or a lower credit spread.

Another way to understand why a callable bond can have negative convexity is to rearrange Equation 17.

$$\text{EffCon} = \frac{\left[(PV_-) - (PV_0)\right] - \left[(PV_0) - (PV_+)\right]}{(\Delta\text{Curve})^2 \times (PV_0)}$$

In the numerator, the first bracketed expression is the increase in price when the benchmark yield curve is lowered. The second expression is the decrease in price when the benchmark yield curve is raised. On a non-callable bond, the increase is always larger than the decrease (in absolute value). This result is the "convexity effect" for the relationship between bond prices and yields-to-maturity. On a callable bond, the increase can be smaller than the decrease (in absolute value). That creates negative convexity, as illustrated in Exhibit 8.

4 INTEREST RATE RISK AND THE INVESTMENT HORIZON

This section explores the effect of yield volatility on the investment horizon, and on the interaction between the investment horizon, market price risk, and coupon reinvestment risk.

4.1 Yield Volatility

An important aspect in understanding the interest rate risk and return characteristics of an investment in a fixed-rate bond is the time horizon. This section considers a short-term horizon. A primary concern for the investor is the change in the price of the bond given a sudden (i.e., same-day) change in its yield-to-maturity. The accrued interest does not change, so the impact of the change in the yield is on the flat price of the bond. Section 4.2 considers a long-term horizon. The reinvestment of coupon interest then becomes a key factor in the investor's horizon yield.

Bond duration is the primary measure of risk arising from a change in the yield-to-maturity. Convexity is the secondary risk measure. In the discussion of the impact on the bond price, the phrase "for a *given* change in the yield-to-maturity" is used repeatedly. For instance, the given change in the yield-to-maturity could be 1 bp, 25 bps, or 100 bps. In comparing two bonds, it is assumed that the "given change" is the same for both securities. When the government bond par curve is shifted up or down by the same amount to calculate effective duration and effective convexity, the events are described as "parallel" yield curve shifts. Because yield curves are rarely (if ever) straight lines, this shift may also be described as a "shape-preserving" shift to the yield curve. The key assumption is that all yields-to-maturity under consideration rise or fall by the same amount across the curve.

Although the assumption of a parallel shift in the yield curve is common in fixed-income analysis, it is not always realistic. In reality, the shape of the yield curve changes based on factors affecting the supply and demand of shorter-term versus longer-term securities. In fact, the term structure of bond yields (also called the "term structure of interest rates") is typically upward sloping. However, the **term structure of yield volatility** may have a different shape depending on a number of factors. The term structure of yield volatility is the relationship between the volatility of bond yields-to-maturity and times-to-maturity.

For example, a central bank engaging in expansionary monetary policy might cause the yield curve to steepen by reducing short-term interest rates. But this policy might cause greater *volatility* in short-term bond yields-to-maturity than in longer-term bonds, resulting in a downward-sloping term structure of yield volatility. Longer-term bond yields are mostly determined by future inflation and economic growth expectations. Those expectations often tend to be less volatile.

The importance of yield volatility in measuring interest rate risk is that bond price changes are products of two factors: (1) the impact *per* basis-point change in the yield-to-maturity and (2) the *number* of basis points in the yield-to-maturity change. The first factor is duration or the combination of duration and convexity, and the second factor is the yield volatility. For example, consider a 5-year bond with a modified duration of 4.5 and a 30-year bond with a modified duration of 18.0. Clearly, for a *given* change in yield-to-maturity, the 30-year bond represents more much more interest rate risk to an investor who has a short-term horizon. In fact, the 30-year bond appears to have *four times* the risk given the ratio of the modified durations. But that assumption neglects the possibility that the 30-year bond might have half the yield volatility of the 5-year bond.

Equation 13, restated here, summarizes the two factors.

$$\%\Delta PV^{Full} \approx \left(-\text{AnnModDur} \times \Delta \text{Yield}\right) + \left[\frac{1}{2} \times \text{AnnConvexity} \times \left(\Delta \text{Yield}\right)^2\right]$$

The estimated percentage change in the bond price depends on the modified duration and convexity as well as on the yield-to-maturity change. Parallel shifts between two bond yields and along a benchmark yield curve are common assumptions in fixed-income analysis. However, an analyst must be aware that non-parallel shifts frequently occur in practice.

EXAMPLE 15

A fixed-income analyst is asked to rank three bonds in terms of interest rate risk. Interest rate risk here means the potential price decrease on a percentage basis given a sudden change in financial market conditions. The increases in the yields-to-maturity represent the "worst case" for the scenario being considered.

Bond	Modified Duration	Convexity	ΔYield
A	3.72	12.1	25 bps
B	5.81	40.7	15 bps
C	12.39	158.0	10 bps

The modified duration and convexity statistics are annualized. ΔYield is the increase in the annual yield-to-maturity. Rank the bonds in terms of interest rate risk.

Solution:

Calculate the estimated percentage price change for each bond:

Bond A:

$$(-3.72 \times 0.0025) + \left[\frac{1}{2} \times 12.1 \times (0.0025)^2\right] = -0.009262$$

Bond B:

$$(-5.81 \times 0.0015) + \left[\frac{1}{2} \times 40.7 \times (0.0015)^2\right] = -0.008669$$

Bond C:

$$(-12.39 \times 0.0010) + \left[\frac{1}{2} \times 158.0 \times (0.0010)^2\right] = -0.012311$$

Based on these assumed changes in the yield-to-maturity and the modified duration and convexity risk measures, Bond C has the highest degree of interest rate risk (a potential loss of 1.2311%), followed by Bond A (a potential loss of 0.9262%) and Bond B (a potential loss of 0.8669%).

4.2 Investment Horizon, Macaulay Duration, and Interest Rate Risk

Although short-term interest rate risk is a concern to some investors, other investors have a long-term horizon. Day-to-day changes in bond prices cause *unrealized* capital gains and losses. Those unrealized gains and losses might need to be accounted for in financial statements. This section considers a long-term investor concerned only with the total return over the investment horizon. Therefore, interest rate risk is important to this investor. The investor faces coupon reinvestment risk as well as market price risk if the bond needs to be sold prior to maturity.

Section 2 included examples of interest rate risk using a 10-year, 8% annual coupon payment bond that is priced at 85.503075 per 100 of par value. The bond's yield-to-maturity is 10.40%. A key result in Example 3 is that an investor with a 10-year time horizon is concerned only with coupon reinvestment risk. This situation assumes, of course, that the issuer makes all of the coupon and principal payments as scheduled. The buy-and-hold investor has a higher total return if interest rates rise (see Example 3) and a lower total return if rates fall (see Example 5). The investor in Examples 4 and

6 has a four-year horizon. This investor faces market price risk in addition to coupon reinvestment risk. In fact, the market price risk dominates because this investor has a higher total return if interest rates fall (see Example 6) and a lower return if rates rise (see Example 4).

Now, consider a third investor who has a seven-year time horizon. If interest rates remain at 10.40%, the future value of reinvested coupon interest is 76.835787 per 100 of par value.

$$\left[8 \times (1.1040)^6\right] + \left[8 \times (1.1040)^5\right] + \left[8 \times (1.1040)^4\right] + \left[8 \times (1.1040)^3\right] +$$
$$\left[8 \times (1.1040)^2\right] + \left[8 \times (1.1040)^1\right] + 8 = 76.835787$$

The bond is sold for a price of 94.073336, assuming that the bond stays on the constant-yield price trajectory and continues to be "pulled to par."

$$\frac{8}{(1.1040)^1} + \frac{8}{(1.1040)^2} + \frac{108}{(1.1040)^3} = 94.073336$$

The total return is 170.909123 (= 76.835787 + 94.073336) per 100 of par value, and the horizon yield, as expected, is 10.40%.

$$85.503075 = \frac{170.909123}{(1 + r)^7}, \quad r = 0.1040$$

Following Examples 3 and 4, assume that the yield-to-maturity on the bond rises to 11.40%. Also, coupon interest is now reinvested each year at 11.40%. The future value of reinvested coupons becomes 79.235183 per 100 of par value.

$$\left[8 \times (1.1140)^6\right] + \left[8 \times (1.1140)^5\right] + \left[8 \times (1.1140)^4\right] + \left[8 \times (1.1140)^3\right] +$$
$$\left[8 \times (1.1140)^2\right] + \left[8 \times (1.1140)^1\right] + 8 = 79.235183$$

After receiving the seventh coupon payment, the bond is sold. There is a capital loss because the price, although much higher than at purchase, is below the constant-yield price trajectory.

$$\frac{8}{(1.1140)^1} + \frac{8}{(1.1140)^2} + \frac{108}{(1.1140)^3} = 91.748833$$

The total return is 170.984016 (= 79.235183 + 91.748833) per 100 of par value and the holding-period rate of return is 10.407%.

$$85.503075 = \frac{170.984016}{(1 + r)^7}, \quad r = 0.10407$$

Following Examples 5 and 6, assume that the coupon reinvestment rates and the bond yield-to-maturity fall to 9.40%. The future value of reinvested coupons is 74.512177.

$$\left[8 + (1.0940)^6\right] + \left[8 + (1.0940)^5\right] + \left[8 + (1.0940)^4\right] + \left[8 + (1.0940)^3\right] +$$
$$\left[8 + (1.0940)^2\right] + \left[8 + (1.0940)^1\right] + 8 = 74.52177$$

The bond is sold at a capital gain because the price is above the constant-yield price trajectory.

$$\frac{8}{(1.0940)^1} + \frac{8}{(1.0940)^2} + \frac{108}{(1.0940)^3} = 96.481299$$

The total return is 170.993476 (= 74.512177 + 96.481299) per 100 of par value, and the horizon yield is 10.408%.

$$85.503075 = \frac{170.993476}{(1 + r)^7}, \quad r = 0.10408$$

These results are summarized in the following table to reveal the remarkable outcome: The total returns and horizon yields are virtually the same. The investor with the 7-year horizon, unlike those having a 4- or 10-year horizon, achieves the same holding-period rate of return whether interest rates rise, fall, or remain the same. Note that the terms "horizon yield" and "holding-period rate of return" are used interchangeably in this reading. Sometimes "horizon yield" refers to yields on bonds that need to be sold at the end of the investor's holding period.

Interest Rate	Future Value of Reinvested Coupon	Sale Price	Total Return	Horizon Yield
9.40%	74.512177	96.481299	170.993476	10.408%
10.40%	76.835787	94.073336	170.909123	10.400%
11.40%	79.235183	91.748833	170.984016	10.407%

This particular bond was chosen as an example to demonstrate an important property of Macaulay duration: For a particular assumption about yield volatility, Macaulay duration indicates the investment horizon for which coupon reinvestment risk and market price risk offset each other. In Section 3.1, the Macaulay duration of this 10-year, 8% annual payment bond is calculated to be 7.0029 years. This is one of the applications for duration in which "years" is meaningful and in which Macaulay duration is used rather than modified duration. The particular assumption about yield volatility is that there is a one-time "parallel" shift in the yield curve that occurs before the next coupon payment date. Exhibit 13 illustrates this property of bond duration, assuming that the bond is initially priced at par value.

Exhibit 13	**Interest Rate Risk, Macaulay Duration, and the Investment Horizon**

A. Interest Rates Rise

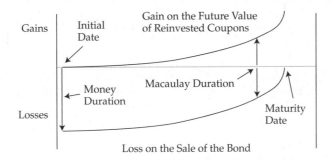

B. Interest Rates Fall

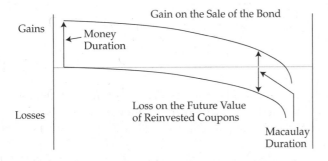

As demonstrated in Panel A of Exhibit 13, when interest rates rise, duration measures the immediate drop in value. In particular, the money duration indicates the change in price. Then as time passes, the bond price is "pulled to par." The gain in the future value of reinvested coupons starts small but builds over time as more coupons are received. The curve indicates the additional future value of reinvested coupons because of the higher interest rate. At some point in the lifetime of the bond, those two effects offset each other and the gain on reinvested coupons is equal to the loss on the sale of the bond. That point in time is the Macaulay duration statistic.

The same pattern is displayed in the Panel B when interest rates fall, which leads to a reduction in the bond yield and the coupon reinvestment rate. There is an immediate jump in the bond price, as measured by the money duration, but then the "pulled to par" effect brings the price down as time passes. The impact from reinvesting at a lower rate starts small but then becomes more significant over time. The loss on reinvested coupons is with respect to the future value if interest rates had not fallen. Once again, the bond's Macaulay duration indicates the point in time when the two effects offset each other and the gain on the sale of the bond matches the loss on coupon reinvestment.

The earlier numerical example and Exhibit 13 allow for a statement of the general relationships among interest rate risk, the Macaulay duration, and the investment horizon.

1 When the investment horizon is greater than the Macaulay duration of a bond, coupon reinvestment risk dominates market price risk. The investor's risk is to lower interest rates.

2 When the investment horizon is equal to the Macaulay duration of a bond, coupon reinvestment risk offsets market price risk.

3 When the investment horizon is less than the Macaulay duration of the bond, market price risk dominates coupon reinvestment risk. The investor's risk is to higher interest rates.

In the numerical example, the Macaulay duration of the bond is 7.0 years. Statement 1 reflects the investor with the 10-year horizon; Statement 2, the investor with the 7-year horizon; and Statement 3, the investor with the 4-year horizon.

The difference between the Macaulay duration of a bond and the investment horizon is called the **duration gap**. The duration gap is a bond's Macaulay duration minus the investment horizon. The investor with the 10-year horizon has a negative duration gap and currently is at risk of lower rates. The investor with the 7-year horizon has a duration gap of zero and currently is hedged against interest rate risk. The investor with the 4-year horizon has a positive duration gap and currently is at risk of higher rates. The word "currently" is important because interest rate risk is connected to an *immediate* change in the bond's yield-to-maturity and the coupon reinvestment rates. As time passes, the investment horizon is reduced and the Macaulay duration of the bond also changes. Therefore, the duration gap changes as well.

EXAMPLE 16

An investor plans to retire in 10 years. As part of the retirement portfolio, the investor buys a newly issued, 12-year, 8% annual coupon payment bond. The bond is purchased at par value, so its yield-to-maturity is 8.00% stated as an effective annual rate.

1 Calculate the approximate Macaulay duration for the bond, using a 1 bp increase and decrease in the yield-to-maturity and calculating the new prices per 100 of par value to six decimal places.

2 Calculate the duration gap at the time of purchase.

3 Does this bond at purchase entail the risk of higher or lower interest rates? Interest rate risk here means an immediate, one-time, parallel yield curve shift.

Solution to 1:

The approximate modified duration of the bond is 7.5361. $PV_0 = 100$, $PV_+ = 99.924678$, and $PV_- = 100.075400$.

$$PV_+ = \frac{8}{(1.0801)^1} + \cdots + \frac{108}{(1.0801)^{12}} = 99.924678$$

$$PV_- = \frac{8}{(1.0799)^1} + \cdots + \frac{108}{(1.0799)^{12}} = 100.075400$$

$$\text{ApproxModDur} = \frac{100.075400 - 99.924678}{2 \times 0.0001 \times 100} = 7.5361$$

The approximate Macaulay duration is 8.1390 (= 7.5361 × 1.08).

Solution to 2:

Given an investment horizon of 10 years, the duration gap for this bond at purchase is negative: 8.1390 − 10 = −1.8610.

> **Solution to 3:**
>
> A negative duration gap entails the risk of lower interest rates. To be precise, the risk is an immediate, one-time, parallel, downward yield curve shift because coupon reinvestment risk dominates market price risk. The loss from reinvesting coupons at a rate lower than 8% is larger than the gain from selling the bond at a price above the constant-yield price trajectory.

CREDIT AND LIQUIDITY RISK

5

The focus of this reading is to demonstrate how bond duration and convexity estimate the bond price change, either in percentage terms or in units of currency, given an assumed yield-to-maturity change. This section addresses the *source* of the change in the yield-to-maturity. In general, the yield-to-maturity on a corporate bond is composed of a government *benchmark* yield and a *spread* over that benchmark. A change in the bond's yield-to-maturity can originate in either component or a combination of the two.

The key point is that for a traditional (option-free) fixed-rate bond, the same duration and convexity statistics apply for a change in the benchmark yield as for a change in the spread. The "building blocks" approach from "Introduction to Fixed-Income Valuation" shows that these yield-to-maturity changes can be broken down further. A change in the benchmark yield can arise from a change in either the expected inflation rate or the expected real rate of interest. A change in the spread can arise from a change in the credit risk of the issuer or in the liquidity of the bond. Therefore, for a fixed-rate bond, the "inflation duration," the "real rate duration," the "credit duration," and the "liquidity duration" are all the same number. The inflation duration would indicate the change in the bond price if expected inflation were to change by a certain amount. In the same manner, the real rate duration would indicate the bond price change if the real rate were to go up or down. The credit duration and liquidity duration would indicate the price sensitivity that would arise from changes in those building blocks in the yield-to-maturity. A bond with a modified duration of 5.00 and a convexity of 32.00 will appreciate in value by about 1.26% if its yield-to-maturity goes down by 25 bps: $(-5.00 \times -0.0025) + [1/2 \times 32.00 \times (-0.0025)^2] = +0.0126$, regardless of the *source* of the yield-to-maturity change.

Suppose that the yield-to-maturity on a corporate bond is 6.00%. If the benchmark yield is 4.25%, the spread is 1.75%. An analyst believes that credit risk makes up 1.25% of the spread and liquidity risk, the remaining 0.50%. Credit risk includes the probability of default as well as the recovery of assets if default does occur. A credit rating downgrade or an adverse change in the ratings outlook for a borrower reflects a higher risk of default. Liquidity risk refers to the transaction costs associated with selling a bond. In general, a bond with greater frequency of trading and a higher volume of trading provides fixed-income investors with more opportunity to purchase or sell the security and thus has less liquidity risk. In practice, there is a difference between the *bid* (or purchase) and the *offer* (or sale) price. This difference depends on the type of bond, the size of the transaction, and the time of execution, among other factors. For instance, government bonds often trade at just a few basis points between the purchase and sale prices. More thinly traded corporate bonds can have a much wider difference between the bid and offer prices.

The problem for a fixed-income analyst is that it is rare for the changes in the components of the overall yield-to-maturity to occur in isolation. In practice, the analyst is concerned with the *interaction* between changes in benchmark yields and spreads, between changes in expected inflation and the expected real rate, and between changes in credit and liquidity risk. For example, during a financial crisis, a "flight to quality" can cause government benchmark yields to fall as credit spreads widen. An unexpected credit downgrade on a corporate bond can result in greater credit as well as liquidity risk.

EXAMPLE 17

The (flat) price on a fixed-rate corporate bond falls one day from 92.25 to 91.25 per 100 of par value because of poor earnings and an unexpected ratings downgrade of the issuer. The (annual) modified duration for the bond is 7.24. Which of the following is *closest* to the estimated change in the credit spread on the corporate bond, assuming benchmark yields are unchanged?

A   15 bps

B   100 bps

C   108 bps

Solution:

Given that the price falls from 92.25 to 91.25, the percentage price decrease is 1.084%.

$$\frac{91.25 - 92.25}{92.25} = -0.01084$$

Given an annual modified duration of 7.24, the change in the yield-to-maturity is 14.97 bps.

$$-0.01084 \approx -7.24 \times \Delta\text{Yield}, \ \Delta\text{Yield} = 0.001497$$

Therefore, the answer is A. The change in price reflects a credit spread increase on the bond of about 15 bps.

SUMMARY

This reading covers the risk and return characteristics of fixed-rate bonds. The focus is on the widely used measures of interest rate risk—duration and convexity. These statistics are used extensively in fixed-income analysis. The following are the main points made in the reading:

- The three sources of return on a fixed-rate bond purchased at par value are (1) receipt of the promised coupon and principal payments on the scheduled dates, (2) reinvestment of coupon payments, and (3) potential capital gains, as well as losses, on the sale of the bond prior to maturity.

- For a bond purchased at a discount or premium, the rate of return also includes the effect of the price being "pulled to par" as maturity nears, assuming no default.

- The total return is the future value of reinvested coupon interest payments and the sale price (or redemption of principal if the bond is held to maturity).

- The horizon yield (or holding period rate of return) is the internal rate of return between the total return and purchase price of the bond.

- Coupon reinvestment risk increases with a higher coupon rate and a longer reinvestment time period.

- Capital gains and losses are measured from the carrying value of the bond and not from the purchase price. The carrying value includes the amortization of the discount or premium if the bond is purchased at a price below or above par value. The carrying value is any point on the constant-yield price trajectory.

- Interest income on a bond is the return associated with the passage of time. Capital gains and losses are the returns associated with a change in the value of a bond as indicated by a change in the yield-to-maturity.

- The two types of interest rate risk on a fixed-rate bond are coupon reinvestment risk and market price risk. These risks offset each other to a certain extent. An investor gains from higher rates on reinvested coupons but loses if the bond is sold at a capital loss because the price is below the constant-yield price trajectory. An investor loses from lower rates on reinvested coupon but gains if the bond is sold at a capital gain because the price is above the constant-yield price trajectory.

- Market price risk dominates coupon reinvestment risk when the investor has a short-term horizon (relative to the time-to-maturity on the bond).

- Coupon reinvestment risk dominates market price risk when the investor has a long-term horizon (relative to the time-to-maturity)—for instance, a buy-and-hold investor.

- Bond duration, in general, measures the sensitivity of the full price (including accrued interest) to a change in interest rates.

- Yield duration statistics measuring the sensitivity of a bond's full price to the bond's own yield-to-maturity include the Macaulay duration, modified duration, money duration, and price value of a basis point.

- Curve duration statistics measuring the sensitivity of a bond's full price to the benchmark yield curve are usually called "effective durations."

- Macaulay duration is the weighted average of the time to receipt of coupon interest and principal payments, in which the weights are the shares of the full price corresponding to each payment. This statistic is annualized by dividing by the periodicity (number of coupon payments or compounding periods in a year).

- Modified duration provides a linear estimate of the percentage price change for a bond given a change in its yield-to-maturity.

- Approximate modified duration approaches modified duration as the change in the yield-to-maturity approaches zero.

- Effective duration is very similar to approximate modified duration. The difference is that approximate modified duration is a yield duration statistic that measures interest rate risk in terms of a change in the bond's own yield-to-maturity, whereas effective duration is a curve duration statistic that measures interest rate risk assuming a parallel shift in the benchmark yield curve.

- Key rate duration is a measure of a bond's sensitivity to a change in the benchmark yield curve at specific maturity segments. Key rate durations can be used to measure a bond's sensitivity to changes in the shape of the yield curve.

- Bonds with an embedded option do not have a meaningful internal rate of return because future cash flows are contingent on interest rates. Therefore, effective duration is the appropriate interest rate risk measure, not modified duration.

- The effective duration of a traditional (option-free) fixed-rate bond is its sensitivity to the benchmark yield curve, which can differ from its sensitivity to its own yield-to-maturity. Therefore, modified duration and effective duration on a traditional (option-free) fixed-rate bond are not necessarily equal.

- During a coupon period, Macaulay and modified durations decline smoothly in a "saw-tooth" pattern, assuming the yield-to-maturity is constant. When the coupon payment is made, the durations jump upward.

- Macaulay and modified durations are inversely related to the coupon rate and the yield-to-maturity.

- Time-to-maturity and Macaulay and modified durations are *usually* positively related. They are *always* positively related on bonds priced at par or at a premium above par value. They are *usually* positively related on bonds priced at a discount below par value. The exception is on long-term, low-coupon bonds, on which it is possible to have a lower duration than on an otherwise comparable shorter-term bond.

- The presence of an embedded call option reduces a bond's effective duration compared with that of an otherwise comparable non-callable bond. The reduction in the effective duration is greater when interest rates are low and the issuer is more likely to exercise the call option.

- The presence of an embedded put option reduces a bond's effective duration compared with that of an otherwise comparable non-putable bond. The reduction in the effective duration is greater when interest rates are high and the investor is more likely to exercise the put option.

- The duration of a bond portfolio can be calculated in two ways: (1) the weighted average of the time to receipt of *aggregate* cash flows and (2) the weighted average of the durations of individual bonds that compose the portfolio.

- The first method to calculate portfolio duration is based on the cash flow yield, which is the internal rate of return on the aggregate cash flows. It cannot be used for bonds with embedded options or for floating-rate notes.

- The second method is simpler to use and quite accurate when the yield curve is relatively flat. Its main limitation is that it assumes a parallel shift in the yield curve in that the yields on all bonds in the portfolio change by the same amount.

- Money duration is a measure of the price change in terms of units of the currency in which the bond is denominated.

- The price value of a basis point (PVBP) is an estimate of the change in the full price of a bond given a 1 bp change in the yield-to-maturity.

- Modified duration is the primary, or first-order, effect on a bond's percentage price change given a change in the yield-to-maturity. Convexity is the secondary, or second-order, effect. It indicates the change in the modified duration as the yield-to-maturity changes.

- Money convexity is convexity times the full price of the bond. Combined with money duration, money convexity estimates the change in the full price of a bond in units of currency given a change in the yield-to-maturity.

- Convexity is a positive attribute for a bond. Other things being equal, a more convex bond appreciates in price more than a less convex bond when yields fall and depreciates less when yields rise.

- Effective convexity is the second-order effect on a bond price given a change in the benchmark yield curve. It is similar to approximate convexity. The difference is that approximate convexity is based on a yield-to-maturity change and effective convexity is based on a benchmark yield curve change.

- Callable bonds have negative effective convexity when interest rates are low. The increase in price when the benchmark yield is reduced is less in absolute value than the decrease in price when the benchmark yield is raised.

- The change in a bond price is the product of (1) the impact per basis-point change in the yield-to-maturity and (2) the number of basis points in the yield change. The first factor is estimated by duration and convexity. The second factor depends on yield volatility.

- The investment horizon is essential in measuring the interest rate risk on a fixed-rate bond.

- For a particular assumption about yield volatility, the Macaulay duration indicates the investment horizon for which coupon reinvestment risk and market price risk offset each other. The assumption is a one-time parallel shift to the yield curve in which the yield-to-maturity and coupon reinvestment rates change by the same amount in the same direction.

- When the investment horizon is greater than the Macaulay duration of the bond, coupon reinvestment risk dominates price risk. The investor's risk is to lower interest rates. The duration gap is negative.

- When the investment horizon is equal to the Macaulay duration of the bond, coupon reinvestment risk offsets price risk. The duration gap is zero.

- When the investment horizon is less than the Macaulay duration of the bond, price risk dominates coupon reinvestment risk. The investor's risk is to higher interest rates. The duration gap is positive.

- Credit risk involves the probability of default and degree of recovery if default occurs, whereas liquidity risk refers to the transaction costs associated with selling a bond.

- For a traditional (option-free) fixed-rate bond, the same duration and convexity statistics apply if a change occurs in the benchmark yield or a change occurs in the spread. The change in the spread can result from a change in credit risk or liquidity risk.

- In practice, there often is interaction between changes in benchmark yields and in the spread over the benchmark.

PRACTICE PROBLEMS

1   A "buy-and-hold" investor purchases a fixed-rate bond at a discount and holds the security until it matures. Which of the following sources of return is *least likely* to contribute to the investor's total return over the investment horizon, assuming all payments are made as scheduled?

   A   Capital gain

   B   Principal payment

   C   Reinvestment of coupon payments

2   Which of the following sources of return is *most likely* exposed to interest rate risk for an investor of a fixed-rate bond who holds the bond until maturity?

   A   Capital gain or loss

   B   Redemption of principal

   C   Reinvestment of coupon payments

3   An investor purchases a bond at a price above par value. Two years later, the investor sells the bond. The resulting capital gain or loss is measured by comparing the price at which the bond is sold to the:

   A   carrying value.

   B   original purchase price.

   C   original purchase price value plus the amortized amount of the premium.

The following information relates to Problems 4–6

An investor purchases a nine-year, 7% annual coupon payment bond at a price equal to par value. After the bond is purchased and before the first coupon is received, interest rates increase to 8%. The investor sells the bond after five years. Assume that interest rates remain unchanged at 8% over the five-year holding period.

4   Per 100 of par value, the future value of the reinvested coupon payments at the end of the holding period is *closest* to:

   A   35.00.

   B   40.26.

   C   41.07.

5   The capital gain/loss per 100 of par value resulting from the sale of the bond at the end of the five-year holding period is *closest* to a:

   A   loss of 8.45.

   B   loss of 3.31.

   C   gain of 2.75.

6   Assuming that all coupons are reinvested over the holding period, the investor's five-year horizon yield is *closest* to:

   A   5.66%.

These questions were developed by Danny Hassett, CFA (Cedar Hill, TX, USA), Lou Lemos, CFA (Louisville, KY, USA), and Bin Wang, CFA (Austin, TX, USA). Copyright © 2013 by CFA Institute.

B 6.62%.

C 7.12%.

---

7 An investor buys a three-year bond with a 5% coupon rate paid annually. The bond, with a yield-to-maturity of 3%, is purchased at a price of 105.657223 per 100 of par value. Assuming a 5-basis point change in yield-to-maturity, the bond's approximate modified duration is *closest* to:

A 2.78.

B 2.86.

C 5.56.

8 Which of the following statements about duration is correct? A bond's:

A effective duration is a measure of yield duration.

B modified duration is a measure of curve duration.

C modified duration cannot be larger than its Macaulay duration.

9 An investor buys a 6% annual payment bond with three years to maturity. The bond has a yield-to-maturity of 8% and is currently priced at 94.845806 per 100 of par. The bond's Macaulay duration is *closest* to:

A 2.62.

B 2.78.

C 2.83.

10 The interest rate risk of a fixed-rate bond with an embedded call option is *best* measured by:

A effective duration.

B modified duration.

C Macaulay duration.

11 Which of the following is *most* appropriate for measuring a bond's sensitivity to shaping risk?

A key rate duration

B effective duration

C modified duration

12 A Canadian pension fund manager seeks to measure the sensitivity of her pension liabilities to market interest rate changes. The manager determines the present value of the liabilities under three interest rate scenarios: a base rate of 7%, a 100 basis point increase in rates up to 8%, and a 100 basis point drop in rates down to 6%. The results of the manager's analysis are presented below:

Interest Rate Assumption	Present Value of Liabilities
6%	CAD 510.1 million
7%	CAD 455.4 million
8%	CAD 373.6 million

The effective duration of the pension fund's liabilities is *closest* to:

A 1.49.

B 14.99.

C 29.97.

13 Which of the following statements about Macaulay duration is correct?

A   A bond's coupon rate and Macaulay duration are positively related.

B   A bond's Macaulay duration is inversely related to its yield-to-maturity.

C   The Macaulay duration of a zero-coupon bond is less than its time-to-maturity.

14 Assuming no change in the credit risk of a bond, the presence of an embedded put option:

A   reduces the effective duration of the bond.

B   increases the effective duration of the bond.

C   does not change the effective duration of the bond.

15 A bond portfolio consists of the following three fixed-rate bonds. Assume annual coupon payments and no accrued interest on the bonds. Prices are per 100 of par value.

Bond	Maturity	Market Value	Price	Coupon	Yield-to-Maturity	Modified Duration
A	6 years	170,000	85.0000	2.00%	4.95%	5.42
B	10 years	120,000	80.0000	2.40%	4.99%	8.44
C	15 years	100,000	100.0000	5.00%	5.00%	10.38

The bond portfolio's modified duration is *closest* to:

A   7.62.

B   8.08.

C   8.20.

16 A limitation of calculating a bond portfolio's duration as the weighted average of the yield durations of the individual bonds that compose the portfolio is that it:

A   assumes a parallel shift to the yield curve.

B   is less accurate when the yield curve is less steeply sloped.

C   is not applicable to portfolios that have bonds with embedded options.

17 Using the information below, which bond has the *greatest* money duration per 100 of par value assuming annual coupon payments and no accrued interest?

Bond	Time-to-Maturity	Price Per 100 of Par Value	Coupon Rate	Yield-to-Maturity	Modified Duration
A	6 years	85.00	2.00%	4.95%	5.42
B	10 years	80.00	2.40%	4.99%	8.44
C	9 years	85.78	3.00%	5.00%	7.54

A   Bond A

B   Bond B

C   Bond C

18 A bond with exactly nine years remaining until maturity offers a 3% coupon rate with annual coupons. The bond, with a yield-to-maturity of 5%, is priced at 85.784357 per 100 of par value. The estimated price value of a basis point for the bond is *closest* to:

A   0.0086.

B   0.0648.

C   0.1295.

19 The "second-order" effect on a bond's percentage price change given a change in yield-to-maturity can be *best* described as:

A duration.

B convexity.

C yield volatility.

20 A bond is currently trading for 98.722 per 100 of par value. If the bond's yield-to-maturity (YTM) rises by 10 basis points, the bond's full price is expected to fall to 98.669. If the bond's YTM decreases by 10 basis points, the bond's full price is expected to increase to 98.782. The bond's approximate convexity is *closest* to:

A 0.071.

B 70.906.

C 1,144.628.

21 A bond has an annual modified duration of 7.020 and annual convexity of 65.180. If the bond's yield-to-maturity decreases by 25 basis points, the expected percentage price change is *closest* to:

A 1.73%.

B 1.76%.

C 1.78%.

22 A bond has an annual modified duration of 7.140 and annual convexity of 66.200. The bond's yield-to-maturity is expected to increase by 50 basis points. The expected percentage price change is *closest* to:

A −3.40%.

B −3.49%.

C −3.57%.

23 Which of the following statements relating to yield volatility is *most* accurate? If the term structure of yield volatility is downward sloping, then:

A short-term rates are higher than long-term rates.

B long-term yields are more stable than short-term yields.

C short-term bonds will always experience greater price fluctuation than long-term bonds.

24 The holding period for a bond at which the coupon reinvestment risk offsets the market price risk is *best* approximated by:

A duration gap.

B modified duration.

C Macaulay duration.

25 When the investor's investment horizon is less than the Macaulay duration of the bond she owns:

A the investor is hedged against interest rate risk.

B reinvestment risk dominates, and the investor is at risk of lower rates.

C market price risk dominates, and the investor is at risk of higher rates.

26 An investor purchases an annual coupon bond with a 6% coupon rate and exactly 20 years remaining until maturity at a price equal to par value. The investor's investment horizon is eight years. The approximate modified duration of the bond is 11.470 years. The duration gap at the time of purchase is *closest* to:

A −7.842.

B   3.470.

C   4.158.

27   A manufacturing company receives a ratings upgrade and the price increases on its fixed-rate bond. The price increase was *most likely* caused by a(n):

    A   decrease in the bond's credit spread.

    B   increase in the bond's liquidity spread.

    C   increase of the bond's underlying benchmark rate.

SOLUTIONS

1 A is correct. A capital gain is least likely to contribute to the investor's total return. There is no capital gain (or loss) because the bond is held to maturity. The carrying value of the bond at maturity is par value, the same as the redemption amount. When a fixed-rate bond is held to its maturity, the investor receives the principal payment at maturity. This principal payment is a source of return for the investor. A fixed-rate bond pays periodic coupon payments, and the reinvestment of these coupon payments is a source of return for the investor. The investor's total return is the redemption of principal at maturity and the sum of the reinvested coupons.

2 C is correct. Because the fixed-rate bond is held to maturity (a "buy-and-hold" investor), interest rate risk arises entirely from changes in coupon reinvestment rates. Higher interest rates increase income from reinvestment of coupon payments, and lower rates decrease income from coupon reinvestment. There will not be a capital gain or loss because the bond is held until maturity. The carrying value at the maturity date is par value, the same as the redemption amount. The redemption of principal does not expose the investor to interest rate risk. The risk to a bond's principal is credit risk.

3 A is correct. Capital gains (losses) arise if a bond is sold at a price above (below) its constant-yield price trajectory. A point on the trajectory represents the carrying value of the bond at that time. That is, the capital gain/loss is measured from the bond's carrying value, the point on the constant-yield price trajectory, and not from the original purchase price. The carrying value is the original purchase price plus the amortized amount of the discount if the bond is purchased at a price below par value. If the bond is purchased at a price above par value, the carrying value is the original purchase price minus (not plus) the amortized amount of the premium. The amortized amount for each year is the change in the price between two points on the trajectory.

4 C is correct. The future value of reinvested cash flows at 8% after five years is closest to 41.07 per 100 of par value.

$$\left[7 \times (1.08)^4\right] + \left[7 \times (1.08)^3\right] + \left[7 \times (1.08)^2\right] + \left[7 \times (1.08)^1\right] + 7 = 41.0662$$

The 6.07 difference between the sum of the coupon payments over the five-year holding period (35) and the future value of the reinvested coupons (41.07) represents the "interest-on-interest" gain from compounding.

5 B is correct. The capital loss is closest to 3.31 per 100 of par value. After five years, the bond has four years remaining until maturity and the sale price of the bond is 96.69, calculated as:

$$\frac{7}{(1.08)^1} + \frac{7}{(1.08)^2} + \frac{7}{(1.08)^3} + \frac{107}{(1.08)^4} = 96.69$$

The investor purchased the bond at a price equal to par value (100). Because the bond was purchased at a price equal to its par value, the carrying value is par value. Therefore, the investor experienced a capital loss of 96.69 − 100 = −3.31.

6 B is correct. The investor's five-year horizon yield is closest to 6.62%. After five years, the sale price of the bond is 96.69 (from problem 5) and the future value of reinvested cash flows at 6% is 41.0662 (from problem 4) per 100 of par value. The total return is 137.76 (= 41.07 + 96.69), resulting in a realized five-year horizon yield of 6.62%:

$$100.00 = \frac{137.76}{(1+r)^5}, \quad r = 0.0662$$

7   A is correct. The bond's approximate modified duration is closest to 2.78. Approximate modified duration is calculated as:

$$\text{ApproxModDur} = \frac{(PV_-) - (PV_+)}{2 \times (\Delta \text{Yield}) \times (PV_0)}$$

Lower yield-to-maturity by 5 bps to 2.95%:

$$PV_- = \frac{5}{(1+0.0295)^1} + \frac{5}{(1+0.0295)^2} + \frac{5+100}{(1+0.0295)^3} = 105.804232$$

Increase yield-to-maturity by 5 bps to 3.05%:

$$PV_+ = \frac{5}{(1+0.0305)^1} + \frac{5}{(1+0.0305)^2} + \frac{5+100}{(1+0.0305)^3} = 105.510494$$

$PV_0 = 105.657223, \Delta \text{Yield} = 0.0005$

$$\text{ApproxModDur} = \frac{105.804232 - 105.510494}{2 \times 0.0005 \times 105.657223} = 2.78$$

8   C is correct. A bond's modified duration cannot be larger than its Macaulay duration. The formula for modified duration is:

$$\text{ModDur} = \frac{\text{MacDur}}{1+r}$$

where r is the bond's yield-to-maturity per period. A bond's yield-to-maturity has an effective lower bound of 0, and thus the denominator $1 + r$ term has a lower bound of 1. Therefore, ModDur will typically be less than MacDur.

Effective duration is a measure of curve duration. Modified duration is a measure of yield duration.

9   C is correct. The bond's Macaulay duration is closest to 2.83. Macaulay duration (MacDur) is a weighted average of the times to the receipt of cash flow. The weights are the shares of the full price corresponding to each coupon and principal payment.

Period	Cash Flow	Present Value	Weight	Period × Weight
1	6	5.555556	0.058575	0.058575
2	6	5.144033	0.054236	0.108472
3	106	84.146218	0.887190	2.661570
		94.845806	1.000000	2.828617

Thus, the bond's Macaulay duration (MacDur) is 2.83.

Alternatively, Macaulay duration can be calculated using the following closed-form formula:

$$\text{MacDur} = \left\{ \frac{1+r}{r} - \frac{1 + r + [N \times (c - r)]}{c \times [(1+r)^N - 1] + r} \right\} - (t/T)$$

$$\text{MacDur} = \left\{ \frac{1.08}{0.08} - \frac{1.08 + \left[3 \times (0.06 - 0.08)\right]}{0.06 \times \left[(1.08)^3 - 1\right] + 0.08} \right\} - 0$$

$$\text{MacDur} = 13.50 - 10.67 = 2.83$$

10 A is correct. The interest rate risk of a fixed-rate bond with an embedded call option is best measured by effective duration. A callable bond's future cash flows are uncertain because they are contingent on future interest rates. The issuer's decision to call the bond depends on future interest rates. Therefore, the yield-to-maturity on a callable bond is not well defined. Only effective duration, which takes into consideration the value of the call option, is the appropriate interest rate risk measure. Yield durations like Macaulay and modified durations are not relevant for a callable bond because they assume no changes in cash flows when interest rates change.

11 A is correct. Key rate duration is used to measure a bond's sensitivity to a shift at one or more maturity segments of the yield curve which result in a change to yield curve shape. Modified and effective duration measure a bond's sensitivity to parallel shifts in the entire curve.

12 B is correct. The effective duration of the pension fund's liabilities is closest to 14.99. The effective duration is calculated as follows:

$$\text{EffDur} = \frac{(PV_-) - (PV_+)}{2 \times (\Delta \text{Curve}) \times (PV_0)}$$

$PV_0 = 455.4$, $PV_+ = 373.6$, $PV_- = 510.1$, and $\Delta \text{Curve} = 0.0100$.

$$\text{EffDur} = \frac{510.1 - 373.6}{2 \times 0.0100 \times 455.4} = 14.99$$

13 B is correct. A bond's yield-to-maturity is inversely related to its Macaulay duration: The higher the yield-to-maturity, the lower its Macaulay duration and the lower the interest rate risk. A higher yield-to-maturity decreases the weighted average of the times to the receipt of cash flow, and thus decreases the Macaulay duration.

A bond's coupon rate is inversely related to its Macaulay duration: The lower the coupon, the greater the weight of the payment of principal at maturity. This results in a higher Macaulay duration. Zero-coupon bonds do not pay periodic coupon payments; therefore, the Macaulay duration of a zero-coupon bond is its time-to-maturity.

14 A is correct. The presence of an embedded put option reduces the effective duration of the bond, especially when rates are rising. If interest rates are low compared with the coupon rate, the value of the put option is low and the impact of the change in the benchmark yield on the bond's price is very similar to the impact on the price of a non-putable bond. But when benchmark interest rates rise, the put option becomes more valuable to the investor. The ability to sell the bond at par value limits the price depreciation as rates rise. The presence of an embedded put option reduces the sensitivity of the bond price to changes in the benchmark yield, assuming no change in credit risk.

15 A is correct. The portfolio's modified duration is closest to 7.62. Portfolio duration is commonly estimated as the market-value-weighted average of the yield durations of the individual bonds that compose the portfolio.

The total market value of the bond portfolio is 170,000 + 120,000 + 100,000 = 390,000.

The portfolio duration is 5.42 × (170,000/390,000) + 8.44 × (120,000/390,000) + 10.38 × (100,000/390,000) = 7.62.

16 A is correct. A limitation of calculating a bond portfolio's duration as the weighted average of the yield durations of the individual bonds is that this measure implicitly assumes a parallel shift to the yield curve (all rates change by the same amount in the same direction). In reality, interest rate changes frequently result in a steeper or flatter yield curve. This approximation of the "theoretically correct" portfolio duration is *more* accurate when the yield curve is flatter (less steeply sloped). An advantage of this approach is that it can be used with portfolios that include bonds with embedded options. Bonds with embedded options can be included in the weighted average using the effective durations for these securities.

17 B is correct. Bond B has the greatest money duration per 100 of par value. Money duration (MoneyDur) is calculated as the annual modified duration (AnnModDur) times the full price (PV^{Full}) of the bond including accrued interest. Bond B has the highest money duration per 100 of par value.

$$MoneyDur = AnnModDur \times PV^{Full}$$

$$MoneyDur \text{ of Bond A} = 5.42 \times 85.00 = 460.70$$

$$MoneyDur \text{ of Bond B} = 8.44 \times 80.00 = 675.20$$

$$MoneyDur \text{ of Bond C} = 7.54 \times 85.78 = 646.78$$

18 B is correct. The PVBP is closest to 0.0648. The formula for the price value of a basis point is:

$$PVBP = \frac{(PV_-) - (PV_+)}{2}$$

where:

PVBP = price value of a basis point
PV_- = full price calculated by lowering the yield-to-maturity by one basis point
PV_+ = full price calculated by raising the yield-to-maturity by one basis point

Lowering the yield-to-maturity by one basis point to 4.99% results in a bond price of 85.849134:

$$PV_- = \frac{3}{(1 + 0.0499)^1} + \cdots + \frac{3 + 100}{(1 + 0.0499)^9} = 85.849134$$

Increasing the yield-to-maturity by one basis point to 5.01% results in a bond price of 85.719638:

$$PV_+ = \frac{3}{(1 + 0.0501)^1} + \cdots + \frac{3 + 100}{(1 + 0.0501)^9} = 85.719638$$

$$PVBP = \frac{85.849134 - 85.719638}{2} = 0.06475$$

Alternatively, the PVBP can be derived using modified duration:

$$\text{ApproxModDur} = \frac{(PV_-) - (PV_+)}{2 \times (\Delta\text{Yield}) \times (PV_0)}$$

$$\text{ApproxModDur} = \frac{85.849134 - 85.719638}{2 \times 0.0001 \times 85.784357} = 7.548$$

PVBP = 7.548 × 85.784357 × 0.0001 = 0.06475

19 B is correct. Convexity measures the "second order" effect on a bond's percentage price change given a change in yield-to-maturity. Convexity adjusts the percentage price change estimate provided by modified duration to better approximate the true relationship between a bond's price and its yield-to-maturity which is a curved line (convex).

Duration estimates the change in the bond's price along the straight line that is tangent to this curved line ("first order" effect). Yield volatility measures the magnitude of changes in the yields along the yield curve.

20 B is correct. The bond's approximate convexity is closest to 70.906. Approximate convexity (ApproxCon) is calculated using the following formula:

$$\text{ApproxCon} = [PV_- + PV_+ - (2 \times PV_0)]/(\Delta\text{Yield}^2 \times PV_0)$$

where:

PV_- = new price when the yield-to-maturity is decreased
PV_+ = new price when the yield-to-maturity is increased
PV_0 = original price
ΔYield = change in yield-to-maturity

$$\text{ApproxCon} = [98.782 + 98.669 - (2 \times 98.722)]/(0.001^2 \times 98.722) = 70.906$$

21 C is correct. The expected percentage price change is closest to 1.78%. The convexity-adjusted percentage price change for a bond given a change in the yield-to-maturity is estimated by:

$$\%\Delta PV^{Full} \approx [-\text{AnnModDur} \times \Delta\text{Yield}] + [0.5 \times \text{AnnConvexity} \times (\Delta\text{Yield})^2]$$

$$\%\Delta PV^{Full} \approx [-7.020 \times (-0.0025)] + [0.5 \times 65.180 \times (-0.0025)^2] = 0.017754,$$ or 1.78%

22 B is correct. The expected percentage price change is closest to −3.49%. The convexity-adjusted percentage price change for a bond given a change in the yield-to-maturity is estimated by:

$$\%\Delta PV^{Full} \approx [-\text{AnnModDur} \times \Delta\text{Yield}] + [0.5 \times \text{AnnConvexity} \times (\Delta\text{Yield})^2]$$

$$\%\Delta PV^{Full} \approx [-7.140 \times 0.005] + [0.5 \times 66.200 \times (0.005)^2] = -0.034873,$$ or −3.49%

23 B is correct. If the term structure of yield volatility is downward-sloping, then short-term bond yields-to-maturity have greater volatility than for long-term bonds. Therefore, long-term yields are more stable than short-term yields. Higher volatility in short-term rates does not necessarily mean that the level of short-term rates is higher than long-term rates. With a downward-sloping term structure of yield volatility, short-term bonds will not always experience greater price fluctuation than long-term bonds. The estimated percentage change in a bond price depends on the modified duration and convexity as well as on the yield-to-maturity change.

24 C is correct. When the holder of a bond experiences a one-time parallel shift in the yield curve, the Macaulay duration statistic identifies the number of years necessary to hold the bond so that the losses (or gains) from coupon reinvestment offset the gains (or losses) from market price changes. The duration gap is the difference between the Macaulay duration and the investment horizon. Modified duration approximates the percentage price change of a bond given a change in its yield-to-maturity.

25 C is correct. The duration gap is equal to the bond's Macaulay duration minus the investment horizon. In this case, the duration gap is positive, and price risk dominates coupon reinvestment risk. The investor risk is to higher rates.

The investor is hedged against interest rate risk if the duration gap is zero; that is, the investor's investment horizon is equal to the bond's Macaulay duration. The investor is at risk of lower rates only if the duration gap is negative; that is, the investor's investment horizon is greater than the bond's Macaulay duration. In this case, coupon reinvestment risk dominates market price risk.

26 C is correct. The duration gap is closest to 4.158. The duration gap is a bond's Macaulay duration minus the investment horizon. The approximate Macaulay duration is the approximate modified duration times one plus the yield-to-maturity. It is 12.158 (= 11.470 × 1.06).

Given an investment horizon of eight years, the duration gap for this bond at purchase is positive: 12.158 − 8 = 4.158. When the investment horizon is less than the Macaulay duration of the bond, the duration gap is positive, and price risk dominates coupon reinvestment risk.

27 A is correct. The price increase was most likely caused by a decrease in the bond's credit spread. The ratings upgrade most likely reflects a lower expected probability of default and/or a greater level of recovery of assets if default occurs. The decrease in credit risk results in a smaller credit spread. The increase in the bond price reflects a decrease in the yield-to-maturity due to a smaller credit spread. The change in the bond price was not due to a change in liquidity risk or an increase in the benchmark rate.

Fundamentals of Credit Analysis

by Christopher L. Gootkind, CFA

LEARNING OUTCOMES

Mastery	The candidate should be able to:
☐	a. describe credit risk and credit-related risks affecting corporate bonds;
☐	b. describe seniority rankings of corporate debt and explain the potential violation of the priority of claims in a bankruptcy proceeding;
☐	c. distinguish between corporate issuer credit ratings and issue credit ratings and describe the rating agency practice of "notching";
☐	d. explain risks in relying on ratings from credit rating agencies;
☐	e. explain the components of traditional credit analysis;
☐	f. calculate and interpret financial ratios used in credit analysis;
☐	g. evaluate the credit quality of a corporate bond issuer and a bond of that issuer, given key financial ratios of the issuer and the industry;
☐	h. describe factors that influence the level and volatility of yield spreads;
☐	i. calculate the return impact of spread changes;
☐	j. explain special considerations when evaluating the credit of high yield, sovereign, and municipal debt issuers and issues.

INTRODUCTION

With bonds outstanding worth many trillions of US dollars, the debt markets play a critical role in the global economy. Companies and governments raise capital in the debt market to fund current operations; buy equipment; build factories, roads,

The author would like to thank several of his Fixed Income Research colleagues at Loomis, Sayles & Company for their assistance with this reading: Paul Batterton, Diana Leader-Cramer, Diana Monteith, Shannon O'Mara, CFA, and Laura Sarlo, CFA.

bridges, airports, and hospitals; acquire assets, and so on. By channeling savings into productive investments, the debt markets facilitate economic growth. Credit analysis has a crucial function in the debt capital markets—efficiently allocating capital by properly assessing credit risk, pricing it accordingly, and repricing it as risks change. How do fixed-income investors determine the riskiness of that debt, and how do they decide what they need to earn as compensation for that risk?

This reading will cover the basic principles of credit analysis, which may be broadly defined as the process by which credit risk is evaluated. Readers will be introduced to such concepts as the definition of credit risk, credit ratings, components of traditional credit analysis, measures of cash flow, key financial metrics and ratios, bond issuer creditworthiness comparisons within a given industry as well as across industries, the pricing of credit risk in the bond market, and the effects of changes in prices on holding period return.

The reading focuses primarily on analysis of corporate debt; however, credit analysis of sovereign and sub-sovereign (municipal) government bonds will also be addressed. Structured finance, a segment of the debt markets that includes securities backed by pools of assets, such as residential and commercial mortgages as well as other consumer loans, will not be covered here.

The key components of credit risk—default probability and loss severity—are introduced in the next section along with such credit-related risks as spread risk, credit migration risk, and liquidity risk. Section 3 discusses the relationship between credit risk and the capital structure of the firm. Credit ratings and the role of credit rating agencies are addressed in Section 4. Section 5 focuses on the process of analyzing the credit risk of corporations, whereas Section 6 examines the impact of credit spreads on risk and return. Special considerations applicable to the analysis of (i) high-yield (low-quality) corporate bonds and (ii) government bonds are presented in Section 7. Section 8 gives a brief summary, and a set of review questions concludes the reading.

2 CREDIT RISK

Credit risk is the risk of loss resulting from the borrower (issuer of debt) failing to make full and timely payments of interest and/or principal. Credit risk has two components. The first is known as **default risk**, or **default probability**, which is the probability that a borrower defaults—that is, fails to meet its obligation to make full and timely payments of principal and interest, according to the terms of the debt security. The second component is **loss severity** (also known as "loss given default") in the event of default—that is, the portion of a bond's value (including unpaid interest) an investor loses. A default can lead to losses of various magnitudes. In most instances, in the event of default, bondholders will recover some value, so there will not be a total loss on the investment. Thus, credit risk is reflected in the distribution of potential losses that may arise if the investor is not paid in full and on time. Although it is sometimes important to consider the entire distribution of potential losses and their respective probabilities,[1] it is often convenient to summarize the risk with a single default probability and loss severity and to focus on the **expected loss**:

Expected loss = Default probability × Loss severity given default

---

[1] As an example, careful attention to the full distribution of potential losses is important in analyzing credit risk in structured finance products because the various tranches usually share unequally in the credit losses on the underlying loans or securities. A particular tranche typically bears none of the losses up to some level of underlying losses, then it bears all of the underlying losses until the tranche is wiped out. Losses on a "thin" tranche are very likely to be either 0 percent or 100 percent, with relatively small probabilities on intermediate loss severities. This situation is not well described by a single "average" loss severity.

The loss severity, and hence the expected loss, can be expressed as either a monetary amount (e.g., €450,000) or as a percentage of the principal amount (e.g., 45 percent). The latter form is generally more useful for analysis because it is independent of the amount of investment. Loss severity is often expressed as (1 − Recovery rate), where the recovery rate is the percentage of the principal amount recovered in the event of default.

Because default risk (default probability) is quite low for most good quality debt issuers, bond investors tend to focus primarily on assessing this likelihood and devote less effort to assessing the potential loss severity arising from default. However, as an issuer's default risk rises, investors will focus more on what the recovery rate might be in the event of default. This issue will be discussed in more detail later. Other important forms of credit-related risk include the following:

- **Spread risk**. Corporate bonds and other "credit-risky" debt instruments typically trade at a yield premium, or spread, to bonds that have been considered "default-risk free," such as US Treasury bonds or German government bonds. Yield spreads, expressed in basis points, widen based on two primary factors: (1) a decline in an issuer's creditworthiness, sometimes referred to as credit migration or downgrade risk, and (2) an increase in **market liquidity risk**. These two risks are separate but frequently related.

- **Credit migration risk** or **downgrade risk**. This is the risk that a bond issuer's creditworthiness deteriorates, or migrates lower, leading investors to believe the risk of default is higher and thus causing the yield spreads on the issuer's bonds to widen and the price of its bonds to fall. The term "downgrade" refers to action by the major bond rating agencies, whose role will be covered in more detail in Section 4.

- **Market liquidity risk**. This is the risk that the price at which investors can actually transact—buying or selling—may differ from the price indicated in the market. To compensate investors for the risk that there may not be sufficient market liquidity for them to buy or sell bonds in the quantity they desire, the spread or yield premium on corporate bonds includes a market liquidity component, in addition to a credit risk component. Unlike stocks, which trade on exchanges, most markets bonds trade primarily over the counter, through broker–dealers trading for their own accounts. Their ability and willingness to make markets, as reflected in the bid–ask spread, is an important determinant of market liquidity risk. The two main issuer-specific factors that affect market liquidity risk are (1) the size of the issuer (that is, the amount of publicly traded debt an issuer has outstanding) and (2) the credit quality of the issuer. In general, the less debt an issuer has outstanding, the less frequently its debt trades, and thus the higher the market liquidity risk. And the lower the quality of the issuer, the higher the market liquidity risk.

During times of financial stress or crisis, such as in late 2008, market liquidity can decline sharply, causing yield spreads on corporate bonds, and other credit-risky debt, to widen and their prices to drop. Some research has been done on trying to quantify market liquidity risk,[2] and more is likely to be done in the aftermath of the financial crisis.

---

2 For example, see Francis A. Longstaff, Sanjay Mithal, and Eric Neis, "Corporate Yield Spreads: Default Risk or Liquidity? New Evidence from the Credit-Default Swap Market," NBER Working Paper No. 10418 (April 2004).

EXAMPLE 1

Defining Credit Risk

1 Which of the following *best* defines credit risk?
   A The probability of default times the severity of loss given default
   B The loss of principal and interest payments in the event of bankruptcy
   C The risk of not receiving full interest and principal payments on a timely basis

2 Which of the following is the *best* measure of credit risk?
   A The expected loss
   B The severity of loss
   C The probability of default

3 Which of the following is NOT credit or credit-related risk?
   A Default risk
   B Interest rate risk
   C Downgrade or credit migration risk

Solution to 1:

C is correct. Credit risk is the risk that the borrower will not make full and timely payments.

Solution to 2:

A is correct. The expected loss captures both of the key components of credit risk: (the product of) the likelihood of default and the loss severity in the event of default. Neither component alone fully reflects the risk.

Solution to 3:

B is correct. Bond price changes due to general interest rate movements are not considered credit risk.

---

3   CAPITAL STRUCTURE, SENIORITY RANKING, AND RECOVERY RATES

The various debt obligations of a given borrower will not necessarily all have the same **seniority ranking**, or priority of payment. In this section, we will introduce the topic of an issuer's capital structure and discuss the various types of debt claims that may arise from that structure, as well as their ranking and how those rankings can influence recovery rates in the event of default.

3.1 Capital Structure

The composition and distribution across operating units of a company's debt and equity—including bank debt, bonds of all seniority rankings, preferred stock, and common equity—is referred to as its **capital structure**. Some companies and industries have straightforward capital structures, with all the debt equally ranked and issued by one main operating entity. Other companies and industries, due to their frequent acquisitions and divestitures (e.g., media companies or conglomerates) or high levels of regulation (e.g., banks and utilities), tend to have more complicated capital structures. Companies in these industries often have many different subsidiaries, or operating companies, that have their own debt outstanding and parent holding companies that also issue debt, with different levels or rankings of seniority. Similarly, the cross-border operations of multi-national corporations tend to increase the complexity of their capital structures.

3.2 Seniority Ranking

Just as borrowers can issue debt with many different maturity dates and coupons, they can also have many different rankings in terms of seniority. The ranking refers to the priority of payment, with the most senior or highest-ranking debt having the first claim on the cash flows and assets of the issuer. This level of seniority can affect the value of an investor's claim in the event of default and restructuring. Broadly, there is **secured debt** and **unsecured debt**. Unsecured bonds are often referred to as debentures. Secured debt means the debtholder has a direct claim—a pledge from the issuer—on certain assets and their associated cash flows. Unsecured bondholders have only a general claim on an issuer's assets and cash flow. In the event of default, unsecured debtholders' claims rank below (i.e., get paid after) those of secured creditors[3] under what's known as the **priority of claims**.

Exhibit 1   Seniority Ranking

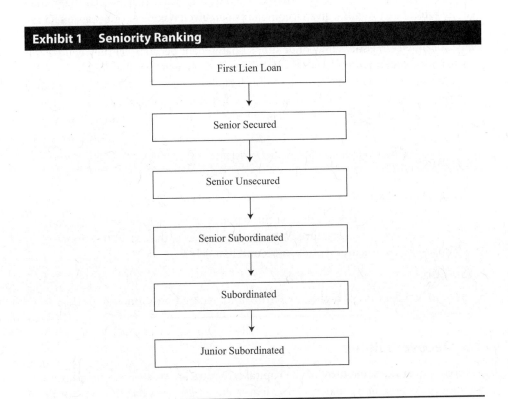

Within each category of debt, there are finer gradations of types and rankings. Within secured debt, there is first mortgage or first lien debt, which is the highest-ranked debt in terms of priority of repayment. **First mortgage debt** refers to the pledge of a specific property (e.g., a power plant for a utility or a specific casino for a

---

3 The term "creditors" is used throughout this reading to mean holders of debt instruments, such as bonds and bank loans. Unless specifically stated, it does not include such obligations as trade credit, tax liens, or employment-related obligations.

gaming company). **First lien debt** refers to a pledge of certain assets that could include buildings but might also include property and equipment, licenses, patents, brands, and so on. There can also be **second lien**, or even third lien, secured debt, which, as the name implies, has a secured interest in the pledged assets but ranks below first lien debt in both collateral protection and priority of payment.

Within unsecured debt, there can also be finer gradations and seniority rankings. The highest-ranked unsecured debt is senior unsecured debt. It is the most common type of all corporate bonds outstanding. Other, lower-ranked debt includes **subordinated debt** and junior subordinated debt. Among the various creditor classes, these obligations have among the lowest priority of claims and frequently have little or no recovery in the event of default. That is, their loss severity can be as high as 100 percent. (See Exhibit 1 for seniority ranking.) For regulatory and capital purposes, banks in Europe and the United States have issued debt and debt-like securities that rank even lower than subordinated debt[4] and are intended to provide a capital cushion in times of financial distress. Many of them did not work as intended during the financial crisis that began in 2008, and most were phased out, potentially to be replaced by more effective instruments that automatically convert to equity in certain circumstances.

There are many reasons why companies issue—and investors buy—debt with different seniority rankings. Issuers are interested in optimizing their cost of capital—finding the right mix of the various types of both debt and equity—for their industry and type of business. Issuers may offer secured debt because that is what the market (i.e., investors) may require, given a company's perceived riskiness, or because secured debt is generally lower cost due to the reduced credit risk inherent in its higher priority of claims. Or, issuers may offer subordinated debt because (1) they believe it is less expensive than issuing equity[5] (and doesn't dilute existing shareholders) and is typically less restrictive than issuing senior debt and (2) investors are willing to buy it because they believe the yield being offered is adequate compensation for the risk they perceive. Credit risk versus return will be discussed in more detail later in the reading.

EXAMPLE 2

Seniority Ranking

The Acme Company has senior unsecured bonds as well as both first and second lien debt in its capital structure. Which ranks higher with respect to priority of claims: senior unsecured bonds or second lien debt?

Solution:

Second lien debt ranks higher, by virtue of its secured position.

3.3 Recovery Rates

All creditors at the same level of the capital structure are treated as one class; thus, a senior unsecured bondholder whose debt is due in 30 years has the same pro rata claim in bankruptcy as one whose debt matures in six months. This provision is referred to as bonds ranking **pari passu** ("on an equal footing") in right of payment.

---

4 These have various names such as hybrids, trust preferred, and upper and lower Tier 2 securities. In some cases, the non-payment or deferral of interest does not constitute an event of default, and in other cases, they might convert into perpetual securities—that is, securities with no maturity date.

5 Debtholders require a lower return than equity holders because they have prior claims to an issuer's cash flow and assets. That is, the cost of debt is lower than the cost of equity. In most countries, this cost differential is even greater due to the tax deductibility of interest payments.

Defaulted debt will often continue to be traded by investors and broker–dealers based on their assessment that either in liquidation of the bankrupt company's assets or in some form of reorganization, the bonds will have some recovery value. In the case of reorganization, or restructuring (whether through formal bankruptcy or on a voluntary basis), new debt, equity, cash, or some combination thereof could be issued in exchange for the original defaulted debt.

As discussed, recovery rates vary by seniority of ranking in a company's capital structure, under the priority of claims treatment in bankruptcy. Over many decades, there have been enough defaults to generate statistically meaningful historical data on recovery rates by seniority ranking. Exhibit 2 provides recovery rates by seniority ranking for North American non-financial companies.[6] For example, as shown in Exhibit 2, investors on average recovered 51.6 percent of the value of senior unsecured debt that defaulted in 2009 but only 28.0 percent of the value of senior subordinated issues that defaulted that year.

Exhibit 2	Average Corporate Debt Recovery Rates Measured by Ultimate Recoveries					
	Emergence Year*			**Default Year**		
Seniority ranking	**2010**	**2009**	**1987–2010**	**2010**	**2009**	**1987–2010**
Senior secured	64.4%	59.0%	63.5%	56.3%	65.6%	63.5%
Senior unsecured	51.0%	48.3%	49.2%	26.5%	51.6%	49.2%
Senior subordinated	20.5%	26.2%	29.4%	21.7%	28.0%	29.4%
Subordinated	53.4%	34.3%	29.3%	0.0%	58.3%	29.3%
Junior subordinated	NA	0.5%	18.4%	NA	0.0%	18.4%

* Emergence year is typically the year the defaulted company emerges from bankruptcy. Default year data refer to the recovery rate of debt that defaulted in that year (i.e., 2009 and 2010) or range of years (i.e., 1987–2010). Data are for North American nonfinancial companies. NA indicates not available.
Source: Based on data from Moody's Investors Service, Inc.'s Ultimate Recovery Database.

There are a few things worth noting:

1 **Recovery rates can vary widely by industry.** Companies that go bankrupt in industries that are in secular decline (e.g., newspaper publishing) will most likely have lower recovery rates than those that go bankrupt in industries merely suffering from a cyclical economic downturn.

2 **Recovery rates can also vary depending on when they occur in a credit cycle.**[7] As shown in Exhibit 3, at or near the bottom of a credit cycle—which is almost always closely linked with an economic cycle—recoveries will tend

---

6 The recovery rates shown for default years 2009 and 2010 should be viewed as preliminary because some of the numbers are based on the relatively small number of defaults for which final recovery had been determined at the time of the Moody's study. For example, the 2010 senior unsecured recovery rate reflects only two bonds.
7 Credit cycles describe the changing availability—and pricing—of credit. When the economy is strong or improving, the willingness of lenders to extend credit, and on favorable terms, is high. Conversely, when the economy is weak or weakening, lenders pull back, or "tighten" credit, by making it less available and more expensive. This frequently contributes to asset values, such as real estate, declining, causing further economic weakness send higher defaults. Central banks frequently survey banks to assess how "tight" or "loose" their lending standards are. This information, as well as the level and direction of corporate bond default rates, helps provide a good sense of where one is in the credit cycle.

to be lower than at other times in the credit cycle. This is because there will be many companies closer to, or already in, bankruptcy, causing valuations to be depressed.

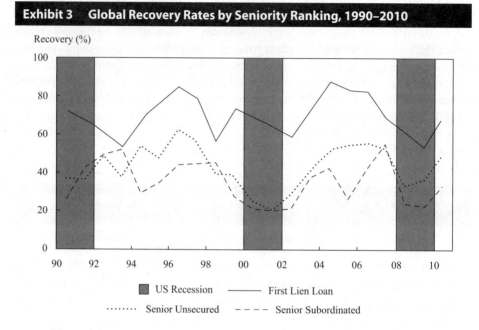

Exhibit 3   Global Recovery Rates by Seniority Ranking, 1990–2010

Source: Based on data from Moody's Investors Service, Inc's Ultimate Recovery Database.

3   **These recovery rates are averages**. In fact, there can be large variability, both across industries, as noted above, as well as across companies within a given industry. Factors might include composition and proportion of debt across an issuer's capital structure. An abundance of secured debt will lead to smaller recovery rates on lower-ranked debt.

Understanding recovery rates is important because they are a key component of credit analysis and risk. Recall that the best measure of credit risk is expected loss—that is, probability of default times loss severity given default. And loss severity equals (1 – Recovery rate). Having an idea how much one can lose in the event of default is a critical factor in valuing credit, particularly lower-quality credit, as the default risk rises.

Priority of claims: Not always absolute. The priority of claims in bankruptcy—the idea that the highest-ranked creditors get paid out first, followed by the next level, and on down, like a waterfall—is well established and is often described as "absolute." In principle, in the event of bankruptcy or liquidation:

■   Creditors with a secured claim have the right to the value of that specific property before any other claim. If the value of the pledged property is less than the amount of the claim, then the difference becomes a senior unsecured claim.

■   Unsecured creditors have a right to be paid in full before holders of equity interests (common and preferred shareholders) receive value on their interests.

■   Senior creditors take priority over junior (i.e., subordinated) creditors. A creditor is senior unless expressly subordinated.

In practice, however, more junior creditors and even shareholders may receive some consideration without more senior creditors being paid in full. Why might this be the case? In bankruptcy, there are different classes of claimants, and all classes that are impaired (that is, receive less than full claim) get to vote to confirm the plan of reorganization. This vote is subject to the absolute priority of claims. Either by consent of the various parties or by the judge's order, however, absolute priority may not be strictly enforced in the final plan. There may be disputes over the value of various assets in the bankruptcy estate (e.g., what is a plant, or a patent portfolio, worth?) or the present value or timing of payouts. For example, what is the value of the new debt I'm receiving for my old debt of a reorganized company before it emerges from bankruptcy?

Resolution of these disputes takes time, and cases can drag on for months and years. In the meantime, during bankruptcy, substantial expenses are being incurred for legal and accounting fees, and the value of the company may be declining as key employees leave, customers go elsewhere, and so on. Thus, to avoid the time, expense, and uncertainty over disputed issues, such as the value of property in the estate, the legality of certain claims, and so forth, the various claimants have a strong incentive to negotiate and compromise. This frequently leads to more junior creditors and other claimants (e.g., even shareholders) receiving more consideration than they are legally entitled to.

It's worth noting that in the United States, the bias is toward reorganization and recovery of companies in bankruptcy, whereas in other jurisdictions, such as the United Kingdom, the bias is toward liquidation of companies in bankruptcy and maximizing value to the banks and other senior creditors. It's also worth noting that bankruptcy and bankruptcy laws are very complex and can vary greatly by country, so it is difficult to generalize about how creditors will fare. As shown in the earlier chart, there is huge variability in recovery rates for defaulted debt. Every case is different.

EXAMPLE 3

Priority of Claims

1 Under which circumstance is a subordinated bondholder *most likely* to recover some value in a bankruptcy without a senior creditor getting paid in full? When:

 A absolute priority rules are enforced.

 B the various classes of claimants agree to it.

 C the company is liquidated rather than reorganized.

2 In the event of bankruptcy, claims at the same level of the capital structure are:

 A on an equal footing, regardless of size, maturity, or time outstanding.

 B paid in the order of maturity from shortest to longest, regardless of size or time outstanding.

 C paid on a first-in, first-out (FIFO) basis so that the longest-standing claims are satisfied first, regardless of size or maturity.

Solution to 1:

B is correct. All impaired classes get to vote on the reorganization plan. Negotiation and compromise are often preferable to incurring huge legal and accounting fees in a protracted bankruptcy process that would otherwise reduce the value of the estate for all claimants. This process may allow junior creditors (e.g., subordinated bondholders) to recover some value even though more senior creditors do not get paid in full.

Solution to 2:

A is correct. All claims at the same level of the capital structure are pari passu (on an equal footing).

4   RATINGS AGENCIES, CREDIT RATINGS, AND THEIR ROLE IN THE DEBT MARKETS

The major credit ratings agencies—Moody's Investors Service ("Moody's"), Standard & Poor's ("S&P"), and to a somewhat lesser extent, Fitch Ratings ("Fitch")—play a central, if somewhat controversial, role in the credit markets. For the vast majority of outstanding bonds, at least two of the agencies provide ratings: a symbol-based measure of the potential risk of default of a particular bond or issuer of debt. In the public and quasi-public bond markets,[8] issuers won't offer, and investors won't buy, bonds that do not carry ratings from Moody's and/or S&P (and Fitch). This practice applies for all types of bonds—government or sovereign, government related,[9] supra-national,[10] corporate, municipal, and mortgage- and asset-backed debt. How did the ratings agencies attain such a dominant position in the credit markets? What are credit ratings, and what do they mean? How does the market use credit ratings? What are the risks of relying solely or excessively on credit ratings?

The history of the major ratings agencies goes back more than 100 years. John Moody began publishing credit analysis and opinions on US railroads in 1909. S&P published its first ratings in 1916. They have grown in size and prominence since then. Many bond investors like the fact that there are independent analysts who meet with the issuer and often have access to material, non-public information, such as financial projections that investors cannot receive, to aid in the analysis. What has also proven very attractive to investors is that credit ratings provide direct and easy comparability of the relative credit riskiness of all bond issuers, within and across industries and bond types, although there is some debate about ratings comparability across the types of bonds.[11]

Several factors have led to the near universal use of credit ratings in the bond markets and the dominant role of the major credit rating agencies. These factors include the following:

- Independent assessment of credit risk
- Ease of comparison across bond issuers, issues, and market segments
- Regulatory and statutory reliance and usage[12]

---

8 That is, underwritten by investment banks, as opposed to privately placed on a "best efforts" basis.

9 These are government agencies or instrumentalities that may have implicit or explicit guarantees from the government. Examples include Ginnie Mae in the United States and *Pfandbriefe* in Germany.

10 Supranationals are international financial institutions, such as the International Bank for Reconstruction and Development ("World Bank"), the Asian Development Bank, and the European Investment Bank, that are established by treaty and owned by several member governments.

11 Investigations conducted after the late 2008/early 2009 financial crisis suggested that, for a given rating category, municipal bonds have experienced a lower historical incidence of default than corporate debt.

12 It is common for regulations to make reference to ratings issued by recognized credit ratings agencies. In light of the role played by the agencies in the sub-prime mortgage crisis, however, some jurisdictions (e.g., the United States) are moving to remove such references. Nonetheless, the so-called Basel III global framework for bank supervision developed beginning in 2009 retains such references.

- Issuer payment for ratings[13]
- Huge growth of debt markets
- Development and expansion of bond portfolio management and the accompanying bond indices.

However, in the aftermath of the financial crisis of 2008–2009, when the rating agencies were blamed for at least contributing to the crisis with their overly optimistic ratings on securities backed by subprime mortgages, there were attempts to reduce the role and dominant positions of the major credit rating agencies. New rules, regulations, and legislation were passed to require the agencies to be more transparent, reduce conflicts of interest, and stimulate more competition. Challenging the hegemony of Moody's, S&P, and Fitch, additional credit rating agencies have emerged, while existing ones that have a strong presence in their home markets but are not so well known globally, such as Dominion Bond Rating Service (DBRS) in Canada and Mikuni & Co. in Japan, have tried to raise their profiles. The market dominance of the biggest credit rating agencies, however, remains largely intact.

4.1 Credit Ratings

The three major global credit rating agencies—Moody's, S&P, and Fitch—use similar, symbol-based ratings that are basically an assessment of a bond issue's risk of default. Exhibit 4 shows their long-term ratings ranked from highest to lowest.[14]

Exhibit 4	Long-Term Ratings Matrix: Investment Grade vs. Non-Investment Grade			
		Moody's	**S&P**	**Fitch**
Investment Grade	High-Quality Grade	Aaa	AAA	AAA
		Aa1	AA+	AA+
		Aa2	AA	AA
		Aa3	AA–	AA–
	Upper-Medium Grade	A1	A+	A+
		A2	A	A
		A3	A–	A–
	Low-Medium Grade	Baa1	BBB+	BBB+
		Baa2	BBB	BBB
		Baa3	BBB–	BBB–

(continued)

---

13 The "issuer pay" model allows the distribution of ratings to a broad universe of investors and undoubtedly facilitated widespread reliance on ratings. It is controversial, however, because some believe it creates a conflict of interest among the rating agency, the investor, and the issuer. Studies suggest, however, that ratings are not biased upward and alternate payment models, such as "investor pays," have their own shortcomings, including the "free rider" problem inherent in a business where information is widely available and freely shared. So, despite its potential problems, and some calls for a new payment model, the "issuer pay" model remains entrenched in the market.

14 The rating agencies also provide ratings on short-term debt instruments, such as bank deposits and commercial paper. However, they use different scales: From the highest to lowest rating, Moody's uses P-1, P-2, P-3; S&P uses A-1+, A-1, A-2, A-3; Fitch uses F-1, F-2, F-3. Below that is not prime. Short-term ratings are typically used by money market funds, with the vast majority of the instruments they own rated in the highest (or in the case of S&P, the highest or second-highest) category. These top ratings basically map to a single-A or higher long-term rating.

Exhibit 4   (Continued)

		Moody's	S&P	Fitch
Non-Investment Grade "Junk" or "High Yield"	Low Grade or Speculative Grade	Ba1	BB+	BB+
		Ba2	BB	BB
		Ba3	BB–	BB–
		B1	B+	B+
		B2	B	B
		B3	B–	B–
		Caa1	CCC+	CCC+
		Caa2	CCC	CCC
		Caa3	CCC–	CCC–
		Ca	CC	CC
		C	C	C
	Default	C	D	D

Bonds rated triple-A (Aaa or AAA) are said to be "of the highest quality, with minimal credit risk"[15] and thus have extremely low probabilities of default. Double-A (Aa or AA) rated bonds are referred to as "high-quality grade" and are also regarded as having very low default risk. Bonds rated single-A are referred to as "upper-medium grade." Baa (Moody's) or BBB (S&P and Fitch) are called "low-medium grade." Bonds rated Baa3/BBB– or higher are called "investment grade." Bonds rated Ba1 or lower by Moody's and BB+ or lower by S&P and Fitch, respectively, have speculative credit characteristics and increasingly higher default risk. As a group, these bonds are referred to in a variety of ways: "low grade," "speculative grade," "non-investment grade," "below investment grade," "high yield," and, in an attempt to reflect the extreme level of risk, some observers refer to these bonds as "junk bonds." The D rating is reserved for securities that are already in default in S&P's and Fitch's scales. For Moody's, bonds rated C are likely, but not necessarily, in default. Generally, issuers of bonds rated investment grade are more consistently able to access the debt markets and can borrow at lower interest rates than those rated below investment grade.

In addition, rating agencies will typically provide outlooks on their respective ratings—positive, stable, or negative—and may provide other indicators on the potential direction of their ratings under certain circumstances, such as "On Review for a Downgrade" or "On CreditWatch for an Upgrade."[16] It should also be noted that, in support of the ratings they publish, the rating agencies also provide extensive written commentary and financial analysis on the obligors they rate, as well as summary industry statistics.

4.2 Issuer vs. Issue Ratings

Rating agencies will typically provide both issuer and issue ratings, particularly as they relate to corporate debt. Terminology used to distinguish between issuer and issue ratings includes corporate family rating (CFR) and corporate credit rating (CCR) or issuer credit rating and issue credit rating. An issuer credit rating is meant to address

---

15 Moody's Investors Service, "Ratings Symbols and Definitions" (July 2011).
16 Additional detail on their respective ratings definitions, methodologies, and criteria can be found on each of the major rating agency's websites: www.moodys.com, www.standardandpoors.com, and www.fitch.com.

an obligor's overall creditworthiness—its ability and willingness to make timely payments of interest and principal on its debt. The issuer credit rating usually applies to its senior unsecured debt.

Issue ratings refer to specific financial obligations of an issuer and take into consideration such factors as ranking in the capital structure (e.g., secured or subordinated). Although **cross-default provisions**, whereby events of default such as non-payment of interest[17] on one bond trigger default on all outstanding debt,[18] implies the same default probability for all issues, specific issues may be assigned different credit ratings—higher or lower—due to a ratings adjustment methodology known as **notching**.

Notching. For the rating agencies, likelihood of default is the primary factor in assigning their ratings. However, there are secondary factors as well. These factors include the priority of payment in the event of a default (e.g., secured versus senior unsecured versus subordinated) as well as potential loss severity in the event of default. Another rating factor is so-called **structural subordination**, which can arise when a corporation with a holding company structure has debt at both its parent holding company and operating subsidiaries. Debt at the operating subsidiaries will get serviced by the cash flow and assets of the subsidiaries before funds can be passed ("upstreamed") to the holding company to service debt at that level.

Recognizing these different payment priorities, and thus the potential for higher (or lower) loss severity in the event of default, the rating agencies have adopted a notching process whereby their credit ratings on issues can be moved up or down from the issuer rating (senior unsecured). As a general rule, the higher the senior unsecured rating, the smaller the notching adjustment will be. The reason behind this is that the higher the rating, the lower the perceived risk of default, so the need to "notch" the rating to capture the potential difference in loss severity is greatly reduced. For lower-rated credits, however, the risk of default is greater and thus the potential difference in loss from a lower (or higher) priority ranking is a bigger consideration in assessing an issue's credit riskiness. Thus, the rating agencies will typically apply larger rating adjustments. For example, S&P applies the following notching guidelines:

> As default risk increases, the concern over what can be recovered takes on greater relevance and, therefore, greater rating significance. Accordingly, the LGD [Loss Given Default] aspect of ratings is given more weight as one moves down the rating spectrum. For example, subordinated debt can be rated up to two notches below a noninvestment grade corporate credit rating, but one notch at most if the corporate credit rating is investment grade. (In the same vein, issues of companies with an 'AAA' rating need not be notched at all.)[19]

Exhibit 5 is an example of S&P's notching criteria, as applied to United Rentals, Inc. (URI). URI is a US-based equipment rental company whose corporate credit—and senior unsecured—rating is single-B. Note how the company's subordinated debt is rated two notches lower, at CCC+.

Exhibit 5	URI's S&P Ratings Detail, 27 May 2011
Corporate credit rating	B/Stable/–
Preferred stock (1 issue)	CCC

(continued)

---

17 This issue will be covered in greater detail in the section on covenants.

18 Nearly all bonds have a cross-default provision. Rare exceptions to this cross-default provision include the deeply subordinated, debt-like securities referenced earlier in this reading.

19 Standard & Poor's, "Rating Each Issue," in *Corporate Ratings Criteria 2008* (New York: Standard and Poor's, 2008):89.

Exhibit 5 (Continued)	
Senior unsecured (2 issues)	B
Subordinated (4 issues)	CCC+

Source: Based on data from Standard & Poor's Financial Services, LLC.

4.3 Risks in Relying on Agency Ratings

The dominant position of the rating agencies in the global debt markets, and the near-universal use of their credit ratings on debt securities, suggests that investors believe they do a good job assessing credit risk. In fact, with a few exceptions (e.g., too high ratings on US subprime mortgage-backed securities issued in the mid-2000s, which turned out to be much riskier than expected), their ratings have proved quite accurate as a relative measure of default risk. For example, Exhibit 6 shows historical S&P one-year global corporate default rates by rating category from 1991 to 2010.[20]

Exhibit 6	Global Corporate Annual Default Rates by Rating Category (%)						
	AAA	AA	A	BBB	BB	B	CCC/C
1991	0.00	0.00	0.00	0.55	1.68	13.84	33.87
1992	0.00	0.00	0.00	0.00	0.00	6.99	30.19
1993	0.00	0.00	0.00	0.00	0.70	2.62	13.33
1994	0.00	0.00	0.14	0.00	0.27	3.08	16.67
1995	0.00	0.00	0.00	0.17	0.98	4.59	28.00
1996	0.00	0.00	0.00	0.00	0.67	2.91	4.17
1997	0.00	0.00	0.00	0.25	0.19	3.49	12.00
1998	0.00	0.00	0.00	0.41	0.97	4.61	42.86
1999	0.00	0.17	0.18	0.19	0.95	7.28	32.35
2000	0.00	0.00	0.26	0.37	1.25	7.73	34.12
2001	0.00	0.00	0.35	0.33	3.13	11.24	44.55
2002	0.00	0.00	0.00	1.01	2.81	8.11	44.12
2003	0.00	0.00	0.00	0.23	0.56	4.01	32.93
2004	0.00	0.00	0.08	0.00	0.53	1.56	15.33
2005	0.00	0.00	0.00	0.07	0.20	1.73	8.94
2006	0.00	0.00	0.00	0.00	0.30	0.81	12.38
2007	0.00	0.00	0.00	0.00	0.19	0.25	15.09
2008	0.00	0.38	0.38	0.48	0.78	3.98	26.26
2009	0.00	0.00	0.22	0.54	0.72	10.38	48.68
2010	0.00	0.00	0.00	0.00	0.55	0.80	22.27
Mean	0.00	0.03	0.08	0.23	0.87	5.00	25.91

---

20 S&P uses a static pool methodology here. It measures the percentage of issues that defaulted in a given calendar year based on how they were rated at the beginning of the year.

Exhibit 6	(Continued)						
	AAA	AA	A	BBB	BB	B	CCC/C
Max	0.00	0.38	0.38	1.01	3.13	13.84	48.68
Min	0.00	0.00	0.00	0.00	0.00	0.25	4.17

Source: Based on data from Standard & Poor's Financial Services, LLC.

As Exhibit 6 shows, the highest-rated bonds have extremely low default rates. With very few exceptions, the lower the rating, the higher the annual rate of default, with bonds rated CCC and lower experiencing the highest default rates by far. There are limitations and risks, however, to relying on credit rating agency ratings, including the following:

1 **Credit ratings can be very dynamic**. That is, over a long time period (e.g., many years), credit ratings can migrate—move up or down—significantly from the time of bond issuance. Using Standard & Poor's data, Exhibit 7 shows the average three-year migration (or "transition") by rating from 1981 to 2010. Note that the higher the credit rating, the greater the ratings stability. Even for AAA rated credits, however, only about 70 percent (70 percent in the United States and 68 percent globally) of the time did ratings remain in that rating category over a three-year period. (Of course, AAA rated credits can have their ratings move in only one direction—down.) A very small fraction of AAA rated credits became non-investment grade or defaulted within three years. For single-B rated credits, only about 40 percent (40 percent in the United States and 39 percent globally) of the time did ratings remain in that rating category over three-year periods. This observation about the dynamism of credit ratings isn't meant to be a criticism of the rating agencies. It is meant to demonstrate that creditworthiness can and does change—up or down—and that bond investors should not assume an issuer's credit rating will remain the same from time of purchase through the entire holding period.

Exhibit 7	Average Three-Year Corporate Transition Rates, 1981–2010 (%)								
From/To	AAA	AA	A	BBB	BB	B	CCC/C	D	NR*
United States									
AAA	69.75	16.60	2.47	0.38	0.21	0.13	0.13	0.17	10.15
AA	1.32	65.46	17.75	2.52	0.47	0.42	0.04	0.20	11.82
A	0.11	4.34	67.32	12.05	1.79	0.69	0.14	0.42	13.16
BBB	0.04	0.47	8.61	62.21	8.03	2.47	0.35	1.22	16.60
BB	0.02	0.10	0.78	10.95	43.95	13.59	1.40	5.60	23.61
B	0.01	0.06	0.42	1.08	10.06	40.27	4.94	15.79	27.37
CCC/C	0.00	0.00	0.38	0.98	1.97	12.19	13.47	43.98	27.02
Global									
AAA	68.09	18.85	2.46	0.34	0.14	0.08	0.11	0.14	9.78
AA	1.30	65.78	18.59	2.24	0.37	0.26	0.03	0.15	11.29
A	0.08	4.53	67.31	11.84	1.42	0.57	0.12	0.34	13.80
BBB	0.03	0.41	8.90	61.42	7.44	2.12	0.36	1.20	18.12
BB	0.01	0.07	0.67	11.31	43.97	12.06	1.37	5.17	25.37

(continued)

Exhibit 7   (Continued)

From/To	AAA	AA	A	BBB	BB	B	CCC/C	D	NR*
B	0.01	0.05	0.34	1.08	10.90	38.93	4.61	15.25	28.84
CCC/C	0.00	0.00	0.29	0.91	2.05	16.04	12.39	40.47	27.85

*NR means not rated—that is, certain corporate issuers were no longer rated by S&P. This could occur for a variety of reasons, including issuers paying off their debt and no longer needing ratings.
Source: Based on data from Standard & Poor's Financial Services, LLC.

2   **Rating agencies are not infallible**. The mis-rating of billions of dollars of subprime-backed mortgage securities is one example. Other examples include the mis-ratings of US companies Enron and WorldCom and European issuer Parmalat. Like many investors, the rating agencies did not see the accounting fraud being committed in those companies.

3   **Other types of so-called idiosyncratic or event risk are difficult to capture in ratings**. Examples of this include litigation risk, such as that which can affect tobacco companies, or environmental and business risks faced by chemical companies and utility power plants. This would also include such unpredictable events as the earthquake and tsunami that hit Japan in March 2011 and its credit impact on debt issuer Tokyo Electric Power Company (TEPCO). Leveraged transactions, such as debt-financed acquisitions and large stock buybacks, are often difficult to anticipate and thus to capture in credit ratings.

4   **Ratings tend to lag market pricing of credit**. Bond prices and credit spreads frequently move more quickly because of changes in perceived creditworthiness than rating agencies change their ratings (or even outlooks) up or down. Bond prices and relative valuations can move every day, whereas bond ratings, appropriately, don't change that often. Even over long time periods, however, credit ratings can badly lag changes in bond prices. Exhibit 8 shows the price and Moody's rating of a bond from US automaker Ford Motor Company before, during, and after the financial crisis in 2008. Note how the bond's price moved down sharply well before Moody's downgraded its credit rating—multiple times—and also how the bond's price began to recover—and kept recovering—well before Moody's upgraded its credit rating on Ford debt.

Exhibit 8   Ford Motor Company Senior Unsecured Debt: Price vs. Moody's Rating Since 2005

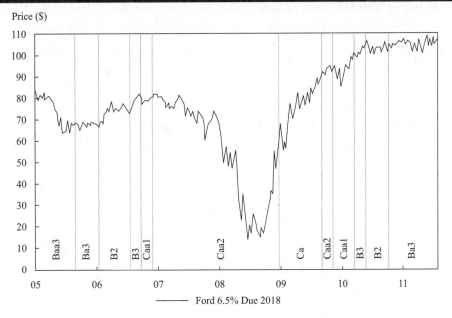

Sources: Data based on Bloomberg Finance L.P. and Moody's Investors Service.

Moreover, particularly for certain speculative-grade credits, two bonds with similar ratings may trade at very different valuations. This is partly a result of the fact that credit ratings primarily try to assess the risk of default, whereas for low-quality credits, the market begins focusing more on expected loss (default probability times loss severity). So, bonds from two separate issuers with comparable (high) risk of default but different recovery rates may have similar ratings but trade at significantly different dollar prices.[21]

Thus, bond investors who wait for rating agencies to change their ratings before making buy and sell decisions in their portfolios may be at risk of underperforming other investors who make portfolio decisions in advance of—or not solely based on—rating agency changes.

As described, there are risks in relying on credit rating agency ratings when investing in bonds. Thus, while the credit rating agencies will almost certainly continue to play a significant role in the bond markets, it's important for investors to perform their own credit analyses and draw their own conclusions regarding the credit risk of a given debt issue or issuer.

EXAMPLE 4

Credit Ratings

1   Using the S&P ratings scale, investment grade bonds carry which of the following ratings?

   A   AAA to EEE

---

21 See Christopher L. Gootkind, "Improving Credit Risk Analysis," in *Fixed-Income Management for the 21st Century* (Charlottesville, VA: Association for Investment Management and Research, 2002).

    B BBB– to CCC

    C AAA to BBB–

2 Using both Moody's and S&P ratings, which of the following pairs of ratings is considered high yield, also known as "below investment grade," "speculative grade," or "junk"?

    A Baa1/BBB–

    B B3/CCC+

    C Baa3/BB+

3 What is the difference between an issuer rating and an issue rating?

    A The issuer rating applies to all of an issuer's bonds, whereas the issue rating considers a bond's seniority ranking.

    B The issuer rating is an assessment of an issuer's overall creditworthiness, whereas the issue rating is always higher than the issuer rating.

    C The issuer rating is an assessment of an issuer's overall creditworthiness, typically reflected as the senior unsecured rating, whereas the issue rating considers a bond's seniority ranking (e.g., secured or subordinated).

4 Based on the practice of notching by the rating agencies, a subordinated bond from a company with an issuer rating of BB would likely carry what rating?

    A B+

    B BB

    C BBB–

5 The fixed-income portfolio manager you work with asked you why a bond from an issuer you cover didn't rise in price when it was upgraded by Fitch from B+ to BB. Which of the following is the *most likely* explanation?

    A Bond prices never react to rating changes.

    B The bond doesn't trade often so the price hasn't adjusted to the rating change yet.

    C The market was expecting the rating change, and so it was already "priced in" to the bond.

6 Amalgamated Corp. and Widget Corp. each have bonds outstanding with similar coupons and maturity dates. Both bonds are rated B2, B–, and B by Moody's, S&P, and Fitch, respectively. The bonds, however, trade at very different prices—the Amalgamated bond trades at €89, whereas the Widget bond trades at €62. What is the *most likely* explanation of the price (and yield) difference?

    A Widget's credit ratings are lagging the market's assessment of the company's credit deterioration.

    B The bonds have similar risks of default (as reflected in the ratings), but the market believes the Amalgamated bond has a higher expected loss in the event of default.

    C The bonds have similar risks of default (as reflected in the ratings), but the market believes the Widget bond has a higher expected recovery rate in the event of default.

Solution to 1:

C is correct.

Solution to 2:

B is correct. Note that issuers with ratings such as Baa3/BB+ (answer C) are called "crossovers" because one rating is investment grade (the Moody's rating of Baa3) and the other is high yield (the S&P rating of BB+).

Solution to 3:

C is correct.

Solution to 4:

A is correct. The subordinated bond would have its rating notched lower than the company's BB rating, probably by two notches, reflecting the higher weight given to loss severity for below-investment-grade credits.

Solution to 5:

C is correct. The market was anticipating the rating upgrade and had already priced it in. Bond prices often do react to rating changes, particularly multi-notch ones. Even if bonds don't trade, their prices adjust based on dealer quotations given to bond pricing services.

Solution to 6:

A is correct. Widget's credit ratings are probably lagging behind the market's assessment of its deteriorating creditworthiness. Answers B and C both state the situation backwards. If the market believed that the Amalgamated bond had a higher expected loss given default, then that bond would be trading at a lower, not a higher, price. Similarly, if the market believed that the Widget bond had a higher expected recovery rate in the event of default, then that bond would be trading at a higher, not a lower, price.

TRADITIONAL CREDIT ANALYSIS: CORPORATE DEBT SECURITIES

5

The goal of credit analysis is to assess an issuer's ability to satisfy its debt obligations, including bonds and other indebtedness, such as bank loans. These debt obligations are contracts, the terms of which specify the interest rate to be paid, the frequency and timing of payments, the maturity date, and the covenants that describe the permissible and required actions of the borrower. Because corporate bonds are contracts, enforceable by law, credit analysts generally assume an issuer's willingness to pay and concentrate instead on assessing its ability to pay. Thus, the main focus in credit analysis is to understand a company's ability to generate cash flow over the term of its debt obligations. In so doing, analysts must assess both the credit quality of the company and the fundamentals of the industry in which the company operates. Traditional credit analysis considers the sources, predictability, and sustainability of cash generated by a company to service its debt obligations. This section will focus on corporate credit analysis; in particular, it will emphasize non-financial companies. Financial institutions have very different business models and funding profiles from industrial and utility companies.

5.1 Credit Analysis vs. Equity Analysis: Similarities and Differences

The above description of credit analysis suggests credit and equity analyses should be very similar; in many ways, they are. There are motivational differences, however, between equity and fixed-income investors that are an important aspect of credit analysis. Strictly speaking, management works for the shareholders of a company. Its primary objective is to maximize the value of the company for its owners. In contrast, management's legal duty to its creditors—including bondholders—is to meet the terms of the governing contracts. Growth in the value of a corporation from rising profits and cash flow accrues to the shareholders, while the best outcome for bondholders is to receive full, timely payment of interest and repayment of principal when due. Conversely, shareholders are more exposed to the decline in value as a company's future earnings power and cash flow decline because bondholders have a priority claim on cash flow and assets. Should a company's earnings power and cash flow decline to the extent that it can no longer make its debt payments, however, then bondholders are at risk of loss as well.

In summary, in exchange for a priority claim on cash flow and assets, bondholders do not share in the growth in value of a company (except to the extent that its creditworthiness improves) but have downside risk in the event of default. In contrast, shareholders have theoretically unlimited upside opportunity, but in the event of default, their investment is typically wiped out before the bondholders suffer a loss. This is very similar to the type of payoff patterns seen in financial options. In fact, in recent years, a great deal of credit modeling has been predicated on a sophisticated application of financial option theory and mathematics. Although it is beyond the scope of this present introduction to the subject, it is an expanding area of interest to both institutional investors and rating agencies.

Thus, although the analysis is similar in many respects for both equity and credit, equity analysts are interested in the strategies and investments that will increase a company's value and grow earnings per share. They then compare that earnings power and growth potential with that of other companies in a given industry. Credit analysts will look more at the downside risk by measuring and assessing the sustainability of a company's cash flow relative to its debt levels and interest expense. Importantly for credit analysts, the balance sheet will show the composition of an issuer's debt—the overall amount, how much is coming due and when, and the distribution by seniority ranking. In general, equity analysts will focus more on income and cash flow statements, whereas credit analysts tend to focus more on the balance sheet and cash flow statements.

5.2 The Four Cs of Credit Analysis: A Useful Framework

Traditionally, it has been convenient to consider what is often called the "four Cs of credit analysis":[22]

- Capacity
- Collateral
- Covenants
- Character

---

[22] There is no unique list of Cs. In addition to those listed here, one may see "capital" and/or "conditions" on a particular author's list of four (or five) Cs. Conditions typically refers to overall economic conditions. Capital refers to the company's accumulated capital and its specific capital assets and is essentially subsumed within the categories of capacity and collateral. Keep in mind that the list of Cs is a convenient way to summarize the important aspects of the analysis, not a checklist to be applied mechanically.

Capacity refers to the ability of the borrower to make its debt payments on time; this is the focus of this section. **Collateral** refers to the quality and value of the assets supporting the issuer's indebtedness. **Covenants** are the terms and conditions of lending agreements that the issuer must comply with. **Character** refers to the quality of management. Each of these will now be covered in greater detail.

5.2.1 *Capacity*

Capacity is the ability of a borrower to service its debt. To determine that, credit analysis, in a process similar to equity analysis, starts with industry analysis and then turns to examination of the specific issuer (company analysis).

Industry structure.   A useful framework for analyzing industry structure was developed by business school professor and consultant Michael Porter.[23] The framework looks at the five major forces of competition in an industry:

1 **Power of suppliers.** An industry that relies on just a few suppliers has greater credit risk than an industry that has multiple suppliers. Industries and companies with just a few suppliers have limited negotiating power to keep them from raising prices to their customers, whereas industries that have many suppliers can play them off against each other to keep prices in check.

2 **Power of buyers/customers.** Industries that rely heavily on just a few main customers have greater risk because the negotiating power lies with the buyers. For example, a toolmaker that sells 50 percent of its products to one large global retailer has limited negotiating power with its principal customer.

3 **Barriers to entry.** Industries with high entry barriers tend to have lower risk than industries with low entry barriers because competition may not be as fierce and pricing power is strong or at least sufficient. High entry barriers can take many forms, including high capital investment, such as in aerospace; large, established distribution systems, such as in auto dealerships; patent protection, such as in technology or pharmaceutical industries; or a high degree of regulation, such as in utilities.

4 **Substitution risk.** Industries (and companies) that offer products and services that provide great value to their customers, and for which there are not good or cost-competitive substitutes, typically have strong pricing power, generate substantial cash flows, and represent less credit risk than other industries or companies. Certain (patent-protected) drugs are an example, as are large jet airplanes. Over time, however, disruptive technologies and inventions can increase substitution risk. For example, years ago, airplanes began displacing many trains and steamships. Newspapers were considered to have a nearly unassailable market position until television and then the internet became substitutes for how people received news and information. Over time, recorded music has shifted from records to tapes, to compact discs, to mp3s and other forms of digital media.

5 **Level of competition.** Industries with heavy competition—characterized by a large number of participants, none of whom has significant market share—tend to have less cash flow predictability and, therefore, represent higher credit risk than industries with less competition. Regulation can play an important role in competition as well. For example, regulated utilities typically have a monopoly

---

23 Michael E. Porter, *Competitive Strategy: Techniques for Analyzing Industries and Competitors* (New York; The Free Press, 1980).

position in a given market, which results in relatively stable and predictable cash flows. (They often carry higher debt levels, however, as a result of that monopoly position and the more stable cash flows.)

It is also important to consider how companies in an industry generate revenues and earn profits. Is it an industry with high fixed costs and capital investment or one with modest fixed costs? These structures generate revenues and earn profits in very different ways. Two of the best examples of industries with high fixed costs, also referred to as "having high operating leverage," are airlines and hotels. Many of their costs are fixed—running a hotel, flying a plane—so they cannot easily cut costs. If an insufficient number of people stay at a company's hotel, or fly in its planes, then the company will have trouble covering its fixed costs and will be at risk of losing lots of money. With high occupancy, however, revenues are strong, fixed costs get more than covered, and the company can earn substantial profits.

Industry fundamentals.   After understanding an industry's structure, the next step is to assess its fundamentals, including its sensitivity to macroeconomic factors, its growth prospects, its profitability, and its business need—or lack thereof—for strong credit quality. Judgments about these can be made by looking at the following:

- *Cyclical or non-cyclical.* This is a crucial assessment because industries that are cyclical—that is, have greater sensitivity to broader economic performance—have more volatile revenues, margins, and cash flows and thus are inherently riskier than non-cyclical industries. Consumer product and health care companies are typically considered non-cyclical, whereas auto and steel companies can be very cyclical. Companies in cyclical industries should carry lower levels of debt relative to their ability to generate cash flow over an economic cycle than companies in less-cyclical or non-cyclical industries.

- *Growth prospects.* Although growth is typically a greater focus for equity analysts than for credit analysts, bond investors have an interest in growth as well. Industries that have little or no growth tend to consolidate via mergers and acquisitions. Depending upon how these are financed (e.g., using stock or debt) and the economic benefits (or lack thereof) of the merger, they may or may not be favorable to corporate bond investors. Weaker competitors in slow-growth industries may begin to struggle financially, adversely affecting their creditworthiness.

- *Published industry statistics.* Analysts can get a strong sense of an industry's fundamentals and performance by researching statistics that are published by and available from a number of different sources, including the rating agencies, investment banks, industry publications, and frequently, government agencies.

Company fundamentals.   Following analysis of an industry's structure and fundamentals, the next step is to assess the fundamentals of the company: the corporate borrower. Analysts should examine the following:

- Competitive position
- Track record/operating history
- Management's strategy and execution
- Ratios and ratio analysis

Competitive position.   Based on their knowledge of the industry structure and fundamentals, analysts assess a company's competitive position within the industry. What is its market share? How has it changed over time: Is it increasing, decreasing, holding steady? Is it well above (or below) its peers? How does it compare with respect to cost structure? How might it change its competitive position? What sort of financing might that require?

Track record/Operating history. How has the company performed over time? It's useful to go back several years and analyze the company's financial performance, perhaps during times of both economic growth and contraction. What are the trends in revenues, profit margins, and cash flow? Capital expenditures represent what percent of revenues? What are the trends on the balance sheet—use of debt versus equity? Was this track record developed under the current management team? If not, when did the current management team take over?

Management's strategy and execution. What is management's strategy for the company: to compete and to grow? Does it make sense, and is it plausible? How risky is it, and how differentiated is it from its industry peers? Is it venturing into unrelated businesses? Does the analyst have confidence in management's ability to execute? What is management's track record, both at this company and at previous ones? Credit analysts also want to know and understand how management's strategy will affect its balance sheet. Does management plan to manage the balance sheet prudently, in a manner that doesn't adversely affect bondholders? Analysts can learn about management's strategy from reading comments, discussion, and analysis that are included with financial statements filed with appropriate regulators, listening to conference calls about earnings or other big announcements (e.g., acquisitions), going to company websites to find earnings releases and copies of slides of presentations at various industry conferences, visiting and speaking with the company, and so on.

EXAMPLE 5

Industry and Company Analysis

1 Given a hotel company, a chemical company, and a consumer products company, which is *most likely* to be able to support a high debt load over an economic cycle?

   A The hotel company, because people need a place to stay when they travel.

   B The chemical company, because chemicals are a key input to many products.

   C The consumer products company, because consumer products are typically resistant to recessions.

2 Why do heavily regulated monopoly companies, such as utilities, carry high debt loads?

   A Regulators require them to carry high debt loads.

   B They generate strong and stable cash flows, enabling them to support high levels of debt.

   C They are not very profitable and need to borrow heavily to maintain their plant and equipment.

3 XYZ Corp. manufactures a commodity product in a highly competitive industry in which no company has significant market share and where there are low barriers to entry. Which of the following *best* describes XYZ's ability to take on substantial debt?

   A Its ability is very limited because companies in industries with those characteristics generally cannot support high debt loads.

> **B**   Its ability is strong because companies in industries with those charac-
> teristics generally have high margins and cash flows that can support
> significant debt.
>
> **C**   We don't have enough information to answer the question.
>
> ## Solution to 1:
>
> C is correct. Consumer products companies are considered non-cyclical, whereas
> hotel and chemical companies are more cyclical and thus more vulnerable to
> economic downturns.
>
> ## Solution to 2:
>
> B is correct. Because such monopolies' financial returns are generally dictated
> by the regulators, they generate consistent cash flows and are, therefore, able to
> support high debt levels. In addition, significant barriers to entry arising from
> high capital investment requirements and the regulatory process can contribute
> to debt capacity.
>
> ## Solution to 3:
>
> A is correct. Companies in industries with those characteristics typically have
> low margins and limited cash flow and thus cannot support high debt levels.

Ratios and ratio analysis.   To provide context and metrics to the analysis and understanding of a company's fundamentals—based on the industry in which it operates, its
competitive position, its strategy and execution—a number of financial ratios derived
from the company's principal financial statements are examined: the income statement,
balance sheet, and cash flow statement. Credit analysts calculate a number of ratios
to assess the financial health of a company, identify trends over time, and compare
companies across an industry to get a sense of relative creditworthiness. Note that
typical values of these ratios vary widely from one industry to another because of different industry characteristics previously identified: competitive structure, economic
cyclicality, regulation, and so on.

  We will categorize the key credit analysis ratios into three different groups:

- Profitability and cash flow
- Leverage
- Coverage

Profitability and cash flow measures.   It is from profitability and cash flow generation
that companies can service their debt. Credit analysts typically look at operating profit
margins and operating income to get a sense of a company's underlying profitability
and see how it varies over time. Operating income is defined as operating revenues
minus operating expenses and is commonly referred to as "earnings before interest
and taxes" (EBIT). Credit analysts focus on EBIT because it is useful to determine a
company's performance prior to costs arising from its capital structure (i.e., how much
debt it carries versus equity). And "before taxes" is used because interest expense is
paid before income taxes are calculated.

  There are several measures of cash flow used in credit analysis; some are more
conservative than others because they make certain adjustments for cash that gets used
in managing and maintaining the business or in making payments to shareholders.

- **Earnings before interest, taxes, depreciation, and amortization (EBITDA).**
  EBITDA is a commonly used measure of cash flow that takes operating
  income and adds back depreciation and amortization expense because those

are non-cash items. This is a somewhat crude measure of cash flow because it excludes certain cash-related expenses of running a business, such as capital expenditures and changes in (non-cash) working capital. Thus, despite its popularity as a cash flow metric, analysts look at other measures in addition to EBITDA.

■ **Funds from operations (FFO).** Standard & Poor's defines funds from operations as net income from continuing operations plus depreciation, amortization, deferred income taxes, and other non-cash items.[24]

■ **Free cash flow before dividends.**[25] This measures excess cash flow generated by the company (excluding non-recurring items) before payments to shareholders or that could be used to pay down debt or pay dividends. It includes net income plus depreciation and amortization minus capital expenditures minus increase (plus decrease) in non-cash working capital, and excludes non-recurring items. Companies that have negative free cash flow before payments to shareholders will be consuming cash they have or will need to rely on additional financing—from banks, bond investors, or equity investors. This obviously represents higher credit risk.

■ **Free cash flow after dividends.** This measure just takes the preceding calculation and subtracts dividend payments. If this number is positive, it represents cash that could be used to pay down debt or build up cash on the balance sheet. Either outcome is a form of deleveraging, which is favorable from a credit risk standpoint. Some credit analysts will calculate net debt by subtracting balance sheet cash from total debt, although they shouldn't assume the cash will be used to pay down debt. Actual debt paid down from free cash flow is a stronger form of deleveraging. Some analysts will also deduct stock buybacks to get the "truest" form of free cash flow that can be used to de-lever on either a gross or net debt basis; however, others view stock buybacks as more discretionary and as having less certain timing than dividends, and thus treat those two forms of shareholder payments differently when calculating free cash flow.

Leverage ratios. There are a few measures of leverage used by credit analysts. The most common are the debt/capital, debt/EBITDA, and FFO/debt ratios. Note that many analysts adjust a company's reported debt levels for debt-like liabilities, such as underfunded pensions and other retiree benefits, as well as operating leases. When adjusting for leases, analysts will typically add back the imputed interest or rent expense to various cash flow measures.

■ **Debt/capital.** Capital is calculated as total debt plus shareholders equity. This ratio shows the percent of a company's capital base that is financed with debt. A lower percentage of debt indicates lower credit risk. This traditional ratio is generally used for investment-grade corporate issuers. Where goodwill or other intangible assets are significant (and subject to obsolescence, depletion, or other forms of devaluation), it is often informative to also compute the debt to capital ratio after assuming a write-down of the after-tax value of such assets.

---

[24] The funds from operations differs only slightly from the better known cash flow from operations in that it excludes working capital changes. The idea behind using FFO in credit analysis is to take out the near-term swings and seasonality in working capital that can potentially distort the amount of operating cash flow a business is generating. Over time, the working capital swings are expected to even out. Analysts tend to look at both FFO and cash flow from operations, particularly for businesses with large working capital swings (e.g., very cyclical manufacturing companies).

[25] In other parts of the CFA curriculum, this is referred to as free cash flow to the firm (FCFF). These can be regarded as interchangeable.

- **Debt/EBITDA.** This ratio is a common leverage measure. Analysts use it on a "snapshot" basis, as well as to look at trends over time and at projections and to compare companies in a given industry. Rating agencies often use it as a trigger for rating actions, and banks reference it in loan covenants. A higher ratio indicates more leverage and thus higher credit risk. Note that this ratio can be very volatile for companies with high cash flow variability, such as those in cyclical industries and with high operating leverage (fixed costs).

- **FFO/debt.** Credit rating agencies like using this leverage ratio. They publish key median and average ratios, such as this one, by rating category so analysts can get a sense of why an issuer is assigned a certain credit rating, as well as where that rating may migrate based on changes to such key ratios as this one.

Coverage ratios. Coverage ratios measure an issuer's ability to meet—to "cover"—its interest payments. The two most common are the EBITDA/interest expense and EBIT/interest expense ratios.

- **EBITDA/interest expense.** This measurement of interest coverage is a bit more liberal than the one that uses EBIT because it does not subtract out the impact of (non-cash) depreciation and amortization expense. A higher ratio indicates better credit quality.

- **EBIT/interest expense.** Because EBIT does not include depreciation and amortization, it is considered a more conservative measure of interest coverage. This ratio is now used less frequently than EBITDA/interest expense.

Exhibit 9 is a good example of the key average credit ratios by rating category for industrial companies over a three-year period, as published by Standard & Poor's.

Exhibit 9	Industrial Comparative Ratio Analysis							
Credit Rating	EBITDA Margin (%)	Return on Capital (%)	EBIT Interest Coverage (x)	EBITDA Interest Coverage (x)	FFO/Debt (%)	Free Operations Cash Flow/ Debt (%)	Debt/ EBITDA (x)	Debt/Debt plus Equity (%)
AAA								
US	29.6	36.8	60.2	68.0	251.1	197.0	0.4	15.7
EMEA	NA	NA	NA	NA	NA	NA	NA	NA
AA								
US	24.6	24.5	16.8	20.5	69.9	52.3	1.2	36.0
EMEA	25.2	21.7	14.4	17.6	163.9	82.5	0.9	23.7
A								
US	24.2	21.0	22.0	29.0	96.7	65.9	1.5	36.0
EMEA	21.5	17.1	9.0	12.3	92.8	60.1	1.6	34.5
BBB								
US	21.8	16.1	8.8	12.2	54.0	32.8	2.7	46.3
EMEA	19.7	13.1	5.3	7.9	52.1	23.7	2.6	44.9
BB								
US	23.4	11.8	4.1	6.2	35.7	13.6	3.3	54.9
EMEA	20.3	11.0	5.3	7.2	31.8	9.7	3.3	51.0
B								

Credit Rating	EBITDA Margin (%)	Return on Capital (%)	EBIT Interest Coverage (x)	EBITDA Interest Coverage (x)	FFO/Debt (%)	Free Operations Cash Flow/ Debt (%)	Debt/ EBITDA (x)	Debt/Debt plus Equity (%)
US	19.4	8.0	1.6	2.9	17.5	5.1	6.6	84.0
EMEA	20.5	6.8	1.7	3.4	19.1	2.2	7.0	78.4

Notes: Data are as of 24 August 2011. EMEA is Europe, Middle East, and Africa.
Source: Based on data from Standard & Poor's Financial Services, LLC.

Comments on issuer liquidity.   An issuer's access to liquidity is also an important consideration in credit analysis. Companies with strong liquidity represent lower credit risk than those with weak liquidity, other factors being equal. The financial crisis of 2008–2009 showed companies and investors that access to liquidity via the debt and equity markets should not be taken for granted, particularly for those that do not have strong balance sheets or steady operating cash flow.

When assessing an issuer's liquidity, credit analysts tend to look at the following:

- **Cash on the balance sheet.** Cash holdings provide the greatest assurance of having sufficient liquidity to make promised payments.

- **Net working capital.** The big US automakers used to have enormous negative working capital, despite having high levels of cash on the balance sheet. This proved disastrous when the financial crisis hit in 2008 and the economy contracted sharply. Auto sales—and thus revenues—fell, the auto companies cut production, and working capital consumed billions of dollars in cash as accounts payable came due when the companies most needed liquidity.

- **Operating cash flow.** Analysts will project this figure out a few years and consider the risk that it may be lower than expected.

- **Committed bank lines.** Committed but untapped lines of credit provide contingent liquidity in the event that the company is unable to tap other, potentially cheaper, financing in the public debt markets.

- **Debt coming due and committed capital expenditures in the next one to two years.** Analysts will compare the sources of liquidity with the amount of debt coming due as well as with committed capital expenditures to ensure that companies can repay their debt and still invest in the business if the capital markets are somehow not available.

As will be discussed in more detail in the section on special considerations for high-yield credits, issuer liquidity is a bigger consideration for high-yield companies than for investment grade companies.

EXAMPLE 6

Watson Pharmaceuticals, Inc. is a US-based specialty health care company. As a credit analyst, you have been asked to assess its creditworthiness—on its own, relative to another competitor and its overall industry, and compared with a similarly rated company in a different industry. Using the financial statements provided in Exhibits 10 through 13 for the three years ending 31 December 2008, 2009, and 2010, address the following:

1   Calculate Watson Pharmaceuticals' operating profit margin, EBITDA, and free cash flow. (Note: The company did not pay dividends in 2008–2010.)

2   Determine Watson's leverage ratios: debt/EBITDA, debt/capital, free cash flow/debt.

3   Calculate Watson's interest coverage using both EBIT and EBITDA.

4   Using the statistics provided on the pharmaceutical industry and on competitor Johnson & Johnson, compare the credit ratios of Watson and Johnson & Johnson and explain the relative creditworthiness and ratings of the two companies.

5   Contrast the credit ratios of Watson with Luxembourg-based ArcelorMittal, one of the world's largest global steelmakers. Comment on the volatility of the credit ratios of the two companies. Which company looks to be more cyclical? What industry factors might explain some of the differences? In comparing the creditworthiness of these two companies, what other factors might be considered to offset greater volatility of credit ratios?

Exhibit 10A   Watson Pharmaceuticals' Financial Statements

Consolidated Statements of Operations (dollars in millions except per share amounts)	Years Ended December 31		
	2008	2009	2010
Net revenues	2,535.5	2,793.0	3,566.9
Operating expenses:			
Cost of sales (excludes amortization)	1,502.8	1,596.8	1,998.5
Research and development	170.1	197.3	296.1
Selling and marketing	232.9	263.1	320.0
General and administrative	190.5	257.1	436.1
Amortization	80.7	92.6	180.0
Loss on asset sales and impairments	0.3	2.2	30.8
Total operating expenses	2,177.3	2,409.1	3,261.5
Operating income	358.2	383.9	305.4
Other (expense) income:			
Interest income	9.0	5.0	1.6
Interest expense	(28.2)	(34.2)	(84.1)
Other income	19.3	7.9	27.7
Total other (expense) income, net	0.1	(21.3)	(54.8)
Income before income taxes and non-controlling interest	358.3	362.6	250.6
Provision for income taxes	119.9	140.6	67.3

(Continued)

Consolidated Statements of Operations (dollars in millions except per share amounts)	Years Ended December 31		
	2008	2009	2010
Net income	238.4	222.0	183.3
Loss attributable to noncontrolling interest	—	—	1.1
Net income attributable to common shareholders	238.4	222.0	184.4

Source: Based on data from Watson Pharmaceuticals' Company Annual Report (2010).

Exhibit 10B   Watson Pharmaceuticals' Financial Statements

Consolidated Balance Sheets (dollars in millions)	Years Ended December 31		
	2008	2009	2010
ASSETS			
Current assets:			
Cash and cash equivalents	507.6	201.4	282.8
Marketable securities	13.2	13.6	11.1
Accounts receivable	305.0	517.4	560.9
Inventories, net	473.1	692.3	631.0
Prepaid expenses and other current assets	48.5	213.9	134.2
Deferred tax assets	111.0	130.9	179.4
Total current assets	**1,458.4**	**1,769.5**	**1,799.4**
Property and equipment, net	658.5	694.2	642.3
Investments and other assets	80.6	114.5	84.5
Deferred tax assets	52.3	110.8	141.0
Product rights and other intangibles, net	560.0	1,713.5	1,632.0
Goodwill	868.1	1,501.0	1,528.1
Total assets	**3,677.9**	**5,903.5**	**5,827.3**
LIABILITIES AND EQUITY			
Current liabilities:			
Accounts payable and accrued expenses	381.3	614.3	741.1
Income taxes payable	15.5	78.4	39.9
Short-term debt and current portion of long-term debt	53.2	307.6	—
Deferred tax liabilities	15.9	31.3	20.8
Deferred revenue	16.1	16.3	18.9
Total current liabilities	**482.0**	**1,047.9**	**820.7**

(continued)

(Continued)

Consolidated Balance Sheets	Years Ended December 31		
(dollars in millions)	2008	2009	2010
Long-term debt	824.7	1,150.2	1,016.1
Deferred revenue	30.1	31.9	18.2
Other long-term liabilities	4.9	118.7	183.1
Other taxes payable	53.3	76.0	65.1
Deferred tax liabilities	174.3	455.7	441.5
Total liabilities	**1,569.3**	**2,880.4**	**2,544.7**
Equity:			
Preferred stock	—	—	—
Common stock	0.4	0.4	0.4
Additional paid-in capital	995.9	1,686.9	1,771.8
Retained earnings	1,418.1	1,640.1	1,824.5
Accumulated other comprehensive (loss) income	(3.2)	1.9	(2.5)
Treasury stock, at cost (9.7 and 9.6 shares held, respectively)	(302.6)	(306.2)	(312.5)
Total stockholders' equity	**2,108.6**	**3,023.1**	**3,281.7**
Noncontrolling interest	—	—	0.9
Total equity	**2,108.6**	**3,023.1**	**3,282.6**
Total liabilities and equity	**3,677.9**	**5,903.5**	**5,827.3**

Source: Based on data from Watson Pharmaceuticals' Company Annual Report (2010).

Exhibit 10C   Watson Pharmaceuticals' Financial Statements

Consolidated Statements of Cash Flow	Years Ended December 31		
(dollars in millions)	2008	2009	2010
Cash flows from operating activities:			
Net income	238.4	222.0	183.3
Reconciliation to net cash provided by operating activities:			
Depreciation	90.0	96.4	101.9
Amortization	80.7	92.6	180.0
Provision for inventory reserve	45.7	51.0	50.0
Share-based compensation	18.5	19.1	23.5
Deferred income tax (benefit) provision	3.5	(19.0)	(118.3)
(Gain) loss on sale of securities	(9.6)	1.1	(27.3)
Loss on asset sales and impairment	0.3	2.6	29.8
Increase in allowance for doubtful accounts	1.2	3.4	9.5

(Continued)

Consolidated Statements of Cash Flow (dollars in millions)	Years Ended December 31		
	2008	**2009**	**2010**
Accretion of preferred stock and contingent payment consideration	—	2.2	38.4
Other, net	(13.9)	(7.6)	11.3
Changes in working capital	(38.2)	(87.0)	88.9
Net cash provided by operating activities	416.6	376.8	571.0
Cash flows from investing activities:			
Additions to property and equipment	(63.5)	(55.4)	(56.6)
Additions to product rights and other intangibles	(37.0)	(16.5)	(10.9)
Additions to marketable securities	(8.2)	(8.0)	(5.5)
Additions to long-term investments	—	—	(43.7)
Proceeds from sale of property and equipment	—	3.0	2.7
Proceeds from sale of marketable securities	6.7	9.0	9.5
Proceeds from sale of investments	8.2	—	95.4
Acquisition of business, net of cash acquired	—	(968.2)	(67.5)
Other investing activities, net	0.4	—	2.5
Net cash used in investing activities	(93.4)	(1,036.1)	(74.1)
Cash flows from financing activities:			
Proceeds from issuance of long-term debt	—	1,109.9	—
Principal payments on debt	(95.6)	(786.6)	(459.7)
Proceeds from borrowings on short-term debt	67.9	—	—
Proceeds from stock plans	8.4	33.4	54.7
Repurchase of common stock	(0.9)	(3.6)	(6.3)
Net cash provided by (used in) financing activities	(20.2)	353.1	(411.3)
Effect of currency exchange rate changes	—	—	(4.2)
Net increase (decrease) in cash and cash equivalents	303.0	(306.2)	81.4
Cash and cash equivalents at beginning of period	204.6	507.6	201.4
Cash and cash equivalents at end of period	507.6	201.4	282.8

Source: Based on data from Watson Pharmaceuticals' Company Annual Report (2010).

Exhibit 11   Johnson & Johnson's Credit Ratios

	2008	2009	2010
Operating margin	25.1%	25.2%	26.8%
Debt/EBITDA	0.6x	0.8x	0.9x
EBITDA/Interest	43.3x	40.7x	42.8x
FCF/Debt	58.1%	61.1%	48.9%
Debt/Capital	21.8%	22.3%	22.9%

Source: Company Filings, Loomis, Sayles & Company.

Exhibit 12   Pharmaceuticals: US Industry Credit Ratios (average of past three fiscal years as of 27 June 2011)

	Corp. Credit Rating[a]	Return on Capital (%)	EBIT Interest Coverage (x)	EBITDA Interest Coverage (x)	FFO/ Debt (%)	Free Operating Cash Flow/Debt (%)	Debt/ EBITDA (x)	Debt/ Debt plus Equity (%)
Abbott Laboratories	AA/ Stable/ A-1+	23.7	12.4	15.7	65.4	48.4	1.3	36.3
Allergan, Inc.	A+/ Stable/ A-1	17.0	12.8	16.9	51.2	37.3	1.4	30.5
Axcan Intermediate Holdings Inc.	BB−/ Stable/−	14.0	2.2	3.1	20.2	18.6	2.7	55.2
Bristol-Myers Squibb	A+/ Stable/ A-1	31.7	14.3	15.0	105.3	82.8	0.7	23.0
Catalent	B+/ Stable/−	2.5	0.5	1.8	4.0	2.0	8.9	82.5
Eli Lilly and Company	AA/ Stable/ A-1+	39.6	18.6	22.7	116.6	101.9	0.7	33.1
Johnson & Johnson	AAA/ Stable/ A-1+	31.8	30.9	36.4	209.6	175.7	0.4	14.0
King Pharmaceuticals, Inc.	BB/ Stable/−	16.0	10.9	14.9	68.3	58.2	1.2	26.3
Merck & Co., Inc.	AA−/ Positive/ A-1+	28.2	22.3	20.2	150.8	114.1	0.6	12.1
Mylan Inc.	BB/ Stable/−	7.5	2.0	3.1	11.7	4.4	5.6	63.5
Pfizer Inc.	AA/ Stable/ A-1+	22.5	21.4	25.9	141.9	179.6	0.4	12.2

Exhibit 12   (Continued)

	Corp. Credit Rating[a]	Return on Capital (%)	EBIT Interest Coverage (x)	EBITDA Interest Coverage (x)	FFO/ Debt (%)	Free Operating Cash Flow/Debt (%)	Debt/ EBITDA (x)	Debt/ Debt plus Equity (%)
Valeant Pharmaceuticals International	BB–/ Stable/–	15.1	3.3	4.9	22.0	21.1	2.9	67.0
Watson Pharmaceuticals, Inc.	BBB–/ Stable/–	11.5	9.5	14.2	39.4	29.4	2.0	33.6
Median		17.0	12.4	15.0	65.4	48.4	1.3	33.1

[a] As of June 27, 2010.
Source: Standard and Poor's Financial Services LLC (S&P).

Exhibit 13   ArcelorMittal Credit Ratios

	2008	2009	2010
Operating margin	10.2%	–2.4%	4.6%
Debt/EBITDA	2.0x	8.0x	3.3x
EBITDA/Interest	7.4x	1.1x	3.6x
FCF/Debt	20.0%	13.0%	–2.1%
Debt/Capital	36.5%	27.5%	28.2%

Source: Company Filings, Loomis, Sayles & Company.

Solutions:

1   Operating profit margin (%) = Operating income/Revenue

   2008: 358.2/2535.5 = 0.141 or 14.1 percent

   2009: 383.9/2793.0 = 0.137 or 13.7 percent

   2010: 305.4/3566.9 = 0.086 or 8.6 percent

   EBITDA = Operating income + Depreciation + Amortization

   2008: 358.2 + 90.0 + 80.7 = 528.9

   2009: 383.9 + 96.4 + 92.6 = 572.9

   2010: 305.4 + 101.9 + 180.0 = 587.3

   FCF = Cash flow from operations – Capital expenditures – Dividends

   2008: 416.6 – (63.5 + 37.0 – 0.0) – 0 = 316.1

   2009: 376.8 – (55.4 + 16.5 – 3.0) – 0 = 307.9

   2010: 571.0 – (56.6 + 10.9 – 2.7) – 0 = 506.2

where

Capital expenditures = Additions to property and equipment + Additions
                            to product rights and intangibles – Proceeds of
                            sale of property and equipment

Note that "Additions to product rights and intangibles" is included in capital expenditures here because such activities are likely to be both material and recurring for a health care/drug company. For other types of businesses, the analyst might elect to exclude this item from capital expenditures when calculating FCF.

2   Debt/EBITDA

Total debt = Short-term debt and Current portion of long-term debt + Long-term debt

2008: Debt: 53.2 + 824.7 = 877.9

Debt/EBITDA: 877.9/528.9 = 1.7x

2009: Debt: 307.6 + 1150.2 = 1457.8

Debt/EBITDA: 1457.8/572.9 = 2.5x

2010: Debt: 0 + 1016.1 = 1016.1

Debt/EBITDA: 1016.1/587.3 = 1.7x

Debt/Capital (%)

Capital = Debt + Equity

2008: Capital: 877.9 + 2108.6 = 2986.5

Debt/Capital: 877.9/2986.5 = 29.4 percent

2009: Capital: 1457.8 + 3023.1 = 4480.9

Debt/Capital: 1457.8/4480.9 = 32.5 percent

2010: Capital: 1016.1 + 3282.6 = 4298.7

Debt/Capital: 1016.1/4298.7 = 23.6 percent

FCF/Debt (%)

2008: 316.1/877.9 = 36.0 percent

2009: 307.9/1457.8 = 21.1 percent

2010: 506.2/1016.1 = 49.8 percent

3   EBIT/Interest expense

2008: 358.2/28.2 = 12.7x

2009: 383.9/34.2 = 11.2x

2010: 305.4/84.1 = 3.6x

EBITDA/Interest expense

2008: 528.9/28.2 = 18.8x

2009: 572.9/34.2 = 16.8x

2010: 587.3/84.1 = 7.0x

4   Based just on these credit ratios, Johnson & Johnson (J&J) has a higher operating margin, better leverage ratios, a much better Debt/EBITDA, a better FCF/debt over the three years (though slightly lower in 2010), a lower debt/capital (although pretty close in 2010), and a much better interest coverage as measured by EBITDA/interest. Collectively, those ratios suggest J&J is a stronger credit than Watson.

Watson Pharmaceuticals' Credit Ratios	2008	2009	2010
Operating margin	14.1%	13.7%	8.6%
Debt/EBITDA	1.7x	2.5x	1.7x
EBITDA/Interest	18.8x	16.8x	7.0x
FCF/Debt	36.0%	21.1%	49.8%
Debt/Capital	29.4%	32.5%	23.6%

Johnson & Johnson's Credit Ratios	2008	2009	2010
Operating margin	25.1%	25.2%	26.8%
Debt/EBITDA	0.6x	0.8x	0.9x
EBITDA/Interest	43.3x	40.7x	42.8x
FCF/Debt	58.1%	61.1%	48.9%
Debt/Capital	21.8%	22.3%	22.9%

5   By the five credit ratios shown in the tables, Watson has a higher and less volatile operating margin than ArcelorMittal, lower leverage (except debt/capital in 2009), and higher interest coverage. Based on the volatility of its cash flow and operating margin, Arcelor appears to be a much more cyclical credit. Coupled with its higher debt levels, one would expect Arcelor to have a lower credit rating. To mitigate the impact of its more volatile credit ratios, Arcelor might have very high levels of liquidity. Its size and global diversity may also be a "plus." In addition, it could have favorable supplier and customer contracts, and/or its profitability might be improving as, for example, competitors that are sub-scale and/or employing aggressively low pricing strategies are forced to retrench or exit the industry.

Watson Pharmaceuticals' Credit Ratios	2008	2009	2010
Operating margin	14.1%	13.7%	8.6%
Debt/EBITDA	1.7x	2.5x	1.7x
EBITDA/Interest	18.8x	16.8x	7.0x
FCF/Debt	36.0%	21.1%	49.8%
Debt/Capital	29.4%	32.5%	23.6%

ArcelorMittal's Credit Ratios	2008	2009	2010
Operating margin	10.2%	−2.4%	4.6%
Debt/EBITDA	2.0x	8.0x	3.3x
EBITDA/Interest	7.4x	1.1x	3.6x
FCF/Debt	20.0%	13.0%	−2.1%
Debt/Capital	36.5%	27.5%	28.2%

5.2.2 Collateral

Collateral, or asset value, analysis is typically emphasized more with weaker credit quality companies. As discussed earlier, credit analysts focus primarily on probability of default, which is mostly about an issuer's ability to generate sufficient cash flow to support its debt payments, as well as its ability to refinance maturing debt. Only when the default probability rises to a sufficient level do analysts typically consider asset or collateral value in the context of loss severity in the event of default.

Analysts do think about the value and quality of a company's assets; however, these are difficult to observe directly. Factors to consider include the nature and amount of intangible assets on the balance sheet. Some assets, such as patents, are clearly valuable and can be sold if necessary to cover liabilities. Goodwill, on the other hand, is not considered a high-quality asset. In fact, sustained weak financial performance most likely implies that a company's goodwill will be written down, reinforcing its poor quality. Another factor to consider is the amount of depreciation an issuer takes relative to its capital expenditures: Low capital expenditures relative to depreciation expense could imply that management is insufficiently investing in its business, which will lead to lower-quality assets, potentially reduced future operating cash flow, and higher loss severity in the event of default.

A market-based signal that credit analysts use to impute the quality of a publicly traded company's assets, and its ability to support its debt, is equity market capitalization. For instance, a company whose stock trades below book value may have lower-quality assets than is suggested by the amount reported on the balance sheet.

As economies become more service- and knowledge-based and those types of companies issue debt, it's important to understand that these issuers rely more on human and intellectual capital than on "hard assets." In generating profits and cash flow, these companies are not as asset intensive. One example would be software companies. Another example would be investment management firms. Human- and intellectual- capital-based companies may generate a lot of cash flow, but their collateral value is questionable, unless there are patents and other forms of intellectual property and "intangible capital" that may not appear directly on the balance sheet but could be valuable in the event of financial distress or default.

Regardless of the nature of the business, the key point of collateral analysis is to assess the value of the assets relative to the issuer's level—and seniority ranking—of debt.

5.2.3 *Covenants*

Covenants are meant to protect creditors while also giving management sufficient flexibility to operate its business on behalf of and for the benefit of the shareholders. They are integral to credit agreements, whether they are bonds or bank loans, and they spell out what the issuer's management is (1) obligated to do and (2) limited in doing. The former are called "affirmative covenants," whereas the latter are called "negative" or "restrictive covenants." Obligations would include such duties as making interest and principal payments and filing audited financial statements on a timely basis. Covenants might also require a company to redeem debt in the event of the company being acquired[26] or to keep the ratio of debt to EBITDA below some prescribed amount. The limitations might include a cap on the amount of cash that can be paid out to shareholders relative to earnings, or perhaps on the amount of additional secured debt that can be issued. Covenant violations can be an event of default unless they are cured in a short time or a waiver is granted.

For corporate bonds, covenants are described in the bond **prospectus**, the document that is part of a new bond issue. The prospectus describes the terms of the bond issue, as well as supporting financial statements, to help investors perform their analyses and make investment decisions as to whether or not to submit orders to buy the new bonds. Actually, the **bond indenture** is the governing legal credit agreement and is typically incorporated by reference in the prospectus.

---

26 This is often referred to as a "change of control" covenant.

Covenants are an important but underappreciated part of credit analysis. Strong covenants protect bond investors from the possibility of management taking actions that would hurt an issuer's creditworthiness. For example, without appropriate covenants management might pay large dividends, undertake stock buybacks well in excess of free cash flow, sell the company in a leveraged buyout,[27] or take on a lot of secured debt that structurally subordinates unsecured bondholders. All of these actions would enrich shareholders at the expense of bondholders. Recall that management works for the shareholders and that bonds are contracts, with management's only real obligation to creditors being to uphold the terms of the contract. Weak covenants pose additional risks to bond investors.

The bond-buying investor base is very large and diverse, particularly for investment-grade debt. It includes insurance companies, investment management firms, pension funds, mutual funds, hedge funds, sovereign wealth funds, and so on. Although there are some very large investment firms, the buyer base is fragmented and does not—and legally cannot—act as a syndicate. Thus, bondholders are generally not able to negotiate strong covenants on most new bond issues. Therefore, covenants provide limited protection to investment-grade bondholders and often only somewhat stronger protection to high-yield investors. Covenants on new bond issues tend to be stronger during weak economic or market conditions because investors seek more protection during such times. There are a few organized institutional investor groups focused on strengthening covenants: the Credit Roundtable[28] in the United States and the European Model Covenant Initiative in the United Kingdom.

Covenant language is often very technical and written in "legalese," so it can be helpful to have an in-house person with a legal background to review and interpret the specific covenant terms and wording. One might also use a third-party service specializing in covenant analysis, such as Covenant Review.[29]

We will go into more detail on specific covenants in the section on special considerations for high-yield bonds.

5.2.4 *Character*

The character of a corporate borrower can also be difficult to observe. The analysis of character as a factor in credit analysis dates to when loans were made to companies owned by individuals. Most corporate bond issuers are now publicly owned by shareholders or privately owned by pools of capital, such as private equity firms. Management often has little ownership in a corporation, so analysis and assessment of character is different than it would be for owner-managed firms. Credit analysts can make judgments about management's character in the following ways:

- An assessment of the soundness of management's strategy.

- Management's track record in executing past strategies, particularly if they led to bankruptcy or restructuring. A company run by executives whose prior positions/ventures resulted in significant distress might still be able to borrow in the debt markets, but it would likely have to borrow on a secured basis and/or pay a higher rate of interest.

- Use of aggressive accounting policies and/or tax strategies. Examples might include using a significant amount of off-balance-sheet financing, capitalizing versus immediately expensing items, timing revenue recognition, and/or frequently changing auditors. These are potential warning flags to other behaviors or actions that may adversely impact an issuer's creditworthiness.

---

27 A leveraged buyout (LBO) is an acquisition of a company by private investors using high levels of debt and relatively little equity.

28 See www.creditroundtable.org.

29 See www.covenantreview.com.

■ Any history of fraud or malfeasance—a major warning flag to credit analysts.

■ Previous poor treatment of bondholders—for example, management actions that resulted in major credit rating downgrades. These actions might include a debt-financed acquisition, a large special dividend to shareholders, or a major debt-financed stock buyback program.

EXAMPLE 7

The Four Cs

1   Which of the following would not be a bond covenant?

   A   The issuer must file financial statements with the bond trustee on a timely basis.

   B   The company can buy back as much stock as it likes.

   C   If the company offers security to any creditors, it must offer security to this bond issue.

2   Why should credit analysts be concerned if a company's stock trades below book value?

   A   It means the company is probably going bankrupt.

   B   It means the company will probably incur lots of debt to buy back its undervalued stock.

   C   It's a signal that the company's asset value on its balance sheet may be impaired and have to be written down, suggesting less collateral protection for creditors.

3   If management is of questionable character, how can investors incorporate this assessment into their credit analysis and investment decisions?

   A   They can choose not to invest based on the increased credit risk.

   B   They can insist on getting collateral (security) and/or demand a higher return.

   C   They can choose not to invest or insist on additional security and/or higher return.

Solution to 1:

B is correct. Covenants describe what the borrower is (1) obligated to do or (2) limited in doing. It's the absence of covenants that would permit a company to buy back as much stock as it likes. A requirement that the company offer security to this bond issue if it offers security to other creditors (answer C) is referred to as a "negative pledge."

Solution to 2:

C is correct.

Solution to 3:

C is correct. Investors can always say no if they are not comfortable with the credit risk presented by a bond or issuer. They may also decide to lend to a borrower with questionable character only on a secured basis and/or demand a higher return for the perceived higher risk.

CREDIT RISK VS. RETURN: YIELDS AND SPREADS 6

The material in this section applies to all bonds subject to credit risk. For simplicity, in what follows all such bonds are sometimes referred to as "corporate" bonds.

As in other types of investing, taking more risk in credit offers higher potential return, but with more volatility and less certainty of earning that return. Using credit ratings as a proxy for risk, Exhibit 14 shows the composite yield to maturity[30] for bonds of all maturities within each rating category in the US and European bond markets according to Barclays Capital, one of the largest providers of fixed-income market indices.

Exhibit 14 Corporate Yields by Rating Category as of 30 June 2011									
Barclays Capital Indices	Investment Grade					Non-Investment Grade			
	AAA (%)	AA (%)	A (%)	BBB (%)	BB (%)	B (%)	CCC (%)	CC (%)	D (%)
US	3.09	3.10	3.64	4.35	6.50	7.93	10.27	14.11	22.73
Pan European	3.33	3.58	4.14	4.98	6.90	8.67	17.12	13.81	54.80

Source: Based on data from Barclays Capital.

Note that the lower the credit quality, the higher the quoted yield. The realized yield, or return, will almost always be different because of changes in interest rates and the various forms of credit risk discussed earlier. For example, in the aggregate credit losses will "eat up" some of the yield premium offered by lower-quality bonds versus higher-quality credits. Trailing 12-month returns by credit rating category, and the volatility (standard deviation) of those returns, are shown in Exhibit 15.

---

30 High-yield bonds are often quoted on a "yield to call" (YTC) or "yield to worst" (YTW) basis because so many of them are callable before maturity, whereas most investment-grade bonds are non-callable, or at least callable at such punitive premiums that issuers are not likely to exercise that option.

Exhibit 15	US Trailing 12-Month Returns by Rating Category, 31 December 1996–30 June 2011

	Aaa	Aa	A	Baa	Ba	B	Caa
Avg. Return:	6.18%	6.63%	6.52%	7.33%	8.58%	6.93%	8.10%
Max. Return:	16.08%	19.30%	29.39%	36.43%	50.80%	52.10%	97.47%
Min. Return:	−4.17%	−5.47%	−14.98%	−15.70%	−22.12%	−31.47%	−44.35%
Avg. Volatility:	4.02%	4.45%	5.18%	5.51%	6.31%	8.11%	12.63%

Source: Based on data from Barclays Capital and Loomis, Sayles & Company.

As shown in the exhibit, the higher the credit risk, the greater the return potential and the higher the volatility of that return. This pattern is consistent with other types of investing that involves risk and return (although average returns on single-B rated bonds appear anomalous in this example).

For extremely liquid bonds that are deemed to have virtually no default risk (e.g., German government bonds, or *Bunds*), the yield is a function of real interest rates plus an expected inflation rate and a maturity premium. Of course, those factors are present in corporate bonds as well. In addition, the yield on corporate bonds will include a liquidity premium and a credit spread intended to compensate investors for these additional risks as well as for the expected level of credit losses. Thus, the yield on a corporate bond can be decomposed as

Yield on corporate bond = Real risk-free interest rate + Expected inflation rate + Maturity premium + Liquidity premium + Credit spread

Changes in any of these components will alter the yield, price, and return on the bond.

Investors in corporate bonds focus primarily on the yield spread relative to a comparable, default-free bond, which is composed of the liquidity premium and the credit spread:

Yield spread = Liquidity premium + Credit spread

The market's willingness to bear risk will affect each of these components. In general, however, it is not possible to directly observe the market's assessment of the components separately—analysts can only observe the total yield spread.

Spreads on all corporate bonds can be affected by a number of factors, with lower-quality issuers typically experiencing greater spread volatility. These factors, which are frequently linked, include the following:

- **Credit cycle.** As the credit cycle improves, credit spreads will narrow. Conversely, a deteriorating credit cycle will cause credit spreads to widen. Spreads are tightest at or near the top of the credit cycle, when financial markets believe risk is low, whereas they are widest at or near the bottom of the credit cycle, when financial markets believe risk is high.

- **Broader economic conditions.** Not surprisingly, weakening economic conditions will push investors to desire a greater risk premium and drive overall credit spreads wider. Conversely, a strengthening economy will cause credit spreads to narrow because investors anticipate credit metrics will improve due to rising corporate cash flow, thus reducing the risk of default.

- **Financial market performance overall, including equities.** In weak financial markets, credit spreads will widen, whereas in strong markets, credit spreads will narrow. In a steady, low-volatility environment, credit spreads will typically also narrow, as investors tend to "reach for yield."

- **Broker–dealers' willingness to provide sufficient capital for market making.** Bonds trade primarily over the counter, so investors need broker–dealers to commit capital for market-making purposes. During the financial crisis in 2008–2009, several large broker–dealer counterparties either failed or were taken over by another. This, combined with financial and regulatory stresses faced by virtually all the other broker–dealers, greatly reduced the total capital available for making markets and the willingness to buy/sell credit-risky bonds. Future regulatory reform may well lead to persistent or even permanent reductions in broker-provided capital.

- **General market supply and demand.** In periods of heavy new issue supply, credit spreads will widen if there is insufficient demand. In periods of high demand for bonds, spreads will move tighter.

Each of the first four factors played a role during the financial crisis of 2008–2009, causing spreads to widen dramatically, as shown in Exhibit 16, before narrowing sharply as governments intervened and markets stabilized. This is shown in two panels—one for investment grade, another for high yield—because of the much greater spread volatility in high-yield bonds, particularly CCC rated credits. This spread volatility is reflected in the different spread ranges on the y-axes. OAS is option-adjusted spread, which incorporates the value of the embedded call option in certain corporate bonds that issuers have the right to exercise before maturity.[31]

---

31 The details of valuing bonds with embedded options and the calculation of OAS are covered in Level II of the CFA curriculum.

Exhibit 16   US Investment-Grade and High-Yield Corporate Spreads

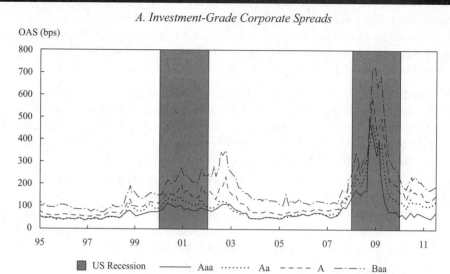

A. Investment-Grade Corporate Spreads

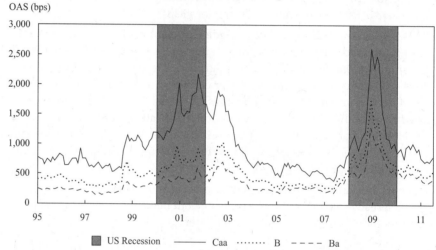

B. High-Yield Corporate Spreads

Sources: Based on data from Barclays Capital and Loomis Sayles & Company.

EXAMPLE 8

Yield Spreads

1 Which bonds are likely to exhibit the greatest spread volatility?

   A Bonds from issuers rated AA

   B Bonds from issuers rated BB

   C Bonds from issuers rated A

2 If investors become increasingly worried about the economy—say, as shown by declining stock prices—what is the *most likely* impact on credit spreads?

   A There will be no change to credit spreads. They aren't affected by equity markets.

     B   Narrower spreads will occur. Investors will move out of equities into debt securities.

     C   Wider spreads will occur. Investors are concerned about weaker creditworthiness.

Solution to 1:

B is correct. Lower-quality bonds exhibit greater spread volatility than higher-quality bonds. All of the factors that affect spreads—the credit cycle, economic conditions, financial performance, market-making capacity, and supply/demand conditions—will tend to have a greater impact on the pricing of lower-quality credits.

Solution to 2:

C is correct. Investors will require higher yields as compensation for the greater credit losses that are likely to occur in a weakening economy.

We have discussed how yield spreads on credit-risky debt obligations, such as corporate bonds, can fluctuate based on a number of factors, including changes in the market's view of issuer-specific or idiosyncratic risk. The next question to ask is how these spread changes affect the price of and return on these bonds.

Although bond investors do concern themselves with default risks, recall that the probability of default for higher-quality bonds is typically very low: For investment-grade bonds, annual defaults are nearly always well below 1 percent (recall Exhibit 6). On the other hand, default rates can be very high for lower-quality issuers, although they can vary widely depending upon the credit cycle, among other things. What most investors in investment-grade debt focus on more than default risk is spread risk—that is, the effect on prices and returns from changes in spreads.

The return impact from spread changes is driven by two main factors: the modified duration (price sensitivity with respect to changes in interest rates) of the bond and the magnitude of the spread change. The effect on return to the bondholder depends on the holding period used for calculating the return.

The simplest example is that of a small, instantaneous change in the yield spread. In this case, the return impact, i.e., the percentage change in price (including accrued interest), can be approximated by

$$\text{Return impact} \approx -\text{MDur} \times \Delta\text{Spread}$$

where MDur is the modified duration. The negative sign in this equation reflects the fact that because bond prices and yields move in opposite directions, narrower spreads have a positive impact on bond prices and thus returns, whereas wider spreads have a negative impact on bond returns. Note that if the spread change is expressed in basis points, then the return impact will also be in basis points, whereas if the spread change is expressed as a decimal, the return impact will also be expressed as a decimal. Either way, the result is easily re-expressed as a percent.

For larger spread changes (and thus larger yield changes), the impact of convexity needs to be incorporated into the approximation:

$$\text{Return impact} \approx -(\text{MDur} \times \Delta\text{Spread}) + \tfrac{1}{2}\text{Cvx} \times (\Delta\text{Spread})^2$$

In this case, one must be careful to ensure that convexity (denoted by Cvx) is appropriately scaled to be consistent with the way the spread change is expressed. In general, for bonds without embedded options, one can scale convexity so that it has the same order of magnitude as the duration squared and then express the spread change as a decimal. For example, for a bond with duration of 5.0 and reported convexity of 0.235, one would re-scale convexity to 23.5 before applying the formula. For a 1 percent (i.e., 100 bps) increase in spread, the result would be

Return impact = $(-5.0 \times 0.01) + \frac{1}{2} \times 23.5 \times (0.01)^2 = -0.048825$ or -4.8825 percent

The return impact of instantaneous spread changes is illustrated in Exhibit 17 using two bonds from British Telecom, the UK telecommunications company. The bonds, denominated in British pounds, are priced to provide a certain spread over British government bonds (gilts) of a similar maturity. From the starting spread, in increments of 25 bps and for both wider and narrower spreads, the new price and actual return for each spread change are calculated. In addition, the exhibit shows the approximate returns with and without the convexity term. As can be seen, the approximation using only duration is reasonably accurate for small spread changes but for larger changes, the convexity term generally provides a meaningful improvement.

Exhibit 17   Impact of Duration on Price for a Given Change in Spread

Issuer: British Telecom, 8.625%, maturing on 26 March 2020

Price: £129.475	Modified Duration: 6.084	Spread to Gilt Curve: 248 b.p.
Accrued interest: 6.3	Convexity: 47.4	YTM: 4.31

	Scenarios								
Spread Δ (b.p.)	−100	−75	−50	−25	0	25	50	75	100
Spread (b.p.)	148	173	198	223	248	273	298	323	348
New Price (£)	137.90	135.73	133.60	131.52	129.48	127.47	125.51	123.59	121.71
New Price + Accrued (£)	144.20	142.03	139.90	137.82	135.78	133.77	131.81	129.89	128.01
Price Δ (£)	8.43	6.26	4.13	2.05	0.00	−2.01	−3.96	−5.88	−7.77
Return (%)									
Actual	6.21%	4.61%	3.04%	1.51%	0.00%	−1.48%	−2.92%	−4.33%	−5.72%
Approx: Dur only	6.08%	4.56%	3.04%	1.52%	0.00%	−1.52%	−3.04%	−4.56%	−6.08%
Approx: Dur & Cvx	6.32%	4.70%	3.10%	1.54%	0.00%	−1.51%	−2.98%	−4.43%	−5.85%

Issuer: British Telecom, 6.375%, maturing on 23 June 2037

Price: £110.093	Modified Duration: 13.064	Spread to Gilt Curve: 247 b.p.
Accrued interest: 3.117	Convexity: 253.5	YTM: 5.62

	Scenarios								
Spread Δ (b.p.)	−100	−75	−50	−25	0	25	50	75	100
Spread (b.p.)	147	172	197	222	247	272	297	322	347
New Price (£)	125.99	121.72	117.65	113.78	110.09	106.58	103.23	100.04	97.00
New Price + Accrued (£)	129.11	124.84	120.77	116.90	113.21	109.70	106.35	103.16	100.11
Price Δ (£)	15.90	11.63	7.56	3.69	0.00	−3.51	−6.86	−10.05	−13.10
Return (%)									
Actual	14.04%	10.27%	6.68%	3.26%	0.00%	−3.10%	−6.06%	−8.88%	−11.57%

Exhibit 17   (Continued)

	Scenarios								
Approx: Dur only	13.06%	9.80%	6.53%	3.27%	0.00%	−3.27%	−6.53%	−9.80%	−13.06%
Approx: Dur & Cvx	14.33%	10.51%	6.85%	3.35%	0.00%	−3.19%	−6.22%	−9.09%	−11.80%

Source: Based on data from Bloomberg Finance, L.P. (settle date is 19 December 2011).

Note that the price change for a given spread change is higher for the longer-duration bond—in this case, the 2037 maturity British Telecom bond—than for the shorter-duration bond. Longer-duration corporate bonds are referred to as having "higher spread sensitivity"; that is, their prices, and thus returns, are more volatile with respect to changes in spread. It is essentially the same concept as duration for any bond: The longer the duration of a bond, the greater the price volatility for a given change in interest rates/yields.

In addition, investors want to be compensated for the fact that the further one is from a bond's maturity (i.e., the longer the bond), the greater the uncertainty about an issuer's future creditworthiness. Based on credit analysis, an investor might be confident that an issuer's risk of default is relatively low in the near term; however, looking many years into the future, the investor's uncertainty grows because of factors that are increasingly difficult, if not impossible, to forecast (e.g., poor management strategy or execution, technological obsolescence, natural or man-made disasters, corporate leveraging events). This increase in credit risk over time can be seen in Exhibit 18. Note that in this Standard & Poor's study,[32] one-year default rates for the 2010 issuance pool are 0 percent for all rating categories of B+ or higher. The three-year default rates for bonds issued in 2008 are materially higher, and the observed defaults include bonds originally rated up to BBB− (i.e., low investment grade). The 10-year default rates for bonds issued in 2001 are appreciably higher than the 3-year default rates, and the defaults include bonds initially rated as high as A+ (i.e., solid investment grade). In addition to the risk of default rising over time, the data also show quite conclusively that the lower the credit rating, the higher the risk of default. Finally, note the very high risk of default for bonds rated CCC or lower over all time horizons. This is consistent with Exhibit 7 earlier in the reading, which showed significant three-year ratings variability ("migration"), with much of the migration to lower credit ratings (i.e., higher risk of default).

Exhibit 18   Default Rate by Rating Category (%) (Non-financials)

Credit Rating	1 Year (2010 pool)	3 Year (2008 pool)	10 Year (2001 pool)
AAA	0.00	0.00	0.00
AA+	0.00	0.00	0.00
AA	0.00	0.00	0.00
AA−	0.00	0.00	0.00
A+	0.00	0.00	1.76

(continued)

---

32 From S&P, "2010 Annual Global Corporate Default Study and Ratings Transitions," Standard & Poor's report (30 March 2011). Detailed descriptions of the underlying methodology are available in Appendix I of the report.

Exhibit 18   (Continued)

Credit Rating	1 Year (2010 pool)	3 Year (2008 pool)	10 Year (2001 pool)
A	0.00	0.00	1.70
A–	0.00	0.00	0.87
BBB+	0.00	0.00	5.03
BBB	0.00	0.00	4.55
BBB–	0.00	1.04	12.80
BB+	0.00	2.12	15.38
BB	0.00	3.53	19.91
BB–	0.00	6.14	26.84
B+	0.00	12.73	33.69
B	0.76	22.08	39.02
B–	2.07	25.23	55.83
CCC/C	21.99	56.63	65.31

Source: Based on data from S&P, "2010 Annual Global Corporate Default Study and Ratings Transitions," Standard & Poor's report (30 March 2011).

It is also worth noting that bid–ask spreads (in yield terms) translate into higher transaction costs for longer-duration bonds; investors want to be compensated for that as well. For these reasons, spread curves (often called **credit curves**), like yield curves, are typically upward sloping. That is, longer-maturity bonds of a given issuer typically trade at wider spreads than shorter-maturity bonds to their respective comparable-maturity government bonds.[33] Exhibit 19, using the US telecommunications company AT&T as an example, shows the upward-sloping credit curve by plotting the yields of its bonds versus their maturity. (As a large and frequent issuer, AT&T has many bonds outstanding across the yield curve.)

---

33 There are some exceptions to this—bonds that trade at a high premium price over par due to having coupons that are well above the bond's yield to maturity and bonds that trade at distressed levels due to credit concerns. Many investors are averse to paying high premium prices for bonds that have credit risk because of the greater potential price decline—towards a recovery price in the event of default—from a credit-adverse event. Thus, high-coupon intermediate-maturity bonds can trade at similar or wider spreads to longer-maturity bonds. For distressed credits, the high risk of default causes all bonds for a given issuer to migrate toward the same expected recovery price. In this case, the shorter-maturity and shorter-duration bonds will have a higher quoted yield to maturity, and wider spread, than the longer-maturity and longer-duration bonds. This follows from the return impact formulas. The shorter the duration, the higher the yield (including spread) must go to bring the price down to a given expected recovery price.

Exhibit 19   AT&T Credit Curve vs. US Treasury Curve

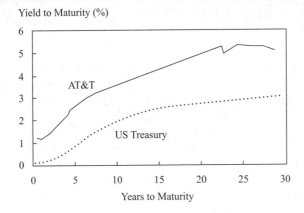

Source: Based on data from Bloomberg Finance, L.P., as of 5 October 2011.

EXAMPLE 9

Return Impact

Calculate the return impact on a 10-year corporate bond with a 4.75 percent coupon priced at 100, with an instantaneous 50 bps widening in spread due to the issuer's announcement that it was adding substantial debt to finance an acquisition, resulting in a two-notch downgrade by the rating agencies. The bond has a modified duration of 7.9 and its convexity is 74.9.

Solution:

The impact from the 50 bps spread widening is:

$$\text{Return impact} \approx -(\text{MDur} \times \Delta\text{Spread}) + \tfrac{1}{2}\,\text{Cvx} \times (\Delta\text{Spread})^2$$
$$= -(0.0050 \times 7.9) + (0.5 \times 74.9) \times (0.0050)^2$$
$$= -0.0386, \text{ or } -3.86 \text{ percent}$$

Because yields and bond prices move in opposite directions, the wider spread caused the bond price to fall. Using a bond-pricing calculator, the exact return is −3.85 percent, so this approximation was very accurate.

In summary, spread changes can have a significant impact on the performance of credit-risky bonds over a given holding period, and the higher the modified duration of the bond(s), the greater the price impact from changes in spread. Wider spreads hurt bond performance, whereas narrower spreads help bond performance. For bond investors who actively manage their portfolios (i.e., don't just buy bonds and hold them to maturity), forecasting spread changes and expected credit losses on both individual bonds and their broader portfolios is an important strategy for enhancing investment performance.

7 SPECIAL CONSIDERATIONS OF HIGH-YIELD, SOVEREIGN, AND MUNICIPAL CREDIT ANALYSIS

Thus far, we have focused primarily on basic principles of credit analysis and investing with emphasis on higher-quality, investment-grade corporate bonds. Although many of these principles are applicable to other credit-risky segments of the bond market, there are some differences in credit analysis that need to be considered. This section focuses on special considerations in evaluating the credit of debt issuers from the following three market segments: high-yield corporate bonds, sovereign bonds, and municipal bonds.

7.1 High Yield

Recall that high-yield, or non-investment-grade, corporate bonds are those rated below Baa3/BBB– by the major rating agencies. These bonds are sometimes referred to as "junk bonds" because of the higher risk inherent in their weak balance sheets and/or poor or less-proven business prospects.

There are many reasons companies are rated below investment grade, including

- Highly leveraged capital structure
- Weak or limited operating history
- Limited or negative free cash flow
- Highly cyclical business
- Poor management
- Risky financial policies
- Lack of scale and/or competitive advantages
- Large off-balance-sheet liabilities
- Declining industry (e.g., newspaper publishing)

Companies with weak balance sheets and/or business profiles have lower margin for error and greater risk of default relative to higher-quality investment-grade names. And the higher risk of default means more attention must be paid to recovery analysis (or loss severity, in the event of default). Consequently, high-yield analysis typically is more in-depth than investment-grade analysis and thus has special considerations. This includes the following:

- Greater focus on issuer liquidity and cash flow
- Detailed financial projections
- Detailed understanding and analysis of the debt structure
- Understanding of an issuer's corporate structure
- Covenants
- Equity-like approach to high yield analysis

Liquidity. Liquidity—that is, having cash and/or the ability to generate or raise cash—is important to all issuers. It is absolutely critical for high-yield companies. Investment-grade companies typically have substantial cash on their balance sheets, generate a lot of cash from operations relative to their debt (or else they wouldn't be investment grade!), and/or are presumed to have alternate sources of liquidity, such as bank lines and commercial paper.[34] For these reasons, investment-grade companies can more easily roll over (refinance) maturing debt. On the other hand, high-yield companies may not have those options available. For example, there is no high-yield commercial paper market, and bank credit facilities often carry tighter restrictions for high-yield companies. Both bad company-specific news and difficult financial market conditions can lead to high-yield companies being unable to access the debt markets. And although the vast majority of investment-grade corporate debt issuers have publicly traded equity and can thus use that equity as a financing option, many high-yield companies are privately held and thus don't have access to public equity markets.

Thus, issuer liquidity is a key focus in high-yield analysis. Sources of liquidity, from strongest to weakest, are the following:

1 Cash on the balance sheet

2 Working capital

3 Operating cash flow

4 Bank credit facilities

5 Equity issuance

6 Asset sales

Cash on the balance sheet is easy to see and self-evident as a source for repaying debt.[35] As mentioned earlier in this reading, working capital can be a large source or use of liquidity, depending on its amount, its use in a company's cash-conversion cycle, and its role in a company's operations. Operating cash flow is a ready source of liquidity as sales turn to receivables, which turn to cash over a fairly short time period. Bank lines, or credit facilities, can be an important source of liquidity, though there may be some covenants relating to the use of the bank lines which are crucial to know and will be covered a little later. Equity issuance may not be a reliable source of liquidity because an issuer is private or because of poor market conditions if a company does have publicly traded equity. Asset sales are the least reliable source of liquidity because both the potential value and the actual time of closing can be highly uncertain.

The amount of these liquidity sources should be compared with the amount and timing of upcoming debt maturities. A large amount of debt coming due in the next 6–12 months alongside low sources of liquidity will be a warning flag for bond investors and could push an issuer into default because investors may choose not to buy new bonds intended to pay off the existing debt. Insufficient liquidity—that is, running out of cash or no longer having access to external financing to refinance or pay off existing debt—is the principal reason issuers default. Although liquidity is important for industrial companies, it is an absolute necessity for financial firms, as seen in the case of Lehman Brothers and other troubled firms during the financial crisis of 2008. Financial institutions are highly levered and often highly dependent on funding longer-term assets with short-term term liabilities.

Financial Projections. Because high-yield companies have less room for error, it's important to forecast, or project, future earnings and cash flow out several years, perhaps including several scenarios, to assess whether the issuer's credit profile is stable, improving, or declining and thus whether it needs other sources of liquidity or is at

---

34 Commercial paper (CP) is short-term funding—fewer than 270 days—used by many large, investment-grade corporations on a daily basis. In practice, issuance of CP requires solid, long-term, investment-grade ratings, mostly A rated or better, with a much smaller market for BBB rated companies.

35 Note that some cash may be "trapped" in other countries for certain tax, business, or regulatory reasons, and may not be easily accessible, or repatriation—bringing the money back to the home country—could trigger cash tax payments.

risk of default. Ongoing capital expenditures and working capital changes should be incorporated as well. Special emphasis should be given to realistic "stress" scenarios that could expose a borrower's vulnerabilities.

Debt Structure.   High-yield companies tend to have many layers of debt in their capital structures, with varying levels of seniority and, therefore, different potential recovery rates in the event of default. (Recall the historical table of default recovery rates based on seniority in Exhibit 2.) A high-yield issuer will often have at least some of the following types of obligations in its debt structure:

- (Secured) Bank debt[36]
- Second lien debt
- Senior unsecured debt
- Subordinated debt, which may include convertible bonds[37]
- Preferred stock[38]

The lower the ranking in the debt structure, the lower the credit rating and the lower the expected recovery in the event of default. In exchange for these associated higher risks, investors will normally demand higher yields.

As discussed in Section 5, the standard leverage calculation used by credit analysts is debt/EBITDA and is quoted as a multiple (e.g., "5.2x levered"). For an issuer with several layers of debt with different expected recovery rates, high-yield analysts should calculate leverage at each level of the debt structure.

EXAMPLE 10

Debt Structure and Leverage

Freescale Semiconductor specializes in semiconductors that are used in autos, communication equipment, and industrial machinery. This high-yield-rated company's debt structure is complicated because of the many levels of seniority that resulted from the company's 2006 leveraged buyout by a consortium of private equity firms. Exhibit 20 is a simplified depiction of the company's debt structure, as well as some key credit-related statistics.

Exhibit 20	Freescale Semiconductor Debt and Leverage Structure as of Year-End 2010
Financial Information ($ millions)	
Cash	$ 1,050
Total debt	$ 7,611
Net debt	$ 6,561
Interest expense	$ 590
EBITDA	$ 990

---

[36] Because of the higher risk of default, in most instances bank debt will be secured for high-yield issuers.
[37] Convertible bonds are debt instruments that give holders the option to convert to a fixed number of shares of common stock. They can be at any level of the capital structure but are frequently issued as senior subordinated debt.
[38] Preferred stock has elements of both debt and equity. It typically receives a fixed payment like a bond does and has higher priority of claims than common stock. As a type of equity, however, it is subordinated to all forms of debt.

> ### Exhibit 20   (Continued)
>
> **Debt Structure ($ millions)**
>
> | | |
> |---|---:|
> | Secured debt (bank loan and bonds) | $ 4,899 |
> | Senior unsecured bonds | $ 1,948 |
> | Subordinated bonds | $ 764 |
> | TOTAL DEBT | $ 7,611 |
>
> *Source:* Company Filings, Loomis Sayles & Company.

Using the information provided, address the following:

1 Calculate the total financial leverage through each level of debt, including total gross leverage.

2 Calculate the net leverage through the total debt structure.

3 Why might Freescale have so much secured debt relative to unsecured debt (both senior and subordinated)? (Note: This question draws on concepts from earlier sections.)

Solutions to 1 and 2:

	Gross Leverage (Debt/EBITDA)	Net Leverage (Debt – Cash)/ EBITDA
Secured debt leverage		
(Total secured debt/EBITDA)		
4899/990	4.9x	
Senior unsecured leverage		
(Secured debt + Senior unsecured debt)/EBITDA		
(4899 + 1948)/990	6.9x	
Total leverage (includes subordinated)		
(Total debt/EBITDA)		
7611/990	7.7x	
Net leverage (leverage net of cash through entire debt structure)		
(Total debt – Cash)/EBITDA		6.6x

Solution to 3:

Freescale might have that much secured debt because (1) it was less expensive than issuing more unsecured debt on which investors would have demanded a higher yield and/or (2) given the riskiness of the business (semiconductors that are sold into cyclical industries, such as autos), the operating leverage of the business model, and the riskiness of the balance sheet (lots of debt from a leveraged buyout), investors would only lend the company money on a secured basis.

High-yield companies that have a lot of secured debt (typically bank debt) relative to unsecured debt are said to have a "top-heavy" capital structure. With this structure, there is less capacity to take on more bank debt in the event of financial stress. Along with the often more stringent covenants associated with bank debt and its generally shorter maturity compared with other forms of debt, this means that these issuers are more susceptible to default, as well as to lower recovery for the various less secured creditors.

Corporate Structure.   Many debt-issuing corporations, including high-yield companies, utilize a holding company structure with a parent and several operating subsidiaries. Knowing where an issuer's debt resides (parent versus subsidiaries) and how cash can move from subsidiary to parent ("upstream") and vice versa ("downstream") should be key components of the analysis of high-yield issuers.

In a holding company structure, the parent owns stock in its subsidiaries. Typically, the parent doesn't generate much of its own earnings or cash flow but instead receives funds from its subsidiaries in the form of dividends from their earnings. And the subsidiaries' dividends are generally paid out of earnings after they satisfy of all their other obligations, such as debt payments. To the extent that their earnings and cash flow are weak, subsidiaries may be limited in their ability to pay dividends to the parent. Moreover, subsidiaries that carry a lot of their own debt may have restrictions or limitations on how much cash they can provide to the parent via dividends or another form, such as an intercompany loan. These restrictions and limitations on cash moving between parent and subsidiaries can have a major impact on their respective abilities to meet their debt obligations. The parent's reliance on cash flow from its subsidiaries means the parent's debt is structurally subordinated to the subsidiaries' debt and thus will usually have a lower recovery rating in default.

For companies with very complex holding companies, there may also be one or more intermediate holding companies, each carrying their own debt, and in some cases, they may not own 100 percent of the subsidiaries' stock. This structure is sometimes seen in high-yield companies that have been put together through many mergers and acquisitions or that were part of a leveraged buyout.[39]

Exhibit 21 returns to United Rentals, Inc. (URI), a high-yield company highlighted earlier as an example of the credit rating agency notching process. URI has a capital structure consisting of a parent company that has debt—in this case, convertible senior notes—as well as subsidiaries with outstanding debt. And in the case of URI's United Rentals North America subsidiary, it has several layers of debt by seniority.

---

39 For holding companies with complex corporate structures, such as multiple subsidiaries with their own capital structures, a default in one subsidiary may not trigger a cross-default. Astute analysts will look for that in indentures and other legal documentation.

Exhibit 21   URI's Capital Structure

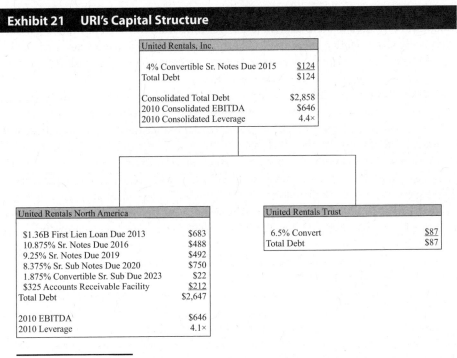

Sources: Based on data from company filings and Loomis, Sayles & Company.

Thus, high-yield investors should analyze and understand an issuer's corporate structure, including the distribution of debt between the parent and its subsidiaries. Leverage ratios should be calculated at each of the debt-issuing entities, as well as on a consolidated basis.

Also important is that although the debt of an operating subsidiary may be "closer to" and better secured by particular assets of the subsidiary, the credit quality of a parent company might still be superior. The parent company could, while being less directly secured by any particular assets, still benefit from the diversity and availability of all the cash flows in the consolidated system. In short, credit quality is not simply an automatic analysis of debt provisions and liens.

Covenant Analysis.   As discussed earlier, analysis of covenants is very important for all bonds. It is especially important for high-yield credits because of their reduced margin of safety. Key covenants for high-yield issuers may include the following:

- Change of control put
- Restricted payments
- Limitations on liens and additional indebtedness
- Restricted versus unrestricted subsidiaries

Under the **change of control put**, in the event of an acquisition (a "change of control"), bondholders have the right to require the issuer to buy back their debt (a "put option"), often at par or at some small premium to par value. This covenant is intended to protect creditors from being exposed to a weaker, more indebted borrower as a result of acquisition. For investment-grade issuers, this covenant typically has a two-pronged test: acquisition of the borrower and a consequent downgrade to a high-yield rating.

The **restricted payments** covenant is meant to protect creditors by limiting how much cash can be paid out to shareholders over time. The restricted payments "basket" is typically sized relative to an issuer's cash flow and debt outstanding—or is being raised—and is an amount that can grow with retained earnings or cash flow, giving management more flexibility to make pay-outs.

The **limitations on liens** covenant is meant to put limits on how much secured debt an issuer can have. This covenant is important to unsecured creditors who are structurally subordinated to secured creditors; the higher the amount of debt that is layered ahead of them, the less they stand to recover in the event of default.

With regard to **restricted versus unrestricted subsidiaries**, issuers may classify certain of their subsidiaries as restricted and others as unrestricted as it pertains to offering guarantees for their holding company debt. These subsidiary guarantees can be very useful to holding company creditors because they put their debt on equal standing (pari passu) with debt at the subsidiaries instead of with structurally subordinated debt. Restricted subsidiaries should be thought of as those that are designated to help service parent-level debt, typically through guarantees. They tend to be an issuer's larger subsidiaries and have significant assets, such as plants and other facilities, and/or cash flow. There may be tax or legal (e.g., country of domicile) reasons why certain subsidiaries are restricted while others are not. Analysts should carefully read the definitions of restricted versus unrestricted subsidiaries in the indenture because sometimes the language is so loosely written that the company can reclassify subsidiaries from one type to another with a simple vote by a board of directors or trustees.

For high-yield investors, it is also important to know what covenants are in an issuer's bank credit agreements. These agreements are typically filed with the securities commission in the country where the loan document was drafted. Bank covenants can be more restrictive than bond covenants and may include so-called **maintenance covenants**, such as leverage tests, whereby the ratio of, say, debt/EBITDA may not exceed "x" times. In the event a covenant is breached, the bank is likely to block further loans under the agreement until the covenant is cured. If not cured, the bank may accelerate full payment of the facility, triggering a default.

Equity-like approach to high-yield analysis.   High-yield bonds are sometimes thought of as a "hybrid" between higher-quality bonds, such as investment-grade corporate debt, and equity securities. Their more volatile price and spread movements are less influenced by interest rate changes than are higher-quality bonds, and they show greater correlation with movements in equity markets. Indeed, as shown in Exhibit 22, historical returns on high-yield bonds and the standard deviation of those returns fall somewhere between investment-grade bonds and equities.

Exhibit 22   US Trailing 12-Month Returns by Asset Class, 31 December 1988–30 June 2011

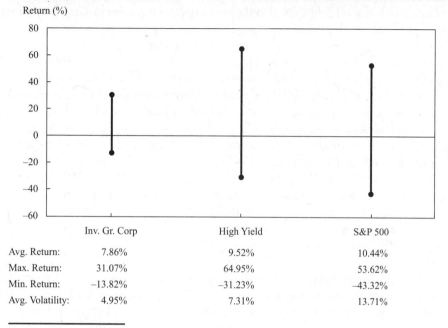

	Inv. Gr. Corp	High Yield	S&P 500
Avg. Return:	7.86%	9.52%	10.44%
Max. Return:	31.07%	64.95%	53.62%
Min. Return:	−13.82%	−31.23%	−43.32%
Avg. Volatility:	4.95%	7.31%	13.71%

Sources: Based on data from Barclays, Haver Analytics, and Loomis, Sayles & Company.

Consequently, an equity market-like approach to analyzing a high-yield issuer can be useful. One approach is to calculate an issuer's enterprise value. Enterprise value (EV) is usually calculated by adding equity market capitalization and total debt and then subtracting excess cash.[40,41] Enterprise value is a measure of what a business is worth (before any takeover premium) because an acquirer of the company would have to either pay off or assume the debt and it would receive the acquired company's cash.

Bond investors like using EV because it shows the amount of equity "cushion" beneath the debt. It can also give a sense of (1) how much more leverage management might attempt to put on a company in an effort to increase equity returns or (2) how likely—and how expensive—a credit-damaging leveraged buyout might be. Similar to how stock investors look at equity multiples, bond investors may calculate and compare EV/EBITDA and debt/EBITDA across several issuers as part of their analysis. Narrow differences between the EV/EBITDA and debt/EBITDA ratios for a given issuer indicate a small equity cushion and, therefore, potentially higher risk for bond investors.

7.2 Sovereign Debt

Governments around the world issue debt to help finance their general operations, including current expenses such as wages for government employees, and investments in long-term assets such as infrastructure and education. Government bonds in developed countries (such as the United States) have traditionally been viewed as the default risk-free rate off of which all other credits are priced. Fiscal challenges in developed countries exacerbated by the 2008 crisis, however, have called into question

---

40 Excess cash takes total cash and subtracts any negative working capital.

41 Unlike the vast majority of investment-grade companies, many high-yield issuers do not have publicly traded equity. For those issuers, one can use comparable public company equity data to estimate EV.

the notion of a "risk-free rate," even for some of the highest-quality government borrowers. As their capital markets have developed, an increasing number of sovereigns have been able to issue both external debt (denominated in hard currency, often the US dollar) as well as local debt (issued in the sovereign's own currency). Generally, weaker sovereigns can only access international (that is, non-local) debt markets by issuing bonds in foreign currencies that are viewed to be safer stores of value. Local—also known as internal—debt is somewhat easier to service because the debt is typically denominated in the country's own currency, subject to its own laws, and the central bank can print additional money to service the government's local debt. Twenty years ago, many emerging market countries[42] could only issue external debt. Today, many are able to issue local debt and have successfully built domestic yield curves of local bonds across the maturity spectrum. All sovereigns are best able to service both external and local debt if they run "twin surpluses"—that is, a government budget surplus as well as a current account surplus. Running a current account surplus means the country is a net exporter of capital to the world and is not dependent on external financing.

Despite ongoing financial globalization and the development of local bond markets, sovereign defaults continue. Defaults are often precipitated by such events as war, political upheaval, major currency devaluation, a sharp deterioration in trade, or dramatic price declines in a country's key commodity exports. But default risks for some developed countries escalated after 2009 as government revenues dropped precipitously following the financial crisis, expenditures surged, and financial markets focused on the long-term sustainability of public finances, given aging populations and rising social security needs. Some of the weaker and more highly indebted members of the eurozone became unable to access the debt markets at economical rates and had to seek loans from the International Monetary Fund (IMF) and the European Union. These weaker governments had previously been able to borrow at much lower rates because of their membership in the European Union and adoption of the euro. Intra-eurozone yield spreads widened and countries were shut out of markets, however, as the global financial crisis exacted a high toll on their public finances and, in some cases, their banking systems, which became contingent liabilities for the sovereigns. In Ireland, the government guaranteed most bank liabilities, causing the country's debt burden to increase dramatically.

Like corporate analysis, sovereign credit analysis is based on a combination of qualitative and quantitative factors. Ultimately, the two key issues for sovereign analysis are 1) a government's ability to pay and 2) its willingness to pay. Willingness to pay is important because, due to the principle of sovereign immunity, investors are generally unable to force a sovereign to pay its debts.

To illustrate the most important considerations in sovereign credit analysis, we present a basic framework for evaluating sovereign credit and assigning sovereign debt ratings.[43] The framework highlights the specific characteristics analysts should expect in a top-quality sovereign credit. Some of these are self-explanatory (e.g., absence of corruption). For others, a brief rationale and/or range of values is included to clarify interpretation. Most, but not all, of these items are included in rating agency Standard & Poor's methodology.

Political and economic profile

- *Institutional effectiveness and political risks*

---

42 There is no commonly accepted definition of emerging market countries. The World Bank considers GDP/Capita to be a useful measure, with below-average GDP/Capita likely indicating an emerging market. Other factors include the degree of openness and maturity of the economy, as well as a country's political stability.
43 This outline was developed from the detailed exposition of Standard & Poor's methodology given in "Sovereign Government Rating Methodology and Assumptions," June 2011.

- *Effectiveness, stability, and predictability of policy making and institutions*
    - Successful management of past political, economic, and/or financial crises
    - Ability and willingness to implement reforms to address fiscal challenges
    - Predictable policy framework
    - Absence of challenges to political institutions
    - Checks and balances in the system
    - Absence of corruption
    - Unbiased law enforcement and respect for rule of law and property rights
    - Independent/ unfettered media and sources of economic data
- *Perceived commitment to honor debts*
- *Economic structure and growth prospects*
    - Income per capita: More prosperous countries generally have a broader and deeper tax base with which to support debt.
    - Trend growth prospects: Trend GDP growth is primarily a reflection of productivity. Above-average trend growth indicates greater ability to service debt from future revenue and, therefore, greater creditworthiness.
    - Sources and stability of growth: Stable, broad-based growth and absence of excessive private sector credit expansion indicate stronger sovereign credit.
    - Size of the public sector relative to private sector: A smaller, leaner public sector is more likely to be able to enact necessary changes because it should be less beholden to special interest groups, including public employee unions.
    - Growth and age distribution of population: A relatively young and growing population contributes to trend GDP growth and an expanding tax base and mitigates the burden of social services, health care, and pensions, which are disproportionately costly for aging populations.

Flexibility and performance profile

- *External liquidity and international investment position*
    - Status of currency: Sovereigns that control a reserve currency or a very actively traded currency are able to use their own currency in many international transactions and are less vulnerable to adverse shifts in global investor portfolios.
    - External liquidity: Countries with a substantial supply of foreign exchange (foreign exchange reserves plus current account receipts) relative to projected external funding needs (current account payments plus debt maturities) are less vulnerable to interruption of external liquidity.
    - External debt: Countries with low external debt relative to current account receipts are better able to service their foreign currency debt. This is similar to that of a coverage ratio for a corporation.
- *Fiscal performance, flexibility, and debt burden*
    - Trend change in general government debt as a percent of GDP: Stable or declining debt as a percent of GDP indicates a strong credit; a rising ratio is ultimately unsustainable and is, therefore, a sign of diminishing creditworthiness.

- Perceived willingness and ability to increase revenue or cut expenditure to ensure debt service.

- General government interest expense as a percent of revenue: Less than 5 percent is good; greater than 15 percent is poor.

- Net general government debt as a percent of GDP: Less than 30 percent is good; more than 100 percent is poor.

- Contingent liabilities arising from financial sector, public enterprises, and guarantees: Less than 30 percent of GDP is good; more than 80 percent is very poor.

■ *Monetary flexibility*

  - *Ability to use monetary policy to address domestic economic objectives* (e.g., growth)

    ■ Exchange rate regime: A freely floating currency allows maximum effectiveness for monetary policy. A fixed-rate regime limits effectiveness and flexibility. A hard peg, such as a currency board or monetary union, affords no independent monetary policy.

  - *Credibility of monetary policy*

    ■ Operationally independent central bank: An independent central bank is less likely to "debase the currency" by excessive money creation (e.g., in order to fund government deficits).

    ■ Clear central bank mandate/objectives

    ■ Track record of low and stable inflation

    ■ Central government's ability to issue substantial long-term, fixed-rate debt in local currency: This is a sign of market confidence in the currency as a store of value.

  - *Effectiveness of monetary policy transmission via domestic capital markets*

    ■ Well-developed banking system

    ■ Active money market and corporate bond market

    ■ Greater reliance on market-based policy tools (e.g., open market operations) and limited reliance on blunt, administrative policy tools (e.g., reserve requirements)

In light of a sovereign government's various powers—taxation, regulation, monetary policy, and ultimately, the sovereign's ability to "print money" to repay debt—within its own economy, it is virtually always at least as good a credit in its local currency as it is in foreign currency. Thus, credit rating agencies often distinguish between local and foreign currency bonds, with local currency ratings as much as two notches higher. Of course, if a sovereign were to rely heavily on printing money to repay debt, it would fuel high inflation or hyperinflation and increase default risk on local debt as well.[44]

EXAMPLE 11

Sovereign Debt

Exhibit 23 shows several key sovereign statistics for Portugal.

---

[44] According to Reinhart and Rogoff in their book *This Time is Different*, between 1800 and 2009 there have been more than 250 defaults on external sovereign debt and at least 68 defaults on internal debt. Reinhart and Rogoff use a broader definition of default that includes very high levels of inflation (more than 20 percent).

€ (billions), except where noted	2005	2006	2007	2008	2009	2010
Exhibit 23 Key Sovereign Statistics for Portugal						
Nominal GDP	153.7	160.3	169.3	171.2	168.6	172.6
Population (millions)	10.6	10.6	10.6	10.6	10.6	10.6
Unemployment (%)	8.6	8.6	8.9	8.5	10.6	12.0
Exports as share GDP (%)	20.3	22.2	22.6	22.6	18.8	21.3
Current account as share GDP (%)	−10.3	−10.7	−10.1	−12.6	−10.9	−10.0
Government revenues	61.3	64.8	69.7	70.7	67.0	71.8
Government expenditures	70.4	71.4	75.1	77.1	84.1	88.7
Budget balance (surplus/deficit)	−9.0	−6.5	−5.4	−6.4	−17.1	−16.9
Government interest payments	3.8	4.2	5.1	5.3	4.9	5.2
Primary balance (surplus/deficit)	−5.3	−2.2	−0.4	−1.1	−12.2	−11.7
Government debt	96.5	102.4	115.6	123.1	139.9	161.3
Interest rate on new debt (%)	3.4	3.9	4.4	4.5	4.2	5.4

Sources: Based on data from Haver Analytics, Eurostat, and Instituto Nacional de Estatistica (Portugal).

1 Calculate the government debt/GDP ratio for Portugal over the years 2005–2010.

2 Calculate GDP/Capita for the same period.

3 Based on those calculations, as well as other data from Exhibit 23, what can you say about Portugal's credit trend?

Solutions to 1 and 2:

	2005	2006	2007	2008	2009	2010
Gross government debt/GDP	63%	64%	68%	72%	83%	93%
GDP/Capita	14,500	15,123	15,972	16,151	15,906	16,283

Solution to 3:

The credit trend is deteriorating. Government debt/GDP is rising rapidly. The government is running a budget deficit, and the country is running a sizable current account deficit, which means it must attract funding from outside the country. Interest payments are generally rising, as is the interest rate on new debt.

7.3 Municipal Debt

While sovereigns are the largest issuers of government debt, non-sovereign—sometimes called sub-sovereign—government entities issue bonds as well. This would include state, provincial, and local governments (e.g., cities, towns, and counties, often referred to as municipalities) as well as the various agencies and authorities they create. For example, the City of Tokyo (Tokyo Metropolitan Government) has debt outstanding, as does the Lombardy region in Italy, the City of Buenos Aires in Argentina, and the State of California in the United States.

When people talk about municipal debt securities, however, they are usually referring to the US municipal bond market because of its size. This market is approximately $3.7 trillion in size, roughly 10 percent of the total US bond market,[45] and is composed of both tax-exempt[46] and, to a lesser extent, taxable bonds issued by state and local governments and their agencies. Municipal borrowers may also issue bonds on behalf of private entities, such as non-profit colleges or hospitals. Historically, for any given rating category, these bonds have much lower default rates than corporate bonds with the same ratings. For example, according to Moody's Investors Service, the 10-year average cumulative default rate from 1970 through 2009 was 0.09 percent for municipal bonds, compared with an 11.06 percent 10-year average cumulative default rate for all corporate debt.[47] The majority of municipal bonds are either general obligation bonds or revenue bonds.

General obligation (GO) bonds are unsecured bonds issued with the full faith and credit of the issuing government, typically a city, county, or state. These bonds are supported by the taxing authority of the issuer. The credit analysis of GO bonds has some similarities to sovereign debt analysis (e.g., the ability to levy and collect taxes and fees to help service debt). Almost without exception, however, municipalities must balance their operating budgets (i.e., exclusive of long-term capital projects) annually and they have no ability to use monetary policy the way many sovereigns can. The economic analysis focuses on employment, per capita income (and changes in it over time), per capita debt (and changes in it over time), the tax base (depth, breadth, diversification, stability, etc.), demographics, and net population growth, as well as an analysis of whether the state or municipality has the infrastructure and location to attract and support new jobs. Analysis should look at the volatility and variability of revenues during times of both economic strength and weakness. An overreliance on one or two types of tax revenue—particularly a volatile one, such as capital gains taxes or sales taxes—can signal increased credit risk. Pensions and other post-retirement obligations may not show up directly on the state or municipality's balance sheet, and many of these entities have underfunded pensions that need to be addressed. Adding the unfunded pension and post-retirement obligations to the debt reveals a more realistic picture of the issuer's debt and longer-term obligations. The relative ease or difficulty in managing the annual budgeting process and the government's ability to operate consistently within its budget are also important credit analysis considerations.

Disclosure by state and local governments varies widely, with some of the smaller issuers providing limited financial information. Reporting requirements are inconsistent, so the financial reports may not be available for six months or more after the closing of a reporting period.

---

45 Securities Industry and Financial Markets Association (SIFMA), "Outstanding US Bond Market Data," (Q3 2011).

46 Tax exempt refers to the fact that interest received on these bonds is not subject to US federal income taxes and, in many cases, is exempt for in-state residents from state and local taxes as well.

47 Moody's Investors Service, "US Municipal Bond Defaults and Recoveries, 1970–2009," Moody's Special Comment (February 2010).

Exhibit 24 compares several key debt statistics from two of the largest states in the United States: California and Texas. California has one of the lowest credit ratings of any of the states, whereas Texas has one of the highest. Note the higher debt burden (and ranking) across several measures: Total debt, Debt/Capita, Debt/Personal income, and debt as a percent of state GDP. What is not shown here is that California also has a higher tax burden and greater difficulty balancing its budget on an annual basis than Texas.

Exhibit 24 Municipal Debt Comparison: California vs. Texas		
	California	Texas
Ratings:		
Moody's Investors Service	A1	Aaa
Standard & Poor's	A–	AA+
Fitch	A–	AAA
Unemployment rate (%)	12.40	8.20
Personal income per capita ($)	43,641	37,774
Debt burden, net ($/rank):		
Total (millions)	94,715 (1)	15,433 (9)
Per capita	2,542 (8)	612 (39)
As a percent of 2009 personal income	6.00 (9)	1.60 (40)
As a percent of 2010 GDP	4.73 (8)	1.05 (41)

Sources: Based on data from the US Bureau of Labor Statistics (as of 2010), the US Census Bureau (as of 2008), and Moody's Investors Service (as of 2010).

Revenue bonds are issued for specific project financing (e.g., financing for a new sewer system, a toll road, bridge, hospital, a sports arena, etc.). Revenue bonds have a higher degree of risk than GO bonds because they are dependent on a single source of revenue. The analysis of these bonds is a combination of an analysis of the project and the finances around the particular project. The project analysis focuses on the need and projected utilization of the project, as well as on the economic base supporting the project. The financial analysis has some similarities to the analysis of a corporate bond in that it is focused on operating results, cash flow, liquidity, capital structure, and the ability to service and repay the debt. A key credit metric for revenue-backed municipal bonds is the debt service coverage ratio (DSCR), which measures how much revenue is available to cover debt payments (principal and interest) after operating expenses. Many revenue bonds have a minimum DSCR covenant; the higher the DSCR, the stronger the creditworthiness.

CONCLUSION AND SUMMARY

8

In this reading, we introduced readers to the basic principles of credit analysis. We described the importance of the credit markets and the various types of credit risk. We discussed the role and importance of credit ratings and the methodology associated with assigning ratings, as well as the risks of relying on credit ratings. The reading covered the key components of credit analysis and the financial ratios used to help measure creditworthiness.

We also discussed risk versus return when investing in credit and how spread changes affect holding period returns. In addition, we addressed the special considerations to take into account when doing credit analysis of high-yield companies, sovereign borrowers, and municipal bonds.

- Credit risk is the risk of loss resulting from the borrower failing to make full and timely payments of interest and/or principal.

- The key components of credit risk are risk of default and loss severity in the event of default. The product of the two is expected loss. Investors in higher-quality bonds tend not to focus on loss severity because default risk for those securities is low.

- Loss severity equals (1 – Recovery rate).

- Other forms of credit-related risk include downgrade risk (also called credit migration risk) and market liquidity risk. Either of these can cause yield spreads—yield premiums—to rise and bond prices to fall.

- Downgrade risk refers to a decline in an issuer's creditworthiness. Downgrades will cause its bonds to trade at wider yields and thus lower prices.

- Market liquidity risk refers to a widening of the bid–ask spread on an issuer's bonds. Lower-quality bonds tend to have greater market liquidity risk than higher-quality bonds, and during times of market or financial stress, market liquidity risk rises.

- The composition of an issuer's debt and equity is referred to as its "capital structure." Debt ranks ahead of all forms of equity with respect to priority of payment, and within the debt component of the capital structure, there can be varying levels of seniority.

- With respect to priority of claims, secured debt ranks ahead of unsecured debt, and within unsecured debt, senior debt ranks ahead of subordinated debt. In the typical case, all of an issuer's bonds have the same probability of default due to cross-default provisions in most indentures. Higher priority of claim means higher recovery rate—lower loss severity—in the event of default.

- For issuers with more complex corporate structures—for example, a parent holding company that has operating subsidiaries—debt at the holding company is structurally subordinated to the subsidiary debt, although the possibility of more diverse assets and earnings streams from other sources could still result in the parent having higher effective credit quality than a particular subsidiary.

- Recovery rates can vary greatly by issuer and industry. They are influenced by the composition of an issuer's capital structure, where in the economic and credit cycle the default occurred, and what the market's view of the future prospects are for the issuer and its industry.

- The priority of claims in bankruptcy is not always absolute. It can be influenced by several factors, including some leeway accorded to bankruptcy judges, government involvement, or a desire on the part of the more senior creditors to settle with the more junior creditors and allow the issuer to emerge from bankruptcy as a going concern, rather than risking smaller and delayed recovery in the event of a liquidation of the borrower.

- Credit rating agencies, such as Moody's, Standard & Poor's, and Fitch, play a central role in the credit markets. Nearly every bond issued in the broad debt markets carries credit ratings, which are opinions about a bond issue's creditworthiness. Credit ratings enable investors to compare the credit risk of debt issues and issuers within a given industry, across industries, and across geographic markets.

- Bonds rated Aaa to Baa3 by Moody's and AAA to BBB− by Standard & Poor's (S&P) and/or Fitch (higher to lower) are referred to as "investment grade." Bonds rated lower than that—Ba1 or lower by Moody's and BB+ or lower by S&P and/or Fitch—are referred to as "below investment grade" or "speculative grade." Below-investment-grade bonds are also called "high-yield" or "junk" bonds.

- The rating agencies rate both issuers and issues. Issuer ratings are meant to address an issuer's overall creditworthiness—its risk of default. Ratings for issues incorporate such factors as their rankings in the capital structure.

- The rating agencies will notch issue ratings up or down to account for such factors as capital structure ranking for secured or subordinated bonds, reflecting different recovery rates in the event of default. Ratings may also be notched due to structural subordination.

- There are risks in relying too much on credit agency ratings. Because creditworthiness is dynamic, initial/current ratings do not necessarily reflect the evolution of credit quality over an investor's holding period. Importantly, bond ratings do not always capture price risk because valuations often adjust before ratings change and the notching process may not adequately reflect the price decline of a bond that is lower ranked in the capital structure. Similarly, because ratings primarily reflect the probability of default but not necessarily the severity of loss given default, bonds with the same rating may have significantly different expected losses (default probability times loss severity). And like analysts, credit rating agencies may have difficulty forecasting certain credit-negative outcomes, such as adverse litigation, leveraging corporate transactions, and such low likelihood/high severity events as earthquakes and hurricanes.

- The role of corporate credit analysis is to assess the company's ability to make timely payments of interest and repay principal at maturity. Analysts focus on an issuer's ability to generate cash flow by doing an assessment of the company as well as the industry in which it operates.

- Credit analysis is similar to equity analysis. It is important to understand, however, that bonds are contracts and that management's duty to bondholders and other creditors is limited to the terms of the contract. In contrast, management's duty to shareholders is to act in their best interest by trying to maximize the value of the company—perhaps even at the expense of bondholders at times.

- Credit analysts tend to focus more on the downside risk given the asymmetry of risk/return, whereas equity analysts focus more on upside opportunity from earnings growth, and so on.

- The "4 Cs" of credit analysis—capacity, collateral, covenants, and character—provide a useful framework for evaluating credit risk.

- Credit analysis focuses on an issuer's ability to generate cash flow. The analysis starts with an industry assessment—structure and fundamentals—and continues with an analysis of an issuer's competitive position, management strategy, and track record. Key credit ratios focus on debt leverage and interest coverage and use such measures as EBITDA, free cash flow, funds from operations, balance sheet debt, and adjustments, such as leases, pensions, and other retiree benefits.

- Credit ratios are used to calculate an issuer's creditworthiness, as well as to compare its credit quality with peer companies.

- An issuer's ability to access liquidity is also an important consideration in credit analysis.

- The higher the credit risk, the greater the offered/required yield and potential return demanded by investors. Over time, bonds with more credit risk offer higher returns but with greater volatility of return than bonds with lower credit risk.

- The yield on a credit-risky bond comprises the yield on a default risk–free bond with a comparable maturity plus a yield premium, or "spread," that comprises a credit spread and a liquidity premium. That spread is intended to compensate investors for credit risk—risk of default and loss severity in the event of default—and the credit-related risks that can cause spreads to widen and prices to decline—downgrade or credit migration risk, as well as market liquidity risk.

  Yield spread = Liquidity premium + Credit spread.

- In times of financial market stress, the liquidity premium can increase sharply, causing spreads to widen on all credit-risky bonds, with lower-quality issuers most affected. In times of credit improvement or stability, however, credit spreads can narrow sharply as well, providing attractive investment returns.

- Credit curves—the plot of yield spreads for a given bond issuer across the yield curve—are typically upward sloping, with the exception of high premium-priced bonds and distressed bonds, where credit curves can be inverted because of the fear of default, when all creditors at a given ranking in the capital structure will receive the same recovery rate without regard to debt maturity.

- The impact of spread changes on holding period returns for credit-risky bonds are a product of two primary factors: the basis point spread change and the sensitivity of price to yield as reflected by (end-of-period) modified duration and convexity. Spread narrowing enhances holding period returns, whereas spread widening has a negative impact on holding period returns. Longer-duration bonds have greater price and return sensitivity to changes in spread than shorter-duration bonds.

  Return impact ≈ $-(MDur \times \Delta Spread) + \frac{1}{2}Cvx \times (\Delta Spread)^2$

- For high-yield bonds, with their greater risk of default, more emphasis should be placed on an issuer's sources of liquidity, as well as on its debt structure and corporate structure. Credit risk can vary greatly across an issuer's debt structure depending on the seniority ranking. Many high-yield companies often have complex capital structures, resulting in different levels of credit risk depending on where the debt resides.

- Covenant analysis is especially important for high-yield bonds. Key covenants include payment restrictions, limitation on liens, change of control, coverage maintenance tests (often limited to bank loans), and any guarantees from restricted subsidiaries. Covenant language can be very technical and legalistic, so it may help to seek legal or expert assistance.

- An equity-like approach to high-yield analysis can be helpful. Calculating and comparing enterprise value with EBITDA and debt/EBITDA can show a level of equity "cushion" or support beneath an issuer's debt.

- Sovereign credit analysis includes assessing both an issuer's ability and willingness to pay its debt obligations. Willingness to pay is important because, due to sovereign immunity, a sovereign government cannot be forced to pay its debts.

- In assessing sovereign credit risk, a helpful framework is to focus on five broad areas: (1) institutional effectiveness and political risks, (2) economic structure and growth prospects, (3) external liquidity and international investment position, (4) fiscal performance, flexibility, and debt burden, and (5) monetary flexibility.

- Among the characteristics of a high-quality sovereign credit are the absence of corruption and/or challenges to political framework; governmental checks and balances; respect for rule of law and property rights; commitment to honor debts; high per capita income with stable, broad-based growth prospects; control of a reserve or actively traded currency; currency flexibility; low external debt and external financing needs relative to external receipts; stable or declining ratio of debt to GDP; low debt service as a percent of revenue; low ratio of net debt to GDP; operationally independent central bank; track record of low and stable inflation; and a well-developed banking system and active money market.

- In the United States, there are two basic kinds of municipal debt: general obligation bonds and revenue-backed bonds.

- General obligation (GO) bonds are backed by the taxing authority of the issuing municipality (e.g., state or city). The credit analysis of GO bonds has some similarities to sovereign analysis—debt burden per capita versus income per capita, tax burden, demographics, and economic diversity. Underfunded and "off-balance-sheet" liabilities, such as pensions for public employees and retirees, are debt-like in nature.

- Revenue-backed bonds support specific projects, such as toll roads, bridges, airports, and other infrastructure. The creditworthiness comes from the revenues generated by usage fees and tolls levied.

PRACTICE PROBLEMS

1	The risk that a bond's creditworthiness declines is *best* described by:

   A	credit migration risk.

   B	market liquidity risk.

   C	spread widening risk.

2	Stedsmart Ltd and Fignermo Ltd are alike with respect to financial and operating characteristics, except that Stedsmart Ltd has less publicly traded debt outstanding than Fignermo Ltd. Therefore, Stedsmart Ltd is *most likely* to have:

   A	no market liquidity risk.

   B	lower market liquidity risk.

   C	higher market liquidity risk.

3	In the event of default, debentures' claims will *most likely* rank:

   A	above that of secured debt holders.

   B	below that of secured debt holders.

   C	the same as that of secured debt holders.

4	In the event of default, the recovery rate of which of the following bonds would *most likely* be the highest?

   A	First mortgage debt

   B	Senior unsecured debt

   C	Junior subordinate debt

5	During bankruptcy proceedings of a firm, the priority of claims was not strictly adhered to. Which of the following is the *least likely* explanation for this outcome?

   A	Senior creditors compromised.

   B	The value of secured assets was less than the amount of the claims.

   C	The judge's order resulted in actual claims not adhering to strict priority of claims.

6	Although rating agencies assess the creditworthiness of debt issuers and issues, the *least likely* reason that a fixed income analyst should conduct an independent analysis of credit risk is because rating agencies:

   A	may at times mis-rate issues.

   B	often lag the market in pricing credit risk.

   C	cannot foresee future debt-financed acquisitions.

7	Jaco Meyer, a credit analyst, is analyzing the human capital of a company. Such an analysis will *most likely* give Meyer insight into the:

   A	quality of the company's management.

   B	strength of the company's balance sheet.

   C	power of the company's customers.

8	If goodwill makes up a large percentage of a company's total assets, this *most likely* indicates that:

   A	the company has low free cash flow before dividends.

B there is a low likelihood that the market price of the company's common stock is below book value.

C a large percentage of the company's assets are of low quality.

9 In order to analyze the **collateral** of a company a credit analyst should assess the:

A cash flows of the company.

B soundness of management's strategy.

C value of the company's assets in relation to the level of debt.

10 In order to determine the **capacity** of a company, it would be *most* appropriate to analyze the:

A company's strategy.

B growth prospects of the industry.

C aggressiveness of the company's accounting policies.

11 A credit analyst is evaluating the credit worthiness of three companies: a construction company, a travel and tourism company, and a beverage company. Both the construction and travel and tourism companies are cyclical, whereas the beverage company is non-cyclical. The construction company has the highest debt level of the three companies. The highest credit risk is *most likely* exhibited by the:

A construction company.

B beverage company.

C travel and tourism company.

12 Based on the information provided in Exhibit 1, the EBITDA interest coverage ratio of Adidas AG is *closest* to:

A 7.91x.

B 10.12x.

C 12.99x.

Exhibit 1	Adidas AG Excerpt from Consolidated Income Statement Year Ending 31 December 2010 (€ in millions)
Gross profit	5,730
Royalty and commission income	100
Other operating income	110
Other operating expenses	5,046
Operating profit	894
Interest income	25
Interest expense	113
Income before taxes	806
Income taxes	238
Net income	568

Additional information:
Depreciation and amortization: €249 million

Source: Adidas AG Annual Financial Statements, December 2010

13 The following information is from the annual report of Adidas AG for December 2010:

- Depreciation and amortization: €249 million
- Total assets: €10,618 million
- Total debt: €1,613 million
- Shareholders' equity: €4,616 million

The debt/capital ratio of Adidas AG is *closest* to:

A 15.19%.

B 25.90%.

C 34.94%.

14 Funds from operations (FFO) of Pay Handle Ltd increased in 2011. In 2011 the total debt of the company remained unchanged, while additional common shares were issued. Pay Handle Ltd's ability to service its debt in 2011, as compared to 2010, *most likely*:

A improved.

B worsened.

C remained the same.

15 Based on the information in Exhibit 2, Grupa Zywiec SA's credit risk is *most likely*:

A lower than the industry.

B higher than the industry.

C the same as the industry.

Exhibit 2	European Food, Beverage, and Tobacco Industry and Grupa Zywiec SA Selected Financial Ratios for 2010				
	Total debt/Total capital (%)	FFO/Total debt (%)	Return on capital (%)	Total debt/ EBITDA (x)	EBITDA interest coverage (x)
Grupa Zywiec SA	47.1	77.5	19.6	1.2	17.7
Industry Median	42.4	23.6	6.55	2.85	6.45

16 Based on the information in Exhibit 3, the credit rating of Davide Campari-Milano S.p.A. is *most likely*:

A lower than Associated British Foods plc.

B higher than Associated British Foods plc.

C the same as Associated British Foods plc.

Exhibit 3   European Food, Beverage, and Tobacco Industry; Associated British Foods plc; and Davide Campari-Milano S.p.A Selected Financial Ratios, 2010

Company	Total debt/ total capital (%)	FFO/ total debt (%)	Return on capital (%)	Total debt/ EBITDA (x)	EBITDA interest coverage (x)
Associated British Foods plc	0.2	84.3	0.1	1.0	13.9
Davide Campari-Milano S.p.A.	42.9	22.9	8.2	3.2	3.2
European Food, Beverage, and Tobacco Median	**42.4**	**23.6**	**6.55**	**2.85**	**6.45**

17 Holding all other factors constant, the *most likely* effect of low demand and heavy new issue supply on bond yield spreads is that yield spreads will:

   A widen.

   B tighten.

   C not be affected.

18 A credit analyst is assessing a two-year, 13.5% coupon bond with a 1.77 duration. Because of a recent slump in operating revenue, the bond's yield to maturity has increased from 7.20% to 7.50%. The impact of the change in yield to maturity on the return of the bond is *closest* to:

   A 0.53%.

   B −0.53%.

   C −0.60%.

SOLUTIONS

1 A is correct. Credit migration risk or downgrade risk refers to the risk that a bond issuer's creditworthiness may deteriorate or migrate lower. The result is that investors view the risk of default to be higher, causing the spread on the issuer's bonds to widen.

2 C is correct. Market liquidity risk refers to the risk that the price at which investors transact may be different from the price indicated in the market. Market liquidity risk is increased by (1) less debt outstanding and/or (2) a lower issue credit rating. Because Stedsmart Ltd is comparable to Fignermo Ltd except for less publicly traded debt outstanding, it should have higher market liquidity risk.

3 B is correct. Secured debt holders have a direct claim on certain assets and their associated cash flows whereas unsecured debt holders only have a general claim on the issuer's assets and cash flow.

4 A is correct. First mortgage debt is the highest ranked debt in terms of priority of claims and is considered secured debt. First mortgage debt will also have the expected highest recovery rate. First mortgage debt refers to the pledge of specific property. Neither senior unsecured nor junior subordinate debt has any claims on specific assets.

5 B is correct. Whether or not secured assets are sufficient for the claims, this would not influence priority of claims. The difference between pledge assets and the claim becomes senior unsecured debt and still adheres to the guidelines of priority of claims.

6 C is correct. Neither an analyst nor ratings agencies can anticipate unexpected events.

7 B is correct. An analysis of the human capital of a company is the purpose of assessing the strength of its balance sheets or, stated differently, the value and quality of assets supporting the issuer's indebtedness (i.e., collateral).

8 C is correct. Goodwill is viewed as a lower quality asset compared with tangible assets that can be sold and more easily converted into cash.

9 C is correct. The value of assets in relation to the level of debt is important to assess the collateral of the company; that is, the quality and value of the assets that support the debt levels of the company.

10 B is correct. The growth prospects of the industry provide the analyst insight regarding the capacity of the company.

11 A is correct. The construction company is both highly leveraged which increases credit risk and in a highly cyclical industry which results in more volatile earnings. The beverage company is in a non-cyclical industry with less volatile earnings.

12 B is correct. The interest expense is €113 million and EBITDA = Operating profit + Depreciation and amortization = €894 + 249 million = €1,143 million. EBITDA interest coverage = EBITDA/Interest expense = 1,143/113 = 10.12 times.

13 B is correct. Total debt is €1,613 million with Total capital = Total debt + Shareholders' equity = €1,613 + 4,616 = €6,229 million. The Debt/Capital ratio = 1,613/6,229 = 25.90%.

14 A is correct. If the debt of the company remained unchanged but FFO increased, more cash is available to service debt compared to the previous year. Additionally, the debt/capital ratio has improved. It would imply that the ability of Pay Handle Ltd to service their debt has improved.

15 A is correct. Based on four of the five credit ratios, Grupa Zywiec SA's credit quality is superior to that of the industry.

16 A is correct. Davide Campari-Milano S.p.A. has more financial leverage and less interest coverage than Associated British Foods plc, which implies greater credit risk.

17 A is correct. Low demand implies wider yield spreads, while heavy supply will widen spreads even further.

18 B is correct. Return impact $\approx -(\Delta \text{Spread} \times \text{Duration}_{\text{End}})$

Higher credit risk implies widening of the spread by 30 basis points and a lower return.

Return impact = $-(30 \text{ basis points} \times 1.77 \text{ years}) = -53.1$ basis points = -0.531%

Glossary

A priori probability   A probability based on logical analysis rather than on observation or personal judgment.

Abnormal profit   Equal to accounting profit less the implicit opportunity costs not included in total accounting costs; the difference between total revenue (TR) and total cost (TC).

Abnormal return   The amount by which a security's actual return differs from its expected return, given the security's risk and the market's return.

Absolute advantage   A country's ability to produce a good or service at a lower absolute cost than its trading partner.

Absolute dispersion   The amount of variability present without comparison to any reference point or benchmark.

Absolute frequency   The number of observations in a given interval (for grouped data).

Accelerated book build   An offering of securities by an investment bank acting as principal that is accomplished in only one or two days.

Accelerated methods   Depreciation methods that allocate a relatively large proportion of the cost of an asset to the early years of the asset's useful life.

Account   With the accounting systems, a formal record of increases and decreases in a specific asset, liability, component of owners' equity, revenue, or expense.

Accounting (or explicit) costs   Payments to non-owner parties for services or resources they supply to the firm.

Accounting loss   When accounting profit is negative.

Accounting profit   Income as reported on the income statement, in accordance with prevailing accounting standards, before the provisions for income tax expense. Also called *income before taxes* or *pretax income*.

Accounts payable   Amounts that a business owes to its vendors for goods and services that were purchased from them but which have not yet been paid.

Accounts receivable   Amounts customers owe the company for products that have been sold as well as amounts that may be due from suppliers (such as for returns of merchandise). Also called *commercial receivables* or *trade receivables*.

Accounts receivable turnover   Ratio of sales on credit to the average balance in accounts receivable.

Accrued expenses   Liabilities related to expenses that have been incurred but not yet paid as of the end of an accounting period—an example of an accrued expense is rent that has been incurred but not yet paid, resulting in a liability "rent payable." Also called *accrued liabilities*.

Accrued interest   Interest earned but not yet paid.

Accrued revenue   Revenue that has been earned but not yet billed to customers as of the end of an accounting period.

Accumulated depreciation   An offset to property, plant, and equipment (PPE) reflecting the amount of the cost of PPE that has been allocated to current and previous accounting periods.

Acid-test ratio   A stringent measure of liquidity that indicates a company's ability to satisfy current liabilities with its most liquid assets, calculated as (cash + short-term marketable investments + receivables) divided by current liabilities.

Acquisition method   A method of accounting for a business combination where the acquirer is required to measure each identifiable asset and liability at fair value. This method was the result of a joint project of the IASB and FASB aiming at convergence in standards for the accounting of business combinations.

Action lag   Delay from policy decisions to implementation.

Active investment   An approach to investing in which the investor seeks to outperform a given benchmark.

Active return   The return on a portfolio minus the return on the portfolio's benchmark.

Active strategy   In reference to short-term cash management, an investment strategy characterized by monitoring and attempting to capitalize on market conditions to optimize the risk and return relationship of short-term investments.

Activity ratio   The ratio of the labor force to total population of working age. Also called *participation ratio*.

Activity ratios   Ratios that measure how efficiently a company performs day-to-day tasks, such as the collection of receivables and management of inventory. Also called *asset utilization ratios* or *operating efficiency ratios*.

Add-on rates   Bank certificates of deposit, repos, and indices such as Libor and Euribor are quoted on an add-on rate basis (bond equivalent yield basis).

Addition rule for probabilities   A principle stating that the probability that A or B occurs (both occur) equals the probability that A occurs, plus the probability that B occurs, minus the probability that both A and B occur.

Agency RMBS   In the United States, securities backed by residential mortgage loans and guaranteed by a federal agency or guaranteed by either of the two GSEs (Fannie Mae and Freddie Mac).

Agency bonds   See *quasi-government bond*.

Aggregate demand   The quantity of goods and services that households, businesses, government, and foreign customers want to buy at any given level of prices.

Aggregate demand curve   Inverse relationship between the price level and real output.

Aggregate income   The value of all the payments earned by the suppliers of factors used in the production of goods and services.

Aggregate output   The value of all the goods and services produced in a specified period of time.

Aggregate supply   The quantity of goods and services producers are willing to supply at any given level of price.

Aggregate supply curve   The level of domestic output that companies will produce at each price level.

Aging schedule   A breakdown of accounts into categories of days outstanding.

All-or-nothing (AON) orders   An order that includes the instruction to trade only if the trade fills the entire quantity (size) specified.

Allocationally efficient   Said of a market, a financial system, or an economy that promotes the allocation of resources to their highest value uses.

Allowance for bad debts   An offset to accounts receivable for the amount of accounts receivable that are estimated to be uncollectible.

Alternative investment markets   Market for investments other than traditional securities investments (i.e., traditional common and preferred shares and traditional fixed income instruments). The term usually encompasses direct and indirect investment in real estate (including timberland and farmland) and commodities (including precious metals); hedge funds, private equity, and other investments requiring specialized due diligence.

Alternative trading systems   Trading venues that function like exchanges but that do not exercise regulatory authority over their subscribers except with respect to the conduct of the subscribers' trading in their trading systems. Also called *electronic communications networks* or *multilateral trading facilities*.

American depository receipt   A US dollar-denominated security that trades like a common share on US exchanges.

American depository share   The underlying shares on which American depository receipts are based. They trade in the issuing company's domestic market.

American-style   Said of an option contract that can be exercised at any time up to the option's expiration date.

Amortisation   The process of allocating the cost of intangible long-term assets having a finite useful life to accounting periods; the allocation of the amount of a bond premium or discount to the periods remaining until bond maturity.

Amortised cost   The historical cost (initially recognised cost) of an asset, adjusted for amortisation and impairment.

Amortizing bond   Bond with a payment schedule that calls for periodic payments of interest and repayments of principal.

Amortizing loans   Loan with a payment schedule that calls for periodic payments of interest and repayments of principal.

Annual percentage rate   The cost of borrowing expressed as a yearly rate.

Annuity   A finite set of level sequential cash flows.

Annuity due   An annuity having a first cash flow that is paid immediately.

Anticipation stock   Excess inventory that is held in anticipation of increased demand, often because of seasonal patterns of demand.

Antidilutive   With reference to a transaction or a security, one that would increase earnings per share (EPS) or result in EPS higher than the company's basic EPS—antidilutive securities are not included in the calculation of diluted EPS.

Arbitrage   1) The simultaneous purchase of an undervalued asset or portfolio and sale of an overvalued but equivalent asset or portfolio, in order to obtain a riskless profit on the price differential. Taking advantage of a market inefficiency in a risk-free manner. 2) The condition in a financial market in which equivalent assets or combinations of assets sell for two different prices, creating an opportunity to profit at no risk with no commitment of money. In a well-functioning financial market, few arbitrage opportunities are possible. 3) A risk-free operation that earns an expected positive net profit but requires no net investment of money.

Arbitrage-free pricing   The overall process of pricing derivatives by arbitrage and risk neutrality. Also called the *principle of no arbitrage*.

Arbitrageurs   Traders who engage in arbitrage. See *arbitrage*.

Arc elasticity   An elasticity based on two points, in contrast with (point) elasticity. With reference to price elasticity, the percentage change in quantity demanded divided by the percentage change in price between two points for price.

Arithmetic mean   The sum of the observations divided by the number of observations.

Arms index   A flow of funds indicator applied to a broad stock market index to measure the relative extent to which money is moving into or out of rising and declining stocks.

Ascending price auction   An auction in which an auctioneer calls out prices for a single item and potential buyers bid directly against each other, with each subsequent bid being higher than the previous one.

Asian call option   A European-style option with a value at maturity equal to the difference between the stock price at maturity and the average stock price during the life of the option, or $0, whichever is greater.

Ask   The price at which a dealer or trader is willing to sell an asset, typically qualified by a maximum quantity (ask size). See *offer*.

Ask size   The maximum quantity of an asset that pertains to a specific ask price from a trader. For example, if the ask for a share issue is $30 for a size of 1,000 shares, the trader is offering to sell at $30 up to 1,000 shares.

Asset allocation   The process of determining how investment funds should be distributed among asset classes.

Asset beta   The unlevered beta; reflects the business risk of the assets; the asset's systematic risk.

Asset class   A group of assets that have similar characteristics, attributes, and risk/return relationships.

Asset swap   Converts the periodic fixed coupon of a specific bond to a Libor plus or minus a spread.

Asset utilization ratios   Ratios that measure how efficiently a company performs day-to-day tasks, such as the collection of receivables and management of inventory.

Asset-backed securities   A type of bond issued by a legal entity called a *special purpose vehicle* (SPV), on a collection of assets that the SPV owns. Also, securities backed by receivables and loans other than mortgage loans.

Asset-based loan   A loan that is secured with company assets.

Asset-based valuation models   Valuation based on estimates of the market value of a company's assets.

Assets   Resources controlled by an enterprise as a result of past events and from which future economic benefits to the enterprise are expected to flow.

Assignment of accounts receivable   The use of accounts receivable as collateral for a loan.

At the money   An option in which the underlying's price equals the exercise price.

At-the-money   Said of an option in which the underlying's price equals the exercise price.

Auction   A type of bond issuing mechanism often used for sovereign bonds that involves bidding.

Autarkic price   The price of a good or service in an autarkic economy.

Autarky   A state in which a country does not trade with other countries.

Automated Clearing House (ACH)   An electronic payment network available to businesses, individuals, and financial institutions in the United States, US Territories, and Canada.

Automatic stabilizer   A countercyclical factor that automatically comes into play as an economy slows and unemployment rises.

Available-for-sale Debt and equity securities not classified as either held-to-maturity or held-for-trading securities. The investor is willing to sell but not actively planning to sell. In general, available-for-sale securities are reported at fair value on the balance sheet.

Average fixed cost Total fixed cost divided by quantity.

Average life See *weighted average life*.

Average product Measures the productivity of inputs on average and is calculated by dividing total product by the total number of units for a given input that is used to generate that output.

Average revenue Quantity sold divided into total revenue.

Average total cost Total costs divided by quantity.

Average variable cost Total variable cost divided by quantity.

Back simulation Another term for the historical method of estimating VAR. This term is somewhat misleading in that the method involves not a *simulation* of the past but rather what *actually happened* in the past, sometimes adjusted to reflect the fact that a different portfolio may have existed in the past than is planned for the future.

Back-testing With reference to portfolio strategies, the application of a strategy's portfolio selection rules to historical data to assess what would have been the strategy's historical performance.

Backup lines of credit A type of credit enhancement provided by a bank to an issuer of commercial paper to ensure that the issuer will have access to sufficient liquidity to repay maturing commercial paper if issuing new paper is not a viable option.

Balance of payments A double-entry bookkeeping system that summarizes a country's economic transactions with the rest of the world for a particular period of time, typically a calendar quarter or year.

Balance of trade deficit When the domestic economy is spending more on foreign goods and services than foreign economies are spending on domestic goods and services.

Balance sheet The financial statement that presents an entity's current financial position by disclosing resources the entity controls (its assets) and the claims on those resources (its liabilities and equity claims), as of a particular point in time (the date of the balance sheet). Also called *statement of financial position* or *statement of financial condition*.

Balance sheet ratios Financial ratios involving balance sheet items only.

Balanced With respect to a government budget, one in which spending and revenues (taxes) are equal.

Balloon payment Large payment required at maturity to retire a bond's outstanding principal amount.

Bank discount basis A quoting convention that annualizes, on a 360-day year, the discount as a percentage of face value.

Bar chart A price chart with four bits of data for each time interval—the high, low, opening, and closing prices. A vertical line connects the high and low. A cross-hatch left indicates the opening price and a cross-hatch right indicates the close.

Barter economy An economy where economic agents as house-holds, corporations, and governments "pay" for goods and services with another good or service.

Base rates The reference rate on which a bank bases lending rates to all other customers.

Basic EPS Net earnings available to common shareholders (i.e., net income minus preferred dividends) divided by the weighted average number of common shares outstanding.

Basis point Used in stating yield spreads, one basis point equals one-hundredth of a percentage point, or 0.01%.

Basket of listed depository receipts An exchange-traded fund (ETF) that represents a portfolio of depository receipts.

Bearer bonds Bonds for which ownership is not recorded; only the clearing system knows who the bond owner is.

Behavioral equations With respect to demand and supply, equations that model the behavior of buyers and sellers.

Behavioral finance A field of finance that examines the psychological variables that affect and often distort the investment decision making of investors, analysts, and portfolio managers.

Behind the market Said of prices specified in orders that are worse than the best current price; e.g., for a limit buy order, a limit price below the best bid.

Benchmark A comparison portfolio; a point of reference or comparison.

Benchmark issue The latest sovereign bond issue for a given maturity. It serves as a benchmark against which to compare bonds that have the same features but that are issued by another type of issuer.

Benchmark rate Typically the yield-to-maturity on a government bond having the same, or close to the same, time-to-maturity.

Benchmark spread The yield spread over a specific benchmark, usually measured in basis points.

Bermuda-style Said of an option contract that can be exercised on specified dates up to the option's expiration date.

Bernoulli random variable A random variable having the outcomes 0 and 1.

Bernoulli trial An experiment that can produce one of two outcomes.

Best bid The highest bid in the market.

Best effort offering An offering of a security using an investment bank in which the investment bank, as agent for the issuer, promises to use its best efforts to sell the offering but does not guarantee that a specific amount will be sold.

Best offer The lowest offer (ask price) in the market.

Beta A measure of systematic risk that is based on the covariance of an asset's or portfolio's return with the return of the overall market.

Bid The price at which a dealer or trader is willing to buy an asset, typically qualified by a maximum quantity.

Bid size The maximum quantity of an asset that pertains to a specific bid price from a trader.

Bid–ask spread The difference between the prices at which dealers will buy from a customer (bid) and sell to a customer (offer or ask). It is often used as an indicator of liquidity.

Bid–offer spread The difference between the prices at which dealers will buy from a customer (bid) and sell to a customer (offer or ask). It is often used as an indicator of liquidity.

Bilateral loan A loan from a single lender to a single borrower.

Binomial model A model for pricing options in which the underlying price can move to only one of two possible new prices.

Binomial random variable The number of successes in n Bernoulli trials for which the probability of success is constant for all trials and the trials are independent.

Binomial tree The graphical representation of a model of asset price dynamics in which, at each period, the asset moves up with probability p or down with probability $(1 - p)$.

Block brokers   A broker (agent) that provides brokerage services for large-size trades.

Blue chip   Widely held large market capitalization companies that are considered financially sound and are leaders in their respective industry or local stock market.

Bollinger Bands   A price-based technical analysis indicator consisting of a moving average plus a higher line representing the moving average plus a set number of standard deviations from average price (for the same number of periods as used to calculate the moving average) and a lower line that is a moving average minus the same number of standard deviations.

Bond   Contractual agreement between the issuer and the bondholders.

Bond equivalent yield   A calculation of yield that is annualized using the ratio of 365 to the number of days to maturity. Bond equivalent yield allows for the restatement and comparison of securities with different compounding periods.

Bond indenture   The governing legal credit agreement, typically incorporated by reference in the prospectus.

Bond market vigilantes   Bond market participants who might reduce their demand for long-term bonds, thus pushing up their yields.

Bond yield plus risk premium approach   An estimate of the cost of common equity that is produced by summing the before-tax cost of debt and a risk premium that captures the additional yield on a company's stock relative to its bonds. The additional yield is often estimated using historical spreads between bond yields and stock yields.

Bonus issue of shares   A type of dividend in which a company distributes additional shares of its common stock to shareholders instead of cash.

Book building   Investment bankers' process of compiling a "book" or list of indications of interest to buy part of an offering.

Book value   The net amount shown for an asset or liability on the balance sheet; book value may also refer to the company's excess of total assets over total liabilities. Also called *carrying value*.

Boom   An expansionary phase characterized by economic growth "testing the limits" of the economy.

Bottom-up analysis   With reference to investment selection processes, an approach that involves selection from all securities within a specified investment universe, i.e., without prior narrowing of the universe on the basis of macroeconomic or overall market considerations.

Break point   In the context of the weighted average cost of capital (WACC), a break point is the amount of capital at which the cost of one or more of the sources of capital changes, leading to a change in the WACC.

Breakeven point   The number of units produced and sold at which the company's net income is zero (revenues = total costs); in the case of perfect competition, the quantity where price, average revenue, and marginal revenue equal average total cost.

Bridge financing   Interim financing that provides funds until permanent financing can be arranged.

Broad money   Encompasses narrow money plus the entire range of liquid assets that can be used to make purchases.

Broker   1) An agent who executes orders to buy or sell securities on behalf of a client in exchange for a commission. 2) See *futures commission merchants*.

Brokered market   A market in which brokers arrange trades among their clients.

Broker–dealer   A financial intermediary (often a company) that may function as a principal (dealer) or as an agent (broker) depending on the type of trade.

Budget constraint   A constraint on spending or investment imposed by wealth or income.

Budget surplus/deficit   The difference between government revenue and expenditure for a stated fixed period of time.

Business risk   The risk associated with operating earnings. Operating earnings are uncertain because total revenues and many of the expenditures contributed to produce those revenues are uncertain.

Buy-side firm   An investment management company or other investor that uses the services of brokers or dealers (i.e., the client of the sell side firms).

Buyback   A transaction in which a company buys back its own shares. Unlike stock dividends and stock splits, share repurchases use corporate cash.

Buyout fund   A fund that buys all the shares of a public company so that, in effect, the company becomes private.

CBOE Volatility Index   A measure of near-term market volatility as conveyed by S&P 500 stock index option prices.

CD equivalent yield   A yield on a basis comparable to the quoted yield on an interest-bearing money market instrument that pays interest on a 360-day basis; the annualized holding period yield, assuming a 360-day year.

Call   An option that gives the holder the right to buy an underlying asset from another party at a fixed price over a specific period of time.

Call market   A market in which trades occur only at a particular time and place (i.e., when the market is called).

Call money rate   The interest rate that buyers pay for their margin loan.

Call option   An option that gives the holder the right to buy an underlying asset from another party at a fixed price over a specific period of time.

Call protection   The time during which the issuer of the bond is not allowed to exercise the call option.

Callable bond   A bond containing an embedded call option that gives the issuer the right to buy the bond back from the investor at specified prices on pre-determined dates.

Callable common shares   Shares that give the issuing company the option (or right), but not the obligation, to buy back the shares from investors at a call price that is specified when the shares are originally issued.

Candlestick chart   A price chart with four bits of data for each time interval. A candle indicates the opening and closing price for the interval. The body of the candle is shaded if the opening price was higher than the closing price, and the body is clear if the opening price was lower than the closing price. Vertical lines known as wicks or shadows extend from the top and bottom of the candle to indicate the high and the low prices for the interval.

Cannibalization   Cannibalization occurs when an investment takes customers and sales away from another part of the company.

Capacity   The ability of the borrower to make its debt payments on time.

Capital account   A component of the balance of payments account that measures transfers of capital.

Capital allocation line   (CAL) A graph line that describes the combinations of expected return and standard deviation of return available to an investor from combining the optimal portfolio of risky assets with the risk-free asset.

Capital asset pricing model (CAPM) An equation describing the expected return on any asset (or portfolio) as a linear function of its beta relative to the market portfolio.

Capital budgeting The allocation of funds to relatively long-range projects or investments.

Capital consumption allowance A measure of the wear and tear (depreciation) of the capital stock that occurs in the production of goods and services.

Capital deepening investment Increases the stock of capital relative to labor.

Capital expenditure Expenditure on physical capital (fixed assets).

Capital lease See *finance lease.*

Capital market expectations An investor's expectations concerning the risk and return prospects of asset classes.

Capital market line (CML) The line with an intercept point equal to the risk-free rate that is tangent to the efficient frontier of risky assets; represents the efficient frontier when a risk-free asset is available for investment.

Capital market securities Securities with maturities at issuance longer than one year.

Capital markets Financial markets that trade securities of longer duration, such as bonds and equities.

Capital rationing A capital rationing environment assumes that the company has a fixed amount of funds to invest.

Capital restrictions Controls placed on foreigners' ability to own domestic assets and/or domestic residents' ability to own foreign assets.

Capital stock The accumulated amount of buildings, machinery, and equipment used to produce goods and services.

Capital structure The mix of debt and equity that a company uses to finance its business; a company's specific mixture of long-term financing.

Capital-indexed bonds Type of index-linked bond. The coupon rate is fixed but is applied to a principal amount that increases in line with increases in the index during the bond's life.

Captive finance subsidiary A wholly-owned subsidiary of a company that is established to provide financing of the sales of the parent company.

Carry The net of the costs and benefits of holding, storing, or "carrying" an asset.

Carrying amount The amount at which an asset or liability is valued according to accounting principles.

Carrying value The net amount shown for an asset or liability on the balance sheet; book value may also refer to the company's excess of total assets over total liabilities. For a bond, the purchase price plus (or minus) the amortized amount of the discount (or premium).

Cartel Participants in collusive agreements that are made openly and formally.

Cash In accounting contexts, cash on hand (e.g., petty cash and cash not yet deposited to the bank) and demand deposits held in banks and similar accounts that can be used in payment of obligations.

Cash conversion cycle A financial metric that measures the length of time required for a company to convert cash invested in its operations to cash received as a result of its operations; equal to days of inventory on hand + days of sales outstanding – number of days of payables. Also called *net operating cycle.*

Cash equivalents Very liquid short-term investments, usually maturing in 90 days or less.

Cash flow additivity principle The principle that dollar amounts indexed at the same point in time are additive.

Cash flow from operating activities The net amount of cash provided from operating activities.

Cash flow from operations The net amount of cash provided from operating activities.

Cash flow yield The internal rate of return on a series of cash flows.

Cash market securities Money market securities settled on a "same day" or "cash settlement" basis.

Cash markets See *spot markets.*

Cash prices See *spot prices.*

Cash-settled forwards See *non-deliverable forwards.*

Central bank funds market The market in which deposit-taking banks that have an excess reserve with their national central bank can loan money to banks that need funds for maturities ranging from overnight to one year. Called the Federal or Fed funds market in the United States.

Central bank funds rates Interest rates at which central bank funds are bought (borrowed) and sold (lent) for maturities ranging from overnight to one year. Called Federal or Fed funds rates in the United States.

Central banks The dominant bank in a country, usually with official or semi-official governmental status.

Certificate of deposit An instrument that represents a specified amount of funds on deposit with a bank for a specified maturity and interest rate. It is issued in small or large denominations, and can be negotiable or non-negotiable.

Change in polarity principle A tenet of technical analysis that once a support level is breached, it becomes a resistance level. The same holds true for resistance levels; once breached, they become support levels.

Change in quantity supplied A movement along a given supply curve.

Change in supply A shift in the supply curve.

Change of control put A covenant giving bondholders the right to require the issuer to buy back their debt, often at par or at some small premium to par value, in the event that the borrower is acquired.

Character The quality of a debt issuer's management.

Chart of accounts A list of accounts used in an entity's accounting system.

Classified balance sheet A balance sheet organized so as to group together the various assets and liabilities into subcategories (e.g., current and noncurrent).

Clawback A requirement that the GP return any funds distributed as incentive fees until the LPs have received back their initial investment and a percentage of the total profit.

Clearing The process by which the exchange verifies the execution of a transaction and records the participants' identities.

Clearing instructions Instructions that indicate how to arrange the final settlement ("clearing") of a trade.

Clearinghouse An entity associated with a futures market that acts as middleman between the contracting parties and guarantees to each party the performance of the other.

Closed economy An economy that does not trade with other countries; an *autarkic economy.*

Closed-end fund A mutual fund in which no new investment money is accepted. New investors invest by buying existing shares, and investors in the fund liquidate by selling their shares to other investors.

Coefficient of variation (CV) The ratio of a set of observations' standard deviation to the observations' mean value.

Coincident economic indicators Turning points that are usually close to those of the overall economy; they are believed to have value for identifying the economy's present state.

Collateral The quality and value of the assets supporting an issuer's indebtedness.

Collateral manager Buys and sells debt obligations for and from the CDO's portfolio of assets (i.e., the collateral) to generate sufficient cash flows to meet the obligations to the CDO bondholders.

Collateral trust bonds Bonds secured by securities such as common shares, other bonds, or other financial assets.

Collateralized bond obligations A structured asset-backed security that is collateralized by a pool of bonds.

Collateralized debt obligation Generic term used to describe a security backed by a diversified pool of one or more debt obligations.

Collateralized debt obligations A securitized pool of fixed-income assets.

Collateralized loan obligations A structured asset-backed security that is collateralized by a pool of loans.

Collateralized mortgage obligation A security created through the securitization of a pool of mortgage-related products (mortgage pass-through securities or pools of loans).

Collateralized mortgage obligation (CMO) A structured asset-backed security that is collateralized by a pool of mortgages.

Collaterals Assets or financial guarantees underlying a debt obligation above and beyond the issuer's promise to pay.

Combination A listing in which the order of the listed items does not matter.

Commercial paper A short-term, negotiable, unsecured promissory note that represents a debt obligation of the issuer.

Commercial receivables Amounts customers owe the company for products that have been sold as well as amounts that may be due from suppliers (such as for returns of merchandise). Also called *trade receivables* or *accounts receivable*.

Committed capital The amount that the limited partners have agreed to provide to the private equity fund.

Committed lines of credit A bank commitment to extend credit up to a pre-specified amount; the commitment is considered a short-term liability and is usually in effect for 364 days (one day short of a full year).

Commodity swap A swap in which the underlying is a commodity such as oil, gold, or an agricultural product.

Common market Level of economic integration that incorporates all aspects of the customs union and extends it by allowing free movement of factors of production among members.

Common shares A type of security that represent an ownership interest in a company.

Common stock See *common shares*.

Common value auction An auction in which the item being auctioned has the same value to each auction participant, although participants may be uncertain as to what that value is.

Common-size analysis The restatement of financial statement items using a common denominator or reference item that allows one to identify trends and major differences; an example is an income statement in which all items are expressed as a percent of revenue.

Company analysis Analysis of an individual company.

Comparable company A company that has similar business risk; usually in the same industry and preferably with a single line of business.

Comparative advantage A country's ability to produce a good or service at a lower relative cost, or opportunity cost, than its trading partner.

Competitive strategy A company's plans for responding to the threats and opportunities presented by the external environment.

Complements Said of goods which tend to be used together; technically, two goods whose cross-price elasticity of demand is negative.

Complete markets Informally, markets in which the variety of distinct securities traded is so broad that any desired payoff in a future state-of-the-world is achievable.

Complete preferences The assumption that a consumer is able to make a comparison between any two possible bundles of goods.

Completed contract A method of revenue recognition in which the company does not recognize any revenue until the contract is completed; used particularly in long-term construction contracts.

Component cost of capital The rate of return required by suppliers of capital for an individual source of a company's funding, such as debt or equity.

Compounding The process of accumulating interest on interest.

Comprehensive income The change in equity of a business enterprise during a period from nonowner sources; includes all changes in equity during a period except those resulting from investments by owners and distributions to owners; comprehensive income equals net income plus other comprehensive income.

Conditional expected value The expected value of a stated event given that another event has occurred.

Conditional probability The probability of an event given (conditioned on) another event.

Conditional variances The variance of one variable, given the outcome of another.

Consistent With reference to estimators, describes an estimator for which the probability of estimates close to the value of the population parameter increases as sample size increases.

Conspicuous consumption Consumption of high status goods, such as a luxury automobile or a very expensive piece of jewelry.

Constant returns to scale The characteristic of constant per-unit costs in the presence of increased production.

Constant-cost industry When firms in the industry experience no change in resource costs and output prices over the long run.

Constant-yield price trajectory A graph that illustrates the change in the price of a fixed-income bond over time assuming no change in yield-to-maturity. The trajectory shows the "pull to par" effect on the price of a bond trading at a premium or a discount to par value.

Constituent securities With respect to an index, the individual securities within an index.

Consumer choice theory The theory relating consumer demand curves to consumer preferences.

Consumer surplus The difference between the value that a consumer places on units purchased and the amount of money that was required to pay for them.

Consumption The purchase of final goods and services by individuals.

Consumption basket A specific combination of the goods and services that a consumer wants to consume.

Consumption bundle A specific combination of the goods and services that a consumer wants to consume.

Contingency provision Clause in a legal document that allows for some action if a specific event or circumstance occurs.

Contingent claims Derivatives in which the payoffs occur if a specific event occurs; generally referred to as options.

Contingent convertible bonds Bonds that automatically convert into equity if a specific event or circumstance occurs, such as the issuer's equity capital falling below the minimum requirement set by the regulators. Also called *CoCos*.

Continuation patterns A type of pattern used in technical analysis to predict the resumption of a market trend that was in place prior to the formation of a pattern.

Continuous random variable A random variable for which the range of possible outcomes is the real line (all real numbers between $-\infty$ and $+\infty$ or some subset of the real line).

Continuous time Time thought of as advancing in extremely small increments.

Continuous trading market A market in which trades can be arranged and executed any time the market is open.

Continuously compounded return The natural logarithm of 1 plus the holding period return, or equivalently, the natural logarithm of the ending price over the beginning price.

Contra account An account that offsets another account.

Contract rate See *mortgage rate*.

Contraction The period of a business cycle after the peak and before the trough; often called a *recession* or, if exceptionally severe, called a *depression*.

Contraction risk The risk that when interest rates decline, the security will have a shorter maturity than was anticipated at the time of purchase because borrowers refinance at now-available lower interest rates.

Contractionary Tending to cause the real economy to contract.

Contractionary fiscal policy A fiscal policy that has the objective to make the real economy contract.

Contracts for differences See *non-deliverable forwards*.

Contribution margin The amount available for fixed costs and profit after paying variable costs; revenue minus variable costs.

Convenience yield A non-monetary advantage of holding an asset.

Conventional bond See *plain vanilla bond*.

Conventional cash flow A conventional cash flow pattern is one with an initial outflow followed by a series of inflows.

Convergence The tendency for differences in output per capita across countries to diminish over time; in technical analysis, a term that describes the case when an indicator moves in the same manner as the security being analyzed.

Conversion price For a convertible bond, the price per share at which the bond can be converted into shares.

Conversion ratio For a convertible bond, the number of common shares that each bond can be converted into.

Conversion value For a convertible bond, the current share price multiplied by the conversion ratio.

Convertible bond Bond that gives the bondholder the right to exchange the bond for a specified number of common shares in the issuing company.

Convertible preference shares A type of equity security that entitles shareholders to convert their shares into a specified number of common shares.

Convexity adjustment For a bond, one half of the annual or approximate convexity statistic multiplied by the change in the yield-to-maturity squared.

Core inflation The inflation rate calculated based on a price index of goods and services except food and energy.

Correlation A number between -1 and $+1$ that measures the comovement (linear association) between two random variables.

Correlation coefficient A number between -1 and $+1$ that measures the consistency or tendency for two investments to act in a similar way. It is used to determine the effect on portfolio risk when two assets are combined.

Cost averaging The periodic investment of a fixed amount of money.

Cost of capital The rate of return that suppliers of capital require as compensation for their contribution of capital.

Cost of carry See *carry*.

Cost of debt The cost of debt financing to a company, such as when it issues a bond or takes out a bank loan.

Cost of goods sold For a given period, equal to beginning inventory minus ending inventory plus the cost of goods acquired or produced during the period.

Cost of preferred stock The cost to a company of issuing preferred stock; the dividend yield that a company must commit to pay preferred stockholders.

Cost recovery method A method of revenue recognition in which the seller does not report any profit until the cash amounts paid by the buyer—including principal and interest on any financing from the seller—are greater than all the seller's costs for the merchandise sold.

Cost structure The mix of a company's variable costs and fixed costs.

Cost-push Type of inflation in which rising costs, usually wages, compel businesses to raise prices generally.

Counterparty risk The risk that the other party to a contract will fail to honor the terms of the contract.

Coupon rate The interest rate promised in a contract; this is the rate used to calculate the periodic interest payments.

Cournot assumption Assumption in which each firm determines its profit-maximizing production level assuming that the other firms' output will not change.

Covariance A measure of the co-movement (linear association) between two random variables.

Covariance matrix A matrix or square array whose entries are covariances; also known as a variance–covariance matrix.

Covenants The terms and conditions of lending agreements that the issuer must comply with; they specify the actions that an issuer is obligated to perform (affirmative covenant) or prohibited from performing (negative covenant).

Covered bond Debt obligation secured by a segregated pool of assets called the cover pool. The issuer must maintain the value of the cover pool. In the event of default, bondholders have recourse against both the issuer and the cover pool.

Covered call An option strategy involving the holding of an asset and sale of a call on the asset.

Credit With respect to double-entry accounting, a credit records increases in liability, owners' equity, and revenue accounts or decreases in asset accounts; with respect to borrowing, the willingness and ability of the borrower to make promised payments on the borrowing.

Credit analysis The evaluation of credit risk; the evaluation of the creditworthiness of a borrower or counterparty.

Credit curve A curve showing the relationship between time to maturity and yield spread for an issuer with comparable bonds of various maturities outstanding, usually upward sloping.

Credit default swap (CDS) A type of credit derivative in which one party, the credit protection buyer who is seeking credit protection against a third party, makes a series of regularly scheduled payments to the other party, the credit protection seller. The seller makes no payments until a credit event occurs.

Credit derivatives A contract in which one party has the right to claim a payment from another party in the event that a specific credit event occurs over the life of the contract.

Credit enhancements Provisions that may be used to reduce the credit risk of a bond issue.

Credit migration risk The risk that a bond issuer's creditworthiness deteriorates, or migrates lower, leading investors to believe the risk of default is higher. Also called *downgrade risk*.

Credit risk The risk of loss caused by a counterparty's or debtor's failure to make a promised payment. Also called *default risk*.

Credit scoring model A statistical model used to classify borrowers according to creditworthiness.

Credit spread option An option on the yield spread on a bond.

Credit tranching A structure used to redistribute the credit risk associated with the collateral; a set of bond classes created to allow investors a choice in the amount of credit risk that they prefer to bear.

Credit-linked coupon bond Bond for which the coupon changes when the bond's credit rating changes.

Credit-linked note Fixed-income security in which the holder of the security has the right to withhold payment of the full amount due at maturity if a credit event occurs.

Credit-worthiness The perceived ability of the borrower to pay what is owed on the borrowing in a timely manner; it represents the ability of a company to withstand adverse impacts on its cash flows.

Cross-default provisions Provisions whereby events of default such as non-payment of interest on one bond trigger default on all outstanding debt; implies the same default probability for all issues.

Cross-price elasticity of demand The percent change in quantity demanded for a given small change in the price of another good; the responsiveness of the demand for Product A that is associated with the change in price of Product B.

Cross-sectional analysis Analysis that involves comparisons across individuals in a group over a given time period or at a given point in time.

Cross-sectional data Observations over individual units at a point in time, as opposed to time-series data.

Crossing networks Trading systems that match buyers and sellers who are willing to trade at prices obtained from other markets.

Crowding out The thesis that government borrowing may divert private sector investment from taking place.

Cumulative distribution function A function giving the probability that a random variable is less than or equal to a specified value.

Cumulative preference shares Preference shares for which any dividends that are not paid accrue and must be paid in full before dividends on common shares can be paid.

Cumulative relative frequency For data grouped into intervals, the fraction of total observations that are less than the value of the upper limit of a stated interval.

Cumulative voting Voting that allows shareholders to direct their total voting rights to specific candidates, as opposed to having to allocate their voting rights evenly among all candidates.

Currencies Monies issued by national monetary authorities.

Currency option bonds Bonds that give the bondholder the right to choose the currency in which he or she wants to receive interest payments and principal repayments.

Currency swap A swap in which each party makes interest payments to the other in different currencies.

Current account A component of the balance of payments account that measures the flow of goods and services.

Current assets Assets that are expected to be consumed or converted into cash in the near future, typically one year or less. Also called *liquid assets*.

Current cost With reference to assets, the amount of cash or cash equivalents that would have to be paid to buy the same or an equivalent asset today; with reference to liabilities, the undiscounted amount of cash or cash equivalents that would be required to settle the obligation today.

Current government spending With respect to government expenditures, spending on goods and services that are provided on a regular, recurring basis including health, education, and defense.

Current liabilities Short-term obligations, such as accounts payable, wages payable, or accrued liabilities, that are expected to be settled in the near future, typically one year or less.

Current ratio A liquidity ratio calculated as current assets divided by current liabilities.

Current yield The sum of the coupon payments received over the year divided by the flat price; also called the *income* or *interest yield* or *running yield*.

Curve duration The sensitivity of the bond price (or the market value of a financial asset or liability) with respect to a benchmark yield curve.

Customs union Extends the free trade area (FTA) by not only allowing free movement of goods and services among members, but also creating a common trade policy against nonmembers.

Cyclical See *cyclical companies*.

Cyclical companies Companies with sales and profits that regularly expand and contract with the business cycle or state of economy.

Daily settlement See *mark to market* and *marking to market*.

Dark pools Alternative trading systems that do not display the orders that their clients send to them.

Data mining The practice of determining a model by extensive searching through a dataset for statistically significant patterns. Also called *data snooping*.

Data snooping See *data mining*.

Date of book closure The date that a shareholder listed on the corporation's books will be deemed to have ownership of the shares for purposes of receiving an upcoming dividend; two business days after the ex-dividend date.

Date of record The date that a shareholder listed on the corporation's books will be deemed to have ownership of the shares for purposes of receiving an upcoming dividend; two business days after the ex-dividend date.

Day order An order that is good for the day on which it is submitted. If it has not been filled by the close of business, the order expires unfilled.

Days in receivables Estimate of the average number of days it takes to collect on credit accounts.

Days of inventory on hand (DOH) An activity ratio equal to the number of days in the period divided by inventory turnover over the period.

Day's sales outstanding Estimate of the average number of days it takes to collect on credit accounts.

Dead cross A technical analysis term that describes a situation where a short-term moving average crosses from above a longer-term moving average to below it; this movement is considered bearish.

Deadweight loss A net loss of total (consumer and producer) surplus.

Dealers A financial intermediary that acts as a principal in trades.

Dealing securities Securities held by banks or other financial intermediaries for trading purposes.

Debentures Type of bond that can be secured or unsecured.

Debit With respect to double-entry accounting, a debit records increases of asset and expense accounts or decreases in liability and owners' equity accounts.

Debt incurrence test A financial covenant made in conjunction with existing debt that restricts a company's ability to incur additional debt at the same seniority based on one or more financial tests or conditions.

Debt-rating approach A method for estimating a company's before-tax cost of debt based upon the yield on comparably rated bonds for maturities that closely match that of the company's existing debt.

Debt-to-assets ratio A solvency ratio calculated as total debt divided by total assets.

Debt-to-capital ratio A solvency ratio calculated as total debt divided by total debt plus total shareholders' equity.

Debt-to-equity ratio A solvency ratio calculated as total debt divided by total shareholders' equity.

Declaration date The day that the corporation issues a statement declaring a specific dividend.

Decreasing returns to scale Increase in cost per unit resulting from increased production.

Decreasing-cost industry An industry in which per-unit costs and output prices are lower when industry output is increased in the long run.

Deductible temporary differences Temporary differences that result in a reduction of or deduction from taxable income in a future period when the balance sheet item is recovered or settled.

Default probability The probability that a borrower defaults or fails to meet its obligation to make full and timely payments of principal and interest, according to the terms of the debt security. Also called *default risk*.

Default risk The probability that a borrower defaults or fails to meet its obligation to make full and timely payments of principal and interest, according to the terms of the debt security. Also called *default probability*.

Default risk premium An extra return that compensates investors for the possibility that the borrower will fail to make a promised payment at the contracted time and in the contracted amount.

Defensive companies Companies with sales and profits that have little sensitivity to the business cycle or state of the economy.

Defensive interval ratio A liquidity ratio that estimates the number of days that an entity could meet cash needs from liquid assets; calculated as (cash + short-term marketable investments + receivables) divided by daily cash expenditures.

Deferred coupon bond Bond that pays no coupons for its first few years but then pays a higher coupon than it otherwise normally would for the remainder of its life. Also called *split coupon bond*.

Deferred income A liability account for money that has been collected for goods or services that have not yet been delivered; payment received in advance of providing a good or service.

Deferred revenue A liability account for money that has been collected for goods or services that have not yet been delivered; payment received in advance of providing a good or service.

Deferred tax assets A balance sheet asset that arises when an excess amount is paid for income taxes relative to accounting profit. The taxable income is higher than accounting profit and income tax payable exceeds tax expense. The company expects to recover the difference during the course of future operations when tax expense exceeds income tax payable.

Deferred tax liabilities A balance sheet liability that arises when a deficit amount is paid for income taxes relative to accounting profit. The taxable income is less than the accounting profit and income tax payable is less than tax expense. The company expects to eliminate the liability over the course of future operations when income tax payable exceeds tax expense.

Defined benefit pension plans Plan in which the company promises to pay a certain annual amount (defined benefit) to the employee after retirement. The company bears the investment risk of the plan assets.

Defined contribution pension plans Individual accounts to which an employee and typically the employer makes contributions, generally on a tax-advantaged basis. The amounts of contributions are defined at the outset, but the future value of the benefit is unknown. The employee bears the investment risk of the plan assets.

Defined-benefit plan A pension plan that specifies the plan sponsor's obligations in terms of the benefit to plan participants.

Defined-contribution plan A pension plan that specifies the sponsor's obligations in terms of contributions to the pension fund rather than benefits to plan participants.

Deflation Negative inflation.

Degree of confidence The probability that a confidence interval includes the unknown population parameter.

Degree of financial leverage (DFL) The ratio of the percentage change in net income to the percentage change in operating income; the sensitivity of the cash flows available to owners when operating income changes.

Degree of operating leverage (DOL) The ratio of the percentage change in operating income to the percentage change in units sold; the sensitivity of operating income to changes in units sold.

Degree of total leverage The ratio of the percentage change in net income to the percentage change in units sold; the sensitivity of the cash flows to owners to changes in the number of units produced and sold.

Degrees of freedom (df) The number of independent observations used.

Demand   The willingness and ability of consumers to purchase a given amount of a good or service at a given price.

Demand and supply analysis   The study of how buyers and sellers interact to determine transaction prices and quantities.

Demand curve   Graph of the inverse demand function.

Demand function   A relationship that expresses the quantity demanded of a good or service as a function of own-price and possibly other variables.

Demand shock   A typically unexpected disturbance to demand, such as an unexpected interruption in trade or transportation.

Demand-pull   Type of inflation in which increasing demand raises prices generally, which then are reflected in a business's costs as workers demand wage hikes to catch up with the rising cost of living.

Dependent   With reference to events, the property that the probability of one event occurring depends on (is related to) the occurrence of another event.

Depository bank   A bank that raises funds from depositors and other investors and lends it to borrowers.

Depository institutions   Commercial banks, savings and loan banks, credit unions, and similar institutions that raise funds from depositors and other investors and lend it to borrowers.

Depository receipt   A security that trades like an ordinary share on a local exchange and represents an economic interest in a foreign company.

Depreciation   The process of systematically allocating the cost of long-lived (tangible) assets to the periods during which the assets are expected to provide economic benefits.

Depression   See *contraction*.

Derivative pricing rule   A pricing rule used by crossing networks in which a price is taken (derived) from the price that is current in the asset's primary market.

Derivatives   A financial instrument whose value depends on the value of some underlying asset or factor (e.g., a stock price, an interest rate, or exchange rate).

Descending price auction   An auction in which the auctioneer begins at a high price, then lowers the called price in increments until there is a willing buyer for the item being auctioned.

Descriptive statistics   The study of how data can be summarized effectively.

Development capital   Minority equity investments in more mature companies that are looking for capital to expand or restructure operations, enter new markets, or finance major acquisitions.

Diffuse prior   The assumption of equal prior probabilities.

Diffusion index   Reflects the proportion of the index's components that are moving in a pattern consistent with the overall index.

Diluted EPS   The EPS that would result if all dilutive securities were converted into common shares.

Diluted shares   The number of shares that would be outstanding if all potentially dilutive claims on common shares (e.g., convertible debt, convertible preferred stock, and employee stock options) were exercised.

Diminishing balance method   An accelerated depreciation method, i.e., one that allocates a relatively large proportion of the cost of an asset to the early years of the asset's useful life.

Diminishing marginal productivity   Describes a state in which each additional unit of input produces less output than previously.

Direct debit program   An arrangement whereby a customer authorizes a debit to a demand account; typically used by companies to collect routine payments for services.

Direct financing leases   A type of finance lease, from a lessor perspective, where the present value of the lease payments (less receivable) equals the carrying value of the leased asset. The revenues earned by the lessor are financing in nature.

Direct format   With reference to the cash flow statement, a format for the presentation of the statement in which cash flow from operating activities is shown as operating cash receipts less operating cash disbursements. Also called *direct method*.

Direct method   See *direct format*.

Direct taxes   Taxes levied directly on income, wealth, and corporate profits.

Direct write-off method   An approach to recognizing credit losses on customer receivables in which the company waits until such time as a customer has defaulted and only then recognizes the loss.

Disbursement float   The amount of time between check issuance and a check's clearing back against the company's account.

Discount   To reduce the value of a future payment in allowance for how far away it is in time; to calculate the present value of some future amount. Also, the amount by which an instrument is priced below its face (par) value.

Discount interest   A procedure for determining the interest on a loan or bond in which the interest is deducted from the face value in advance.

Discount margin   See *required margin*.

Discount rates   In general, the interest rate used to calculate a present value. In the money market, however, discount rate is a specific type of quoted rate.

Discounted cash flow models   Valuation models that estimate the intrinsic value of a security as the present value of the future benefits expected to be received from the security.

Discouraged worker   A person who has stopped looking for a job or has given up seeking employment.

Discrete random variable   A random variable that can take on at most a countable number of possible values.

Discriminatory pricing rule   A pricing rule used in continuous markets in which the limit price of the order or quote that first arrived determines the trade price.

Diseconomies of scale   Increase in cost per unit resulting from increased production.

Dispersion   The variability around the central tendency.

Display size   The size of an order displayed to public view.

Distressed investing   Investing in securities of companies in financial difficulties. Private equity funds typically buy the debt of mature companies in financial difficulties.

Divergence   In technical analysis, a term that describes the case when an indicator moves differently from the security being analyzed.

Diversification ratio   The ratio of the standard deviation of an equally weighted portfolio to the standard deviation of a randomly selected security.

Dividend   A distribution paid to shareholders based on the number of shares owned.

Dividend discount model   (DDM) A present value model that estimates the intrinsic value of an equity share based on the present value of its expected future dividends.

Dividend discount model based approach An approach for estimating a country's equity risk premium. The market rate of return is estimated as the sum of the dividend yield and the growth rate in dividends for a market index. Subtracting the risk-free rate of return from the estimated market return produces an estimate for the equity risk premium.

Dividend payout ratio The ratio of cash dividends paid to earnings for a period.

Dividend yield Annual dividends per share divided by share price.

Divisor A number (denominator) used to determine the value of a price return index. It is initially chosen at the inception of an index and subsequently adjusted by the index provider, as necessary, to avoid changes in the index value that are unrelated to changes in the prices of its constituent securities.

Domestic content provisions Stipulate that some percentage of the value added or components used in production should be of domestic origin.

Double bottoms In technical analysis, a reversal pattern that is formed when the price reaches a low, rebounds, and then sells off back to the first low level; used to predict a change from a downtrend to an uptrend.

Double coincidence of wants A prerequisite to barter trades, in particular that both economic agents in the transaction want what the other is selling.

Double declining balance depreciation An accelerated depreciation method that involves depreciating the asset at double the straight-line rate. This rate is multiplied by the book value of the asset at the beginning of the period (a declining balance) to calculate depreciation expense.

Double top In technical analysis, a reversal pattern that is formed when an uptrend reverses twice at roughly the same high price level; used to predict a change from an uptrend to a downtrend.

Double-entry accounting The accounting system of recording transactions in which every recorded transaction affects at least two accounts so as to keep the basic accounting equation (assets = liabilities + owners' equity) in balance.

Down transition probability The probability that an asset's value moves down in a model of asset price dynamics.

Downgrade risk The risk that a bond issuer's creditworthiness deteriorates, or migrates lower, leading investors to believe the risk of default is higher. Also called *credit migration risk*.

Drag on liquidity When receipts lag, creating pressure from the decreased available funds.

Drawdown A reduction in net asset value (NAV).

DuPont analysis An approach to decomposing return on investment, e.g., return on equity, as the product of other financial ratios.

Dual-currency bonds Bonds that make coupon payments in one currency and pay the par value at maturity in another currency.

Duration gap A bond's Macaulay duration minus the investment horizon.

Dutch Book theorem A result in probability theory stating that inconsistent probabilities create profit opportunities.

Dutch auction An auction in which the auctioneer begins at a high price, then lowers the called price in increments until there is a willing buyer for the item being auctioned.

Early repayment option See *prepayment option*.

Earnings per share The amount of income earned during a period per share of common stock.

Earnings surprise The portion of a company's earnings that is unanticipated by investors and, according to the efficient market hypothesis, merits a price adjustment.

Economic costs All the remuneration needed to keep a productive resource in its current employment or to acquire the resource for productive use; the sum of total accounting costs and implicit opportunity costs.

Economic indicator A variable that provides information on the state of the overall economy.

Economic loss The amount by which accounting profit is less than normal profit.

Economic order quantity–reorder point (EOQ–ROP) An approach to managing inventory based on expected demand and the predictability of demand; the ordering point for new inventory is determined based on the costs of ordering and carrying inventory, such that the total cost associated with inventory is minimized.

Economic profit Equal to accounting profit less the implicit opportunity costs not included in total accounting costs; the difference between total revenue (TR) and total cost (TC). Also called *abnormal profit* or *supernormal profit*.

Economic rent The surplus value that results when a particular resource or good is fixed in supply and market price is higher than what is required to bring the resource or good onto the market and sustain its use.

Economic stabilization Reduction of the magnitude of economic fluctuations.

Economic union Incorporates all aspects of a common market and in addition requires common economic institutions and coordination of economic policies among members.

Economics The study of the production, distribution, and consumption of goods and services; the principles of the allocation of scarce resources among competing uses. Economics is divided into two broad areas of study: macroeconomics and microeconomics.

Economies of scale Reduction in cost per unit resulting from increased production.

Effective annual rate The amount by which a unit of currency will grow in a year with interest on interest included.

Effective annual yield (EAY) An annualized return that accounts for the effect of interest on interest; EAY is computed by compounding 1 plus the holding period yield forward to one year, then subtracting 1.

Effective convexity A *curve convexity* statistic that measures the secondary effect of a change in a benchmark yield curve on a bond's price.

Effective duration The sensitivity of a bond's price to a change in a benchmark yield curve.

Effective interest rate The borrowing rate or market rate that a company incurs at the time of issuance of a bond.

Efficient market A market in which asset prices reflect new information quickly and rationally.

Elastic Said of a good or service when the magnitude of elasticity is greater than one.

Elasticity The percentage change in one variable for a percentage change in another variable; a measure of how sensitive one variable is to a change in the value of another variable.

Elasticity of supply A measure of the sensitivity of quantity supplied to a change in price.

Electronic communications networks See *alternative trading systems*.

Electronic funds transfer (EFT) The use of computer networks to conduct financial transactions electronically.

Elliott wave theory   A technical analysis theory that claims that the market follows regular, repeated waves or cycles.

Embedded option   Contingency provisions that provide the issuer or the bondholders the right, but not the obligation, to take action. These options are not part of the security and cannot be traded separately.

Empirical probability   The probability of an event estimated as a relative frequency of occurrence.

Employed   The number of people with a job.

Endogenous variables   Variables whose equilibrium values are determined within the model being considered.

Enterprise value   A measure of a company's total market value from which the value of cash and short-term investments have been subtracted.

Equal weighting   An index weighting method in which an equal weight is assigned to each constituent security at inception.

Equilibrium condition   A condition necessary for the forces within a system to be in balance.

Equipment trust certificates   Bonds secured by specific types of equipment or physical assets.

Equity   Assets less liabilities; the residual interest in the assets after subtracting the liabilities.

Equity risk premium   The expected return on equities minus the risk-free rate; the premium that investors demand for investing in equities.

Equity swap   A swap transaction in which at least one cash flow is tied to the return to an equity portfolio position, often an equity index.

Equity-linked note   Type of index-linked bond for which the final payment is based on the return of an equity index.

Estimate   The particular value calculated from sample observations using an estimator.

Estimation   With reference to statistical inference, the subdivision dealing with estimating the value of a population parameter.

Estimator   An estimation formula; the formula used to compute the sample mean and other sample statistics are examples of estimators.

Eurobonds   Type of bond issued internationally, outside the jurisdiction of the country in whose currency the bond is denominated.

European-style   Said of an option contract that can only be exercised on the option's expiration date.

Event   Any outcome or specified set of outcomes of a random variable.

Ex-date   The first date that a share trades without (i.e. "ex") the dividend.

Ex-dividend date   The first date that a share trades without (i.e. "ex") the dividend.

Excess kurtosis   Degree of peakedness (fatness of tails) in excess of the peakedness of the normal distribution.

Excess supply   A condition in which the quantity ready to be supplied is greater than the quantity demanded.

Exchanges   Places where traders can meet to arrange their trades.

Execution instructions   Instructions that indicate how to fill an order.

Exercise   The process of using an option to buy or sell the underlying.

Exercise price   The fixed price at which an option holder can buy or sell the underlying. Also called *strike price, striking price,* or *strike.*

Exercise value   The value obtained if an option is exercised based on current conditions. Also known as *intrinsic value.*

Exhaustive   Covering or containing all possible outcomes.

Exogenous variables   Variables whose equilibrium values are determined outside of the model being considered.

Expansion   The period of a business cycle after its lowest point and before its highest point.

Expansionary   Tending to cause the real economy to grow.

Expansionary fiscal policy   Fiscal policy aimed at achieving real economic growth.

Expected inflation   The level of inflation that economic agents expect in the future.

Expected loss   Default probability times Loss severity given default.

Expected value   The probability-weighted average of the possible outcomes of a random variable.

Expenses   Outflows of economic resources or increases in liabilities that result in decreases in equity (other than decreases because of distributions to owners); reductions in net assets associated with the creation of revenues.

Experience curve   A curve that shows the direct cost per unit of good or service produced or delivered as a typically declining function of cumulative output.

Export subsidy   Paid by the government to the firm when it exports a unit of a good that is being subsidized.

Exports   Goods and services that an economy sells to other countries.

Extension risk   The risk that when interest rates rise, fewer prepayments will occur because homeowners are reluctant to give up the benefits of a contractual interest rate that now looks low. As a result, the security becomes longer in maturity than anticipated at the time of purchase.

Externality   An effect of a market transaction that is borne by parties other than those who transacted.

Extra dividend   A dividend paid by a company that does not pay dividends on a regular schedule, or a dividend that supplements regular cash dividends with an extra payment.

FIFO method   The first in, first out, method of accounting for inventory, which matches sales against the costs of items of inventory in the order in which they were placed in inventory.

FX swap   The combination of a spot and a forward FX transaction.

Face value   The amount of cash payable by a company to the bondholders when the bonds mature; the promised payment at maturity separate from any coupon payment.

Factor   A common or underlying element with which several variables are correlated.

Factor markets   Markets for the purchase and sale of factors of production.

Fair value   The amount at which an asset could be exchanged, or a liability settled, between knowledgeable, willing parties in an arm's-length transaction; the price that would be received to sell an asset or paid to transfer a liability in an orderly transaction between market participants.

Fed funds rate   The US interbank lending rate on overnight borrowings of reserves.

Federal funds rate   The US interbank lending rate on overnight borrowings of reserves.

Fiat money   Money that is not convertible into any other commodity.

Fibonacci sequence   A sequence of numbers starting with 0 and 1, and then each subsequent number in the sequence is the sum of the two preceding numbers. In Elliott Wave Theory, it is believed that market waves follow patterns that are the ratios of the numbers in the Fibonacci sequence.

Fiduciary call   A combination of a European call and a risk-free bond that matures on the option expiration day and has a face value equal to the exercise price of the call.

Fill or kill   See *immediate or cancel order*.

Finance lease   Essentially, the purchase of some asset by the buyer (lessee) that is directly financed by the seller (lessor). Also called *capital lease*.

Financial account   A component of the balance of payments account that records investment flows.

Financial flexibility   The ability to react and adapt to financial adversities and opportunities.

Financial leverage   The extent to which a company can effect, through the use of debt, a proportional change in the return on common equity that is greater than a given proportional change in operating income; also, short for the financial leverage ratio.

Financial leverage ratio   A measure of financial leverage calculated as average total assets divided by average total equity.

Financial risk   The risk that environmental, social, or governance risk factors will result in significant costs or other losses to a company and its shareholders; the risk arising from a company's obligation to meet required payments under its financing agreements.

Financing activities   Activities related to obtaining or repaying capital to be used in the business (e.g., equity and long-term debt).

Firm commitment offering   See *underwritten offering*.

First lien debt   Debt secured by a pledge of certain assets that could include buildings, but may also include property and equipment, licenses, patents, brands, etc.

First mortgage debt   Debt secured by a pledge of a specific property.

First price sealed bid auction   An auction in which envelopes containing bids are opened simultaneously and the item is sold to the highest bidder.

First-degree price discrimination   Where a monopolist is able to charge each customer the highest price the customer is willing to pay.

Fiscal multiplier   The ratio of a change in national income to a change in government spending.

Fiscal policy   The use of taxes and government spending to affect the level of aggregate expenditures.

Fisher effect   The thesis that the real rate of interest in an economy is stable over time so that changes in nominal interest rates are the result of changes in expected inflation.

Fisher index   The geometric mean of the Laspeyres index.

Fixed charge coverage   A solvency ratio measuring the number of times interest and lease payments are covered by operating income, calculated as (EBIT + lease payments) divided by (interest payments + lease payments).

Fixed costs   Costs that remain at the same level regardless of a company's level of production and sales.

Fixed price tender offer   Offer made by a company to repurchase a specific number of shares at a fixed price that is typically at a premium to the current market price.

Fixed rate perpetual preferred stock   Nonconvertible, noncallable preferred stock that has a fixed dividend rate and no maturity date.

Fixed-for-floating interest rate swap   An interest rate swap in which one party pays a fixed rate and the other pays a floating rate, with both sets of payments in the same currency. Also called *plain vanilla swap* or *vanilla swap*.

Flags   A technical analysis continuation pattern formed by parallel trendlines, typically over a short period.

Flat price   The full price of a bond minus the accrued interest; also called the *quoted* or *clean* price.

Float   In the context of customer receipts, the amount of money that is in transit between payments made by customers and the funds that are usable by the company.

Float factor   An estimate of the average number of days it takes deposited checks to clear; average daily float divided by average daily deposit.

Float-adjusted market-capitalization weighting   An index weighting method in which the weight assigned to each constituent security is determined by adjusting its market capitalization for its market float.

Floaters   See *floating-rate notes*.

Floating-rate notes   A note on which interest payments are not fixed, but instead vary from period to period depending on the current level of a reference interest rate.

Flotation cost   Fees charged to companies by investment bankers and other costs associated with raising new capital.

Foreclosure   Allows the lender to take possession of a mortgaged property if the borrower defaults, and then sell it to recover funds.

Foreign currency reserves   Holding by the central bank of non-domestic currency deposits and non-domestic bonds.

Foreign direct investment   Direct investment by a firm in one country (the source country) in productive assets in a foreign country (the host country).

Foreign exchange gains (or losses)   Gains (or losses) that occur when the exchange rate changes between the investor's currency and the currency that foreign securities are denominated in.

Foreign portfolio investment   Shorter-term investment by individuals, firms, and institutional investors (e.g., pension funds) in foreign financial instruments such as foreign stocks and foreign government bonds.

Forward commitments   Class of derivatives that provides the ability to lock in a price to transact in the future at a previously agreed-upon price.

Forward contract   An agreement between two parties in which one party, the buyer, agrees to buy from the other party, the seller, an underlying asset at a later date for a price established at the start of the contract.

Forward curve   A series of forward rates, each having the same timeframe.

Forward market   For future delivery, beyond the usual settlement time period in the cash market.

Forward price   The fixed price or rate at which the transaction scheduled to occur at the expiration of a forward contract will take place. This price is agreed on at the initiation date of the contract.

Forward rate   The interest rate on a bond or money market instrument traded in a forward market. A forward rate can be interpreted as an incremental, or marginal, return for extending the time-to-maturity for an additional time period.

Forward rate agreements   A forward contract calling for one party to make a fixed interest payment and the other to make an interest payment at a rate to be determined at the contract expiration.

Fractile   A value at or below which a stated fraction of the data lies.

Fractional reserve banking   Banking in which reserves constitute a fraction of deposits.

Free cash flow   The actual cash that would be available to the company's investors after making all investments necessary to maintain the company as an ongoing enterprise (also referred to as free cash flow to the firm); the internally generated funds that can be distributed to the company's investors (e.g., shareholders and bondholders) without impairing the value of the company.

Free cash flow to equity (FCFE)   The cash flow available to a company's common shareholders after all operating expenses, interest, and principal payments have been made, and necessary investments in working and fixed capital have been made.

Free cash flow to the firm (FCFF)   The cash flow available to the company's suppliers of capital after all operating expenses have been paid and necessary investments in working capital and fixed capital have been made.

Free float   The number of shares that are readily and freely tradable in the secondary market.

Free trade   When there are no government restrictions on a country's ability to trade.

Free trade areas   One of the most prevalent forms of regional integration, in which all barriers to the flow of goods and services among members have been eliminated.

Free-cash-flow-to-equity models   Valuation models based on discounting expected future free cash flow to equity.

Frequency distribution   A tabular display of data summarized into a relatively small number of intervals.

Frequency polygon   A graph of a frequency distribution obtained by drawing straight lines joining successive points representing the class frequencies.

Full price   The price of a security with accrued interest; also called the *invoice* or *dirty* price.

Fundamental analysis   The examination of publicly available information and the formulation of forecasts to estimate the intrinsic value of assets.

Fundamental value   The underlying or true value of an asset based on an analysis of its qualitative and quantitative characteristics. Also called *intrinsic value.*

Fundamental weighting   An index weighting method in which the weight assigned to each constituent security is based on its underlying company's size. It attempts to address the disadvantages of market-capitalization weighting by using measures that are independent of the constituent security's price.

Funds of hedge funds   Funds that hold a portfolio of hedge funds.

Future value (FV)   The amount to which a payment or series of payments will grow by a stated future date.

Futures contract   A variation of a forward contract that has essentially the same basic definition but with some additional features, such as a clearinghouse guarantee against credit losses, a daily settlement of gains and losses, and an organized electronic or floor trading facility.

Futures price   The agreed-upon price of a futures contract.

G-spread   The yield spread in basis points over an actual or interpolated government bond.

GDP deflator   A gauge of prices and inflation that measures the aggregate changes in prices across the overall economy.

Gains   Asset inflows not directly related to the ordinary activities of the business.

Game theory   The set of tools decision makers use to incorporate responses by rival decision makers into their strategies.

General equilibrium analysis   An analysis that provides for equilibria in multiple markets simultaneously.

General partner   The partner that runs the business and theoretically bears unlimited liability.

Geometric mean   A measure of central tendency computed by taking the nth root of the product of n non-negative values.

Giffen good   A good that is consumed more as the price of the good rises.

Gilts   Bonds issued by the UK government.

Giro system   An electronic payment system used widely in Europe and Japan.

Global depository receipt   A depository receipt that is issued outside of the company's home country and outside of the United States.

Global minimum-variance portfolio   The portfolio on the minimum-variance frontier with the smallest variance of return.

Global registered share   A common share that is traded on different stock exchanges around the world in different currencies.

Gold standard   With respect to a currency, if a currency is on the gold standard a given amount can be converted into a prespecified amount of gold.

Golden cross   A technical analysis term that describes a situation where a short-term moving average crosses from below a longer-term moving average to above it; this movement is considered bullish.

Good-on-close   An execution instruction specifying that an order can only be filled at the close of trading. Also called *market on close.*

Good-on-open   An execution instruction specifying that an order can only be filled at the opening of trading.

Good-till-cancelled order   An order specifying that it is valid until the entity placing the order has cancelled it (or, commonly, until some specified amount of time such as 60 days has elapsed, whichever comes sooner).

Goods markets   Markets for the output of production.

Goodwill   An intangible asset that represents the excess of the purchase price of an acquired company over the value of the net assets acquired.

Government equivalent yield   A yield that restates a yield-to-maturity based on 30/360 day-count to one based on actual/actual.

Greenmail   The purchase of the accumulated shares of a hostile investor by a company that is targeted for takeover by that investor, usually at a substantial premium over market price.

Grey market   The forward market for bonds about to be issued. Also called "when issued" market.

Gross domestic product   The market value of all final goods and services produced within the economy in a given period of time (output definition) or, equivalently, the aggregate income earned by all households, all companies, and the government within the economy in a given period of time (income definition).

Gross margin   Sales minus the cost of sales (i.e., the cost of goods sold for a manufacturing company).

Gross profit   Sales minus the cost of sales (i.e., the cost of goods sold for a manufacturing company).

Gross profit margin   The ratio of gross profit to revenues.

Grouping by function   With reference to the presentation of expenses in an income statement, the grouping together of expenses serving the same function, e.g. all items that are costs of goods sold.

Grouping by nature   With reference to the presentation of expenses in an income statement, the grouping together of expenses by similar nature, e.g., all depreciation expenses.

Growth cyclical   A term sometimes used to describe companies that are growing rapidly on a long-term basis but that still experience above-average fluctuation in their revenues and profits over the course of a business cycle.

Growth investors   With reference to equity investors, investors who seek to invest in high-earnings-growth companies.

Haircut   See *repo margin*.

Harmonic mean   A type of weighted mean computed by averaging the reciprocals of the observations, then taking the reciprocal of that average.

Head and shoulders pattern   In technical analysis, a reversal pattern that is formed in three parts: a left shoulder, head, and right shoulder; used to predict a change from an uptrend to a downtrend.

Headline inflation   The inflation rate calculated based on the price index that includes all goods and services in an economy.

Hedge funds   Private investment vehicles that typically use leverage, derivatives, and long and short investment strategies.

Hedge portfolio   A hypothetical combination of the derivative and its underlying that eliminates risk.

Held for trading   Debt or equity financial assets bought with the intention to sell them in the near term, usually less than three months; securities that a company intends to trade. Also called *trading securities*.

Held-to-maturity   Debt (fixed-income) securities that a company intends to hold to maturity; these are presented at their original cost, updated for any amortization of discounts or premiums.

Herding   Clustered trading that may or may not be based on information.

Hidden order   An order that is exposed not to the public but only to the brokers or exchanges that receive it.

High water marks   The highest value, net of fees, which a fund has reached. It reflects the highest cumulative return used to calculate an incentive fee.

Histogram   A bar chart of data that have been grouped into a frequency distribution.

Historical cost   In reference to assets, the amount paid to purchase an asset, including any costs of acquisition and/or preparation; with reference to liabilities, the amount of proceeds received in exchange in issuing the liability.

Historical equity risk premium approach   An estimate of a country's equity risk premium that is based upon the historical averages of the risk-free rate and the rate of return on the market portfolio.

Historical simulation   Another term for the historical method of estimating VAR. This term is somewhat misleading in that the method involves not a *simulation* of the past but rather what *actually happened* in the past, sometimes adjusted to reflect the fact that a different portfolio may have existed in the past than is planned for the future.

Holder-of-record date   The date that a shareholder listed on the corporation's books will be deemed to have ownership of the shares for purposes of receiving an upcoming dividend; two business days after the ex-dividend date.

Holding period return   The return that an investor earns during a specified holding period; a synonym for total return.

Holding period yield (HPY)   The return that an investor earns during a specified holding period; holding period return with reference to a fixed-income instrument.

Homogeneity of expectations   The assumption that all investors have the same economic expectations and thus have the same expectations of prices, cash flows, and other investment characteristics.

Horizon yield   The internal rate of return between the total return (the sum of reinvested coupon payments and the sale price or redemption amount) and the purchase price of the bond.

Horizontal analysis   Common-size analysis that involves comparing a specific financial statement with that statement in prior or future time periods; also, cross-sectional analysis of one company with another.

Horizontal demand schedule   Implies that at a given price, the response in the quantity demanded is infinite.

Household   A person or a group of people living in the same residence, taken as a basic unit in economic analysis.

Hurdle rate   The rate of return that must be met for a project to be accepted.

Hypothesis   With reference to statistical inference, a statement about one or more populations.

Hypothesis testing   With reference to statistical inference, the subdivision dealing with the testing of hypotheses about one or more populations.

I-spread   The yield spread of a specific bond over the standard swap rate in that currency of the same tenor.

IRR rule   An investment decision rule that accepts projects or investments for which the IRR is greater than the opportunity cost of capital.

Iceberg order   An order in which the display size is less than the order's full size.

If-converted method   A method for accounting for the effect of convertible securities on earnings per share (EPS) that specifies what EPS would have been if the convertible securities had been converted at the beginning of the period, taking account of the effects of conversion on net income and the weighted average number of shares outstanding.

Immediate or cancel order   An order that is valid only upon receipt by the broker or exchange. If such an order cannot be filled in part or in whole upon receipt, it cancels immediately. Also called *fill or kill*.

Impact lag   The lag associated with the result of actions affecting the economy with delay.

Imperfect competition   A market structure in which an individual firm has enough share of the market (or can control a certain segment of the market) such that it is able to exert some influence over price.

Implicit price deflator for GDP   A gauge of prices and inflation that measures the aggregate changes in prices across the overall economy.

Implied forward rates   Calculated from spot rates, an implied forward rate is a break-even reinvestment rate that links the return on an investment in a shorter-term zero-coupon bond to the return on an investment in a longer-term zero-coupon bond.

Implied volatility   The volatility that option traders use to price an option, implied by the price of the option and a particular option-pricing model.

Import license   Specifies the quantity of a good that can be imported into a country.

Imports   Goods and services that a domestic economy (i.e., house-holds, firms, and government) purchases from other countries.

In the money   Options that, if exercised, would result in the value received being worth more than the payment required to exercise.

In-the-money   Options that, if exercised, would result in the value received being worth more than the payment required to exercise.

Incentive fee (or performance fee)   Funds distributed by the general partner to the limited partner(s) based on realized profits.

Income   Increases in economic benefits in the form of inflows or enhancements of assets, or decreases of liabilities that result in an increase in equity (other than increases resulting from contributions by owners).

Income constraint   The constraint on a consumer to spend, in total, no more than his income.

Income elasticity of demand   A measure of the responsiveness of demand to changes in income, defined as the percentage change in quantity demanded divided by the percentage change in income.

Income statement   A financial statement that provides information about a company's profitability over a stated period of time. Also called *statement of operations* or *profit and loss statement.*

Income tax paid   The actual amount paid for income taxes in the period; not a provision, but the actual cash outflow.

Income tax payable   The income tax owed by the company on the basis of taxable income.

Income trust   A type of equity ownership vehicle established as a trust issuing ownership shares known as units.

Increasing marginal returns   Where the marginal product of a resource increases as additional units of that input are employed.

Increasing returns to scale   Reduction in cost per unit resulting from increased production.

Increasing-cost industry   An industry in which per-unit costs and output prices are higher when industry output is increased in the long run.

Incremental cash flow   The cash flow that is realized because of a decision; the changes or increments to cash flows resulting from a decision or action.

Indenture   Legal contract that describes the form of a bond, the obligations of the issuer, and the rights of the bondholders. Also called the *trust deed.*

Independent   With reference to events, the property that the occurrence of one event does not affect the probability of another event occurring.

Independent projects   Independent projects are projects whose cash flows are independent of each other.

Independently and identically distributed (IID)   With respect to random variables, the property of random variables that are independent of each other but follow the identical probability distribution.

Index of Leading Economic Indicators   A composite of economic variables used by analysts to predict future economic conditions.

Index-linked bond   Bond for which coupon payments and/or principal repayment are linked to a specified index.

Indexing   An investment strategy in which an investor constructs a portfolio to mirror the performance of a specified index.

Indifference curve   A curve representing all the combinations of two goods or attributes such that the consumer is entirely indifferent among them.

Indifference curve map   A group or family of indifference curves, representing a consumer's entire utility function.

Indirect format   With reference to cash flow statements, a format for the presentation of the statement which, in the operating cash flow section, begins with net income then shows additions and subtractions to arrive at operating cash flow. Also called *indirect method.*

Indirect method   See *indirect format.*

Indirect taxes   Taxes such as taxes on spending, as opposed to direct taxes.

Industry   A group of companies offering similar products and/or services.

Industry analysis   The analysis of a specific branch of manufacturing, service, or trade.

Inelastic   Insensitive to price changes.

Inelastic supply   Said of supply that is insensitive to the price of goods sold.

Inferior goods   A good whose consumption decreases as income increases.

Inflation   The percentage increase in the general price level from one period to the next; a sustained rise in the overall level of prices in an economy.

Inflation Reports   A type of economic publication put out by many central banks.

Inflation premium   An extra return that compensates investors for expected inflation.

Inflation rate   The percentage change in a price index—that is, the speed of overall price level movements.

Inflation uncertainty   The degree to which economic agents view future rates of inflation as difficult to forecast.

Inflation-linked bond   Type of index-linked bond that offers investors protection against inflation by linking the bond's coupon payments and/or the principal repayment to an index of consumer prices. Also called *linkers.*

Information cascade   The transmission of information from those participants who act first and whose decisions influence the decisions of others.

Information-motivated traders   Traders that trade to profit from information that they believe allows them to predict future prices.

Informationally efficient market   A market in which asset prices reflect new information quickly and rationally.

Initial margin   The amount that must be deposited in a clearinghouse account when entering into a futures contract.

Initial margin requirement   The margin requirement on the first day of a transaction as well as on any day in which additional margin funds must be deposited.

Initial public offering   (IPO) The first issuance of common shares to the public by a formerly private corporation.

Installment method   With respect to revenue recognition, a method that specifies that the portion of the total profit of the sale that is recognized in each period is determined by the percentage of the total sales price for which the seller has received cash.

Installment sales   With respect to revenue recognition, a method that specifies that the portion of the total profit of the sale that is recognized in each period is determined by the percentage of the total sales price for which the seller has received cash.

Intangible assets   Assets lacking physical substance, such as patents and trademarks.

Interbank market The market of loans and deposits between banks for maturities ranging from overnight to one year.

Interbank money market The market of loans and deposits between banks for maturities ranging from overnight to one year.

Interest Payment for lending funds.

Interest coverage A solvency ratio calculated as EBIT divided by interest payments.

Interest rate A rate of return that reflects the relationship between differently dated cash flows; a discount rate.

Interest rate swap A swap in which the underlying is an interest rate. Can be viewed as a currency swap in which both currencies are the same and can be created as a combination of currency swaps.

Interest-only mortgage A loan in which no scheduled principal repayment is specified for a certain number of years.

Intergenerational data mining A form of data mining that applies information developed by previous researchers using a dataset to guide current research using the same or a related dataset.

Intermarket analysis A field within technical analysis that combines analysis of major categories of securities—namely, equities, bonds, currencies, and commodities—to identify market trends and possible inflections in a trend.

Intermediate goods and services Goods and services purchased for use as inputs to produce other goods and services.

Internal rate of return (IRR) The discount rate that makes net present value equal 0; the discount rate that makes the present value of an investment's costs (outflows) equal to the present value of the investment's benefits (inflows).

Interpolated spread The yield spread of a specific bond over the standard swap rate in that currency of the same tenor.

Interquartile range The difference between the third and first quartiles of a dataset.

Interval With reference to grouped data, a set of values within which an observation falls.

Interval scale A measurement scale that not only ranks data but also gives assurance that the differences between scale values are equal.

Intrinsic value See *exercise value*.

Inventory The unsold units of product on hand.

Inventory blanket lien The use of inventory as collateral for a loan. Though the lender has claim to some or all of the company's inventory, the company may still sell or use the inventory in the ordinary course of business.

Inventory investment Net change in business inventory.

Inventory turnover An activity ratio calculated as cost of goods sold divided by average inventory.

Inverse demand function A restatement of the demand function in which price is stated as a function of quantity.

Investing activities Activities which are associated with the acquisition and disposal of property, plant, and equipment; intangible assets; other long-term assets; and both long-term and short-term investments in the equity and debt (bonds and loans) issued by other companies.

Investment banks Financial intermediaries that provide advice to their mostly corporate clients and help them arrange transactions such as initial and seasoned securities offerings.

Investment opportunity schedule A graphical depiction of a company's investment opportunities ordered from highest to lowest expected return. A company's optimal capital budget is found where the investment opportunity schedule intersects with the company's marginal cost of capital.

Investment policy statement (IPS) A written planning document that describes a client's investment objectives and risk tolerance over a relevant time horizon, along with constraints that apply to the client's portfolio.

Investment property Property used to earn rental income or capital appreciation (or both).

January effect Calendar anomaly that stock market returns in January are significantly higher compared to the rest of the months of the year, with most of the abnormal returns reported during the first five trading days in January. Also called *turn-of-the-year effect*.

Joint probability The probability of the joint occurrence of stated events.

Joint probability function A function giving the probability of joint occurrences of values of stated random variables.

Just-in-time (JIT) method Method of managing inventory that minimizes in-process inventory stocks.

Key rate duration A method of measuring the interest rate sensitivities of a fixed-income instrument or portfolio to shifts in key points along the yield curve.

Keynesians Economists who believe that fiscal policy can have powerful effects on aggregate demand, output, and employment when there is substantial spare capacity in an economy.

Kondratieff wave A 54-year long economic cycle postulated by Nikolai Kondratieff.

Kurtosis The statistical measure that indicates the peakedness of a distribution.

LIFO layer liquidation With respect to the application of the LIFO inventory method, the liquidation of old, relatively low-priced inventory; happens when the volume of sales rises above the volume of recent purchases so that some sales are made from relatively old, low-priced inventory. Also called *LIFO liquidation*.

LIFO method The last in, first out, method of accounting for inventory, which matches sales against the costs of items of inventory in the reverse order the items were placed in inventory (i.e., inventory produced or acquired last are assumed to be sold first).

Labor force The portion of the working age population (over the age of 16) that is employed or is available for work but not working (unemployed).

Labor markets Markets for labor services.

Labor productivity The quantity of goods and services (real GDP) that a worker can produce in one hour of work.

Laddering strategy A form of active strategy which entails scheduling maturities on a systematic basis within the investment portfolio such that investments are spread out equally over the term of the ladder.

Lagging economic indicators Turning points that take place later than those of the overall economy; they are believed to have value in identifying the economy's past condition.

Laspeyres index A price index created by holding the composition of the consumption basket constant.

Law of demand The principle that as the price of a good rises, buyers will choose to buy less of it, and as its price falls, they will buy more.

Law of diminishing returns The smallest output that a firm can produce such that its long run average costs are minimized.

Law of one price   The condition in a financial market in which two equivalent financial instruments or combinations of financial instruments can sell for only one price. Equivalent to the principle that no arbitrage opportunities are possible.

Law of supply   The principle that a rise in price usually results in an increase in the quantity supplied.

Lead underwriter   The lead investment bank in a syndicate of investment banks and broker–dealers involved in a securities underwriting.

Leading economic indicators   Turning points that usually precede those of the overall economy; they are believed to have value for predicting the economy's future state, usually near-term.

Legal tender   Something that must be accepted when offered in exchange for goods and services.

Lender of last resort   An entity willing to lend money when no other entity is ready to do so.

Leptokurtic   Describes a distribution that is more peaked than a normal distribution.

Lessee   The party obtaining the use of an asset through a lease.

Lessor   The owner of an asset that grants the right to use the asset to another party.

Letter of credit   Form of external credit enhancement whereby a financial institution provides the issuer with a credit line to reimburse any cash flow shortfalls from the assets backing the issue.

Level of significance   The probability of a Type I error in testing a hypothesis.

Leverage   In the context of corporate finance, leverage refers to the use of fixed costs within a company's cost structure. Fixed costs that are operating costs (such as depreciation or rent) create operating leverage. Fixed costs that are financial costs (such as interest expense) create financial leverage.

Leveraged buyout   (LBO) A transaction whereby the target company management team converts the target to a privately held company by using heavy borrowing to finance the purchase of the target company's outstanding shares.

Liabilities   Present obligations of an enterprise arising from past events, the settlement of which is expected to result in an outflow of resources embodying economic benefits; creditors' claims on the resources of a company.

Life-cycle stage   The stage of the life cycle: embryonic, growth, shakeout, mature, declining.

Likelihood   The probability of an observation, given a particular set of conditions.

Limit down   A limit move in the futures market in which the price at which a transaction would be made is at or below the lower limit.

Limit order   Instructions to a broker or exchange to obtain the best price immediately available when filling an order, but in no event accept a price higher than a specified (limit) price when buying or accept a price lower than a specified (limit) price when selling.

Limit order book   The book or list of limit orders to buy and sell that pertains to a security.

Limit up   A limit move in the futures market in which the price at which a transaction would be made is at or above the upper limit.

Limitations on liens   Meant to put limits on how much secured debt an issuer can have.

Limited partners   Partners with limited liability. Limited partnerships in hedge and private equity funds are typically restricted to investors who are expected to understand and to be able to assume the risks associated with the investments.

Line chart   In technical analysis, a plot of price data, typically closing prices, with a line connecting the points.

Linear interpolation   The estimation of an unknown value on the basis of two known values that bracket it, using a straight line between the two known values.

Linear scale   A scale in which equal distances correspond to equal absolute amounts. Also called *arithmetic scale*.

Linker   See *inflation-linked bond*.

Liquid market   Said of a market in which traders can buy or sell with low total transaction costs when they want to trade.

Liquidating dividend   A dividend that is a return of capital rather than a distribution from earnings or retained earnings.

Liquidation   To sell the assets of a company, division, or subsidiary piecemeal, typically because of bankruptcy; the form of bankruptcy that allows for the orderly satisfaction of creditors' claims after which the company ceases to exist.

Liquidity   The ability to purchase or sell an asset quickly and easily at a price close to fair market value. The ability to meet short-term obligations using assets that are the most readily converted into cash.

Liquidity premium   An extra return that compensates investors for the risk of loss relative to an investment's fair value if the investment needs to be converted to cash quickly.

Liquidity ratios   Financial ratios measuring the company's ability to meet its short-term obligations.

Liquidity trap   A condition in which the demand for money becomes infinitely elastic (horizontal demand curve) so that injections of money into the economy will not lower interest rates or affect real activity.

Load fund   A mutual fund in which, in addition to the annual fee, a percentage fee is charged to invest in the fund and/or for redemptions from the fund.

Loan-to-value ratio   The ratio of a property's purchase price to the amount of its mortgage.

Lockbox system   A payment system in which customer payments are mailed to a post office box and the banking institution retrieves and deposits these payments several times a day, enabling the company to have use of the fund sooner than in a centralized system in which customer payments are sent to the company.

Locked limit   A condition in the futures markets in which a transaction cannot take place because the price would be beyond the limits.

Lockup period   The minimum period before investors are allowed to make withdrawals or redeem shares from a fund.

Logarithmic scale   A scale in which equal distances represent equal proportional changes in the underlying quantity.

London Interbank Offered Rate   (Libor) Collective name for multiple rates at which a select set of banks believe they could borrow unsecured funds from other banks in the London interbank market for different currencies and different borrowing periods ranging from overnight to one year.

London interbank offered rate   (Libor or LIBOR) Collective name for multiple rates at which a select set of banks believe they could borrow unsecured funds from other banks in the London interbank market for different currencies and different borrowing periods ranging from overnight to one year.

Long   The buyer of a derivative contract. Also refers to the position of owning a derivative.

Long position   A position in an asset or contract in which one owns the asset or has an exercisable right under the contract.

Long-lived assets   Assets that are expected to provide economic benefits over a future period of time, typically greater than one year. Also called *long-term assets*.

Long-run average total cost curve   The curve describing average total costs when no costs are considered fixed.

Long-run industry supply curve   A curve describing the relationship between quantity supplied and output prices when no costs are considered fixed.

Long-term contract   A contract that spans a number of accounting periods.

Longitudinal data   Observations on characteristic(s) of the same observational unit through time.

Look-ahead bias   A bias caused by using information that was unavailable on the test date.

Loss severity   Portion of a bond's value (including unpaid interest) an investor loses in the event of default.

Losses   Asset outflows not directly related to the ordinary activities of the business.

Lower bound   The lowest possible value of an option.

M^2   A measure of what a portfolio would have returned if it had taken on the same total risk as the market index.

Macaulay duration   The approximate amount of time a bond would have to be held for the market discount rate at purchase to be realized if there is a single change in interest rate. It indicates the point in time when the coupon reinvestment and price effects of a change in yield-to- maturity offset each other.

Macroeconomics   The branch of economics that deals with aggregate economic quantities, such as national output and national income.

Maintenance covenants   Covenants in bank loan agreements that require the borrower to satisfy certain financial ratio tests while the loan is outstanding.

Maintenance margin   The minimum amount that is required by a futures clearinghouse to maintain a margin account and to protect against default. Participants whose margin balances drop below the required maintenance margin must replenish their accounts.

Maintenance margin requirement   The margin requirement on any day other than the first day of a transaction.

Management buy-ins   Leveraged buyout in which the current management team is being replaced and the acquiring team will be involved in managing the company.

Management buyout   (MBO) An event in which a group of investors consisting primarily of the company's existing management purchase all of its outstanding shares and take the company private.

Management fee   A fee based on assets under management or committed capital, as applicable. Also called *base fee*.

Manufacturing resource planning (MRP)   The incorporation of production planning into inventory management. A MRP analysis provides both a materials acquisition schedule and a production schedule.

Margin   The amount of money that a trader deposits in a margin account. The term is derived from the stock market practice in which an investor borrows a portion of the money

required to purchase a certain amount of stock. In futures markets, there is no borrowing so the margin is more of a down payment or performance bond.

Margin bond   A cash deposit required by the clearinghouse from the participants to a contract to provide a credit guarantee. Also called a *performance bond*.

Margin call   A request for the short to deposit additional funds to bring their balance up to the initial margin.

Margin loan   Money borrowed from a broker to purchase securities.

Marginal cost   The cost of producing an additional unit of a good.

Marginal probability   The probability of an event *not* conditioned on another event.

Marginal product   Measures the productivity of each unit of input and is calculated by taking the difference in total product from adding another unit of input (assuming other resource quantities are held constant).

Marginal propensity to consume   The proportion of an additional unit of disposable income that is consumed or spent; the change in consumption for a small change in income.

Marginal propensity to save   The proportion of an additional unit of disposable income that is saved (not spent).

Marginal rate of substitution   The rate at which one is willing to give up one good to obtain more of another.

Marginal revenue   The change in total revenue divided by the change in quantity sold; simply, the additional revenue from selling one more unit.

Marginal revenue product   The amount of additional revenue received from employing an additional unit of an input.

Marginal value   The added value from an additional unit of a good.

Marginal value curve   A curve describing the highest price consumers are willing to pay for each additional unit of a good.

Mark to market   The revaluation of a financial asset or liability to its current market value or fair value.

Market   A means of bringing buyers and sellers together to exchange goods and services.

Market anomaly   Change in the price or return of a security that cannot directly be linked to current relevant information known in the market or to the release of new information into the market.

Market bid–ask spread   The difference between the best bid and the best offer.

Market discount rate   The rate of return required by investors given the risk of the investment in a bond; also called the *required yield* or the *required rate of return*.

Market equilibrium   The condition in which the quantity willingly offered for sale by sellers at a given price is just equal to the quantity willingly demanded by buyers at that same price.

Market float   The number of shares that are available to the investing public.

Market liquidity risk   The risk that the price at which investors can actually transact—buying or selling—may differ from the price indicated in the market.

Market mechanism   The process by which price adjusts until there is neither excess supply nor excess demand.

Market model   A regression equation that specifies a linear relationship between the return on a security (or portfolio) and the return on a broad market index.

Market multiple models   Valuation models based on share price multiples or enterprise value multiples.

Market order   Instructions to a broker or exchange to obtain the best price immediately available when filling an order.

Market rate of interest   The rate demanded by purchases of bonds, given the risks associated with future cash payment obligations of the particular bond issue.

Market structure   The competitive environment (perfect competition, monopolistic competition, oligopoly, and monopoly).

Market value   The price at which an asset or security can currently be bought or sold in an open market.

Market-capitalization weighting   An index weighting method in which the weight assigned to each constituent security is determined by dividing its market capitalization by the total market capitalization (sum of the market capitalization) of all securities in the index. Also called *value weighting*.

Market-on-close   An execution instruction specifying that an order can only be filled at the close of trading.

Market-oriented investors   With reference to equity investors, investors whose investment disciplines cannot be clearly categorized as value or growth.

Marketable limit order   A buy limit order in which the limit price is placed above the best offer, or a sell limit order in which the limit price is placed below the best bid. Such orders generally will partially or completely fill right away.

Markowitz efficient frontier   The graph of the set of portfolios offering the maximum expected return for their level of risk (standard deviation of return).

Matching principle   The accounting principle that expenses should be recognized when the associated revenue is recognized.

Matching strategy   An active investment strategy that includes intentional matching of the timing of cash outflows with investment maturities.

Matrix pricing   Process of estimating the market discount rate and price of a bond based on the quoted or flat prices of more frequently traded comparable bonds.

Maturity premium   An extra return that compensates investors for the increased sensitivity of the market value of debt to a change in market interest rates as maturity is extended.

Maturity structure   A factor explaining the differences in yields on similar bonds; also called *term structure*.

Mean absolute deviation   With reference to a sample, the mean of the absolute values of deviations from the sample mean.

Mean excess return   The average rate of return in excess of the risk-free rate.

Mean–variance analysis   An approach to portfolio analysis using expected means, variances, and covariances of asset returns.

Measure of central tendency   A quantitative measure that specifies where data are centered.

Measure of value   A standard for measuring value; a function of money.

Measurement scales   A scheme of measuring differences. The four types of measurement scales are nominal, ordinal, interval, and ratio.

Measures of location   A quantitative measure that describes the location or distribution of data; includes not only measures of central tendency but also other measures such as percentiles.

Median   The value of the middle item of a set of items that has been sorted into ascending or descending order; the 50th percentile.

Medium of exchange   Any asset that can be used to purchase goods and services or to repay debts; a function of money.

Medium-term note   A corporate bond offered continuously to investors by an agent of the issuer, designed to fill the funding gap between commercial paper and long-term bonds.

Menu costs   A cost of inflation in which businesses constantly have to incur the costs of changing the advertised prices of their goods and services.

Mesokurtic   Describes a distribution with kurtosis identical to that of the normal distribution.

Mezzanine financing   Debt or preferred shares with a relationship to common equity due to a feature such as attached warrants or conversion options and that is subordinate to both senior and high yield debt. It is referred to as mezzanine because of its location on the balance sheet.

Microeconomics   The branch of economics that deals with markets and decision making of individual economic units, including consumers and businesses.

Minimum efficient scale   The smallest output that a firm can produce such that its long run average cost is minimized.

Minimum-variance portfolio   The portfolio with the minimum variance for each given level of expected return.

Minsky moment   Named for Hyman Minksy: A point in a business cycle when, after individuals become overextended in borrowing to finance speculative investments, people start realizing that something is likely to go wrong and a panic ensues leading to asset sell-offs.

Mismatching strategy   An active investment strategy whereby the timing of cash outflows is not matched with investment maturities.

Modal interval   With reference to grouped data, the most frequently occurring interval.

Mode   The most frequently occurring value in a set of observations.

Modern portfolio theory   (MPT) The analysis of rational portfolio choices based on the efficient use of risk.

Modified duration   A measure of the percentage price change of a bond given a change in its yield-to-maturity.

Momentum oscillators   A graphical representation of market sentiment that is constructed from price data and calculated so that it oscillates either between a high and a low or around some number.

Monetarists   Economists who believe that the rate of growth of the money supply is the primary determinant of the rate of inflation.

Monetary policy   Actions taken by a nation's central bank to affect aggregate output and prices through changes in bank reserves, reserve requirements, or its target interest rate.

Monetary transmission mechanism   The process whereby a central bank's interest rate gets transmitted through the economy and ultimately affects the rate of increase of prices.

Monetary union   An economic union in which the members adopt a common currency.

Money   A generally accepted medium of exchange and unit of account.

Money convexity   For a bond, the annual or approximate convexity multiplied by the full price.

Money creation   The process by which changes in bank reserves translate into changes in the money supply.

Money duration   A measure of the price change in units of the currency in which the bond is denominated given a change in its yield-to-maturity.

Money market   The market for short-term debt instruments (one-year maturity or less).

Money market securities   Fixed-income securities with maturities at issuance of one year or less.

Money market yield   A yield on a basis comparable to the quoted yield on an interest-bearing money market instrument that pays interest on a 360-day basis; the annualized holding period yield, assuming a 360-day year.

Money multiplier   Describes how a change in reserves is expected to affect the money supply; in its simplest form, 1 divided by the reserve requirement.

Money neutrality   The thesis that an increase in the money supply leads in the long-run to an increase in the price level, while leaving real variables like output and employment unaffected.

Money-weighted return   The internal rate of return on a portfolio, taking account of all cash flows.

Moneyness   The relationship between the price of the underlying and an option's exercise price.

Monopolist   Said of an entity that is the only seller in its market.

Monopolistic competition   Highly competitive form of imperfect competition; the competitive characteristic is a notably large number of firms, while the monopoly aspect is the result of product differentiation.

Monopoly   In pure monopoly markets, there are no substitutes for the given product or service. There is a single seller, which exercises considerable power over pricing and output decisions.

Monte Carlo simulation   An approach to estimating a probability distribution of outcomes to examine what might happen if particular risks are faced. This method is widely used in the sciences as well as in business to study a variety of problems.

Mortgage loan   A loan secured by the collateral of some specified real estate property that obliges the borrower to make a predetermined series of payments to the lender.

Mortgage pass-through security   A security created when one or more holders of mortgages form a pool of mortgages and sell shares or participation certificates in the pool.

Mortgage rate   The interest rate on a mortgage loan; also called *contract rate*.

Mortgage-backed securities   Debt obligations that represent claims to the cash flows from pools of mortgage loans, most commonly on residential property.

Mortgage-backed security   Debt obligations that represent claims to the cash flows from pools of mortgage loans, most commonly on residential property.

Moving average   The average of the closing price of a security over a specified number of periods. With each new period, the average is recalculated.

Moving-average convergence/divergence oscillator   (MACD) A momentum oscillator that is constructed based on the difference between short-term and long-term moving averages of a security's price.

Multi-factor model   A model that explains a variable in terms of the values of a set of factors.

Multi-market indices   Comprised of indices from different countries, designed to represent multiple security markets.

Multi-step format   With respect to the format of the income statement, a format that presents a subtotal for gross profit (revenue minus cost of goods sold).

Multilateral trading facilities   See *alternative trading systems*.

Multinational corporation   A company operating in more than one country or having subsidiary firms in more than one country.

Multiplication rule for probabilities   The rule that the joint probability of events A and B equals the probability of A given B times the probability of B.

Multiplier models   Valuation models based on share price multiples or enterprise value multiples.

Multivariate distribution   A probability distribution that specifies the probabilities for a group of related random variables.

Multivariate normal distribution   A probability distribution for a group of random variables that is completely defined by the means and variances of the variables plus all the correlations between pairs of the variables.

Muni   A type of non-sovereign bond issued by a state or local government in the United States. It very often (but not always) offers income tax exemptions.

Municipal bonds   A type of non-sovereign bond issued by a state or local government in the United States. It very often (but not always) offers income tax exemptions.

Mutual fund   A professionally managed investment pool in which investors in the fund typically each have a pro-rata claim on the income and value of the fund.

Mutually exclusive projects   Mutually exclusive projects compete directly with each other. For example, if Projects A and B are mutually exclusive, you can choose A or B, but you cannot choose both.

n Factorial   For a positive integer n, the product of the first n positive integers; 0 factorial equals 1 by definition. n factorial is written as n!.

NPV rule   An investment decision rule that states that an investment should be undertaken if its NPV is positive but not undertaken if its NPV is negative.

Narrow money   The notes and coins in circulation in an economy, plus other very highly liquid deposits.

Nash equilibrium   When two or more participants in a non-coop-erative game have no incentive to deviate from their respective equilibrium strategies given their opponent's strategies.

National income   The income received by all factors of production used in the generation of final output. National income equals gross domestic product (or, in some countries, gross national product) minus the capital consumption allowance and a statistical discrepancy.

Natural rate of unemployment   Effective unemployment rate, below which pressure emerges in labor markets.

Negative externality   A negative effect (e.g., pollution) of a market transaction that is borne by parties other than those who transacted; a spillover cost.

Neo-Keynesians   A group of dynamic general equilibrium models that assume slow-to-adjust prices and wages.

Net book value   The remaining (undepreciated) balance of an asset's purchase cost. For liabilities, the face value of a bond minus any unamortized discount, or plus any unamortized premium.

Net exports   The difference between the value of a country's exports and the value of its imports (i.e., value of exports minus imports).

Net income   The difference between revenue and expenses; what remains after subtracting all expenses (including depreciation, interest, and taxes) from revenue.

Net operating cycle   An estimate of the average time that elapses between paying suppliers for materials and collecting cash from the subsequent sale of goods produced.

Net present value (NPV) The present value of an investment's cash inflows (benefits) minus the present value of its cash outflows (costs).

Net profit margin An indicator of profitability, calculated as net income divided by revenue; indicates how much of each dollar of revenues is left after all costs and expenses. Also called *profit margin* or *return on sales*.

Net realisable value Estimated selling price in the ordinary course of business less the estimated costs necessary to make the sale.

Net revenue Revenue after adjustments (e.g., for estimated returns or for amounts unlikely to be collected).

Net tax rate The tax rate net of transfer payments.

Neutral rate of interest The rate of interest that neither spurs on nor slows down the underlying economy.

New Keynesians A group of dynamic general equilibrium models that assume slow-to-adjust prices and wages.

New classical macroeconomics An approach to macroeconomics that seeks the macroeconomic conclusions of individuals maximizing utility on the basis of rational expectations and companies maximizing profits.

New-issue DRP Dividend reinvestment plan in which the company meets the need for additional shares by issuing them instead of purchasing them.

No-load fund A mutual fund in which there is no fee for investing in the fund or for redeeming fund shares, although there is an annual fee based on a percentage of the fund's net asset value.

Node Each value on a binomial tree from which successive moves or outcomes branch.

Nominal GDP The value of goods and services measured at current prices.

Nominal rate A rate of interest based on the security's face value.

Nominal risk-free interest rate The sum of the real risk-free interest rate and the inflation premium.

Nominal scale A measurement scale that categorizes data but does not rank them.

Non-accelerating inflation rate of unemployment Effective unemployment rate, below which pressure emerges in labor markets.

Non-agency RMBS In the United States, securities issued by private entities that are not guaranteed by a federal agency or a GSE.

Non-cumulative preference shares Preference shares for which dividends that are not paid in the current or subsequent periods are forfeited permanently (instead of being accrued and paid at a later date).

Non-current assets Assets that are expected to benefit the company over an extended period of time (usually more than one year).

Non-current liabilities Obligations that broadly represent a probable sacrifice of economic benefits in periods generally greater than one year in the future.

Non-current liability Obligations that broadly represent a probably sacrifice of economic benefits in periods generally greater than one year in the future.

Non-cyclical A company whose performance is largely independent of the business cycle.

Non-deliverable forwards Cash-settled forward contracts, used predominately with respect to foreign exchange forwards. Also called *contracts for differences*.

Non-participating preference shares Preference shares that do not entitle shareholders to share in the profits of the company. Instead, shareholders are only entitled to receive a fixed dividend payment and the par value of the shares in the event of liquidation.

Non-recourse loan Loan in which the lender does not have a shortfall claim against the borrower, so the lender can look only to the property to recover the outstanding mortgage balance.

Non-renewable resources Finite resources that are depleted once they are consumed, such as oil and coal.

Non-satiation The assumption that the consumer could never have so much of a preferred good that she would refuse any more, even if it were free; sometimes referred to as the "more is better" assumption.

Non-sovereign bonds A bond issued by a government below the national level, such as a province, region, state, or city.

Non-sovereign government bonds A bond issued by a government below the national level, such as a province, region, state, or city.

Nonconventional cash flow In a nonconventional cash flow pattern, the initial outflow is not followed by inflows only, but the cash flows can flip from positive (inflows) to negative (outflows) again (or even change signs several times).

Noncurrent assets Assets that are expected to benefit the company over an extended period of time (usually more than one year).

Nonparametric test A test that is not concerned with a parameter, or that makes minimal assumptions about the population from which a sample comes.

Nonsystematic risk Unique risk that is local or limited to a particular asset or industry that need not affect assets outside of that asset class.

Normal distribution A continuous, symmetric probability distribution that is completely described by its mean and its variance.

Normal good A good that is consumed in greater quantities as income increases.

Normal profit The level of accounting profit needed to just cover the implicit opportunity costs ignored in accounting costs.

Notching Ratings adjustment methodology where specific issues from the same borrower may be assigned different credit ratings.

Notes payable Amounts owed by a business to creditors as a result of borrowings that are evidenced by (short-term) loan agreements.

Notice period The length of time (typically 30 to 90 days) in advance that investors may be required to notify a fund of their intent to redeem.

Notional principal An imputed principal amount.

Number of days of inventory An activity ratio equal to the number of days in a period divided by the inventory ratio for the period; an indication of the number of days a company ties up funds in inventory.

Number of days of payables An activity ratio equal to the number of days in a period divided by the payables turnover ratio for the period; an estimate of the average number of days it takes a company to pay its suppliers.

Number of days of receivables Estimate of the average number of days it takes to collect on credit accounts.

Objective probabilities Probabilities that generally do not vary from person to person; includes a priori and objective probabilities.

Off-the-run Seasoned government bonds are off-the-run securities; they are not the most recently issued or the most actively traded.

Offer The price at which a dealer or trader is willing to sell an asset, typically qualified by a maximum quantity (ask size).

Official interest rate An interest rate that a central bank sets and announces publicly; normally the rate at which it is willing to lend money to the commercial banks. Also called *official policy rate* or *policy rate*.

Official policy rate An interest rate that a central bank sets and announces publicly; normally the rate at which it is willing to lend money to the commercial banks.

Oligopoly Market structure with a relatively small number of firms supplying the market.

On-the-run The most recently issued and most actively traded sovereign securities.

One-sided hypothesis test A test in which the null hypothesis is rejected only if the evidence indicates that the population parameter is greater than (smaller than) θ_0. The alternative hypothesis also has one side.

One-tailed hypothesis test A test in which the null hypothesis is rejected only if the evidence indicates that the population parameter is greater than (smaller than) θ_0. The alternative hypothesis also has one side.

Open economy An economy that trades with other countries.

Open interest The number of outstanding contracts in a clearinghouse at any given time. The open interest figure changes daily as some parties open up new positions, while other parties offset their old positions.

Open market operations The purchase or sale of bonds by the national central bank to implement monetary policy. The bonds traded are usually sovereign bonds issued by the national government.

Open-end fund A mutual fund that accepts new investment money and issues additional shares at a value equal to the net asset value of the fund at the time of investment.

Open-market DRP Dividend reinvestment plan in which the company purchases shares in the open market to acquire the additional shares credited to plan participants.

Operating activities Activities that are part of the day-to-day business functioning of an entity, such as selling inventory and providing services.

Operating breakeven The number of units produced and sold at which the company's operating profit is zero (revenues = operating costs).

Operating cash flow The net amount of cash provided from operating activities.

Operating cycle A measure of the time needed to convert raw materials into cash from a sale; it consists of the number of days of inventory and the number of days of receivables.

Operating efficiency ratios Ratios that measure how efficiently a company performs day-to-day tasks, such as the collection of receivables and management of inventory.

Operating lease An agreement allowing the lessee to use some asset for a period of time; essentially a rental.

Operating leverage The use of fixed costs in operations.

Operating profit A company's profits on its usual business activities before deducting taxes. Also called *operating income*.

Operating profit margin A profitability ratio calculated as operating income (i.e., income before interest and taxes) divided by revenue. Also called *operating margin*.

Operating risk The risk attributed to the operating cost structure, in particular the use of fixed costs in operations; the risk arising from the mix of fixed and variable costs; the risk that a company's operations may be severely affected by environmental, social, and governance risk factors.

Operational independence A bank's ability to execute monetary policy and set interest rates in the way it thought would best meet the inflation target.

Operationally efficient Said of a market, a financial system, or an economy that has relatively low transaction costs.

Opportunity cost The value that investors forgo by choosing a particular course of action; the value of something in its best alternative use.

Option A financial instrument that gives one party the right, but not the obligation, to buy or sell an underlying asset from or to another party at a fixed price over a specific period of time. Also referred to as *contingent claim* or *option contract*.

Option contract See *option*.

Option premium The amount of money a buyer pays and seller receives to engage in an option transaction.

Option-adjusted price The value of the embedded option plus the flat price of the bond.

Option-adjusted spread OAS = Z-spread – Option value (in basis points per year).

Option-adjusted yield The required market discount rate whereby the price is adjusted for the value of the embedded option.

Order A specification of what instrument to trade, how much to trade, and whether to buy or sell.

Order precedence hierarchy With respect to the execution of orders to trade, a set of rules that determines which orders execute before other orders.

Order-driven markets A market (generally an auction market) that uses rules to arrange trades based on the orders that traders submit; in their pure form, such markets do not make use of dealers.

Ordinal scale A measurement scale that sorts data into categories that are ordered (ranked) with respect to some characteristic.

Ordinary annuity An annuity with a first cash flow that is paid one period from the present.

Ordinary shares Equity shares that are subordinate to all other types of equity (e.g., preferred equity). Also called *common stock* or *common shares*.

Organized exchange A securities marketplace where buyers and seller can meet to arrange their trades.

Other comprehensive income Items of comprehensive income that are not reported on the income statement; comprehensive income minus net income.

Other receivables Amounts owed to the company from parties other than customers.

Out of the money Options that, if exercised, would require the payment of more money than the value received and therefore would not be currently exercised.

Out-of-sample test A test of a strategy or model using a sample outside the time period on which the strategy or model was developed.

Out-of-the-money Options that, if exercised, would require the payment of more money than the value received and therefore would not be currently exercised.

Outcome A possible value of a random variable.

Over-the-counter (OTC) markets A decentralized market where buy and sell orders initiated from various locations are matched through a communications network.

Overbought A market condition in which market sentiment is thought to be unsustainably bullish.

Oversold A market condition in which market sentiment is thought to be unsustainably bearish.

Own-price The price of a good or service itself (as opposed to the price of something else).

Own-price elasticity of demand The percentage change in quantity demanded for a percentage change in own price, holding all other things constant.

Owner-of-record date The date that a shareholder listed on the corporation's books will be deemed to have ownership of the shares for purposes of receiving an upcoming dividend; two business days after the ex-dividend date.

Owners' equity The excess of assets over liabilities; the residual interest of shareholders in the assets of an entity after deducting the entity's liabilities. Also called *shareholders' equity*.

Paasche index An index formula using the current composition of a basket of products.

Paired comparisons test A statistical test for differences based on paired observations drawn from samples that are dependent on each other.

Paired observations Observations that are dependent on each other.

Pairs arbitrage trade A trade in two closely related stocks involving the short sale of one and the purchase of the other.

Panel data Observations through time on a single characteristic of multiple observational units.

Par curve A sequence of yields-to-maturity such that each bond is priced at par value. The bonds are assumed to have the same currency, credit risk, liquidity, tax status, and annual yields stated for the same periodicity.

Par value The amount of principal on a bond.

Parallel shift A parallel yield curve shift implies that all rates change by the same amount in the same direction.

Parameter A descriptive measure computed from or used to describe a population of data, conventionally represented by Greek letters.

Parametric test Any test (or procedure) concerned with parameters or whose validity depends on assumptions concerning the population generating the sample.

Pari passu On an equal footing.

Partial duration See *key rate duration*.

Partial equilibrium analysis An equilibrium analysis focused on one market, taking the values of exogenous variables as given.

Participating preference shares Preference shares that entitle shareholders to receive the standard preferred dividend plus the opportunity to receive an additional dividend if the company's profits exceed a pre-specified level.

Pass-through rate The coupon rate of a mortgage pass-through security.

Passive investment A buy and hold approach in which an investor does not make portfolio changes based on short-term expectations of changing market or security performance.

Passive strategy In reference to short-term cash management, it is an investment strategy characterized by simple decision rules for making daily investments.

Payable date The day that the company actually mails out (or electronically transfers) a dividend payment.

Payment date The day that the company actually mails out (or electronically transfers) a dividend payment.

Payments system The system for the transfer of money.

Payout Cash dividends and the value of shares repurchased in any given year.

Payout policy A company's set of principles guiding payouts.

Peak The highest point of a business cycle.

Peer group A group of companies engaged in similar business activities whose economics and valuation are influenced by closely related factors.

Pennants A technical analysis continuation pattern formed by trendlines that converge to form a triangle, typically over a short period.

Per capita real GDP Real GDP divided by the size of the population, often used as a measure of the average standard of living in a country.

Per unit contribution margin The amount that each unit sold contributes to covering fixed costs—that is, the difference between the price per unit and the variable cost per unit.

Percentage-of-completion A method of revenue recognition in which, in each accounting period, the company estimates what percentage of the contract is complete and then reports that percentage of the total contract revenue in its income statement.

Percentiles Quantiles that divide a distribution into 100 equal parts.

Perfect competition A market structure in which the individual firm has virtually no impact on market price, because it is assumed to be a very small seller among a very large number of firms selling essentially identical products.

Perfectly elastic Said of a good or service that is infinitely sensitive to a change in the value of a specified variable (e.g., price).

Perfectly inelastic Said of a good or service that is completely insensitive to a change in the value of a specified variable (e.g., price).

Performance appraisal The evaluation of risk-adjusted performance; the evaluation of investment skill.

Performance bond See *margin bond*.

Performance evaluation The measurement and assessment of the outcomes of investment management decisions.

Performance measurement The calculation of returns in a logical and consistent manner.

Period costs Costs (e.g., executives' salaries) that cannot be directly matched with the timing of revenues and which are thus expensed immediately.

Periodicity The assumed number of periods in the year, typically matches the frequency of coupon payments.

Permanent differences Differences between tax and financial reporting of revenue (expenses) that will not be reversed at some future date. These result in a difference between the company's effective tax rate and statutory tax rate and do not result in a deferred tax item.

Permutation An ordered listing.

Perpetual bonds Bonds with no stated maturity date.

Perpetuity A perpetual annuity, or a set of never-ending level sequential cash flows, with the first cash flow occurring one period from now. A bond that does not mature.

Personal consumption expenditures All domestic personal consumption; the basis for a price index for such consumption called the PCE price index.

Personal disposable income   Equal to personal income less personal taxes.

Personal income   A broad measure of household income that includes all income received by households, whether earned or unearned; measures the ability of consumers to make purchases.

Plain vanilla bond   Bond that makes periodic, fixed coupon payments during the bond's life and a lump-sum payment of principal at maturity. Also called *conventional bond.*

Planning horizon   A time period in which all factors of production are variable, including technology, physical capital, and plant size.

Platykurtic   Describes a distribution that is less peaked than the normal distribution.

Point and figure chart   A technical analysis chart that is constructed with columns of X's alternating with columns of O's such that the horizontal axis represents only the number of changes in price without reference to time or volume.

Point estimate   A single numerical estimate of an unknown quantity, such as a population parameter.

Point of sale (POS)   Systems that capture transaction data at the physical location in which the sale is made.

Policy rate   An interest rate that a central bank sets and announces publicly; normally the rate at which it is willing to lend money to the commercial banks.

Population   All members of a specified group.

Population mean   The arithmetic mean value of a population; the arithmetic mean of all the observations or values in the population.

Population standard deviation   A measure of dispersion relating to a population in the same unit of measurement as the observations, calculated as the positive square root of the population variance.

Population variance   A measure of dispersion relating to a population, calculated as the mean of the squared deviations around the population mean.

Portfolio company   In private equity, the company that is being invested in.

Portfolio demand for money   The demand to hold speculative money balances based on the potential opportunities or risks that are inherent in other financial instruments.

Portfolio planning   The process of creating a plan for building a portfolio that is expected to satisfy a client's investment objectives.

Position   The quantity of an asset that an entity owns or owes.

Positive externality   A positive effect (e.g., improved literacy) of a market transaction that is borne by parties other than those who transacted; a spillover benefit.

Posterior probability   An updated probability that reflects or comes after new information.

Potential GDP   The level of real GDP that can be produced at full employment; measures the productive capacity of the economy.

Power of a test   The probability of correctly rejecting the null—that is, rejecting the null hypothesis when it is false.

Precautionary money balances   Money held to provide a buffer against unforeseen events that might require money.

Precautionary stocks   A level of inventory beyond anticipated needs that provides a cushion in the event that it takes longer to replenish inventory than expected or in the case of greater than expected demand.

Preference shares   A type of equity interest which ranks above common shares with respect to the payment of dividends and the distribution of the company's net assets upon liquidation. They have characteristics of both debt and equity securities. Also called *preferred stock.*

Preferred stock   See *preference shares.*

Premium   In the case of bonds, premium refers to the amount by which a bond is priced above its face (par) value. In the case of an option, the amount paid for the option contract.

Prepaid expense   A normal operating expense that has been paid in advance of when it is due.

Prepayment option   Contractual provision that entitles the borrower to prepay all or part of the outstanding mortgage principal prior to the scheduled due date the principal must be repaid. Also called *early repayment option.*

Prepayment penalty mortgages   Mortgages that stipulate a monetary penalty if a borrower prepays within a certain time period after the mortgage is originated.

Prepayment risk   The uncertainty that the cash flows will be different from the scheduled cash flows as set forth in the loan agreement due to the borrowers' ability to alter payments.

Present value (PV)   The present discounted value of future cash flows: For assets, the present discounted value of the future net cash inflows that the asset is expected to generate; for liabilities, the present discounted value of the future net cash outflows that are expected to be required to settle the liabilities.

Present value models   Valuation models that estimate the intrinsic value of a security as the present value of the future benefits expected to be received from the security. Also called *discounted cash flow models.*

Pretax margin   A profitability ratio calculated as earnings before taxes divided by revenue.

Price   The market price as established by the interactions of the market demand and supply factors.

Price elasticity of demand   Measures the percentage change in the quantity demanded, given a percentage change in the price of a given product.

Price floor   A minimum price for a good or service, typically imposed by government action and typically above the equilibrium price.

Price index   Represents the average prices of a basket of goods and services.

Price limits   Limits imposed by a futures exchange on the price change that can occur from one day to the next.

Price multiple   A ratio that compares the share price with some sort of monetary flow or value to allow evaluation of the relative worth of a company's stock.

Price priority   The principle that the highest priced buy orders and the lowest priced sell orders execute first.

Price relative   A ratio of an ending price over a beginning price; it is equal to 1 plus the holding period return on the asset.

Price return   Measures *only* the price appreciation or percentage change in price of the securities in an index or portfolio.

Price return index   An index that reflects *only* the price appreciation or percentage change in price of the constituent securities. Also called *price index.*

Price stability   In economics, refers to an inflation rate that is low on average and not subject to wide fluctuation.

Price takers   Producers that must accept whatever price the market dictates.

Price to book value   A valuation ratio calculated as price per share divided by book value per share.

Price to cash flow   A valuation ratio calculated as price per share divided by cash flow per share.

Price to earnings ratio   (P/E ratio or P/E) The ratio of share price to earnings per share.

Price to sales   A valuation ratio calculated as price per share divided by sales per share.

Price value of a basis point   A version of money duration, it is an estimate of the change in the full price of a bond given a 1 basis point change in the yield-to-maturity.

Price weighting   An index weighting method in which the weight assigned to each constituent security is determined by dividing its price by the sum of all the prices of the constituent securities.

Priced risk   Risk for which investors demand compensation for bearing (e.g. equity risk, company-specific factors, macroeconomic factors).

Primary bond markets   Markets in which issuers first sell bonds to investors to raise capital.

Primary capital markets (primary markets)   The market where securities are first sold and the issuers receive the proceeds.

Primary dealers   Financial institutions that are authorized to deal in new issues of sovereign bonds and that serve primarily as trading counterparties of the office responsible for issuing sovereign bonds.

Primary market   The market where securities are first sold and the issuers receive the proceeds.

Prime brokers   Brokers that provide services including custody, administration, lending, short borrowing, and trading.

Principal   The amount of funds originally invested in a project or instrument; the face value to be paid at maturity.

Principal amount   Amount that an issuer agrees to repay the debt holders on the maturity date.

Principal business activity   The business activity from which a company derives a majority of its revenues and/or earnings.

Principal value   Amount that an issuer agrees to repay the debt holders on the maturity date.

Principle of no arbitrage   See *arbitrage-free pricing*.

Prior probabilities   Probabilities reflecting beliefs prior to the arrival of new information.

Priority of claims   Priority of payment, with the most senior or highest ranking debt having the first claim on the cash flows and assets of the issuer.

Private equity securities   Securities that are not listed on public exchanges and have no active secondary market. They are issued primarily to institutional investors via non-public offerings, such as private placements.

Private investment in public equity   An investment in the equity of a publicly traded firm that is made at a discount to the market value of the firm's shares.

Private placement   Typically a non-underwritten, unregistered offering of securities that are sold only to an investor or a small group of investors. It can be accomplished directly between the issuer and the investor(s) or through an investment bank.

Private value auction   An auction in which the value of the item being auctioned is unique to each bidder.

Probability   A number between 0 and 1 describing the chance that a stated event will occur.

Probability density function   A function with non-negative values such that probability can be described by areas under the curve graphing the function.

Probability distribution   A distribution that specifies the probabilities of a random variable's possible outcomes.

Probability function   A function that specifies the probability that the random variable takes on a specific value.

Producer price index   Reflects the price changes experienced by domestic producers in a country.

Producer surplus   The difference between the total revenue sellers receive from selling a given amount of a good and the total variable cost of producing that amount.

Production function   Provides the quantitative link between the level of output that the economy can produce and the inputs used in the production process.

Production opportunity frontier   Curve describing the maximum number of units of one good a company can produce, for any given number of the other good that it chooses to manufacture.

Productivity   The amount of output produced by workers in a given period of time—for example, output per hour worked; measures the efficiency of labor.

Profit   The return that owners of a company receive for the use of their capital and the assumption of financial risk when making their investments.

Profit and loss (P&L) statement   A financial statement that provides information about a company's profitability over a stated period of time.

Profit margin   An indicator of profitability, calculated as net income divided by revenue; indicates how much of each dollar of revenues is left after all costs and expenses.

Profitability ratios   Ratios that measure a company's ability to generate profitable sales from its resources (assets).

Project sequencing   To defer the decision to invest in a future project until the outcome of some or all of a current project is known. Projects are sequenced through time, so that investing in a project creates the option to invest in future projects.

Promissory note   A written promise to pay a certain amount of money on demand.

Property, plant, and equipment   Tangible assets that are expected to be used for more than one period in either the production or supply of goods or services, or for administrative purposes.

Prospectus   The document that describes the terms of a new bond issue and helps investors perform their analysis on the issue.

Protective put   An option strategy in which a long position in an asset is combined with a long position in a put.

Pseudo-random numbers   Numbers produced by random number generators.

Public offer   See *public offering*.

Public offering   An offering of securities in which any member of the public may buy the securities. Also called *public offer*.

Pull on liquidity   When disbursements are paid too quickly or trade credit availability is limited, requiring companies to expend funds before they receive funds from sales that could cover the liability.

Pure discount bonds   See *zero-coupon bonds*.

Pure discount instruments   Instruments that pay interest as the difference between the amount borrowed and the amount paid back.

Pure-play method   A method for estimating the beta for a company or project; it requires using a comparable company's beta and adjusting it for financial leverage differences.

Put   An option that gives the holder the right to sell an underlying asset to another party at a fixed price over a specific period of time.

Put option An option that gives the holder the right to sell an underlying asset to another party at a fixed price over a specific period of time.

Put/call ratio A technical analysis indicator that evaluates market sentiment based upon the volume of put options traded divided by the volume of call options traded for a particular financial instrument.

Putable bonds Bonds that give the bondholder the right to sell the bond back to the issuer at a predetermined price on specified dates.

Putable common shares Common shares that give investors the option (or right) to sell their shares (i.e., "put" them) back to the issuing company at a price that is specified when the shares are originally issued.

Put–call parity An equation expressing the equivalence (parity) of a portfolio of a call and a bond with a portfolio of a put and the underlying, which leads to the relationship between put and call prices.

Put–call–forward parity The relationship among puts, calls, and forward contracts.

Quantile A value at or below which a stated fraction of the data lies. Also called *fractile*.

Quantitative easing An expansionary monetary policy based on aggressive open market purchase operations.

Quantity The amount of a product that consumers are willing and able to buy at each price level.

Quantity demanded The amount of a product that consumers are willing and able to buy at each price level.

Quantity equation of exchange An expression that over a given period, the amount of money used to purchase all goods and services in an economy, $M \times V$, is equal to monetary value of this output, $P \times Y$.

Quantity theory of money Asserts that total spending (in money terms) is proportional to the quantity of money.

Quartiles Quantiles that divide a distribution into four equal parts.

Quasi-fixed cost A cost that stays the same over a range of production but can change to another constant level when production moves outside of that range.

Quasi-government bonds A bond issued by an entity that is either owned or sponsored by a national government. Also called *agency bond*.

Quick assets Assets that can be most readily converted to cash (e.g., cash, short-term marketable investments, receivables).

Quick ratio A stringent measure of liquidity that indicates a company's ability to satisfy current liabilities with its most liquid assets, calculated as (cash + short-term marketable investments + receivables) divided by current liabilities.

Quintiles Quantiles that divide a distribution into five equal parts.

Quota rents Profits that foreign producers can earn by raising the price of their goods higher than they would without a quota.

Quotas Government policies that restrict the quantity of a good that can be imported into a country, generally for a specified period of time.

Quote-driven market A market in which dealers acting as principals facilitate trading.

Quoted interest rate A quoted interest rate that does not account for compounding within the year. Also called *stated annual interest rate*.

Quoted margin The specified yield spread over the reference rate, used to compensate an investor for the difference in the credit risk of the issuer and that implied by the reference rate.

Random number An observation drawn from a uniform distribution.

Random number generator An algorithm that produces uniformly distributed random numbers between 0 and 1.

Random variable A quantity whose future outcomes are uncertain.

Range The difference between the maximum and minimum values in a dataset.

Ratio scales A measurement scale that has all the characteristics of interval measurement scales as well as a true zero point as the origin.

Real GDP The value of goods and services produced, measured at base year prices.

Real income Income adjusted for the effect of inflation on the purchasing power of money.

Real interest rate Nominal interest rate minus the expected rate of inflation.

Real risk-free interest rate The single-period interest rate for a completely risk-free security if no inflation were expected.

Realizable (settlement) value With reference to assets, the amount of cash or cash equivalents that could currently be obtained by selling the asset in an orderly disposal; with reference to liabilities, the undiscounted amount of cash or cash equivalents expected to be paid to satisfy the liabilities in the normal course of business.

Rebalancing Adjusting the weights of the constituent securities in an index.

Rebalancing policy The set of rules that guide the process of restoring a portfolio's asset class weights to those specified in the strategic asset allocation.

Recession A period during which real GDP decreases (i.e., negative growth) for at least two successive quarters, or a period of significant decline in total output, income, employment, and sales usually lasting from six months to a year.

Recognition lag The lag in government response to an economic problem resulting from the delay in confirming a change in the state of the economy.

Record date The date that a shareholder listed on the corporation's books will be deemed to have ownership of the shares for purposes of receiving an upcoming dividend; two business days after the ex-dividend date.

Recourse loan Loan in which the lender has a claim against the borrower for any shortfall between the mortgage balance outstanding and the proceeds received from the sale of the property.

Redemption yield See *yield to maturity*.

Redemptions Withdrawals of funds by investors.

Refinancing rate A type of central bank policy rate.

Registered bonds Bonds for which ownership is recorded by either name or serial number.

Relative dispersion The amount of dispersion relative to a reference value or benchmark.

Relative frequency With reference to an interval of grouped data, the number of observations in the interval divided by the total number of observations in the sample.

Relative price The price of a specific good or service in comparison with those of other goods and services.

Relative strength analysis   A comparison of the performance of one asset with the performance of another asset or a benchmark based on changes in the ratio of the securities' respective prices over time.

Relative strength index   A technical analysis momentum oscillator that compares a security's gains with its losses over a set period.

Renewable resources   Resources that can be replenished, such as a forest.

Rent   Payment for the use of property.

Reorganization   Agreements made by a company in bankruptcy under which a company's capital structure is altered and/or alternative arrangements are made for debt repayment; US Chapter 11 bankruptcy. The company emerges from bankruptcy as a going concern.

Replication   The creation of an asset or portfolio from another asset, portfolio, and/or derivative.

Repo   A form of collateralized loan involving the sale of a security with a simultaneous agreement by the seller to buy the same security back from the purchaser at an agreed-on price and future date. The party who sells the security at the inception of the repurchase agreement and buys it back at maturity is borrowing money from the other party, and the security sold and subsequently repurchased represents the collateral.

Repo margin   The difference between the market value of the security used as collateral and the value of the loan. Also called *haircut*.

Repo rate   The interest rate on a repurchase agreement.

Repurchase agreement   A form of collateralized loan involving the sale of a security with a simultaneous agreement by the seller to buy the same security back from the purchaser at an agreed-on price and future date. The party who sells the security at the inception of the repurchase agreement and buys it back at maturity is borrowing money from the other party, and the security sold and subsequently repurchased represents the collateral.

Repurchase date   The date when the party who sold the security at the inception of a repurchase agreement buys the security back from the cash lending counterparty.

Repurchase price   The price at which the party who sold the security at the inception of the repurchase agreement buys the security back from the cash lending counterparty.

Required margin   The yield spread over, or under, the reference rate such that an FRN is priced at par value on a rate reset date.

Required rate of return   See *market discount rate*.

Required yield   See *market discount rate*.

Required yield spread   The difference between the yield-to-maturity on a new bond and the benchmark rate; additional compensation required by investors for the difference in risk and tax status of a bond relative to a government bond. Sometimes called the *spread over the benchmark*.

Reservation prices   The highest price a buyer is willing to pay for an item or the lowest price at which a seller is willing to sell it.

Reserve requirement   The requirement for banks to hold reserves in proportion to the size of deposits.

Residual claim   The owners' remaining claim on the company's assets after the liabilities are deducted.

Resistance   In technical analysis, a price range in which selling activity is sufficient to stop the rise in the price of a security.

Restricted payments   A bond covenant meant to protect creditors by limiting how much cash can be paid out to shareholders over time.

Retail method   An inventory accounting method in which the sales value of an item is reduced by the gross margin to calculate the item's cost.

Retracement   In technical analysis, a reversal in the movement of a security's price such that it is counter to the prevailing longterm price trend.

Return on assets (ROA)   A profitability ratio calculated as net income divided by average total assets; indicates a company's net profit generated per dollar invested in total assets.

Return on equity (ROE)   A profitability ratio calculated as net income divided by average shareholders' equity.

Return on sales   An indicator of profitability, calculated as net income divided by revenue; indicates how much of each dollar of revenues is left after all costs and expenses.

Return on total capital   A profitability ratio calculated as EBIT divided by the sum of short- and long-term debt and equity.

Return-generating model   A model that can provide an estimate of the expected return of a security given certain parameters and estimates of the values of the independent variables in the model.

Revaluation model   The process of valuing long-lived assets at fair value, rather than at cost less accumulated depreciation. Any resulting profit or loss is either reported on the income statement and/or through equity under revaluation surplus.

Revenue   The amount charged for the delivery of goods or services in the ordinary activities of a business over a stated period; the inflows of economic resources to a company over a stated period.

Reversal patterns   A type of pattern used in technical analysis to predict the end of a trend and a change in direction of the security's price.

Reverse repo   A repurchase agreement viewed from the perspective of the cash lending counterparty.

Reverse repurchase agreement   A repurchase agreement viewed from the perspective of the cash lending counterparty.

Reverse stock split   A reduction in the number of shares outstanding with a corresponding increase in share price, but no change to the company's underlying fundamentals.

Revolving credit agreements   The strongest form of short-term bank borrowing facilities; they are in effect for multiple years (e.g., 3–5 years) and may have optional medium-term loan features.

Ricardian equivalence   An economic theory that implies that it makes no difference whether a government finances a deficit by increasing taxes or issuing debt.

Risk averse   The assumption that an investor will choose the least risky alternative.

Risk aversion   The degree of an investor's inability and unwillingness to take risk.

Risk budgeting   The establishment of objectives for individuals, groups, or divisions of an organization that takes into account the allocation of an acceptable level of risk.

Risk management   The process of identifying the level of risk an entity wants, measuring the level of risk the entity currently has, taking actions that bring the actual level of risk to the desired level of risk, and monitoring the new actual level of risk so that it continues to be aligned with the desired level of risk.

Risk premium   An extra return expected by investors for bearing some specified risk.

Risk tolerance The amount of risk an investor is willing and able to bear to achieve an investment goal.

Risk-neutral pricing Sometimes said of derivatives pricing, uses the fact that arbitrage opportunities guarantee that a risk-free portfolio consisting of the underlying and the derivative must earn the risk-free rate.

Risk-neutral probabilities Weights that are used to compute a binomial option price. They are the probabilities that would apply if a risk-neutral investor valued an option.

Robust The quality of being relatively unaffected by a violation of assumptions.

Rule of 72 The principle that the approximate number of years necessary for an investment to double is 72 divided by the stated interest rate.

Running yield See *current yield.*

Safety stock A level of inventory beyond anticipated needs that provides a cushion in the event that it takes longer to replenish inventory than expected or in the case of greater than expected demand.

Safety-first rules Rules for portfolio selection that focus on the risk that portfolio value will fall below some minimum acceptable level over some time horizon.

Sales Generally, a synonym for revenue; "sales" is generally understood to refer to the sale of goods, whereas "revenue" is understood to include the sale of goods or services.

Sales returns and allowances An offset to revenue reflecting any cash refunds, credits on account, and discounts from sales prices given to customers who purchased defective or unsatisfactory items.

Sales risk Uncertainty with respect to the quantity of goods and services that a company is able to sell and the price it is able to achieve; the risk related to the uncertainty of revenues.

Sales-type leases A type of finance lease, from a lessor perspective, where the present value of the lease payments (less receivable) exceeds the carrying value of the leased asset. The revenues earned by the lessor are operating (the profit on the sale) and financing (interest) in nature.

Salvage value The amount the company estimates that it can sell the asset for at the end of its useful life. Also called *residual value.*

Sample A subset of a population.

Sample excess kurtosis A sample measure of the degree of a distribution's peakedness in excess of the normal distribution's peakedness.

Sample kurtosis A sample measure of the degree of a distribution's peakedness.

Sample mean The sum of the sample observations, divided by the sample size.

Sample selection bias Bias introduced by systematically excluding some members of the population according to a particular attribute—for example, the bias introduced when data availability leads to certain observations being excluded from the analysis.

Sample skewness A sample measure of degree of asymmetry of a distribution.

Sample standard deviation The positive square root of the sample variance.

Sample statistic A quantity computed from or used to describe a sample.

Sample variance A sample measure of the degree of dispersion of a distribution, calculated by dividing the sum of the squared deviations from the sample mean by the sample size minus 1.

Sampling The process of obtaining a sample.

Sampling distribution The distribution of all distinct possible values that a statistic can assume when computed from samples of the same size randomly drawn from the same population.

Sampling error The difference between the observed value of a statistic and the quantity it is intended to estimate.

Sampling plan The set of rules used to select a sample.

Saving In economics, income not spent.

Say's law Named for French economist J.B. Say: All that is produced will be sold because supply creates its own demand.

Scenario analysis Analysis that shows the changes in key financial quantities that result from given (economic) events, such as the loss of customers, the loss of a supply source, or a catastrophic event; a risk management technique involving examination of the performance of a portfolio under specified situations. Closely related to stress testing.

Screening The application of a set of criteria to reduce a set of potential investments to a smaller set having certain desired characteristics.

Scrip dividend schemes Dividend reinvestment plan in which the company meets the need for additional shares by issuing them instead of purchasing them.

Sealed bid auction An auction in which bids are elicited from potential buyers, but there is no ability to observe bids by other buyers until the auction has ended.

Search costs Costs incurred in searching; the costs of matching buyers with sellers.

Seasoned offering An offering in which an issuer sells additional units of a previously issued security.

Second lien A secured interest in the pledged assets that ranks below first lien debt in both collateral protection and priority of payment.

Second price sealed bid An auction (also known as a Vickery auction) in which bids are submitted in sealed envelopes and opened simultaneously. The winning buyer is the one who submitted the highest bid, but the price paid is equal to the second highest bid.

Second-degree price discrimination When the monopolist charges different per-unit prices using the quantity purchased as an indicator of how highly the customer values the product.

Secondary bond markets Markets in which existing bonds are traded among investors.

Secondary market The market where securities are traded among investors.

Secondary precedence rules Rules that determine how to rank orders placed at the same time.

Sector A group of related industries.

Sector indices Indices that represent and track different economic sectors—such as consumer goods, energy, finance, health care, and technology—on either a national, regional, or global basis.

Secured bonds Bonds secured by assets or financial guarantees pledged to ensure debt repayment in case of default.

Secured debt Debt in which the debtholder has a direct claim—a pledge from the issuer—on certain assets and their associated cash flows.

Securitization A process that involves moving assets into a special legal entity, which then uses the assets as guarantees to secure a bond issue.

Securitized assets Assets that are typically used to create asset backed bonds, for example when a bank securitizes a pool of loans the loans are said to be securitized.

Securitized bonds   Bonds created from a process that involves moving assets into a special legal entity, which then uses the assets as guarantees to secure a bond issue.

Security characteristic line   A plot of the excess return of a security on the excess return of the market.

Security market index   A portfolio of securities representing a given security market, market segment, or asset class.

Security market line   (SML) The graph of the capital asset pricing model.

Security selection   The process of selecting individual securities; typically, security selection has the objective of generating superior risk-adjusted returns relative to a portfolio's benchmark.

Self-investment limits   With respect to investment limitations applying to pension plans, restrictions on the percentage of assets that can be invested in securities issued by the pension plan sponsor.

Sell-side firm   A broker or dealer that sells securities to and provides independent investment research and recommendations to investment management companies.

Semi-strong-form efficient market   A market in which security prices reflect all publicly known and available information.

Semiannual bond basis yield   An annual rate having a periodicity of two; also known as a *semiannual bond equivalent yield*.

Semiannual bond equivalent yield   See *semiannual bond basis yield*.

Semideviation   The positive square root of semivariance (sometimes called *semistandard deviation*).

Semilogarithmic   Describes a scale constructed so that equal intervals on the vertical scale represent equal rates of change, and equal intervals on the horizontal scale represent equal amounts of change.

Semivariance   The average squared deviation below the mean.

Seniority ranking   Priority of payment of various debt obligations.

Sensitivity analysis   Analysis that shows the range of possible outcomes as specific assumptions are changed.

Separately managed account   (SMA) An investment portfolio managed exclusively for the benefit of an individual or institution.

Serial maturity structure   Structure for a bond issue in which the maturity dates are spread out during the bond's life; a stated number of bonds mature and are paid off each year before final maturity.

Settlement   The process that occurs after a trade is completed, the securities are passed to the buyer, and payment is received by the seller.

Settlement date   Date when the buyer makes cash payment and the seller delivers the security.

Settlement price   The official price, designated by the clearinghouse, from which daily gains and losses will be determined and marked to market.

Share repurchase   A transaction in which a company buys back its own shares. Unlike stock dividends and stock splits, share repurchases use corporate cash.

Shareholder wealth maximization   To maximize the market value of shareholders' equity.

Shareholder-of-record date   The date that a shareholder listed on the corporation's books will be deemed to have ownership of the shares for purposes of receiving an upcoming dividend; two business days after the ex-dividend date.

Shareholders' equity   Assets less liabilities; the residual interest in the assets after subtracting the liabilities.

Sharpe ratio   The average return in excess of the risk-free rate divided by the standard deviation of return; a measure of the average excess return earned per unit of standard deviation of return.

Shelf registration   Type of public offering that allows the issuer to file a single, all-encompassing offering circular that covers a series of bond issues.

Short   The seller of an asset or derivative contract. Also refers to the position of being short an asset or derivative contract.

Short position   A position in an asset or contract in which one has sold an asset one does not own, or in which a right under a contract can be exercised against oneself.

Short selling   A transaction in which borrowed securities are sold with the intention to repurchase them at a lower price at a later date and return them to the lender.

Short-run average total cost curve   The curve describing average total costs when some costs are considered fixed.

Short-run supply curve   The section of the marginal cost curve that lies above the minimum point on the average variable cost curve.

Shortfall risk   The risk that portfolio value will fall below some minimum acceptable level over some time horizon.

Shutdown point   The point at which average revenue is less than average variable cost.

Simple interest   The interest earned each period on the original investment; interest calculated on the principal only.

Simple random sample   A subset of a larger population created in such a way that each element of the population has an equal probability of being selected to the subset.

Simple random sampling   The procedure of drawing a sample to satisfy the definition of a simple random sample.

Simple yield   The sum of the coupon payments plus the straight-line amortized share of the gain or loss, divided by the flat price.

Simulation   Computer-generated sensitivity or scenario analysis that is based on probability models for the factors that drive outcomes.

Simulation trial   A complete pass through the steps of a simulation.

Single price auction   A Dutch auction variation, also involving a single price, is used in selling US Treasury securities.

Single-step format   With respect to the format of the income statement, a format that does not subtotal for gross profit (revenue minus cost of goods sold).

Sinking fund arrangement   Provision that reduces the credit risk of a bond issue by requiring the issuer to retire a portion of the bond's principal outstanding each year.

Skewed   Not symmetrical.

Skewness   A quantitative measure of skew (lack of symmetry); a synonym of skew.

Small country   A country that is a price taker in the world market for a product and cannot influence the world market price.

Solvency   With respect to financial statement analysis, the ability of a company to fulfill its long-term obligations.

Solvency ratios   Ratios that measure a company's ability to meet its long-term obligations.

Sovereign bonds   A bond issued by a national government.

Sovereign yield spread   An estimate of the country spread (country equity premium) for a developing nation that is based on a comparison of bonds yields in country being analyzed and a developed country. The sovereign yield spread is the difference between a government bond yield in the country being analyzed, denominated in the currency of the developed country, and the Treasury bond yield on a similar maturity bond in the developed country.

Sovereigns A bond issued by a national government.

Spearman rank correlation coefficient A measure of correlation applied to ranked data.

Special dividend A dividend paid by a company that does not pay dividends on a regular schedule, or a dividend that supplements regular cash dividends with an extra payment.

Special purpose entity A non-operating entity created to carry out a specified purpose, such as leasing assets or securitizing receivables; can be a corporation, partnership, trust, limited liability, or partnership formed to facilitate a specific type of business activity. Also called *special purpose vehicle* or *variable interest entity*.

Special purpose vehicle See *special purpose entity*.

Specific identification method An inventory accounting method that identifies which specific inventory items were sold and which remained in inventory to be carried over to later periods.

Speculative demand for money The demand to hold speculative money balances based on the potential opportunities or risks that are inherent in other financial instruments. Also called *portfolio demand for money*.

Speculative money balances Monies held in anticipation that other assets will decline in value.

Split coupon bond See *deferred coupon bond*.

Sponsored A type of depository receipt in which the foreign company whose shares are held by the depository has a direct involvement in the issuance of the receipts.

Spot curve A sequence of yields-to-maturity on zero-coupon bonds. Sometimes called *zero* or *strip curve* because coupon payments are "stripped" off of the bonds.

Spot markets Markets in which assets are traded for immediate delivery.

Spot prices The price of an asset for immediately delivery.

Spot rates A sequence of market discount rates that correspond to the cash flow dates; yields-to-maturity on zero-coupon bonds maturing at the date of each cash flow.

Spread In general, the difference in yield between different fixed income securities. Often used to refer to the difference between the yield-to-maturity and the benchmark.

Spread over the benchmark See *required yield spread*.

Spread risk Bond price risk arising from changes in the yield spread on credit-risky bonds; reflects changes in the market's assessment and/or pricing of credit migration (or downgrade) risk and market liquidity risk.

Stable With reference to an equilibrium, one in which price, when disturbed away from the equilibrium, tends to converge back to it.

Stackelberg model A prominent model of strategic decision-making in which firms are assumed to make their decisions sequentially.

Stagflation When a high inflation rate is combined with a high level of unemployment and a slowdown of the economy.

Standard cost With respect to inventory accounting, the planned or target unit cost of inventory items or services.

Standard deviation The positive square root of the variance; a measure of dispersion in the same units as the original data.

Standard normal distribution The normal density with mean (μ) equal to 0 and standard deviation (σ) equal to 1.

Standardizing A transformation that involves subtracting the mean and dividing the result by the standard deviation.

Standing limit orders A limit order at a price below market and which therefore is waiting to trade.

Stated annual interest rate A quoted interest rate that does not account for compounding within the year. Also called *quoted interest rate*.

Statement of cash flows A financial statement that reconciles beginning-of-period and end-of-period balance sheet values of cash; provides information about an entity's cash inflows and cash outflows as they pertain to operating, investing, and financing activities. Also called *cash flow statement*.

Statement of changes in equity (statement of owners' equity) A financial statement that reconciles the beginning-of-period and end-of-period balance sheet values of shareholders' equity; provides information about all factors affecting shareholders' equity. Also called *statement of owners' equity*.

Statement of financial condition The financial statement that presents an entity's current financial position by disclosing resources the entity controls (its assets) and the claims on those resources (its liabilities and equity claims), as of a particular point in time (the date of the balance sheet).

Statement of financial position The financial statement that presents an entity's current financial position by disclosing resources the entity controls (its assets) and the claims on those resources (its liabilities and equity claims), as of a particular point in time (the date of the balance sheet).

Statement of operations A financial statement that provides information about a company's profitability over a stated period of time.

Statement of owners' equity A financial statement that reconciles the beginning of-period and end-of-period balance sheet values of shareholders' equity; provides information about all factors affecting shareholders' equity. Also called *statement of changes in shareholders' equity*.

Statement of retained earnings A financial statement that reconciles beginning-of-period and end-of-period balance sheet values of retained income; shows the linkage between the balance sheet and income statement.

Statistic A quantity computed from or used to describe a sample of data.

Statistical inference Making forecasts, estimates, or judgments about a larger group from a smaller group actually observed; using a sample statistic to infer the value of an unknown population parameter.

Statistically significant A result indicating that the null hypothesis can be rejected; with reference to an estimated regression coefficient, frequently understood to mean a result indicating that the corresponding population regression coefficient is different from 0.

Statutory voting A common method of voting where each share represents one vote.

Step-up coupon bond Bond for which the coupon, which may be fixed or floating, increases by specified margins at specified dates.

Stock dividend A type of dividend in which a company distributes additional shares of its common stock to shareholders instead of cash.

Stock-out losses Profits lost from not having sufficient inventory on hand to satisfy demand.

Stop order An order in which a trader has specified a stop price condition. Also called *stop-loss order*.

Stop-loss order See *stop order*.

Store of value The quality of tending to preserve value.

Store of wealth   Goods that depend on the fact that they do not perish physically over time, and on the belief that others would always value the good.

Straight-line method   A depreciation method that allocates evenly the cost of a long-lived asset less its estimated residual value over the estimated useful life of the asset.

Strategic analysis   Analysis of the competitive environment with an emphasis on the implications of the environment for corporate strategy.

Strategic asset allocation   The set of exposures to IPS-permissible asset classes that is expected to achieve the client's long-term objectives given the client's investment constraints.

Strategic groups   Groups sharing distinct business models or catering to specific market segments in an industry.

Street convention   Yield measure that neglects weekends and holidays; the internal rate of return on cash flows assuming payments are made on the scheduled dates, even when the scheduled date falls on a weekend or holiday.

Stress testing   A set of techniques for estimating losses in extremely unfavorable combinations of events or scenarios.

Strong-form efficient market   A market in which security prices reflect all public and private information.

Structural (or cyclically adjusted) budget deficit   The deficit that would exist if the economy was at full employment (or full potential output).

Structural subordination   Arises in a holding company structure when the debt of operating subsidiaries is serviced by the cash flow and assets of the subsidiaries before funds can be passed to the holding company to service debt at the parent level.

Subjective probability   A probability drawing on personal or subjective judgment.

Subordinated debt   A class of unsecured debt that ranks below a firm's senior unsecured obligations.

Subordination   A common structure in securitization, which leads to the creation of more than one bond class or tranche. Bond classes differ as to how they will share any losses resulting from defaults of the borrowers whose loans are in the pool of loans.

Substitutes   Said of two goods or services such that if the price of one increases the demand for the other tends to increase, holding all other things equal (e.g., butter and margarine).

Sunk cost   A cost that has already been incurred.

Supernormal profit   Equal to accounting profit less the implicit opportunity costs not included in total accounting costs; the difference between total revenue (TR) and total cost (TC).

Supply   The willingness of sellers to offer a given quantity of a good or service for a given price.

Supply curve   The graph of the inverse supply function.

Supply function   The quantity supplied as a function of price and possibly other variables.

Supply shock   A typically unexpected disturbance to supply.

Support   In technical analysis, a price range in which buying activity is sufficient to stop the decline in the price of a security.

Support tranche   A class or tranche in a CMO that protects the PAC tranche from prepayment risk.

Supranational bonds   A bond issued by a supranational agency such as the World Bank.

Surety bond   Form of external credit enhancement whereby a rated and regulated insurance company guarantees to reimburse bondholders for any losses incurred up to a maximum amount if the issuer defaults.

Survey approach   An estimate of the equity risk premium that is based upon estimates provided by a panel of finance experts.

Survivorship bias   The bias resulting from a test design that fails to account for companies that have gone bankrupt, merged, or are otherwise no longer reported in a database.

Sustainable growth rate   The rate of dividend (and earnings) growth that can be sustained over time for a given level of return on equity, keeping the capital structure constant and without issuing additional common stock.

Sustainable rate of economic growth   The rate of increase in the economy's productive capacity or potential GDP.

Swap contract   An agreement between two parties to exchange a series of future cash flows.

Syndicated loans   Loans from a group of lenders to a single borrower.

Syndicated offering   A bond issue that is underwritten by a group of investment banks.

Systematic risk   Risk that affects the entire market or economy; it cannot be avoided and is inherent in the overall market. Systematic risk is also known as non diversifiable or market risk.

Systematic sampling   A procedure of selecting every kth member until reaching a sample of the desired size. The sample that results from this procedure should be approximately random.

t-Test   A hypothesis test using a statistic (t-statistic) that follows a t-distribution.

TRIN   A flow of funds indicator applied to a broad stock market index to measure the relative extent to which money is moving into or out of rising and declining stocks.

Tactical asset allocation   The decision to deliberately deviate from the strategic asset allocation in an attempt to add value based on forecasts of the near-term relative performance of asset classes.

Target balance   A minimum level of cash to be held available—estimated in advance and adjusted for known funds transfers, seasonality, or other factors.

Target capital structure   A company's chosen proportions of debt and equity.

Target independent   A bank's ability to determine the definition of inflation that they target, the rate of inflation that they target, and the horizon over which the target is to be achieved.

Target semideviation   The positive square root of target semivariance.

Target semivariance   The average squared deviation below a target value.

Tariffs   Taxes that a government levies on imported goods.

Tax base   The amount at which an asset or liability is valued for tax purposes.

Tax expense   An aggregate of an entity's income tax payable (or recoverable in the case of a tax benefit) and any changes in deferred tax assets and liabilities. It is essentially the income tax payable or recoverable if these had been determined based on accounting profit rather than taxable income.

Tax loss carry forward   A taxable loss in the current period that may be used to reduce future taxable income.

Taxable income   The portion of an entity's income that is subject to income taxes under the tax laws of its jurisdiction.

Taxable temporary differences   Temporary differences that result in a taxable amount in a future period when determining the taxable profit as the balance sheet item is recovered or settled.

Technical analysis   A form of security analysis that uses price and volume data, which is often displayed graphically, in decision making.

Technology   The process a company uses to transform inputs into outputs.

Technology of production   The "rules" that govern the transformation of inputs into finished goods and services.

Tenor   The time-to-maturity for a bond or derivative contract. Also called *term to maturity*.

Term maturity structure   Structure for a bond issue in which the bond's notional principal is paid off in a lump sum at maturity.

Term structure   See *maturity structure*.

Term structure of credit spreads   The relationship between the spreads over the "risk-free" (or benchmark) rates and times-to-maturity.

Term structure of yield volatility   The relationship between the volatility of bond yields-to-maturity and times-to-maturity.

Terminal stock value   The expected value of a share at the end of the investment horizon—in effect, the expected selling price. Also called *terminal value*.

Terminal value   The expected value of a share at the end of the investment horizon—in effect, the expected selling price.

Terms of trade   The ratio of the price of exports to the price of imports, representing those prices by export and import price indices, respectively.

Theory of the consumer   The branch of microeconomics that deals with consumption—the demand for goods and services—by utility-maximizing individuals.

Theory of the firm   The branch of microeconomics that deals with the supply of goods and services by profit-maximizing firms.

Third-degree price discrimination   When the monopolist segregates customers into groups based on demographic or other characteristics and offers different pricing to each group.

Time tranching   The creation of classes or tranches in an ABS/MBS that possess different (expected) maturities.

Time value   The difference between the market price of the option and its intrinsic value, determined by the uncertainty of the underlying over the remaining life of the option.

Time value decay   Said of an option when, at expiration, no time value remains and the option is worth only its exercise value.

Time value of money   The principles governing equivalence relationships between cash flows with different dates.

Time-period bias   The possibility that when we use a time-series sample, our statistical conclusion may be sensitive to the starting and ending dates of the sample.

Time-series data   Observations of a variable over time.

Time-weighted rate of return   The compound rate of growth of one unit of currency invested in a portfolio during a stated measurement period; a measure of investment performance that is not sensitive to the timing and amount of withdrawals or additions to the portfolio.

Top-down analysis   With reference to investment selection processes, an approach that starts with macro selection (i.e., identifying attractive geographic segments and/or industry segments) and then addresses selection of the most attractive investments within those segments.

Total comprehensive income   The change in equity during a period resulting from transaction and other events, other than those changes resulting from transactions with owners in their capacity as owners.

Total costs   The summation of all costs, where costs are classified according to fixed or variable.

Total expenditure   The total amount spent over a time period.

Total factor productivity   A scale factor that reflects the portion of growth that is not accounted for by explicit factor inputs (e.g. capital and labor).

Total fixed cost   The summation of all expenses that do not change when production varies.

Total invested capital   The sum of market value of common equity, book value of preferred equity, and face value of debt.

Total probability rule   A rule explaining the unconditional probability of an event in terms of probabilities of the event conditional on mutually exclusive and exhaustive scenarios.

Total probability rule for expected value   A rule explaining the expected value of a random variable in terms of expected values of the random variable conditional on mutually exclusive and exhaustive scenarios.

Total product   The aggregate sum of production for the firm during a time period.

Total return   Measures the price appreciation, or percentage change in price of the securities in an index or portfolio, plus any income received over the period.

Total return index   An index that reflects the price appreciation or percentage change in price of the constituent securities plus any income received since inception.

Total return swap   A swap in which one party agrees to pay the total return on a security. Often used as a credit derivative, in which the underlying is a bond.

Total revenue   Price times the quantity of units sold.

Total surplus   The difference between total value to buyers and the total variable cost to sellers; made up of the sum of consumer surplus and producer surplus.

Total variable cost   The summation of all variable expenses.

Tracking error   The standard deviation of the differences between a portfolio's returns and its benchmark's returns; a synonym of active risk.

Tracking risk   The standard deviation of the differences between a portfolio's returns and its benchmark's returns; a synonym of active risk. Also called *tracking error*.

Trade creation   When regional integration results in the replacement of higher cost domestic production by lower cost imports from other members.

Trade credit   A spontaneous form of credit in which a purchaser of the goods or service is financing its purchase by delaying the date on which payment is made.

Trade diversion   When regional integration results in lower-cost imports from non-member countries being replaced with higher-cost imports from members.

Trade payables   Amounts that a business owes to its vendors for goods and services that were purchased from them but which have not yet been paid.

Trade protection   Government policies that impose restrictions on trade, such as tariffs and quotas.

Trade receivables Amounts customers owe the company for products that have been sold as well as amounts that may be due from suppliers (such as for returns of merchandise) Also called *commercial receivables* or *accounts receivable*.

Trade surplus (deficit) When the value of exports is greater (less) than the value of imports.

Trading securities Securities held by a company with the intent to trade them. Also called *held-for-trading securities*.

Traditional investment markets Markets for traditional investments, which include all publicly traded debts and equities and shares in pooled investment vehicles that hold publicly traded debts and/or equities.

Transactions money balances Money balances that are held to finance transactions.

Transactions motive In the context of inventory management, the need for inventory as part of the routine production–sales cycle.

Transfer payments Welfare payments made through the social security system that exist to provide a basic minimum level of income for low-income households.

Transitive preferences The assumption that when comparing any three distinct bundles, A, B, and C, if A is preferred to B and simultaneously B is preferred to C, then it must be true that A is preferred to C.

Transparency Said of something (e.g., a market) in which information is fully disclosed to the public and/or regulators.

Treasury Inflation-Protected Securities A bond issued by the United States Treasury Department that is designed to protect the investor from inflation by adjusting the principal of the bond for changes in inflation.

Treasury shares Shares that were issued and subsequently repurchased by the company.

Treasury stock Shares that were issued and subsequently repurchased by the company.

Treasury stock method A method for accounting for the effect of options (and warrants) on earnings per share (EPS) that specifies what EPS would have been if the options and warrants had been exercised and the company had used the proceeds to repurchase common stock.

Tree diagram A diagram with branches emanating from nodes representing either mutually exclusive chance events or mutually exclusive decisions.

Trend A long-term pattern of movement in a particular direction.

Treynor ratio A measure of risk-adjusted performance that relates a portfolio's excess returns to the portfolio's beta.

Triangle patterns In technical analysis, a continuation chart pattern that forms as the range between high and low prices narrows, visually forming a triangle.

Trimmed mean A mean computed after excluding a stated small percentage of the lowest and highest observations.

Triple bottoms In technical analysis, a reversal pattern that is formed when the price forms three troughs at roughly the same price level; used to predict a change from a downtrend to an uptrend.

Triple tops In technical analysis, a reversal pattern that is formed when the price forms three peaks at roughly the same price level; used to predict a change from an uptrend to a downtrend.

Trough The lowest point of a business cycle.

True yield The internal rate of return on cash flows using the actual calendar including weekends and bank holidays.

Trust deed See *indenture*.

Trust receipt arrangement The use of inventory as collateral for a loan. The inventory is segregated and held in trust, and the proceeds of any sale must be remitted to the lender immediately.

Turn-of-the-year effect Calendar anomaly that stock market returns in January are significantly higher compared to the rest of the months of the year, with most of the abnormal returns reported during the first five trading days in January.

Two-fund separation theorem The theory that all investors regardless of taste, risk preferences, and initial wealth will hold a combination of two portfolios or funds: a risk-free asset and an optimal portfolio of risky assets.

Two-sided hypothesis test A test in which the null hypothesis is rejected in favor of the alternative hypothesis if the evidence indicates that the population parameter is either smaller or larger than a hypothesized value.

Two-tailed hypothesis test A test in which the null hypothesis is rejected in favor of the alternative hypothesis if the evidence indicates that the population parameter is either smaller or larger than a hypothesized value.

Two-week repo rate The interest rate on a two-week repurchase agreement; may be used as a policy rate by a central bank.

Type I error The error of rejecting a true null hypothesis.

Type II error The error of not rejecting a false null hypothesis.

Unanticipated (unexpected) inflation The component of inflation that is a surprise.

Unbilled revenue Revenue that has been earned but not yet billed to customers as of the end of an accounting period. Also called *accrued revenue*.

Unclassified balance sheet A balance sheet that does not show subtotals for current assets and current liabilities.

Unconditional probability The probability of an event *not* conditioned on another event.

Underemployed A person who has a job but has the qualifications to work a significantly higher-paying job.

Underlying An asset that trades in a market in which buyers and sellers meet, decide on a price, and the seller then delivers the asset to the buyer and receives payment. The underlying is the asset or other derivative on which a particular derivative is based. The market for the underlying is also referred to as the *spot market*.

Underwriter A firm, usually an investment bank, that takes the risk of buying the newly issued securities from the issuer, and then reselling them to investors or to dealers, thus guaranteeing the sale of the securities at the offering price negotiated with the issuer.

Underwritten offering A type of securities issue mechanism in which the investment bank guarantees the sale of the securities at an offering price that is negotiated with the issuer. Also known as *firm commitment offering*.

Unearned fees Unearned fees are recognized when a company receives cash payment for fees prior to earning them.

Unearned revenue A liability account for money that has been collected for goods or services that have not yet been delivered; payment received in advance of providing a good or service. Also called *deferred revenue* or *deferred income*.

Unemployed People who are actively seeking employment but are currently without a job.

Unemployment rate The ratio of unemployed to the labor force.

Unexpected inflation The component of inflation that is a surprise.

Unit elastic   An elasticity with a magnitude of 1.

Unit labor cost   The average labor cost to produce one unit of output.

Unit normal distribution   The normal density with mean (μ) equal to 0 and standard deviation (σ) equal to 1.

Unitary elastic   An elasticity with a magnitude of 1.

Units-of-production method   A depreciation method that allocates the cost of a long-lived asset based on actual usage during the period.

Univariate distribution   A distribution that specifies the probabilities for a single random variable.

Unlimited funds   An unlimited funds environment assumes that the company can raise the funds it wants for all profitable projects simply by paying the required rate of return.

Unsecured debt   Debt which gives the debtholder only a general claim on an issuer's assets and cash flow.

Unsponsored   A type of depository receipt in which the foreign company whose shares are held by the depository has no involvement in the issuance of the receipts.

Unstable   With reference to an equilibrium, one in which price, when disturbed away from the equilibrium, tends not to return to it.

Up transition probability   The probability that an asset's value moves up.

Utility function   A mathematical representation of the satisfaction derived from a consumption basket.

Utils   A unit of utility.

Validity instructions   Instructions which indicate when the order may be filled.

Valuation allowance   A reserve created against deferred tax assets, based on the likelihood of realizing the deferred tax assets in future accounting periods.

Valuation ratios   Ratios that measure the quantity of an asset or flow (e.g., earnings) in relation to the price associated with a specified claim (e.g., a share or ownership of the enterprise).

Value at risk   (VAR) A money measure of the minimum value of losses expected during a specified time period at a given level of probability.

Value investors   With reference to equity investors, investors who are focused on paying a relatively low share price in relation to earnings or assets per share.

Variable costs   Costs that fluctuate with the level of production and sales.

Variable-rate note   Similar to a floating-rate note, except that the spread is variable rather than constant.

Variance   The expected value (the probability-weighted average) of squared deviations from a random variable's expected value.

Variation margin   Additional margin that must be deposited in an amount sufficient to bring the balance up to the initial margin requirement.

Veblen good   A good that increases in desirability with price.

Venture capital   Investments that provide "seed" or start-up capital, early-stage financing, or mezzanine financing to companies that are in the early stages of development and require additional capital for expansion.

Venture capital fund   A fund for private equity investors that provides financing for development-stage companies.

Vertical analysis   Common-size analysis using only one reporting period or one base financial statement; for example, an income statement in which all items are stated as percentages of sales.

Vertical demand schedule   Implies that some fixed quantity is demanded, regardless of price.

Volatility   As used in option pricing, the standard deviation of the continuously compounded returns on the underlying asset.

Voluntarily unemployed   A person voluntarily outside the labor force, such as a jobless worker refusing an available vacancy.

Voluntary export restraint   A trade barrier under which the exporting country agrees to limit its exports of the good to its trading partners to a specific number of units.

Vote by proxy   A mechanism that allows a designated party—such as another shareholder, a shareholder representative, or management—to vote on the shareholder's behalf.

Warehouse receipt arrangement   The use of inventory as collateral for a loan; similar to a trust receipt arrangement except there is a third party (i.e., a warehouse company) that supervises the inventory.

Warrant   Attached option that gives its holder the right to buy the underlying stock of the issuing company at a fixed exercise price until the expiration date.

Waterfall   The provision in an ABS that describes the flow of payments between bond classes.

Weak-form efficient market hypothesis   The belief that security prices fully reflect all past market data, which refers to all historical price and volume trading information.

Wealth effect   An increase (decrease) in household wealth increases (decreases) consumer spending out of a given level of current income.

Weighted average cost method   An inventory accounting method that averages the total cost of available inventory items over the total units available for sale.

Weighted average cost of capital   A weighted average of the aftertax required rates of return on a company's common stock, preferred stock, and long-term debt, where the weights are the fraction of each source of financing in the company's target capital structure.

Weighted average coupon rate   Weighting the mortgage rate of each mortgage loan in the pool by the percentage of the mortgage outstanding relative to the outstanding amount of all the mortgages in the pool.

Weighted average life   Measure that gives investors an indication of how long they can expect to hold the MBS before it is paid off; the convention-based average time to receipt of all principal repayments. Also called *average life*.

Weighted average maturity   Weighting the remaining number of months to maturity for each mortgage loan in the pool by the amount of the outstanding mortgage balance.

Weighted mean   An average in which each observation is weighted by an index of its relative importance.

Wholesale price index   Reflects the price changes experienced by domestic producers in a country.

Winner's curse   The tendency for the winner in certain competitive bidding situations to overpay, whether because of overestimation of intrinsic value, emotion, or information asymmetries.

Winsorized mean   A mean computed after assigning a stated percent of the lowest values equal to one specified low value, and a stated percent of the highest values equal to one specified high value.

Working capital   The difference between current assets and current liabilities.

Working capital management   The management of a company's short-term assets (such as inventory) and short-term liabilities (such as money owed to suppliers).

World price   The price prevailing in the world market.

Yield   The actual return on a debt security if it is held to maturity.

Yield duration   The sensitivity of the bond price with respect to the bond's own yield-to-maturity.

Yield to maturity   Annual return that an investor earns on a bond if the investor purchases the bond today and holds it until maturity. It is the discount rate that equates the present value of the bond's expected cash flows until maturity with the bond's price. Also called *yield-to-redemption* or *redemption yield*.

Yield to redemption   See *yield to maturity*.

Yield-to-worst   The lowest of the sequence of yields-to-call and the yield-to-maturity.

Zero volatility spread (Z-spread)   Calculates a constant yield spread over a government (or interest rate swap) spot curve.

Zero-coupon bonds   Bonds that do not pay interest during the bond's life. It is issued at a discount to par value and redeemed at par. Also called *pure discount bonds*.

Index